BRICKS
TO BABEL

BRICKS TO BABEL

In his introduction, Arthur Koestler refers to his new work as an omnibus in which the author acts as guide. It is, in fact, a conducted tour of his writings and consists of extensive passages linked by a commentary to put them in perspective. The result conveys a fascinating picture of the development of one of the most wide-ranging thinkers and writers of our time, a kind of intellectual odyssey, published in the year of his seventy-fifth birthday, of a man who has throughout his life been pursuing clues which might contribute to the diagnosis – and the solution – of the human predicament.

Book One, entitled "In Search of Utopia", describes his early search for and later scepticism about political solutions, above all his youthful period as an undercover Communist. There is, therefore, a considerable amount of autobiographical material from *Arrow in the Blue* and *The Invisible Writing* and also, of course, from *Dialogue with Death*, spelling out the profound effect which ninety days in the death cell in Franco's Spain had upon him. Interwoven with it are colourful accounts of life in a Palestine Kibbutz in the 1920s and the developments which led to the founding of the State of Israel. His disenchantment with Communism is reflected in the extracts from his famous novels, *The Gladiators*, *Darkness at Noon* and *Arrival and Departure*.

Some thirty years ago came the fundamental change when Koestler abandoned politics and turned to science and philosophy. This is reflected in Book Two, "In Search of a Synthesis". Here we find his important and far-reaching research into the mind of man – notably his theory of creativity in science and art (*The Act of Creation*) – and the reverse side of the coin, the pathology of the human mind (*The Ghost in the Machine*), exemplified in the tendency of our species to destroy itself. Short cuts to a solution, such as contemporary versions of Eastern mysticism, are studied and rejected, but his final section ("A Glance through the Keyhole") catches a glimpse of a new form of mysticism – or cosmic consciousness – which might emerge from the infinite vista of the subatomic and extra-galactic worlds. There is some comfort (he writes) in the thought that in the universe we are not alone, but surrounded by our elders and betters.

Books by Arthur Koestler

Novels
The Gladiators
Darkness at Noon
Arrival and Departure
Thieves in the Night
The Age of Longing
The Call-Girls

Autobiography
Dialogue with Death
Scum of the Earth
Arrow in the Blue
The Invisible Writing
The God that Failed (with others)

Essays
The Yogi and the Commissar
Insight and Outlook
Promise and Fulfilment
The Trail of the Dinosaur
Reflections on Hanging
The Sleepwalkers
The Lotus and the Robot
The Act of Creation
The Ghost in the Machine
Drinkers of Infinity
The Case of the Midwife Toad
The Roots of Coincidence
The Challenge of Chance
(with *Sir Alister Hardy and Robert Harvie*)
The Heel of Achilles
Suicide of a Nation? (ed.)
Beyond Reductionism: The Alpbach Symposium
(ed. with J. R. Smythies)
The Thirteenth Tribe
Life After Death
(with Arnold Toynbee and others)
Janus – A Summing Up

Theatre
Twilight Bar

ARTHUR KOESTLER

BRICKS
TO BABEL

A Selection from 50 Years of His Writings,
Chosen and with
New Commentary by the Author

Random House   New York

Library of Congress Cataloging in Publication Data
Koestler, Arthur, 1905-
Bricks to Babel.
Bibliography: p.
Includes index.
I. Title.
PR602. 04B7 1981   828'.91209 80-6020
ISBN 0-394-51897-7

Manufactured in the United States of America
2 4 6 8 9 7 5 3
First American Edition 1981

CONTENTS

To Cynthia

PREFACE

This book belongs to the category known as an omnibus. It is defined in the *Concise Oxford Dictionary* as a "volume containing several stories, plays, etc., by a single author published at a low price [sic] to be within the reach of all".

As a rule, such books are compiled by an editor, who selects the items to be included and provides the commentaries. In this case, however, it is the author himself who made the selection and supplies a running commentary. To stick to the metaphor, this omnibus provides a guided tour, with the author acting as guide, pointing out the sights and deciding where to stop for a closer view.

At the time when I embarked on it, this seemed a sensible idea: after all nobody knows the landscape to be covered by the tour, its history and hidden beauties, more thoroughly and intimately than the author who created them. But soon the hideous truth dawned on me that the petrol for the omnibus was rationed; it could only cover a fraction of the landscape, as a simple calculation will show. The thirty published books, listed in the Bibliography on page 687, add up to roughly 9000 pages. The present volume, to be manageable, was not to exceed 700 pages. That meant that only 7·5 per cent of the total could be included in it; and, what is worse, that 92·5 per cent had to be left out.

The process of selection and elimination was guided by considerations not always easy to reconcile. In the first place, the volume had to be divided about equally into two parts, "Book One" and "Book Two", which correspond to the two fundamentally different periods in the author's life and work. The first – "In Search of Utopia" – was centred on politics, the second – "In Search of a Synthesis" – was devoted to science and philosophy. This vocational change occurred in my late forties, and as it was fairly unusual in our specialised age, it led to some odd consequences. Thus I sometimes meet young people who had read in college *The Sleepwalkers* or some other book on natural philosophy written after the "vocational change", and who had no idea that the same author once wrote political novels – and I meet other, more elderly people, who have read a novel called *Darkness at Noon* but never heard of any of the books written in the second period. It makes me feel sometimes as if I had undergone a change of sex. Yet one of the main purposes of this omnibus is to reflect the inseparability of the "two cultures" and the search for a synthesis which would reveal the unitary structure underlying both.

The next point to stress is that an omnibus is not an autobiography, but a selection from an author's writings. However, this author's writings include four volumes of autobiography* which themselves form an integral part of his work. I have described them as "a typical case-history of a Central European member of the educated middle classes, born in the first years of our century" – and therein lies their documentary value. It also explains why extracts from *Arrow in the Blue* and *The Invisible Writing* occupy a relatively large space in Book One. But it should be remembered that they were written when the author was still in his forties, whereas now he is in his seventies. Thus his early years are brought to light like one of those Russian dolls, enclosed in a larger doll, which is enclosed in – and so forth.

The Invisible Writing ends with the author's escape from occupied France and his settling in England, in 1940, at the age of thirty-five. My friends and publishers have frequently urged me to continue the autobiography, but from 1940 onward my life ceased to be a "typical case-history", or of any public interest, and I preferred to concentrate instead on a selection of published works – hence the present volume.

The painful process of selection and elimination became much easier once I had decided to keep polemical texts to a minimum. A considerable part of *The Ghost in the Machine, Janus* and other works is devoted to polemics against Skinnerian Behaviourism and the inadequacies of the Neo-Darwinian theory of evolution. I felt that in the long run it did not matter much if these critical parts were omitted (except for the occasional aside), as the orthodox doctrines they attacked are crumbling anyway, and in a decade or two will have vanished into limbo, as other orthodoxies have in the past. I regret nevertheless that in this process of elimination some items I was – rightly or wrongly – particularly fond of, had to fall by the wayside – including a whole book, *The Case of the Midwife Toad*. It was mainly devoted to a refutation of

Dialogue with Death, Scum of the Earth, Arrow in the Blue and *The Invisible Writing*.

the arrogant Neo-Darwinian claim that evolution, from amoeba to man, can be satisfactorily explained by chance mutations plus natural selection – and to a partial vindication of the Lamarckian claim that some of the skills and acquired characteristics of the parents are transmitted to their offspring – in other words, that evolution is based on cumulative experience and not on a game of blind man's buff.*

The conflicting claims of chronological order versus thematic unity posed the worst problems. In Book One chronological order is more or less preserved; but even so Part One and Part Five, both concerned with the same theme, had to be separated to avoid confusing the reader. Vice versa, some chapters in Book Two, dealing with theoretical subjects, are mosaics – or collages – of excerpts from several books, often written years apart, on the same theme. The Chronology at the end of the book is intended to enable the reader to restore at a glance the temporal sequence of events and the circumstances in which the works quoted were written.

Another problem was balance. The Procrustean solution of chopping off from each of the books quoted in this volume a piece of the same length would obviously not do. Some of the novels readily yielded a more or less self-contained episode; in the case of others (*The Gladiators*, for instance) much longer extracts were needed to convey something of their atmosphere. With the non-fiction books similar problems arose; they could at least be partly

*As this volume goes to press, the scientific establishment has been shaken by the experiments of a young Australian immunologist, E. J. Steele, which seem to confirm that acquired immunity against certain diseases in mice can be transmitted from one generation to the next. Steele's book, *Somatic Selection and Adaptive Evolution* (Toronto, 1979), bears the provocative sub-title "On the Inheritance of Acquired Characters". Nevertheless Steele's results were published in the Proceedings of the National Academy of Science of the USA and in leading scientific journals, and endorsed by several Nobel laureates in biology, among them Sir Peter Medawar, who wrote that, if the results are confirmed, they will "represent one of the landmarks in the history of biology". I was both surprised and cheered to learn from Steele's preface that what had caused him to embark on his revolutionary experiments was a book of mine. "When I finished reading Koestler's recent book *Janus – A Summing Up*", he wrote, "his philosophy provided that necessary inspiration to tackle, in a rational way, a long held dissatisfaction with the conventional Darwinian explanation of evolution." I mention this episode as an example that trespassers can occasionally fulfil a useful function and that cobblers need not always stick to their last.

overcome by using condensations and abstracts of earlier books in later ones. But in other cases this technique could not be applied; for instance, the excerpt from *Reflections on Hanging*, which at first glance may seem disproportionately long, would lose its impact (such as it may have) by being further compressed and stripped of detail. Thus the amount of space allocated to this or that subject does not necessarily reflect the importance attributed to it by the author, but is also influenced by the nature of the material.

I must ask the reader's indulgence for occasional repetitions – which are unavoidable in a collection of texts which often overlap.

The texts quoted are set in Roman type; the author's comments, written in 1979–80, are set in italics.

The source references refer only to chapters in the books quoted, but not to pages – as the pagination of reprints and paperbacks often differs from the pagination in the first editions.

BOOK ONE

In Search of Utopia

But, although M. de Pontverre was
a good man, he was certainly not a
virtuous man; on the contrary, he
was an enthusiast.

ROUSSEAU Confessions

PART ONE

PROMISED LAND

Chapter 1

ARROW IN THE BLUE

I was born in Budapest, in the fifth year of this century, the only child of a Hungarian father and a Viennese mother. My father was a prosperous industrialist until he went bankrupt during the inflation following the First World War. Up to 1914 we lived in Budapest; during the war years partly, and after the war permanently, in Vienna.

My childhood and youth are described in Arrow in the Blue. The following extract is condensed from chapters VI and XII:

It is reported that John Stuart Mill wrote Latin verse at the age of three. I can offer no equally impressive feat. Still, my first words in French, also pronounced at the age of three, are reliably recorded. They were addressed to a new governess and consisted in the laconic statement: "*Mademoiselle, pantalons mouillés.*"

I learnt avidly, read greedily, developed an early passion for mathematics, physics, and the construction of mechanical toys. When, around ten, I became an expert in changing fuses and repairing electric lamps and shortly after built a submarine which navigated in our bathtub, it was decided in concurrence with my own wishes that I should study engineering and physics. Accordingly, when I finished elementary school, I was sent to the *Real-schule*, which I attended for the next seven years, first in Hungary, then in Austria.

The educational system of the Austro–Hungarian Monarchy provided three types of secondary schools for pupils from the age of ten to eighteen: the *Gymnasium*, which prepared for a career in the humanities, with emphasis on Latin and Greek; the *Real-schule*, which specialised in science and modern languages; and the *Real-Gymnasium*, a mixture of the two. I went to the *Real-schule* which suited me perfectly.

From my childhood to my university days, mathematics and science were my principal interests, and chess my main hobby. I was particularly fascinated by geometry, algebra, and physics because I was convinced – much as the Pythagoreans and the alchemists had been – that these disciplines contained the clue to the mystery of existence. I believed that the problems of the universe were hidden in some well-defined secret, like the combination-lock of a safe, or the philosopher's stone. To devote oneself to the solution of this secret seemed the only purpose worth living for.

It is difficult to convey a child's delight and excitement in penetrating the mysteries of the Pythagorean triangle, or of Kepler's laws of planetary movement, or of Planck's theory of quanta. It is the excitement of the explorer who, even though his goal is limited and specialised, is always driven by an unconscious, childlike hope of stumbling upon the ultimate mystery. The Phoenician galleys journeyed over uncharted seas to find the Pillars of Hercules, and even Captain Scott may have been unknowingly tempted by the hope that perhaps there really was a hole at the South Pole in which the earth's axis turned on bearings of ice. From the star-gazers of Babylon down to the great artist-scientists of the Renaissance, the urge to explore was one of man's vital drives, and even in Goethe's day it would have been as shocking for an educated person to say that he took no interest in science as to declare that he was bored with art. The increasing volume of facts and the specialisation of research have made this interest gradually dry up and become a monopoly of technicians and specialists. From the middle of the nineteenth century onward, physics, chemistry, biology, and astrophysics began to fade out as ingredients of a rounded education. However, in pre-Relativistic days it was still just possible for the non-specialist to keep abreast of general developments in science. I grew up during the closing years of that era, before science became so formalised and abstract that it was removed from the layman's grasp.

The heroes of my youth were Darwin and Spencer, Kepler, Newton and Mach; Edison, Herz and Marconi – the Buffalo Bills of the frontiers of discovery. And my Bible was Haeckel's *Die Weltraetsel*. In this popular classic of the turn of the century, seven "riddles of the universe" were listed; of these, six appeared "definitely solved" (including the Nature of Matter and the Origin of Life) while the seventh, the question of the Freedom of the Will, was declared to be "a pure dogma, based on an illusion, and having no real existence".

It was very reassuring to know, at the age of fourteen, that the riddles of the universe had all been solved. Nevertheless, there remained a doubt in my mind, for the paradox of infinity and eternity had by some oversight not been included in the list.

Infinity and eternity – there was the rub. One day during the summer holidays, in 1919, I was lying on my back under a blue sky on a hill slope in Buda. My eyes were filled with the unbroken, unending, transparent, complacent, saturated blue above me, and I felt a mystic elation – one of those states of spontaneous illumination which are so frequent in childhood and become rarer and rarer as the years wear on. In the middle of this beatitude, the paradox of spatial infinity suddenly pierced my brain as if it had been stung by a wasp. You could shoot a super-arrow into the blue with a super-force which could carry it beyond the pull of the earth's gravity, past the moon, past the sun's attraction – and what then? It would traverse inter-stellar space, pass other suns, other galaxies, Milky Ways, Honeyed Ways, Acid Ways – and what then? It would go on and on, past the spiral nebulae, and more galaxies and more spiral nebulae, and there would be nothing to stop it, no limit and no end, in space or in time – and the worst of it was that this was not fantasy but true. It was sheer torture to the brain. The sky had no business to look so blue and smug if its smile hid the most awful secret which it was unwilling to yield, just as adults drove one crazy with their smiles when they were determined to withhold a secret, cruelly and lawlessly denying one's most sacred right – the right to know. The right to know was self-evident and inalienable – otherwise one's being here, with eyes to see with, and a mind to think with, made no sense.

The idea that infinity would remain an unsolved riddle was unbearable. The more so as I had learned that a finite quantity like the earth – or like myself reclining on it – shrank to zero when divided by an infinite quantity. So, mathematically, if space was infinite, the earth was zero and I was zero and one's life-span was zero, and a year and a century were zero. It made no sense, there was a miscalculation somewhere, and the answer to the riddle was obviously to be found by reading more books about gravity, electricity, astronomy, and higher mathematics. Had not Haeckel promised that the last riddle would be solved within a few years? Maybe I had been chosen and elected to solve it. This seemed all the more likely to me as nobody else appeared to be as excited about space and the arrow as I was.

The thirst for the absolute is a stigma which marks those unable to find satisfaction in the relative world of the now and here. My obsession with the arrow was the first phase of the quest. When it proved sterile, the Infinite as a target was replaced by Utopias of one kind or another. It was the same quest which drove me to the Promised Land and into the Communist Party.

I have a vivid image of the arrow splitting lengthwise into two. The two halves continue their flight in divergent directions, one symbolising action, the other contemplation. I can remember fairly clearly the moment when the arrow split. It was on a spring morning in 1924. I was sitting on a bench in the *Völksgarten*, one of Vienna's enchanted parks, with a pile of books beside me. On top lay a pamphlet about the latest Arab riots in Palestine, with appalling details of children put to the sword as in the days of Herod, of Jewish settlers being killed after having been blinded and castrated, of the passivity of the British Mandatory Administration and their refusal to allow the Jews to arm in self-defence.

While I was reading the pamphlet, I felt myself choke with impotent anger. Like most people who suffer from Chronic Indignation – as others do from chronic indigestion – I could feel, during an attack, the infusion of adrenalin into the bloodstream, the craving of the muscles for violent action. As the case may be, you begin to tremble, or throw a choleric fit, or write a revolutionary tract, or start growing an ulcer. When I had finished reading the pamphlet and had calmed down a little, I fell into one of my habitual reveries about devoting my life to the cause of the persecuted as a fighter and writer of books which would shake the conscience of the world.

While still in the grip of that dream, I opened the next book in the pile at its marked page. It was Herman Weyl's introduction to Einstein's theory of Relativity. A phrase suddenly struck me and has remained in my memory ever since. It said that the theory of General Relativity led the imagination "across the peaks of glaciers never before explored by any human being". I saw

Einstein's world-shaking formula – Energy equals Mass multiplied by the square of the velocity of light – hovering in a kind of rarified haze over the glaciers, and this image carried a sensation of infinite tranquillity and peace. The martyred pioneers of the Holy Land shrank to insignificance. The fate of these unfortunates had to be viewed with the same serene, detached, meditative eye as that of stars bursting into novae, of sunspots erupting, of forests decaying into swamps. This change in perspective was accompanied by a physiological change. The sensation of choking with indignation was succeeded by the relaxed quietude and self-dissolving stillness of the "oceanic feeling".*

All this sounds rather a mouthful, for to talk about one's own split personality is a special form of vanity – particularly in the case of Central Europeans fed on Goethe's "Two souls, alas, inhabit my breast". But if I am to remain truthful, the separate existence of those "two souls" must be emphasised, for the split remained with me, and the resulting tug-of-war is one of the recurrent *leitmotifs* of this report. It is reflected in the antithetical titles of several books: *The Yogi and the Commissar, Insight and Outlook, Darkness at Noon, Le Zero et l'Infini, Arrival and Departure,* and so on.

At the age of twenty, one year before I was supposed to graduate from the Polytechnic in Vienna, I abandoned my studies and became what in present parlance is called a drop-out. The decision was a sudden one, and its motivation, seen in retrospect, appears to have been not so very different from the seemingly irrational impulses of the young in the last couple of decades. The common denominator is a feeling of absurdity, of living in a world which makes no sense. Bearing this in mind, the following extract from Arrow in the Blue† *may perhaps appear less bizarre:*

One night in October 1925, I came home late after a long discussion on free will and determinism with a Russian student named Orochov. Orochov was a socialist and the nearest incarnation of a Dostoyevskian character that I have met; he seemed to have stepped straight out of *The Possessed.* He was ugly, warm-hearted,

*The term coined by Romain Rolland and used by Freud to denote mystic or religious experience.
†*Ch.* xv

tormented and sincere. A year later he committed suicide to escape the squalor of extreme poverty, by jumping at night from a bridge into the frozen Danube.

During that discussion in Orochov's bare room, he had stubbornly defended the determinist position, while I maintained that, within certain limits, man has freedom of decision and ultimate mastery of his fate. We had had no alcohol, only pints of weak tea, but I went away feeling drunk and elated. It was raining hard and, having no hat or umbrella, I exulted in getting drenched and letting the rain get inside my collar and slide in an icy trickle down my spine. The streets were deserted. I got home and, in a state of manic exaltation, lit a match and slowly burnt my Matriculation Book. This document, in Austria called *Index*, was the student's sacred passport; in it were entered the examinations he had passed, the courses he had attended and other relevant details concerning his studies. The burning of my *Index* was a literal burning of my boats, and the end of my prospective career as a respectable citizen and member of the engineering profession.

The reason for that act of apparent lunacy was a sudden enamouredness with unreason itself. The discussion with Orochov had brought on a condition which I can only describe as a severe shock of "oceanic feeling"; and in that condition all values are reversed. It appeared to me as a self-evident truth that reason was absurd. Already Kant had proved that reason had to abdicate before the problems that really mattered, like eternity and infinity. Einstein had given the *coup de grâce* to commonsense. Freud, in a different sphere, had completed the process. The inflation, with prices of a thousand Kronen for a loaf of bread, had reduced economic standards to complete absurdity. Old G's tragic end had demonstrated what a life guided by homely reason and respectability led up to. Life was a chaos and to embark on a reasonable career in the midst of chaos was madness. All this may sound like a tenuous intellectual construction; but at the time I felt it very intensely — so much so that people who ordered their lives according to the dictates of reason appeared to me as only deserving contempt and pity.

I had no plans except "to lead my own life". In order to do that I had to "get off the track". This metaphorical track I visualised as an endless stretch of steel rails on rotting sleepers. You were born on to a certain track as a train is put on its run according to the timetable; and once on the track, you no longer had free will. Your life was determined, as Orochov maintained, by outside forces:

the rail of steel, stations, shunting points. If you accepted that condition, running on rails became a habit which you could no longer break. The point was to jump off the track before the habit was formed, before you became encased in a rattling prison.

My parents were both of Jewish origin, but completely estranged from the Judaic religion and tradition, and I was brought up in the same assimilated, liberal spirit. Nevertheless, as an undergraduate, I joined a Zionist duelling fraternity, and became one of the founders of the Austrian branch of Jabotinsky's League of Zionist Activists.* Thus I came to Judaism from outside, as it were; a volunteer, rather, than a victim of persecution.

A few months after I broke off my studies, I set out for the Holy Land to join one of the early Kibbutzim – Heftzeba, on Mount Gilboa – to till the soil of Utopia.

The student fraternity turned out in full strength in their colourful regalia on the railway platform and sang the Zionist anthem. Then came the loveliest music to the ears of a young man heading for adventure: the whistle, puff and jolt of the train pulling out of the station.

*Which later gave birth to Begin's terrorist movement, the Irgun.

Chapter 2

KIBBUTZ LIFE IN THE 'TWENTIES*

The Zionist settlers started from the conviction that the Jews could only be reborn as a nation if they acquired a social structure like other nations, with a solid base of farmers and manual labourers. In order to become normal again, they had to reverse the social pyramid of the ghetto where for centuries they had been condemned to the parasitic existence of money-lenders, traders and middlemen. The promised land could only become truly theirs if they tilled its soil with their own hands. "If I spend not my strength I shall not gather the crop," wrote the Hebrew poet Byalik.

This new insight shaped the character of the Zionist movement. The cry "back to the land" did not spring from a romantic whim; it expressed a historical necessity.

Once this necessity was recognised, it was developed with characteristic Jewish exuberance into an almost mystic worship of manual work, of "labour which ennobles". The cult of labour became ideologically fused with Marxist class-concepts, with Tolstoyan ethics and Jewish messianism. This curious blend of national renaissance and socialist Utopia became incarnated in its purest form in the collective settlements or communes, which gave Israel its unique character as a social experiment.

My destination was one of these collective settlements – Kvutsa Heftsebā – in the Valley of Yesreel. Kvutsa means "group" or "community" and was used to designate the older type of collective settlements before being superseded by "Kibbutz". Heftsebā

*From Promise and Fulfilment, ch. IV, and Arrow in the Blue, ch. XVI.

*is the Arab name for the hillside where the settlement was
established.*

The Valley of Yesreel sweeps in a broad arc from the Mediterranean to the Jordan. In Biblical times it was, and it is again today,
the most fertile plain in Palestine. In 1926 it was still mostly a
stony desert, infested with malaria, typhus, and marauding
Bedouin tribesmen. The hills bordering the valley were dotted
with Arab mud villages, dissolving by an act of natural mimicry in
the violet haze of earth and rock. Down in the plain sprawled the
first Jewish pioneer settlements, a conspicuous eyesore with their
white, cubic, concrete buildings. They were a challenge to the
landscape and its native inhabitants.

Heftsebā was at that time the settlement farthest to the east, that
is, deepest in purely Arab territory. It also had the worst climate,
for it lay some three hundred feet below sea level. (The Valley of
Yesreel slopes down towards the east until it reaches the Jordan
valley, the deepest depression in the surface of the earth.) In
summer the heat was stifling, aggravated by the Khamsin, a hot
desert wind with a peculiarly unnerving effect – ancient Turkish
law considered it a mitigating circumstance if a murder was
committed during a Khamsin. Mosquitoes, flies, cockroaches and
bugs of all varieties abounded – the only abundance which nature
provided in that region, for the earth was arid and stony, and had
not seen a plough for a millennium and a half before the settlers of
Heftsebā arrived. The settlers were nearly all lawyers, architects,
docors of philosophy from Vienna and Prague. They had had no
previous experience in agriculture and in hard manual labour.
The settlement was built at the foot of Mount Gilboa, the hill
where Joshua defeated the Amorites and bade the sun stand still.

I arrived at Heftsebā one evening in April, 1926. The first sight
of the settlement was a shock. I had disembarked at Haifa a few
days before, and was still dazed by the picturesque and colourful
oriental scenery of its port and Arab bazaars. Now I found myself
in a rather dismal and slumlike oasis in the wilderness, consisting
of wooden huts, surrounded by dreary vegetable plots. The huts
were not the log cabins made familiar by illustrations of the
American pioneering age, but ramshackle dwellings in which
only the poorest in Europe would live, as an alternative to the
discarded railway carriage. The only buildings made of concrete
were the cowshed and a square, white house where the children of
the settlement lived together, separated from their parents. I don't

know what I had imagined the settlement would look like; but certainly not like this.

It was dinner-time when I arrived; the men and women were assembled in the wooden barrack that served as a communal dining hall. They sat on benches at tables made of rough deal planks on trestles. Most of them were between twenty and thirty but gave the impression of being much older, for they all looked weary and physically exhausted; they slumped over their plates, elbows on table, and spooned their soup in silence, too tired to talk. Their faces were sunburnt but not healthy. Many showed the yellowish tint of malaria; the women's features were coarsened by the climate and hard work. Nobody asked what my business was or took any interest in me as I came in. At least so I thought; only later did I become aware of the silent, intense scrutiny to which the newcomer's smallest actions were subjected by the community.

I asked for Guetig, one of the leaders of the commune [and an Old Boy of my student fraternity], who had been advised of my impending arrival. I was told that he was ill with malaria. Without further comment, the man to whom I had spoken moved closer to his neighbour on the bench to make room for me. I sat down, and from the head of the table a plate of soup and a chunk of bread were passed along, but still neither of my neighbours inquired who I was or what I wanted. It was, and still is, one of the basic rules of the Palestine communes that the wayfarer be given food and a bed without payment or questions asked.

Dinner consisted of onion soup, bread, goat's cheese and olives. The midday meal on the next day was the same; breakfast consisted of tea and a salad of onions and raw vegetables. Meat was served once a week, on the Sabbath.

Eventually I got into conversation with my right-hand neighbour. He was dark and haggard, with thick-lensed glasses on a deeply-furrowed face which expressed strength, intelligence and mildness. His name was Loebl – Dr Loebl, in fact; it appears in the dedication of my novel on Palestine, Thieves in the Night.

I explained to Loebl that I had come with the intention of joining the commune. "For good?" he asked, without looking up from his plate. I said I didn't know; that I would like to work here for a year or two, and later perhaps find a job in Tel Aviv, or go into politics. Loebl said nothing. He was spooning his soup and chewing his bread, concentrating on his food in the manner of men who are engaged in a constant struggle to keep up their physical strength. The gravely ill eat in that way, and people in concentration camps who know that every lost calory is a lost chance of survival. After a while he explained that because of the economic depression there were more candidates for the collective settlements than these could absorb. On seeing my dismayed expression, he added that he would talk to the Secretary – the Secretary is the mayor and leader of the commune – and see whether it could be arranged that I should stay for a few weeks on probation.

Before being accepted as a member of a commune, each candidate has to pass through a probationary stage – a kind of novitiate – during which his physical qualities and social adaptability are weighed and measured by the community. As I found out much later, during that short talk with Loebl I had in fact already been weighed and found wanting. One did not enter a commune, any more than a convent or a monastic order, "for a year or two". In more recent times it has become a custom for young people to spend six months or a year on a collective farm before embarking on a career in the towns. But in the early days, to enter a *Kvutsa* meant dedication for a lifetime.

I was given a bed in a bare, stiflingly hot little room which I shared with two other men. The room was part of a hut, the other half of which was occupied by a married couple. Through the thin wooden partition we could hear every word and every sound as if they lived in the same room with us. This lack of privacy, which extended to the communal shower-room and the communal latrine, was an even greater nervous strain on the settlers than the fight against disease and physical exhaustion. It was a principle of all communes that the care of children and cattle came first, and care of the adult human element later. Thus the first concrete building to be erected had been the cowshed and next had come the children's house; while the men and women of the settlement continued to live in tents and shacks, often for many years. This self-imposed hardship was partly dictated by poverty, partly by the settlers' collectivist ideology. The *Kvutsa* was regarded by its members as a mystic community in which not only property but also one's thoughts, feelings, and the most intimate aspects of life ought to be shared – with the only exclusion of sexual life. Promiscuous tendencies were considered signs of individual selfishness and social maladjustment. Sexual conflicts and tragedies did, of course, occur but they were exceptional – mainly, one may suppose, because the sexual appetites were blunted by fatigue and by the neutralising effect of familiarity.

This, incidentally, led to the curious phenomenon of a kind of
incest-barrier developing between men and women within the
same commune – with a resulting trend toward exogamy, a preference to marry outsiders.

The morning after my arrival I was assigned to work on a steep,
sloping field, which was intended to become a future vegetable
plot. As yet it was only a staked-out stretch of arid waste which
seemed to contain more stones than earth. The stones had to be
picked up one by one and carried away in baskets. When a small
area was cleared of the bigger stones, it was hacked up in ridges
with a hoe. After an hour or two of this work, my hands were
blistered, my head, covered with a wet handkerchief, swam, and
my bones felt as if stretched on the rack. Loebl, who was in charge
of the gang working in that field, watched me out of the corner of
his eye and repeatedly told me to fall out and take a rest. The
second and third days were no better; only towards the end of the
first week did I gradually begin to pick up the rhythm of the work
and the technique of economising energy with every movement.

My probationary period lasted some four or five weeks. I did my
best to hide my aversion for the spade – that rusty, clotted spade,
so different from the gleaming symbol of my dreams of freedom.
But in a small community, where everybody is constantly under
the scrutiny of everybody else, it is impossible to hide any trait of
character; even a passing mood, a momentary shadow of discontent, the first hint of friendship and animosity are immediately
known to all. This is not a result of gossip or spying on each other,
but rather of a kind of sixth sense which the closely knit community develops, and which registered individual disturbances with
the precision of a seismograph. It gives the member of the *Kvutsa* a
curious feeling of being transparent – as if he were living under an
X-ray camera and had nowhere to hide. This leads in most cases
sooner or later to a psychological crisis. About one person out of
every two is unable to stand up to the strain and leaves the *Kvutsa*
in the second or third year. The remaining half become more or
less permanently adjusted; and in another few years they become
unfit for any other form of life.

At the end of my probationary period, Loebl told me with great
gentleness that the Members' Assembly had decided to give preference to two other candidates who were physically and mentally better equipped for *Kvutsa* life than I. I received the news
with mixed feelings of dejection and half-conscious relief. The
handicaps which I have mentioned were real; but had I felt the

true vocation, I would probably have overcome them. At the same time, the collapse of my plans was a bitter disappointment, and though it is obvious that I was completely unfit for that kind of life, it is even today painful to remember that I failed.

No doubt my dismay was partly caused by hurt pride; but to an equal extent by the fact that during those short weeks I had grown very fond of Loebl, Guetig and others, and had come under the strange lure of *Kvutsa* life. The nature of this attraction is difficult to convey. The *Kvutsa* in its early days was a socialist monastery and at the same time a wildly romantic pioneering adventure. To stand guard in the moonlight with an old rifle at the foot of Mount Gilboa was an experience not easy to forget. Nor the bliss of the peaceful Sabbath mornings when physical rest, the clean shirt from the communal laundry, and the meat at dinner were savoured as rare luxuries. Nor the undefinable feeling of growing roots in an untamed spot, and of growing human ties of a quality unknown elsewhere — organic ties as binding as the climbing plants which make separate trees grow into an indivisible living tangle. I believe that never since the primitive Christian communities have such strange brotherhoods existed as in the early days of the communal settlements in Palestine.

Life in a *Kvutsa* meant — and still means in some parts of the country, such as the Negeb Desert — a life of heroic poverty and of grim struggles on the borderline of human endurance. The institutions and amenities of normal society were absent. No uniformed policemen or gendarmes protected the settlers in a hostile land; they had to wield with one hand the plough and with the other the sword, as in the days of Ezra after the return from the Babylonian exile. All forms of hired labour were barred from the communal settlements. So was private property and the use of money. The member of the commune was supposed to work to the limit of his capacity and receive the bare necessities of existence in return. He was housed and fed and provided with soap and toothbrush, working clothes and reading matter, postage stamps and contraceptives, from the communal store, free of charge. His children were brought up under the care of nurses and teachers in the communal children's house. Money was only used by the Treasurer of the commune in his transactions with the outer world; but even these transactions were largely on paper. The necessities of the commune were bought on credit from the co-operative stores of the Hebrew trade unions, and the produce of the commune was sold to another branch of the same co-operative

organisation. Children born and brought up in a collective settlement never saw a banknote or a coin; they had literally no notion
of the value of money and the ways of handling it.

All this led to a curious estrangement from reality. Life in the
Kvutsa was hard, but at the same time free from economic cares,
from the worries of a normal social existence. The commune took
charge of all of man's needs from the cradle to the grave.

At the time of my first stay in Kvutsa Heftsebā, there existed
some twenty or thirty collective settlements in Palestine. When
the independence of Israel was proclaimed, their number had
grown to some one hundred and twenty; as this is written [1951]
there are more than two hundred. Unlike other Utopian experiments, from Spartacus's Sun City to the "New Harmony" of the
Owenites, all of which have collapsed after a short time, the
Palestine communes have succeeded in establishing themselves
as stable forms of rural society; in some of the oldest settlements
the children now belong to the third native generation. Indeed,
the most remarkable thing about the Kvutsa is that is has survived.

It would be a mistake, however, to overestimate the social
significance of these unique communities, or to use them as
models for experiments on a mass scale. The members of the
collective settlements are an élite of volunteers; the rigours of
their existence are self-imposed. It would be impossible to build
any similar society by compulsion, just as it would be impossible
to compel a large section of the population to take monastic vows.
Even the voluntary settlers, with their spirit of fervent self-
sacrifice, had to make concessions and mitigate the harshness of
the original collectivist doctrine. During the forty years which
have elapsed since the first collective settlement was founded in
Dagania on the shores of Lake Tiberias, the structure of the Kvutsa
has undergone a gradual reform. The settlers are now permitted
certain private possessions, from clothing to radio sets and other
small comforts of life. In most collective settlements small children are allowed to live with their parents instead of being segregated in the communal children's house. Some settlements have
ceased to be purely agricultural and run industrial plants and
craft shops of their own. Others allow their members pocket
money which they can spend as they please. Mixed farms, half-
way between collective and co-operative farming, have sprung up
here and there. But this organic evolution does not diminish the
value and achievement of the early pioneers, and the moral inspiration which the budding nation of Israel derived from them.

I have frequently re-visited Hetfsebā – and many other collective settlements – since my abortive attempt to settle in the shadow of Mount Gilboa. The idea of writing a novel around life in a *Kvutsa* attracted me from the beginning; it was the first subject for a novel which occurred to me. It did not materialise until twenty years later, in *Thieves in the Night*, written in 1945.

Chapter 3

THE HORNS OF THE DILEMMA*

The account of Kibbutz life in the previous chapter referred to the relatively peaceful period of the nineteen-twenties. The following extracts from the novel Thieves in the Night *describe the founding of a new Kibbutz in 1937, in the days of growing Arab unrest. It is a nocturnal, paramilitary action, following a set routine, intended to take the Arab villagers in the neighbourhood by surprise. The fortified camp, with its watch-tower, tents, huts, parapets and barbed-wire fences, is erected in a single night, surrounded by the symbolic furrow which, according to Arab custom, indicates effective possession.*

The site of the new settlement in the novel is a few miles from "Gan Tamar", an older Kibbutz which serves as a base for the operation. The account is fictitious, but based on personal experience as a witness of one such episode.

. . .So far, in a seemingly leisurely, almost casual way, everything had gone according to plan.

At 1 a.m. the forty boys of the Haganah, who were to form the vanguard, had assembled in the communal dining-hut of Gan Tamar, the old settlement from where the expedition was to start. In the large, vaulted, empty dining-hall the boys looked very young, awkward and sleepy. They were mostly under nineteen, born in the country, sons and grandsons of the first settlers from Petakh Tikwah, Rishon le Zion, Metullah, Nahalal. Hebrew for them was the native tongue, not a precariously acquired art; the Country their country, neither promise nor fulfilment. Europe for them was a

---

*From Thieves in the Night.

legend of glamour and frightfulness, the new Babylon, land of exile
where their elders sat by the rivers and wept. They were mostly
blond, freckled, broad-featured, heavy-boned and clumsy; farmers' sons, peasant lads, un-Jewish-looking and slightly dull.
They were haunted by no memories and had nothing to forget.
They had no ancient curse upon them and no hysterical hopes; they
had the peasant's love for the land, the schoolboy's patriotism, the
self-righteousness of a very young nation. They were Sabras –
nicknamed after the thorny, rather tasteless fruit of the cactus,
grown on arid earth, tough, hard-living, scant.

There was also a sprinkling of Europeans among them, immigrants from the new Babylon. They had gone through the hard,
ascetic training of Hekhalutz and Hashomer Hatzair, youth movements which united the fervour of a religious order with the
dogmatism of a socialist debating club. Their faces were darker,
narrower, keener; they bore the stigma of the "things to forget". It
was there in the sharper bend of the nasal bone, the bitter sensu-
ousness of fleshier lips, the knowing look in moister eyes. They
looked nervous and overstrung amidst the phlegmatic and sturdy
Sabras; more enthusiastic and less reliable.

They all sat round the raw deal tables of the dining-hall, heavy
with sleep and silent. The naked bulbs suspended on wires from
the ceiling gave a bleak, cheerless light; the chipped salt-cellars
and oil cruets formed pointless little oases on the empty communal
tables.

At last Bauman, the leader of the detachment, arrived. He wore
riding breeches and a black leather jacket – a relic from the
street-fighting in Vienna in 1934, when the malignant dwarf
Dollfuss had ordered his field guns to fire point-blank into the
balconies, lined with geranium-boxes and drying linen, of the
workers' tenements in Floridsdorf, crossing himself after each
salvo. Bauman had received his leather jacket and his illegal but
thorough military training in the ranks of the Schutzbund; he had
the round, jovial face of a Viennese baker's boy; only in the rare
moments when he was tired or angry did it reveal the imprint of the
things to forget. In his case there were two: the fact that his people
had happened to live behind one of those little balconies with the
geranium-boxes; and the warm, moist feeling on his face of the
spittle of a humorous jailer in the prison of Graz every morning at
six o'clock when breakfast was doled out in the cells.

"Well, you lazy bums," Bauman said, "get up; attention; stand
over there."

His Hebrew was rather bumpy. He lined them up along the wall dividing the dining-hall from the kitchen.

"The lorries will be here in twenty minutes," he said, rolling himself a cigarette. "Most of you know what it's all about. The land which we are going to occupy, about fifteen hundred acres, was bought by our National Fund several years ago from an absentee Arab landowner named Zaid Effendi el Mussa, who lives in Beirut and has never seen it. It consists of a hill on which the new settlement, Ezra's Tower, will be erected, of the valley surrounding it and some pastures on nearby slopes. The hill is a mess of rocks and has not seen a plough for the last thousand years, but there are traces of ancient terracing dating back to our days. In the valley a few fields were worked by Arab tenants of Zaid Effendi's, who live in the neighbouring village of Kfar Tabiyeh. They have been paid compensation amounting to about three times the value of the land so that they were able to buy better plots on the other side of their village; one of them has even built himself an ice factory in Jaffa.

"Then there is a Bedouin tribe which, without Zaid Effendi's knowledge, used to graze their camels and sheep each spring on the pastures. Their sheikh has been paid compensation. When all this was settled, the villagers of Kfar Tabiyeh suddenly remembered that part of the hill did not belong to Zaid, but was *masha'a* land, that is communal property of the village. This part consists of a strip about eighty yards in width running straight to the top of the hill and cutting it in two. According to law *masha'a* land can only be sold with the consent of all members of the village. Kfar Tabiyeh has 563 souls distributed over eleven *hamulles* or clans. The elders of each clan had to be bribed separately, and the thumbprints of each of the 563 members obtained, including the babes' and village idiot's. Three villagers had emigrated years ago to Syria; they had to be traced and bribed. Two were in prison, two had died abroad, but there was no documentary proof of their deaths; it had to be obtained. When all was finished, each square foot of arid rock had cost the National Fund about the price of a square foot in the business centres of London or New York. . . ."

He threw his cigarette away and wiped his right cheek with the palm of his hand. It was a habit which originated from his experience with the humorous jailer in Graz.

"It took two years to finish these little formalities. When they were finished, the Arab rebellion broke out. The first attempt to take possession of the place failed. The prospective settlers were received with a hail of stones from the villagers of Kfar Tabiyeh and had to give up. At the second attempt, undertaken in greater strength, they were shot at and lost two men. That was three months ago. You are making today the third attempt, and this time we shall succeed. By tonight the stockade, the watch-tower and the first living-huts will have been erected on the hill.

"Our detachment is going to occupy the site before dawn. A second detachment will accompany the convoy of the settlers which will start two hours later. The Arabs will not know before daybreak. Trouble during the day is unlikely. The critical time will be the first few nights. But by then the Place will be fortified.

"Some of our cautious big-heads in Jerusalem wanted us to wait for quieter times. The Place is isolated, the next Hebrew settlement eleven miles away and there is no road; it is surrounded by Arab villages; it is close to the Syrian frontier from which the terrorists infiltrate. These are precisely the reasons why we have decided not to wait. – That's all. We have five minutes left; single file into the kitchen for coffee."

At 1.20 a.m. Bauman and the forty boys got into three lorries and drove with dimmed headlights out through the gates of the settlement.

*   *   *

The Mukhtar of Kfar Tabiyeh was the only man in the village who slept in pyjamas. The other Mukhtar, who lived at the other end of the village, slept in his clothes on a mat, Bedouin fashion.

At 6.30 a.m. the Mukhtar was woken by Issa, his eldest son. Issa had been standing for quite a while next to the bed not daring to touch his father; his close-set, slightly squinting eyes in the pale, pock-marked face were anxiously fixed on the enormous bulk in the blue-and-yellow striped pyjamas. The Mukhtar had thrown the blanket off in his sleep; his crumpled pyjama-jacket had slipped upward, revealing a strip of brownish skin covered with black fluff just above the navel. Issa averted his eyes from his father's nakedness. He held a small cup of bitter coffee in his hand which would soon get cold and thus lead to violent unpleasantness. His eyes shifted nervously round the whitewashed room, bare except for the bed, the straw mat, some low wicker stools and a flypaper hanging from the ceiling. The wall opposite the bed was adorned with a coloured paper fan and portrait prints of General Allenby and a smirking person in striped trousers with a carnation in his buttonhole, who looked like a ladies' hairdresser from Leeds and at closer scrutiny proved to be Mr Neville Chamberlain. The portraits were each decorated with a bunch of dry cornflower stalks as a token of the Mukhtar's loyalty, and a chain of blue glass beads to protect Mr Chamberlain against the Evil Eye.

The coffee was getting cold. Issa cleared his throat. "Father," he called. "Welcome, Father."

The Mukhtar woke at once, and with one sudden heave got himself into an erect sitting position.

"Welcome twice," he said, reaching for the coffee. He knew that they would not dare to wake him without urgent reason and waited to be told, his heavy bloodshot eyes on his son's insipid face, gulping the bitter coffee with noisy sips.

"Father, they have occupied the Hill of Dogs," said Issa. Hill of Dogs was the name by which the villagers of Kfar Tabiyeh called the Place, derived from some old legendary event which they had forgotten.

The Mukhtar heaved himself out of bed, ignored the slippers which his son held out for him and, barefooted, walked out to the balcony. The sun had risen about an hour ago, and already the air was hot. He leaned heavily with his palms on the parapet of red bricks which, with gaps left between each adjoining pair, made a kind of horizontal lattice. Beyond the Mukhtar's house there were only a few clay huts which formed the outposts of the village, then the sparsely terraced slope down to the valley. The valley was arid and stony with a few patches of black, ploughed-up earth; on its further side rose the equally arid Hill of Dogs. The top of the hill seemed to swarm with tiny black crawling figures. In the midst of that busy antheap something like a vertical match-stick could be made out: the watch-tower.

With slow, deliberate chewing movements the Mukhtar gathered the saliva in his mouth, masticated it and spat over the parapet. He cursed softly and savagely under his breath, then turned to Issa.

"Why are you standing about, you pock-marked mule? Get my war glass."

The youth jumped and returned a moment later with a heavy and impressive telescope of brass. It was a relic of the Turkish Army, in which the Mukhtar had fought as an officer against General Allenby's forces in the First World War. He adjusted the glass and the Hill of Dogs jumped from a distance of two miles to one or two hundred yards. The panelled frame of the watch-tower, now visible in detail, dominated the scene; on its top one could see the

cyclopean reflector-eye which at night would blink its messages to
the intruders' confederates, defiling the peaceful darkness of the
hills. Around the tower there were the messy beginnings of a camp
with tangled barbed wire, trenches and dug-outs, several tents and
the first wall of a pre-fabricated wooden hut in the process of
erection. And all around bustling figures, digging, hammering and
running about in undignified, alien hurry in their loathsome
clothes, bareheaded in open shirts; and their loathsome shameless
women with naked bulging calves and thighs, and nipples bursting through tight shirts – whores, harlots, bitches and daughters of
bitches. . . .

The Mukhtar let the glass sink. His face had become a greyish
yellow, as in an attack of malaria, and his eyes were bloodshot. His
stomach almost turned over at the thought that henceforth every
morning when he got up the first thing to meet his eyes would be
this abomination, this defilement, this brazen challenge of the
intruders. Dogs on the Hill of Dogs, dropping their filth, wallowing
in it, building their citadel of filth. . . . It was finished. The whole
landscape was spoilt. Never again would he, the Mukhtar of Kfar
Tabiyeh, be allowed to enjoy the use of his own balcony. His eyes
would no longer rest in peace on God's creation, watch the fellaheen in the valley walking behind their wooden ploughs in
dignified leisure, watch the sheep flocking over the slopes – they
would be drawn to that one spot in which the whole landscape had
become focused, that poisoned fountain of evil, the well of blasphemy and temptation. . . .

From inside the house he heard the slow clop-clop of the old
man's stick on the stone floor. Issa, who had also heard it, quickly
brought his father's clothes. The Mukhtar got into his long, wide
skirt, pulled the striped vest over his pyjamas, wrapped the kefiyeh
round his head, lifted the coiled agál with both hands into the air
like a crown and adjusted it on top of the kefiyeh. He had just
finished dressing when the old man, stick in front, emerged on the
balcony. Disregarding his son's and grandson's greetings, he
advanced with small firm steps to the parapet, rested his stick on its
top and lifted his blind face towards the hills. "Where?" he asked
with a curt, commanding bellow. His sparse white goat's-beard
stuck out in front, and his bony nose with the hawk's bend seemed
to sniff the air for the smell of the intruders.

"Over there, on the Dogs' Hill," the Mukhtar said submissively,
guiding the stick in the old man's hand towards the spot.

The old man gave no answer; he stood erect and motionless at the parapet, his face lifted to the hills. Issa, avoiding the Mukhtar's eye, had disappeared into the house. The Mukhtar stood behind his father like a waiter in attendance, his big, heavy body slumped into guilty shapelessness. At last he could bear the old man's silence no longer.

"It is not my fault," he said in a throaty, plaintively bumptious voice. "The whole village wanted to sell. They would have sold even against my will, the dogs, and we would have got nothing."

The old man made no answer and no move.

"I only got eight hundred," said the Mukhtar, "and they would have sold anyway. I could do nothing. They cheated us, the swine. In Khubeira they paid six pounds for the dunum and another five hundred to the Mukhtar."

The old man again said nothing and after a while turned round and hobbled back into the house, his stick stepping in front.

The Mukhtar listened to the receding clop-clop on the tiles. By God, he thought, what does he know? He sees nothing and understands nothing of the world. By God. . . .

He retreated into his bedroom without turning again towards the hill; but in the centre of his back, between the shoulder-blades, he felt its contemptuous stare like the stare of the Evil Eye.

*   *   *

Pursuing his thoughts, the Mukhtar had completed his walk and arrived home; he put on his slippers, ordered his water pipe and sat down under Mr Chamberlain's portrait to continue his lonely meditation. The quiet bubbling of the pipe soothed his mind, while his hands were engaged in pushing the yellow amber beads of his rosary. Oh, to wake up in the morning and to look at the hill and to see the watch-tower gone and those creeping insects vanished like jinnis in the light; and to breathe the pure air and behold the peaceful country with its silent hills. . . . By God, it shall be.

Now that he had made up his mind, he felt relaxed and at peace with himself. For beneath the surface of his boisterousness he knew himself to be a weak, corrupt and greedy man; but he also knew that his love for the hills and his country was genuine, and that he would defend it against the intruders with cunning, courage and ruse, with smiles and treachery, and was quite prepared, at least as long as his present mood lasted, to get himself hanged for complicity with the terrorists, and not even to twitch when they slipped the coiled rope over his head.

*   *   *

By 9 a.m. the rough path from the dirt track to the hill top had been sufficiently cleared for the heavy trucks to move up. Their unloading started at once. The empty trucks were formed into a convoy and sent back to Gan Tamar to fetch the rest of the materials. Some of the Helpers were beginning to think of a break, but there was to be none until twelve o'clock.

At 10.45 the watch-post reported the approach of Arabs from the direction of Kfar Tabiyeh. Bauman had already spotted them from the tower. They were a strange procession. In front walked two barefooted children in their loose, striped kaftans which looked like nightgowns. Behind them three or four women in black, also barefooted. Behind these the men, about ten of them, in striped skirts and European jackets, their naked feet in string-laced shoes. They were unarmed except for some shepherds' sticks. They came unhurriedly up the slope; the children's faces looked scared, the women's vacant, the men's watchful and blank.

As they approached the barbed wire, the Hebrews working on the site lifted their heads, gave them a short look and went on working, pretending to ignore their presence. Their faces had become taut and shut; the quiet elation of the work had gone. Bauman and Reuben met the Arabs at the barbed wire. The Arabs came slowly up to them, the women and children falling back, the men approaching the fence with a negligent stroll. They saw the symbolic furrow, and their eyes followed the furrow's course around the site.

"Marhaba," said one of them, "welcome."

"Welcome twice," Reuben said.

The Arabs started moving along the fence towards the end which was not yet fenced in. But where the barbed wire ended the boss of the Haganah stood leaning on their rifles, wooden-faced, barring their way.

"We want to come in," one of the Arabs said. He looked more like a Turk and smiled blandly.

"Two of you are welcome to come in," said Reuben. His Arabic, as his Hebrew, was fluent and businesslike.

"God," cried another Arab, an excitable little man with one eye, "can't we even walk on the land of our fathers and of our own?"

"The land is ours," said Reuben, "and there are people working who should not be disturbed. But if you come in a few days' time you are welcome to share our meal."

"We came to talk," said the Turk, smiling over the stumps of some decaying teeth.

"Then come in and be welcome – the two of you."

"Don't go," said the excitable one. "Who knows what will happen? God, and on our own land. . . ."

"Come, ya Abu Tafidi. We shall go in and talk to them," said the Turk.

"Don't go, ya Abu Tafidi," cried the excitable one. "These men are bad, otherwise they would let us all in."

The Arabs parleyed loudly among themselves, while the Hebrews watched them with expressionless faces. Finally the Turk and Abu Tafidi walked into the camp, while the others squatted down outside the barbed wire. Abu Tafidi was a member of the Mukhtar's clan; in fact he was his cousin, great-uncle and son-in-law all at the same time; and yet, owing to the caprices of heredity, he belonged to a different type. He was a tall and bony old man with a distinguished stoop about his shoulder and a quiet, pensive way of speech. The Turk was fattish, smooth-mannered and jaunty. They exchanged compliments with Bauman and Reuben, sat down at the foot of the tower and started earnestly to discuss the weather and the crops. In due course the Turk came to the point. Smiling, emphatic and with every sign of sincerity, he explained that the settlers – nice, strong young people to whom he wished every good in the world – were victims of a cruel mistake in starting to build on this hill, for the land was not theirs and shortly of course they would have to evacuate it, according to the law. So why not go in peace at once, to avoid unpleasantness and remain friends? – He spoke with great simplicity, in a rapid and friendly way, while his hands milled round in smooth swift gestures as in a deaf-mute pantomime.

Reuben interrupted him. "What is this nonsense about the land not being ours?" he asked evenly.

The Turk laughed as if at an excellent joke. But surely, he explained, they all knew the law – the law of 1935 about the protection of tenants in cases of transfer of land? Of course the settlers knew it, they only played the innocents – and he winked his eye and slapped his knees and shook his finger at Reuben and Bauman, while the old man looked on, silent and impassive. Of course, the Turk went on, the settlers had offered some compensation to the dispossessed tenants, but was it enough? Was it fair? Of course it was not. The law guaranteed protection to dispossessed tenants, and the law was sacred. And if some of the tenants, poor, ignorant, uneducated fools, had in momentary confusion agreed to take some compensation money and signed some paper which they did not understand – what did that mean, and who was to prove that such an agreement was valid? "Oh, come, come," the Turk said with paternal affability, "you are educated young people, you have been to schools and universities, surely you know all this? Surely you want to act according to the law, and avoid trouble and bloodshed?"

Bauman and Reuben both rose at the same time, without having exchanged a glance. "We must get on with our work," said Bauman. "This land has been lawfully acquired, and there is nothing more to be said about it."

The Turk's face had grown a shade darker; it looked as if he had never smiled.

"You young fools and children of death," he said quietly. "You don't know what may happen to you."

"We are prepared," Bauman said curtly.

There was a moment's silence. One of Bauman's boys came up to them, carrying a copper tray with four small cups of unsweetened coffee. The Turk, after a short hesitation, took his cup; the old man refused. They sipped their coffee standing. Then the old man spoke for the first time.

"I know not much about the law," he said; his voice was gentle, almost soft. "A man who is rich and cunning may offer money to another one who is poor and ignorant, and this other man may sell his cattle and his hut. There is no justice in this. This hill belonged to our fathers and our fathers' fathers."

"And before that, it belonged to our fathers' fathers," said Bauman.

"So the books say. But your ancestors lost it. A country which one has lost one cannot buy back with money."

"This hill has borne no crop since our ancestors left it," said Reuben. "You have neglected the land. You let the terraces fall to ruin, and the rain carried the earth away. We shall clean the hill of the stones and bring tractors and fertilisers."

"What the valley bears is enough for us," said the old man. "Where God put stones, man should not carry them away. We shall live as our fathers lived and we do not want your money and your tractors and your fertilisers, and we do not want your women, whose sight offends the eye."

He had spoken angrily, but without raising his voice, as one accustomed to see young men take his words reverently and in blind obedience.

"Our ideas differ," Bauman said with polite finality. "And now I believe we have said all that is to be said."

The old man turned silently on his heels and walked out of the camp. The Turk hesitated, then said with a certain reluctance:

"The fellaheen of Kfar Tabiyeh are peaceful men. There are Arab Patriots in the hills around who are not so peaceful. You have been warned." He lowered his voice and added in a confidential tone: ". . .This warning our Mukhtar charged me to transmit to you, as a sign of his goodwill, although the Patriots would pay him ill if they knew about it."

Bauman chuckled softly. "Your Mukhtar is a wise man," he said. "Nobody likes to see his house blown up by soldiers. Your Mukhtar is like a fox who lives in a hole with two escapes, one to sunrise and one to sunset."

The Turk shrugged. "Peace with you," he said, turning to catch up with the old man.

The Arabs outside the barbed wire rose to their feet. At first they had sat there in tense silence and watched the proceedings under the tower. As the minutes had passed and they saw the Turk laugh and slap his knees in animated talk, they had relaxed. When they were offered coffee on trays which they refused twice and accepted the third time as is befitting, they had relaxed even more. The children had munched oranges and the women, sitting huddled together at a little distance from the men, had started giggling and pointing at the girls with naked legs. Then the men had started chatting with some of the Haganah boys who knew Arabic; the boys, leaning on their rifles, had answered condescendingly and treated them to cigarettes. When the parley at the tower broke up, the excitable one-eyed villager had just started inquiring whether the new settlers would bring a doctor and open a dispensary as the other settlements had done, and whether the doctor would be able to cure his blind eye. Now, as their speakers returned and they saw their dark faces, they surrounded them with the guilty look of children who had been naughty in their parents' absence. The Turk and the old man walked silently through their group. The others formed into pairs behind them, and the procession slowly descended the slope without turning their heads.

The Turk and the old man did not speak until they had almost reached the valley. Then the Turk said:

"The devil may take them away, but he could leave their tractors. They are dogs and sons of bitches but they know how to work. They will grow tomatoes and melons and God knows what out of that stony hill. . . ." He sighed. "We are too lazy, ya Abu; by God. . . ."

The old man turned on him with a hard look.

"You speak like a fool," he said. "Is the hill here for me, or am I here for the hill?"

* * *

After the villagers left, Joseph, who had watched the parley from the top of a truck which he was helping to unload, came up to Bauman. "Listen," he said, "why did you not let them all come in? It was very rude."

Bauman looked at him with a faint smile.

"We are too weak to afford to be polite," he said. "By keeping them out we established ourselves in their eyes as masters of the place. By now they have all unconsciously accepted the fact."

Joseph grinned. "Where did you learn all this psychology, Bauman?" he said.

"Intuition," said Bauman.

"I thought one only had intuitions about people one liked."

"Who told you that I don't like them?" said Bauman.

"I wish my Arabic was as good as yours," said Joseph. "What was the old sheikh explaining so solemnly?"

"He explained that every nation has the right to live according to its own fashion, right or wrong, without outside interference. He explained that money corrupts, fertilisers stink and tractors make a noise, all of which he dislikes."

"And what did you answer?"

"Nothing."

"But you saw his point."

Bauman looked at him steadily:

"We cannot afford to see the other man's point."

But the author of the novel, although an enthusiastic Zionist, could not help seeing the other man's point. For the sentiments voiced by Abu Tafidi were not only those of an uneducated village elder. They were shared by the vast majority of Arabs in Palestine. One of the characters in the novel, the editor of a moderate Arab weekly, has this sudden emotional outburst during a formal luncheon party in the house of a high-ranking British official:

"I care not whether they pay," cried Kamel Effendi. "And I care not for their hospitals and their schools. This is our country, you understand? We want no foreign benefactors. We want not to be patronised. We want to be left alone, you understand! We want to live our own way and we want no foreign teachers and no foreign money and no foreign habits and no smiles of condescension and no pat on the shoulder and no arrogance and no shameless women with wriggling buttocks in our holy places. We want not their honey and we want not their sting, you understand? Neither their honey nor their sting. This you can tell them. If they are thrown out in other countries – very bad, very sorry. Very, very sorry – but not our business. If they want to come here – a few of them, maybe thousand, maybe two thousand – t'faddal, welcome. But then know you are guests and know how to behave. Otherwise – to the devil. Into the sea – and hallass, finished. This is plain language. You tell them."

There was a painful silence while Kamel Effendi wiped his forehead and the Assistant Chief Commissioner stood hovering over the group like an unhappy flamingo. Then Matthews said unexpectedly:

"Yeah – I see your point, Mr Kamel. I guess you are wrong, but wrong in your own right."

Chapter 4

THE POISON OF HOLINESS*

To pick up the chronological thread: with my hopes of joining
Kibbutz Heftsebā shattered, I entered upon a period of semi-
starvation as a Jack of all trades which lasted a little over a year. I
worked as a draughtsman for an Arab architect in Haifa; sold
advertising space for a Hebrew weekly; sold lemonade in the Arab
bazaar; had briefly a job as a land-surveyor's assistant in Tel Aviv
and another with a travel agency. But throughout this period of
drifting I also wrote political articles and travelogues which I
hopefully sent to European newspapers. Some of these were
accepted and thus revived an earlier ambition to become a writer
or journalist.

My opportunity came when the post of Middle East correspondent of the prodigious Ullstein chain of newspapers became
temporarily vacant. The person who had occupied that much-
coveted post, Wolfgang von Weisl, was a friend of mine; he had
been given another assignment and recommended me as his
successor. To my surprise I was accepted – initially on probation,
soon after as a fully accredited correspondent with a generous
salary and headquarters in Jerusalem.

I took up my new post in 1927, just about two years after the
night of the discussion with Orochov and the symbolic burning of
my boats.

My beat included Palestine, Egypt, Transjordan (now Jordan),
Iraq, Syria and the Lebanon. I wrote on an average three full-
length articles a week for the host of newspapers and magazines
owned by Ullsteins. About half of these dealt with politics, the
other half were feature pieces about cabbages and kings: about the

*From Arrow in the Blue, chs. XVIII, XXII, and Thieves in the Night.

Hebrew theatre and the brothels of Beirut, about Byzantine mosaics and Bedouin costumes, about the Queen of Sheba and the potash works on the Dead Sea. . . . One of the idyllic aspects of the Arab countries at that time was that, if you were a visiting European journalist, you went for information straight to the reigning King, Emir or Pasha, and were usually asked to stay for lunch. Thus at the age of twenty-three I could – and did – boast of the acquaintance of King Feisal of Iraq, the Emir Abdulla of Transjordan, the Egyptian Prime Minister, Nahas Pasha, the President of the Lebanese Republic, and so on.

Yet out of the profuse literary output during this period, I have found hardly anything worth preserving. There are not many writers who like to be reminded of their juvenilia. Even E. M. Forster once wrote to me that he could think of his early work "only with rage and shame".

I have always marvelled how a tiny country like Palestine could contain such an enormous contrast as offered by its two principal towns: the haughty melancholia of Jerusalem and the vulgar exuberance of Tel Aviv. Jerusalem, with its Holy Places, monasteries, convents and university, was the spiritual centre, with a mixed Christian, Jewish and Muslim population. Tel Aviv was purely Jewish – the first Hebrew town built since the destruction of the Temple by Titus. It was an ancient dream unexpectedly come true; and as dreams go it was disorderly, irrational, with an occasional tendency to turn into a nightmare. I have tried to convey the atmosphere of the two rival cities in Thieves in the Night:

Each time Joseph came to Tel Aviv he was torn between his conflicting emotions of tenderness and revulsion. Tenderness for the one and only purely Hebrew town in the world, and the jostling vitality of its citizens; revulsion from the dreadful mess they had made of it. It was a frantic, maddening city which gripped the traveller by the buttonhole as soon as he entered it, tugged and dragged him around like a whirlpool, and left him after a few days faint and limp, not knowing whether he should laugh or cry, love or hate it.

The adventure had started at the turn of the century, when the handful of native Jewish families in Arab Jaffa decided to build a

suburb of their own. So they left the Arab port with its labyrinthine bazaars, exotic smells and furtive daggers, and started
building on the yellow sand of the Mediterranean dunes the city
of their dreams: an exact replica of the ghettoes of Warsaw,
Cracow and Lodz. There was a main street named after Dr Herzl
with two rows of exquisitely ugly houses, each of which gave the
impression of an orphanage or police barracks. There was also a
multitude of dingy shops, most of which sold lemonade, buttons
and flypaper.

In the early nineteen-twenties, with the beginnings of Zionist
colonisation, the town spread along the beach. It grew in hectic
jumps with each new wave of immigration – an inland tide of
asphalt and concrete advancing over the dunes. There was no
time for planning and no willingness for it; growth was feverish
and anarchic; the Hill of Spring (which is what Tel Aviv means in
Hebrew) became a maze of peeling stucco, and after the first rains
looked as if it had contracted the measles.

However, life in Tel Aviv during those early days owed its
peculiar character not to the people who had houses built, but to
the workmen who built them. The first Hebrew city was dominated by young workers of both sexes in their teens and twenties.
The streets belonged to them; khaki shirts, shorts and dark sun-
glasses were the fashionable wear, and ties, nicknamed "her-
rings", a rarity. In the evening, when the cool breeze from the sea
relieved the white glare of the day, they walked arm in arm over
the hot asphalt of half-finished boulevards which ended abruptly
in the dunes. At night, they built bonfires and danced the horra on
the beach; and at least once a week they dragged pompous Mayor
Dizengoff or old Chief Rabbi Hertz out of their beds and took them
down to the sea to dance with them. They were hard-working,
sentimental and gay. They were carried by a wave of enthusiasm
which had a crest and no trough.

It was a town sprung to life like a phantom out of the gap of two
thousand years in Jewish history. It was a town whose population
could not quite believe in its own reality, while they watched it
grow with awe and wonder. One day Mayor Dizengoff dropped a
stone into the sea to inaugurate the beginning of work on the
future harbour. When the water had plopped over the symbolic
stone, he turned round and said solemnly: "Citizens, I can still
remember the days when Tel Aviv had no harbour. . . ."*

*Arrow in the Blue, ch. xviii.

However, my job demanded that I live in Jerusalem, and thus to
suffer those periodic bouts of depression to which its citizens
seemed to be prone – I called it the Jerusalem Sadness:

Jerusalem Sadness is a local disease, like Baghdad Boils, due to
the combined effect of the tragic beauty and inhuman atmosphere
of the city. It is the haughty, desolate beauty of a walled-in mountain fortress in the desert. The angry face of Yahveh is brooding
over the hot rocks, which have seen more holy murder, rape and
plunder than any other place on this earth. Its inhabitants are
poisoned by holiness. Josephus Flavius, who was a priest in the
city and suffered from Jerusalem Sadness, has this strange phrase:
"The union of what is divine and what is mortal is disagreeable."
The population of the city is a mosaic; but every portion of it is
disagreeable. Perhaps the most disagreeable are the clergy, Muslim, Christian and Jewish alike. The Muslim clergy in my time
used to call on the average twice a year for a holy blood bath. A
peaceful Arab landlord would joke with the family of his Jewish
tenants some Friday morning during the Ramadan, go to the
Mosque, listen to the Imam, run home and slaughter tenant, wife
and children with a kitchen knife. The Greek, Latin, Syriac, Cop-
tic, Armenian and other Christian clergy would come to blows
over such questions as to "whether the Greeks had a right to place
a ladder on the floor of the Armenian chapel for the purpose of
cleaning the upper part of the chapel above the cornice in the
Basilica of the Nativity in Bethlehem"; and "whether the Greeks
must attach their curtain tight or in natural folds to the lower
Nail No.2 at the foot of the pillar which lies south-east of the
left-hand set of steps leading to the manger" (both examples are
authentic, and I may add to them the regulation "that the Latins
should have their curtain fall naturally down the same pillar,
leaving a space of sixteen centimetres between it and that of the
Greek Orthodox").

The Jewish clergy was engaged in feuds with the Muslims
about rights of way to the Wailing Wall, and among themselves
about the correct method of ritual slaughter; they also encouraged
their orthodox disciples to protect the sanctity of the Sabbath by
beating up the godless who smoked cigarettes in the streets and by
throwing bricks at passing motor cars.

The political atmosphere was just as poisoned. The Husseini
clan murdered members of the Nashashibi clan; during the riot
season they both murdered Jews; the Jewish Parties hated each

other, the British, and the Arabs, in that order; the British sahibs, here called *hawadjas*, behaved as British sahibs used to do.

There were no cafés or night clubs, no cocktail parties, and no night-life of any kind in Jerusalem. People kept to themselves, their church, clan or party. It was an austere, pharisaic town, full of hatred, distrust and phoney relics. I lived at No. 29, Street of the Prophets, at five minutes distance from the Via Dolorosa, another five from the Mosque of Omar where for a shilling you are shown the Archangel Gabriel's footprints on the rock. I have never lived at such close quarters with divinity, and never farther removed from it. The whole unholy history of the city, from David to Herod, from Pilate to the Crusaders, from Titus to Glubb, is an illustration of the destructive power of faith, and the resulting unpleasantness of the union of the mortal and the divine. It is this awareness of defeat, driven home by the haughty silence of the desert, of dry watercourse and arid rock, which causes the Jerusalem Sadness.

Sadness apart, I grew increasingly tired of Palestine. Zionism in 1929 had come to a standstill. Immigration had been reduced to a mere trickle. Nazism, which was to turn it into a flood, was still a monster being hatched in the womb of the future.

I had gone to Palestine as a young enthusiast, driven by a romantic impulse. Instead of Utopia, I had found an extremely complex reality which both attracted and repelled me, but where the repellent effect, for a simple reason, gradually gained the upper hand. The reason was the Hebrew language. It was a petrified language which had been abandoned by the Jews long before the Christian era – in the days of Christ, they spoke Aramaic – and had now been revived by a *tour de force*. By making Hebrew its official language, the small Jewish community of Palestine seemed to have turned its back on Western civilisation.

I felt that to undergo the same process would be spiritual suicide. I was a romantic fool, in love with unreason; but I knew that in a Hebrew-language environment I would always remain a stranger; and at the same time gradually lose touch with European culture. I had left Europe at the age of twenty. Now I was twenty-three and had had my fill of both Arab romantics and Jewish mystique. I was longing for Europe, thirsting for Europe, pining for Europe.*

*Arrow in the Blue, *ch.* xxii.

I asked the Ullsteins for a transfer, and had the good luck to be assigned to Paris. In subsequent years my interest in Zionism faded; it was reawakened, with a vengeance, thirteen years later, when the gas chambers went into action.

PART TWO

LAND OF PROMISE

Chapter 5

MOUNT OF OLIVES TO MONTPARNASSE

My education seems to have proceeded by shocks and jolts. The most delightful of these jolts was the change of scenery from the Judean Desert to the Luxembourg Gardens, from the Holy City to Sodom on the Seine, from the Levantine fringe of civilisation to its luminous centre. After three years of cultural exile and starvation of the senses, the first contact with Paris, at the age of twenty-four, was bound to have the intensity of a chemical reaction.*

I was sent to Paris on a double assignment: as a cultural correspondent to write feature articles, but also to work for the Ullstein News Service. In Jerusalem I had been my own master; in Paris I had to keep strenuous office hours. For several months, when we were short of staff, I was on night duty from 9 p.m. to 11 p.m. and from 4 a.m. to 8 a.m. This schedule confronted me with the problem whether it was preferable to go to bed at midnight and be woken up at 3.15 by the shriek of the alarm clock, or not to go to bed at all. But it also provided the opportunity to become familiar with aspects of Paris which belong to a vanished epoque – as reflected in this "Elegy on Bawdy Houses":†

*Arrow in the Blue, ch. XXII.
†From Arrow in the Blue, ch. XXIV

To stay up, night after night, until 4 a.m. and then go to work is not
easy – not even in Paris, not even at the age of twenty-four. My
companions dropped off one by one, and I was left alone to roam
Montparnasse, until the waiters started putting the chairs upside
down on the tables and throwing sawdust on the floor. So I went
and sat in some all-night *brasserie* on the Boulevard Edgar
Quinet, frequented almost exclusively by tired street-walkers, or
to the *Chope du Nègre* in the Rue du Faubourg Montmartre,
frequented by the same patrons plus their protectors – the
maqueraux and *souteneurs* of all ages, whose main occupation
was to play belotte while keeping an eye on their dames and their
clients. Or I sauntered round the *Halles*, and watched the unloading of the mountains of vegetables and fruit, fish and beef, eggs
and hens, into the giant belly of Paris – envying Zola who wrote
his novel on the *Halles* without ever having been there at night (he
preferred to rely on the eyewitness reports of the Goncourt
brothers).

Sometimes I ate out of sheer despair and boredom two or three
dozen oysters at the *Chien qui Fume*, swilling them down with
Alsatian wine and following this up with onion soup – the traditional fare of revellers who wind up the night at the *Halles*. I
looked at them with the same bitterness as the milkman and the
dustman and the street-cleaner, whose day starts at dawn, watch
those sodden parties in dishevelled evening dress drive past. Like
all professional night-workers I developed a contempt for the
drunk, and a natural *camaraderie* for the pariahs of the entertainment industry – waiters, café artistes, doormen and tarts. As I still
looked like a schoolboy, and was nearly always sober, dragging
myself from one place to another, carrying a book and looking
unhappy and bored, I became soon quite well known among the
tarts and their friends under the name of *le petit journaliste*. They
knew that I was always good for a *café-crème* and a brioche, or for
a *crème de menthe au cassis*, which for some inscrutable reason is
the street-walker's favourite drink. Most of these were tramps by
temperament, morally irresponsible, with a low I.Q., and a tendency to alcoholism, or drug addiction, or more frequently a
pathological addiction to some particularly unattractive, seedy,
weedy, swaggering pimp. The pimps were almost without
exception wholly lacking in masculine sex appeal. They acted
tough without looking it; the predominant type was pigeon-
chested, sallow-faced, with sloping, padded shoulders, short,
bandy-legged. They had no physical prowess and relied, if it came

to a fight, on their switch-blade knives, razors and, rarely, on revolvers. They had no sexual prowess either. Many of them were impotent or nearly so; many suffered from chronic gonorrhoea. And yet one woman after another told me: "You will never understand that. But if he touches me with the palm of his hand I feel more than if other men make love to me with ten horse-powers." (This is not quite idiomatic, but let's leave it at that.)

The secret of this pathological relationship seems to lie chiefly in the pimp's brutality to his women. It is a calculated and nauseating kind of brutality which has its own ritual and cant. There are, of course other factors which vary from case to case, but brutality is the common denominator, and its obvious function is to satisfy the tramp's craving for punishment – a craving the more consistent as it is mostly unconscious. "I will punish you" is a favourite expression in the *souteneur's* vocabulary, and the threat alone seems to have the required effect. "Punishment" consists mostly in slaps, kicks or mere verbal abuse; overtly sadistic practices hardly ever occur. They would defeat the purpose of the relationship, which is based on the axiom that the punishment is an act of justice which the victim deserves for being "bad". In short, the prostitute creates her own ritual of penance; the kick on the shin and the slap in the face represent the act of atonement; the unsavouriness and repellent physique of the protector and avenger are part of the pattern.

The prostitutes who worked in the *maisons clos*, as the brothels were politely called, were of a quite different mettle. They compared to the street-walkers as an élite regiment to a band of mercenaries. They had no *souteneurs*, or, if they got into trouble, took a protector on a strict business basis.

Among the Closed Houses, there were *sérieuse* and less *sérieuse* ones. The serious Houses watched carefully over their reputation; no drunkenness, bawdy behaviour or fleecing of the clients was tolerated; and the girls had to observe a strict code of etiquette. There existed a number of luxury establishments like the "Chabannais", the "Sphinx" or the place in the Rue des Victoires which specialised in *tableaux vivants* – featuring monks, nuns, princes and shepherdesses in Rabelaisian poses. But such establishments, like everything else connected with the tourist industry, were regarded by the trade with some contempt. The serious Houses catered to the people who lived in the *quartier*, had their more or less stable clientèle, reasonable tariffs and a cosy atmosphere where a man could sit for an hour over a glass of

beer or brandy, pay and go home without having been molested —
which is what about half of the guests did. Not infrequently they
brought their wives or mistresses who wanted to satisfy their
curiosity and see a "House" from the inside; only in the cheaper
establishments were female visitors excluded for fear of competition.

The average, serious, well-spoken House had a large parlour on
the ground floor, equipped like a café, with leather benches
around the wall, tables and chairs. The only visible difference
between a House and a café was that the women had little or
nothing on (except of course those who had come as guests); but
one got as quickly accustomed to this as in a nudist colony. There
was little lewdness, hardly any drunkenness, no jealousy and no
quarrels. If a client wished to retire with a lady upstairs, they left
the drawing-room separately, and did or did not reappear later on.
But although these disappearances were obviously the *raison
d'être* of the House, they played no more than a casual part in the
picture — in the same way as people may sit for hours on the
terrace of a café, taking only a sip of coffee or none at all. Abundance of opportunity has an automatically neutralising effect. In
the adolescent's imagination the shared bed of marriage is a scene
of permanent voluptuousness; the Anglo-Saxon idea of a Paris
House was equally wide off the mark.

An anthropological survey, which was never made, would have
shown that the average "serious" woman in a serious Paris House
was twenty-five years old; healthy, thanks to regular medical
inspection and preventive care; that she had a child boarded out
in the country; that she counted on working as a prostitute for five
years and then buying with her savings a shop or a café in a small
provincial town, marrying a substantial widower and living
happily and respectably ever after. Each week she had her fixed
day off; on that day she put on a neat tailored suit, a slightly
dowdy hat, conservative make-up and a mangy fox around her
neck, and spent the day in the country with relatives, or with the
child and its foster parents. The relatives or the foster parents had
no idea what her profession was, and nothing about her dress or
behaviour would distinguish her from the salesgirl in a department store or seamstress in a *maison de couture*, which she
pretended to be. Nor, once her life's ambition was realised, would
there be the slightest sign to distinguish her from the other owners
of millinery shops or cafés in the small town, married to other
substantial widowers. Except, perhaps, that she would have more

understanding of her husband's foibles and whims, and of human nature in general. Among the black-clad, high-bosomed, cosy and energetic women behind the tinkling cash-registers of France there are thousands of ex-prostitutes, and the country is none the worse off for them. Some of them, I am sure, became heroines of the Resistance.

Since the Paris Houses were closed in 1946, they are rapidly becoming a legend. Should the reader detect between these lines a certain nostalgia for them, I plead guilty without embarrassment. For the Houses were an essential part of the Paris landscape, of French life and literature. As regards morality, all the hackneyed but nevertheless valid arguments were on their side: that prostitution is as old as civilisation; that the main effect of legal prohibition – as in the case of the prohibition of liquor – was to force prostitution underground and to produce all the concomitant symptoms of crime, squalor and corruption. The Paris Houses, while they were legal, were neither Sodom nor the idyllic places described in some novels; they were orderly, commercial establishments where sex, deprived of its mystery, was traded as a commodity. It is absurd to expect that in a mercantile society the most potent human urge should escape the process of commercialisation. And once trading in sex is recognised as inevitable, a legal, regulated trade is preferable to the squalor of the black market.

One of the cheapest Paris brothels was in the Rue de Fourcy, in the *Quartier Saint Paul* – the slums between the Hôtel de Ville and the Bastille. It was frequented by factory workers, garage hands, Algerian carpet pedlars, post office clerks and navvies. On Friday evenings, with their week's pay in their pockets, the men formed a long queue on the narrow sidewalk of the little street. They looked like people peacefully waiting for seats in a movie, except that the queue comprised only men. They were smoking, chatting, reading the sports page of *Paris Soir*, chewing *cacahouettes* and sunflower seeds. From time to time the *gérante* put her head out of the door and asked whether there were any clients present for Mademoiselle Josette; and then a man would tranquilly detach himself from the queue and enter the House. The tariff in this House in 1929 was Frs. 4.50 (*serviette comprise*) or the price of a cheap *prix fixe* meal. Here sex was reduced to the equivalent of the Salvation Army soup. It sounds revolting, but it was merely pathetic; and the scene still had considerably more dignity than that of an American strip-tease show. At least the men knew that they would not be cheated, that their hunger would be satisfied; and for them the House in the Rue de Fourcy with its cheap glitter had even an aura of romance. It was their version of the rich man's nightclub; in the name of what moral principle were these carpet pedlars and inmates of the doss-houses deprived of their *prix fixe* paradise?

One of the girls who worked in the Rue de Fourcy was really called Josette. She was young, dark and pretty, born of Italian parents near Marseilles. She reckoned that after another two years she would be in the clear and marry her boy friend – who was in the army and would be discharged at about that time. With her savings they hoped to open a service station somewhere in Provence; and of course he would never know by what means her dowry had been earned. Her working day ended at 4 a.m.; then she would walk in her trim, neat, tailored suit and low-heeled shoes to the vicinity of the Gare de Lyon, where she lived. On her way home she was frequently accosted by late prowlers who took her for a respectable woman. She mostly refused their invitations, though often she was offered ten or twenty times the amount which was the tariff of the House. She did this partly because she was too tired, and partly because keeping up pretences bored and disgusted her.

"I shall never be good at that kind of thing," she explained. "The comedy, the fuss and the chichis disgust me. Here everything is straight and simple. But the moment I put a blouse on, and a skirt over my behind, my price goes up ten times and I become a *femme fatale*. You know why? Because the moment I put my blouse on, this here" (she slapped her pretty bare bosom) "becomes a mystery. Some would pay a hundred francs for a peep down that blouse when here they can have everything for five francs, *serviette comprise*. And they tell me how clever I am, and how *spirituelle* I am, and that I am the woman they always dreamt of. Particularly the English and the Americans on their way home from the *Bal Musette* in the Rue de Lappe. They are so nice and blond and stupid that one feels pity for them. If they had Houses like this in their country they would learn that all the excitement is about nothing – so much noise for an omelette. They tell me half the English are impotent, or paederasts or *des mélancoliques*. It is because they see a mystery where there is only a corset with elastic panels. *O les pauvres malheureux....*"

In between the strenuous office hours and night shifts, I wrote on an average two feature articles per month for the *Vossische Zeitung*, the Ullsteins' most venerable liberal daily, roughly comparable to the *Manchester Guardian* of the period. I wrote about surrealist films (Bunuel's classic *Un Chien Andalou* had just come out), and about the Pitoefs' theatre; about the fantastic scandal of the *Gazette du Franc* and the fantastic disappearance of the White Russian General Kutiepof (who had been kidnapped by the GPU – a fact which, as a good Progressive, I refused to believe). I also wrote about the Piccolis' famous marionette theatre which for a while I frequented as a hobby; about spring in Paris, the first French talkies, Maeterlinck's latest book, and the Duc de Broglie's theory of matter-waves which won him the Nobel Prize for Physics in 1929.

That last article had a decisive influence on my fortunes. I had called on de Broglie less than an hour after the newsflash from Stockholm had reached our office, and before he himself had received confirmation of the award. He was happy as a schoolboy, made no effort to conceal it, and asked me twice: "Are you quite sure that it is true and not a hoax?" One or two journalists had already telephoned and asked him idiotic questions about sun-spots and death-rays; so he was much relieved to discover that I had been a student of science and took a passionate interest in physics. We talked for three or four hours — de Broglie was then thirty-seven, and an exceptional combination of genius and charm – after which I worked through the night in a state of exaltation.

The article was a popular exposé of the revolutionary implications of the de Broglie–Schrödinger theory of wave-mechanics; it appeared a few days later in the Vossische and occupied a whole page. As a result, the Ullsteins decided that I had a knack for popularising scientific subjects; and as the Science Editor of the Vossische, Professor Joel, was nearing retirement age, they offered me that job, which I accepted with enthusiasm. On revienttoujours à son premier amour – the arrow in the blue reasserted its magic attraction.

I took up my new job in Berlin in September, 1930; the first honeymoon with Paris had lasted just over a year. I did not suspect that three years later I would be back, as a penniless refugee.

Chapter 6

THE CHINAMAN'S NOD*

Black Friday, October 24, 1929, came soon after I had taken up my
post in Paris. Its significance escaped us almost entirely. It took
several months for its repercussions to make themselves felt in
Europe. Once the first shock-waves of the Depression arrived,
events proceeded rapidly. Unemployment in Germany soared to
the figure of seven million – one-third of the total number of
wage-earners. The strength of the National Socialist Party
increased at the same rate. The foundations were shaken, Europe
ready for the collapse.

I arrived in Berlin on the day of the fateful Reichstag elections,
September 14, 1930.

It was the third turning point in my career, and each of the three
was marked by a symbolic date. I had left the home of my parents
and set out for Palestine on April Fools' Day, 1926. I had arrived in
Paris on the day which commemorates the beginning of the
French Revolution: on Bastille Day, July 14, 1929. And I arrived in
Berlin on the day which heralded the end of the Weimar Republic
and the beginning of the age of barbarism in Europe.

Up to September 14, the National Socialist Party had occupied
twelve seats in the German Parliament. After that day, one
hundred and seven. The parties of the Centre were crushed. The
Democratic Party had all but vanished. The Socialists had lost
nine of their seats. The Communists had increased their vote by 0
per cent, the Nazis by 800 per cent. The final show down was
approaching. It came thirty months later.

The day after the elections, I took up my new job in the impos-

*From Arrow in the Blue, chs. xxv, xxvII, and The God That Failed.

ing building in the Kochstrasse. Everybody there was still dazed. I had to pay courtesy calls on the editors of our four daily papers and of a dozen weeklies and monthlies, all housed in that one labyrinthine building. They shook hands limply, with absent looks. One or two of them said with a wry smile: "Why on earth didn't you stay on in Paris?" The arrival of a new Science editor at that particular moment struck them as exceedingly funny.

After a few days the panic subsided and the people in the Kochstrasse, as everywhere else in Germany, settled down to carry on business as usual in a country that had become a minefield. More than half the people in the Kochstrasse building were Jews. The other half did not fare much better later on. The Ullstein crowd was Dr Goebbels' bête noir. We stood for everything that he hated. We were steeped in German culture, yet immune against German chauvinism through a hereditary Judeo-cosmopolitan touch. We were fervently anti-war, anti-militaristic, anti-reactionary. We were for "Locarno" and for "Rapallo", that is, for Franco-German and Russo-German collaboration. We were for the Kellogg Pact which outlawed war, and for the League of Nations which would punish every possible aggressor, and for Briand's Pan-Europa. Towards England we were cool because it had a Colonial Empire (the French had one too, but nobody took it seriously), and because it kept Europe divided by its "Machiavellian balance-of-power policy". We believed in national self-determination, and in freedom for the colonial peple, and in social progress. In short, we were very enlightened and reasonable. Only, we failed to see that the Age of Reason and Enlightenment was drawing to a close.

Cosmic disturbances sometimes cause a magnetic storm on earth. Man has no organ to detect it, and seafarers often do not realise that their compass has gone haywire. We lived in the midst of such a magnetic storm, but we failed to notice the signs. We did not see that our slogans had lost their bearing and pointed in the wrong directions. We invoked "democracy" solemnly as in a prayer, and watched while the greatest nation of Europe voted, by perfectly democractic methods, its assassins into power. We worshipped the will of The Masses, and their will turned out to be death and self-destruction. We regarded capitalism as an outworn system, and were willing to exchange it for a new form of slavery. We preached tolerance, and the evil which we tolerated destroyed our civilisation.

Individuals reacted to the approaching apocalypse according to

their varied temperaments. There were the professional optimists, and the constitutional optimists. The former fooled their
readers; the latter fooled themselves.

Thirty months is a long time. There were ups and downs.
Elections followed each other at an increasingly feverish rhythm.
The Nazis' votes increased by leaps and bounds, but in between
they suffered minor setbacks and everybody breathed a little more
freely. After the event, people asked themselves: How could we
have been such fools to twiddle our thumbs when the outcome
was so obvious? The answer is that owing to the inertia of human
imagination, to most people it wasn't obvious at all.

Every phase of this process of decomposition was reflected in
the public-opinion factory where I worked. The tone of our papers
changed by perceptible degrees. A regular column began to
appear in the *Vossische Zeitung*, devoted to news about German
ethnic minorities outside the Reich. It signalled the shift of
emphasis from a cosmopolitan to a Pan-Germanistic orientation.

The attitude of the paper towards the Western powers stiffened.
We had always been critical of the Versailles Treaty; now
balanced criticism yielded to self-righteousness. The editorials
became pompous, patriotic and provincial. It was not necessary to
instruct editors and foreign correspondents to change their
course. Once the tone was set, they followed suit – automatically,
by instinct. If one had accused them of having changed their
convictions they would have sincerely and indignantly denied it.

Long before the thirty months had run their course, our *Vossische*, the Bible of German Liberalism, had little more than its
name in common with its former self. Some departmental heads
fought a valiant rearguard battle, but they were the exceptions.
New faces appeared in the house and old members of the staff
vanished. The cold purge dragged on through 1932. Though the
Ullsteins were Jews, they tried to aryanise the firm by degrees, in
an indirect way. The victims of the purge were, as far as I can
remember, all Jews; the newly hired members of the staff all
"Aryans" and sturdy nationalists.

The building in the Kochstrasse became a place of fear and
insecurity which reflected the fear and insecurity of the country in
general. We still walked the long sound-proof corridors with the
important air of cabinet ministers, but we covertly watched each
other, wondering whose turn would come next. In some cases the
colleagues of a man knew that he was due for the axe while the
victim himself was still strutting among them ignorant of his fate.

A gruesome joke which circulated through all editorial offices is symbolic of the atmosphere of the Weimar Republic during its last months:

Under the reign of the second Emperor of the Ming Dynasty there lived an executioner by the name of Wang Lun. He was a master of his art and his fame spread through all the provinces of the Empire. There were many executions in those days, and sometimes there were as many as fifteen or twenty men to be beheaded at one session. Wang Lun's habit was to stand at the foot of the scaffold with an engaging smile, hiding his curved sword behind his back, and while whistling a pleasant tune, to behead his victim with a swift movement as he walked up the steps of the scaffold.

Now this Wang Lun had one secret ambition in his life, but it took him fifty years of strenuous effort to realise it. His ambition was to be able to behead a person with a stroke so swift that, in accordance with the law of inertia, the victim's head would remain poised on his trunk, in the same manner as a plate remains undisturbed on the table if the tablecloth is pulled out under it with a sudden jerk.

Wang Lun's great moment came in the seventy-eighth year of his life. On that memorable day he had to dispatch sixteen clients from this world of shadows to their ancestors. He stood as usual at the foot of the scaffold, and eleven shaven heads had already rolled in the dust after his inimitable master-stroke. His triumph came with the twelfth man. When this man began to ascend the steps of the scaffold, Wang Lun's sword flashed with such lightning speed across his neck that the man's head remained in its place, and he continued to walk up the steps without realising what had happened. When he reached the top of the scaffold, the man addressed Wang Lun as follows:

"O cruel Wang Lun, why do you prolong my agony of waiting when you dealt with the others with such merciful and amiable speed?"

When he heard these words, Wang Lun knew that the ambition of his life had been accomplished. A serene smile appeared on his features; then he said with exquisite courtesy to the waiting man:

"Just kindly nod, please."

We walked along the hushed corridors of our citadel of German democracy, greeting each other with a grinning "Kindly nod, please". And we fingered the back of our necks to make sure that the head was still attached to it.

The Weimar Republic was doomed. It had betrayed its convictions and dishonoured itself without improving its chances of survival. To expect salvation from the Liberal parties was absurd.

Nor was there more to be hoped from the Socialists. Their record for the preceding quarter-century was one of unprincipled opportunism and spineless compromise. In 1912 they had solemnly pledged themselves to make it impossible for their government to go to war; two years later they enthusiastically supported Kaiser Wilhelm's war of conquest. In 1918, when military defeat carried them into power, they missed their historic chance to transform Germany into a truly democratic country. Instead of boldly advancing, they manoeuvred. In the 1932 presidential elections, their candidate was doddering old Field Marshal Hindenburg, the Pétain of Germany. They got him elected, and six months later he called Adolf Hitler into power.

Thus, in 1930, the progressive intellectuals of Germany were only too familiar with the sad record of the Socialist Party. On the other hand, as yet few unfavourable facts about Soviet Communism had become public knowledge. Trotsky, leader of the Opposition, had been exiled; but as revolutions go, exile is a relatively mild punishment. No prominent Soviet politician had been tried in public, no member of the Opposition had been executed. Those were comparatively idyllic days; the purges, the show trials and the Terror only started four years later, after the assassination of Kirov, in December, 1934.

Forced collectivisation of the peasants' land had only just begun. The mass deportations of "Kulaks", the famine and partial depopulation of the countryside were still a matter of the future. The first Five Year Plan had been undertaken in 1929; it was in its second year. It was a gigantic enterprise of truly historic significance. Russia had embarked on "the great experiment"; one could have reservations about the regime, but there was no *prima facie* case for rejecting it out of hand. Only the Conservatives and reactionaries did that, at the same time displaying a benevolent neutrality towards the Italian and German variants of Fascism. There were a few isolated voices among progressive intellectuals – Bertrand Russell and H. G. Wells for instance – who from the beginning had uncompromisingly opposed the Soviet regime; but they were few, and were not listened to.

In 1930, Russia was a decisive asset for the German Communist

Party, whereas today it has become a liability to the Communists of Western Europe. The Socialists had no such asset, only their dismal reputation of having made a mess of their Republic. After the elections of September, 1930, I had seen the Liberal middle class throw all its principles overboard. Active resistance against the Nazis seemed only possible by throwing in one's lot either with the Socialists or the Communists. A comparison of their past records, their vitality and determination eliminated the first, and favoured the second.

I was not alone in arriving at this conclusion. The trend towards polarisation between the two extremist movements bore all the signs of inexorable fatality. The title of H. R. Knickerbocker's famous best-seller of that time, *Germany – Fascist or Soviet?*, was an exact summing up of the situation. There was no "third force", and no third choice.

Chapter 7

WOE TO THE SHEPHERDS*

Against this background, I now made a concentrated effort to study the Marxist interpretation of history and the intricacies of the dialectical method, which enabled one to translate a somewhat abstract philosophy into concrete political action. The impact of dialectical materialism on a scientifically inclined mind amounted to no less than a revelation.

> The bourgeois family will vanish as a matter of course with the vanishing of capital. . . . The bourgeois claptrap about the family and education, about the haloed correlation of parent and child, becomes all the more disgusting the more, by the action of modern industry, all family ties among the proletarians are torn asunder. . . .

Thus the Communist Manifesto. Every page of Marx, and even more of Engels, brought a new discovery, and an intellectual delight. Torn from its context, the above passage sounds ridiculous; as part of a system, which made social philosophy fall into a lucid and comprehensive pattern, the demonstration of the historical relativity of institutions and ideals – of family, class, patriotism, bourgeois morality, sexual taboos – had the intoxicating effect of a sudden liberation from the rusty chains with which a pre-1914 middle-class childhood had cluttered one's mind.

By the time I had finished with Engels's *Feuerbach* and Lenin's *State and Revolution*, something had clicked in my brain and I was shaken by a mental explosion. To say that one had "seen the light" is a poor description of the intellectual rapture which only the convert knows (regardless to what faith he has been converted). The new light seems to pour in from all directions; the whole universe falls into pattern like the stray pieces in a jigsaw

*From The God That Failed *and* Arrow in the Blue, chs. xxviii *and* xxix.

puzzle, assembled by magic at one stroke. There is now an answer to every question; doubts and conflicts are a matter of the tortured past – a past already remote, when one had lived in dismal ignorance in the tasteless, colourless world of those who *don't know*. Nothing henceforth can disturb the convert's inner peace and serenity – except the occasional fear of losing faith again, losing thereby what alone makes life worth living, and falling back into the outer darkness, where there is wailing and gnashing of teeth.

The first, and decisive, effect which the study of Marxist dialectics had on me I can only describe by saying that, without my being aware of it, I had stepped from an open into an intellectually closed world. Marxism, like orthodox Freudianism, like Catholicism, is a closed system. A closed system has three peculiarities. Firstly, it claims to represent a truth of universal validity, capable of explaining all phenomena, and to have a cure for all that ails man. In the second place, it is a system which cannot be refuted by evidence, because all potentially damaging data are automatically processed and reinterpreted to make them fit the expected pattern. The processing is done by sophisticated methods of casuistry, centred on axioms of great emotive power, and indifferent to the rules of common logic; it is a kind of Wonderland croquet, played with mobile hoops. In the third place, it is a system which invalidates criticism by shifting the argument to the subjective motivation of the critic, and deducing his motivation from the axioms of the system itself. The orthodox Freudian school in its early stages approximated a closed system; if you argued that for such and such reasons you doubted the existence of the so-called castration complex, the Freudian's prompt answer was that your argument betrayed an unconscious resistance indicating that you yourself have a castration complex; you were caught in a vicious circle. Similarly, if you argued with a Stalinist that to make a pact with Hitler was not a nice thing to do, he would explain that your bourgeois class-consciousness made you unable to understand the dialectics of history. And if a paranoiac lets you in on the secret that the moon is a hollow sphere filled with aphrodisiac vapours which the Martians have put there to bewitch mankind; and you object that the theory, though attractive, is based on insufficient evidence, he will at once accuse you of being a member of the world conspiracy to suppress the truth. In short, the closed system excludes the possibility of objective argument by two related proceedings: (a) facts are deprived of their value as evidence by scholastic processing; (b) objections are invalidated by shifting the argument to the personal motive behind the objection. This procedure is legitimate according to the closed system's rules of the game which, however absurd they seem to the outsider, have a great coherence and inner consistency.

The atmosphere inside the closed system is highly charged; it is an emotional hothouse. The absence of objectivity in debate is many times compensated by its fervour. The disciple receives a thorough indoctrination, and thorough training in the system's particular method of reasoning. The trained, "closed-minded" theologian, psychoanalyst, or Marxist can at any time make mincemeat of his "open-minded" adversary and thus prove the superiority of his system to the world and to himself. His self-assurance, the radiance of his sincere belief, create a peculiar relationship between the initiate and the potential convert. It is the relationship between the guru and the pupil, between confessor and penitent, analyst and patient, between the militant Party member and the admiring fellow-traveller.

In every conversion to the Communist faith, some guru plays an important part. In most novels by authors who at one time were close to the Communist Party, one finds a key character who reflects the writer's infatuation with the person, or type of person, who attracted him to the movement. In Malraux's *Man's Fate* it is the Russian, Borodin; in Steinbeck's *In Dubious battle* it is Mac; in Hemingway's *To Have and Have Not* it is Captain Morgan; in Sartre's *The Age of Reason* it is Bruneau. An interesting exception is Silone's hero, Peter Spina, who is a self-portrait; for Silone, the son of poor Abruzzi peasants, was perhaps the only one among us who was not a convert but a "natural" Communist. At the opposite end of the scale is Sartre, the professor of philosophy; his guru – honest, hard-fisted Bruneau in *The Age of Reason* – is the archetype of the ideal Proletarian. Worship of the proletarian appears at first sight as a specifically Marxist phenomenon, but is merely a new variant of romantic shepherd cults, peasant cults, noble-savage cults of the past. That, however, did not prevent us Communist writers in the nineteen-thirties from feeling for workers in an automobile factory the same kind of emotion which Proust felt for his duchesses.

My childhood and youth bore a markedly individualistic stamp; on the other hand, my progress towards the Communist Party followed a typical, almost conventional pattern of that time.

There was a mass-migration of the sons and daughters of the European bourgeoise trying to escape from the collapsing world of their parents. The disintegration of the middle strata of society led to the fatal process of polarisation; Fascists and Communists shared about equally the benefits; while the ageing liberals lived on pointlessly like a swarm of tired winter-flies crawling over the dim windows of Europe.

Devotion to pure Utopia, and revolt against a polluted society, are the two poles which provide the tension of all militant creeds. To ask which of the two makes the current flow — attraction by the ideal or repulsion by the social environment — is to ask the old question whether the hen was first or the egg.

It did not require much persuasion to turn me into a rebel. Since my childhood I had been afflicted by Chronic Indignation. Rousseau remarks somewhere that he, too, suffered from this affliction, and explains it as an after-effect of the ignominies and sufferings which he had endured in his childhood. Here he seems, for once, to be unjust to himself, for early suffering may sensitise or thwart a person without turning him into an indignant rebel. This type seems to depend on a specific quality: the gift of projective imagination, or empathy, which compels one to regard an injustice inflicted on others as an indignity to oneself; and vice versa, to perceive an injustice to oneself as part and symbol of a general evil in society. The chronically indignant person is not necessarily quarrelsome, but always a rebel. His incessant campaigns to obtain justice for himself, for one Cause or another, for his friends and protégés (for he always has a large clientèle of protégés to whom he causes more embarrassment than relief) occupy most of his time and make him into a kind of admirable bore.

What distinguishes the chronically indignant rebel from the dedicated revolutionary is that the former is capable of changing causes, the latter not. The rebel turns his indignation now against this injustice, now against another; the revolutionary is a consistent hater who has invested all his powers of hatred in one target. The rebel always has a touch of the quixotic; the revolutionary is a bureaucrat of Utopia. The rebel is an enthusiast; the revolutionary, a fanatic. Robespierre, Marx, Lenin were revolutionaries; Danton, Bakunin, Trotsky were rebels. It is mostly the revolutionaries who alter the material course of history; but some rebels leave a subtler and yet more lasting imprint on it. At any rate, the rebel, for all his tiresome fulminations and enthusiasms, is a more attractive type than the revolutionary.

The ignominies of the colonial administration in Palestine had changed me from a romantic into an active Zionist. The event that aroused my indignation to a pitch never reached before was the American policy of destroying food stocks to keep agricultural prices up during the depression years – at a time when millions of unemployed lived in misery and near starvation. In retrospect, the economic policy which led to these measures is a subject for academic controversy; but in 1931 and 1932, its effect on Europeans was that of a crude and indeed terrifying shock which destroyed what little faith they still had in the existing social order. By 1932, there were seven million unemployed in Germany – which means that one out of every three wage-earners lived on the dole. In Austria, Hungary and the surrounding countries the situation was similar or worse. Meat, coffee, fruit had become unobtainable luxuries for large sections of the population, even the bread on the table was measured out in thin slices; yet the newspapers spoke laconically of millions of tons of coffee being dumped into the sea, of wheat being burned, pigs being cremated, oranges doused with kerosene "to ease conditions on the market". It was a grotesque and incomprehensible paradox – and to the socially conscious a sign of the total breakdown and decomposition of the economic system. Had not Marx foretold that capitalism would perish through its internal contradictions; that the cycle of prosperous periods ending in a crisis would repeat itself in an accelerated rhythm and each crisis be worse – until the last would bring the capitalist system to its end? Clearly, the prophecy was on the point of being fulfilled. When people starve and food is destroyed before their eyes so that their fat exploiters may grow even fatter, then the last judgement must be at hand.

Woe to the shepherds who feed themselves but feed not their flocks! Indignation glowed inside me; I felt like hitting out, shooting from a barricade or throwing sticks of dynamite. At whom? It was an impersonal fury, directed at no individual or group in particular. I did not hate the police, or the factory owners, or the rich – I had at that time a very comfortable income. I found the Brownshirts repellent, but they belonged to a strange and absurd world. My indignation had no personal target; it was directed at the hypocrisy and suicidal stupidity which were driving us all to perdition. In my fantasies no people were killed but huge buildings burst open and their walls came tumbling down as if in an earthquake – Ministries, editorial offices, radio stations, the whole *Sieges Allee* with its hideous statues of princes and field marshals. . . .

Echoes of the indignant wrath of the Hebrew prophets, and of the forthcoming Apocalypse according to St Marx; the sound of the hunger-marchers' boots on the pavement and the smell of wheat being burnt in the fields – all these ingredients fused into an emotional explosion.

Though the mixture which set it off varied from case to case, the reaction was the same for a large number of writers and intellectuals the world over: Barbusse, Romain Rolland, Gide, Malraux in France; Piscator, Becher, Seghers, Brecht in Germany; Auden, Isherwood, Spender, Day Lewis in England; Sinclair, Dos Passos, Steinbeck, Caldwell in the USA – to mention only a few. In the nineteen-thirties conversion to the Communist faith was not a fashion or craze – it was a sincere and spontaneous expression of an optimism born out of despair: a misfired Renaissance, a false dawn of history. To be attracted to the new faith was, I still believe, an honourable error. We were wrong for the right reasons; and I still feel that, with a few exceptions – I have already mentioned Bertrand Russell and H. G. Wells – those who derided the Russian Revolution from the beginning, did so mostly for reasons that were less honourable than our error. There is a world of difference between a disenchanted lover and those incapable of love.

To the psychiatrist, both the craving for Utopia and the rebellion against the *status quo* are symptoms of psychological maladjustment. To the social reformer, both are symptoms of a progressive, rational attitude. The psychiatrist is apt to forget that adjustment to a deformed society creates deformed individuals. The reformer is apt to forget that hatred, even of the objectively hateful, cannot beget a happy society. Hence each of the two attitudes reflects a half-truth. It is true that the case histories of most rebels reveal a neurotic conflict with family and society – but this only proves, to paraphrase Marx, that a moribund society creates its own morbid grave-diggers. It is also true that in the presence of revolting injustice the only honourable attitude is revolt – but if one compares the noble ideals in the name of which revolutions were started with the sorry end to which they came, one realises that a polluted society pollutes even its revolutionary offspring.

In fitting together the two half-truths, the psychiatrist's and the social reformer's, one must conclude that if, on the one hand, oversensitivity to injustice and obsessive cravings for Utopia are signs of a neurotic disposition, society may, on the other hand, reach an impasse where the neurotic rebel creates more rejoicing in heaven than the sane administrator who orders food destroyed under the eyes of starving men. And that, precisely, was the impasse reached by our civilisation in 1931.

Chapter 8

THE PROMETHEAN VISION*

To repeat it once more: revolutionary movements derive their momentum from two forces: they are repelled by the existing order of society and attracted by a Utopian ideal. The preceding extracts dealt with the repellent forces in the nineteen-thirties; those which follow are concerned with the great attractive force that reached its peak during that period: the Soviet myth.

The Soviet myth – as distinct from Soviet reality – acts on its victims both on the rational and the irrational level. The two are so intimately tangled that it is difficult to reconstruct the various stages of becoming a myth-addict in their proper sequence. I remember, however, the first stage with especial clarity. Every comparison between the state of affairs in Russia and in the Western world seemed to speak eloquently in favour of the former. In the West, there was mass unemployment; in Russia, a shortage of manpower. In the West, chronic strikes and social unrest which, in some countries, were threatening to lead to civil war; in Russia, where all factories belonged to the people, the workers vied in socialist competitions for higher production out-puts. In the West, the anarchy of *laissez faire* was drowning the capitalist system in chaos and depression; in Russia, the First Five Year Plan was transforming, by a series of giant strokes, the most backward into the most advanced country of Europe. If History herself were a fellow-traveller, she could not have arranged a more clever timing of events than this coincidence of the gravest crisis of the Western world with the initial phase of Russia's industrial revolution. The contrast between the downward trend

*From Arrow in the Blue, ch. xxx, and The Yogi and the Commissar.

of capitalism and the simultaneous steep rise of planned Soviet economy was so striking and obvious that it led to the equally obvious conclusion: they are the future – we, the past.

The next stage was falling in love with the Five Year Plan. On one-sixth of our sick planet, the most gigantic constructive effort of all times had begun; there Utopia was being built in steel and concrete. Steeped in the Soviet literature of the period whose one and only subject was the building of factories, power stations, tractors, silos and the fulfilment of the Plan, I half-seriously considered writing a modern version of the Song of Songs:

"The eyes of my beloved shine like blast furnaces in the steppe; her lips are boldly drawn like the White Sea Canal; her shoulder is slenderly curved like the Dnieper Dam; her spine is long and straight, like the Turkestan-Siberian railway. . . ." And the foxes, the little foxes that spoilt the vine, were the counter-revolutionary Fascist saboteurs.

It is not easy to recapture that mood today. Irony keeps intruding; the bitterness of later experience is always present. We can add to our knowledge, but we cannot at will subtract from it; no brain surgeon can restore the virginity of an illusion.

When I said that I fell in love with the First Five Year Plan, this was hardly an exaggeration. At twenty-five, I still regarded happiness as a problem in social engineering. Russia had undertaken the greatest engineering experiment in history – at a time when the remaining five-sixths of the world were visibly falling to pieces. Marxist theory and Soviet practice were the admirable and ultimate fulfilment of the nineteenth century's ideal of Progress, to which I owed allegiance. The greatest electric power dam in the world must surely bring the greatest happiness to the greatest number.

Five years earlier I had left home to help with the building of the New Jerusalem. To resurrect the Jewish State after two thousand years had appeared to me not only as a romantic undertaking, but at the same time as a kind of miracle cure for a sick race. I had been disappointed by the provincial chauvinism of Palestine; now a new Zion was in sight, on an infinitely larger, all-embracing scale. It also promised a magic cure – not only for a small ethnic group, but for the whole of mankind. And, just as the new Jewish State was meant to bring back the ancient age of the Prophets, so the Classless Society, according to Marx, would be a revival, at the end of the evolutionary spiral, of the primitive communistic society of a past golden age.

A short time before I actually joined the Communist Party, I planned to throw up my job and to go, for a year or two, as a tractor driver to Russia. The Soviet State needed skilled tractor-men and I had studied engineering; so the plan seemed logical. But the Party officials who took me in hand explained that it was a "typically *petit-bourgeois* romantic idea", so I had to abandon it. I mention this episode because it aimed at an exact, though unconscious repetition of my setting out for *Kvutsa* Heftsebā to become "a drawer of water and hewer of wood". It proves that, living in a disintegrating society, I was thirsting for faith, for an opportunity to build, create and construct.

To create, build, connect and construct . . . that was the lure of the New Faith. The World Revolution was merely an inevitable formality which had to be accomplished before the Classless Society could be built, just as the Last Judgement had to precede the establishment of the Kingdom of Heaven on earth. The rule of the bourgeoisie had of course to be abolished, and its values, codes, taboos and mores thrown on the rubbish heap – in the same way as the bourgeois revolution of 1789 had done away with Feudalism, Aristocracy, the *jus primae noctis*, and all that nonsense. This could not be accomplished without some fighting and bloodshed – but that part of the programme left me rather indifferent. I was only interested in what was to come afterwards; in the building of that Communist society which meant the ultimate fulfilment of man's destiny. It would liberate his immense creative potentialities, now smothered and thwarted by the economic yoke. "The average citizen of the classless society," wrote Trotsky, "will be raised to the level of an Aristotle, a Goethe, a Marx." Once the yoke was shattered, man's Promethean energies would pour forth like lava after a volcanic eruption.

It was a powerful belief, and its loss is a lasting impoverishment. The majority of my comrades were moved by similar notions; at least during the initial stages of their Party career, the Promethean vision dominated the destructive tendency. In later years I saw them change, one by one, as the End receded from their vision, and the Means alone remained. But that we could not foresee when, like the captive Tribe, we set out on our journey leaving the fleshpots of Egypt behind. We did not yet know the desert; we knew only that there was a Promised Land – and that the plagues were descending on Pharaoh according to plan.

In one sense we were in a privileged position. Unlike other revolutionary movements, from early Christianity to the Socialists, whose programmes were purely theoretical blueprints of the future, our Utopia was already incarnated in a real country with real people. Its inaccessibility and remoteness were an additional advantage – it allowed free rein to one's imagination, stimulated by the picturesque costumes and nostalgic songs of the steppes. Progress, Justice, Socialism were abstract slogans that provided no food for dreams, no opportunity for worship and love. But now the homeless, dispersed socialist movement had gained a country, a flag, a sense of power and self-confidence; and even a genuinely beloved father-image in the silhouette of Lenin with the shrewd Mongolian look in his twinkling, humorous eyes. The epic struggle of a great people, fighting its battles of freedom and playing the balalaika in between, satisfied our romantic yearnings and filled us with a new sense of patriotism.

Our fragmentary knowledge of what was happening in Russia assumed the character of a Homeric legend:

The People had come to power on one-sixth of the earth. Private ownership, the greed for power, social distinctions, sexual taboos, had been abolished at one stroke. There were no longer rich and poor, masters and servants, officers and other ranks. The history of *homo sapiens* had started again from scratch. There was thunder behind each of these new decrees, like the voice from Sinai giving the Ten Commandments. Those who listened felt an emotional surge of which they had no longer thought themselves capable. A faith had been released in them, so deeply repressed that they had been unaware of its existence; a hope so deeply buried that they had forgotten it. . . .

In 1930 the Soviet regime was still in its early teens; the reality behind the myth was still difficult to discover for outsiders. Gentle Liberals, who disliked Marx and abhorred violence, came back from guided tours in Russia with a changed, friendly attitude towards "the great Soviet experiment". Worried industrialists and bankers admitted that, after all, "there may be something in it". The various "Societies for promoting Cultural Relations with the USSR" had on their Committees everybody from duchesses to dentists. And the unforgettable Russian films of that epoch received an enthusiastic welcome from critics and public, regardless of their political views.

When I remember films like "Storm over Asia" or "Potemkin", I still believe that they were among the most powerful emotional experiences of my past. To a lesser degree this is also true of the performances of Tairoff's and Meyerhold's theatres touring Europe; and of the books of the new Soviet novelists – of Leonof's *The Thief*, Sholokhov's *Silent Don*, Serafimovich's *The Iron Flood*, and of Isaac Babel's stories of the Civil War. I don't know, and I do not want to know, how I would respond to them today; at the time it looked as if Soviet Russia were on its way to a fresh and radiant culture which in due time – probably at the end of the Second Five Year Plan – would equal the glories of the Renaissance and of the Golden Age of Greece.

And to think that the masterpieces of Eisenstein and Pudovkin were produced by the State; that Stanislavsky and Meyerhold and Wachtangof were employees of the State; that all literature, poetry and prose was published by the State – that is, by the sovereign People, the workers and peasants, the greatest and most original patron of the Arts ever seen! A regime capable of such achievements could inspire only love and admiration, and a new faith in humanity.

It also seemed to me that Communist Russia continued where the Liberal Ullsteins had left off. That super-trust which I had served for the last five years in the Middle East, in Paris and Berlin, and to which I had become intimately attached, had represented in my eyes the embodiment of progressive Liberalism and at the same time of a bold *avant-gardism*. The revolutionary writers and poets of Germany had always been warmly acclaimed on our literary pages. There was in my eyes no break, but a logical continuity between the modernism of Weimar and the new Soviet culture, which seemed destined to become its heir.

Wherever I looked, in every field of social and cultural activity, the Communist movement appeared as the logical extension of the progressive humanistic trend. It was the continuation and fulfilment of the great Judeo-Christian tradition – a new, fresh branch on the tree of Europe's progress through Renaissance and Reformation, through the French Revolution and the Liberalism of the nineteenth century, towards the socialist millennium.

When I ask myself with the melancholy wisdom that comes after the event, how I could have lived for years in this mental trance, I find some comfort in the thought that mediaeval scholasticism and Aristotelian exegesis lasted for a much longer period, and completely befuddled the best brains of that time; and furthermore, that even in our day many approve of the idea that 90 per cent of their contemporaries are designated for an eternal super-Auschwitz by their loving Father in Heaven.

In fine, the mentality of a person who lives inside a closed system of thought, Communist or other, can be summed up in a single formula: He can prove everything he believes, and he believes everything he can prove. The closed system sharpens the faculties of the mind, like an over-efficient grindstone, to a brittle edge; it produces a scholastic, Talmudic, hair-splitting brand of cleverness which affords no protection against committing the crudest imbecilities. People with this mentality are found particularly often among the intelligentsia. I like to call them the "clever imbeciles" – an expression which I do not consider offensive, as I was one of them.

Chapter 9

THE EXPANDING UNIVERSE*

In spite of my premonition that doomsday was approaching, I threw myself with enthusiasm into my new job. It was an ideal job, with unlimited possibilities for roaming through the domains of science and fantasy, from the electron to the spiral nebulae, from experiments in telepathy to the quest for lost Atlantis. To be a science editor sounds like a rather dull occupation; I found it more exciting than that of a foreign correspondent. After four years I had begun to tire of living in a whirl of colourful but undigested impressions, of the superficiality of the type of journalism in which I had been engaged. Now, parallel to the reawakening of political interest, my new job revived the early passion for science as a key to the cosmic mystery:

> Astrophysics is a science which should be pursued in the following manner. Drink some vodka on a clear, cold night, wrap your feet in a warm blanket, sit down on your balcony and stare into the sky. Preferred localities are mountainous regions with a faint thunder of avalanches in the distance; preferred time, the hours of melancholy. If this prescription is not followed, the science in question will appear as a petrified forest of numbers and equations; but he who observes the prescription will experience a curious state of trance. The algebraic signs will change into violin clefs and out of the bizarre equations will emerge the symphony of the rise and decline of the universe . . .

This was the romantic preamble to an article on Professor Piccard's first ascent by balloon into the stratosphere, in May, 1931. Another piece, on the cultivation *in vitro* of living tissues – which, under proper conditions, are potentially immortal – began:

*From Arrow in the Blue, ch. xxxi.

Philosophy is the gaseous state of thought, Science its liquid state, Religion its rigid state. In all three states doubts are expressed regarding the necessity, and even the possibility, of absolute death. We shall discuss this doubt in the liquid state. . . .

The more I became engrossed in historical materialism, in the dry schema of a world governed by the class struggles of Economic Man, the more romantic became, by a kind of rebound, my approach to science. This, however, was not a purely subjective reaction. Just at that time science itself was in the throes of a revolutionary crisis which was rapidly replacing our traditional concepts of reality by a new, wildly futuristic picture of the world. The arrow in the blue no longer pursued its flight in a straight line through infinity; in Einstein's cosmos it followed an elliptical path through the curved space of the universe, and would eventually return to its point of origin from the opposite direction like a traveller on the earth always heading due east.

Even more startling was the discovery that this finite world of ours was expanding at a terrific speed, like, to quote Einstein, "an exploding grenade". This conclusion was reached by direct observations of distant nebulae, whose spectra indicated that they were all running away from us; the farther away they were, the faster they went. So we were living, both in the political and in the physical sense, in an exploding world. I obtained an exclusive interview with Einstein on his return from a visit to Mount Wilson Observatory in 1931, and got my comments straight from the horse's mouth, as it were. Einstein was not in the least disturbed by the fact that our universe was exploding:

"If you just simply take the findings of General Relativity," he explained in his gentle and cosy manner, "and put beside them the empirical findings about the expansion of cosmic matter, then you arrive straight at a solution which shows that the relation between the rate of expansion and the mean density of matter agree quite nicely with what you would expect. . . ." So far so good. ". . . But," Einstein continued, "the speed of this expansion is, according to recent observations, simply dreadful ("fürchterlich gross"). . . ." He agreed that the idea was "not nice at all"; but was confident that "if we keep our eyes open, something will turn up to get us round this difficulty".

During my science editorship, 1930 to 1932, not only was the universe exploding, but the microcosmos, the inside of the atom, was in even worse fermentation. Work on the splitting of the atomic nucleus was making rapid strides. One of the most adventurous efforts in this field was an experiment by three young Berlin physicists – Brasch, Lange and Urban – to smash atoms with lightning from the sky – quite literally. The cyclotron and synchroton were not yet invented, and to split atoms, tensions of several million volts were needed. To obtain these, the three young physicists built a laboratory 5000 feet high in the Italian Alps, on Monte Generoso, and obtained discharges up to fifteen million volts by flying a kite in the thunder-clouds over the peaks. Such a Promethean challenge to the gods could not remain unpunished; one of the three, Kurt Urban, fell off a rock, and was killed.

One of my first science articles in the *Vossische Zeitung* discussed the future of atom splitting – and brought in a shower of protest from German academic circles because it was "so fantastic and utopian":

> . . . If our reading of these phenomena is correct, then we are on the eve of a new era in the history of man, and the technological progress of the last hundred years, which has so radically changed the face of the earth, will be regarded by the future Historian as a mere fumbling prelude. . . . It is significant that the signs of the coming new age should appear in these times of social and political confusion, of a chaotic malaise. . . .

There followed some optimistic speculation about the peaceful uses of atomic energy, and some anxious speculation about destructive chain-reactions which might transform the nucleus:

> . . . into a Pandora's box charged with lightning bolts. Is there no Faustian Earth-Spirit to guard the entrance of the microcosmos, where Nature's most secret forces dance their rounds?

No wonder the Herr Professors didn't like it.

Even more important than this twin-revolution in the realms of the infinitely large and the infinitely small, was the philosophical upheaval which accompanied them, and which became known as "the crisis of causality". Absolute space and absolute time had already gone overboard; the third pillar of our traditional view of the world, the law of causal determination, now followed suit. The so-called Laws of Nature lost their solid character; they could no longer be regarded as expressing certainties, merely statistical probabilities. The rigid causal connections between "cause" and "effect" were loosened, softened up as it were; what the physicist had regarded as universal laws now turned out to be mere rules of the thumb, whose validity was limited to medium-sized phenomena; on the sub-atomic level determinism itself dissolved in a kind of blurred fringe, and all certainty vanished from the universe.

This crisis had been brewing in the physicists' laboratories since the beginning of the century; but its full philosophical implications only became apparent in the late nineteen-twenties. By 1932 the tidy Newtonian view of the universe had been replaced by a kind of expressionistic portrait full of such horrors as "negative energies", "holes in space", and electrons "moving in the opposite sense of time".

At sixteen, I had lived in a neatly arranged, comprehensible clockwork-universe whose last mystery was just about to be solved. At twenty-six I saw the arrogant self-confidence of the nineteenth century scientist collapse. Since the Renaissance, the Ultimate Cause had gradually shifted from the heavens to the atomic nucleus, from the super-human to the sub-human level. But now it became clear that the working of this "destiny from below" was just as unfathomable as "destiny from above" had been. I learnt a decisive lesson in intellectual modesty which, without my noticing it, counterbalanced the "total" explanations offered by Marxist philosophy. At that time there was as yet no conscious conflict between the two; the crusade for Utopia and the quest for Truth, the dubious battles of the day and the vista of eternity, seemed to complement each other.

Writing half a century later, the crisis in physics, and its implications for philosophy – or metaphysics – still remain unresolved. It will return, as a kind of leitmotif, in later chapters of this volume.

As far as a science editor can have a policy, mine was a definite bias towards a "naturalistic" trend [to-day it is called environmentalism] in technology; that is to say,

> towards inventions which tend to exploit natural sources of energy in a clean, direct and elegant manner. In the visions of a naturalistic technology there is no place for such purgatoria as the stokehold of a steamship, or a mining-shaft; the energy supply of the future must come from sources purer, closer to nature, and more powerful; from solar radiations concentrated by giant parabolic mirrors and stored in heat accumulators; from turbines which suckle energy direct from the

great mother of organic life, the ocean; from power-stations fed by the natural movements of rain, river and wind. In other words, technology will be integrated into the natural processes on which all organic life is based. (*Vossische Zeitung*, 1930.)

* * *

In 1931, a polar expedition still had the romantic aura of a boyhood dream; Captain Scott and Commander Peary, Amundsen and Nansen were among the heroes of my schooldays, as Charles Lindbergh and Lawrence of Arabia were to be for the next generation.

The Graf Zeppelin Arctic expedition in July, 1931, was one of the most successful ventures of its kind. It was also the climax of my career as a journalist. The Ullsteins had acquired the news monopoly, and I was the only representative of the world press on board – about the most perfect assignment a newspaperman could pray for. During a non-stop flight of five days and four nights, the expedition accomplished a nearly complete photographic survey of the arctic land-masses between the fortieth and hundred-and-tenth degrees of longitude East (Franz Josef Land, Northern Land, etc.), discovered half a dozen islands, crossed others off the map, filled in one of the last remaining blank spots on the chart, and, in the words of the leader of the expedition, "did in about ninety hours an amount of work which would have taken a combined sea-and-land expedition several years to accomplish without producing equally reliable results".

Some previous arctic air expeditions had ended in disaster. Nobile's airship *Italia* had crashed; Amundsen, searching for the survivors, had for ever vanished together with his plane. The Zeppelin expedition marked the dividing line between the romantic and the scientific era in arctic exploration; that was its historic significance.

Chapter 10

HOW TO FAIL AS A SPY*

On the return of the expedition, I received invitations for lectures from all over Europe. I obtained six weeks' leave and, equipped with my log-book and set of lantern slides, went on a lecture tour through Germany, Denmark, Sweden and Holland. When I got back to Berlin in September, 1931, the Ullsteins offered me the post of foreign editor and assistant editor-in-chief of the *B.Z. am Mittag* – Germany's largest evening paper – in addition to retaining my post as science editor of the *Vossische*. I accepted. It was an unusual – and perhaps symbolic – combination of jobs which involved a considerable amount of work, a high salary, and much professional satisfaction. It lasted for about nine months; half-way through I formally joined the Communist Party.

The political considerations which led up to this decision I have discussed in previous chapters. The peculiar timing of the decisive step is more difficult to explain. It coincided with the most rewarding phase so far attained in my professional career. It seems logical that a person should enlist in a revolutionary movement when he is in despair, starving, frustrated, out of a job. But I was doing fine in this putrid *bourgeois*-capitalist world; in fact I had never done better. And this, perhaps, explains the timing of the decision.

I have always wanted to write a sequel to La Fontaine's fable of the fox and the grapes. The poor fox is constantly mocked by his friends about the sour grapes, until he develops an inferiority complex. Night after night, while the other members of the pack divert themselves by stealing nice, fat hens, he is secretly engaged in taking climbing lessons. After several weeks of dogged effort,

*From Arrow in the Blue, ch. xxxv, The Invisible Writing, ch. i, and The God that Failed.

he finally succeeds in getting at the grapes – only to discovery that they really *are* sour, as he had maintained from the beginning. But who will believe him? He does not even believe himself. The grapes become an obsession with him. He has to climb after them, and eat the beastly fruit for the sole purpose of proving to himself that it is indeed sour. He gets more and more skinny on this diet and, after a nervous breakdown, dies of gastric ulcers.

The parable is meant to illustrate the tragedy of snobs and careerists. The sophisticated snob, *à la* Proust or Evelyn Waugh, knows quite well that duchesses are sour and boring, yet he has to feed on duchesses to prove to himself that they are within his reach. The same goes for all climbers, compelled to go on guzzling the acid grapes until the end.

After my return from the Arctic, I felt suddenly liberated from this compulsion, and the impulse to burn my boats asserted itself once again. I had run away from home just before obtaining my degree. Now I took the plunge, which sooner or later must lead to the loss of my job – and open the way towards a new departure.

Seven years earlier, I had explained my decision to throw up my studies as an enamouredness with unreason itself, as an urge to jump off the track on which my future seemed destined to run like a train from station to station. This time I had an even better alibi. The Weimar Republic seemed to be heading towards civil war. The irrational impulse, which compelled me to throw away the fruit of years of labour, proved in the end eminently rational in a world of mass insanity. Had I behaved reasonably, I would in all likelihood have ended in the crematorium of Auschwitz. The tragic plane on which the world moves in times of upheaval has a logic different from the homely reasoning of the trivial plane. For the average citizen it is difficult if not impossible to make the transition; he suffers passively the unreason of floods, wars and revolutions, while apparently crazy adventurers, artists and other emotionally unbalanced people, accustomed to living on the precarious edge where the tragic and the trivial planes intersect, jump with alacrity from one to the other. They seem to thrive on catastrophes; their folly is their guardian angel.

I applied for membership to the Communist Party on December 31, 1931; the new life was to start with the new calendar year.

The preface to The Invisible Writing, *written in 1952–3, sounds a note of apology concerning the chapters which describe my early*

*Communist days in Berlin and Soviet Russia in the nineteen-
thirties: "I found it impossible to revive the naive enthusiasm of
that period: I could analyse the ashes, but not resurrect the
flame."*

I went to Communism, to quote Pablo Picasso, "as one goes to a
spring of fresh water", and I left Communism as one clambers out
of a poisoned river strewn with the wreckage of flooded cities and
the corpses of the drowned. This, in sum, is my story from 1931 to
1938, from my twenty-sixth to my thirty-third year.

Seven months after I joined the Communist Party I emigrated
from Germany to Soviet Russia. These seven months of transition
are divided into two periods. During the first, I was a secret
member of the Party; during the second, an open one.

My written application for membership of the KPD – *Kom-
munistische Partei Deutschlands* – was addressed to the Central
Committee of the Party. It was answered a week or so later by a
rather mystifying letter, typed on blank paper and bearing an
illegible signature, in which I was invited, "with reference to your
esteemed of December 31" to meet "a representative of our firm"
at the offices of the Schneidermühl paper-mill in Berlin.

The man whom I met at the appointed place and hour was Herr
Ernst Schneller, head of the Department for Agitation and
Propaganda (AGITPROP) of the German Communist Party, and
at the same time chief of one of the Comintern's secret *apparats* or
intelligence networks. In yet another capacity, Schneller was
Reichstagsabgeordneter, a member of the German Parliament.
This double existence as an official dignitary and as an underground conspirator was by no means exceptional. A large proportion of the Communist membership lived, and still lives, to use
French Party slang, *à cheval* – astride the two worlds. Nor is such
an existence considered dishonourable. To exploit fully the constitutional liberties provided by bourgeois society for the purpose
of destroying them is elementary Marxist dialectics.

I had two meetings with Ernst Schneller, and after these I never
saw him again. A few years later he died in a Nazi prison where he
was serving a six-year sentence of hard labour. He was an
insignificant-looking, shy, thin, bony man with a pinched face
and an awkward smile. He told me that he was a vegetarian and
lived mostly on raw vegetables and fruit; also, that he never read
any newspapers except the Party press. At first I took him for a
narrow-minded bureaucrat, but my initial feeling of condescen-

sion soon changed into respect for his quiet and astute manner of arguing. I told him of my desire to throw up my job and go as a tractor-driver to Russia; but within a few hours Schneller had convinced me that I would be more useful to the Party by keeping my membership secret, carrying on as a journalist, influencing, within the limits of my possibilities, the policy of my paper, and passing on to the Party any inside information that came my way. The Party, he explained, though still enjoying the privilege of legality, would probably quite soon be outlawed and forced underground. In that event people like myself, who were in respectable positions and untainted by suspicion, would be even more valuable than at present in the struggle against Fascism and imperialist aggression. Everything he said sounded so plausible that by the end of our first meeting I agreed to his proposal and became, without being fully aware of the fact, a member of the Comintern's intelligence network.

At our second and last meeting, Schneller handed me my Party card, made out under the alias "Ivan Steinberg". He had also brought along a dark, blowsy girl named Paula who would serve as a liaison with my future superior in the *apparat*, named Edgar. Thus from the moment of joining the Party I found myself plunged into a strange world of conspiratorial twilight, populated by "Edgars" and "Paulas" without a surname or address – fleeting, elusive shapes like the phosphorescent creatures of the deep sea.

Edgar and Paula were my only contacts in the *apparat*. We usually met in my flat, where Paula took down on a typewriter what information I was able to supply, while Edgar would pace up and down the room and put in a question now and then to clarify a point. He was a slim, smooth, smiling young man of thirty, blond, with an open face and frank eyes. His real name I only discovered more than twenty years later, in the following footnote in Alexander Weissberg's book, *Conspiracy of Silence* (London, 1952):

In *The God That Failed* Koestler mentions a man named Edgar. . . . "Edgar" was a revolutionary worker from Hamburg. His real name was Fritz Burde. He was a decent fellow and a good comrade. I met him in 1936 in Moscow when he had a high position in the Red Army Intelligence service. . . . For a long time the GPU and the War Commissariat had been fighting for control of this important secret organisation abroad. Once Tukhachevsky was arrested, the GPU had a free hand. They recalled almost all the military secret agents from abroad and arrested them. Fritz Burde was in charge of the secret service of the Red Army in Scandinavia, and when he was recalled with the others he told friends that he was going to his death, but that he had no alternative.

Without knowing what fate had befallen him, I used "Edgar" some ten years later as a model for Bernard, the young Nazi agent in *Arrival and Departure*. I was trying to visualise a handsome and winning Nazi who would capture the reader's sympathy – and found myself describing the smiling appearance and manners of Edgar, the Communist. He fitted the part perfectly.

My contact with the *apparat* remained a peripheral one, and after two or three months came to a dismal end. In my capacity as foreign editor of the *B.Z. am Mittag* I had access to virtually all confidential information of a political nature that converged in that important nerve centre of the Weimar Republic, the Ullsteins. My assistant at that post was a young man of twenty-one, Von E., the son of a retired German ambassador. With only five years separating us, we soon became friends; I preached the Marxist doctrine to Von E., and became the kind of guru to him that others had been to me. After a fortnight or so, he had made sufficient progress to be roped into the service of the Cause. The Von E.'s entertained at their house members of the German general staff and of the diplomatic corps; my young friend's task was to keep his ears open and report to me anything of interest – in particular information relating to "the preparations for the war of aggression against the Soviet Union by Germany and the other imperialistic powers".

For a few weeks all went well. Then young Von E. was seized with remorse, and one morning after a sleepless night, he presented me with an ultimatum: he must either reveal our treasonable activities, or shoot himself. He had written a letter of confession, addressed to the managing director of the firm; but he would only hand the letter in if I gave my consent. He placed the long, hand-written letter on my desk.

Logically this demand made no sense. In the terms of the law, we had committed no punishable offence. We had not stolen military secrets or sold political documents. Von E. had merely passed on some parlour gossip to me which I in turn had related to my political friends. But these arguments failed to impress the young man. To be a Marxist, or a Socialist, he said, was one thing; to pass on information to agents of a foreign power, quite another. It was treason; and whether, in the strictly technical sense, we were spies or not had no bearing on this fact. Unless I consented to his making a full confession, it was impossible for him to go on living.

I did not take young Von E.'s threat entirely seriously, and was unable to convince myself of the reality of the scene. The boy, standing in front of the desk – he had refused to sit down – looked ghastly, with black stubbles on his white face and red, swollen eyes. He was perhaps unconsciously dramatising the situation, and the thrills of self-dramatisation were not unknown to me. On the other hand, he seemed quite capable of carrying the act to the point of really shooting himself. His demand that I shoud expressly consent to his handing in of the letter was quixotic and absurd. Yet I consented without further argument – and without even reading the letter that would inevitably put an end both to my professional career and to my usefulness to the *apparat*.

The only reasonable course would have been to read the letter carefully and discuss its contents in detail; to explain away certain points, ridicule others, and put a harmless interpretation on the rest; to blur and confuse the issue, make young Von E. feel a fool, and then to gain time by asking him to think the matter over. With a certain amount of psychology and persuasion, it would perhaps have been possible to make the young man see matters differently, to make the harsh contours of fact dissolve in doubt and dialectical twilight. Even if I could not save my job, I could save my standing with the *apparat* by putting up a fight and denying Von E.'s accusations. Yet, strangely enough, I could not get myself to argue. The whole scene had a touch of dreamlike unreality; and as I stuffed the letter back into Von E.'s pocket and told him to hand it in with my blessings and to go to hell, I was acting with a dreamy inner certitude that made me indifferent to the consequences.

I had been prepared to sacrifice my future for the Party, but not to throw it away in such an apparently senseless manner. Now, however, after twenty years, it seems to me that my ready consent to Von E.'s denunciation and to the destruction of my career was senseless only in appearance. It seems as if on crucial occasions a type of logic were entering into action entirely different from the reasoning of the "trivial plane". As I look back on my past, I see a blind man painfully groping with his stick along the crowded pavement, while his absent-minded dog trots along on a loose leash and might as well not exist. Yet at the critical moment when the street has to be crossed and the stick becomes useless, the blind man feels a reassuring tug of the leash and knows that his seeing eye has taken over.

In this particular case the blessings of unreason soon became apparent. My quixotic gesture towards Von E. saved me from the imminent danger of becoming a full-fledged *apparatchik* – the Party's homely slang-name for its agents. Some time before the disaster, Edgar had suggested that I go to Japan for the *apparat* under the guise of a news-correspondent. I had agreed at once, and though this scheme did not materialise, some similar assignment was bound to turn up sooner or later. As yet I was still an amateur, drifting on the periphery of the vortex; a few more weeks or months and I would inevitably have been drawn into a zone from which there is no turning back. Thanks to Von E.'s confession, however, I not only lost my job with the Ullsteins but also my usefulness to the *apparat* – and this in a manner which to Edgar and Schneller proved my total unfitness for secret work. They dropped me without ceremony.

A few days after the letter was handed in, the Ullsteins gave me notice on the pretext of reductions in the staff, and offered me a lump sum in compensation for the remaining term of my five-year contract. Not a word was said about Von E. and the Communist Party; they were anxious to avoid a scandal. So was the Party; Edgar instructed me to accept the settlement and leave it at that.

Except on one occasion, I never saw either him or Paula again. Paula was later killed by the SS in Ravensbruck. Edgar's and Schneller's fate I have already mentioned.

Having lost my job, I was free from the fetters of the bourgeois world; having lost my usefulness for the *apparat*, there was no longer any reason for keeping my Party-membership secret. I gave up my flat in the expensive district of Neu-Westend, and moved into an apartment-house on Bonner Platz known as the Red Block, for most of the tenants were penniless writers and artists of radical views. There I joined the local Communist cell and was at last permitted to lead the full life of a regular Party member.

Our cell was one among several thousand in Berlin, and one among the several hundred thousand basic units of the Communist network in the world. Cells exist in every country where the Party is legally tolerated; in countries where Communism is outlawed, a system of "groups of five" or "groups of three" replaces the larger legal units. The term "cell" is not purely metaphorical;

for these are living, pulsating units within a huge, sprawling organism, co-ordinated in their function, governed by a hierarchy of nerve centres, and susceptible to various diseases – to the Titoist virus, to bourgeois infection or Trotskyist cancer. The part of the white phagocytes is played by the various defence mechanisms of the Party, from the Central Control Commission to the GPU.

Our cell comprised about twenty members. The consciousness of being one unit among millions in an organised, disciplined whole was always present. We had among us several *littérateurs*, such as Alfred Kantorowicz and Max Schroeder; a psychoanalyst – Wilhelm Reich, who broke with the Party in 1933 and is now the director of the Institute for Orgone Research in Rangeley, Maine;* several actors from an *avant-garde* theatre called The Mouse Trap; several girls with intellectual ambitions; an insurance agent and a number of working men. In so far as the majority of us were intellectuals, our cell was untypical in its structure, yet entirely typical in its function – that is, in our daily work and routine.

Half of our activities were legal, half illegal. The cell met officially once a week, but the more active members were in daily contact with each other. The official meeting always started with a political lecture by an instructor from District Headquarters (or by the cell leader after he had been briefed at HQ), in which the line was laid down concerning the various questions of the day. This was followed by discussion, but a discussion of a peculiar kind. It is a basic rule of Communist discipline that, once the Party leadership has decided to adopt a certain line regarding a given problem, all criticism of that decision becomes deviationist sabotage. In theory, discussion is permissible before a decision has been reached; in practice decisions are always imposed from above, without previous consultation with the rank and file. One of the slogans of the German Party said: "The front-line is no place for discussions." Another said: "Wherever a Communist happens to be, he is always in the front-line." So our discussions always showed a complete unanimity of opinion.

That last summer of Weimar Germany was for the Party a period of transition; we were preparing to go underground, and accordingly regrouping our cadres. We might be outlawed overnight; everything had to be ready for this emergency. The moment we

*In 1952, when this was written, Reich's career as a cult-figure was still in the future.

were forced into illegality, all Party cells would cease to function, and would be superseded by a new, nationwide structure, the "Groups of Five". The cells, whose membership ranged from ten to thirty comrades, were too large in size for underground work, and offered easy opportunities for *agents provocateurs* and informers. The breaking up of the cadres into Groups of Five meant a corresponding diminution of risks. Only the leader of the Group was to know the identity and addresses of the other four; and he alone was to have contact with the next higher level of the Party hierarchy. If he was arrested, he could only betray the four individuals in his group, and his contact-man.

So, while our cell still continued to function, each member was secretly allotted to a Group of Five, the idea being that none of the groups should know the composition of any other. In fact, as we were all neighbours in the Block, we each knew which Group was secretly meeting in whose flat; and, on the night of the burning of the Reichstag, when Goering dealt his death-blow to the Communist Party, the Groups scattered and the whole elaborate structure collapsed all over the Reich. We had marvelled at the conspiratorial ingenuity of our leaders; and though all of us had to read works on the technique of insurrection and civil warfare, our critical faculties had become so numbed that none of us realised the catastrophic implications of the scheme. These preparations for a long underground existence in decentralised groups meant that our leaders accepted the victory of the Nazis as inevitable. And the breaking up of the cadres into small units indicated that the Party would offer no open, armed resistance to Hitler's bid for power, and was preparing for sporadic small-scale actions instead.

But we, the rank and file, knew nothing of this. During that long, stifling summer of 1932 we fought our ding-dong battles with the Nazis. Hardly a day passed without one or two being killed in Berlin. The main battlefields were the *Bierstuben*, the smoky little taverns of the working-class districts. Some of these served as meeting places for the Nazis, some as meeting-places (*Verkehrslokale*) for us. To enter the wrong pub was to venture into the enemy's lines. From time to time the Nazis would shoot up one of our *Verkehrslokale*. It was done in the classic Chicago tradition: a gang of SA men would drive slowly past the tavern, firing through the glass panes, then vanish at break-neck speed. We had far fewer motor-cars than the Nazis, and retaliation was mostly carried out in cars either stolen, or borrowed from sympathisers. The men who did these jobs were members of the RFB (*Roter Frontkämpfer Bund*), the League of Communist War Veterans. My car was sometimes borrowed by comrades whom I had never seen before, and returned a few hours later with no questions asked and no explanations offered. It was a tiny, red, open Fiat car and most unsuitable for such purposes; but nobody else in our cell had one. It was the last relic of my bourgeois past; now it served as a vehicle for the proletarian revolution. I spent half my time driving it round on various errands: transporting pamphlets and leaflets, shadowing certain Nazi cars whose numbers had been signalled to us, and acting as a security agent. Once I had to transport the equipment of a complete hand-printing press from a railway station to a cellar under a greengrocer's shop.

The RFB men who came to fetch the car for their guerilla expeditions were sometimes rather sinister types from the Berlin underworld. They came, announced by a telephone call or by a verbal message from District HQ, but the same men rarely turned up twice. Sometimes, on missions of a more harmless nature, I was myself ordered to act as driver. We would drive slowly past a number of Nazi pubs to watch the goings-on, or patrol a pub of our own when one of our informers in the Nazi camp warned us of impending attack. This latter kind of mission was unpleasant; we would park, with headlights turned off and engine running, in the proximity of the pub; and at the approach of a car I would hear the click of the safety-catch on my passengers' guns, accompanied by the gentle advice "to keep my chump well down". But I was never involved in any actual shooting.

Once the RFB men who came to fetch the car disguised themselves in my flat before starting out. They stuck on moustaches, put on glasses, dark jackets and bowler hats. I watched them from the window driving off – four stately, bowler-hatted gents in the ridiculous little red car, looking like a party in a funeral procession. They came back four hours later, changed back to normal, and made off with a silent handshake. My instructions, in case the number of the car was taken by the police during some action, were to say that it had been stolen and that I had found it again in a deserted street.

On July 20, 1932, von Papen staged his *coup d'état*: one lieutenant and eight men chased the Socialist government of Prussia from office. It was the beginning of the end. The Socialist Party, with its eight million followers, did nothing. The Socialist-controlled trade unions did not even call a protest strike. Only we, the Communists, called for an immediate general strike. The call fell on deaf ears. Like inflated currency, our verbiage had lost all real meaning for the masses. We lost the battle against Hitler before it was joined. After July 20, 1932, it was evident to all but ourselves that the KPD, strongest among the Communist parties in Europe, was a castrated giant whose brag and bluster only served to cover its lost virility.

A few months later everything was over. Years of preparations for the emergency proved within a few hours totally useless. Thaelmann, leader of the Party, and the majority of his lieutenants were found in their carefully-prepared hide-outs and arrested within the first few days. The Central Committee fled abroad. The long night descended over Germany.

Few among the intellectuals in the Party realised at the time that within the short span of three generations the Communist movement had travelled from the era of the Apostles to that of the Borgias. But the seeds of corruption had already been present in the works of Marx: in the vitriolic tone of his polemics, the abuse heaped on his opponents, the denunciation of rivals and dissenters as traitors to the working class and agents of the bourgeoisie. Proudhon, Dühring, Bakunin, Liebknecht, Lassalle, had been treated by Marx exactly as Trotsky, Bukharin, Zinoviev et alia were treated by Stalin – except that Marx did not have the power to shoot his victims. During these three generations, the uses of the dialectic had also been vastly simplified. It was, for instance, easy to prove scientifically that everybody who disagreed with the Party line was an agent of Fascism because (a) by disagreeing with the line he endangered the unity of the Party; (b) by endangering the unity of the Party he improved the chances of a Fascist victory; hence (c) *objectively* he acted as an agent of Fascism even if *subjectively* he had his kidneys smashed in a Fascist concentration camp. It was equally easy to prove that charity, public or private, was counter-revolutionary because it deceived the masses regarding the true nature of the capitalist system, and thereby contributed to its preservation.

My fanatical allegiance to the Party did not cause complete mental blindness to the more absurd phenomena in my new environment. I noticed that the political instructors sent by District Headquarters to the meetings of our cell knew nothing of the world outside the narrow field of working-class politics – that is, strikes, demonstrations and trade union developments. They did not know or believe that the Christian-Democratic Chancellor Bruenning was genuinely opposed to Hitler, or that there was a difference between a British Tory and a German Nazi. For them, democracy was "a camouflaged form of the dictatorship of the capitalist ruling class" and Fascism "its overt form"; while "the class-content" of both regimes was the same. The political struggles between the various "bourgeois" parties were merely a symptom of the "internal contradictions of the capitalist system"; the real alignment of social forces was along the class frontier. All this to my mind was both true and untrue. It was untrue because it was a crude oversimplification of a complex reality; but in the long view of History nuances did not matter, and my sophistication did not matter, and the dialectical telescope revealed the essential truth.

A special feature of Party life that had a lasting influence on me was worship of the proletariat and contempt for the intelligentsia. Intellectuals of middle-class origin were in the Party on sufferance, not by right; this was constantly rubbed into us. We had to be tolerated, because during the transition period the Party needed the engineers, doctors, scientists and literati of the pre-revolutionary intelligentsia. But we were no more trusted or respected than the so-called "useful Jews" in Hitler's Germany, who were given a distinctive armlet and allowed a short respite before their usefulness expired and they went the way of their kin. The social origin of parents and grandparents is as decisive under a Communist regime as racial origin was under the Nazi regime. Accordingly, Communist intellectuals of middle-class origin were trying by various means to give themselves proletarian airs. They wore coarse polo-sweaters, displayed black fingernails, talked working-class slang. It was one of our undisputed articles of faith that members of the working-class, regardless of their level of intelligence and education, would always have a more "correct" approach to any political problem than the learned intellectual. This was supposed to be due to a kind of instinct rooted in class-consciousness. There is again a distinct parallel here with the Nazis' contempt for "destructive Jewish cleverness" as opposed to the "healthy and natural instinct of the race". That a truck-driver or a dynamo-fitter can be just as neurotic as a literary critic, and that he merely lacks the articulateness to express it, was a much later discovery.

It is relatively easy to explain how a person with my story and background came to become a Communist, but more difficult to convey a state of mind that led a young man of twenty-six to be ashamed of having been to a university, to curse the agility of his brain, the articulateness of his language, to regard such civilised tastes and habits as he had acquired as a constant source of self-reproach, and intellectual self-mutilation as a desirable aim. If it had been possible to lance those tastes and habits like a boil, I would gladly have submitted to the operation.

A recent American study, embracing people from all social classes and races, including Negroes, has shown that the majority of young Americans who joined the Communist Party were prompted not by economic distress, but by some conflict within the family. I have said before that such psychological facts neither prove nor disprove the validity of Marxist theory. But vice versa, it is not Marxist theory in itself which turns people into rebels, but a psychological disposition which makes them susceptible to revolutionary theories. The latter then serve as rationalisations of their personal conflict – which does not exclude the possibility that the rationalisation may be a correct one.

To sum up this aspect of the story. As a child I had been taught that whatever I did was wrong, a pain to others and a disgrace to myself. Now, at twenty-six, the floating mass of anxiety and guilt, always ready to fasten on the first peg in sight, turned against my bourgeois background, my powers of reasoning and capacity for enjoyment. To bask in the sun, to read a novel, to dine in a good restaurant, to go to a picture gallery, became guilty exercises of a privilege that others could not share, frivolous diversions from the class struggle. Middle-class Communists live, like Catholics, in a constant awareness of original sin.

I deplore the logical error that led me into the Communist Party; but I do not regret the spiritual discipline that it imposed. Purgatory is a painful experience; but no one who went through it is likely to wish that it should be erased from his past.

A small episode has stuck in my memory as characteristic of the atmosphere of Berlin during the feverish months of Götterdämmerung that preceded the Nazis' seizure of power. It is hard to believe for anyone who has not experienced the mass-hysteria that conquered the German people during the last days of Weimar. It happened to a colleague of mine at Ullsteins', whose

name has slipped my memory – it sounded something like von
Ehrendorf, so I shall call him that.

During the carnival season of 1932, Ehrendorf went to a dance
and picked up a tall, pretty blonde. She wore a large swastika
brooch on her breast, was about nineteen or twenty, gay, uninhibited and brimful of healthy animal spirits – in short, the ideal
Hitler-Mädchen of the Brave New World. After the dance, Ehrendorf persuaded her to go back with him to his flat, where she met
his advances more than half-way. Then, at the climactic moment,
the girl raised herself on one elbow, stretched out the other arm in
the Roman salute, and breathed in a dying voice a fervent "Heil
Hitler". Poor Ehrendorf nearly had a stroke. When he had
recovered, the blonde sweetie explained to him that she and a
bunch of her girl friends had taken a solemn vow, pledging
themselves "to remember the Fuehrer every time at the most
sacred moment in a woman's life".

A short time before I lost my job, I had organised a caucus of
Communist sympathisers among the Ullstein staff. The group met
once a week in my flat, and comprised about a dozen columnists,
sub-editors, magazine artists, theatre and film critics. Its purpose
was to exchange information, and to counteract the pro-Nazi
tendencies within the trust. Only two of us were members of the
CP – Kantorowicz, who was a free-lance contributor to several
Ullstein papers, and myself; and we were the only ones who
punctually attended the meetings of the caucus, who took the
matter seriously and knew what we were about. We were disciplined members of a civilian army acting under instructions; the
others were free agents, divided and confused, as intellectuals
always are in matters of practical action, anxious "to do something", frightened of the consequences, and given to long,
rambling, pointless arguments.

I reported every week on the antics of the group through Edgar
to the apparat, including brief reports on the background and
character of each of the members. My instructions were to let them
all talk to their hearts' content and just to keep the thing going,
while watching the individual evolution of each member with a
view to his possible future usefulness. By this slow, patient,
apparently aimless method did the apparat cast its net into
thousands of similar "study groups" and "discussion circles" in
universities, editorial offices, government agencies, industrial

enterprises all over the world. It was all perfectly harmless and high-minded; and it produced an astonishing harvest of Alger Hisses, Nunn Mays and Donald MacLeans. Yet such big and dramatic catches were rare; of equal importance were the more intangible results of ideological infiltration, the creation of a mental climate in progressive-liberal circles which ranged from benevolent neutrality to active support of the Great Socialist Experiment, and the equation of all criticism of Russia with a reactionary, Fascist attitude.

Our particular little group was not a successful one, and it petered out after a few months. With the shadow of Hitler lying across the country like a monster-shaped cloud, our motley crowd of intellectuals was too scared to be capable of any clear thought. It was easy to win their sympathy for Russia, but impossible to make them take a determined stand for their own interests in Germany. Whenever Communists took the lead in actions of social protest – in defence of anti-Fascists, Negroes, or in the resistance movements in any part of the world – they certainly acted for devious motives of their own. But at the same time they behaved with courage, discipline and determination, which won them grudging admiration and gave them a considerable moral advantage over their soft and undecided progressive allies. It was this fearless, active, knight-errant aspect of Communism which attracted me and millions of others to the movement, and which compensated us for our disappointments.

I was waiting for my visa to Russia. When I lost my job I had asked the Party for permission to emigrate. This was regarded as a rare privilege, for the duty of every Communist was to work for the Revolution in his own country. However, I still enjoyed a certain reputation as a liberal journalist (the reasons why I had to leave the Ullsteins were not known in public), and the Party was willing to exploit this advantage. It was agreed that I should go to Russia and write a series of articles on the First Five Year Plan, maintaining the fiction that I was still a bourgeois reporter. I accordingly entered into an agreement with a literary agency, the Karl Dunker Verlag,* who undertook to syndicate the series in some twenty newspapers in various European countries. But the months passed by, and my visa did not arrive.

*Not to be confused with the Communist editor, Herman Dunker.

I would probably still be waiting for it if Johannes R. Becher had not arrived in Berlin from Moscow.

Becher, the Communist poet laureate, was President of the "League of Proletarian Revolutionary Writers of Germany". He was a tall, sturdy Bavarian with a fleshy nondescript face, made even more inscrutable by thick-lensed, steel-rimmed spectacles. One could take him for a teacher of mathematics or the director of an insurance company – for anything but a poet. Yet behind this calm poise and neutral facade was a complex and fascinating personality.

Becher became known in Germany in the mad years after the First World War, partly as a young expressionist poet, partly as the lucky survivor of a suicide pact. His outstanding quality was a cynical humour, very unusual in Party circles. Together with this went an astute judgement of men, remarkable cunning in handl-ing situations, and a ruthless capacity for manoeuvring in trou-bled waters. It is probably this combination of abilities, so rare in a poet, that has enabled him to survive the purges and traps which threaten the Communist writer. In the inner circles of the Party he was sometimes called "the tightrope walker".

Becher took a liking to me which I reciprocated and in a manner still do, regardless of the fact that after I left the Party he publicly denounced me as a war criminal, a gangster and a spy, and variously demanded that I should be exterminated or put into a mental asylum. But to issue statements of this kind is no more than an inescapable formality for Party members; the Soviet citi-zen who, as a matter of routine, signs a resolution asking that this or that fallen leader should be "shot as a mad dog" has no ill feeling against the victim and would be surprised if told that the latter resented his performing such a simple act of duty. When one knows the rules of the game one does not take these matters very seriously, and when one's former comrades keep calling one every name out of the zoo there is no need even for forgiveness; one knows that they cannot act otherwise.

So Becher and I got on well, and he procured me an official invitation from MORP, the "International Organisation of Revolutionary Writers", to write a book on the Soviet Union: *Russia through Bourgeois Eyes*. The idea of it was similar to that of the articles for which I had signed up with Dunker: Mr K., a liberal news-correspondent, starts his journey with an anti-Communist bias, is gradually converted by the results of the Five Year Plan, and ends up as a friend and admirer of the Soviet Union. As

MORP was *de facto* a branch of the Comintern, and Becher himself occupied a high position in it, my visa was now at last granted.

I still had my car, the little red Fiat that had rendered such faithful services to the cell. It was known in the Party under the pet name "Gretchen". One day Becher happened to ask me whether I intended to sell Gretchen before I left. I told him that I intended to leave her to the Party.

"The Party," said Becher, "is a large body. The German branch of MORP is affiliated to it. It would be logical to leave Gretchen to us." I agreed that it would be logical. As Becher happened to be chairman of the German branch of MORP, it was also logical that he took personal possession of Gretchen, and a few days after I had left for Russia, he went off in her to find inspiration in the Black Forest. As a sign of his appreciation, he procured me a contract for my book with the Russian State Publishing Trust against a cash advance of three thousand roubles.

By the end of July, 1932, I was at last ready to turn my back on the bourgeois world and head once more for Utopia. It was six months before the Germany of Weimar became Nazi-land.

Chapter 11

A BLINKERED TRAVELLER*

My first destination was not Moscow but Kharkov, then capital of the Soviet Ukraine. I had friends living in that town, who had invited me to stay with them until I found my feet in the new world.

My idea of Russia had been formed entirely by Soviet propaganda. It was the image of a super-America, engaged in the most gigantic enterprise in history, buzzing with activity, efficiency, enthusiasm. The motto of the First Five Year Plan had been to "reach and surpass" the Occident; this task had been completed in four years instead of five. At the frontier I would "change trains for the twenty-first century", as another slogan had promised.

The train puffed slowly across the Ukrainian steppe. It stopped frequently. At every station there was a crowd of peasants in rags, offering ikons and linen in exchange against a loaf of bread. The women were lifting up their infants to the compartment windows – infants pitiful and terrifying with limbs like sticks, puffed bellies, big cadaverous heads lolling on thin necks. I had arrived, unsuspecting, at the peak of the famine of 1932–3, which had depopulated entire districts and claimed several million victims. Its ravages are now officially admitted, but at the time they were kept secret from the world. The scenes at the railway stations all along our journey gave me an inkling of the disaster, but no understanding of its causes and extent. My Russian travelling companions took pains to explain to me that these wretched crowds were *kulaks*, rich peasants who had resisted the collectiv-

*From The Invisible Writing, *Part Two, and* Von Weissen Nächten und Roten Tagen.

isation of the land and whom it had therefore been necessary to evict from their farms.

I reacted to the brutal impact of reality on illusion in a manner typical of the true believer. I was surprised and bewildered – but the elastic shock-absorbers of my Party training began to operate at once. I had eyes to see, and a mind conditioned to explain away what they saw.

To illustrate this point, I shall quote a passage from the travel-book that I started to write a few weeks after my arrival. Working on the book was a means to work all doubts and misgivings out of my system by ridiculing my own bewilderment. It was a strenuous effort, as the style of the excerpt reveals; it is a description of the author's first impressions on Russian soil:

> . . . Let us not deceive ourselves: this writer did not stand up very well to the test of the first few days. He splashed about rather helplessly in the bottomless porridge of impressions which he had found instead of the neat and tidy contours of socialist life anticipated in his imagination. He had visualised the Soviet Union as a kind of gigantic Manhattan with enormous buildings sprouting from the earth like mushrooms after rain, with rivers queuing up before power stations, mountains being tossed into the air by faith, and people breathlessly racing, as in an accelerated film, to fulfil the Plan. Yet the first Soviet town in which he set foot gave the impression of a huge village of seven hundred thousand sleeping souls, lazy as the Orient, timeless as the steppes. From the railway station a heavy peasant crowd was clumping through the dusty streets as if heading for a fair; and this was not a backward village, but the capital of the second largest Republic in the Union. In the antique tram-car the conductress sits ensconced among the passengers, chewing sunflower seeds, and if you ask her for a street she looks at you reproachfully from under her peasant kerchief and shrugs. The droshkys look like relics in a museum: high up on his lofty seat the *isvoschik* wields his whip, cursing the mother and grandmother of his skinny mare; an occasional motorist clatters, wildly hooting, with creaking axles along the unpaved road; stalls with gory posters depicting the tortures of the Inquisition lure the *mushiks* inside to enjoy modern art – which is further represented by the street photographers' backdrops, showing palaces with marble columns and lotus-covered ponds. Foreign newspapers are unobtainable, telegrams travel slower than the trains, a telephone call takes longer than a journey in the tram.
>
> Yet in the centre of this sleepy village with its dusty streets, milling crowds, and overcrowded tram-cars, there is a square with two modern skyscrapers; and next to it the new telephone exchange all in steel and glass; and there is a new model hospital, and the new tractor

factory – the second largest in Europe; and the sports stadium, the amusement park, the worker's club, and so on and so on. . . .

It looks like a film which, through a mistake, has been twice exposed by the photographer: once in the past and once in the future. The two pictures overlap and interlace; the result is chaos. Only slowly does the newcomer learn to sort things out, to distinguish between the two layers, to discover in the confusing maze the dominant pattern. It will take him even longer to understand the people of this country, these men and women who are again a mixture of two different epochs: of the race that plods barefoot through the mud, and another that carries briefcases and wears horn-rimmed lenses. Their heredity is the shapeless vagueness of the steppes; their environment the hard precision of the Plan.

Only slowly does the newcomer learn to think in contradictions; to distinguish, underneath a chaotic surface, the shape of things to come; to realise that in Sovietland the present is a fiction, a quivering membrane stretched between the past and the future. . . .

The chapter from which I have quoted was suppressed by the censor. The book appeared two years later in a mutilated version, with half of its contents cut out, under the title *Red Days and White Nights* (the "White Nights" referred to the Arctic regions). But writing it was occupational therapy: it helped me to rearrange my impressions, to classify everything that shocked me as the "heritage of the past" and everything I liked as the "seeds of the future". By setting up this automatic sorting machine in one's mind, it was still possible in 1932 to live in Russia and yet to remain a Communist.

All the more mentally alert among the Russians had that automatic sorting machine in their heads. They knew that official propaganda was a pack of lies, but justified this by referring to the "backward masses". They knew that the standard of living in the capitalist world was much higher than in Russia, but justified this by saying that the Russians had been even worse off under the Czar. They were nauseated by the adulation of Stalin, but justified it by explaining that the *mushik* needed a new idol to replace the ikon on the wall.

When conditions become insupportable, men react according to their temperament, by rebellion, apathy or self-deception. The Soviet citizen knows that rebellion against the largest and most perfect police machinery in history amounts to suicide. So the majority lives in a state of apathy and cynicism; while the minority lives by self-deception. I belonged to this minority. The Communist mind has perfected the techniques of self-deception in the same manner as its techniques of mass propaganda. The "inner censor" in the mind of the true believer completes the work of the public censor; his self-discipline is as strict as the obedience imposed by the regime; he terrorises his own conscience into submission.

During the first fortnight I visited Kharkov's factories and workers' clubs. My Russian was ungrammatical, but fairly fluent. I had acquired it during my last four months in Berlin by the same pressure-cooker method by which I had learnt modern Hebrew before setting out for Palestine. Thus I was able to get around alone, to travel by tram instead of in official cars, to do my own shopping and talk with everybody with whom I came into contact.

The only public conveyances in Kharkov were old-fashioned electric tram-cars which ran at intervals of twenty to thirty minutes, crammed to three times their normal capacity, covered with grapes of people clinging in acrobatic postures to bumpers, fenders, running boards, windows and roof. On my first journey on a tram not only my wallet was stolen from my hip pocket, but also my fountain pen from my breast pocket and my cigarettes from my trouser pockets; the squeeze was such that they could have cut off my trouser-legs without my feeling it. The chronic overcrowding of public conveyances made Russia into a paradise of pickpockets who displayed a virtuosity as nowhere else. They were mostly *besprisornys*, the notorious waifs and strays who had been roaming about the country like a plague of locusts ever since the Civil War.

Difficult to contemplate without a feeling of constriction in the throat, was the bazaar. This was a permanent market held in a huge, empty square. Those who had something to sell squatted in the dust with their goods spread out before them on a handkerchief or scarf. The goods ranged from a handful of rusty nails to a tattered quilt, or a pot of sour milk sold by the spoon, flies included. You could see an old woman sitting for hours with one painted Easter egg or one small piece of dried-up goat's cheese before her. Or an old man, his bare feet covered with sores, trying to barter his torn boots for a kilo of black bread and a packet of mahorka tobacco. Hemp slippers, and even soles and heels torn off from boots and replaced by a bandage of rags, were frequent items for barter. Some old men had nothing to sell; they sang

Ukrainian ballads and were rewarded by an occasional kopeck. Some of the women had babies lying beside them on the pavement or in their laps, feeding; the fly-ridden infant's lips were fastened to the leathery udder from which it seemed to suck bile instead of milk. A surprising number of men had something wrong with their eyes: a squint, or one pupil gone opaque and milky, or one entire eyeball missing. Most of them had swollen hands and feet; their faces, too, were puffed rather than emaciated, and of that peculiar colour which Tolstoy, talking of a prisoner, describes as "the hue of shoots sprouting from potatoes in a cellar".

The bazaar of Kharkov was one of those scenes one imagines one could paint from memory, even after twenty years. Officially, these men and women were all kulaks who had been expropriated as a punitive measure. In reality, as I was gradually to find out, they were ordinary peasants who had been forced to abandon their villages in the famine-stricken regions. In last year's harvest-collecting campaign the local Party officials, anxious to deliver their quota, had confiscated not only the harvest but also the seed reserves, and the newly established collective farms had nothing to sow with. Their cattle and poultry they had killed rather than surrender it to the kolkhoz; so when the last grain of the secret hoard was eaten, they left the land which no longer was theirs. Entire villages had been abandoned, whole districts depopulated; in addition to the five million kulaks officially deported to Siberia, several million more were on the move. They choked the railway stations, crammed the freight trains, squatted in the markets and public squares, and died in the streets; I have never seen so many and such hurried funerals as during that winter in Kharkov. The exact number of these "nomadised" people was never disclosed and probably never counted; in order of magnitude it must have exceeded the modest numbers involved in the migrations after the fall of the Roman Empire.

My idea for the book, and for the series of articles which would constitute its backbone, was a journey across the Soviet Empire from the extreme north to the frontier of Afghanistan. The Arctic I had visited the year before, as a member of the Graf Zeppelin expedition; this was to provide the contents of the first part of the book. Part two was to be devoted to the achievements of the Five Year Plan in Russia and in the Ukraine; part three to the development of the backward regions of Central Asia. The latter part of the journey took me across the Caucasus into the three Autonomous Soviet Republics of Georgia, Armenia and Azerbeijan; across the Caspian and through Turkestan to Ashkhabad and the oasis of Merv in the Karakum desert; then down to the Afghan frontier and up again to Bokhara, Samarkand and Tashkent; then via Kazakstan back to Moscow. Altogether I spent five months on this journey, travelling by railway, steamship, paddle-steamer, motor car and on horseback. This last means of locomotion was by far the most comfortable; you can't overcrowd a horse. Some of these Central Asian regions had not before been visited by Europeans, except by Russian Government officials.

Yet all this was less exciting than it may sound. Encased as I was in my closed universe, my eyes and mind were focused on statistics, factories, tractor stations and power plants; to landscape and architecture, to flower and bird, I paid little attention. To pay undue attention to relics of the past was a sign of a morbid, sentimental, romantic and escapist attitude. The old folk songs were forbidden; they would have evoked an unhealthy yearning for bygone days. Some classics which expressed a "socially progressive attitude" – for instance, *War and Peace, Oblomov* and *Dead Souls* – were read in school and reprinted in cheap editions by the State Publishing Trust; the rest, including most of Dostoyevsky, were, if not exactly banned, condemned to oblivion by the simple means of not reprinting them. (The State monopoly in publishing is in the long run a more decisive feature of the Communist regime than the concentration camps and even the one-Party system.) The Communist's duty was not to observe the world but to change it; his eyes were to focus on the present and the future, not on the past. The history of mankind would start with the World Revolution; all that went before was merely a barbaric overture.

The same was true of philosophy, architecture and the fine arts; and this attitude was by no means confined to fanatical Party bureaucrats. Professor Landau, the outstanding genius among Russian physicists, once tried to convince me during half an hour that to read any philosopher earlier than Marx was simply a waste of time. Auden's call "to clear from the head of the masses the impressive rubbish" expressed a similar attitude. It was less absurd than it appears today; born out of the despair of world war and civil war, of social unrest and economic chaos, the desire for a complete break with the past, for starting human history from scratch, was deep and genuine. In this apocalyptic climate, dadaism, futurism, surrealism, and Five-Year-Plan-mystique came together in a curious amalgam. Moved by a perhaps similar mood of despair, John Donne had begged: "Moist with a drop of Thy blood my dry soule." The mystic of the nineteen-thirties yearned, as a sign of Grace, for a look at the Dnieper Dam and a 3 per cent increase in the Soviet pig-iron production.

So I set out for Mount Ararat and the city of Bokhara, not to feast my eyes and delve into the past, but to see how they were doing on the Central Asiatic cotton production front. There were of course occasional lapses of discipline, a peep now and then round my self-imposed blinkers; even a travelling salesman may notice that a sunset lends colour to the sky. But on the whole I stuck with a deplorable purposefulness to my programme and spent most of my time visiting factories, *kolkhozi*, workers' clubs, kindergartens and Party offices. The people who took charge of me when I arrived in a new place, knew little or nothing of the history, architecture and pre-revolutionary folklore of their town. They were all members of the Party, schooled by the Party, conditioned by the Party. A seventeenth-century church or a fifteenth-century mosque was for them "just an old building", dismissed with a shrug. If the visitor betrayed interest in a Byzantine mosaic or a carved column, this romantic, bourgeois attitude was passed over with a lenient smile; foreign comrades were expected to be backward in their ideological training.

The Communist writer Anna Saeghers – a woman whom I greatly admired – once made an unguarded remark that has stuck in my memory. She was telling us, a small circle of Party members, about a clandestine meeting of hers with a comrade in a forest in Austria. It had been spring, and despite the circumstances she greatly enjoyed her walk in the woods. When she met the other person, a Party official, he had launched at once into an "analysis of the difficulties confronting the movement and the means of overcoming them". From that moment it had seemed to her that the birds had become silent, and the air had lost its fragrance. She was and is a devoted Communist, and this experience greatly disturbed her. "Why," she asked pathetically, "why is it that the leaves die wherever we go?"

In retrospect my overall impression of life in Soviet Russia has become tinged with the sadness and desolation of this remark.

A vignette from Red Days *may illustrate this mood – and the author's valiant efforts to overcome it by an attitude of cheerful optimism.*

The silk factory in Ashkhabad is the oldest in Turkmenistan; it was founded in 1928. Before that, the word "factory" did not exist in the Turkoman vocabulary. It was the most picturesque factory that I had ever seen, except perhaps for the great pottery in Seville's Triana:

In the little garden which serves as a factory yard, some twenty native factory girls are squatting on the ground, smoking over their bowls of *khok-chai*, the green Persian tea. They all still wear their colourful national costumes, complete with *boerk*. The *boerks* are tall cylindrical hats, wrapped in multi-coloured silks, and adorned with coins and amulets; each must weigh several pounds. They smoke black mahorka, which looks like flaky pipe tobacco and is loosely filled into five-inch-long cornets rolled out of newspaper. Apart from the slow movements required to sip their *khok-chai* and lift the paper cornets to their lips, they are entirely immobile. The sky is blue, the sun stabs down in pitiless rays, a camel ambles past; little white mahorka clouds float out of the immobile girls' nostrils. It looks as if they hadn't moved a limb for the last three hundred years. Then the factory whistle sounds, the girls carry the *chai* bowls unhurriedly to a corner, smooth their medals and amulets and, holding the smoking paper-cones between their teeth, vanish one by one through the concrete vault of the factory gate, tripping along like painted figures on a mediaeval clock-tower. The step across the factory gate takes them in one move from the seventeenth century straight into the twentieth.

You and I, we shall die and never learn what news the first spaceship will bring home from another planet [sic]. We shall not learn what ideas, machines and courting habits the citizens of the future will employ. Our curiosity will never be assuaged. But look at these girls. The fetters which had tied them to mediaeval Islam have suddenly snapped; they rubbed their eyes, sat down in Wells' time machine, and alighted three centuries later. Their curiosity is satisfied. I envy them.

Re-reading, after twenty years, passages like the above from *Red Days*, I am amazed by their naïvety. They express, however, what I believed at the time – or rather one set of beliefs to which I clung

with desperate tenacity. I did not see, because I did not want to
see, that for the tradition-bound people of Asia the enforced
voyage in the time-machine amounted to their deportation into a
disconsolate and incomprehensible world. I saw one half of the
truth – that a storm was brewing over Asia, and that the Revolution of 1917 had merely been the first blast. I did not see the barren
desolation which the storm would leave in its wake everywhere,
from China to Georgia. Nor that it would merely mean a change
from partial enslavement by landlords, tax-collectors and
money-lenders, to total enslavement by the State, which is landlord, tax-collector and money-lender all in one.

By a strange hazard I stumbled on the first great show trial in
Central Asia – a foretaste of things to come.

The only sizeable building in Ashkhabad was the City Soviet,
the equivalent of a Town Hall. The hall was rectangular, with a
raised platform which on other occasions served as a stage for the
performances of the Turkoman National Theatre. On that platform now sat the People's Court, consisting of the Judge, his two
Assessors, the State Prosecutor, the Lawyer for the Defence, a
translator and a stenographer. Facing them sat the audience on
rows of benches. The first three were occupied by the defendants;
there were twenty-nine of them. Behind them sat three militia
men with bayonets fixed on their rifles. Behind these the public:
men, women, and a class of schoolchildren between the age of ten
and fifteen. Only about half of the seats for the public were
occupied. One of the accused was testifying in a droning, monotonous voice. Everybody seemed half asleep – the Court, the
accused and the audience: Turkomans in tall sheepskin hats,
Uzbeks with coloured skull-caps, Russians in cloth-caps, women
with tall boerks or coloured scarves on their heads.

The accused was talking in Turkoman; after each couple of
sentences his statement was translated into Russian. We had
come in near the beginning of his testimony.

His name was Changildi. At the age of seven he had become an
orphan, and was employed as a shepherd by the local Bey. One
day he had stepped on a thistle, and his foot started festering and
had to be amputated. Then he had sold milk, and later had become
an opium smuggler on the Persian frontier. Then he had been
arrested, fined four hundred roubles, and put into prison. Then
Citizen Attakurdov had got him out of prison and made him an

official of the District *Kholhoz* Centre. (Attakurdov, as I gathered, was the principal accused: he was the former Chairman of the Town Soviet and a member of the Central Executive Committee of the Party.) In 1931, Changildi was dismissed from the District *Kholhoz* Centre, but Attakurdov's brother-in-law got him a new job in the RDI.*

As a member of the RDI, Changildi had dissolved a certain *kolkhoz* whose members had embezzled melons to the value of fifteen hundred roubles belonging to the State (in other words, they had eaten the melons instead of surrendering them). However, the members of Attakurdov's clan within the guilty *kolkhoz* got away without punishment because he, Changildi, felt himself indebted to Attakurdov. Moreover, after the *kolkhoz* had been dissolved, and individual property had been restored to its members, he, Changildi, had seen to it that the *kulaks* got the best irrigated plots, whereas the *bedniaks* (poor peasants) only received dry plots. This also was done on Attakurdov's orders. . . .

Gradually, I got the hang of the affair. The trial had been on for several weeks. It was expected that it would last for another number of weeks. The City Hall was the only large public meeting place in Ashkhabad; whenever it was needed for a meeting or a theatre performance, the trial was adjourned. The twenty-nine defendants were accused of Sabotage and Counter-revolutionary Conspiracy.

Attakurdov had been the leading personality in the young Turkmen Soviet Republic. He had been chairman of the Ashkhabad Soviet; his brother-in-law, Ovez Kouliev, chairman of the District RDI; another of his in-laws had been editor of the official Party paper. They were now all in the dock. It looked as if Attakurdov and his clan had been running the Republic, and were responsible for all the troubles that had befallen it.

Changildi's testimony provided a revealing glimpse into the nature of these troubles. An entire *kolkhoz* had been disbanded because of a hundred and fifty melons. Moreover, the collectivised land had been restored to its former owners. If such an event was possible, the collectivisation-programme in Turkmenistan must be in a state of chaos. I did not draw these conclusions; but I vaguely guessed them. I did not doubt that Attakurdov and his

*Workers and Peasants Inspectorate – a permanent control commission of the State administration.

people were guilty men, but at the same time I felt that they were being used as scapegoats.

I stayed at the trial for several hours, but did not return the next day or after. It had been too depressing, and I was avoiding more depressing experiences. There had been an eerie unreality about the proceedings. The defendants, for instance, were allowed to smoke in the courtroom. Everybody else, too, of course. Changildi, the one-legged former opium smuggler, had testified with a dead cigarette stump stuck in his dead, ashen face. The Judge and his Assessors hardly seemed to listen. Now and then, when Changildi broke off, the Judge or the Prosecutor (both of whom were Russians) would prompt him, or ask him a question in an indifferent, remote murmur. Counsel for the Defence (one Counsel for the twenty-nine accused) never opened his mouth. He was the youngest person on the platform, a shy native youth, looking like a bewildered student at an examination who does not quite know what is expected of him next. There was no sign of any interest or tension in the room. The spectators seemed to doze, except when they shook Mahorka into a new paper-cone with slow, lazy movements. The schoolchildren, who sat directly behind the bayonets of the guards, did not giggle or crane their necks. Several of them were asleep. There was an atmosphere of informality and amateurishness about the whole thing which made it quite impossible to believe that twenty-nine men, among them the leading figures of the Republic, were on trial for their lives.

After Changildi's testimony there was a pause. The Judge and the Public Prosecutor exchanged a few casual, whispered words. Then they all sat for several minutes, and nothing happened at all. No word was spoken. Time seemed to have come to a standstill. Some of the defendants now and then shuffled their feet. Then the Judge seemed to come regretfully back to life. He said something to one of the accused in the second row. The man got up obediently like a schoolboy, and said that Attakurdov had told him that the Russian people wanted to oppress the people of Turkmenistan. As he went on denouncing Attakurdov in a flat, impersonal voice, he seemed to vanish as an individual; all that remained of him was a limp puppet without a will of its own, manoeuvred by the arch-fiend, Attakurdov. The latter was apparently the Trotsky, or perhaps the Tito, of Turkmenistan.

From my place all I could see of Attakurdov was an occasional view of the back of his head. It was a round head, with close-cropped dark hair, set on a powerful neck and powerful shoulders. The head never turned or moved.

After some time a little man, who seemed to be something like an usher or clerk, came up to us in the last row and said something to Kikiloff.* Kikiloff said to me smilingly that the Court was inviting me as a "distinguished visitor" to sit on the platform. I had noticed him earlier whispering to the little man; then the latter had walked up to the dais and had whispered to the Judge. So now we had to follow him to the platform. Two chairs were brought, and we had to sit down on them, on the edge of the platform, facing the audience.

As a "foreign delegate" in Russia, I had been in the habit of sitting on platforms at all sorts of meetings and celebrations. But this time I felt a painful embarrassment. As we walked up to our two conspicuous chairs, the Judge seemed to take no notice of us, and neither the accused nor the audience gave any sign of curiosity. The Judge was probably thinking that once this foreigner had managed to butt in, one might as well humour him with a place on the grand-stand; and the others were probably thinking that we were Party officials somehow connected with the case.

I could now see the accused. Attakurdov is described in my notes as having the "round, bloated, greyish-yellow face of a Turkish tax-collector". I do not remember his features. I remember that he gave me one single glance of his flat eyes, penetratingly incurious like a dead man's, which made me avert mine.

I also remember that he wore a high-necked, embroidered Russian shirt, because most of the other accused wore dirty, European shirts with the collars missing. They were a miserable lot – yellow-faced, unshaven, creased and crumpled, like vagabonds on police photographs. Yet these were the men who had, a short while ago, held the highest offices in the Party and State. And, unlike the faces on police photographs which stare with an angry or sullen or frightened look into the camera, the men sitting in front of the guards' bayonets all wore expressions of complete indifference and apathy. So did the spectators behind the guards. In fact, the expressions of the spectators were the same as those of the accused. I must have vaguely felt, even then, that they were all one – the defeated victims, the people down there before us; and that we who faced them from the raised platform were their

*My guide, Shaarieh Kikiloff, President of the Turkoman Writers' Federation.

conquerors and rulers. Not the representatives of the Workers' State and the People's Court; but simply the rulers. They did not hate us; they were too apathetic and resigned even for that. How much of this did I consciously understand at the time? I am unable to decide; but I do remember feeling, while I sat exposed on that raised platform, that not the accused but I was being pilloried.

The trial of Attakurdov and accomplices was an exotic and amateurish forerunner of the great show trials in Moscow. It was still on when I left Ashkhabad, and I never knew its outcome. Back in European Russia I found that nobody had ever heard about it. It had only been reported in the local papers of Turkmenistan, and passed over in silence everywhere else. I had walked into it by pure chance. I wonder how many similar trials had been conducted in the same silence in various parts of the vast Soviet Empire, long before the Moscow purges revealed that weird, Kafka-esque pattern to an incredulous world.

My travelling itinerary completed, I spent the late winter and spring of 1933 in Moscow and Kharkóv (where it was easier to get accommodation) writing Red Days. *In the meantime Hitler had come to power in Germany; without being fully aware of it, I had ceased to be an independent traveller and had become one of the grey horde of Europe's political exiles.*

It was a transformation under anaesthesia, so to speak. For the moment it made no apparent difference to my life; I continued to write Red Days, and my main worry was how to go on working in an unheated room in the grim Ukrainian winter. For, as one of the minor disasters in that disastrous year of famine and general dislocation, the electricity supply of the Ukrainian capital had broken down. In the streets the temperature often sank to fifty and sixty degrees below freezing point. When one tried to smoke in the open air the moisture froze in the cigarette which became hard as a stick and gave one the sensation of chewing nicotined ice-cream. Inside my room, the water was permanently frozen in the tap, and the temperature rarely rose over freezing point. At first I tried to work in bed, but found this too uncomfortable; so I hammered away at the typewriter, wearing mittens, and a kind of quilt-jacket padded with cotton-wool, called a *vatinka*.

The electricity breakdown lasted all through the winter. The Ukrainian capital lived in a more or less permanent blackout, paralysed by hunger, darkness and frost. The only public conveyances, the electric tram-cars – dreadfully overcrowded even in normal times – now only ran during two hours a day, to get the workers to the factories and back. The people in the offices worked by the light of paraffin lamps, or oil wicks when the paraffin ran out, huddled in their quilts, surrounded by little clouds of condensed breath, like saints in heaven. After eight o'clock in the evening the streets lay deserted like an arctic settlement in the polar night.

One day the chambermaid in our privileged Intourist hotel fainted from hunger, and afterwards confessed that she had eaten nothing for three days because, as she had only just arrived from the country, the Co-operative had withheld her three-day ration of 1800 grammes (four pounds) of black bread. The bread ration was at the time 800 grammes per day for industrial workers, 600 grammes for other manual workers, 400 grammes for office employees (one pound = 450 grammes); and bread, plus a few tealeaves and an occasional cabbage or salted herring, was the only food to be had on the ration. In the country the people were dying of hunger; in the towns, they vegetated on the minimum survival level. Life seemed to have come to a standstill, the whole machinery on the verge of collapse.

However, no allusion to the real condition of the country was permitted to appear in the Soviet press. The Government was determined to keep the people in the dark regarding its own situation. This apparently impossible task could only be undertaken in a country where all information was centralised at the top of the pyramid, and all communications were Government monopoly. The Soviet press is, in fact, controlled to a degree which the Nazis were never able to achieve. The effect of this total news-centralisation in a country with vast distances is that the people are kept in ignorance not only of foreign events, but also of everything outside the range of their immediate neighbourhood.

Thus every morning I learned from my Kharkov paper about Plan figures that had been reached and surpassed, about competitions between enthusiastic factory shock-brigades, about awards of the Red Banner, new giant factories in the Urals, and so on; the photographs were either of young people, always laughing and always carrying a banner in their hands, or of some picturesque elder in Uzbekistan, always smiling and always occupied with learning the alphabet. Not one word about the famine, the typhus epidemic, the dying out of entire villages; even the fact that there was no electricity in Kharkov was never mentioned in the Khar-

kov newspaper. It gave one a feeling of dreamlike unreality; the
paper seemed to talk about some different country which had no
point of contact with the daily life that we led. The enormous land
was covered by a blanket of silence, and nobody outside the small
circle of initiates was in a position to form a comprehensive
picture of the situation.

I finished *Red Days* some time in April. I had it typed out, top and
five copies, and sent the various copies to the various State
publishing firms in Moscow, Kharkov, Tiflis and Erivan, who had
signed agreements for the Russian, German, Ukrainian, Georgian
and Armenian editions of the book. I have explained in *The God
That Failed* that these agreements, and the considerable advance
payments that went with them, were not the result of my literary
reputation – I had published no book before – but a direct effect of
a Comintern letter that I carried. When I produced it, in Kharkov
or in Erivan, the Director of the State Publishing Trust in question
could not refuse to sign a contract for the contemplated book,
which was described as "an important contribution to our fight on
the Propaganda Front", without the risk of being accused of
sabotage. It was in this indirect manner that the Comintern
financed my sojourn and travels in Soviet Russia, and similar
methods were employed to oblige visiting authors from abroad
who were not members of the Party. They were, of course,
delighted at the news that the Uzbeks, Tadziks and Eskimos were
all eager to read their books, and they would have been very
indignant at the suggestion that the advance payments from the
various State publishing firms amounted to bribes. This is another
miracle which State control over publishing can achieve.

   In spite of my numerous contracts, however, only one edition of
Red Days did, in fact, appear. This was in German, intended for
the German-speaking national minorities. It is a thin, paper-
bound volume, so thoroughly expurgated that less than half of the
original manuscript was allowed to stand. It was published in
1934, after I had left the Soviet Union. I was never sent a copy, and
did not know for certain whether the book had been published or
not until some thirteen years later – when an unknown American
reader sent me a copy that he had picked up by chance on a tourist
trip to the Soviet Union.

   The Russian edition of the book, which from the point of view of
a writer's prestige was the only one that really counted, never saw

the light of day. Three months after I had delivered the manus-
cript I was informed by one of the higher bureaucrats in the
Moscow Trust that it had been rejected because it was written in
"a too frivolous and light-hearted style". This was, of course, a
bitter disappointment; but at least I had not been accused of any
political deviation, and my Party record remained untarnished.

At about the same time I was informed that the Party had
decided against my staying in Russia. The leaders and intellectuals of the German CP who had managed to escape from the Nazi
terror were all gathering in Paris, which was becoming the centre
of the anti-Fascist propaganda compaign, and I was instructed to
join them.

I received the news with immense relief. I was a Communist,
but I found life in Russia terribly depressing. Only now, with the
prospect of departure before me, did I admit to myself how depressing it had been. The drab streets, the unrelieved shabbiness
and poverty, the grim pomposity of everything said and written,
the all-pervading atmosphere of a reformatory school. The feeling
of being cut off from the rest of the world. The boredom of newspapers which contained nothing critical or controversial, no
crime, no sensation, no gossip, sex, scandal, human interest. The
constant exhortations, the stereotyped uniformity of all and
everything, the external portrait of Big Brother following you
everywhere with his eyes. The overwhelming bleakness of an
industrialised Neanderthal.

Yet there was a vital consideration that helped me, and every
other Communist who visited Russia, to get over the shock. It was
our conviction that conditions in Russia were what they were not
because of any fault in our system, but because of the backward-
ness of the Russian people. In Germany, in Austria or France, the
Revolution would take an entirely different form. There was a
saying among German Communists in Russia that could only be
pronounced in a whisper: "Wir werden es besser machen" – "we
shall know better". In other words, every Communist who had
lived in the Soviet Union for some length of time, returned to his
country as a Titoist at heart.

It was this conviction that "we shall know better" that kept my
faith alive. It was no longer the naïve faith of a year before, when I
had got into the train in Berlin expecting that it would take me
straight to Utopia. It had become a rather wistful, rather esoteric
faith, but all the more elastic. I no longer believed in Communism
because of the Russian example, but in spite of it. And a faith that

is held "in spite of" is always more resilient and less open to disillusion than one that is based on a "because".

My last few weeks in Russia I spent in Moscow. I met a number of men in the higher Comintern and Soviet hierarchy, among them Mikhael Kolzov, Karl Radek and Nicolai Bukharin, all of whom have since met with their fate. Bukharin and Radek both made a deep impression on me, but I only met each of them once and in rather formal circumstances. I have incorporated certain characteristic features of both Radek and Bukharin into the "Rubashov" of *Darkness at Noon*, but after all these years I am quite incapable of disentangling the features of the original models from the composite imaginary feature.

They were all tired men. The higher you got in the hierarchy, the more tired they were. I have nowhere seen such exhausted men as among the higher strata of Soviet politicians, among the Old Bolshevik Guard. It was not only the effect of overwork, nervous strain and apprehension. It was the past that was telling on them, the years of conspiracy, prison and exile; the years of the famine and the Civil War; and sticking to the rules of a game that demanded that at every moment a man's whole life should be at stake. They were indeed "dead men on furlough", as Lenin had called them. Nothing could frighten them any more, nothing surprise them. They had given all they had. History had squeezed them out to the last drop, had burnt them out to the last spiritual calory; yet they were still glowing in cold devotion, like phosphorescent corpses.

Yet it was neither the "dead men on furlough" of the Old Guard, nor the Gletkins of the next generation, who made the most lasting impression on me. At the time of my visit, the Soviet Empire occupied one-sixth of the inhabited earth. It would have been impossible to hold such an immense realm together by terror alone. The apathy and passive acquiescence of the ruled, their self-deceiving hopes and propaganda-fed illusions, facilitated the task of the rulers, but could never have given sufficient coherence to that vast structure. The bureaucracy of Party and State, which represented roughly one-third of the total population, had, of course, a vested interest in defending the system; but the majority of this bureaucracy, on the lower grades of the pyramid, lived just as wretchedly and insecurely as those whom they ruled. There existed another human element which prevented the colossal

machinery from breaking down into its component parts, which
kept the creaking transmissions and the dry bearings somehow
going. It was a certain category of men that I find difficult to
define. I can perhaps best describe them by quoting a Talmudic
legend which I recently read in a novel (Manes Sperber's *To Dusty
Death*). It is called "the legend of the thirty-six just men":

> When I was a child, our Rabbis taught me that if the thirty-six men did
> not exist, mankind couldn't last a day, it would drown in its own
> wrongs. The thirty-six are not marked out by any rank or office. They
> cannot be recognised, they never yield their secret, perhaps they are
> not even aware of it themselves; and yet it is they who, in every
> successive generation justify our existence and who every day save
> the world anew.

I have met them on my travels in every part of the Soviet Union. I
could list up to one hundred such individuals whom I met in the
course of one year. So there must exist thousands, or even tens of
thousands of them.

What did these individuals have in common? They were "not
marked out by rank or office". They had the most varied occupa-
tions. They were not fanatical supporters of the regime. They were
the people who, when I was lost and despairing, restored my faith
in the Soviet Union. They created around themselves little islands
of order and dignity in an ocean of chaos and absurdity. In whatever field they worked, their influence communicated itself to
their surroundings. It is the ensemble of these human islands,
dotted over the Soviet realm, which maintains its coherent structure and prevents it from disintegrating.

These men, whether Communists or not, are "Soviet Patriots"
in the sense in which that word was first used in the French
Revolution. They are neither heroes nor saints, and their civic
virtues all go against the grain of the regime they serve. They are
motivated by a grave sense of responsibility in a country where
everybody fears and evades responsibility; they exercise intiative
and independent judgement where blind obedience is the norm;
they are loyal and devoted to their fellow-beings in a world where
loyalty and devotion are expected only towards one's superiors.
They have personal honour and an unconscious dignity of com-
portment, where these words are objects of ridicule. Though there
are thousands of them, they are a small minority, and always the
first victims of every new purge. Yet they do not die out. Their

existence is very nearly a miracle – a triumph of the indestructible human substance over a de-humanising environment.*

For the pressure of that environment seems almost irresistible – slow and steady like soil erosion, or the action of the tides. It results in that gradual thwarting of the mind which I have tried to describe, and is accompanied by an even more fatal corrosion of the spirit. The result is a gradual dehydration of the soul, a spiritual dearth more frightening than the famine. In the United States, the morticians endeavour to transform the dead, with lipstick and rouge, into horizontal members of a perennial cocktail party. In Soviet Russia the method is simpler: there are no funeral rites, death is stripped of its tragic grandeur, reduced to a mere statistical event. At a Writers' Congress in Moscow, after listening to countless speeches promising universal happiness in the brave new world, André Malraux asked suddenly: "And what about the child run over by a tram-car?" There was a pained silence; then somebody said, amidst general approbation:

"In a perfect, planned socialist transport system there will be no accidents."

I left Russia in the late summer 1933.

A few weeks before my departure, I was sitting on the terrace of the Café Metropole in Moscow, in a mood of suicidal depression. Inside the café the orchestra was playing a popular song of the period; its refrain, in German, ran something like this:

> . . . If you love me, you must steal for me,
> And tell me fairy tales of a happy land. . . .

I had three vodkas, and the last words of the song, together with the sentimental tune and my feeling of misery, had a hypnotic effect. They made me escape into a long day-dream, a "fairy tale of a happy land" as the sloppy refrain had it, and the day-dream led me to an idea for a play. The idea was that a pair of scouts from an alien planet land on earth in search of colonising space for their overcrowded world. They explain that only happy planets have a cosmic right to exist, and give mankind a last chance to organise its happiness within three days – or else it will gently be put out of its miseries, and planet earth turned to better use. Faced with this

*P.S. 1980: Let us remember that this was written in 1953, before the term "dissident" was invented.

ultimatum, the government resigns, the opposition washes its hands of the issue, and the dilettantes, at last take over, appointing a crazy poet called Glowworm to be Dictator of Happiness. And lo, it works, to everybody's surprise: money is abolished, authority is abolished, all taboos are smashed, all curtains raised. Alas, at the end of the three days it transpires that the scouts are impostors; and as there is no longer any need to be happy, the old order is restored and everybody goes back to his former miseries.

I began to write the play then and there, on the paper-napkins of the Café Metropole. It was an unforgivable heresy: "escapism" is almost the deadliest sin for a Communist, and I felt rather like a schoolboy drawing obscene pictures on the blackboard all set for a solemn lesson in History. I finished the play in three weeks, the last act on the train that took me out of Russia. I called it *Twilight Bar*. It was a play without literary pretensions, a flight from the pressure of reality, and I described it accordingly as "An Escapade in Four Acts". It was to have a long and undistinguished stage career.

To obtain my exit permit proved almost as difficult as it had been to obtain my entry visa. When it arrived, the relief was even greater.

Chapter 12

PRISONER IN SPAIN*

The first lap of my journey into exile took me in a third-class compartment through Poland and Czechoslovakia to Vienna. It lasted nearly three days, most of which I spent in typing out *Twilight Bar*, blissfully happy to be back in Europe. The moment we passed the frontier a magic change of atmosphere had taken place. The station buffets were piled with foodstuffs I had not seen for a year – sandwiches with cheese, eggs, sausages and ham; coffee and buns and pastry. There were foreign newspapers, books and magazines on the stalls; the platforms and ticket windows were no longer battlefields; and what struck me most, the people all had different personalities instead of being molecules in a grey, amorphous mass. They were mysteriously alive, they were individuals, and some of them, oh wonder, even had dogs. Nobody in Russia kept a dog – but I only became conscious of that now.

I felt excited like a schoolboy who has escaped from an austere college to a matinée in a circus. It was indeed a childish mood, for from a more adult point of view my prospects were grim. My flat in Berlin and all my possessions had been confiscated by the National-Socialist regime. My career was finished, too: I was a German journalist proscribed in Germany. The roubles that I had earned could not be converted into foreign currency. I was nearly twenty-eight and completely destitute for the second time in my life. The first time this had happened when I had starved in Palestine. That had been seven years earlier. Strangely enough, exactly seven years later I was to find myself shipwrecked for yet a

*From Dialogue With Death, ch. ix, and The Invisible Writing, chs. xxxii and xxxiii.

third time – in 1940, when France collapsed and all I could save was a toothbrush and a diary.

To lose one's home, one's hopes and possessions every seven years seems a rather repetitive and humourless type of behaviour. Insurance companies call a person with that kind of pattern "accident prone" and regard him, with perfect justification, as a bore and a nuisance. The mitigating factors in my case are that when Hitler took power in 1933, and when he conquered Europe seven years later, the majority of Europeans became accident prone. Anglo-Saxon readers (and critics) often miss this obvious point and, rather flatteringly, regard the misadventures of this chronicler as of his own making, an emanation of his perverse mind. In fact, I was luckier than any of the people who have played a part in this book; with few exceptions, they are either dead or have vanished in the dense fogs of the East.

I spent three or four days in Vienna, celebrating a series of sentimental reunions with old friends and girl-friends. It was now quite inconceivable to me that I had ever planned to abandon Europe. But though I had only been away for a year, it was also painfully evident that I was returning to a changed Continent. The malignant tumour that Germany had become was eating into Europe's living tissue. The fall of Austria lay still five years ahead in the future, and was accordingly unimaginable; but parliamentary rule and the freedom of the press had already been strangled by Dollfuss, the bigoted dwarf-dictator. In February, 1934, the rank and file of the Austrian *Schutzbund* (the Socialists' paramilitary organisation) was to rise, leaderless, in revolt. Their bloody defeat marked the end of a century of socialist progress in Central Europe.

I arrived in Paris in the autumn of 1933. The years that followed were filled with hectic political activity. They were the years of the great anti-Fascist crusade which, with drums and fanfares, advanced from defeat to defeat.

First came Hitler's defiant withdrawal from the League of Nations. Then the defeat of the Socialist insurrection in Austria. Then Hitler's victory in the referendum on the future of the Saar. Then Hitler's repudiation of the Treaty of Versailles. Then the Anglo-German naval pact, granting Hitler a larger fleet than France's. Then Hitler's march into the Rhineland. Then Hitler's march into Austria. In between Mussolini's conquest of Abyssinia, and the Japanese conquest of Manchuria, and Franco's victory in Spain. And so on, to Munich and Prague, and to the war which we had foreseen and had been unable to prevent.

For seven years, the statesmen and the people of the West failed to see the obvious, failed to understand the threat to their civilisation, and to eliminate it while it could still be done at a relatively small price. This seven-years' blindness which benighted the West from 1932 to 1939 was one of the remarkable phenomena of History. The attitude of the Conservative forces ranged from inane misconceptions of the nature of Hitler's regime to passive sympathy and active complicity. The various Socialist and Labour parties indulged in rhetorical denunciations of the Fascist danger, and did everything in their power to prevent their countries from arming against it. The Communists exploited the anti-Fascist movement for their own purposes and wound it up with a staggering betrayal. It looked as if they were all partners in a secret European suicide pact.

The only mitigating circumstance the West could plead was its inability to believe in the gory tales of Nazi atrocities and in their fantastic plans for world conquest which sounded like something out of science fiction. When Hitler was beaten, the same psychological block made its appearance with regard to the Stalinite regime; the pattern repeated itself with uncanny precision. But then, it required exceptional powers of imagination for people brought up in the traditions of the West to believe in the reality of the National-Socialist and Communist schemes to enforce the millennium by terror, conspiracy and conquest. This incredulity towards the incredible was the most generalised phenomenon in the Seven Years' Night.

In 1933 and during the next two or three years, the only people with an intimate understanding of what went on in the young Third Reich were a few thousand refugees. In the torture chambers of Columbia House in Berlin, in the newly established concentration camps of Oranienburg and Sachsenhausen, of Dachau and Buchenwald, hundreds of comrades personally known to us were being tortured, murdered, or driven to suicide. For us, the actual deeds and future intentions of this new regime were not a matter of speculation, as they were for the politicians of the West, but an intimate, harrowing reality. This condemned us to the always unpopular, shrill-voiced part of Cassandras. Nobody likes people who run about the streets yelling "Get ready, get ready, the day of wrath is at hand". Least of all when they yell in a foreign accent and, by their strident denunciations of the alleged aggressive intentions of Berlin or Moscow (as the case may be), increase international tension and suspicion. They are quite obviously fanatics, or hysterics, or persecution maniacs.

It is doubly painful to write about these seven years at a time when the mood of Western Europe is bent on repeating the same suicidal errors. The lesson of the 'thirties: that an aggressive, expansive power with a messianic belief in its own mission will expand as long as a power-vacuum exists; that the price of survival is the sacrifice of a distressingly large part of the national income over a distressingly long period; and that appeasement, however seductive and plausible its arguments sound, is not a substitute for military strength but an invitation to war – all this should be only too fresh in Europe's memory; yet an astonishing number of politicians, not to mention millions of common men, seem determined to commit the same errors and re-live the same tragedy again. Anti-Nazi refugees who talked about the German concentration camps and Hitler's plans for world-conquest were regarded as fanatics and fomenters of hatred, as their successors, the refugees from Eastern Europe, are regarded today.* If only the Cassandras and Jeremiahs would shut up, we could have peace for our lifetime!

Against the nightmarish background of Nazi Germany, my doubts and misgivings about Russia paled into insignificance. When you march in a crusade, even in a losing crusade, you are not in a mood for reflection. Reflection only set in, with a vengeance, a few years later, when the Russian purges assumed the proportions of mass terror. But that crisis, which would lead to my break with the Party, was still in the future.

In the meantime, Paris was the centre of the international anti-Fascist movement, in which the German Communists in exile played a leading part. In The Invisible Writing I have described in some detail the activities in which I was involved in this period of transition and abortive hopes: the writing of propaganda pamphlets, editing various émigré newspapers, fund-raising for a variety of causes, liaising with French intellectuals, and so on. As most of these jobs were unpaid, and I was

*Again I must remind the reader that this was written in 1953 – before the Hungarian revolution and the "Prague Spring".

still reluctant to become a professional Party bureaucrat or apparatchik, I secured my financial independence for a while by writing, under the pen-name A. Costler, a popular-science book on sex – one of the first of its kind, I believe, long before the genre became a commercialised industry. (Ironically, it is the only book I wrote that was received with unanimous praise by the critics).* I was paid no royalties, but the modest flat sum I got from the publishers enabled me to embark on an ambitious historical novel on the slave revolt in the first century BC in Rome – The Gladiators – which eventually became the first of a trilogy of novels on the ethics of revolution.

I was immersed in writing The Gladiators when the Spanish Civil War exploded and made the horrors of Nazi Germany and Soviet Russia temporarily fade into the background.

*   *   *

In August, 1936, the first month of the Civil War, I travelled as a special correspondent of the London News Chronicle to General Franco's headquarters, which at the time were in Seville.

The main purpose of the journey was to obtain first-hand evidence of German and Italian military aid to the insurgents. At that early stage of the war, no journalists representing left-wing or liberal newspapers were permitted entry into insurgent territory, but by devious means, which I have described in The Invisible Writing, I succeeded in obtaining in Lisbon a safe-conduct from General Franco's brother, Nicolas Franco, his emissary in Portugal, describing me as a "reliable friend of the National Revolution". After a few days in Seville, I was recognised by a former colleague at Ullsteins, who denounced me as a Communist, so I had to make a hurried exit by taxi to Gibraltar.

Even during this short visit, however, I had ample opportunity to observe the comings and goings of the German pilot-officers of the Kondor Legion billeted at the Hotel Cristina, and the German aircraft on the aerodrome, at a time when Hitler still denied

---

*The Encyclopaedia of Sexual Knowledge (London, 1934). As I have not kept the original reviews, I can only quote from those which appear on the jacket:

"Lucid, unshocked, eminently sensible" (New Statesman and Nation). "Excellent for Doctors and Psychologists ..." (Time and Tide). "Covers the ground thoroughly and gives up-to-date information ..." (The Listener). "Well documented and accurate" (Aldous Huxley). "Gives all the essential knowledge that any layman (or woman) needs on all aspects of the subject" (The Schoolmaster). "This monumental book may be commended" (The Medical Officer).

sending aid to Franco and Franco denied receiving it. Thus the evidence I brought back was worth the trouble; it was used by the "Commission of Inquiry into Alleged Breaches of the Non-Intervention Agreement on Spain" (to which I gave testimony at its public hearings in London), was widely disseminated by the press and incorporated in a propaganda booklet I hurriedly wrote.* I mention this episode, because it explains why, when six months later I was captured by Franco's troops, I was convinced that to be shot, without unpleasant preliminaries, was the best I could hope for.

It happened when, in the beginning of February, 1937, the rebel-army took Malaga. I had been covering the war on the Andalusian front for the News Chronicle, and when the town surrendered, having failed to get out in time, I was arrested by Franco's Military Intelligence, and without interrogation or ceremony, clapped into jail. The following extract is from Dialogue with Death:

Round about midday on Saturday, the fourth day after my arrest, the door of my cell swung open again.

Outside there stood, not the now familiar figures of the warders, but two Civil Guards with rifles and fixed bayonets.

"Venga," they said. "Come."

I still had one last cigarette in my breast pocket. I had had nothing to smoke for three days, but I had been saving this one cigarette for the time when the oily voice should call out ny name. I had racked my brains to discover how to manage to preserve a decent demeanour during those last moments, and had thought that a cigarette might perhaps help.

When I saw the two men standing at the door with their bayonets, I thought that the moment had come to light up. I had just put the cigarette in my mouth when one of the Civil Guards produced a most comforting object from his pocket: a pair of steel handcuffs. I knew that they used a cord to bind the hands of those whom they were taking out to be shot; handcuffs are too precious, and removing them from a corpse is far too arduous a business. The only factory in Spain that manufactures handcuffs is in Bilbao, and Bilbao was at that time still in Government hands. There

*Menschenopfer Unerhört, French translation L'Espagne Ensanglantée, both Editions du Carrefour (Paris, 1937); later incorporated into Spanish Testament (London, 1937).

was an unlimited supply of human cattle for the slaughter on the Spanish market, but a shortage of handcuffs.

At this moment, therefore, the shining steel handcuffs were the most cheering sight I could have wished for. I folded my hands piously, and the handcuffs shut to with a snap. I marvelled at the complicated and skilful mechanism of what seemed such a simple apparatus; on each of the wristlets was a little cog-wheel, to make it adjustable for any size of wrist. The elder of the Civil Guards even enquired whether the catch chafed my wrists – he asked this neither out of friendliness nor ironically, but in the businesslike tones of a tailor fitting a suit. Then we marched off down the corridors and out into the street.

Outside the prison gate stood a big lorry and an elegant little sports car. We made for the sports car. On the bonnet were four copper plaques: the first displayed the Swastika between two wings, the second the Roman fasces, the third the five black arrows of the *Falange Española*, and the fourth the coat of arms of the Bourbon dynasty.

Not even in my wildest dreams had I pictured myself going for a drive in such a symbol-laden vehicle. Actually it all came to nothing; for just as we were getting in, an officer with a riding-crop came rushing up to tell the Civil Guards that he was requisitioning the car, and that the lorry was good enough for us, anyway. My guards seemed put out, but did not dare to protest, and we clambered into the lorry, which was already loaded to capacity with forty prisoners and their armed escorts.

I was so exhilarated by the fresh air and the sudden change of scene after four days of solitary confinement that for the first few moments I gazed round at my fellow prisoners almost gaily; then I noticed that their hands were bound with cords. There were, besides, about ten to fifteen of them tied to each other in a group with longer cords.

We stood closely packed together. As the heavy lorry started up, we had to hold on to each other and to the Civil Guards to keep our balance. There was about the same number of Civil Guards as victims; holding their rifles in one hand, they too sought to steady themselves by putting an arm round the shoulder of a neighbour, regardless of whether he were a fellow guard or a man whom half an hour later they would be shooting, sending a bullet through his eye or his nose.

I still had my unlighted cigarette between my lips. The Civil Guard who had put the handcuffs on me lit a cigarette for himself and was about to give me a light. I told him that it was my last cigarette and that I wanted to keep it for later on, and put it back in my pocket. He rolled me a cigarette and handed round his tobacco-pouch and paper amongst the others, both Civil Guards and prisoners. A Civil Guard helped those whose hands were bound too tightly to roll their cigarettes, holding out the finished article for them to give the final lick.

The Civil Guards looked like Andalusian farm-hands or peasants, and the prisoners too looked like Andalusian farm-hands or peasants. As they stood, clinging to each other on the bouncing lorry, one might have taken them for a charabanc party on an excursion to some green spot in the countryside. Arrived at their destination, the various roles will be assigned: those with the ropes will stand up against a wall, the others will send hot leaden projectiles into their flesh. Naturally both groups would rather play football with each other. But that would not do; God in His wisdom has decided it must be thus and not otherwise; so the surviving half of the party will roll themselves cigarettes and climb back surlily into the lorry.

We exchanged tobacco and clung to each other when the lorry gave a lurch, and each felt the bodily warmth of his neighbour; but no one spoke.

With one exception. One of the Civil Guards, with glasses and a corporal's stripes, who was standing pressed against the barrier in a particularly cramped position, remarked with a grin to the man next to him:

"We shall be a lot more comfortable on the return journey."

But only one or two people heard, and no one answered.

A priest passed and looked at us. We too looked at him.

In the vicinity of the railway station the motorised tumbril drew up, and I and my two guards alighted. The first one jumped down and helped me down, since I could not use my hands, and then the second jumped down after me. The lorry drove on again. The prisoners looked after us, and I could feel envy and contempt in their gaze, and even in the eyes of their guards. We were outsiders, we had broken the bond of a common fate. We all three gazed after the lorry as it disappeared in a cloud of dust. One of my guards turned to me and went through the motions of pulling the trigger of his rifle, to dispel any lingering doubts on my part. Then he rolled cigarettes for the three of us, and we entered the station.

This Civil Guard was a lanky, loose-limbed fellow with an absurd, horse-like face. He had long, yellow, equine teeth, a flat nose, and the good-natured, stupid eyes of a cab-horse. He was called Pedro.

The other was short and sturdy, with a bronzed, lively peasant's face. He was called Luis.

While we stood about in the waiting-room, I asked the lanky Don Pedro where they were taking me. "To Seville," he said, and showed me a typed order in which it was stated that "the individual A.K. is to be brought to Seville under safe escort, and to be delivered up to the special jurisdiction of the Commander of the Southern Fighting Forces of the National Army, General González Queipo de Llano".

I had hoped that I was to be taken to Burgos or Salamanca. Of all the cities of the globe Seville was the one the name of which sounded most unfriendly to my ears. And of all the mighty ones of this world the one whom I had most cause to fear was General González Queipo de Llano.

It was scarcely six months since I had seen him face to face. The interview that he had given me and the brief but unfriendly character-sketch that I had drawn of him had already appeared, not only in the press, but in my book in French. Queipo read French, and the book very likely lay on his desk beside my dossier. I could imagine his face while he read the chapter "Portrait of a Rebel General"; it was his own portrait and a faithful one; so much the worse for me. Now I was under his "special jurisdiction". I felt like the proverbial wanderer in the jungle who had inadvertently trodden on a tiger's tail.

We got into the train. It was an ancient train with a funny little engine and funny little carriages that looked like wooden boxes on wheels. We wormed our way into a third class compartment in which a large peasant family was already installed: father, mother, grandmother, an adolescent daughter and a baby. The family moved up closer to one another and respectfully left the two corner seats by the window to the two Civil Guards. I sat next to the lanky Don Pedro; next to me was the mother with the baby, opposite me the grandmother, and next to her in the corner the adolescent daughter. She was very pretty, and she cast stealthy glances at my grimy, but still recognisably foreign, suit. I kept my hands hidden in my sleeves like a monk, so that the handcuffs were not immediately visible. The train ambled off.

The grandmother had already got into conversation with Don Pedro and Don Luis. At first they talked of the weather, then about the orange crop, then about the war. I learned that Motril had fallen since my arrest, and that the fall of Almería was hourly expected. Both the peasants and my guards avoided taking sides; they referred to Franco's army not as "*los nuestros*", "our people", but as "*Los Nacionales*". The guards referred to the other side as "*los Rojos*" (the Reds) but the grandmother spoke of them as "*los Valencianos*". The family came from Antequera, the village that Pizarro used to raid for cigarettes and seed corn. In the first chaotic days after the insurrection they had fled to Malaga to take refuge with relatives and had been unable to return to their own village, which was on the other side of the Front. Then "*los Nacionales*" had taken Malaga, and now they were returning home.

Don Luis asked the husband what things had been like in Malaga under the Reds.

The man shrugged his shoulders and said that he had never troubled his head about politics.

The grandmother said that it was the foreigners who were to blame for the whole tragedy; on the other side the Russians, and on this side the Germans and Italians. Then she clapped her hand to her mouth, and enquired with a sly, apologetic smile if I were a German airman.

No, I told her, I was an English journalist.

The daughter looked at me with interest. Don Pedro and Don Luis grinned, but tactfully held their tongues.

The grandmother wanted to know what the King of England thought about "all this Spanish business".

I said that His Majesty had not yet come to any final conclusion, for the opinions of his advisers were somewhat contradictory.

Whereupon Don Pedro enquired, giving a crafty wink and baring his equine teeth, whether there were also "Reds" in England. Don Luis too winked at me and burst out into raucous laughter. The both nudged me with their knees, and would obviously have been offended if I had not shared in their mirth. I did my best and joined in. It was a little secret between the three of us.

"In the end," said the grandmother, "he'll turn out to be a Red himself."

This remark released a flood of laughter from Don Pedro and Don Luis, and the grandmother was very proud of her joke.

And since we were all in such a merry mood, she took down from the rack, with the help of the mother, their basket of provisions and a bottle of red wine.

She offered us lovely red pimento sausage and cheese and

white bread and wine. The Civil Guards accepted with alacrity; I refused. The whole family pressed me to eat. I did not move my hands from my sleeves. It was a ghastly situation. The guards looked at each other; then Don Luis resolutely seized me by the arm and removed the handcuffs. The whole family turned to stone.

"Holy Mother of God!" cried the grandmother. She looked at me and added softly:

"Your poor mother!"

Then she passed me sausage and cheese and made the sign of the cross over me.

I began eating, and wiped the beads of sweat from my forehead. The daughter looked away, and flushed a fiery red. The baby, who had crawled on to the floor whilst the food was being unpacked, now crawled up to Don Luis and tried to play with the handcuffs.

It was about four hours before we reached Antequera. It was not on our direct route; the train made endless detours. We ate and drank a great deal, but there was no more conversation. Now and again, when the silence became painful, the taciturn peasant would say from his corner:

"Give the *Inglés* another bit of sausage," or

"Has the *Inglés* had enough wine?"

He never addressed me directly. But the mother, who was at once the friendliest and the stupidest member of the family, said, as she pressed a slice of sweet cake into my hand:

"Eat up, Señor. Who knows how much longer you'll be able to eat!"

Whereat Don Pedro remarked jokingly:

"He's going to be shot tomorrow."

But his joke was coldly received, and Don Pedro grew quite embarrassed, obviously feeling that he had committed a *faux pas*.

At one of the small stations he got out to get some water, giving me his rifle and the handcuffs to hold in the meantime. He did this as though absent-mindedly, in his hurry, but I had a feeling that he was doing it to atone for his previous lapse. He brought back some tobacco and a packet of ten cigarettes at 10 centimos, which he presented to me. I handed them round and everyone took one out of politeness, although they were much inferior to the rolled ones.

In Antequera the family got out with a great deal of bustle and fuss. The grandmother once more made the sign of the cross over me; the peasant, without a word, handed me an orange; the daughter blushed again and avoided looking at me. Then the train went on.

It was late afternoon by now, and we all three stretched ourselves out on the seat and fell asleep.

A few stations later more passengers got in, among them a young man and a somewhat corpulent gentleman of the upper classes. They too began a conversation, and in order to avoid fresh complications I myself explained at once that I was a prisoner, although the handcuffs had not been put on me again. The representative of the upper classes thereupon moved into the furthest corner of the carriage and kept glancing at me as though I were a leper. The young man, who, like the peasants and everyone else on the train, was wearing the Nationalist cockade in his buttonhole, offered me a cigarette, and, noticing that I had no coat and was shivering, his rug. He told me that he was going to Seville because he had been requested to report as a recruit to the Phalange. I asked him why, then, he gave "an enemy" his rug. He shrugged his shoulders and winked ever so slightly. I do not know whether Queipo de Llano will be exactly pleased with this Phalangist; or with some thousands like him.

The handcuffs were not put on me again until we reached Seville.

It was quite late at night by then. Don Pedro and Don Luis were once more full of official solemnity, and we marched in single file into the *gendarmerie* on the station.

There a discussion took place as to what was to be done with me at this late hour – it was a quarter past twelve. There was no official car available, and the trams were no longer running. Don Luis suggested that they should take me to the Phalangist barracks just for the night. This was exactly what I had been dreading. I asked Don Pedro whether they could not take me to the prison instead. He grinned and said: "I suppose you don't like the idea of going to the Phalange?" I said that I didn't. They both grinned and whispered together for a while, and then Don Pedro said they would telephone to General Staff Headquarters, for that was after all the authority to deal with my case. They asked an official for the telephone book; he replied that there wasn't one, but that all official numbers were written up on the wall in the telephone booth. So we went into the booth.

The walls were covered with numbers written in pencil. "Italian Base Headquarters, Number So-and-so," I read. "Italian Infantry Barracks, Number So-and-so." "Italian Infantry Barracks

No. 2, Number So-and-so." "Italian Commissariat, Number So-and-so."

The tourist traffic in the town of Seville had obviously increased since my last visit.

At last our joint efforts resulted in our finding the number of the General Staff of the Southern Forces.

Don Luis telephoned, and half an hour later a car came to the station to fetch us.

We drove through the streets of Seville, past the Hotel Madrid, where I had stayed six months ago, past the Hotel Cristina, where I had met the German pilots, past the Phalangist barracks, where I had seen the blood-bespattered prisoners from the Rio Tinto mines being marched in, to the familiar residence of the "radio General". It was an eerie drive, worse than the drive to the Malaga prison when I had imagined that I was being taken to the cemetery. Don Pedro and Don Luis were silent, and I longed for them never to leave me.

The corridors of Staff Headquarters were nocturnally bleak and deserted. Only in a few rooms were people still working; we were sent from one to another, and no one knew what to do with us. Finally we landed up somewhere in the decoding department. There we found a pleasant official who said we might all three sleep on the floor. Don Luis had already squatted on the floor to take off his boots when an officer appeared and ordered us out. He said I had no business to be in the decoding department; the place for me was the police station. So we wandered off to the police station.

Don Pedro and Don Luis were tired out and in a bad temper; I was obviously a nuisance to them, and they would much rather have let me go. But that would never have done; and so at length we ended up in the police station.

We found ourselves in a smelly office, where a surly fellow noted down particulars of my case, and took my finger prints. Then he called two sergeants. They stood to attention at their Chief's table – two gorillas. They saluted, and one of them asked in an official tone:

"*Una flagelación?*"

Flagelación is the term used for the first beating to which an arrested man is subjected in Spanish police stations. It is an illegal but official practice carried out in most countries of Europe. In France it is called *passer à tabac*, and in Germany *die erste Abreibung*.

Don Luis bent assiduously over to the Chief and whispered a

few words in his ear. All I could catch was: "*Inglés – periodista –* journalist." Whereupon the *flagelación* was dispensed with.

I was greatly relieved, and the two gorillas, balked of their prey, led me into a kind of cage with an iron grille. Don Luis and Don Pedro, a few minutes later, when their official papers had been examined and stamped, came past the cage. I called out to them and thanked them for having been so nice to me on the journey. They grew very embarrassed, and shook hands with me in turn through the grille. The gorillas opened their eyes wide, and my two friends departed.

They were not exceptions; they were two out of twenty-five million for the most part kindly Spaniards. Had they been given orders, before we made friends on the journey, to strike me dead or to shoot me, they would have done so with complete sang-froid. Had they been fellow prisoners, they would have shared their last cigarette with me. Had I, on the other hand, made the railway journey with the two unfriendly gorillas, we would most likely have parted with the same cordial feelings.

I looked at the gorillas and the gorillas looked at me, and I wondered what they would have done to me had the *flagelación* not been called off. As it happened to be called off, they gave me cigarettes with a sheepish grin. I grinned back and thought how little depends on what a man is, and how much on the function which society has given him to fulfil. What difference did it make whether Don Luis and Don Pedro and the gendarmes on the tumbril were endowed with a muscial ear or not, whether they preferred cats or dogs, and whether they were good or bad? Suddenly I seemed to understand why the Anarchist doctrine is so popular in Spain. To the Anarchists the problem is as simple as cracking nuts: just smash the hard shell of social institutions and savour the delicious kernel. A fascinating theory; but it seemed to me rather doubtful whether trees would ever bear nuts without shells.

One is never so curious about the future of humanity as when one is locked up in an iron cage, and would rather think of anything but one's own future. I believe that the only consolation you could give to a condemned man on his way to the electric chair would be to tell him that a comet was on the way which would destroy the world the very next day.

Round about two or three o'clock in the morning a car arrived and transported me, under the escort of the gorillas, right across the sleeping city, across the Guadalquivir and down deserted avenues, to the prison of Seville.

Chapter 13

A TURNING POINT*

I was arrested on February 9, kept for four days *incommunicado* in the prison of Malaga, and was transferred on February 13 to the Central Prison of Seville. I was kept in solitary confinement for three months, and during this period was on hunger strike for twenty-six days.† For the first sixty-four days, I was kept *incommunicado* in my cell and not permitted exercise. After that I remained in solitary confinement but was permitted two hours' exercise a day in the company of three other prisoners. I was exchanged against a hostage held by the Valencia Government on May 14, 1937, after ninety-five days of imprisonment.

I was neither tortured nor beaten, but was a witness to the marching off to execution of my fellow prisoners and, except for the last forty-eight hours, lived in the expectation of sharing their fate.

I was never officially informed that sentence of death had been passed on me. The Franco authorities made ambiguous and contradictory statements, with the apparent intention of confusing the issue. The only authentic information that I was able to obtain later on is the account published by Dr Marcel Junod, Delegate of the International Committee of the Red Cross, who negotiated my exchange, and who had been officially informed that I had been sentenced to death by General Franco.‡ On the other hand, a few days before the exchange was agreed upon, the British Consul in Seville was allowed to visit me in prison and told me that the Foreign Office had asked General Franco for an assurance that I would not be shot, which the latter had refused on the grounds

*From The Invisible Writing, chs. XXXII and XXXIII.
†In two stretches of ten and sixteen days; see Dialogue with Death.
‡Dr Marcel Junod, Warrior Without Weapons (New York, 1951).

that my case was still *sub judice*. I was only interrogated once, immediately before my release, on the capital charge of "complicity in a military rebellion", but that interrogation was obviously a formality.

The only direct communication regarding my fate that I received while actually in prison, reached me on the eleventh day after my arrest. On February 19, three officers of the Phalange, one of them a young woman, visited my cell, identifying themselves as members of General Franco's Press and Propaganda Department. They informed me that I was or would be (the alternative was left in suspense) sentenced to death for espionage, that General Franco might, however, commute my sentence to life imprisonment as an act of clemency. This was followed by an invitation to make a statement concerning my feelings towards General Franco. In momentary weakness I dictated a statement which said that I believed General Franco to be a man of humanitarian outlook whom I could trust implicitly; but when it came to signing it, I had sufficiently recovered to cross the statement out and substitute another to the effect that if General Franco granted a commutation of the sentence I would assume that he was acting from political considerations, and that I would continue to believe in a Socialist conception of the future of humanity.* According to yet another version which Burgos gave out (either to the *News Chronicle* or to a British parliamentary delegation), sentence of death for espionage had already been passed by court-martial in Malaga before I was transferred to Seville.

I have put these contradictory versions down for the record although they were mostly unknown to me at the time; if I had known the details they would only have confirmed me in my expectation that some night or other I would be taken out of my cell and stood against the cemetery wall. During the first few days after the fall of Malaga, prisoners in that town were taken out in batches and shot at any hour of the day; later on in Seville, things settled down to a more orderly routine, and executions were carried out three or four times a week between midnight and 2 a.m.

The proceedings were as a rule smooth and subdued. The victims were not forewarned, and mostly too dazed or proud to

---

*For the text of the statement, see *Dialogue with Death*. It was never used by Franco's Propaganda Department.

make a scene when they were led out of their cells by the guards, accompanied by the priest, to the waiting lorry. A few of them sang, some wept, muffled cries of "*madre*" and "*socorro*" were frequent. Sometimes I saw the whole procession – the priest, the guards and the victim – quickly pass in front of my spyhole, but mostly I only heard them, ear pressed against the cell door. Sometimes the victims were fetched from the mass detention cells on the second floor, or from a different wing; sometimes from among the *incommunicados* of the death row where I was housed; it was impossible to discover the system. On one night, Thursday, April 15, the inmates of cells 39, 41 and 42 on my left and right were all marched off, with only my own cell No. 40 spared, after the warder had put his key, no doubt by mistake, into my own lock, and then withdrawn it.

Most of the victims were recently captured militiamen on whom a membership card of the Anarchist or Communist Party or Trade Union, or some other compromising document had been found. They had appeared for a few minutes before a court-martial, and had then been taken back to prison before sentence was passed. The sentence was mostly death by shooting. This was in a number of cases commuted to long-term imprisonment, in which case the prisoner was officially informed, and transferred to a penitentiary. If, on the other hand, the sentence was confirmed, the prisoner only learnt it when they came to fetch him at night. Sometimes his uncertainty lasted several weeks or months. The record was four and a half months, held by a militia Captain.

Another form of execution which Franco had revived, as Hitler had revived decapitation by the axe, was the *vile garotte*, the strangling machine familiar from Goya's drawings. The victim, tied to a post in a sitting position, was slowly choked to death between an iron collar round his throat and a vice being turned through the post against the back of his neck. The man who in *Dialogue with Death* is called "The Consumptive" was executed by this method a few days after I was released. He was one of the three men with whom I took my exercise, the former leader of an Anarchist group of *vigilantes* in Madrid, Garcia Attadel. It was Garcia who told me that the garotte had been revived, but he pretended not to believe that it was actually used.

Nobody was tortured or beaten within the prison of Seville during my stay: these practices were confined to police stations and Phalange barracks. The guards were on the whole humane, the food adequate and, except for those of us who were kept *incommunicado*, the prisoners were permitted during most of the day to take exercise and play games in the open patio.

This, I believe, is about all that I need to repeat here regarding the external conditions and events of the period covered by *Dialogue with Death*, and I can now proceed to certain psychological developments which I have not discussed in the earlier book.

Firstly, during the whole period of solitary confinement, I was, of course, often apprehensive and fearful, but it was a rational and, as it were, healthy fear, not the obsessional and morbid variety. I slept well, except on the nights when I listened to my comrades being led to execution, and even on these nights I found sleep later on. I had consistently pleasant dreams, often of Grecian landscapes and beautiful but sexless women. I had hours of acute despair, but these were hours, and in between were entire days of a newly discovered peace, and even happiness.

This paradox may partly be explained as the effect of a craving for punishment. The neurotic type of anxiety is the irrational anticipation of an unknown punishment for an unknown crime. Now retribution had come in a concrete, tangible form for a concrete tangible offence; the cards were on the table. Whether I was technically guilty of espionage before the law was beside the point; I had gained entry to the enemy camp through false pretenses and I had done everything in my power to damage their cause. My condition was thus a logical consequence of a consciously taken risk, the whole situation was clean, proper and equitable.

Two years after Spain, I was interned for six months in a French concentration camp, and another year later detained for several weeks in an English prison. These later imprisonments involved no danger of life, and regarding privileges and physical comfort, conditions were less harsh than in Seville. Yet on these later occasions I knew that I was innocent and that my confinement was stupid and unjust; this knowledge made these relatively comfortable detentions mentally unbearable and spiritually sterile. In Le Vernet and in Pentonville I knew that I would eventually get out and resume life. In cell No. 40 in Seville the best I could hope for was commutation of the death sentence, and an amnesty after three or five years in a penitentiary; yet I was more at peace with the world and myself in cell No. 40. I am stressing this contrast because it seems to indicate that the craving for justice is more than a product of rational considerations; that it is rooted in layers of the psyche which a pragmatic or hedonistic psychology cannot penetrate.

It could not even be said, I mused, while pacing up and down cell No.40, that the punishment was out of proportion with the offence. A civil war, like a revolution, applies harsher standards than international law. The deception I had used in Lisbon had been a particularly infamous one. In *L'Espagne Ensanglantée* I had accused the opponent of committing certain atrocities though I doubted the authenticity of the documentation from Communist sources that I used; it seemed quite proper that I should now be called to verify the missing evidence through first-hand experience. The chapter in the book on General Queipo de Llano, based on a fraudulently obtained interview, was a portrait drawn with a poisoned pen. Now it formed part of the dossier against me on General Queipo de Llano's desk, on whose jurisdiction my fate depended. There was in all this a neat, symmetrical design. A design, however, does not necessarily presuppose a designer. The symmetry of crystals is the product of electro-chemical forces. Nature favours symmetry, tends organically towards symmetry. Justice is a concept of ethical symmetry, and therefore an essentially natural concept – like the design of a crystal.

Thus justice began to assume in my musings a new, double significance as an organic need and as an ethical absolute based on the concept of symmetry. It could not be reduced to utilitarian considerations, nor to any theological assumptions. The notion of "divine justice" appeared as a lamentable caricature of it, with its dangling carrot and whip – the unconscious source of all *Angst*. I congratulated myself on the disappearance of anxiety, and attributed it to this newly discovered concept of justice. Some die with their boots clean, some with their minds clean; I did not want any mystic mud splashed over the mind's polish. Even less tempting was the thought of Dostoyevsky's sudden conversion in front of the firing squad. That classic episode came often to my mind; I regarded it as an example of the cowardly surrender of the intellect, not to divine grace but to the trembling fear of the flesh. My prison diary in *Dialogue with Death* contains this half serious prayer:

Grant me, O Lord, the right to continued discontent, to curse my work, not to answer letters, and to be a trial to my friends. Am I to swear to grow a better man if this cup is let to pass from me? We both of us know, Lord, that such vows, extracted under duress, are never kept. Do not blackmail me, Lord God, and do not try to make a saint of me; Amen.

The reflections that I have put down so far were all still on the rational level; but as we proceed to others in an inward direction, they will become more embarrassing and more difficult to put into words. They will also contradict each other – for we are moving here through strata that are held together by the cement of contradiction.

On the day when I was arrested in Malaga, there had been three occasions when I believed that my execution was imminent. The first time in the *sala* of the Villa Santa Lucia, with three guns digging into my ribs; the second time, when the car had stopped on the improvised execution ground on the Camino Nuevo; the third time when, after being told that I would be shot at night, they took me out of the police station at nightfall and put me into a lorry, with five men behind me, their rifles across their knees; so that I thought we were driving to the cemetery, whereas we only drove to the prison.

On all three occasions I had benefited from the well-known phenomenon of split consciousness, a dreamlike, dazed self-estrangement which separated the conscious self from the acting self – the former becoming a detached observer, the latter an automaton, while the air hums in one's ears as in the hollow of a sea shell. It is not bad at all; the unpleasant part is the subsequent reunion of the split halves, bringing the full impact of reality in its wake.

The events of this day, and of the next three days with their mass executions, had apparently caused a loosening up of psychic strata close to rock-bottom, which laid them temporarily open to that new type of experience that I am leading up to.

I met with it for the first time a day or two after I had been transferred to Seville. I was standing at the recessed window of cell No. 40 and, with a piece of spring that I had extracted from the wire mattress, was scratching mathematical formulae on the wall. Mathematics, in particular analytical geometry, had been the favourite hobby of my youth, neglected later on for many years. I was trying to remember how to derive the formula of the hyperbola, and was stumped; then I tried the elipse and the parabola, and to my delight succeeded. Next I went on to recall Euclid's proof that the number of primes is infinite.

"Primes" are numbers which are not divisible, like 3, 17, and so on. One would imagine that, as we ascend the scale of numbers, primes would get rarer, crowded out by the ever-increasing products of small numbers, and that finally we would arrive at a very high number which would be the highest prime, the last numerical virgin. Euclid's proof demonstrates in a simple and elegant way that this is not so, and that to whatever astronomical regions we ascend, we shall always find numbers which are not the product of smaller ones, but are generated by immaculate conception, as it were.* Since I had become acquainted with Euclid's proof at school, it had always filled me with a deep satisfaction that was aesthetic rather than intellectual. Now, as I recalled the method and scratched the symbols on the wall, I felt the same enchantment.

And then, for the first time, I suddenly understood the reason for this enchantment: the scribbled symbols on the wall represented one of the rare cases where a meaningful and comprehensible statement about the infinite is arrived at by precise and finite means. The infinite is a mystical mass shrouded in a haze; and yet it was possible to gain some knowledge of it without losing oneself in treacly ambiguities. The significance of this swept over me like a wave. The wave had originated in an articulate verbal insight; but this evaporated at once, leaving in its wake only a wordless essence, a fragrance of eternity, a quiver of the arrow in the blue. I must have stood there for some minutes, entranced, with a wordless awareness that "this is perfect – perfect"; until I noticed some slight mental discomfort nagging at the back of my mind – some trivial circumstance that marred the perfection of the moment. Then I remembered the nature of that annoyance: I was, of course, in prison and might be shot. But this was immediately answered by a feeling whose verbal translation would be: "So what? is that all? have you got nothing more serious to worry about?" – an answer so spontaneous, fresh and amused as if the intruding annoyance had been the loss of a collar-stud. Then I was floating on my back in a river of peace,

---

*For the benefit of amateurs, here is the proof:
Assume that P is the hypothetically highest prime; then imagine a number equal $1 \times 2 \times 3 \times 4 \ldots \times P$. This number is expressed by the numerical symbol (P!). Now add to it 1: (P! + 1). This number is obviously not divisible by P or any number less than P (because these are all contained in (P!)). Hence (P!+1) is either a prime higher than P or it contains a prime factor higher than P. – QED.

under bridges of silence. It came from nowhere and flowed nowhere. Then there was no river and no I. The I had ceased to exist.

It is extremely embarrassing to write down a phrase like that when one has read *The Meaning of Meaning* and nibbled at logical positivism and aims at verbal precision and dislikes nebulous gushing. Yet, "mystical" experiences, as we dubiously call them, are not nebulous, vague or maudlin – they only become so when we debase them by verbalisation. However, to communicate what is incommunicable by its nature, one must somehow put it into words, and so one moves in a vicious circle. When I say "the I had ceased to exist", I refer to a concrete experience that is verbally as incommunicable as the feeling aroused by a piano concerto, yet just as real – only much more real. In fact, its primary mark is the sensation that this state is more real than any other one has experienced before – that for first time the veil has fallen and one is in touch with "real reality", the hidden order of things, the X-ray texture of the world, normally obscured by layers of irrelevancy.

What distinguishes this type of experience from the emotional entrancements of music, landscapes, or love, is that the former has a definitely intellectual, or rather noumenal, content. It is meaningful, though not in verbal terms. Verbal transcriptions that come nearest to it are: the unity and interlocking of everything that exists, an inter-dependence like that of gravitational fields or communicating vessels. The "I" ceases to exist because it has, by a kind of mental osmosis, established communication with, and been dissolved in, the universal pool. It is this process of dissolution and limitless expansion which is sensed as the "oceanic feeling", as the draining of all tension, the absolute catharsis, the peace that passeth all understanding.

The coming-back to the lower order of reality I found to be gradual, like waking up from anaesthesia. There was the equation of the parabola scratched on the dirty wall, the iron bed and the iron table and the strip of blue Andalusian sky. But there was no unpleasant hangover as from other modes of intoxication. On the contrary: there remained a sustained and invigorating, serene and fear-dispelling after-effect that lasted for hours and days. It was as if a massive dose of vitamins had been injected into the veins. Or, to change the metaphor, I resumed my travels through my cell like an old car with its batteries freshly recharged.

Whether the experience had lasted for a few minutes or an hour,

I never knew. In the beginning it occurred two or even three times a week, then the intervals became longer. It could never be voluntarily induced. After my liberation it recurred at even longer intervals, perhaps once or twice in a year. But by that time the groundwork for a change of personality had been completed. I shall henceforth refer to these experiences as "the hours by the window".

Religious conversion on the deathbed or in the death-cell is an almost irresistible temptation. That temptation has two sides.

One plays on crude fear, on the hope for individual salvation through unconditional surrender of the critical faculties to some archaic form of demonology. The other side is more subtle. Faced with the Absolute, the ultimate *nada*, the mind may become receptive to mystic experience. These one may regard as "real" in the sense of subjective pointers to an objective reality *ipso facto* eluding comprehension. But because the experience is inarticulate, has no sensory shape, colour or words, it lends itself to transcription in many forms, including visions of the Cross or of the goddess Kali; they are like dreams of a person born blind, and may assume the intensity of a revelation. Thus a genuine mystic experience may mediate a *bona fide* conversion to practically any creed, Christianity, Buddhism, or Fire-Worship.

I was thus waging a two-front war against the concise, rational, materialistic way of thinking which, in thirty-two years of training in mental cleanliness, had become a habit and a necessity like bodily hygiene – and against the temptation to surrender and creep back into the warm protective womb of faith. With those nightly, muffled "*madres*" and "*socorros*" in one's ear, the latter solution appeared as attractive and natural as taking cover from a pointed gun.

The "hours by the window", which had started with the rational reflection that finite statements about the infinite were possible – and which in fact represented a series of such statements on a non-rational level – had filled me with a direct certainty that a higher order of reality existed, and that it alone invested existence with meaning. I came to call it later on "the reality of the third order". The narrow world of sensory perception constituted the first order; this perceptual world was enveloped by the conceptual world which contained phenomena not directly perceivable, such as gravitation, electromagnetic fields, and curved space. The second order of reality filled in the gaps and gave meaning to the absurd patchiness of the sensory world.

In the same manner, the third order of reality enveloped, inter-penetrated, and gave meaning to the second. It contained "occult" phenomena which could not be apprehended or explained either on the sensory or on the conceptual level, and yet occasionally invaded them like spiritual meteors piercing the primitive's vaulted sky. Just as the conceptual order showed up the illusions and distortions of the senses, so the "third order" disclosed that time, space and causality, that the isolation, sepa-rateness and spatio-temporal limitations of the self were merely optical illusions on the next higher level. If illusions of the first type were taken at face value, then the sun was drowning every night in the sea and a mote in the eye was larger than the moon; and if the conceptual world was mistaken for ultimate reality, the world became an equally absurd tale, told by an idiot or by idiot-electrons which caused little children to be run over by motor cars, and little Andalusian peasants to be shot through heart, mouth and eyes, without rhyme or reason. Just as one could not feel the pull of a magnet with one's skin, so one could not hope to grasp in cognate terms the nature of ultimate reality. It was a text written in invisible ink; and though one could not read it, the knowledge that it existed was sufficient to alter the texture of one's existence, and make one's actions conform to the text.

I liked to spin out this metaphor. The captain of a ship sets out with a sealed order in his pocket which he is only permitted to open on the high seas. He looks forward to that moment which will end all uncertainty; but when the moment arrives and he tears the envelope open, he only finds an invisible text which defies all attempts at chemical treatment. Now and then a word becomes visible, or a figure denoting a meridian; then it fades again. He will never know the exact wording of the order; nor whether he has complied with it or failed in his mission. But his awareness of the order in his pocket, even though it cannot be deciphered, makes him think and act differently from the captain of a pleasure-cruiser or of a pirate ship.

I also liked to think that the founders of religions, prophets, saints and seers had at moments been able to read a fragment of the invisible text; after which they had so much padded, drama-tised and ornamented it, that they themselves could no longer tell what parts of it were authentic.

In *Dialogue with Death*, there are only a few allusions to all this; partly, because at the time when I wrote it the war in Spain was still on and I was reluctant to indulge in introspection; and partly because I was still too shattered and confused to give a clear account, even to myself, of what had happened in cell No. 40.

When, after sixty-four days in the cell, I was for the first time allowed out for exercise and made my first contact with other prisoners, there were three of them in the patio: Garcia Attadel; his former secretary, a Cuban; and a young Andalusian peasant. The peasant was called Nicholas: he was short, thin, with a stubby face and gentle eyes. He was illiterate, spoke to the three of us in a shy, deferential voice, and explained that he had hoped, when the war was over, to learn to read and write. He had been in the Anarchist militia, and had been captured a few days before on the Almeria front. The next day when I was let out into the patio, Nicholas was no longer there; he had been shot during the night.

From then on I lived in the constant fear that on the next occasion Garcia and the Cuban would also have vanished. Garcia was gaunt, with a narrow and fierce Castilian face; the Cuban was dapper, round-eyed, and had the swaggering gait of a dandy. The three of us were exercised during the siesta hour, between one and three, when the other prisoners were locked in their cells. As the morning progressed and the hour of exercise drew nearer, I would become more and more anxious and worried. I was tempted to pray for them, but that would have been another surrender. And yet, in a completely irrational manner, I felt convinced that their fate partly depended on me, and that my willingness for sacrifice could somehow protect them.

I then began to probe into myself to discover the exact amount of sacrifice that I was willing to make. This led to quite grotesque reflections: I found that I was willing to give one limb for each, but only in the form of one leg and one arm and not both of the same kind; that under torture I would soon break down and forsake them; and that I was willing to give my life for their joint lives, but not for a single one. Already in Malaga I had become prone to strange preoccupations of a similar kind; when I heard the oily voice read out the lists, I felt an obsessive urge to share in imagination the fate of those who were taken out, to live and re-live the scene of their execution in every detail – for I was convinced that this act of solidarity and identification would make death easier for them.

No doubt, a childish hope made me unconsciously believe that so much altruism and nobility of feeling would be recognised and duly rewarded by some superior power. But this is, I believe, only part of the truth. For there was another, more genuine element in these self-probings. There came, for instance, a day when I found that I was ready to give my life for either Garcia or the Cuban, not two for one, but one for one, and without bargaining conditions. Moreover, I felt that this would be something perfectly easy and natural, like sharing our last cigarettes. I could now no longer understand that I had ever felt otherwise. For it struck me as self-evident, in the manner of twice two being four, that we were all responsible for each other – not only in the superficial sense of social responsibility, but because, in some inexplicable manner, we partook of the same substance or identity, like Siamese twins or communicating vessels. I knew that all these comparisons were awkward and false, and the experience nevertheless true. When I had broken my last cigarette into halves and shared it with little Nicholas, he never thanked me because he knew that his pleasure in inhaling the smoke was mine, that to give was to take, because we were all attached to the same umbilical cord, and were all lying together in the same pulsating womb of transition. If every-body were an island, how could the world be a concern of his?

I was quite aware of the fact that solitary confinement is a spiritual hot-house. On the other hand, my predicament was merely an extreme form of the predicament inherent in the human condition. The difference, whether measured in terms of freedom, or fear, or of life-span expectation, was a difference in degree, not in kind. The problem of the nature of the bonds which united me with my fellow prisoners reflected in a concentrated form the basic problem from which all systems of social ethics are derived. And my seemingly absurd and overstrung preoccupations had, I felt, a desperately direct bearing on the state of our society and on applied politics.

My Party comrades, for instance, would say that the question whether A should sacrifice his life for B, depended entirely on the relative social value of A and B. If Comrade Arturo was more useful in the struggle against Fascism than little Nicholas, then, in a critical situation, it would be for Nicholas to lay down his life for Arturo, but not the other way round. Moreover, if the latter, led by mystic sentimentality, were to sacrifice himself for Nicholas, this would weaken the cause he was serving, and would constitute an objectively harmful, anti-social act. From there it followed that not only one, but a thousand or a hundred thousand Nicholases could and would be sacrificed if the cause was supposed to demand it. For in this view Nicholas existed merely as a social abstraction, a mathematical unit, obtained by dividing a mass of ten thousand militiamen by ten thousand.

But that equation did not work:

> The Party denied the free will of the individual – and at the same time it exacted his willing self-sacrifice. It denied his capacity to choose between two alternatives – and at the same time it demanded that he should always choose the right one. It denied his power to distinguish between good and evil – and at the same time it spoke accusingly of guilt and treachery. The individual stood under the sign of economic fatality, a wheel in a clockwork which had been wound up for all eternity and could not be stopped or influenced – and the Party demanded that the wheel should revolt against the clockwork and change its course. There was somewhere an error in the calculation; the equation did not work out. – (*Darkness at Noon*).

I remembered a phrase of Malraux's from *Les Conquérants*: "Une vie ne vaut rien, mais rien ne vaut une vie.' In the social equation, the value of a single life is nil; in the cosmic equation it is infinite. Now every schoolboy knows that if you smuggle either a nought or the infinite into a finite calculation, the equation will be disrupted and you will be able to prove that three equals five, or five hundred. Not only Communism, but any political movement which implicitly relies on utilitarian ethics, must become a victim to the same fatal error. It is a fallacy as naive as a mathematical teaser, and yet its consequences lead straight to Goya's "Disasters", of the reign of the garotte, the torture-chambers of the Inquisition, or the cellars of the Lubianka. Whether the road is paved with quotations from Rousseau, Marx, Christ or Mohammed, makes little difference.

I feel that this present account gives a far too tidy and logical description of a spiritual crisis with its ups and downs, advances and relapses; its oscillation between new certainties and old doubts; its sudden illuminations, followed by long periods of inner darkness, petty resentments and fear. I do not believe that anybody, except a very primitive person, can be reborn in one night, as so many tales of sudden conversions will have it. I do believe that one can suddenly "see the light" and undergo a change that will alter the course of one's life. But a change of this kind takes place at the core of the individual, and it will take a long time to seep through to the periphery, until the entire personality becomes impregnated with it. A conversion which, after the first genuine crisis, saves further labour by buying a whole package of ready-made beliefs, and replaces one set of dogmas by another, can hardly be an inspiring example to those who cling to a minimum standard of intellectual honesty. Nor do I believe that a true spiritual transformation can be the result of a process of conscious reasoning, working its way downward, as it were. It begins on the level where the unconscious axioms of faith, the innate standards of value, are located. It starts, as it were, in the boiler-room, at the fuse-boxes and gas-mains which control life in the house; the intellectual re-furnishing comes afterwards. Some eminent converts of our time seem to have left it all to the decorators; and the Christian love they show their neighbours is about as convincing as a Communist peace offensive.

It was easier to reject the utilitarian concept of ethics than to find a substitute for it. Perhaps the solution was to be found in a reversal of Bentham's maxim: – the least suffering for the smallest number. It sounded attractive – up to a point. But beyond that point lay quietism, stagnation and resignation. To change from Lenin's way to Gandhi's way was again tempting, yet it was another short-cut, a toppling over from one extreme to the other. Perhaps the solution lay in a new form of synthesis between saint and revolutionary, between the active and the contemplative life; or perhaps we lived in an era of transition comparable to the last centuries of the Roman Empire, which admitted of no solution at all.

In the years that followed I wrote several books in which I attempted to assimilate the experiences of cell No. 40. In *The Gladiators* (about half of which was written after Seville) and *Darkness at Noon*, which was the next book, I tried to come to intellectual terms with the intuitive glimpses gained during the "hours at the window". Both novels were variations on the same theme: the problem of Ends and Means, the conflict between morality and social expediency. The third novel of that trilogy, *Arrival and Departure*, was a rejection of the ethical neutrality of science as expressed in the psychiatrist's claim to be able to "reduce" courage, dedication and self-sacrifice to neurotic motives. Finally, in *The Yogi and the Commissar*, I tried once more to digest, in the form of essays this time, the meaning of the solitary dialogue of cell No.40. This book, written in 1943, closed the cycle; it had taken five years to digest the hours by the window.

PART THREE

THE GOD
THAT FAILED

Chapter 14

THE GLADIATORS*

I finished The Gladiators, *the first novel of the trilogy, in July, 1938, a few months after my formal break with the Communist Party. I had started writing it four years earlier, when my progressive disillusionment with the Party had reached an acute state. In* The Invisible Writing *I have described the casual incident which made me embark on writing a historical novel on the slave revolution in the first century BC:*

The day after [some trouble with the Party bureaucracy] I was moved by a momentary curiosity to look up the name "Spartacus" in a German Encyclopaedia. The German Communist Party is the offspring of a revolutionary group that called itself "*Spartakus Bund*", founded in 1917 by Karl Liebknecht and Rosa Luxemburg. The name "Spartacus" was accordingly a household word among Communists; but, like most Communists, I had only the vaguest notion who Spartacus was. I knew that he had led some sort of a revolution in antiquity, and that was about all. It was one of those blind spots in one's education which one always means to cure by looking the subject up, but somehow one never gets round to doing it.

So I opened Volume II, *Seefeld to Traun*, of *Meyers Lexikon*, and read the following:

*From The Invisible Writing, ch. xxiv, and The Gladiators.

Spartacus, leader of the Slaves' or Gladiators' War 73–71 BC, a free-born Thracian, was sent, as a Roman prisoner of war, to the Gladiators' Training School in Capua, fled from there in 73 with seventy of his comrades, occupied Mt Vesuvius, defeated the Praetor Varinius, and saw his following grow to 70,000 men. He now took possession of Southern Italy and four times defeated the Romans, until in 71 the Praetor M. Licinius Crassus drove him to the south-western tip of Italy; he fell at Petelia, together with 60,000 slaves. The prisoners were crucified, the survivors who had succeeded in breaking through were annihilated by Pompeius (q.v.) in the foothills of the Alps. Bibl.: Hartwig, *Der Sklavenkrieg.*

This laconic text took such a hold on my imagination that I resolved on the spot to add to my unpublished manuscripts yet another one, by writing a historical novel. It took four years to write, involved me in a mammoth research task, gave me a new outlook on history, and was my first novel to appear in print. The following weeks I spent mostly at the *Bibliothèque Nationale*, in front of one of the green-shaded desk-lamps, digging into Roman history, the condition of slaves in antiquity, the regulations concerning gladiators' fights, the folklore of Thrace and Gaul, the economy of the Roman state, the topography of Mount Vesuvius, and so on. During the next few months I read more history than I had done since my school-days, and wrote the first eight chapters – about one-third of the book.

But the remaining two-thirds took several years; constant interruptions, ranging from Party activities and journalism to Seville jail, turned the writing of it into a kind of obstacle race. After each interruption, the return to the first century BC brought peace and relief. I have tried to explain the reasons in the postscript (to the Danube edition) of the novel:

It was not so much an escape as a form of occupational therapy which helped me to clarify my ideas; for there existed some obvious parallels between the first pre-Christian century and the present. It had been a century of social unrest, of revolutions and mass-upheavals. Their causes had an equally familiar ring: the breakdown of traditional values, the abrupt transformation of the economic system, unemployment, corruption, and a decadent ruling class. Only against this background could it be understood that a band of seventy circus fighters could grow within a few months into an army, and for two years hold half Italy under its sway.

But why, then, did the revolution go to pieces? The reasons were complex, but one factor stood out clearly: Spartacus was a victim of the "law of detours", which compels the leader on the road to Utopia to be "ruthless for the sake of pity". Yet he shrinks from taking the last step – the purge of the dissidents and the establishment of a ruthless tyranny; and through this refusal he dooms his revolution to defeat. In *Darkness at Noon*, the Bolshevik Commissar Rubashov goes the opposite way and follows the "law of detours" to the end – only to discover that it was "a defective compass which led to such a winding, twisted course, that the goal finally disappeared in the mist". Thus the two novels complement each other – both roads end in a tragic *cul-de-sac*.

The sources give no indication of the programme or common idea that held the Slave Army together; yet a number of hints indicate that it must have been a kind of "socialist" programme, which asserted that all men were born equal, and denied that the distinction between free men and slaves was part of the natural order. And there are further hints to the effect that at one time Spartacus tried to found somewhere in Calabria a Utopian community – the Sun City – based on common property. Now such ideas were entirely alien to the Roman proletariat before the advent of Christianity. This led to the fairly plausible guess that the Spartacists had been inspired by the same source as the Nazarenes a century later: the Messianism of the Hebrew prophets. There must have been, in the motley crowd of runaway slaves, quite a number of Palestinian origin; and these may have acquainted Spartacus with the prophecies relating to the Son of Man, sent "to comfort the captives, to open the eyes of the blind, to free the oppressed". Every mass movement eventually picks up the ideology or mystique best fitted to its purpose. I assumed that among the numerous cranks, reformers and sectarians whom his horde attracted, Spartacus chose as his mentor and guide a member of the Judaic sect of the Essenes – the only sizeable civilised community that practised primitive Communism at that time, and taught that "what is mine is thine, and what is thine is mine". What Spartacus, after his initial victories, needed most was a programme and credo that would hold his mob together. It seemed to me that the philosophy most likely to appeal to the largest number of the dispossessed must have been the same which a century later found its sublime expression in the Sermon on the Mount – and which Spartacus, the Slave Messiah, had tried to implement.

In contrast to these speculations, I felt the need to draw the known historical background with a strict, indeed pedantic accuracy. This led me into the study of such intricate subjects as the nature and shape of Roman underwear, and their complicated ways of fastening clothes by buckles, belts and sashes. In the end, not a word of all this found its way into the novel, and clothes are hardly mentioned in the text; but I found it impossible to write a scene if I could not visualise how the characters were dressed, and how their garments were held together. Similarly, the months spent in studying Roman exports, imports, taxation and related matters yielded less than three pages of the novel, where Crassus explains to the younger Cato the economic policies of Rome in cynically Marxist terms.

The Gladiators, written in German before I switched to English, was translated by Edith Simon (who has subsequently become one of the most imaginative writers of historical novels).

The extract that follows is the (slightly compressed) opening scene of The Gladiators:

Prologue: The Dolphins

It is night still.

Still no cock has crowed.

But Quintus Apronius, First Scribe of the Market Court of Capua, is used to the fact that clerks have to be earlier risers than cocks. He groans as his toes fish for the sandals on the grimy wooden floor. Once again the sandals stand the wrong way, toes facing bed: the young day's first offence; how many more are to come?

He shuffles along to the window, looks down into the courtyard, a deep shaft surrounded by five storeys. A bony old woman comes climbing up the fire escape: Pomponia, his housekeeper and only slave, brings breakfast and the pail of hot water. She is punctual, he will say that for her. Punctual, old and bony.

The water is lukewarm, breakfast awful: second vexation. But then the Dolphins swim across his mind, the anticipation of his day's splendid climax chases a smile across his face. Pomponia prattles and nags as she bustles about the room, brushing his clothes, helping to adjust the complicated pleats of his clerk's habit. In worried dignity he descends the fire escape, cautiously snatching up his gown, that its hem may not sweep the rungs; he knows that, broom in hand, Pomponia is watching him from the window.

It dawns. Still holding on to his robe, he edges along the houses, for a continuous train of ox- and horse-carts migrates through the narrow alley, with much rumbling and gee-ups: the Driving of Vehicles Through the Streets of Capua During the Day is Strictly Prohibited.

A group of workmen is coming towards him along the street that divides the perfume- and ointment-stalls from the fish market. They are municipal slaves, ruffians staring woodenly with unshaven faces. Harassed, he flattens himself still closer to the housefront, gathers his cloak, mutters with scorn. The slaves march past, two of them jostle against him, unmindful and unrepentant. The Scribe quivers with rage, yet he dare not say anything: the men are unshackled – cursed newfangled slackness – and the overseers dally far behind the gang.

At last they have all passed, Apronius may go on his way; but his day is spoilt. Times are growing more and more menacing, it is five years since Great Dictator Sulla's death, and once more the world is off its hinges. Only five years – yet again there is free corn for lazybones and loiterers; People's Tribunes and demagogues may once more hold forth with their blood-curdling speeches. Bereft of its leader, the nobility compromises; and once more the rabble rears its head.

Quintus Apronius, First Scribe of the Market Court, feels that his day is definitely spoilt; thinking of the Dolphins even, splendid climax of his day, fails to cheer him. A wooden hoarding attracts his gaze; scriptors are busy adorning it with a new announcement. It is a very grand announcement, nearly finished: on top is painted a crimson sun with many rays bristling in all directions. Underneath, Director Lentulus Batuatus, owner of the city's greatest school of gladiators, is proud to invite the gracious Capuan public to a super-performance. The festival will take place the day after tomorrow in any weather, for the director Batuatus, heedless of enormous expense, will have awnings spread over the arena, designed to keep possible rain, not to mention sun, off the honoured public. Moreover, perfume will be sprayed throughout the auditorium during the intervals.

Quake and hurry thither, ye lovers of festive games, esteemed citizens of Capua; ye who witnessed the feats of a Pacidejanus, winner in a

hundred and six combats, ye who once admired invincible Car-
pophore, do not miss this singular opportunity of seeing the famous
fighters from Lentulus Batuatus's school fight and die. . . .

Follows the lengthy list of the performing teams, the main feature
being a fight between the Gallic gladiator Crixus and the Thracian
ring-bearer Spartacus. The notice further announces that one
hundred and fifty novices will duel AD GLADIUM, man against man;
one hundred and fifty more AD BESTIARIUM, man against beast.
During the noon-interval, and while the arena is disinfected,
dwarfs, cripples, women and clowns are to fight mock-duels.
Tickets from three Asses to fifty Sestertii may be booked in
advance at Titus's bakery, in the open-air baths of Hermios, as
well as from the authorised agents who may be found at the
entrance to the Minerva Temple.

Quintus Apronius mutters with scorn; in Rome they have long
ago changed over to the system of free games, offered by ambitious politicians as electioneering stunts. But in this backward
provincial city of Capua everyone has actually got to pay for his
bit of fun. Apronius decides to ask Director Lentulus Batuatus,
whom he knows by sight, for a free ticket. The games-director, one
of Capua's most distinguished citizens, is also an *habitué* of the
Dolphins; time and again Apronius had intended to make his
acquaintance.

Slightly cheered by this resolution, Apronius continues on his
way; a few moments later he has reached his destination, Minerva
Temple Hall, where the Municipal Market Court is in session.

The sun rises, the colleagues appear; sleepy minor clerks first,
grumpily on their dignity. Two parties in a law-suit are already
there, fishmongers quarrelling about a stand in the market; they
are told to wait outside until the beadle calls them in. The officials
move drowsily around the hall, push benches about, arrange the
documents on the president's desk. Quintus Apronius enjoys a
certain amount of respect among his colleagues, due partly to his
seventeen years of service, partly to his position of an Honorary
Secretary to a Sociability-and-Funeral-Club.

Even now he is busy trying to recruit a younger colleague to his
club, the "Worshippers of Diana and Antinous"; he explains the
club-rules with benevolent condescension. New members have to
pay an entrance fee of one hundred Sestertii, the annual subscrip-
tion is fifteen Sestertii, payable in monthly instalments of five
Asses. The club fund, on the other hand, pays three hundred

Sestertii towards the cremation of each deceased member; suicides are excepted. Fifty Sestertii are deducted for the funeral train and divided among them on arrival at the pyre.

Whosoever starts a quarrel at one of the socials is fined four Sestertii, whosoever starts to fight pays twelve Sestertii, whosoever insults the chairman twenty. The banquets are seen to by four annually replaced members who have to provide rugs or bolsters for the dining sofas, hot water and crockery, as well as four amphorae of decent wine, and one loaf at two Asses and four sardines for each member. Quintus Apronius has talked himself quite pink, but his colleague, instead of feeling honoured, merely says he will think it over. Disappointed and irritated, Apronius turns his back on the irreverent youth.

Other officials are filing in, ever higher and mightier ones, up to the Municipal Councillor who acts as judge. Graciously he takes leave of his suite, patronisingly he nods at Apronius who is busy fussing about chair and documents for him. Adversaries and public stream inside, the session has begun, and with it Apronius's business, profession and hobby: Writing. His pinched face lights up; with tender pleasure he traces word after word on that nice virgin parchment – no one writes such an ornate hand, no one takes minutes as efficiently as Apronius, who has gained his superiors' implicit confidence in seventeen years of service. Opponents get personal, attorneys talk, witnesses are examined, experts interrogated, documents pile up, laws and lawlets are read out – all of this is but a pretext to let Apronius prove the Fine Art of minute-writing; he is the true hero of this stage, the others are mere crowd. As the sun beams its noon and the beadle announces the court's adjournment, Apronius has long forgotten what the suit was all about. But the unusually successful flourish which closed his record of the defendant's speech still undulates behind his eyelids.

He neatly stacks records and documents, salutes the Councillor respectfully, the colleagues affably; pressing his pleats to his hips he leaves the scene of his official activities. He strides towards the Tavern of the Twin-Wolves in the Oscian quarter, where a table is reserved for the Worshippers of Diana and Antinous. For the last seven years, ever since the day of his promotion to First Scribe of the Market Court, he has eaten his midday meal here, a meal specially and personally prepared by the proprietor according to a prescribed diet, for Apronius has stomach trouble; but there is no extra charge.

The meal is over. Apronius superintends the washing of his private drinking bowl, snips the crumbs off his dress, departs from the Tavern of the Twin-Wolves and betakes himself to the New Steambaths.

Here too the attendant welcomes the regular guest with deference, hands him the key to Apronius's reserved locker, receives with a forgiving smile the tip of two Asses. The spacious marble hall swarms with life as usual, groups lounge in gossip, news and compliments are exchanged; public speakers, ambitious poets and other opportunists lecture in the arch-roofed shelter, interrupted by their public with heckling, applause and laughter. Apronius enjoys having his intellect titillated in advance of the manifold physical delights of the baths. He joins one group, then another, one ear half-catches a few phrases of an attack on abortion and the falling birthrate; he turns an indignant back as soon as the next speaker has quite finished a dirty story; gown snatched up, he saunters forth, towards a third group. In its centre is a fat real estate agent and broker. He carries on an obscure little bank somewhere in the Oscian quarter, and is trying to hook himself customers by extolling the shares of a new resin refinery in Bruttium. Out of the purest philanthropy he urges the listener to buy at once, resin is a good proposition, resin has a future. Apronius pulls a wry face, mutters with scorn, walks on.

Of course, the largest audience, quite an assembly, has collected round that petty lawyer and author Fulvius again, that dangerous agitator. He speaks dryly and complacently as though quoting a cookery book; and yet those imbeciles seem to lap it up. Full of resentment, pleated robe held high, Apronius squeezes into the listening crowd; not from curiosity, but because he knows well that anger before bath is good for his digestion.

– Doomed is the Roman Republic, declares the lawyer in his scholarly manner of stating dry fact. Once upon a time Rome was an agricultural state, now the peasantry has been bled empty, the State with it. The world expanded, cheap corn was imported from all lands: farmers had to sell their fields and live on alms; cheap slave labour was imported from all lands: artisans starved and workmen went abegging. Rome was flooded with corn, it rotted in the granaries; and for the poor there was no bread. Rome was full of working hands, they opened begging or closed to fists; no hands were wanted. The necessity for a fundamental change had been obvious to all thinking men for nearly a century. But wherever such wisdom aired itself it was killed, together with its progenitor.

"We live," remarks Fulvius, and gravely strokes his indented pate, "in a century of abortive revolutions. . . ."

Apronius has heard enough. Truly, that kind of talk undermines the very base of civilisation. Trembling with wrath and concealing his secret satisfaction – for he can feel anger doing its intended work – Quintus Apronius finally walks inside, to his favourite station: the Hall of the Dolphins.

This is a well-lit room, at once pleasant and severe. All along its marble walls are high marble chairs of utilitarian construction, the elbow-pieces of which represent dolphins, carved by a master hand. These are the seats of lofty wisdom exchanged by neighbours in circumspect discourse, where thoughts fly high as bowels ease. For, to combine both activities harmoniously is the purpose of the Hall of Dolphins.

The Scribe Quintus Apronius's annoyance yields to a gala-mood; and his joy multiplies at the sight of a well-known, well-fed figure enthroned between two dolphins: Lentulus Batuatus, owner of the gladiator-school. The marble seat next to him has just been vacated; Apronius lifts his folds ceremoniously, squats down with a grunt of happiness, and tenderly strokes a dolphin's head with each hand.

That revolutionist has really provoked a most effective wrath. In pious emotion Apronius pays the dolphins their toll, and watches his neighbour out of the corner of his eye. The director's brow appears clouded, and all does not seem to be going well with his physical endeavours. Apronius braces himself and sighs sympathetically that the chief thing in life is after all a good digestion; and that for a long time he has been evolving a theory: all rebellious discontent is actually caused by an irregular digestion, or, to be more exact, by chronic constipation. As a matter of fact, he goes on, he has been considering to make this the subject of a philosophical pamphlet which he hopes to write as soon as his time permits it.

The impresario brushes him with a casual look, nods, answers sullenly that this is quite possible.

– Not only possible, it's an established fact, says Apronius heatedly. And he would pledge himself to explain many an historical incident simply by means of his theory – incidents whose importance has been exaggerated beyond proportion by seditious philosophers.

But all his fervour does not succeed in rousing his neighbour. As far as he is concerned, the director grumbles, he has always fed his people decently, and he has been employing the best of doctors to watch over their physical condition and their diet. And yet, in spite of all that, the wretches have repaid his expensive trouble with the basest ingratitude.

– Apronius inquires compassionately whether Lentulus has business worries; his hopes for a free ticket dwindle sadly.

– Indeed he has, moans the impresario, there is no point in keeping it a secret any longer; seventy of his best gladiators have run away during the night, and the police have found no trace of them in spite of their efforts.

And once started off, the corpulent man with the untarnished business reputation gives way to his chagrin and lets himself go in a lengthy lament on how times are bad and business worse.

The Scribe Apronius listens reverently, his torso bent forward in an attitude of extreme attention, his garments gathered up with affected fingertips. He knows that, apart from the public respect he enjoys on account of his prosperous ventures, Lentulus has also had a remarkable political career in Rome. He came to Capua only two years ago, and founded his gladiator-school which already enjoys an excellent reputation. His business connections spread, net-like, all over Italy and the provinces; his agents buy the human raw material at the Deli slave market and sell it, transformed into model-gladiators, to Spain, Sicily and the Asiatic courts, after one year's thorough training. Lentulus owes his success mainly to his integrity; his establishment employs only renowned trainers, medical specialists superintend the pupils' diet and exercise. But above all, he has succeeded in impressing on his men as an iron rule that, once beaten, they should never ask to be spared, should cut a good figure whilst being finished off and not disgust the audience with any sort of fuss.

"Anyone can live – but dying is an art and takes some learning," he kept on admonishing his gladiators. It was due to that very attribute, their delicate dying discipline, that Lentulus's gladiators fetched an average of 50 per cent more than those from any other school.

And yet, even Lentulus is affected by these unpleasant times; flattered and compassionate, the Scribe listens to the great man's plaint:

"You see, my good man," explains Lentulus, "most games contractors are going through a crisis at present, which is entirely the public's fault. The public no longer appreciates qualified, carefully trained fighters and the trouble, the expense, involved in manufacturing them. Quantity is indeed supplanting quality, the public demands that each performance close with one of those disgusting mass-executions of men by beasts, and all that sort of thing. Have you any idea what that means for the business? Quite simply this: in the classic duel form AD GLADIUM, the losses are obviously one out of two, which means, in other words, that the consumption amounts to 50 per cent. Add a safety margin of 10 per cent for fatally wounded cases – and we arrive at a material-consumption of 60 per cent per show. Right you are – here we have the classic calculation on which we base our balance sheet.

"But now the public comes along and demands animal stunts. They will insist on the picturesque, and of course it never occurs to them that exposing my gladiators AD BESTIARIUM raises consumption to 85 or 90 per cent. Only a few days ago my son's tutor, an extremely able mathematician, worked out that even the best gladiator's chance to survive three years' active service is about one in twenty-five. Logically this means that the contractor must make up for the amount spent on each man's training in one and a half or two performances, to name an average."

Apronius sees his hopes for a free ticket lie dead and buried, and on top of that he is apparently expected to supply comfort. "Well, surely you will be able to get over that loss of a mere fifty men," he says encouragingly.

– "Seventy," the director corrects him, exasperated. "And seventy of the best. One of them is Crixus, my Gallic gladiator-trainer, you've probably seen him at work: a gloomy-looking, heavy man with a seal's-head and slow, dangerous movements. A dead loss. And Castus, the little fellow, agile, malignant, sharp as a jackal. And quite a number of other eminent fighters: Ursus, a giant of a man; Spartacus, a quiet, appealing character who always wore a pretty fur-skin round his shoulders; Oenomaus, a promising debutant; and many more. First-class material, I assure you, and very pleasant-spoken people."

The impresario's voice takes on a positively pathetic tone as he recites his list of lost ones. "Now I'll have to reduce admission by 50 per cent; and already I've had several hundred tickets distributed among paid enthusiasts and free-ticket-scroungers."

Apronius swallows and hastens to raise the conversation to a more generally philosophical level. It must be a rather queer feeling for those gladiators, he reflects, to go on living from performance to performance, always in the shadow of death. He, Quintus Apronius, finds it difficult to imagine himself in the state of mind of one of those creatures.

Lentulus smiles; he is used to laymen asking him such questions.

"One gets used to it, you know," he says. "You as an official have no idea how quickly men get used to the most extraordinary conditions. It's like war; and anyway, fate may overtake every one of us any day. Besides, these people, who have the assurance of a firm roof over their heads and of good, healthy food, really have a far better time of it than me with the entire responsibility resting on my shoulders. Believe me, sometimes I almost envy my pupils."

Apronius confirms with nods that a pupil's life seems indeed to have its points.

"But, you see, man is never satisfied; it seems to be human nature," the contractor continues talking pessimism. Particularly just before a performance, he adds, there is always a certain amount of unrest among the men. This time it had got round somehow that, by public request, the director was forced to expose the surviving AD GLADIUM-victors to renewed fighting AD BESTIARIUM. Naturally the men rather disliked the idea of it; there were some positively embarrassing scenes and last night, in a manner so far inexplicable, the said incident took place.

Despite the fact that he, Lentulus Batuatus himself, is the principal victim, he cannot but agree to some extent with the men's indignation. For the public's behaviour aggravates even him, Lentulus, far more than the business aspect; there is, for example, the latest superstitious belief that fresh gladiators' blood cures certain female complaints. He will spare himself and his esteemed listener a description of the scenes that have been enacted since in the arena. As for his own health, it has been so shattered by all these happenings that he cannot without nausea hear the word "blood" pronounced, and his physician has seriously counselled him to visit a hydropathic institution at Baiae or Pompeii in the near future.

The director sighs and closes his tale with a resigned gesture which might equally point to the vanity of his physical endeavours or the general state of the world.

Apronius rises from his marble seat, rearranges the pleats of his gown, makes his adieux. During his dinner at the Tavern of the Twin-Wolves he remains grumpy and preoccupied, and actually forgets to superintend the washing of his drinking-bowl.

Dusk veils the narrow criss-cross streets of the Oscian quarter as he sets out for home. Not for one single moment does the thought that he failed to get a free ticket leave his saddened mind. He is gorged with bitterness as he clambers up the fire escape to his apartment; what good are seventeen years of service? – an outcast from the feast of life, not even the crumbs stray your way.

Mechanically he lets the clothes down his gaunt body, re-pleats them carefully and lays them out on the wobbly tripod; then extinguishes the light. Rhythmically thudding footsteps echo from the street: the municipal building-slaves are returning from work. He can see their ill-boding, numbed faces as when they pushed him aside and went on without apologising.

Quintus Apronius, First Scribe of the Market Court, stares sadly into his bedroom's night. Is this what one labours for, a whole toilsome life long full of grievance and privation? Can there be gods in such a world?

Since his childhood Apronius has never been so near to tears. In vain he waits for sleep to come, scared of the dreams it will bring. For he knows they will be nasty dreams.

There are three more "Dolphin" episodes in the novel. Their ironic style was intended to provide a counterpoint to the main narrative – the latrine smells, as it were, wafting through history. The narrative itself attempts to reconstruct the fortunes of the horde of slaves and malcontents, which grows like an avalanche; their victories over the Roman legions, their fratricidal quarrels and gradual transformation from a destructive band of brigands into the semblance of a disciplined army.

After a year of aimless forays criss-crossing southern Italy, the leaders of the movement decide to settle on the Gulf of Tarentum, and to build a township of their own – the Sun City. As a site they have chosen the vicinity of the ancient, highly civilised and decadent Greek colony of Thurium. The extracts which follow are from the concluding part of the novel which describes the rise and fall of the Sun City – the Slaves' Utopia of antiquity.

Hegio, a citizen of Thurium, awoke before sunrise in the consciousness that this was the break of a festive day; the house was to be decorated with sprigs and garlands to celebrate the entry of the Prince of Thrace, the new Hannibal. He resolved to go to the vineyards early to fetch vines and mistletoe. He glanced at his sleeping wife, slipped into his sandals, ascended to the flat roof of his house.

As yet it was still dark and chilly, but the sea, which formed a steep vault over his horizon, was already beginning to change colour. Hegio loved this hour dearly, loved its brilliance and its scents. The breath of the sea under the sunny blast of noon differed from its tang at night. At night it smelled of crystalline coolness, like salt and stars; the morning gave it the fragrance of seaweed, and noon the stench of fish and steaming decay. He sniffed the sea air and looked across at the mountains – first to the north where, if he was not mistaken, traces of snow whitened the peaks of the Lucanian Apennines, though it might have been the morning mist. Then he turned south, to the distant, violet bulk of Sila – he was a shareholder of the Pitch and Resin Production Company there. In fallow magnificence the mountains encircled the valley of the Crathis, but the east was guarded by the dome of sea whose extreme brim began at last to smoulder, and broke into flame under the touch of the still invisible disk.

One cock crowed, then a second; finally all the cocks of Thurium competed eagerly in their officious, alarmist cheers to the rising sun. Hegio decided that only Roman fowls could crow so discordantly and vaingloriously; in his Attic homeland even the cocks' voices held more harmony.

> "Harsh to the ear of the Greek sounds
> the crow of the cocks of Latinum,"

he improvised.

He did not like the Romans. He did not despise them, but their coarse conceit and pressing self-assurance made him smile. Efficiency oozed out of their every pore. Despite this he, Hegio, a man who traced his ancestors back to Trojan warriors, had married a Roman. She lay downstairs on the marriage bed, moist with the sweat of a satisfied matron in her slumber. Her satisfaction was not derived from the festive day which would bring Spartacus, Thracian Prince, second Hannibal – but from the fact that he, Hegio, descendant of Trojan heroes, had done his conjugal duty last night after a long interval.

The sea, now fully ablaze, sent its smell into his nostrils; he seemed at once boyish and senile in his eagerness. He liked the mild moon-scents better than the blaze of sun, and the cool charm of Greek youths gave him more delight than did the dutiful pleasures of procreation with his matron.

What was the use? The entire Attic family tree was not worth five vines, nor a single share of the Pitch and Resin Production Company. At the foot of the pale mountain lay the ruins of legen-

dary Sybaris, the fairy-city, built by his ancestors in ancient times.
Greek colonists of refined customs, with silver coins, harps, and a
knowledge of geometry, they had owned the whole strip of South
Italian coast, and that at a time when the Latins, clad in bearskins,
were busy climbing trees.

The cocks crowed a second time, and someone came puffing up
the stairs. It was the matron.

"What are you doing on the roof so early in the morning?" she
asked with that kindly sternness which is so suitable in the treatment of the very young and very old.

"I am looking, my dear, merely looking." He did not mind being
taken for a child or an aged man; the creased face on his lean body
crumpled into boyishly sly wrinkles.

"What's there to look at?" the matron said disapprovingly. She
yawned and stood by his side at the edge of the roof, her hand on
his shoulder. That shoulder was boyish and bony; recollecting the
events of the night she shivered pleasantly under the frost of
dawn.

They gazed down at the town. She was still asleep, a large
village of stone rather than a town, a white village of many pillars,
lovely and very sad in her morning stillness. Her lanes twisted
between the walls like dried-up creeks. The houses were flat-
roofed and huddled confidently against the hillside. But on top of
the hill the village grew into a proper town with wide, square-cut
avenues, in her centre the market place and fountain. After
Sybaris had been destroyed, Hippodamus, famed architect, had
designed this heart of the city according to carefully drawn and
coloured plans. Chalk-white houses stood between blue mountains and blue sea. Thus Thurium had been created, the new city
of the Sybarites, now very old as well. All the original families
were very old; they had many ancestors and few children. They
spoke a purer Greek than the Greeks themselves, now extinct
everywhere except in Alexandria; they were descended from Trojan knights, or at least from that man Smyndirides whose bed was
spoilt for him by a crumpled rose leaf beneath his sheet.

Now and then they married the daughters of the Roman colonists who had been forced on them by the Senate as a punishment
for their siding with Hannibal and against Rome during the last
Punic war. Those colonists had their own quarter north-east of the
town, they multiplied rapidly, worked hard and well, and were
heartily hated; it was said that they blew their noses on their
elbows. They had had the presumption to re-name the town:

"Copia" was the name of the Roman quarter, the whole of Thurium was now supposed to bear that new name; all official documents called her thus. Naturally the old families persisted in calling their town by her proper name, Attica remained Attica, Thurium stayed Thurium. And naturally they were going to side with Spartacus, that new Hannibal, no matter whether he was Carthagian or Thracian; the main thing was that he knocked a few teeth out of those capable elbow-snufflers. The entire town looked forward to his entry with the joy of children or the aged.

The city awoke by degrees; the first few shepherds, unwashed early-birds, drove their sleep-warmed goats through the narrow alleys. The scattered goats' bells tingled absentmindedly, the shepherds whistled shrilly on their short flutes. The sea waved its morning fumes across the roof: seaweed and sands. Far away, on the fields by the hills, grazed herds of white buffalo; they mingled with the morning mist by the river, and the steers, white as chalky Lucania herself, stared with stiffly raised heads at the Apennines.

"Come and have breakfast," said the matron.

Hegio smiled: "I'm going to the river to fetch sprigs and leaves for the Entry."

"Surely not before breakfast," said the matron.

"I shall take the boys with me," said Hegio, "afterwards they can help us decorating."

"The boys will stay here," said the matron.

She was a colonist's daughter. The colonists were against the Thracian Prince. They went about with gloomy frowns on their hostile patriotic countenances. Perhaps they were afraid.

"Then I'll have to go on my own," said Hegio.

"In your nightdress?" asked the matron.

"I'll put something on. You'll see how many sprigs I shall bring home."

He climbed down the stairs, the matron followed with slight snorts of irritation. Downstairs Publibor, the only slave of the household, brought the dog his breakfast.

"You're going with me to the river," said Hegio to his slave. "We're going to get sprigs and leaves. You're coming too," he said to the dog, a calf-sized brute who pulled at his chain, yapping and howling.

They were off: Hegio came first, the slave a few paces behind; the dog frolicked in front, let them pass ahead, only to overtake them again at a furious rate. At the outskirts of the town, where garden walls were no longer of stone but of sun-dried clay and dung, they encountered Tyndarus the greengrocer, who was pushing a cart laden with fresh lettuces and herbs to the city.

"Where to, so early?" asked the greengrocer.

"I, my slave and my dog are going to get leaves and sprigs for the entry of the Thracian Prince," said Hegio.

"Between you and me," said Tyndarus and propped his cart against a wall, "I hear he hasn't much claim to any title. People say he used to be a gladiator and bandit, if not worse."

"Nonsense," said Hegio. "There's always tittle-tattling about those in power. At any rate, he struck Rome a whacking blow. A second Hannibal, that's what he is, and anyhow, it is a change."

"Quite," said the greengrocer who liked to keep in with everybody. "But they do say he's going to give all slaves equal civic rights, that he's going to rob people of their money and houses, and that he'll turn everything topsy-turvy."

"Nonsense," said Hegio and turned to his young slave. "Would you like to leave service and lead a new life?"

"I would," said Publibor.

"There, you see," said the greengrocer and harnessed himself to his cart again. "It is a dangerous affair, I told you so."

Hegio was enjoying himself. "What cheek!" he said. "Only because the matron is a trifle strict and moody? I don't have an easy time of it, either. Do I not treat you well?"

"You do."

The boy looked at him seriously. He seemed to take everything seriously. He had a serious face. Hegio had never noticed before that he had a face at all. This made him thoughtful.

"Didn't I even permit you to join a cremation society?"

"You did."

"He is in the same society as I," said the greengrocer. "We had a general meeting the day before yesterday."

"There you are," said Hegio, surprised. "Just like a free man."

"It is my only privilege," said Publibor.

"Your only one?" said Hegio, more surprised. "Well yes, perhaps so, according to the law. But it is something. And I shall leave you your freedom in my will. Do I live too long for your liking?"

"You do, master."

Hegio grinned, the greengrocer sighed:

"What did I tell you? I said this was dangerous. I should have him whipped."

"Is freedom of such importance to you, then?" said Hegio. "If you ask me, it's only an illusion. Didn't you admit just now that you're having a good time with me?"

"I did."

"You've saved money."

"I have."

"That's the worst of it," said the greengrocer. "In the old days that would have been impossible. Private property creates an appetite for more. I should take his savings away and have him flogged."

"That might be an idea," said Hegio, taking his departure. "In the meantime we will go and get sprigs and leaves for the entry of the Prince of Thrace."

When they had gathered enough vines and leafy branches they sat down near one of the grazing herds by the river Crathis. The dog was tired too, he lay on his belly, his front legs spaced out gracefully like those of the Sphinx of Thebes.

"Look here," said Hegio to his slave. "Here we sit, two people by a river, not far from stately mountains. Are you really waiting for my death?"

The youth looked at him and said:

"Are you really my lord, and am I really your property?"

"I'm afraid so," said Hegio. "It's a fact, from whatever angle you look at it. Even now, while we're alone together, sitting by a river with stately mountains before our eyes, even now you feel each of your words to be cheek and presumption, and I believe mine to be full of gracious condescension. Tell the truth: is it not so?"

"It is," said the youth after a pause.

"Let us proceed then," said Hegio. "Anything that exists is real, you can't get round it. Here I sit in the sun and roast my back, you sit in the shade and freeze. True, it is an unjust division, but it happens to be so, and the gods must have had some idea at the back of their minds when they made it so. Had they thought of the reverse, the reverse it would have been. Reality is rather a forceful argument, don't you think?"

"I do," said the slave. "But if I gave you just a little push I should be sitting in the sun and you would be in the river, O master."

"Why don't you do it then?" asked Hegio smilingly. "Do try. Or do you fear the whip?"

For the first time the boy averted his eyes. He said nothing.

"Well?" asked Hegio. "Why don't you? Here we sit, two people by a river, and you are the stronger. If you kill me and run to the Thracian, you need not even fear punishment. Why don't you do it?"

The lad was silent and pulled out handfuls of grass, his eyes cast down.

"Right here the great Pythagoras taught that the rulers should receive divine adoration and the servants the treatment of cattle. Do you agree with that?"

"I do not," said Publibor.

"In that case, why don't you throw me in the river, especially as nothing can happen to you if you do? Why don't you make use of your strength? Why does your soul feel shamed now, and why is mine filled with exalted emotion and condescension? Or is it not so?"

"It is," said the slave. After a while he added:

"It is only habit."

"Do you think so? Do you think the Thracian will import new habits? If he did, he would be greater than Hannibal. There is nothing greater than to change the habits of thought."

"Yes," said the slave.

"Where did you get all these thoughts, anyway?" asked Hegio. "You've always been hard-working and dumb, I never noticed that you had a face, that you could smile. Maybe laugh – yes. But smile – tell me, do you know how that is done?"

The slave was silent. Hegio regarded him attentively.

"Are you wishing for my death now?" he asked. "The impatient cannot smile. Look at those pebbles at the bottom of the river: the water is transparent, you can even see blades of grass down there. When the water brushes over the pebbles and grass, it gives the faintest humming sound. Can you see and hear such things?"

"I cannot, master. I never had time to lie in the grass."

"Blind and deaf and gloomy you go through this world of ours, and you wait for my death, though I have eyes to see and know all of the many scents of the sea. That is the cause of your shame and the source of my condescension. A man in misfortune is never lovable."

The slave tore out bushels of grass. After a while he said:

"You said yourself I was the stronger."

"Yes, but since when have you known that? It is not as obvious a thought as it seems to be. The matron has beaten you frequently, not very hard, it is true, but she did beat you, and it has never occurred to you that you were stronger than she."

"It did not," said the slave. And after a pause: "That was habit."

"And now? Has the Thracian suddenly informed you of your strength? People say his agents and emissaries are everywhere, inciting the serfs. Is that true?"

"It is."

"And you believe in his teachings?"

"I do."

"And do all of your kind believe in him?"

"Many."

"Why not all of them?"

"The old habits are too strong."

"What does he look like, that Slave-Hannibal of yours?"

"He wears the skin of a beast and rides a white horse, and a guard of strong men carries the fasces before him."

"Just like the Roman Imperators, eh?"

"No, for his ensigns are not silver eagles, but broken chains."

"An original idea," said Hegio. "I do believe both of us can safely expect some pleasant diversion. Don't you think so?"

"I do, master," said the slave, gazing at him earnestly.

For a while they were silent, lay back on the grass and looked at the mountains that had shed their morning veils and enclosed the horizon with their naked, powerful blue. The sun had broken away from the sea, rose higher, warmed the air and sucked in the scent of morn in the fields. In the olive and lemon orchards people were bent on their work today as on all other days.

Before they started on their way home, Hegio said:

"It is strange to think that the Thracian will arrive this very day, that he will probably change everything, yet neither you nor I can really believe in it. It is the same as with war: everybody discusses it, some are for it, some against, but no one honestly believes that it will eventually materialise; and when it is really upon them, they are astounded that they were right. There is no surprise greater than that of the prophet whose prophecies come true. For there is a great laziness of habit in the thoughts of man, and a smiling voice deeply buried inside him, which whispers that

Tomorrow will be just like Today and Yesterday. And, against his better judgement, he believes it. And that is really a mercy, for otherwise he could not live with the knowledge of his certain death.

"And now come on, let us go and decorate the house, so that we may greet the Prince of Thrace as is his due."

The sun rose higher, and the city was full of joyous activity; the citizens of Thurium adorned their houses with vines and garlands. They shoved and jostled each other in the streets. The Roman colonists stood apart and scowled patriotically. Perhaps they were afraid.

Nor was the Council of Thurium entirely happy. True, this strange Imperator had struck Rome a whacking blow and they were pleased with him for that. They were less pleased with him in all other respects. He called himself "Liberator of Slaves, Leader of the Oppressed". You could, of course, interpret it symbolically, especially with reference to an alliance with the Greek cities of the south, groaning under the Roman yoke; had not Thurium and the other South Italian cities once sided with Hannibal? But Hannibal had been a prince in his native country, whereas this man Spartacus was a Prince only by the grace of Thurium's Senate for reasons of urban self-respect: the descendants of Trojan warriors could hardly form an alliance with a vagabond gladiator. And form an alliance they must, else it would be the end of Thurium; to be quite honest, the Council had been surprised and overjoyed when the gladiator did as much as enter negotiations. Finally a treaty had been signed whose main points were as follows:

Outside the city of Thurium, in the plain which stretched between the rivers Sybaris and Crathis, protected by mountains on one side and by sea on the other, the Slave Army will erect its permanent camp and build a city with the name of "Sun City". The Corporation of Thurium will cede to the Thracian Prince all fields and pastureland in the said area; likewise the Corporation shall undertake the maintenance of the Slave Army until the latter is provided with food by the produce of its own soil. Spartacus's soldiers, on the other hand, after the Army's ceremonial entry into Thurium – which is to be of merely symbolical import – will molest the city no further.

"They must be coming any minute now," said the greengrocer Tyndarus to Hegio.

They had been waiting for over an hour, wedged in the convivial crowd which hemmed the wide avenue that led to the agora, waiting for the Entry of the Thracian Prince. Over their heads garlands hung down the white house-fronts; over the houses a blazing sun stood in the skies; and across the roofs the sea blew its midday breath, reeking of fish and decay. The citizens of Thurium were waiting and gossiping and pressing together and sweating a great deal.

But when the sun stood vertically above them, the great moment came at last.

"They're coming!" cried Hegio's little boy, "they're coming!"

They were really coming, a slow cloud of dust at the far end of the avenue. The citizens giggled, groaned, pushed one another, surged forward. Blustering officials pushed them back. They were coming.

"How many are they?" asked Tyndarus the greengrocer and craned his neck.

"A hundred thousand," screamed the little boy who was very well-informed, "a hundred thousand robbers, and they'll turn everything upside-down."

"As many as that can't possibly pass here," said Tyndarus. "They would clog up the whole city."

"Only their show-troops will take part in the Entry," said his left-hand neighbour. "The rest will have to stay outside. That's how it has been settled."

"Settled, indeed," sighed Tyndarus. "And you think they'll abide by it?"

The cloud of dust was coming closer. The citizens of Thurium craned their necks. Most of them were dressed in white; the young women wore thin, airy garments. The self-important officials scurried back and forth.

By and by they could distinguish the foremost ranks of the Slave Army, two rows of ten strong-boned, bull-necked men, their heavy boots spurring the dust. They did not glance to right or left, Thurium did not interest them; they carried the fasces and, in the place of the axes, broken iron chains.

A few of the citizens cheered tentatively but the majority did not follow suit. The citizens were painfully surprised, the grave and dingy procession disappointed them.

And now, right behind the stamping men, they beheld the

white horse, and on it the Thracian Prince in his fur-skin. By his side rode a fat man with a doleful face and dangling moustaches. He rode his horse as though it were a mule. The purple velum was borne in front of them.

The citizens knew what was expected of them: they yelled, waved their hands and flapped their sleeves. The Imperator acknowledged their cheers, raised his arm in salute; but he did not smile and his eyes were not friendly. Still the citizens liked him quite well; they were not exactly bowled over, but they quite liked him. The fat man with the moustaches they liked far less. He did not even acknowledge their cheering, looked straight ahead with unfocused eyes. The crowd on his side receded a little as he passed. His face impressed itself on their memories far deeper than the Imperator's; years later they would still remember it.

The march towards the market place quickened as though the strangers wanted to get the Entry over and done with. Boisterous mass-feeling had been nipped in the bud.

Behind the leaders came more infantry, raking the dust and glancing woodenly out of dirty faces. What strange soldiers they were, these new allies who had given the Romans so sound a beating. What strange ensigns they carried ahead, how solemn and how sinister: crude wooden crosses. The bearers staggered under them and had to crush the shafts to their chests in order not to fall under their weight. And solemn and sinister the broken fetters and iron chains recurred. The leader of a troop of particularly ruffianly characters, a pock-marked lout, carried a giant muraena-eel with a human head made of rags in its jaws. Hegio's little boy stretched on tiptoe and asked in his shrill little voice:

"What's that, Father? Are there fish who eat people?"

The greengrocer clapped his hand over the child's mouth:

"Hush, my boy, hush, hush," he said. "You mustn't ask questions, otherwise the soldiers will be cross."

For the crowd had gradually grown very quiet. The citizens had given up banter and acclamation, the smiles had been wiped off their faces. Frightened, the boy stopped talking. Only the thunder of the marching Army was heard in the avenue, their feet made the dust whirl up and envelop them in a vaporous cloud.

Cavalry came riding past now, men on small Lucanian horses; but Hegio's little boy, whom toy-soldiers had instructed as to the proper looks of classified professional warriors, was by no means the only one to wonder, for even the peace-loving citizens were amazed, nay, horrified, by the unmilitary appearance of their new allies. Not only did almost the entire heavy cavalry lack armour for man and beast – at most one or the other was protected by a clanging bit of tin tied with hempen cord to arm or leg; not only were most of their lances wooden, their shields of reed and hide; not only did most of them flourish scythes, pitchforks and axes instead of swords; no: not even uniforms did they have, nor glittering helmets! Some were bare-headed and waved slings, others wore black felt hats, bleached and so worn that the brims fell like fringes into their bearded faces, their shirts and linen blouses were equally tattered; but half of them wore nothing from the girdle up, rode past with tanned and shaggy chests, shamelessly naked between matted beard and belt.

A moan passed over the queue, and many men of Thurium averted their heads in shame; but the women had glinting eyes and sighed. A matron fainted and had to be carried away.

And the new allies went past; more infantry came marching and tramped the dust, glanced woodenly out of dirty faces. Those who passed now were organised according to nationalities: coarse Gauls and Germans with moustaches; tall Thracians with luminous eyes and peculiarly springy walk; Barbarians from Numidia and Asia whose skin was dark and dry; black men with earrings and thick lips moistly open over bared teeth.

"What a mess!" the greengrocer whispered to Hegio.

"A lively change, I think," smiled Hegio and bent down to the little boy: "Don't you like it? Isn't it rather gay and colourful?"

"Yes, it is," nodded the boy. "Just like a circus."

"Hush," said the greengrocer, "that's the very thing you mustn't say."

A new cloud of dust approached, and oxcarts came, loaded with the sick and wounded. They lay with their backs on filthy blankets; some gazed quietly up at the sky, others writhed in pain, others again stuck out their tongues and grimaced. Their faces were speckled with flies which crawled into their eye-sockets. Hegio's little boy began to cry.

"What do they show us all that for?" asked the greengrocer. "Are these part of their show-troops?"

Three more carts went by, in better condition than the rest, and drawn by oxen. On each of the carts lay one corpse covered with swarms of flies, the ensign of the broken chain at his head. They sent out fetid smells.

And that was the end of the procession.

The crowds had thinned out a little, but most of the citizens had not dared to go away. Fear kept them at their places. Even now, when the entertainment was finished, they remained in the streets, recovering from the shock.

The months went by. The citizens of Thurium calmed down; no soldier of the slave army approached their walls. Outside, on the plain between the rivers Crathis and Sybaris, they were building their fortified camp, the Sun City.

It was nearly spring at that time. Aromatic fumes rose up from the soil, the stormy March breezes blew from the sea. Slaves with axes scrambled up the mountains so furry with trees, and, returning with timber trunks lugged by white buffaloes, they sawed planks and beams for the first granaries and dining halls of their new town. The Celts dug firm, tough clay from the banks of the river Crathis, moulded bricks and dried them in the sun; for the Celts all wanted to live in brick houses. The Thracians sewed tents of blackened goat-skins, plaited pliant twigs into hoops for the frames of their roofs, and laid the floor with soft carpets so that talk might be quiet and sedate when they had guests. The Lucanians and Samnites mixed peat with dung and rubble, and formed their tiny conical houses from the paste; they sprinkled the floor with chaff and straw, and their houses smelled wholesomely of stable. The black men with the earrings twined rushes into an ingenious mesh, and tied the braid to pegs; their huts looked fragile and toy-like, but they stood fast and dry in storm and rain.

The sun was shining, the earth steaming, crops sprouting from the clods. The town grew rapidly as though the sun had coaxed her from the soil, fertile with rottenness, bursting with long restrained live juices. There were seventy thousand of them, marked with the brand, cast out by fortune and scattered over the earth; now they were building their own town. They lugged tree-trunks, carried stone blocks, hammered, glued, sawed. It was going to be a very marvellous town, property of the destitute, home of the homeless, refuge of the wretched. Each one built his house, and the house was his.

The city grew. A stretch of land had been allotted to every tribe, Celts, Thracians, Syrians, Africans; each might build his house as he liked. But the ground-plan was uniform, designed according to the strict Roman rules of camp construction, with straight walls and straight, parallel streets. Outer rampart and moat formed a severe square in the plain between Crathis and Sybaris, at the foot of the valiant, nicked, blue mountains. Austere and defiant, the Slave Town lay embedded in the plain, her four gates guarded by forbidding sentries, silent and bull-necked; before each gate the ensign of the town, the broken chain, looked far into the country. On a hill in the centre of the town stood the great tent with the purple velum, the Imperator's tent, from which issued the new laws to rule the town. The hill was encircled by the dens of his captains, the gladiators; the community buildings formed a second, wider ring around it: tool-sheds and sword-smithies, granaries, corrals, communal dining-halls. For each might build his house as he liked in the allotments, but corn and cattle, arms, tools and the yield of all labour were common property. And the new laws decreed by the Imperator on the very founding of the city, recorded by Fulvius the Lawyer of Capua, read as follows:

1. No longer shall man distress and oppress his neighbour with covetousness and greed in his struggle for the necessities of life; for the Communal Brotherhood undertakes to care for all.

2. Nor shall anyone serve the other from now on, nor the strong subject the weak, nor he who won a sack of meal enslave him who took no booty; for all shall serve the Communal Brotherhood.

3. Therefore no man shall hoard victuals to last for more than one half day, nor amass in his house any other goods or merchandise; for all will be fed with the acquirements of all in the great dining halls, as behoves brethren.

4. Likewise, the requirements of all as regards material for building or weapons, and the well-being of life and limb, will be met, in return for labour done by each one according to his abilities, to further common welfare, be it by the building of houses or the forging of swords, cultivating the soil or tending the flocks. And each one shall do the work he is suited to in strength and ability, and there shall be no differentiation in the sharing out of all worldly goods, but all will share and share alike.

5. Therefore the possibility shall be abolished of one gaining advantages by imposing on the other in buying and selling, or of his gaining possession of property beyond his share in the shape

of notes of hand or coin. Therefore the Lucanian Brotherhood will abolish the use of gold and silver coins, and those of lesser metals; and whosoever is discovered in the possession of such shall incur the penalty of ejection and death.

Such were the laws decreed by Spartacus to rule life in the growing Sun City. Very novel laws they were – and yet as old as the hills. When they had first started to build the camp and dug in the earth, they had found the ruins of mythical Sybaris – those weather-beaten walls had seen the age of Saturn whose memory is longingly cherished by the people, the age that was ruled by justice. They had found inscriptions dealing with the hero Lykurgos and the Spartan state of communal store houses and dining-halls – these new laws of Spartacus, was it not as though corroded stone decreed them here and now? It was the soul and spirit of a country which had borne the ancestors of Thurium's citizens. But that a nondescript Thracian Prince, if a Prince he was and not a circus-gladiator, that such a man should suddenly appear from nowhere, defeat the Romans and build a city in which all these unworldly dreams became real as orders of the day – that was indeed an extravagant spectacle.

And yet the city grew.

Sternly and squarely walled, she grew, and her straight streets grew, her stone houses and dining-halls. New, just and inexorable were her laws. On a hill in the centre of the town, guarded by a double line of sentinels, stood the Imperator's tent from which issued the laws. In an out-of-the-way spot, in the corner of the North Gate wall, stood the crosses for those who broke the laws.

Several died there every day in the interest of common welfare, with fractured limbs and black tongues; and in their last tremors they cursed the tent with the purple velum and the Sun State.

It was too good to last.

In spring, when March blew reckless breezes and the crops sprouted from the clods, they had built their city; now it was summer, and the heat had set in.

The soil cracked, its saps dried up. The sea was like lead, reflecting the heaven's blast in unbearable glitter. The mould pulverished into dust, the dust covered everything once moist and green with a floury powder. The brooks shrank, slowed, died the dry death.

The white buffaloes lay in the shade with heaving flanks. Men and women, too, grew slothful; first their bodies, then their minds.

Life in the town took its course. The shepherds drove the cattle to the meadows, farm-hands, weeders, mowers went about their work, the women cooked, the children played in the dust, the law-breakers died on the stakes by the North Gate. It was as though everything had been like this for years. In the evenings people told each other stories about the wicked time of slavery; it lay behind them, and now only half of it was true.

When the Slave Town had seen five months pass, food grew scarce, the granaries stood empty, and the meals inside the dining-halls became scantier. General feeling sank rapidly.

Young Publibor (who had deserted his master and joined the Slave Army) noticed it every time he entered the dining-hall. As before, six of them dipped into the soup in the joint bowl, but it was only half-full; the wooden ladles travelled considerably faster and clanged together more often. The greatest dexterity was exhibited by the rhetorician Zozimos; his ladle travelled the road between pot and mouth twice as often as the others' in the same space of time; his sleeves fluttered, and in addition he talked almost incessantly. His most frequent topic was the posts by the North Gate which had lately increased in number.

"Discipline and warning, indeed," scoffed Zozimos. "Did we fight and endure the most unusual hardships in order to exchange the old yoke for a new one? In the old days your belly growled with wrath, now it growls with discipline. Life in the Sun Town has become jaded and narrow; enthusiasm and fraternity of yore – what has become of them? The old chasm between leaders and common people has opened again, the Imperator meets only with Councillors and diplomats – to whose entertainment, I might add, the scarcity of provisions does not seem to apply; but no matter. Of course, we have learnt that it is all done to further higher interests and our own welfare – things that we unfortunately don't know anything about. So we must needs be herded like sheep who would not find the way to the pasture on their own; well and good, let us suppose that it is so. But the meadow is barren, and the sheep start bleating angrily as one might expect. And now listen well, my lad, listen to what else happens, for this is the important point. Suddenly, you see, the shepherd begins to talk to the sheep as though they were reasoning creatures, and talks to them of patience and discipline and lofty reasons, and declares that those who will not understand and go on bleating, must be slaughtered to serve a higher cause.

"That's what the philosophers call a paradoxon. Can you reply to this, my lad?"

No, Publibor could not. He muttered hastily:

"Still, the Imperator surely means well, whatever he does."

But these seemed to be the very words the other had been waiting for. He even put his spoon down and, gesticulating frantically, fairly pounced on poor Publibor:

"He means well, you say? Of course he means well, that's the worst of it. There is no more dangerous tyrant than he who is convinced he is the selfless guardian of the people. For the damage done by the congenitally wicked tyrant is confined to the field of his personal interests and his personal cruelty; but the well-meaning tyrant who has a lofty reason for everything, can do unlimited damage. Just think of the God Jehovah, my lad: ever since the unfortunate Hebrews chose to adhere to Him, they've had one calamity after the other, from lofty reasons every time, because he means so well. Give me our old bloodthirsty gods every time: you throw them a sacrifice now and then, and they leave you in peace."

To this naturally Publibor could not say anything either. But that was unnecessary anyhow, for Zozimos talked on irrepressibly. Publibor noticed that the other men at the table who never used to listen to the rhetorician and had always got up as soon as they had finished their meal, were now staying on and listening attentively.

"But," Zozimos went on, "we aren't talking of gods but of human beings. And I tell you, it is dangerous to combine so much power in the fist, and so many lofty reasons in the head, of one single person. In the beginning the head will always order the fist to strike from lofty reasons; later on the fist strikes of its own accord and the head supplies the lofty reasons afterwards; and the person does not even notice the difference. That's human nature, my lad. Many a man has started out as a friend of the people and ended up as a tyrant; but history gives not a single example of a man starting out as a tyrant and ending up as a friend of the

people. Therefore I tell you again: there is nothing so dangerous as
a dictator who means well.''

*As discontent grows in the Sun City, a band of three thousand
unruly Germans and Gauls, led by Spartacus's rival, the savage
Crixus, decide in secret to raid and plunder nearby Metapontum,
the richest town in Lucania.*

The night is very dark, you cannot even see the mountains' outlines. The sirocco charges darkness with heat, men and women
groan in their sleep, afflicted with nightmares. In the tent with the
purple velum the Imperator sits in his corner behind the oil lamp,
opposite him the lawyer Fulvius, reading in a husky voice the
Council of Thurium's report on the causes of the irregularities in
the delivery of turnips.

But at this hour the three thousand conspirators had already left
the camp and were trotting at full speed along the highway which
followed the edge of the twinkling sea to the town Metapontum.

The town of Metapontum also traced her foundation to the Trojan
wars; the faded records in the Magistrate's archives stated that
Nestor, leader of the Pylians, had built her when his warriors had
conquered this land of wine and beef, and brought unto the Italian
Barbarians Asiatic splendour, arts and sciences. A wonderful coin
collection was kept under lock and key in the Magistrate's library,
behind coloured Phoenician glass; they were unlike the clumsy,
thick pieces of Roman silver, stamped on one side only, which
could be easily forged in lesser metals if the State had a mind to do
so – no, they were flat, thin silver discs, voluptuously smooth,
with neat and dainty inscriptions in whose elucidation the
philologists could prove their sagacity. The town had lived
through eight centuries, survived dozens of invasions, always
smilingly submissive to the victor, taming him with her graceful
compliance. She had opened her gates to Hannibal as well as
Pythagoras, hunted out by the Crotoniates; had bowed to numerous masters and numerous deities; her cellars hoarded opulent
sweet wine, white cows turned on the spits over her hearths. None
of her prophets, augurs or astronomers had predicted her ghastly
end.

It happened after sunset, after a day that had been like all other
days. The gates had not been closed yet, farmers were still bent on

their work in the fields. Already they unharnessed the buffaloes from the ploughs, led the thirsty beasts to their water troughs, shouldered their tools on their peaceable way home, when a cloud of dust blotted out the southern highway. Curious, they looked and wondered what it could be that rolled toward their walls, howling and with clattering hoofs. But already the cattle roared plaintively, and broke loose and galloped across the fields. The dismayed farmers sped after their cattle, and the riders on foaming horses sped after the farmers; iron bit hotly into their skulls before they knew what was happening. Thus the massacre began outside the walls and rolled on into the town through every gate at once, and drowned her with a deluge of fire and blood which lasted the whole night through. But the night was dark because the moon had taken a trip, and hour followed hour without the outcry of the murdered city weakening or pausing; for the cries of fury, death and lust were mingling in a horrible chorus which strangled the thundering of the surf. When the cocks crowed for the second time, the whole city was burning away, from the harbour to the Latin Gate; and when the sun raised his head at last from the waves, he looked pale and weary and screened his face with the veil which rose black and flaky from the pillars of flame. All the cities the slaves had sacked in the course of their campaign had suffered and been maimed through the wrath of the oppressed; but the town Metapontum suffered only for one night, for in the morning the town Metapontum was no more.

Trojan warriors had founded her, for eight centuries she had given herself smilingly to every conqueror, the spits over her hearths had never stopped turning. Now she had been erased from the surface of the inhabited earth. Charred walls left for weather to gnaw, cindery flesh dispersed by the winds, dully iridescent lumps of silver coins and coloured Phoenician glass were all that remained.

When, towards morning, they broke the news to the Imperator in his tent, he understood at once that this meant the end of the Sun City.

Spartacus tries to restore discipline by draconic measures, and fails. The slave army splits into warring factions. He has a last chance to regain control by liquidating his rivals. In the hour of decision he is lying in his tent, the wine-horn by his side.

He had not been drunk for a long time, ever since the night after the victory of Vesuvius; but he knew that drunkenness lifted the weight off you and the thoughts in your head began to smile.

He lay on his back, the drinking horn beside him and his hands linked behind his neck, and he waited.

But drunkenness did not come to him. Only foggy images came, rose from a deep shaft inside him and looked into his closed eyes.

Who cast the die, decided a man's life before he was born? He gave noses unto all of them, stuck eyeballs into them, guts and sex, without much difference. But he set them apart in their mothers' wombs already; some were never to smile, nor be smiled at, others were lifted into the light of day, and for them shone the sun. And they had set out, a sinister multitude, had torn asunder the cellar walls and broken the iron chains, to bask their skin in the sun. Now, so they thought and blinked, now everything will be all right, the smell of ignominy will evaporate from our bodies, we will not exude it any more. But the bright world without walls was not for them to enjoy, they were far too unaccustomed to the light. They kicked and struggled like blind men, whatever they grasped they broke to bits. One had to watch over them as over wild beasts, one had to guide them.

First he had guided them upon the straight, wild road, and they had sown fire, reaped hatred and ashes. It had been the wrong road. Then he had led them along smooth highways, winding and roundabout, hard to follow with the eye; and the goal had vanished from their sight. And again they kicked and struggled like blind men, the stench of ignominy never left them, their wolf's claws grew again. . . . He realised with acrid clarity that now and here, at this moment, the future was being determined. If he gave the orders expected of him – if he did, a fresh and bloody massacre would rack the camp, and he would probably prevail – a much hated, much feared victor and absolute leader of the revolution. That would be the bloody detour which alone could lead to salvation.

But he no longer has the will, nor the taste for that kind of salvation. He is a burnt-out case – as so many of his followers, who called themselves Spartakists, were to become two thousand years later. The dilemma which defeated him remained unsolved.

After a protracted agony, the demoralised remains of the Slave

Army are annihilated by the Roman legions under Crassus. Spar-
tacus himself is killed in the battle by the Silarus. The last chapter
of the novel – "The Crosses" – describes the aftermath:

The Italian insurrection was over. Fifteen thousand corpses lay
strewn about the hilly land by the river Silarus; four thousand
women, and the old and infirm who had not taken part in the
battle and had failed to kill themselves in time, were taken alive
by the Romans. Rome breathed with relief, the weight off her
chest; and a manhunt chased through the whole land, unequalled
in the annals of Italy.

The herdsmen of the Lucanian highlands, the farmers and petty
tenants of Apulia, were quarry and prey for Crassus's legions.
Whosoever owned less than one acre or two cows was suspect of
revolutionary sympathies, was killed or kidnapped; a quarter of
the Italian slave population was extirpated. The rebels had
squirted blood over the country, the conquerors turned it into a
slaughterhouse. In small troops they marched through villages,
singing patriotic songs, erected the crosses in the market place,
raped the women, hamstrung the cattle; at night the huts and
slave barracks blazed in flames, torches of victory. A kind of
drunkenness had taken hold of Italy; she extolled the generalis-
simo who had helped to conquer the might of Darkness – general
Pompeius.

Pompeius and his army had returned from Spain just in time to
encounter a small band of fugitives by the Apennines. He
destroyed them and allowed his Legions to participate in the
manhunt, in order to reward them for the hardships they had
undergone in Spain; whereupon he reported to the Senate that,
although it was Crassus, his rival, who had defeated the Slaves,
he, Pompeius, had stamped out the very roots of revolution.

Pompeius got his triumphal entry; he arrived in Rome on
a chariot drawn by four white palfreys. He displayed the laurels
in his right, the ebony mace in his left hand; his inane face
was rouged, the people roared, and the only thing that jarred
his smugness was the fact that the State-slave behind him
who held the golden crown of Jove above his head reiterated a
bit too often the traditional phrase: "Remember that you are a
mortal."

All Crassus got was an ovation, the entry on foot, followed by a
few soldiers; the only special favour granted him was the permission to wear a laurel wreath instead of the ordinary myrtle wreath.

And yet the banker Crassus's march home was a spectacle which sent a tremor through the world, and the like of which it had never seen before. Pompeius's parade began on the Campus Martius and ended, two miles farther, before the Capitol; Crassus had caused two rows of wooden crosses to hem the two hundred miles of Appian Way of his homeward march. Six thousand captive slaves, their hands and feet pierced by nails, hung, at regular intervals of fifty metres, on both sides of the highway, in uninterrupted sequence from Capua to Rome.

Crassus's progress was slow; he rested often. He had sent ahead his regiment of engineers to construct the posts before he arrived; he himself carried the prisoners with him, bundled in groups and tied together with long ropes. Before his army stretched the road, endless and hemmed with empty crosses; behind his army, every cross bore a hanging man.

Crassus took his time. He approached the capital at a leisurely rate, interrupting his march three times a day. During the rest-periods lots were drawn to decide the succession of prisoners to be crucified from here to their next station. The army marched fifteen miles per day, and left behind five hundred crucified per day as their living mile-stones.

The news of his progress caused sensation in the capital. The entire aristocratic youth, and whoever could afford it by hook or by crook, rode to meet Crassus's army in order to see for themselves; a ceaseless stream of tourists, in showy state carriages or hired coaches, on horseback or borne in sedan chairs, drifted south along the Appian Way. Crassus would receive the more eminent among them in his tent during the rest periods, chew candied dates, look sulkily at his visitors and ask them whether they had enjoyed Pompeius's triumphal entry as much as this. And only then did the ingenuity of Crassus's idea dawn on the visitors: Rome had denied Crassus a triumphal entry; now Crassus made Rome meet him in homage on the very road.

It was getting on towards spring. The sun diffused some heat already, but not enough as yet to grant the mercy of a quick death to the people on the crosses left behind Crassus's army. Only a few of them succeeded in bribing a soldier of the rearguard to come back at night and kill them. For Crassus had forbidden any initiative in that direction; although he had no particular inclination to cruelty, he liked an idea to be carried out meticulously, without anything to mar the purity of its effect. But, as he was by no means devoid of humane considerations, he had chosen the method of nailing, which tended to hasten death, rather than the customary stringing up.

The army's march from Capua to Rome took twelve days; and on every one of them it left behind five hundred crucified at regular, tape-measured intervals. The feebler delinquents lived for a few hours only, the more tenacious for several days. If a man was lucky a nail pierced an artery, and he quickly bled to death, but usually only the bones of hands and feet were splintered, and if he fainted in the process, he came to again when they raised the cross, to curse the lords of creation. Many tore at their nails, some to break loose, some to bleed more rapidly; but they realised that torment puts a limit to even the strongest of wills. Many attempted to shatter their skulls against the posts; but they had to realise that of all living creatures it is yourself that is most difficult to kill.

It was getting on towards spring. Day relieved night and night relieved day; and still they lived on, imprisoned by their torment and pain; and gangrene made their flesh rot away, and their tongues swelled, and the beasts and birds of earth and air came close to them, growling, spitting, and flapping their wings. Day relieved night and night relieved day, and the earth would not open up and the sun would not cease travelling the skies. And that which was happening to them was not happening as in a mirage of fever, but in that reality from which one cannot wake; and they did not suffer in remembrance nor in anticipation, but suffered it in the present, here and now.

Chapter 15

DARKNESS AT NOON

The extracts which follow are taken from the Postscript to the Danube edition of Darkness at Noon. *The Postscript provides some of the historical background of the period in which the novel was written. The novel was first published in December 1940. The Postscript was added in 1973.*

Darkness at Noon is the second novel of a trilogy which revolves around the central theme of revolutionary ethics, and of political ethics in general: the problem whether, or to what extent, a noble end justifies ignoble means, and the related conflict between morality and expediency. This may sound like an abstract conundrum, yet every politician is confronted with it at some stage of his career; and for the leaders of a revolutionary movement, from the slave revolt in the first century BC to the Old Bolsheviks of the nineteen-thirties and the radical New Left of the nineteen-seventies, the problem assumes a stark reality, which is both immediate and timeless. It was the realisation of this timeless aspect of Stalin's regime of terror which made me write *Darkness at Noon* in the form of a parable – albeit thinly disguised – without explicitly naming persons or countries; and which made Orwell, in writing *Nineteen Eighty-Four*, adopt a similar technique.

I joined the Communist Party in 1931, at the age of twenty-six. Altogether I remained a member of the Party for seven years. My progressive disillusionment reached an acute stage in 1935, the year when the Great Purge started, which was to sweep most of my comrades away. But a year later the Spanish Civil War broke out; this and other distractions postponed the final break with the Party until 1938.

The decisive event which led to it was the trial of the so-called "Anti-Soviet Bloc of Rightists and Trotskyists" which was staged in the spring of that year in Moscow. It surpassed in absurdity and horror everything that had gone before. The defendants were: Nikolai Bukharin, President of the Communist International (in succession to Zinoviev who had been executed two years earlier); Christian Rakovsky, former head of the Ukrainian Soviet Republic, former Soviet Ambassador to England and France; Nikolai Krestinsky, predecessor of Stalin as General Secretary of the Communist Party of the Ukrainian Soviet Republic, former Soviet Ambassador to Germany; Alexei Rykov, successor of Lenin as President of the Council of People's Commissars. Finally Yagoda, organiser of the previous Moscow trials, head of the GPU in succession to Med:'nsky, whom Yagoda confessed to having poisoned. He also confessed that he had poisoned the writer Maxim Gorky.*

To fathom the depths of absurdity reached in this trial one should bear in mind that it made the preceding show-trials appear as invalid, because the alleged evidence had been supplied by the self-confessed saboteur and poisoner at the head of the GPU; and that, if one was to believe the accused men's confessions, both the Soviet Union and the Communist International had been, during the first fifteen years of their existence, headed by agents of the German and British Intelligence Services.

At the same time news kept coming in about the arrest of virtually all my friends and comrades of the German, Austrian, Hungarian and Spanish Communist parties who had sought refuge in the Soviet Union (see The Invisible Writing). The mills of Gulag were grinding at a terrifying speed, driven by a gale of collective insanity, tearing the fabric of our Utopia to shreds. I lived through my last weeks as a member of the Party like a person who knows that there is a painful and critical operation waiting for him which is being postponed from day to day. Shortly after the execution of Bukharin (whom Lenin had called "the darling of the Party") I wrote my letter of resignation to the Central Committee of the German CP.

The postscript to the novel continues:

---

*Yagoda's successor, Yeshov, was liquidated as a "saboteur of Soviet justice" in 1939; Yeshov's successor, Beria, was liquidated as a "degenerate saboteur of Soviet justice" in 1953. Thus all the heads of the Russian State Police during these twenty-five years were successively executed as poisoners, spies and traitors.

The final break with the movement left me with a sense of loneliness and emptiness. As a loyal member of the Party, I had been taught to regard writing as a means of serving the Cause; now I came to regard it as occupational therapy and a purpose in itself. *The Gladiators*, suspended during the Spanish prison interlude, was finished in the summer of 1938; a week later I started on *Darkness at Noon*.

The novel, as outlined in a short synopsis that I wrote for the publishers, Jonathan Cape, was to be about people in prison in a totalitarian country. There were to be four or five characters who, under sentence of death, re-value their lives; each one discovers that he is guilty, though not of the crimes for which he is going to die. The common denominator of their guilt is having sacrificed morality to expediency in the interest of the Cause. Now they too must die, because their death is expedient to the Cause, by the hands of men who subscribe to the same principles. The title of the novel was to be the *The Vicious Circle*.

When I began writing it, I had no notion of the plot, and only one character was established in my mind. He was to be a member of the Old Bolshevik Guard, his manner of thinking modelled on Nikolai Bukharin's, his personality and physical appearance a synthesis of Leon Trotsky and Karl Radek. I saw him as clearly as a hallucination – short, stocky, with a pointed goatee, rubbing his pince-nez against his sleeve as he paced up and down the cell.

The opening sequence seemed quite obvious. When his own people come to arrest him, Rubashov is asleep and dreaming about the last time when he was arrested in the enemy's country; sleep-dazed, he is unable to decide which of the two hostile dictators is reaching out for him this time, and which of the two omnipresent oil-prints is hanging over his bed. Curiously, this symbolic assertion of the basic sameness of the two totalitarian regimes was written a year before the Hitler–Stalin pact, at a time when, though no longer a Party member, I would still have indignantly rejected the suggestion that there was nothing to choose between Soviet Russia and Nazi Germany.

Once the opening scene was written, I did not have to search for plot and incident; they were waiting among the stored memories of seven years, which, while the lid was down on them, had undergone a kind of fermentation. Now that the pressure was lifted, they came bubbling up. A multitude of harrowing episodes, the significance of which my indoctrinated mind had managed to explain away, were now falling into pattern. I did not worry about what would happen next in the book; I just waited for it to happen. I knew, for instance, that in the end Rubashov would break down and confess to his imaginary crimes; but I had only a vague and general notion of the reasons which would induce him to do so. These reasons emerged step by step during the interrogations of Rubashov by Ivanov and Gletkin. The questions and answers in this dialogue were determined by the mental climate of the period; they were not invented but deduced from that ideological framework which held both the accused and the accuser, the victim and the executioner in its grip. According to the rules of the game they could only argue and act as they did.

To the Western mind, unacquainted with the system and the rules, the confessions in the Trials appeared as one of the great enigmas of our time. Why had the Old Bolsheviks, heroes and leaders of the revolution, who had so often braved death that they called themselves "dead men on furlough", confessed to these absurd and hair-raising lies? If one discounted those who were merely trying to save their necks, like Radek; and those who were mentally broken like Zinoviev; or trying to shield their families like Kameniev who was said to be particularly devoted to his son — then there still remained a hard core of men like Bukharin, Piatakov, Mrachkovsky, Smirnov, and at least a score of others with a revolutionary past of thirty, forty years behind them, the veterans of Czarist prisons and Siberian exile, whose total and gleeful self-abasement remained inexplicable. It was this "hard core" that Rubashov was meant to represent.

The extracts from the novel which follow may provide some glimpses into the particular method of reasoning by which the "hard core" of dedicated Old Bolsheviks was induced to confess to crimes they never committed:

From the diary of N.S. Rubashov, on the fifth day of imprisonment

. . . It is said that No. 1 [Stalin] has Machiavelli's *Prince* lying by his bedside. So he should: since then, nothing really important has been said about the rules of political ethics. We were the first to replace the nineteenth century's liberal ethics of "fair play" by the revolutionary ethics of the twentieth century. In that also we were right: a revolution conducted according to the rules of

cricket is an absurdity. Politics can be relatively fair in the breathing spaces of history; at its critical turning points there is no
other rule possible than the old one, that the end justifies the
means. We were neo-Machiavellians in the name of universal
reason – that was our greatness. That is why we will be absolved
by history.

Yet for the moment we are thinking and acting on credit. Since
we have thrown overboard all conventions and rules of cricket-
morality, our sole guiding principle is that of consequent logic.
We are under the terrible compulsion to follow our thought
through to its final consequence and to act in accordance with it.

A short time ago, our leading agriculturist, B., was shot with
thirty of his collaborators because he maintained the opinion that
nitrate artificial manure was superior to potash. No. 1 is all for
potash; therefore B. and the thirty had to be liquidated as
saboteurs. In a nationally centralised agriculture, the alternative
of nitrate or potash is of enormous importance: it can decide the
issue of the next war. If No. 1 was in the right, history will absolve
him, and the execution of the thirty-one men will be a mere
bagatelle. If he was wrong. . . .

It is that alone that matters: who is objectively in the right. The
cricket-moralists are agitated by quite another problem: whether
B. was subjectively in good faith when he recommended nitrate. If
he was in good faith, then he should be acquitted and allowed to
continue making propaganda for nitrate, even if the country
should be ruined by it. . . .

That is, of course, complete nonsense. For us the question of
subjective good faith is of no interest. He who is in the wrong must
pay; he who is in the right will be absolved. That is the law of
historical credit; it was our law.

History has taught us that often lies serve her better than the
truth; for man is sluggish and has to be led through the desert for
forty years before each step in his development. And he has to be
driven through the desert with threats and promises, by imaginary terrors and imaginary consolations, so that he should not sit
down prematurely to rest and divert himself by worshipping
golden calves.

We have learnt history more thoroughly than the others. We
differ from all others in our logical consistence. We know that
virtue does not matter to history, and that crimes remain
unpunished; but that every error has its consequences and avenges
itself unto the seventh generation. Therefore we concentrated all

our efforts on preventing error and destroying the very seeds of it.
Each wrong idea we follow is a crime committed against future
generations. Therefore we have to punish wrong ideas as others
punish crime. We were compared to the inquisition because, like
them, we persecuted the seeds of evil not only in men's deeds, but
in their thoughts. We admitted no private sphere, not even inside
a man's skull. Our minds were so tensely charged that the slightest collision caused a mortal short-circuit. Thus we were fated to
mutual destruction.

I was one of those. I have thought and acted as I had to; I
destroyed people whom I was fond of, and gave power to others I
did not like. History put me where I stood; I have exhausted the
credit accorded to me; if I was right I have nothing to repent of; if
wrong, I will pay.

But how can the present decide what will be judged truth in the
future? We are doing the work of prophets without their gift. We
replaced vision by logical deduction; but although we all started
from the same point of departure, we came to divergent results.
Proof disproved proof, and finally we had to resort to faith – to
axiomatic faith in the rightness of one's own reasoning. That is the
crucial point. We have thrown all ballast overboard; only one
anchor holds us: faith in one's self.

No. 1 has faith in himself, tough, slow, sullen and unshakable.
He has the most solid anchor-chain of all. Mine has worn thin in
the last few years. . . .

The fact is: I no longer believe in my infallibility. That is why I
am lost.

*The GPU official Ivanov, who is in charge of his case, has served
under Rubashov in the Civil War, and was once his devoted
friend. His interrogation of Rubashov gradually changes into an
impassioned dialogue. Ivanov defends No. 1's terror regime and
mocks Rubashov's moral scruples:*

"I would like to write a Passion play in which God and the Devil
fight for the soul of Saint Rubashov. After a life of sin, he has
turned to God – to a God with the double chin of bourgeois
liberalism and the charity of Salvation Army soups. Satan, on the
contrary, is thin, ascetic and a fanatical devotee of logic. He reads
Machiavelli, Ignatius of Loyola, Marx and Hegel; he is cold and
unmerciful to mankind, out of a kind of mathematical merciful-
ness. He is damned always to do that which is most repugnant to

him: to become a slaughterer, in order to abolish slaughtering, to whip people with knouts so that they may learn not to let themselves be whipped, to strip himself of every scruple in the name of a higher scrupulousness, and to challenge the hatred of mankind because of his love for it – an abstract and geometric love. *Apage Satanas!* Comrade Rubashov prefers to become a martyr. . . .

"If I had a spark of pity, I would now leave you alone. But I have not a spark of pity. I drink; for a time I drugged myself; but the vice of pity I have up till now managed to avoid. The smallest dose of it, and you are lost. Weeping over humanity and bewailing oneself – you know our race's pathological leaning to it. Our greatest poets destroyed themselves by this poison.

"My point is that one should not regard the world as a sort of metaphysical brothel for emotions. Sympathy, conscience, disgust, despair, repentance and atonement are for us repellent debauchery. To sit down and let oneself be hypnotised by one's own navel, to turn up one's eyes and humbly offer the back of one's neck to the executioner – that is an easy solution. The greatest temptation for the like of us is: to renounce violence, to repent, to make peace with oneself. Most great revolutionaries fell before this temptation, from Spartacus to Danton and Dostoyevsky; they are the classical examples of betrayal of the cause. As long as chaos dominates the world, every compromise with one's own conscience is perfidy. When the accursed inner voice speaks to you, hold your hands over your ears. . . ."

Rubashov looked through the window. The melted snow had again frozen and sparkled, an irregular surface of yellow-white crystals. The sentinel on the wall marched up and down with shouldered rifle. The sky was clear but moonless; above the machine-gun turret shimmered the Milky Way.

Rubashov shrugged his shoulders. "Let's admit," he said, "that humanism and politics, respect for the individual and social progress, are incompatible. Let's admit that Gandhi is a catastrophe for India; that chasteness in the choice of means leads to political impotence. In negatives we agree. But look where the other alternative has led us. . . ."

"Well," asked Ivanov. "Where?"

Rubashov rubbed his pince-nez on his sleeve, and looked at him shortsightedly. "What a mess," he said, "what a mess we have made of our golden age."

Ivanov smiled. "Maybe," he said happily. "But look at the Gracchi and Saint-Just and the Commune of Paris. Up to now, all revolutions have been made by moralising dilettantes. They were always in good faith and perished because of their dilettantism. We for the first time are consistent. . . ."

"Yes," said Rubashov. "So consistent, that in the interests of a just distribution of land we deliberately let die of starvation about five million farmers and their families in one year. So consistent were we in the liberation of human beings from the shackles of industrial exploitation that we sent about ten million people to do forced labour in the Arctic regions and the jungles of the East, under conditions similar to those of antique galley slaves. So consistent that, to settle a difference of opinion, we know only one argument: death, whether it is a matter of manure or the Party line to be followed in Indo-China. Our engineers work with the constant knowledge that an error in calculation may take them to prison or the scaffold; our poets settle discussions on questions of style by denunciations to the Secret Police, because the expressionists consider the naturalistic style counter-revolutionary, and vice versa. Acting in the interest of the coming generations, we have laid such privations on the present one that its average length of life is shortened by a quarter. In order to defend the existence of the country, we have had to make laws which are in every point contrary to the aims of the Revolution. The people's standard of living is lower than it was before the Revolution; labour conditions are harder, the discipline more inhuman, the piece-work drudgery worse than in colonial countries with native coolies; our sexual laws are more narrow-minded that those of England, our leader-cult more Byzantine than that of the reactionary dictatorships. Our press and our schools cultivate Chauvinism, militarism, dogmatism, conformism and ignorance. The arbitrary power of the Government is unlimited, and unexampled in history; freedom of the press, of opinion and of movement are as thoroughly exterminated as though the proclamation of the Rights of Man had never been. We have built up the most gigantic police apparatus, with informers made a national institution, and with the most refined scientific system of physical and mental torture. We whip the groaning masses of the country towards a theoretical future happiness, which only we can see. For the energies of this generation are exhausted; they were spent in the Revolution; for this generation is bled white and there is nothing left of it but a moaning, numbed, apathetic lump of sacrificial flesh. . . . Those are the consequences of our consequentiality. You called it vivisection morality. To me it sometimes seems as though the experimenters had torn the skin off the victim and left it standing with bared tissues, muscles and nerves. . . ."

"Well, and what of it?" said Ivanov happily. "Don't you find it wonderful? Has anything more wonderful ever happened in history? We are tearing the old skin off mankind and giving it a new one. That is not an occupation for people with weak nerves; but there was once a time when it filled you with enthusiasm. What has so changed you that you are now as pernickety as an old maid?"

"To continue with the same metaphor," replied Rubashov, "I see the flayed body of this generation: but I see no trace of the new skin. We all thought one could treat history like one experiments in physics. The difference is that in physics one can perform the experiment a thousand times, but in history only once. Danton and Saint-Just can be sent to the scaffold only once."

"And what follows?" asked Ivanov. "Should we sit with idle hands because the consequences of an act are never quite to be foreseen, and hence all action is evil? We vouch for every act with our heads – more cannot be expected of us. In the opposite camp they are not so scrupulous. Any old idiot of a general can experiment with thousands of living bodies; and if he makes a mistake, he will at most be retired. The forces of reaction and counter-revolution have no scruples or ethical problems. Imagine a Sulla, a Galliffet, a Koltschak reading Raskolnikov. Such peculiar birds as you are found only in the trees of revolution. For the others it is easier. . . ."

He looked at his watch. The cell window had turned a dirty grey; the newspaper which was stuck over the broken pane swelled and rustled in the morning breeze. On the rampart opposite, the sentry was still doing his hundred steps up and down.

"For a man with your past," Ivanov went on, "this sudden revulsion against experimenting is rather naive. Every year several million people are killed quite pointlessly by epidemics and other natural catastrophes. And we should shrink from sacrificing a few hundred thousand for the most promising experiment in history? Not to mention the legions of those who die of undernourishment and tuberculosis in coal and quicksilver mines, rice-fields and cotton plantations. No one takes any notice of them; nobody asks why or what for; but if here we shoot a few thousand objectively harmful people, the humanitarians all over the world foam at the mouth. Yes, we liquidated the parasitic part of the peasantry and let it die of starvation. It was a surgical operation which had to be done once and for all; but in the good old days before the Revolution just as many died in any dry year — only senselessly and pointlessly. The victims of the Yellow River floods in China amount sometimes to hundreds of thousands. Nature is generous in her senseless experiments on mankind. Why should mankind not have the right to experiment on itself?"

Finally, convinced by Ivanov's arguments, and even more by their echo reverberating in his own mind — for both are based on the same moral philosophy — Rubashov decides to capitulate: that is, to make a public statement of loyalty to No. 1. He composes a long, carefully formulated letter addressed to the Public Prosecutor of the Republic, which ends with the sentence:

"The undersigned, N.S. Rubashov, former member of the Central Committee of the Party, former Commissar of the People, former Commander of the 2nd Division of the Revolutionary Army, bearer of the Revolutionary Order for Fearlessness before the Enemy of the People, has decided, in consideration of the reasons exposed above, utterly to renounce his oppositional attitude and to denounce publicly his errors."

But in the meantime Ivanov himself is arrested (and subsequently shot) for having treated Rubashov too leniently and having expressed "cynical doubts about his guilt". The investigation is now taken over by Gletkin, Ivanov's former subordinate. Unlike Ivanov, Gletkin belongs to the new generation of "Neanderthal men" (as Rubashov calls them), with no memories or ties to a world which has vanished: "They need not deny their past, because they had none. They were born without umbilical cord, without frivolity, without melancholy."
Gletkin uses on Rubashov one of the notorious GPU techniques: depriving the accused of sleep by day-and-night interrogation while facing a dazzling light, until he becomes physically debilitated and mentally confused.* The main charges against Rubashov are that he had incited a young admirer working in the Kremlin kitchens to poison No. 1; that he had conspired with a foreign power to overthrow the regime; and, thrown in for good

*I knew about these and other GPU methods of what has come to be called brain-washing from private sources (see The Invisible Writing, ch. xxxvii). At the time when the novel was published (1940) they were received with general disbelief.

*measure, industrial sabotage. The charges are so absurd that
Ivanov had not even bothered to read them out in detail. Gletkin
opens the proceedings by doing so:*

Gletkin had stopped reading and was looking at him. After a few
seconds of silence, Gletkin said, in his usual even tone, more as a
statement than a question:
    "You have heard the accusation and plead guilty."
    Rubashov tried to look into his face. He could not and had to
shut his eyes again against the glare of the lamp. He had had a
biting answer on his tongue; instead he said, so quietly that the
thin secretary had to stretch out her head to hear:
    "I plead guilty to not having understood that fatal compulsion
behind the policy of the Government, and to have therefore held
oppositional views. I plead guilty to having followed sentimental
impulses, and in so doing to have been led into contradiction with
historical necessity. I have lent my ear to the laments of the
sacrificed, and thus became deaf to the arguments which proved
the necessity to sacrifice them. I plead guilty to having rated the
question of guilt and innocence higher than that of utility and
harmfulness. Finally, I plead guilty to having placed the idea of
man above the idea of mankind. . . ."
    Rubashov paused and again tried to open his eyes. He blinked
over to the secretary's corner, his head turned away from the light.
She had just finished taking down what he had said; he believed he
saw an ironic smile on her pointed profile.
    "I know," Rubashov went on, "that my aberration, if carried
into effect, would have been a mortal danger to the Revolution.
Every opposition at the critical turning-points of history, carries
in itself the germ of a split in the Party, and hence the germ of civil
war. Humanitarian weakness towards the immature masses is
suicide for the Revolution. And yet my oppositional attitude was
based on a craving for just these methods – in appearance so
desirable, actually so deadly. On a demand for a liberal reform of
the dictatorship; for a broader democracy, for the abolition of the
Terror, and a loosening of the rigid organisation of the Party. I
admit that these demands, in the present situation, are objectively
harmful and therefore counter-revolutionary in character. . . ."
    He paused again, as his throat was dry and his voice had
become husky. He heard the scratching of the secretary's pencil in
the silence; he raised his head a little, with eyes shut, and went on:
    "In this sense, and in this sense only, can you call me a

counter-revolutionary. With the absurd criminal charges made in the accusation, I have nothing to do."

And yet in the end, physically exhausted and mentally defeated, he confesses to all of them:

"The question of motive is the last," said Gletkin.

Rubashov passed his hand over his temples. "You know my motives as well as I do," he said. "You know that I acted neither out of a 'counter-revolutionary mentality', nor was I in the service of a foreign Power. What I thought and what I did, I thought and did according to my own conviction and conscience."

Gletkin had pulled a dossier out of his drawer. He went through it, pulled out a sheet and read in his monotonous voice:

". . . For us the question of subjective good faith is of no interest. He who is in the wrong, must pay; he who is in the right will be absolved. That was our law. . . .' You wrote that in your diary shortly after your arrest."

Rubashov felt behind his eyelids the flickering of the light. In Gletkin's mouth the sentence he had thought and written, acquired a naked sound – as though a confession, intended only for the anonymous priest, had been registered on a gramophone record, which now was repeating it in its cracked voice.

"I don't see," Rubashov said, "how it can serve the Party that her members have to grovel in the dust before all the world. I have pleaded guilty to having pursued a false and objectively harmful policy. Isn't that enough for you?"

He put on his pince-nez, blinked helplessly past the lamp, and ended in a hoarse voice:

"After all, the name N.S. Rubashov is itself a piece of Party history. By dragging it through the dirt, you besmirch the history of the Revolution."

Gletkin looked through the dossier.

"To that I can also reply with a citation from your own writings. You wrote:

" 'It is necessary to hammer every sentence into the masses by repetition and simplification. What is presented as right must shine like gold; what is presented as wrong must be black as pitch. For consumption by the masses, the political processes must be coloured like ginger-bread figures at a fair.' "

Rubashov was silent. Then he said:

"So that is what you are aiming at: I am to play the Devil in your

Punch and Judy show – howl, grind my teeth and put out my tongue – and voluntarily, too. Danton and his friends were spared that, at least."

Gletkin shut the cover of the dossier. He bent forward a bit and settled his cuffs:

"Your testimony at the trial will be the last service you can do the Party."

Rubashov did not answer. He kept his eyes shut and relaxed under the rays of the lamp like a tired sleeper in the sun; but there was no escape from Gletkin's voice.

"Your Danton and the Convention," said the voice, "were just a gallant play compared to what is at stake here. I have read books about it: these people wore powdered pigtails and declaimed about their personal honour. To them, it only mattered to die with a noble gesture, regardless of whether this gesture did good or harm."

Rubashov said nothing. There was a buzzing and humming in his ears; Gletkin's voice was above him; it came from every side of him; it hammered mercilessly on his aching skull.

"You know what is at stake," Gletkin went on. "For the first time in history, a revolution has not only conquered power, but also kept it. We have made our country a bastion of the new era. It covers a sixth of the world and contains a tenth of the world's population."

Gletkin's voice now sounded at Rubashov's back. He had risen and was walking up and down the room. It was the first time this had happened. His boots creaked at every step, his starched uniform crackled, and a sourish smell of sweat and leather became noticeable.

"When our Revolution had succeeded in our country, we believed that the rest of the earth would follow suit. Instead, came a wave of reaction, which threatened to swamp us. There were two currents in the Party. One consisted of adventurers, who wanted to risk what we had won to promote the revolution abroad. You belonged to them. We recognized this current to be dangerous, and have liquidated it."

Rubashov wanted to raise his head and say something. Gletkin's steps resounded in his skull. He was too tired. He let himself fall back, and kept his eyes shut.

"The leader of the Party," Gletkin's voice went on, "had the wider perspective and the more tenacious tactics. He realized that everything depended on surviving the period of world reaction and preserving the bastion. He had realized that it might take ten, perhaps twenty, perhaps fifty years, until the world was ripe for a fresh wave of revolution. Until then we stand alone. Until then we have only one duty: not to perish."

A sentence swam vaguely in Rubashov's memory: "It is the Revolutionary's duty to preserve his own life." Who had said that? He, himself? Ivanov? It was in the name of that principle that he had sacrificed Arlova. And where had it led him?

". . . Not to perish," sounded Gletkin's voice. "The bulwark must be held, at any price and with any sacrifice. The leader of the Party recognized this principle with unrivalled clear-sightedness, and has consistently applied it. The policy of the International had to be subordinated to our national policy. Whoever did not understand this necessity had to be destroyed. Whole sets of our best functionaries in Europe had to be physically liquidated. We did not recoil from crushing our own organizations abroad when the interests of the Bastion required it. We did not recoil from co-operation with the police of reactionary countries in order to suppress revolutionary movements which came at the wrong moment. We did not recoil from betraying our friends and compromising with our enemies, in order to preserve the Bastion. That was the task which history had given us, the representatives of the first victorious revolution. The shortsighted, the aesthetes, the moralists did not understand. But the leader of the Revolution understood that all depended on one thing: to be the better stayer."

Gletkin interrupted his pacing through the room. He stopped behind Rubashov's chair. The scar on his shaven skull shone sweatily. He panted, wiped his skull with his handkerchief, and seemed embarrassed at having broken his customary reserve. He sat down again behind the desk and settled his cuffs. He turned down the light a little, and continued in his usual expressionless voice:

"The Party's line was sharply defined. Its tactics were determined by the principle that the end justifies the means – all means, without exception. In the spirit of this principle, the Public Prosecutor will demand your life, Citizen Rubashov.

"Your faction, Citizen Rubashov, is beaten and destroyed. You wanted to split the Party, although you must have known that a split in the Party meant civil war. You know of the dissatisfaction amongst the peasantry, which has not yet learnt to understand the sense of the sacrifices imposed on it. In a war which may be only a few months away, such currents can lead to a catastrophe. Hence the imperious necessity for the Party to be united. It must be as if cast from one mould – filled with blind discipline and absolute trust. You and your friends, Citizen Rubashov, have made a rent in the Party. If your repentance is real, then you must help us to heal this rent. I have told you, it is the last service the Party will ask you.

"Your task is simple. You have set it yourself: to gild the Right, to blacken the Wrong. The policy of the opposition is wrong. Your task is therefore to make the opposition contemptible; to make the masses understand that opposition is a crime and that the leaders of the opposition are criminals. That is the simple language which the masses understand. If you begin to talk of your complicated motives, you will only create more confusion amongst them. Your task, Citizen Rubashov, is to avoid awakening sympathy and pity. Sympathy and pity for the opposition are a danger to the country.

"Comrade Rubashov, I hope that you have understood the task which the Party has set you."

It was the first time that Gletkin had called Rubashov "Comrade". Rubashov raised his head quickly. He felt a hot wave rising in him, against which he was helpless. His chin shook slightly while he was putting on his pince-nez.

"I understand."

"Observe," Gletkin went on, "that the Party holds out to you no prospect of reward. Some of the accused have been made amenable by physical pressure. Others, by the promise to save their heads – or the heads of their relatives who had fallen into our hands as hostages. To you, Comrade Rubashov, we propose no bargain and we promise nothing."

"I understand," Rubashov repeated.

Gletkin glanced at the dossier.

"There is a passage in your journal which impressed me," he went on. "You wrote: 'I have thought and acted as I had to. If I was right, I have nothing to repent of; if wrong, I shall pay.' "

He looked up from the dossier and looked Rubashov fully in the face:

"You were wrong, and you will pay, Comrade Rubashov. The Party promises only one thing: after the victory, one day when it can do no more harm, the material of the secret archives will be published. Then the world will learn what was in the background of this Punch and Judy show – as you called it – which we had to act for them according to history's text-book. . . ."

He hesitated a few seconds, settled his cuffs and ended rather awkwardly, while the scar on his skull reddened:

"And then you, and some of your friends of the older generation, will be given the sympathy and pity which are denied to you today."

While he was speaking, he had pushed the prepared statement over to Rubashov, and laid his fountain-pen beside it. Rubashov stood up and said with a strained smile:

"I have always wondered what it was like when the Neanderthalers became sentimental. Now I know."

"I do not understand," said Gletkin, who had also stood up.

Rubashov signed the statement.

He is duly sentenced to death and awaits his execution:

Rubashov wandered through his cell. In the old days he would have shamefacedly denied himself this sort of childish musing. Now he was not ashamed. In death the metaphysical became real. He stopped at the window and leaned his forehead against the pane. Over the machine-gun tower one could see a patch of blue. It was pale, and reminded him of that particular blue which he had seen overhead when as a boy he lay on the grass of his father's estate, watching the poplar branches slowly moving against the sky. Apparently even a patch of blue sky was enough to induce the "oceanic feeling". He had read that, according to the latest discoveries of astrophysics, the volume of the world was finite – though space had no boundaries, it was self-contained, like the surface of a sphere. He had never been able to understand that; but now he felt an urgent desire to understand. He now also remembered where he had read about it: during his first arrest in Germany, comrades had smuggled a sheet of the illegally printed Party organ into his cell; at the top were three columns about a strike in a spinning-mill; at the bottom of a column, as a stop-gap, was printed in tiny letters the discovery that the universe was finite, and halfway through it the page was torn off. He had never found out what had been in the torn-off part.

Rubashov stood by the window and tapped on the empty wall with his pince-nez. As a boy he had really meant to study astronomy, and now for forty years he had been doing something else. Why had not the Public Prosecutor asked him: "Defendant Rubashov, what about the infinite?" He would not have been able to answer – and there, there lay the real source of his guilt. . . . Could there be a greater?

When he had read that newspaper notice, then also alone in his cell, with joints still sore from the last bout of torture, he had fallen into a queer state of exaltation – the "oceanic feeling" had swept him away. Afterwards he had been ashamed of himself. The Party disapproved of such states. It called them *petit-bourgeois* mysticism, refuge in the ivory tower. It called them "escape from the task", "desertion of the class struggle". The oceanic feeling was counter-revolutionary.

For in a struggle one must have both legs firmly planted on the earth. The Party taught one how to do it. The infinite was a politically suspect quantity, the individual a suspect quality. The Party did not recognise its existence. The definition of the individual was: a multitude of one million divided by one million.

The Party denied the free will of the individual – and at the same time it exacted his willing self-sacrifice. It denied his capacity to choose between two alternatives – and at the same time it demanded that he should always choose the right one. It denied his power to distinguish between good and evil – and at the same time it thundered against traitors and criminals. The individual stood under the sign of historic determinism, a wheel in a clockwork which had been wound up for all eternity and could not be stopped or influenced – and the Party demanded that the wheel should revolt against the clockwork and change its course. There was somewhere an error in the calculation; the equation did not work out.

It was quiet in the cell. Rubashov heard only the creaking of his steps on the tiles. Six and a half steps to the door, whence they must come to fetch him, six and half steps to the window, behind which night was falling. Soon it would be over. But when he asked himself, for what actually are you dying?, he found no answer.

I shall now revert to the Postscript to the Danube edition of the novel:

The material of the secret archives, to which Gletkin consolingly refers, has not yet been published. But some of it has leaked out, as it was inevitable in the long run. Perhaps the most revealing is General Krivitsky's account of the method by which Mrachkovsky, one of the accused at the first show trial, was induced to confess.

General Walter Krivitsky was the head of Soviet Military Intelligence (Fourth Bureau of the Red Army) for Western Europe till he broke with the regime in 1937. It was the first case of desertion of a top-ranking official in the Soviet Union's foreign intelligence network. On two occasions the GPU tried to assassinate him in France; on the third, in the United States, they succeeded. His death was made to appear as suicide. General Krivitsky was found shot through the head, apparently by his own hand, in a room in a small Washington hotel where he had never stayed before. He had repeatedly warned his family and friends never to believe, if he were to be found dead, that he had committed suicide. There is an old GPU saying: "Any fool can commit a murder, but it takes an artist to commit a natural death."

I have never met General Krivitsky; those of my friends who knew him admired his courage and integrity. His book *I was Stalin's Agent* was published in December, 1939 – at a time when I had finished *Darkness at Noon* except for the last, post-interrogation part. I only read Krivitsky's book several years later, for when I had finished *Darkness at Noon* I became allergic, for a long time, to the whole subject.

First, here is Krivitsky's short summing up of the problem in a chapter of his book called "Why did they Confess?":

> How were the confessions obtained? . . . A bewildered world watched the builders of the Soviet Government flagellate themselves for crimes which they never could have committed, and which have been proved to be fantastic lies. Ever since, the riddle of the confessions has puzzled the Western world. But the confessions never presented a riddle to those of us who had been on the inside of the Stalin machine.
>
> Although several factors contributed to bringing the men to the point of making these confessions, they made them at the last in the sincere conviction that this was their sole remaining service to the Party and the revolution. They sacrificed honour as well as life to defend the hated regime of Stalin, because it contained the last faint gleam of hope for that better world to which they had consecrated themselves in early youth. . . .

Krivitsky proceeds to point out that this explanation applies only to a certain type of accused (whom I have called "the hard core"); and then gives the following account of the way Mrachkovsky was persuaded to confess:*

*Krivitsky's account is considerably shortened in the quotation that follows.

Mrachkovsky had been a member of the Bolshevik Party since 1905. He was the son of a revolutionist exiled to Siberia by the Czar. He himself had been arrested many times by the Czarist police. During the civil war, after the Soviet Revolution, Mrachkovsky organised in the Urals a volunteer corps which performed wonderful feats in defeating the counter-revolutionary armies of Admiral Kolchak. He acquired the reputation of an almost legendary hero in the period of Lenin and Trotsky.

By June 1935, all the preparations for the first show trial had been completed. The confessions of fourteen prisoners had been secured. The leading characters, Zinoviev and Kamenev, had been cast for their roles and had rehearsed their lines. But there were two men in this batch of marked victims who had failed to come across with their confessions. One of these was Mrachkovsky. The other was his colleague Ivan N. Smirnov, a co-founder of the Bolshevik Party, leader of the Fifth Army during the civil war.

Stalin did not want to proceed to the trial without these two men. They had been grilled for months, they had been subjected to all the physical third degree practices of the Ogpu, but still refused to sign confessions. The chief of the Ogpu suddenly called upon my comrade, Sloutski, to take over the interrogation of Mrachkovsky, and to "break down" this man – for whom Sloutski had, as it chanced, a profound respect. Both of us wept when Sloutski told me of his experience as an inquisitor.

"I began the examination cleanly shaven," he said. "When I had finished it, I had grown a beard."

Sloutski began to talk about the internal and international situations of the Soviet Government, of the perils from within and without, of the enemies within the Party undermining the Soviet power, of the need to save the Party at all costs as the only saviour of the revolution.

"I told him," Sloutski reported to me, "that I was personally convinced that he, Mrachkovsky, was not a counter-revolutionist. I took from my desk the confessions of his imprisoned comrades, and showed them to him as evidence of how low they had fallen in their opposition to the Soviet system.

"For three full days and nights we talked and argued. During all this time Mrachkovsky did not sleep a wink. Altogether I snatched about three to four hours of sleep during this whole period of my wrestling with him."

There followed days and nights of argument which brought Mrachkovsky to the realisation that nobody else but Stalin could guide the Bolshevik Party. Mrachkovsky was a firm believer in the one-party system of government, and he had to admit that there was no Bolshevik group strong enough to reform the Party machine from within, or to overthrow Stalin's leadership. True, there was deep discontent in the country, but to deal with it outside the Bolshevik ranks would

mean the end of the proletarian dictatorship to which Mrachkovsky
was loyal.

Both the prosecuting examiner and his prisoner agreed that all
Bolsheviks must submit their will and their ideas to the will and ideas
of the Party. They agreed that one had to remain within the Party even
unto death, or dishonour, or death with dishonour, if it became necessary for the sake of consolidating the Soviet power. It was for the Party
to show the confessors consideration for their acts of self-sacrifice if it
chose.

"I brought him to the point where he began to weep," Sloutski
reported to me. "I wept with him when we arrived at the conclusion
that all was lost, that there was nothing left in the way of hope or faith,
that the only thing to do was to make a desperate effort to forestall a
futile struggle on the part of the discontented masses. For this the
Government must have public 'confessions' by the opposition leaders.

"By the end of the fourth day he signed the whole confession made
by him at the public trial.

"I went home. For a whole week I was unfit for any work. I was unfit
to live."

When I read this account, years after *Darkness at Noon* was
written, I had a sickening feeling of *déjà vu*. The resemblance in
atmosphere and content to the first interrogation of Rubashov by
Ivanov in the novel was striking. The similarity between Ivanov's
and Sloutski's line of argument was easy to explain: both the
novel and the real event were determined by the same framework
of ideas and circumstances. But there were similarities of detail
and nuance which went beyond that. In both cases the interrogation opens with accuser and accused indulging in sentimental
reminiscences of the Civil War; in both cases the accuser has
served under the accused's command; as a result of the Civil War,
one in each pair of antagonists has a game leg; in both cases the
interrogator is in turn liquidated himself. As I read on, I had the
impression of meeting the *Doppelgaengers*, the spectral doubles
of Rubashov and Ivanov – a ghostly, ectoplasmic regurgitation of
the characters of the novel.

Krivitsky had never read *Darkness at Noon*; he was dead by the
time it appeared in print.

As I have repeatedly pointed out, the method by which a Mrachkovsky, a Bukharin or Rubashov was induced to confess, could
only be applied to a certain type of Old Bolshevik with an absolute
loyalty to the Party. With other defendants, other methods of

pressure were used which varied from case to case. Yet, in the controversy around the book, it was constantly alleged that I explained *all* confessions by the same method. In fact, of the three prisoners that appear in the novel, Rubashov alone confesses in self-sacrificing devotion to the Party; Harelip confesses because he is kept under torture; the illiterate peasant confesses without even understanding the charge. Moreover, on page 227 of the novel, Gletkin himself enumerates the various methods by which others were made to confess; in yet another passage (p. 242) it is Rubashov who reflects that "some were silenced by physical fear, some hoped to save their heads. . . ." etc., etc.

Yet when, twenty years after the novel was written, Kruschev, in his historic speech at the Twentieth Party Congress, denounced Stalin's crimes, some untiring controversialists regarded it as proof that "the Rubashov theory of the confessions" was wrong — all the confessions had been obtained by the much simpler, old-fashioned method of torture, blackmail and bribery; had not Kruschev himself said so? The obvious answer is that the leader of a country can hardly be expected to divulge intimate details of the methods employed by its secret police. Perhaps the most effective amongst these were the various techniques of inducing mental breakdowns. It was successfully applied for the first time in the Moscow show trials of the 'thirties, and after the war in other Punch and Judy shows staged in several satellite countries — such as the 1952 trial of Slanski and Clementis in Czechoslovakia, and the Rajk trial in Hungary. It was a versatile psychological technique which could be combined with physical torture or the administration of drugs, and could be further varied according to the victims' personality, powers of resistance and ethical beliefs. For the vast majority of the victims physical ill-treatment, threats and promises were sufficient to make them confess having stolen the Eiffel Tower and sold it as scrap metal. *Darkness at Noon*, however, is chiefly concerned with a historically significant minority, the élite of Old Bolsheviks, the men who made the Russian Revolution, changed the destiny of the world, then sank into the mud of utter self-debasement. They, the Bukharins, the Zinovievs and Piatakovs, were fallen giants, and it would be the ultimate injustice to misinterpret the motives for which they died. Their fantastic self-accusations were not prompted by beatings and the promise of country *datchas*. They died for reasons which reflected an ideology running amuck, but within the logic of their own faith. The Gletkins, cool practitioners of inquisitorial dialectics, succeeded in breaking the Rubashovs down by exploiting the weakness of the flesh and at the same time appealing to the noblest aspects of man: his sense of duty and self-sacrifice. Those critics who failed to appreciate this and considered the "Rubashov theory of the confessions" as too far-fetched, seemed to have common sense on their side, but had no inkling of the magic power of totalitarian ideologies. Since the majority of politicians in the West belong to this category, they failed to grasp the lesson and the warning that it implied.

I have spoken of reality regurgitating fiction in Krivitsky's account. But this was not the only occasion when it happened. In November, 1952, twelve years after the publication of Darkness at Noon, the last survivor among my intimate Party comrades, Otto Katz alias André Simon, was hanged in Prague.

Otto had been one of the most brilliant propagandists and operators of the Communist International, author of the famous *The Brown Book of the Hitler Terror*, producer of Soviet propaganda films, dispenser of secret funds to French newspapers and politicians, roving ambassador of the Comintern who made frequent trips to London and Hollywood to organise "anti-Fascist" front committees.* He had political contacts everywhere among fellow-travellers and progressive intellectuals. He was handsome, charming and attractive to women – particularly to certain middle-aged spinsters of the English Labour Party who wielded some political influence. When I was imprisoned in the Spanish Civil War, he engineered an international campaign for my liberation, which probably saved my head.

Otto had spent the war years in Mexico. Then he had gone back to his native country, Czechoslovakia. After the Communist coup of 1948 he had been appointed editor of the official Party organ, *Pravo Lidu*, and later on Chief of the Press Department at the Foreign Ministry. In 1952 the great purge that swept through the satellite countries, swept him away too. He was one of the nine accused in the Slansky-Clementis trial, charged with being a British spy, a saboteur and – of all things – a Zionist agent. He confessed to everything and was executed by hanging.

As I read the terrible report of Otto's confession, I received an additional shock. In his last statement before the Tribunal, Otto

*Cf. The Invisible Writing, ch. xviii.

quoted Rubashov's last speech as textually as he could probably remember it. Otto's concluding words were:

"I ... belong to the gallows. The only service I can still render is to serve as a warning example to all who, by origin or character, are in danger of following the same path to hell. The sterner the punishment ..." (Voice falls too low to be intelligible).*

Rubashov's last speech, with its emphasis on "rendering a last service" and "serving as a warning example" was a paraphrase of Bukharin's confession at the Moscow trial of 1938 – and Otto knew that. The phrasing by Otto of his last statement was clearly intended as a camouflaged message, to indicate that he, too, had been brought to confess to crimes as imaginary as Bukharin's and Rubashov's. Perhaps he believed that I could do for him what he had done for me when I had been in a similar, yet less hopeless predicament; perhaps he hoped that his influential former friends in London, Paris and Hollywood, who had once admired and fêted the author of the Brown Book, the propagandist for the anti-Fascist cause, would raise their voices in protest. When a man is going to be hanged, he tends to over-estimate the interest which the world takes in his windpipe. Not one voice was raised among the editors, journalists, social hostesses and film-stars who had swarmed round Otto in the romantic, pink days of the "People's Front". His last message was like a scribbled SOS in a bottle washed ashore by the sea, and left to bob among the drift-wood.

*BBC Monitoring Report of last statement by Otto Katz at the Slansky-Clementis trial, November 23, 1952.

Chapter 16

ARRIVAL AND DEPARTURE

Arrival and Departure, published in 1943, is the third novel of the trilogy on ends and means and the related conflict between morality and expediency. The Gladiators and Darkness at Noon were concerned with its disastrous impact on history, past and present; in Arrival and Departure the conflict is transposed to the plane of individual psychology.

Peter Slavek, a young university student in a Central European country under a semi-Fascist dictatorship, starts on his career as a revolutionary without much insight into the unconscious motives of his actions. He arrives as a stowaway in war-time Portugal, intending to get to England and join the RAF; however, he is also sorely tempted to follow his girl-friend Odette to America, which at that time is still a neutral haven. He has withstood torture and imprisonment with great courage, but now, faced with an insoluble dilemma, he suffers a mental and physical breakdown (a so-called hysterical conversion paralysis affecting one leg). He undergoes treatment by a psychotherapist – Dr Sonia Bolgar, a compatriot and former friend of his parents, who is carrying on her practice in Lisbon, while waiting for her American visa. On the analyst's couch Peter is made to re-live his harrowing experiences under the Nazi terror in Eastern Europe,* but also some even more traumatic episodes from his early childhood which left a lasting mark on him. In the course of the treatment Peter is led to discover that his crusading zeal was motivated by unconscious guilt:

He realised that under Sonia's influence the proud structure of his values had collapsed, and imperative exclamation marks had

*These were based on factual events and included accounts of the early stages of the Holocaust, which were at the time met with general disbelief.

been bent into question marks. What, after all, was courage? A matter of glands, nerves, reactions conditioned by heredity and early experiences. A drop of iodine less in the thyroid gland, a sadistic governess or over-protective aunt, a slight variation in the electric resistance of neural pathways, and the hero became a coward, the patriot a traitor. Touched with the magic wand of cause and effect, the actions of men were emptied of their so-called moral content as a Leyden jar is discharged by the touch of a conductor. . . .

. . . Sonia talked for a long time. She began by exposing the false trails, demolishing meaningless catchwords like "courage", "sacrifice", or "the just cause". History, she explained, was not an epos, but a chain of accidents. In the Spanish war, so close to Peter's heart, both sides had fought with equal courage; at all times people had sacrificed themselves for good or bad, enlightened or stupid causes with the same fervour. Thus, if one wanted to explain why Peter had behaved as he did, one had to discard from the beginning his so-called convictions and ethical beliefs. They were mere pretexts of the mind, phantoms projected by more intimate events. It did not matter whether he was a hero of the Proletariat or a martyr of the Catholic Church; the real clue was this suspect craving for martyrdom.

At the conclusion of the treatment Peter's symptoms vanish and Sonia appears to have convinced Peter to say his farewell to arms, to join Odette in the States before his visa expires, and to adopt the ways of down-to-earth reasonableness and expediency. For in the type of therapy practised by her school, and in the philosophy that it implies, there is no provision made for ethical values; its aim is to induce the patient to make his peace with reality; and if the reality is Nazi-occupied Europe, it just cannot be helped.

Yet in the end, Sonia is defeated. She has to leave for the States; Peter is supposed to follow in the next boat but, left to himself, is again assailed by doubts. He carries on an endless imaginary dialogue with her:

"Why do people look at me in such an odd way?" – "They don't. It's your imagination." – "They ask themselves: What is he doing here? Why does he not go to where he belongs?" – "But you belong nowhere, you fool." – "How can one live, belonging nowhere?" – "You belong to yourself. That is the gift I made you." – "I don't want it. Your gift is out of season." – "Then what do you

want?" – "Not to be ashamed of myself." – "What are you
ashamed of?" – "Of walking through the parks while others get
drowned or burned alive; of belonging to myself while everybody
belongs to something else." – "Do you still believe in their big
words and pretty flags?" – "No, I don't." – "Are you not glad that I
opened your eyes?" – "Yes, I am." – "What were your beliefs?" –
"Illusions." – "Your courage?" – "Vanity." – "Your loyalty?" –
"Atonement." – "Why then do you want to start all over again?" –
"Why indeed? That should be your job to explain."

But that precisely was the point which Sonia could not explain,
for apparently it was placed on a plane beyond her reasoning, and
perhaps beyond reasoning altogether.

*Thus in the last minute Peter changes his mind – or rather some
untouchable core inside him, a core apparently "beyond the
reach of cause and effect", changes his mind for him. The novel
ends with his being dropped by parachute to join the resistance
movement in his native country. In his farewell letter to Odette,
written at the aerodrome before the start of his mission, there is a
key passage which reads:*

"Today I am going to fly off at a tangent from the twisting path. I
have not many illusions about the reasons why I am doing it, nor
about the cause which I serve. As children we used to be given a
curious kind of puzzle to play with. It was a print showing a tangle
of very thin blue and red lines. If you just looked at it you couldn't
make out anything. But if you covered it with a piece of transparent red tissue-paper, the red lines of the drawing disappeared and
the blue lines formed a picture – it was a clown in a circus holding
a hoop and a little dog jumping through it. And if you covered the
same drawing with blue tissue-paper, a roaring lion appeared
chasing the clown across the ring. You can play the same trick on
every mortal, living or dead. You can look at him through Sonia's
tissue-paper and write a biography of Napoleon in terms of his
pituitary gland as has been done; the fact that he incidentally
conquered Europe will appear as a mere symptom of the activities
of those two tiny lobes, the size of a pea. You can explain the
message of the Prophets as epileptic foam and the Sistine
Madonna as the projection of an incestuous dream. The method is
correct and the picture in itself complete. But beware of the
arrogant error of believing that it is the only one. The picture you
get through the blue tissue-paper will be no less true and com-

plete. The clown and the lion are both there, interwoven in the
same pattern.''

The implied message he is trying to convey – though he himself
only half understands it – is also hinted at earlier on, in two
parables which Peter wrote at the height of the crisis after Sonia's
departure (in his student days, he was a budding poet). The first
parable is about a young man sitting on a beach and drawing with
his stick triangles in the sand:

''. . . He did not see the sea-gulls circling above his head, nor the
galleys and triremes moving softly along the water's skyline; he
wore a strange, loose gown and his face was set in a dumb,
anguished gaze on his figures in the sand, while his lips mumbled
unintelligible words. An old man with shrewd, wrinkled eyes sat
down at the other end of the bench; and after watching for a while
the young man's antics, spoke to him in a gentle voice:
   '' 'What, my friend, are you doing with your stick?'
   ''The young man jumped as if caught at a shameful or criminal
occupation. 'I am drawing triangles,' he said, blushing foolishly.
   '' 'And why, after having drawn one, do you wipe it out with
your hand, and then draw a new one which is just like the other?'
   '' 'I don't know. I believe these triangles hold a secret, and I
want to discover it.'
   '' 'A secret? . . . Tell me, my friend, do you perchance suffer
from bad dreams? Do you cry out sometimes in your sleep?'
   '' 'I do, ever and anon.'
   '' 'And what is the dream that haunts you, and makes you cry
out in the night?'
   ''The young man blushed once more all over his face.
   '' 'I always dream that I and my dear wife Celia are watching the
athletic games where my friend Porphyrius is performing; he
throws the discus, but in the wrong direction, and the heavy thing
comes whirling through the air and hits my poor wife on the head,
who thereupon faints with a mysterious smile on her lips. . . .'
   ''The old man chuckled and laid his hand on the other's
shoulder.
   '' 'My dear friend,' he said, 'you are lucky that fate made me
cross your path, for I am a teller of oracles, a solver of riddles, a
helper of the afflicted. This will cost you a drachma, but it will be
worth it. And now listen:
   '' 'I have noticed that while you were telling your dream, your

hand again inadvertently began drawing in the sand. When you mentioned yourself, you drew a straight line. When you mentioned friend Porphyrius, you drew a second one at right angles to the first; and when you mentioned your wife Celia, you completed the triangle by drawing the hypotenuse which connects the other two. Thus your dream becomes perfectly transparent. Your mind is harassed by a disquietude which you have been hiding, even from yourself; and the secret of the triangle you are trying to discover can easily be solved by questioning your servants about your wife's private life.'

"The young man jumped to his feet. 'Praised be the gods that you have solved the riddle which haunted my mind! Instead of going on drawing those foolish triangles, as I have done for the past two years, I shall now go home and give Celia a sound thrashing, as befits a reasonable man.'

"He stamped with his sandals on the last figure he had drawn, then, gathering up his robe, walked away with hurried steps along the beach. He felt happy and relieved; that dark, inexplicable urge to draw triangles in the sand had left him for ever; and thus the Theorem of Pythagoras was never discovered."

In other words, the wise old head-shrinker under the blue Aegean skies quite correctly diagnosed that poor Pythagoras was labouring under an obsession which drove him to search for the secret of the triangle; what he failed to realise was that, whatever the young man's unconscious motives – whether jealousy, ambition, or an ailing liver – the results of his search must be judged by their mathematical merits and not by his private motivations – judged in the terms of Euclid, and not of Freud. The old man in the parable sees only the clown, but not the lion; he is a forerunner of that "reductionist" philosophy which came into full bloom in our time.

Peter's second parable is a somewhat whimsical variation on the theme of the individual's ultimate responsibility for his actions:

The Last Judgement

"The gong struck three times; its vibrations expanded in concentric spheres through the darkness, and a voice announced:

" 'Gentlemen, the last judgement.'

"The defendants yawned; they took their places in the narrow carriages; the tiny locomotive shrieked and they departed. It was the train of a Scenic Railway, and it carried them through a dark, winding tunnel. On both sides of the tunnel there were brightly illuminated grottos, isolated by glass panels like shop windows; behind the glass ingenious automata, like figures on a mediaeval clock, enacted charades from the defendants' past. At first they were of a harmlessly embarrassing nature; but as the tunnel burrowed deeper down into the earth, the scenes became obscene and violent; and the monotonous movements of the automata, repeating the same action over and over again, multiplied its horror and shame. Still further down the figures began to lose their human shape; hairy, ape-like, club-armed creatures slew, raped, grimaced, and danced in solemn silence behind the glass. The passengers in the train whimpered and groaned; their cries and gasping breath filled the sultry air of the tunnel; they tried to close their eyes, but the glaring light of the grottos penetrated through their eyelids and they were forced to see.

"After some time the train halted and the passengers alighted on a platform in front of a cathedral. Its door was open and they could see that the Court was already assembled at the other end of the nave. The interior of the cathedral was dim and filled with the thunder of the organ. They marched through the door in single file, and the music subsided. As each defendant advanced through the central aisle, he saw that a large audience filled the rows. The backs of their heads were all alike, but he could not turn to look at their faces; and as he advanced, the judge and the magistrates receded, so that he could not see their faces either.

"Meanwhile the trial of the first defendant had begun. He stood facing the Court, a lean ascetic man with a stoop.

" 'How do you do?' asked the Judge in a terrible voice, which echoed throughout the dome.

" 'Humbly, my Lord,' said the defendant. But his voice was thin, it collapsed in the air without resounding and fell with broken wings on the marble slabs before his feet.

" 'Bad echo,' roared the Judge. 'However, proceed.'

" 'He has sacrificed his fortune to help the poor,' said Counsel for the Defence. His face resembled the defendant's, but there was more fat on his body and more righteousness in his voice.

" 'On what did you dine tonight?' roared the Judge.

" 'On a glass of milk and a crust of bread, my Lord,' said the defendant.

"The Prosecutor rose. He too resembled the defendant, but he looked even more haggard and his voice was like a lash.

" 'A child starved in China while he guzzled his milk and bread,' he shouted.

" 'Condemned!' roared the Judge; and the audience echoed in awestricken voices:

" 'Condemned, condemned.'

"The defendant walked slowly out of the cathedral and sat down in his old seat in the train, burying his face in his hands.

"The next defendant was a jovial, guileless man with a paunch. He advanced beaming all over his face, and as he advanced, the opposing Counsel changed in appearance; they again both resembled the accused, only the Defender looked even more guileless and had a bigger paunch.

" 'On what did you dine tonight?' roared the Judge.

" 'Well, my Lord,' said the defendant, 'we thought we might start with some fresh salmon, this being the season, and a bottle of hock, to keep it swimming and cool.'

" 'Enough,' roared the Judge. 'What has the Defence to say?'

" 'He has a blessed digestion,' the Defender nodded earnestly, crossing his hands on his belly. 'And what is the charge, anyway?'

"The Judge turned towards the prosecution; but the Prosecutor's seat was empty.

" 'Acquitted in the absence of a charge,' he roared; and the audience repeated joyously:

" 'Acquitted, acquitted.'

"The defendant, with a respectful bow, walked out and sat down in his old seat in the train, where he soon fell asleep.

"The next defendant advanced, and again the opposing Counsel were transformed to his likeness. He was a man of bold and reckless appearance, and as soon as he faced the Court, the Prosecutor rose:

" 'I accuse this man,' he said in a mild, angelical voice, "of murder, arson, and treachery.'

" 'We confess proudly to all our acts,' the Defender shouted. 'We did it in the service of our cause.'

" 'He never listened to our voice except when asleep,' complained the Prosecutor.

" 'He always obeyed ours when lucid and awake,' boasted the Defender.

" 'He sowed evil everywhere on his way,' complained the Prosecutor, beating his chest.

" 'So that good may be reaped in due time,' cried the Defender.

" 'Have you seen the harvest?' roared the Judge.

" 'Not yet,' said the accused man. 'But. . . .'

" 'Condemned owing to lack of evidence,' roared the Judge; the audience echoed and the defendant, with a defiant smile, walked out of Court and back to the train.

"The next defendant was a very old man, walking on a gnarled stick, and as he advanced, silence fell upon the cathedral. He stood, with his head bent, oblivious of his surroundings, as if listening to some sound which he alone could hear; but presently the silence became so deep that the others heard it too. It was a strange, thin sound, which rose and died at intervals, as if somebody were testing the keys of an old clavichord.

" 'What's he doing?' asked the Judge.

" 'He is tuning his heart,' said the Defender.

" 'But he's got no tuning fork,' objected the Judge.

" 'He is trying to adjust it to the celestial key,' explained the Defender. 'When he succeeds, his self will expand and become dissolved in the universal spirit.'

"The Prosecutor rose. He was even older than the defendant, his bloodless lips were curved by bitterness and disappointment.

" 'I accuse this man,' he said wearily, 'of passive complicity in every murder and crime of present, past, and future.'

" 'He never killed a fly,' said the Defender.

" 'The flies he did not kill brought pestilence to a whole province,' said the Prosecutor.

" 'Look at him and listen,' whispered the Defender.

"The old man had suddenly lifted his head, and his face was luminous with the smile of the blind. Judge and audience strained their ears, but the vibration of the chord had become so high-pitched that they could no longer decide whether they really heard something or were fooled by the ringing of their ears.

" 'Condemned because of the presence of doubt,' said the Judge; the audience echoed and the defendant, his smile extinguished and his head drooping again, hobbled slowly back to his seat in the train.

"The Court sat all night and accused after accused advanced to face judgement, some trembling, some with feigned jauntiness, some in humble submission, others with jerking eyebrows and twitching faces; and though the Prosecutor spoke mostly in whispers, the verdict for almost all was "condemned". There were those who had been right for the wrong reasons and those

who had been wrong for the right reasons; there were those who
had mortified their bodies, but the scars of their self-chastisement
were not deep enough, and those who had reaped the fruits of the
flesh, but their enjoyment had been found wanting. Some were
punished because they issued orders, others because they obeyed;
some because they clung to their lives, others because they died
bravely for the wrong cause; the afflicted were punished for their
afflictions and the healthy for their health. Their sentence pronounced, they all resumed their old places in the train; and
presently the last one in the queue, a young man with a timid
expression, advanced along the empty aisle to face the Court.

" 'Who is this?' roared the Judge.

" 'A crusader who lost his cross,' said the Prosecutor.

" 'A crusader in search of a cross,' said the Defender.

" 'Well, we can't supply him with one,' roared the Judge. 'That
would make things too easy.'

" 'Easy, my Lord?' the Defender remarked bitterly. 'Look at all
the clanking metal the Prosecution hung on his chest.'

" 'We had to counter-balance his buoyant mind,' said the Prosecutor. 'The defence put too many bubbles into his brain.'

" 'He can't float with all this ballast,' complained the Defender.

" 'There are times to float and times to sink,' remarked the Judge
impatiently, for he had other business to attend to that night.

" 'Timely or not, most of my clients float,' the Defender
remarked contentedly.

" 'Only those who sink will be saved,' said the Prosecutor.

" 'Enough,' said the Judge. He turned to the defendant:'Until
those two agree, there will be no peace for you. The sentence is:
Purgatory on probation.'

" 'On probation,' echoed the audience.

" 'But I have already been in Purgatory,' the young man
remarked meekly.

" 'Never mind,' said the Judge, 'some remain on probation all
their lives.'

" 'All their lives,' echoed the audience.

" 'They are the eternal adolescents through whom the race
matures.'

" 'Matures, matures, matures,' the audience chanted sleepily.

" 'The sitting is closed for today,' roared the Judge, and the
Court rose.

"As the young man turned to walk down the nave towards the
door, he saw for the first time that not only the Prosecutor and

Defender, but also all the faces in the audience were made after his own image. His heart contracted in despair.

" 'Am I alone?' he asked.

"And the audience answered:

" 'There is no one else under this dome.'

"At last they were all seated, the locomotive whistled and the train departed in the direction from which they had come. But now the grottos were extinguished, the tunnel was grey with the light of dawn, and the passengers were asleep. The young man nudged his neighbour.

" 'What strange Court was that?' he asked.

" 'Why, the Supreme Court,' said his neighbour. 'Have you never been there before?'

" 'No,' said the young man. 'Does one return there?'

" 'Every night,' said the other drowsily.

" 'And every time they try you anew?'

" 'It is always the Last Judgement,' said the man and went back to sleep.

"But after a while the young man woke him again:

" 'How is it,' he asked, 'that all these people go back in the same train?'

" 'What else did you expect?' asked his neighbour.

" 'But some were condemned, some were acquitted, others are on probation, and yet it doesn't seem to make any difference?'

" 'Doesn't it?' said his neighbour, yawning.

" 'If it makes no difference, why should I submit to their rules?'

" 'Because it is the Last Judgement,' said the other and went to sleep again.

"After some time the train emerged from the tunnel and halted. The passengers stretched, got out, and without a backward look hastily dispersed in all directions. The morning was grey and chilly; each went to his day's work or leisure; and already they had forgotten that at night they would meet again in the train."

Whatever bizarre shape the court proceedings take, the individual's ultimate responsibility for his actions is irreducible. He is his own accuser and defender, judge, audience and executioner. That is the stern philosophy at which Peter seems to have arrived, redeemed by a touch of Galgenhumor – *the humour of the gallows. He has realised that ethical imperatives, intuitive* insights, *artistic values cannot be explained (or explained away) by "reducing" them to reflexes, childhood traumas, frustrated sex and ultimately to electro-chemical processes. All these are part of the personality, but the whole is more than the sum of its parts, and cannot be completely reduced to its parts without taking it apart and thus destroying its unique pattern of wholeness.*

This view of the irreducibility of values from higher to lower levels in the existential hierarchy is not exactly new, but it ran counter to the prevailing currents of the time – Marxism, Freudianism, Behaviourism, Logical Positivism, and Materialism in general. A novel is not a philosophical treatise, and thus the intended message of Peter Slavek's story could only be hinted at in an implicit, oblique way. But I have subsequently endeavoured to clarify and elaborate it – as we shall see in Book Two.

In the novel, the hero's fate remained undecided. Reality gave it a different twist. I am quoting from the Postscript to the Danube edition:

Peter Slavek was modelled on a young Hungarian friend of mine, the Communist poet Endre Havas, whom I knew during the war in London. Though at one time he too had been disillusioned by the Communist Party, he rejoined it in the days of the Battle of Stalingrad, and after the war went back to Hungary. In 1949, during the great purge which followed the show trial of the former Minister for Foreign Affairs, Laszlo Rajk (who was hanged and posthumously rehabilitated), Havas was arrested, together with virtually all Party intellectuals who had spent the years of the war in the West. He was accused of being a spy, but persisted in his refusal to sign the usual confession. Several of his fellow prisoners, who were released during the revolution of 1956, and escaped to England, reported his end. Havas had gone insane under protracted physical torture.* He would crawl on all fours shouting "Help, help. Long live Stalin". He died in the prison infirmary in

---

*One of the witnesses was Paul Ignotus, former Hungarian Press Attaché in London, who was also imprisoned after the Rajk purge. In his book *Political Prisoner* (London, 1959) he writes: "Havas, with his conspicuous appearance and the typical awkwardness of an intellectual, was a tempting target. They dragged him about and played football with his body. He was left lying in his excrement for days."

1952 or 1953. After the thaw he, too was posthumously rehabilitated as one of the victims of the "Stalin personality cult", and a
biographical note, accompanied by his photograph, appeared in
the official *Encyclopaedia of Hungarian Literature*.

PART FOUR

FIGHTING THE COLD WAR

Chapter 17

BECOMING ANGLICISED

By jumping from Darkness at Noon *straight to* Arrival and Departure, *I have once more put thematic continuity before chronological order. I had started writing* Darkness at Noon *in the summer of 1935 in Paris, and finished writing* Arrival and Departure *in the summer of 1943 in London. This gap in the chronology is filled, as far as the author's adventures are concerned, by* Scum of the Earth — *an eye-witness account of the collapse of France, the events which led up to it, and its tragic aftermath.* Scum of the Earth *was written after my escape to England – and was my first book written in English. The events it described were briefly as follows.*

Shortly after the outbreak of the war I was arrested by the French Police as a suspected Communist – though I had ceased to be one eighteen months before. (It should be remembered that, since Stalin was at that time Hitler's ally, all Communists were suspected of sympathising with the enemy.) I spent four months in the notorious "camp for undesirable aliens" at Le Vernet, in the foothills of the Pyrenees; was released, thanks to the intervention of English politicians, and finished Darkness at Noon *just before the fall of Paris. On the day of the capitulation of France, I enlisted in the Foreign Legion, which enabled me to change my name to the more melodious Albert Dubert, taxi driver from Bern, Switzerland, and thus disappear from the Gestapo's wanted list. After a short and undistinguished career as a Legionnaire, I joined an escape party of British officers in Marseilles. Equipped*

with faked papers, which were easy to come by in those days of
chaos and demoralisation, we travelled to Casablanca, and from
there on a fishing boat to neutral Lisbon.

As an anti-climax to this escape story, I was kept waiting in
Lisbon for a visa to England which never came. The Home Office
was either too busy with the war, or they too thought that I was
still a Communist. This delay provided me with the local colour
for Peter Slavek's stay in Portugal (the "Neutralia" of Arrival and
Departure); but I was getting impatient, and after six weeks of
waiting I boarded a plane bound for England without an entry
permit. We landed in Bristol where I was promptly arrested – as I
had expected in view of the parachute scare and Fifth Column
mania, which were rampant at the time. I was taken under escort
to London, spent two nights at Cannon Row Police Station and six
weeks in Pentonville Prison, until the Home Office found time to
establish my identity and bona fides and set me free.

The extracts which follow are taken from the last chapter of The
Invisible Writing:

If I should write a Baedeker of the prisons of Europe, I would mark
Pentonville with three stars. It is the most decent gaol I have been
in, though the plumbing leaves much to be desired. In Seville the
installations were more modern, with wash-basins and water-
closets in each cell, and you were allowed to buy wine with your
meals, but the inmates were shot and garrotted without much ado.
In Pentonville we only had one hanging during my stay – a
German spy* – but on that morning the guards walked on tiptoe
and there was a hush in the whole, large building. It was nice to
know that you were in a place where putting a man to death was
still regarded as a solemn and exceptional event. It made all the
difference; it was, as a matter of fact, what this war was about. . . .

I was released from Pentonville a few days before Christmas,
1940, equipped with a National Registration Card as proof that I
had regained my identity, and the right to exist.

At this point ends this typical case-history of a Central European member of the educated middle classes, born in the first
years of our century.

Thus the autobiography stops in 1940, with its subject's arrival

---

*This execution was actually described by Pierrepoint, the hangman, in his
evidence before the Royal Commission on Capital Punishment. See Reflections
on Hanging, ch. I.

and settling down in England. It has, however, an epilogue, in which I tried to describe the effects which this metamorphosis of a Continental into an English writer had on me. The motto of the epilogue, quoted from an essay by the former Literary Editor of the New Statesman and Nation, accurately reflects the attitude of the English literary élite to the intruder; though it is only fair to add that others gave him a most generous welcome.

The Invisible Writing: Epilogue

"Of living English novelists I like Koestler the best." This was said to me recently by a friend in France, where *Darkness at Noon* has, in translation, enjoyed a sensational success. "He is wonderfully living," I answered, "but he is not English; he is not a novelist; and how far is he, as a writer, even likeable?"

RAYMOND MORTIMER "The Art of Arthur Koestler", *Cornhill*, November, 1946

The day after I was released from Pentonville, I went to the Recruiting Office to enlist in the Army. I was told that it would take about two months before I was called up. I used this interval to write an account of the collapse of France: *Scum of the Earth* – the first book that I wrote in English. When the call up order arrived in the middle of February, I needed just another fortnight to finish the book, and my publisher wrote to the Recruiting Office to ask whether it would be possible to obtain a deferment. The answer he received deserves to be quoted in full:

> No.3 Centre
> London Recruiting Division
> Duke's Road, WC1
> Euston 5741
> 12th February, 1941

Jonathan Cape, Esq.,
Jonathan Cape Ltd,
30 Bedford Square, WC1

re Arthur Koestler

I am in receipt of your letter of the 11th instant contents of which have been noted.

As requested, I am therefore postponing Mr Koestler's calling up, and would suggest that he calls at this Centre when he is at liberty to join His Majesty's Forces.

> Illegible signature
> Major
> A.R.O.

Having read this remarkable document, I was more than ever convinced that England must lose the war. It took me a month instead of a fortnight to finish *Scum of the Earth*; I had already learnt not to hurry, and that it was bad form to appear too eager. The process of growing roots had begun.

Up to this turning point, my life had been a phantom-chase after the arrow in the blue, the perfect cause, the blueprint of Utopia. Now, with unintentional irony, I adopted as my home a country where arrows are only used on dart-boards, suspicious of all causes, contemptuous of systems, bored by ideologies, sceptical about Utopias, rejecting all blueprints, enamoured of its leisurely muddle, incurious about the future, devoted to its past. A country neither of Yogis nor of Commissars, but of potterers-in-the-garden and stickers-in-the-mud, where strikers played soccer with the Police and Socialists wore peer's crowns. I was intrigued by a civilisation whose social norms were a reversal of mine: which admired "character" instead of "brains", stoicism instead of temperament, nonchalance instead of diligence, the tongue-tied stammer instead of the art of eloquence. I was even more intrigued by the English attitude to the outside world, which I summed up in a maxim: "Be kind to the foreigner, the poor chap can't help it." Most of the friendly natives on whom I tried this nodded in modest agreement; so few saw the joke that I began to wonder whether it was a joke after all.

In short, I was attracted by those obvious features of English life which have always fascinated the stranger. But this attraction gradually wore off, and yielded to exasperation with the land of virtue and gloom which England became under the Labour Government of the post-war era. So, at the end of 1947, after seven years in England, I went tramping again. During the next four and half years I lived in France and the United States, and travelled in a number of other countries. It was during this long absence from England that I became conscious of living *abroad*. In England, I felt a stranger – abroad, an Englishman. In 1952, at the age of forty-seven years, I returned to England, and bought a house in one of London's old squares, in which I shall live happily ever after, until the Great Mushroom appears in the skies.

The reasons why all the places where I have lived long before England have now become "abroad" – which is the ultimate test of belonging to a country – are difficult for me to analyse. There is, for instance, language. Since 1940 I have been writing in English, thinking in English, and reading mostly English literature.

Language serves not only to express thought, but to mould it; the adoption of a new language, particularly by a writer, means a gradual and unconscious transformation of his patterns of thinking, his style and his tastes, his attitudes and reactions. In short, he acquires not only a new medium of communication but a new cultural background. For several years, while I thought in English, I continued to talk French, German and Hungarian in my sleep. Now this occurs only rarely.

The process of changing languages is a fascinating one, and as I have gone through it twice (first from Hungarian to German, then from German to English) I hope to give one day a detailed account of the psychological problems that it involves. One curious aspect of it, from the writer's point of view, is what one may call "the rediscovery of the cliché". Every cliché, even the broken heart and the eternal ocean, was once an original find; and when you begin writing and thinking in a new language, you are apt to invent all by yourself images and metaphors which you think are highly original without realising that they are hoary clichés. It is rather like the sad story of the man in a remote village in Russia, who just after the First World War invented a machine with two wheels and a saddle on which a person could ride quicker than he could walk; and who, when he rode to town on his machine and saw that the streets were full of bicycles, fell down and died of shock. Something similar happened to me when I finished the first novel that I wrote in English (*Arrival and Departure*), with a sentence whose poetic ring made me rather proud:

"... at night, under the incurious stars."

It is still there, on the last page of the book, a verbal bicycle.

Another symptom of growing roots is the homesickness that accompanies prolonged absence. I am talking of the kind of homesickness which is not necessarily focused on persons and places, but a rather diffuse nostalgia for a specific human climate. The buffetings of the past by prison guards, policemen and totalitarian bureaucrats have left their scar: an oversensitivity which reacts to slight traces of aggression or mere uncouthness in the casual contacts of the day, as a Geiger counter registers radioactivity in the air. If one is afflicted in this manner, the mood of an hour or a morning is decided by the rudeness of a taxi-driver, the temper of the charwoman, the smile of the traffic-cop, by waiters, telephone operators, the man at the petrol pump, the girl in the department store. One lives immersed in this anonymous mass; it is like a liquid medium through which one moves without being aware of it; yet its temperature and the amount of friction that it offers, constantly influence one's condition and outlook. In this respect, I have found the human climate of England particularly congenial and soothing – a kind of Davos for internally bruised veterans of the totalitarian age. Its atmosphere contains fewer germs of aggression and brutality per cubic foot in a crowded bus, pub, queue or street than in any other country in which I have lived. I felt a growing conviction that, to quote Orwell, "this nation of flower-lovers and stamp-collectors, pigeon-fanciers, amateur carpenters, coupon-snippers, darts-players and crossword-puzzle fans" lived, in its muddled ways, closer to the text of the invisible writing than any other.

"If I find Mr Koestler's writing unlikeable, it is because he accepts as normal what I believe and hope is abnormal," wrote Mr Raymond Mortimer in an essay from which I quote again, because he seems to me fairly representative of the general attitude of men of letters in his country and generation. I can see their point on the question of likeableness only too well, but on the question of what is *normal* I disagree with them. For the life that I have described was indeed, up to 1940, the typical case-history of a Central European member of the intelligentsia in the totalitarian age. It was entirely normal for a writer, an artist, politician or teacher with a minimum of integrity to have several narrow escapes from Hitler and/or Stalin; to be chased and exiled, and to get acquainted with prisons and concentration camps. It was by no means abnormal for them, in the early 'thirties, to regard Fascism as the main threat, and to be attracted, in varying degrees, by "the great social experiment" in Russia. Even today, about one quarter of the electorate in France and Italy regard it as "normal" to vote for the Communist Party. Even today the displaced persons, the scum of the earth of the post-war era, number several millions. Finally, it was quite normal for six million European Jews to end their lives in a gas chamber.

The awareness that the first thirty-five years of my life were a typical sample of our time, and the chronicler's urge to preserve the sample, were my main reasons for writing these memoirs. Yet the majority of well-meaning citizens of the country in which I

live, believe and hope that prisons and firing squads and gas
chambers and Siberian slave camps just "do not happen" to
ordinary people unless they are deliberately looking for trouble.
This protective filter of the mind which, when reality becomes too
shocking, only allows a thin trickle of it to pass, has its useful
function in keeping us all sane; yet at times it can become rather
exasperating. In 1943, the literary monthly *Horizon* published a
chapter from *Arrival and Departure* which described an episode
in the mass-killings. I received a number of letters, some of them
accusing me of atrocity-mongering to satisfy my morbid imagination; others naïvely asking whether or not the episode had some
factual basis. I had just received the news that several members of
my family were among the victims, and this may explain the
following outburst:

*A collective Answer to some Inquiries.**

Dear Sir
In your letter you asked me the idiotic question whether the events
described in *The Mixed Transport* were "based on fact" or "artistic
fiction".

   Had I published a chapter on Proust and mentioned his homo-
sexuality, you would never have dared to ask a similar question,
because you consider it your duty "to know" although the evidence of
this particular knowledge is less easily accessible than that of the
massacre of three million humans. You would blush if you were found
out not to have heard the name of any second-rate contemporary
writer, painter or composer; you would blush if found out having
ascribed a play by Sophocles to Euripides; but you don't blush and you
have the brazenness to ask whether it is true that you are the contemporary of the greatest massacre in recorded history.

   If you tell me that you don't read newspapers, White Books,
documentary pamphlets obtainable at W. H. Smith bookstalls – why
on earth do you read *Horizon* and call yourself a member of the
intelligentsia? I can't even say that I am sorry to be rude. There is no
excuse for you – for it is your duty to know and to be haunted by your
knowledge. As long as you don't feel, against reason and independently of reason, ashamed to be alive while others are put to death; not
guilty, sick, humiliated because you were spared, you will remain
what you are, an accomplice by omission.

Yours truly,
A.K.

*Horizon, December 1943.

I am quoting this grossly unfair letter, written under emotional strain, because it shows that the process of acclimatisation was not quite as smooth and idyllic as it might appear from the preceding pages; and that has remained true to this day. The smug contentment that I feel each time I arrive at the Passport Control at Dover, joining the queue which says "For British Subjects" and casting a cold eye at the queue "For Foreigners" (the poor chaps can't help it), alternates with moods of impatience and fits of exasperation. But a relationship without ambivalence would be lacking in spice.*

The irony of this relationship is reflected in the sales figures of my books, which are proportionately lower for England than for any other country including Iceland. However, I have gradually become reconciled to the fact that in England I am read only by highbrows, and even by them only as a penance. For I realise that the reasons why the English find my books unlikeable are to be found in precisely that lotus-eating disposition which attracts me to them. Their supreme gift of looking at reality through a soothing filter, their contempt for systems and ideologies, is reflected in their dislike of the *roman a thèse*, the political and ideological novel, of anything didactic and discursive in art, of any form of literary sermonising. In addition to this native trend, English literary criticism has, since the collapse of the "socially conscious" literature of the 'thirties, developed what seems to me an ultra-Flaubertian tendency – "Flaubertian" in a sense in which the author of *Bouvard et Pécuchet* never was one. It was largely because of this trend that Orwell, too, remained a lifelong outsider in his country, though he came from solid British stock, and not from Budapest; even H. G. Wells died in the literary doghouse.

On the whole, I find life in the doghouse quite cosy, and at any rate a good cure for one's vanity – which, when one thinks one has purged and cauterised it finally out of one's system, pops up again like intermittent fever.

---

*Let me remind the reader that the above was written in 1953. In subsequent years, the "moods of impatience and exasperation" steadily increased and occasionally gained the upper hand – see for instance Reflections on Hanging (1955) and Suicide of a Nation? (1963).

Chapter 18

THE YOGI AND THE COMMISSAR

There ought to be a corollary to Parkinson's Law: "the less time you have, the more work you can fit into it". The war kept everybody in England busy – or turned them into busybodies, the two often being undistinguishable. I had a spell in the Pioneer Corps (at the time the only unit in the British Army in which foreigners could enlist), "Digging for Victory" as the recruiting posters said, i.e., building road blocks, digging trenches and other 1914 style earthworks against the expected Panzer invasion; then travelling all over the country as an Army lecturer to somnolent audiences. Later I worked for the Ministry of Information, wrote scripts for propaganda films, radio programmes for the BBC, and leaflets to be dropped by the RAF on Germany; and also did my night stints as an Air Raid Warden and Auxiliary Ambulance Driver. In between these meritorious contributions to the War Effort I wrote Arrival and Departure, *and a number of articles or essays for the* New York Times Magazine, Horizon, Tribune, *etc., of which a selection appeared in* The Yogi and the Commissar – And Other Essays *(1945). The extracts in this chapter are taken from that volume.*

From the Preface to the Dabube edition (1965):

On re-reading these essays after twenty years or more, they appear inevitably dated, though some of them have kept a tenuous hold on life by popping up from time to time in various anthologies. The key pieces represent a kind of parallel commentary on the themes that dominate the trilogy of novels – *The Gladiators,*

Darkness at Noon, Arrival and Departure – which I completed
about the time when some of these essays were written.

The essays include some forecasts of political trends (such as
the Cold War and the division of Europe) which at the time were
indignantly and almost unanimously rejected in the euphoria of
approaching victory. And yet it required no prophetic gifts, only a
sober assessment of the facts, to draw the obvious conclusions.

Not all the essays in The Yogi and the Commissar *are political.
Several are devoted to literary criticism, but into these, too, politics intrude – as shown, for instance, by the following lecture read
to the International PEN Congress in London, 1941. It is at the
same time a thinly veiled attack on the aestheticist, pseudo-
Flaubertian attitudes of the English literary establishment –
alluded to in the previous chapter – which was smugly reasserting itself, in the middle of the war, after the collapse of the
pseudo-Marxist movement ("Auden–Isherwood–Spender") of
the 'thirties:*

The Novelist's Temptations

One of the great Russians – I think it was Turgenev – could only
write with his feet in a bucket of hot water under his desk, facing
the open window of his room. I believe that this position is typical
for the novelist. The hot water bucket stands for inspiration, the
subconscious, the creative source, or whatever you like to call it.
The open window stands for the world outside, the raw material
for the artist's creation.

The strongest temptation which the world outside the window
exerts on the writer is to draw the curtains and close the shutters.
Now this apparently so simple reaction has various interesting
aspects. Perhaps the most dangerous one is that the gesture seems
so natural. The writer needs concentration; his nerves are easily
upset. He must make an immense and ever-renewed effort to bear
the open window, to let those piercing screams into the room, the
laughter, the groaning, and those ephemeral battle cries.

Another aspect of the temptation to close the window is that it
does not at all resemble the traditional form of temptation, but
rather the opposite. The tempter does not appeal to base mortal
desires but to the loftiest regions of the spirit. His lures are: Peace,
Beauty, perhaps even communion with God. The fiend does not

ask you for your soul, he wants to make you a gift of it. He whispers: "Shut the window. The world is a hopeless case. Action is evil. Responsibility is evil. Draw the curtains, forget those savage battle cries, fill your ears with stillness, and bathe your smarting eyes in the dim light of eternity."

Behind the closed shutters strange and sometimes beautiful constructions come to life, the growths of the hothouse, plots and characters hatched in the hothouse. The ivory tower was only one passing form of closed-shutter-interior. There are others; for the decoration of the room with the drawn curtains is subject to the fashions of the time, although fashion and time itself are supposed to be locked out. The ivory tower was an aesthete's creation; others are modelled on moral principles. Their inhabitants don't fiddle while Rome burns, they pray. The room with the drawn curtains may be changed into the nave of a cathedral where the bearded Russian novelist sings hymns of atonement for his revolutionary past; or a sort of introspective deep-sea-aquarium populated by monsters in phosphorescent light; or the padded cell. The latest transformation seems to be an exotic hermitage fit for Yogi exercises. So much for Temptation No. 1.

In Temptation No. 2 the action of the open window on the novelist is experienced not in the form of pressure but of suction. The man behind his desk is tempted, not to close the shutters but to lean right out of the window. He is so fascinated by the events in the street that he begins to gesticulate, shout, and declaim. Before, we had the case of an unimpaired creative force, but no vision of reality; here we have the case of raw vision undigested by the creative process. In leaning too far out of the window our author has taken his feet out the hot water bucket; in technical terms, he has ceased to be a novelist and has become a reporter. The Pink Decade was a period in which novels read like dispatches by war correspondents from the fronts of the class struggle.

Apparently it is very difficult to keep the window open and your feet in the hot water bucket at the same time. Therefore most novelists adopt a compromise, and this compromise is the essence of Temptation No. 3.

In this case the curtains are closed, but the novelist has made a small circular hole in the fabric, with a telescope pushed through, focused on a house and a garden, and a girl with a bunch of roses in her hand, waiting for her betrothed. She is not necessarily the wish-dream-girl of suburban circulating libraries – she may be a very sophisticated young lady with, in her free hand, a volume of

Proust. "Isn't she lovely?" asks our author – who may be a very good author recommended by the Book Society. "Isn't she *alive*? Her name is Sylvia." And indeed we must admit that garden, girl, and roses are perfectly lifelike in spite of the fact that they were produced by the hole-in-the-curtain method. We watch them with admiration until about page twenty-five; and then we horrify the author with the question: "Excuse me, but haven't you forgotten the factory chimney in the background, the splitting of the atom, and the concentration camps?" "Are you crazy?" retorts our author. "Do you expect me to drag a German refugee into my picture, with scars on his back?"

The answer, of course, is that we do not want to *drag* anything into the picture. But there is an alternative in our minds which does require an answer: either Sylvia knows about the concentration camps and still goes on standing there with roses in her hand – then this adds an important feature to her character, not necessarily a derogatory feature, but an important one. Or she has never heard or read about them, then this again gives us a clue. And these clues are essential because they show us her relations, or absence of relations, to the essential facts of her time. But these essentials being shielded from the author by the curtain with the one tiny hole – how can he show her to us in true perspective? We do not miss the factory chimney in the picture – we miss it in the author's mind. It is the author's ignorance of what is going on behind the veiled parts of the window which deprives the picture of its width and depth, of perspective and proportion, and which makes me feel that the longer we look at the young lady in her garden, the more she resembles a figure at Madame Tussaud's.

The perfect novel, then, indeed presupposes that the author should have an all-embracing knowledge of the essential currents of his time. This knowledge is not for actual use – that would produce an encyclopaedia, not a novel. It is for use by implication. It has to act as a catalytic agent, as the saliva in the process of creative assimilation.

But is not all this rather abstract? In hundreds of novels, with some quite good novels among them, the young lady still stands triumphantly in her garden and still clasps those roses in her outstretched hand. Our objection to her is that the author did not, or did not want to, see her in the perspective of her environment, the world of the split atom and the flame-throwers. But what if the narrow surroundings which conditioned her character bear in fact no relation whatever to those unpleasant events which we obstinately call the essentials? Do not millions of Sylvias exist unscorched by flame-throwers and the problems of their time? And is it not possible to write quite good books about them?

Let us imagine a human being living on an island isolated from the rest of the world, and with no knowledge of the rest of the world. His *real* character is conditioned by his immediate environment. Yet as a character in a novel the most interesting thing about him will be his ignorance of the world. We see him in the specific novel-perspective: that is, *we know more about him than he knows about himself.* We have included in our vision the background of towns, mountains, and rivers unknown to him. In other words: his character in the novel is conditioned not by his island-surroundings alone, but by distant surroundings with which he has no point of contact whatsoever. And are the concentration camps less real or significant than the rivers and mountains?

The novelist's quality depends on the width and depth of his vision. His window has to be filled with an all embracing view even if his subject is only a garden with a girl in it. His ears have to be filled with the harmonies and discords of the great symphony, even if his attention is concentrated on the voice of a single flute. "Where there is hope in the air he will hear it; where there is agony about he will feel it" (C. Day Lewis).

Being a contemporary of ours, what he feels will be mainly agony. When I think of the species Novelist, I am always reminded of certain strange practices of the Australian white ant. The normal ants of this species are not able to benefit by the food within their reach owing to an insufficiency of their digestive apparatus. They would all die of starvation but for the existence of certain specialised workers who gather the harvest, select, devour and digest the food, and feed all the others, the queen, the workers, and the winged adults, with the contents of their stomachs. In some species these workers never leave the nest; they hang head downwards in the dark vaults and tunnels of the termitary, and in the absence of other receptacles become living reservoirs, cisterns, honey-pots – with enormous elastic, distended bellies into which the harvest is poured, to be pumped out when folk are hungry.

Hanging head downwards in the dark vaults of our termitary, feeding warriors and winged adults with the assimilated products of a bitter and poisonous harvest, the artist of today is inclined towards rather sinister thoughts. At times he feels as if he were the only adult surrounded by beings still at the stage of befouling themselves. Hence his urge and duty in a world where nobody is well: *the duty not to accept.*

In fact all the temptations I mentioned have a common denominator: the temptation to accept. To close the window *pour embrasser l'absolu*, means to accept the madness outside as incurable, to shirk responsibility. To leave the window ajar and hide the more unpleasant sights means acceptance by complacency. Complacency is passive complicity, and in this sense all art is propaganda, by omission or commission. But only in this sense. Conscious propaganda means the artist's abdication and is only another form of escape – into the happy fields of dilettantism where all problems are easily solved.

The artist is no leader; his mission is not to solve but to expose, not to preach but to demonstrate. The healing, the teaching and preaching he must leave to others; but by exposing the truth by special means unavailable to them, he creates the emotional urge for healing.

The title of the collection refers to two essays, "The Yogi and the Commissar I" and "The Yogi and the Commissar II", which are the first and the last items in that volume. The first – from which the excerpt that follows is taken – intends to be no more than a dramatisation of a fundamental problem of our time, without offering any solutions:

The Yogi and the Commissar I*

I like to imagine an instrument which would enable us to break up patterns of social behaviour as the physicist breaks up a beam of rays. Looking through this sociological spectroscope we would see spread out under the diffraction grating the rainbow-coloured spectrum of all possible human attitudes to life. The whole distressing muddle would become neat, clear and comprehensible.

At one end of the spectrum, obviously on the infra-red end, we would see the Commissar. The Commissar believes in Change from Without. He believes that all the pests of humanity, includ-

*First published in *Horizon* (London), June 1942.

ing constipation and the Oedipus complex, can and will be cured by Revolution, that is, by a radical reorganisation of the system of production and distribution of goods; that this end justifies the use of all means, including violence, ruse, treachery and poison; that logical reasoning is an unfailing compass and the Universe a kind of very large clockwork in which a very large number of electrons once set in motion will forever revolve in their predictable orbits; and that whosoever believes in anything else is an escapist. This end of the spectrum has the lowest frequency of vibrations and is, in a way, the coarsest component of the beam; but it conveys the maximum amount of heat.

At the other end of the spectrum, where the waves become so short and of such high frequency that the eye no longer sees them, colourless, warmthless but all-penetrating, crouches the Yogi, melting away in the ultra-violet. He has no objection to calling the universe a clockwork, but he thinks that it could be called, with about the same amount of truth, a musical-box or a fishpond. He believes that the End is unpredictable and that the Means alone count. He rejects violence under any circumstances. He believes that logical reasoning gradually loses its reliability as a compass as the mind approaches the magnetic pole of the Absolute, which alone matters. He believes that nothing can be improved by exterior organisation and everything by individual effort from within; and that whosoever believes in anything else is an escapist. He believes that the debt-servitude imposed upon the peasants of India by the money-lenders should be abolished not by financial legislation but by spiritual means. He believes that each individual is alone, but attached to the all-one by an invisible umbilical cord; that his creative forces, his goodness, trueness and usefulness can only be nourished by the sap which reaches him through this cord; and that his sole task during his earthly life is to avoid any action, emotion or thought which might lead to a breaking of the cord. This avoidance has to be maintained by a difficult, elaborate technique, the only kind of technique which he accepts.

Between these two extremes are spread out in a continuous sequence the spectral lines of the more sedate human attitudes. The more we approach its centre, the more blurred and woolly the spectrum becomes. On the other hand, this increase of wool on the naked spectral bodies makes them look more decent, and intercourse with them more civilised. You cannot argue with a naked Commissar — he starts at once to beat his chest and next he strangles you, whether you be friend or foe, in his deadly embrace. You cannot argue with the ultra-violet skeleton either, because words mean nothing to him. You can argue with post-war planners, Fabians, Quakers, liberals and philanthropists. But the argument will lead nowhere, for the real issue remains between the Yogi and the Commissar, between the fundamental conceptions of Change from Without and Change from Within.

It is easy to say that all that is wanted is a synthesis – the synthesis between saint and revolutionary; but so far this has never been achieved. What has been achieved are various motley forms of compromise – the blurred intermediary bands of the spectrum – compromise but not synthesis. Apparently the two elements do not mix, and this may be one of the reasons why we have made such a mess of our History. The Commissar's emotional energies are fixed on the relation between individual and society, the Yogi's on the relation between the individual and the absolute. Again it is easy to say that all that is wanted is a little mutual effort. One might as well ask a fish to make a little effort towards becoming a bird, and vice versa. . . .

So much for "The Yogi and the Commissar I".

"The Yogi and the Commissar II" was written two years later (in 1944) and belongs to an altogether different category. It proposes not only some tentative answers to the dilemma dramatised in the first essay, but also to some other ethical and philosophical problems which will be discussed at greater length and more thoroughly in Book Two of this selection. Thus it would be pointless to quote excerpts from "The Yogi and the Commissar II" in the present context, but I would like to mention that this essay contains the seeds of most of the theories developed in later works.

To return to the realities of the war: three articles written in 1943–4 for the New York Times Sunday Magazine are reprinted in The Yogi and the Commissar under the heading "Exhortations". The following brief extracts are perhaps of a certain period interest: they reflect the feeling of helplessness while confronted with evil on an unprecedented scale in the present – and facing another, no less fearful threat in the future.

On Disbelieving Atrocities*

There is a dream which keeps coming back to me at almost regular intervals; it is dark, and I am being murdered in some kind of thicket or brushwood; there is a busy road at no more than ten yards' distance; I scream for help but nobody hears me, the crowd walks past, laughing and chatting. . . .

We, the screamers, have been at it now for about ten years. We started on the night when the epileptic van der Lubbe set fire to the German Parliament; we said that if you don't quench those flames at once, they will spread all over the world; you thought we were maniacs. At present we have the mania of trying to tell you about the killing of the total Jewish population of Europe. So far three million have died. It is the greatest mass-killing in recorded history; and it goes on daily, hourly, as regularly as the ticking of your watch. I have photographs before me on the desk while I am writing this, and that accounts for my emotion and bitterness. People have died to smuggle them out of Poland; they thought it was worth while. But the other day I met one of the best-known American journalists over here. He told me that in the course of some recent public opinion survey nine out of ten average American citizens, when asked whether they believed that the Nazis commit atrocities, answered that it was all propaganda lies, and that they didn't believe a word of it. As to this country, I have been lecturing now for three years to the troops, and their attitude is the same. . . . And meanwhile the watch goes on ticking. What can the screamers do but go on screaming, until they get blue in the face?

Knights in Rusty Armour †

I have been asked by the editor of this paper to write an article, "based on personal experience, on what gives men faith to fight to the end for the democratic way". I quote the question because I feel that, in a negative form, it contains in itself part of the answer. Most of the men whom I have seen dying or going to their death on battlefields, in hospitals, prisons and concentration camps since Badajoz certainly did not part from life out of enthusiasm for an abstract "democratic way". Take one of the great epics of this war:

*New York Times, January, 1944.
†New York Times, January, 1943.

the tiny Greek army, of which nobody ever heard before, beating up Mussolini's crack regiments. It was almost a miracle – and yet the Greeks fought under the Fascist dictatorship of the late Metaxas, a tyranny so stupid and narrow that it put Plato's *Republic* on the list of forbidden books. Again, take the latest miracle, the defence of Stalingrad. We look with humility, gratitude and admiration at the men and women of the Soviet State. Those who try to divide us from them are playing Hitler's game; but those who pretend that Uncle Joe Stalin's ways are democratic ways either are trying to be very clever or are just innocent fools. . . .

The Fraternity of Pessimists*

In this war we are fighting against a total lie in the name of a half-truth. This is a more modest formulation than those currently used, but if we tentatively accept it, the present will probably appear less confused and the future less depressing.

We call Nazism's New Order a total lie because it denies the specific ethos of our species, because by proclaiming that might is right it reduced Civil Law to Jungle Law, and by proclaiming that race is all it reduced Sociology to Zoology. With such a philosophy there can be no compromise.

We, on the other hand, live in a climate of half-truths. We fight against Racialism and yet racial discrimination is far from abolished in the Anglo-Saxon countries; we fight for Democracy and yet our mightiest ally is a dictatorship where at least two of the Four Freedoms are not operating. But such is the sticky, all-pervading influence of our climate that even to mention these facts, undeniable though they are, has the effect of a provocation.

"So why rub it in?" some will probably say. "This is a battlefield, not a public confessional." The answer is that on both sides of the Atlantic people are getting more restive the nearer victory approaches. There is a strange mood of uneasiness every-where – the hangover seems to precede the celebration. . . .

As we have seen, The Yogi and the Commissar *was a miscellane-ous collection; but it contained three consecutive essays of altogether one hundred pages, which formed its hard core and*

*New York Times Magazine, November, 1943.

account for its impact on the fellow-travelling intelligentsia in England, France and the United States. The first of these essays, "Anatomy of a Myth", discussed the psychological roots of the progressive Left's willingness to be deceived about the true nature of Stalin's regime; the second, "Soviet Myth and Reality", gave a detailed account, mainly based on official Soviet sources,* (Government decrees, statistics, etc.) of that regime; the third, "The End of an Illusion", from which the following extracts are taken, analysed the methods of Soviet expansionism, foretold the enslavement of Central and Eastern Europe, and the defensive character of Western policy:

Among the three victorious powers Russia represents the most vigorous expansive force. As a world power it arrives on the stage young and full of ruthless dynamism. With its nationalised economy, centralised power, and totalitarian methods, the USSR presents an aspect of massive compactness compared with the loosely knit, extended and decentralised British Empire – rather like a giant battering ram facing the long, crumbling walls and moats of an ancient fortress. This does not mean that the ram will actually attack the wall; it only means that the men behind the ram and the men behind the moat, however amicable their relations, both know at the back of their minds the potentialities of the situation. And these potentialities must inevitably translate themselves into acute pressure.

According to the laws of least resistance, this pressure will be the stronger the more exposed and vulnerable the point of attack: that is, in the Middle East, the Mediterranean and on the Continent of Europe. Expressed by a polite euphemism, the aim of this pressure is to procure "zones of influence". But the definition of this term depends entirely on the balance of forces. Where the balance is nearly equal, such zones merely mean trading facilities and political treaties; e.g., Britain and Portugal. A tilt of the scales, and the same term means the use of airfields and strategic bases; the "zone of influence" has become a satellite country. One further tilt, and we get puppet governments and all but official incorporation into the bigger state: e.g., Japan and Manchukuo. Finally, direct incorporation either by military conquest or by terror referendum: e.g., Eastern Poland and the Baltic States.

*I was much indebted to Mrs Margaret Dewar for her research into the original sources.

When people talk of "expansion", even the politically educated are apt to think in antiquated terms. The Nazis spoke of the Russians as "Asiatic hordes" and tried to scare us with the anachronistic picture of Stalin-Genghis Khan riding with his Cossacks to Boulogne; in Conservative clubland the danger of a Russian conquest of Czechoslovakia is conceived of in the old-fashioned terms of straightforward military conquest. Hence the general incredulity regarding the real perspectives of Russian expansion on the Continent. The possibilities of modern political warfare by internal disruption and vassalisation were by no means exhausted by Hitler and are not yet appreciated in their true significance.

The question "how far Stalin *intends* to go" is naive and meaningless. The expansion of great Empires follows certain dynamic laws. A great power surrounded by a political vacuum will expand its zones of influence until it feels a growing pressure of resistance. There is no possibility of saturation in a vacuum.

To repeat what I said in the Preface – it required no prophetic gifts, only a sober assessment of the facts, to draw the obvious conclusions. Yet it was precisely the will to get at the facts which was lacking, in particular among liberals and the Left. To mention an example, characteristic of the political climate among French intellectuals at the time – the late war and early post-war years: Sartre's monthly, Les Temps Modernes, *published a series of articles under the title* Le Yogi et le Prolétaire *(a polemical paraphrase of* The Yogi and the Commissar). *The author of the series, which was later published as a book,* was Professor Merleau-Ponty, successor to Henri Bergson's Chair of Philosophy at the Collège de France. The author defended every measure taken by the Soviet regime, including the Stalin-Hitler alliance, as Historic Necessity, condemned Anglo-American policy as Imperialist Aggression, and denounced criticism of the Soviet regime as "an implicit act of war".†*

On a less exalted level, the attacks in Communist Party publications were more personal and virulent. An example of this category was Jean Kannapa's book Le Traître et le Prolétaire – ou l'Entreprise Koestler and Co. Ltd‡ *(another paraphrase of* The

---

*Humanisme et Terreur *(Paris, 1947).*
†*It should be mentioned in fairness that towards the end of his life Merleau-Ponty recanted his views and parted company with Marxism.*
‡*Paris, 1950.*

Yogi and the Commissar). *The next lower level was exemplified by a front-page article in the French CP's weekly paper L'Action, which informed its readers that the little villa in the region of Fontainebleau, which I owned for a while after the war, was a training centre for "Fascist thugs to form a terrorist militia". This was followed up by the Party's Sunday paper Humanité Dimanche, which published a map of the area, obligingly marking the exact location of the villa by an arrow.*

It was inevitable that, as one of the early critics of Stalin's terror regime, I should be branded as a cold warrior. I may as well add that I have worn that brand-mark with pride, as a distinction second only to the tattooed number on the arms of survivors of Nazi concentration camps.

Chapter 19

THE RIGHT TO SAY "NO"

The next collection of essays was The Trail of the Dinosaur, published in 1955. The bulk of it was devoted to the Cold War.

The first item in the collection is the opening talk of a BBC Third Programme series of broadcasts under the ambitious title "The Challenge of our Time". The time was actually the spring of 1947; the euphoria of victory was wearing off, but the most influential among the intellectuals of the West (such as Sartre and Merleau-Ponty in France, and Professor Bernal in England, celebrated as a latter-day Socrates) were, as already said, still loath to part with their illusions about the nature of the Soviet regime. The radio talk provided a welcome opportunity for attacking Bernal's typical "ends-justify-means" approach to ethics.

The Challenge of our Time

I would like to start with a story which you all know, but it will lead us straight to the heart of our problem.

On the 18th of January, 1912, Captain Scott and his four companions reached the South Pole, after a march of sixty-nine days. On the return journey Petty Officer Evans fell ill, and became a burden to the party. Captain Scott had to make a decision. Either he carried the sick man along, slowed down the march and risked perdition for all; or he let Evans die alone in the wilderness and tried to save the rest of his team. Scott took the first course; they dragged Evans along until he died. The delay proved fatal. The blizzards overtook them; Oates, too, fell ill and sacrificed himself; their rations were exhausted; and the frozen bodies of the four men were found six months later only ten miles, or one day's march, from the next depot which they had been unable to reach. Had they sacrificed Evans, they would probably have been saved.

This dilemma, which faced Scott under eighty degrees of latitude, symbolises the eternal predicament of man, the tragic conflict inherent in his nature. It is the conflict between expediency and morality. I shall try to show that this conflict is at the root of our political and social crisis, that it contains in a nutshell the challenge of our time.

Scott had the choice between two roads. Let us follow each of them into their logical extensions. First, the road of expediency, where the traveller is guided by the principle that the End justifies the Means. He starts with throwing Evans to the wolves, as the sacrifice of one comrade is justified by the hope of saving four. As the road extends into the field of politics, the dilemma of Captain Scott becomes the dilemma of Mr Chamberlain. Evans is Czechoslovakia; the sacrifice of this small nation will buy the safety of bigger ones – or so it is hoped. We continue on the straight, logical metal road which now leads us from Munich No. 1 to Munich No. 2: the Hitler–Stalin Pact of 1939, where the Poles go the way the Czechs have gone. By that time the number of individual Evanses is counted by the million: in the name of expediency the German Government decides to kill all incurables and mentally deficients. They are a drag on the nation's sledge and rations are running short. After the incurables come those with bad heredity – Gypsies and Jews: six millions of them. Finally, in the name of expediency, the Western democracies let loose the first atomic bombs on the crowded towns of Hiroshima and Nagasaki, and thus implicitly accept the principle of total and indiscriminate warfare which they hitherto condemned. We continue on our logical road, which has now become a steep slope, into the field of party politics. If you are convinced that a political opponent will lead your country into ruin and plunge the world into a new war – is it not preferable that you should forget your scruples and try to discredit him by revelations about his private life, frame him, blacken him, purge him, censor him, deport him, liquidate him? Unfortunately, your opponent will be equally convinced that you are harmful, and use the same methods against you. Thus, the logic of expediency leads to the atomic disintegration of morality, a kind of radio-active decay of all values.

And now let us turn to the second alternative before Scott. This road leads into the opposite direction; its guiding principles are: respect for the individual, the rejection of violence, and the belief that the Means determine the End. We have seen what happened to Scott's expedition because he did *not* sacrifice Evans. And we can imagine what would have happened to the people of India had Mr Gandhi been allowed to have his saintly way of non-resistance to the Japanese invader; or what would have been the fate of this country had it embraced pacifism, and with it the Gestapo with headquarters in Whitehall.

The fact that both roads lead to disaster, creates a dilemma which is inseparable from man's condition; it is not an invention of the philosophers, but a conflict which we face at each step in our daily affairs. Each of us has sacrificed his Evans at one point or another of his past. And it is a fallacy to think that the conflict can always be healed by that admirable British household ointment called "the reasonable compromise". Compromise is a useful thing in minor dilemmas of daily routine; but each time we face major decisions, the remedy lets us down. Neither Captain Scott nor Mr Chamberlain could fall back on a reasonable compromise. The more responsible the position you hold, the sharper you feel the horns of the dilemma. When a decision involves the fate of a great number of people, the conflict grows proportionately. The technological progress of our age has enormously increased the range and consequence of man's actions, and has thus amplified his inherent dilemma to gigantic proportions. This is the reason for our awareness of a crisis. We resemble the patient who hears for the first time, magnified by a loudspeaker, the erratic thundering of his heart.

The dilemma admits no final solution. But each period has to attempt a temporary solution adapted to its own conditions. That attempt has to proceed in two steps. The first is to realise that a certain admixture of ruthlessness is inseparable from human progress. Without the rebellion of the Barons, there would be no Magna Carta; without the storming of the Bastille, no proclamation of the Rights of Man. The more we have moral values at heart, the more we should beware of crankiness. The trouble with some well-meaning ethical movements is that they have so many sectarians and quietists and cranks in their midst.

But the second and more important step is to realise that the End only justifies the Means within very narrow limits. A surgeon is justified in inflicting pain because the results of the operation are reasonably predictable; but drastic large-scale operations on the social body involve many unknown factors, lead to unpredictable results, and one never knows at what point the surgeon's lancet turns into the butcher's hatchet. Or, to change the metaphor: ruthlessness is like arsenic; injected in very small doses it is a stimulant to the social body, in large quantities it is deadly poison. And today we are all suffering from moral arsenic poisoning.

The symptoms of this disease are obvious in the political and social field; they are less obvious but no less dangerous in the field of science and philosophy. Let me quote as an example the opinions of one of our leading physicists, Professor J. D. Bernal. In an article called "Belief and Action" recently published by the *Modern Quarterly*, he says that "the new social relations" require "a radical change in morality", and that the virtues "based on excessive concern with individual rectitude" need readjustment by a "change from individual to collective morality". "Because collective action is the only effective action, it is the only virtuous action," says Professor Bernal. Now let us see what this rather abstract statement really means. The only practical way for Tom, Dick or Harry to take "effective collective action" is to become a member of an army, political party or movement. His choice will be determined (a) by his nationality, and (b) by his political opinions or prejudices. Once he has joined the collective of his choice, he has to subordinate his "individual rectitude" to the interests of the group or party. This is precisely what, for instance, the accused in the Belsen Trial did. Their excuse was that they had to service the gas chambers and push the victims into them out of loyalty to their party, because their individual responsibility was subordinated to collective responsibility. Counsel for the Defence of Irma Greese could have quoted verbatim Professor Bernal's reflections on ethics – though politically Bernal is a staunch opponent of Nazism and supports, to quote his own words, "the theories of Marx and the practice of Lenin and Stalin". His article actually contains some reservations to the effect that there should be no question of "blind and obedient carrying out of orders", which, he says, leads to the *Führerprinzip*. He does not seem to have noticed that blind obedience plus the *Führerprinzip* are nowhere more in evidence today than in the Party to which Professor Bernal's sympathies belong. In short, I believe that much confusion could be avoided if some scientists would stick to their electrons.

I am not sure whether what philosophers call ethical absolutes exist, but I am sure that we have to act as if they existed. Words and deeds must again be judged on their own merits and not as mere expedients to serve distant and nebulous aims. These worm-eaten ladders lead to no paradise.

In the spring of 1948, I travelled in the United States on a lecture tour to raise funds for the "International Rescue and Relief Committee", in aid of refugees from totalitarian countries. The following is a compressed version of an ex tempore lecture given in Carnegie Hall, New York, printed in The Trail of the Dinosaur. *Its aggressive tone reflects the speaker's irritation with the naïvety and ignorance of the fellow-travelling American "Progressives", who struck me as a leftist mirror-image of Sinclair Lewis's immortal Babbitt.*

The Seven Deadly Fallacies

The war hysteria from which a considerable number of people seem to suffer here in the United States is not a sign of mature awareness. Nor is the mentality of appeasement. Appeasement of an expanding power creates a fog in which neither of the opponents knows where he is; and so the world slides into war, without either of the opponents wanting it. Appeasement means playing poker; a firm, clearly outlined, principled policy means playing chess.

These are platitudes, the type of platitude which every reader of the *New Republic* or the *New Statesman and Nation* knew by heart in the nineteen-thirties. Today they have forgotten it, and arguing against them means regressing to the kindergarten level. I hope that in this meeting we shall remain at least on the level of the primary school. So I shall take it for granted henceforth that war hysteria and appeasement are our Scylla and Charybdis, and that the liberal's precarious task is to navigate like Ulysses between the two.

Allow me, as an aid to navigation, to point out some of the logical fallacies and emotional eddies in which young idealists frequently get shipwrecked. I have listed for myself seven of them – the seven deadly fallacies of what you may allow me to call Left Babbittism. Here they are:

First is the *confusion of Left and East*. Some sections of the reactionary Press are unable or unwilling to distinguish between liberals, New Dealers, Social Democrats and Communists; they

are all damned Reds. Naturally we are indignant at such poisonous imbecility. But the Left itself is partly responsible for this
confusion. The Babbitt of the Left assumes that there is a continuous spectrum stretching from pale pink liberals to red socialists
and so on to infra-red Communists. It is time that he got it into his
head that Moscow is not to his left but to his east. The Soviet
Union is not a socialist country, and Cominform policy is not
socialist policy. So let us bear in mind that "East is east and Left is
left" and if the twain sometimes still meet, the meeting is purely
coincidental.

The second fallacy is the *soul-searching fallacy*. The other day
there was a press conference at which I mentioned that the frightened people in Italy and France look upon you Americans as their
only hope of salvation, both from the economic point of view,
and from the military point of view. Thereupon one of the repor-
ters present said, "Do you really believe that we can help Europe
with our dirty hands?" I asked: "What do you mean by 'dirty
hands'?" He said: "Well, I mean our policy in Greece, and in
Palestine, and backing up Franco, and the way we treat Negroes
and Jews. We are dirty all over, and when we pose as defenders of
democracy it is sheer hypocrisy."

The answer to this fallacy is to project the argument back to
1938. Then it would have run as follows: "We have no right to
fight Hitler's plan of sending the Jews to the gas chambers so long
as there are 'restricted' hotels in America and so long as Negroes
do not have absolute equality here. Once American democracy
has become a perfect democracy, then and then only shall we have
a right to defend what remains of Europe. And if Europe goes to
the dogs before we have finished, that's just too bad and cannot be
helped."

Third, and closely related to the soul-searching fallacy, is the
fallacy of the false equation. Its European version runs: "Soviet
totalitarianism is bad. American imperialism is equally bad.
There is nothing to choose between them, so let us stay in No
Man's Land." To prove that the American system is "just as bad"
as the Russian system, to make the two sides of the equation
balance, your purist has recourse to half-conscious little subter-
fuges. He equates the Hollywood purges with the Moscow purges.
He has never lived under a totalitarian regime, so when he draws
comparisons he does not know what he is talking about. His
conscience is in revolt against the appalling slums of Chicago, in
which the Negro workers of the slaughter-house industry live like

rats. I have spent a few days in Chicago, and I was appalled by what I saw and heard and smelled. Do not think I am a naïve tourist, a romantic admirer of your system. But now compare your treatment of racial minorities at its worst, with the Soviet treatment of the minorities of the Crimean Republic, the Chechen Republic, the Volga-German Republic, whose total populations were deported because they had, as the official Soviet communiqué said, "Proved themselves unreliable during the war". Even the babes in their cradles were unreliable and had to go to Siberia. In Chicago I saw men on strike, and sympathised with them. In Russia strikes, or incitement to strike, are qualified as high treason and punished by the maximum penalty. In American elections political machines corrupt and distort the People's will. In Russian elections 99½ per cent vote for the one official list – the remaining ½ per cent presumably being in bed with influenza. Your enlightened Babbitt equates an imperfect democracy with a perfect totalitarian regime; his philosophy boils down to the maxim that there is nothing to choose between a flea-bite and leprosy.

Fallacy number four is the *anti-anti attitude*. It runs: "I am not a Communist. In fact, I dislike Communist politics, but I don't want to be identified with anti-Communist witchhunting. Hence I am neither a Communist nor an anti-Communist, but an anti-anti-Communist. If William Randolph Hearst says that twice two is four, I shall automatically hold that twice two is five, or at least four and a half."

Don't laugh, for the roots of this fallacy are very deep in all of us, myself included. I remember how painful it was when a doddering elder in a London club walked up to me and said with a tap on my shoulder: "Well, young man, I am glad that at last you have come round to see reason. I myself knew twenty-five years ago what Bolshevism means, and it's never too late to repent."

You can't help this sort of thing; you can't help people being right for the wrong reasons. In the last war we fought in the name of democracy in an alliance with Dictator Metaxas of Greece, Dictator Chiang Kai-shek and Dictator Stalin. But there is a fundamental difference between a war-time alliance, and political identification with one's allies. Being allied to Chiang did not mean that we wished to imitate the Chinese regime. Being against our will in one camp with the Hearst press or Senator McCarthy does not mean that we identify ourselves with their ideas and methods. This fear of finding oneself in bad company is not an expression of political purity; it is an expression of a lack of self-confidence. If you are sure of yourself – politically and ideologically – you will no longer be frightened to say that twice two makes four, even if Colonel McCormick says the same.

Fallacy number five is the *sentimental fallacy*. For years we were allied to the Russians in the struggle against Nazism, and now when we have to part company, the roots of past loyalty are difficult to tear out. Our bedfellows of yesterday do not share this sentimental squeamishness. Over the slightest disagreement they will denounce us as Fascists, traitors and cannibals. These emotional ties are one-way ties.

Fallacy number six is the *fallacy of the perfect cause*. It is related to number two, the soul-searching fallacy. Only absolutely clean hands have a right to reach out to protect and save what remains of Europe. Only an absolutely perfect cause is worth fighting for. And the search for the perfect cause becomes an excuse for quietism.

History knows no perfect causes, no situation of white against black. Eastern totalitarianism is black; its victory would mean the end of our civilisation. Western democracy is not white but grey. To live, even to die for a perfect cause is a luxury permitted to few. In 1942 or 1943 I published an article which began with the words: "In this war we are fighting a total lie in the name of a half-truth." The total lie was Hitler's New Order. The half-truth was our democracy. Today we face a similar emergency and a similar predicament. Once more the choice before us is merely that between a grey twilight and total darkness. But ask the refugees who manage to escape, at the risk of their lives, from behind the Iron Curtain into our grey twilight world whether this choice is worth fighting for. They know. You don't.

The last fallacy, number seven, is the *confusion between short-term and long-term aims*. It is the most dangerous of all. By long-term aims I mean the age-old struggle for reform, for social justice, for a more equitable system of government. By short-term aims I mean the necessity of fighting an immediate emergency.

The danger of confusion is twofold. Your leftist Babbitt may refuse to fight against the short-term emergency until he has finished the job of creating a perfect government in his own country, in a century or two. The opposite danger is to become so obsessed with the immediate emergency, that all principles of the long-term struggle are thrown overboard. Ex-Communists and disappointed radicals are in particular danger of toppling over to the second extreme. It is essential that we should keep in mind that there are two distinct levels involved in our struggle; that to defend our system against a deadly threat does not imply acceptance of everything in this system, does not imply giving up the long-term fight to improve it; and vice versa, that our criticism of the shortcomings of this system does not free us from the duty to defend it, despite its ambiguous greyness, against the total corruption of the human ideal.

This talk was mainly addressed to the progressive Left. I may have been harsh to the Left Babbitt; it was a brotherly harshness. To the Babbitt of the Right I have nothing to say; we have no language in common.

The power-vacuum which two world wars have created in Central and Western Europe, has inescapably linked your fate with that of the European Continent. I feel the enormous burden which is falling on your shoulders. For there will either be a *Pax Americana* in the world, or there will be no pax. Never has such a burden and such a responsibility been borne by any single nation in history. It is the more unfair to you as yours is an adolescent civilisation, with adolescent enthusiasms and adolescent pimples. The task of the progressive intelligentsia of your country is to help the rest of the nation to face its enormous responsibilities. It is time for the American liberal to grow up.

In June, 1950, at the height of the Cold War (or, more correctly, the First Cold War) an impressive gathering of several hundred writers, scholars and scientists took place in Berlin: the Congress for Cultural Freedom, under the patronage of Bertrand Russell, Benedetto Croce, John Dewey, Karl Jaspers and Jacques Maritain.

The Congress was held shortly after the end of the Russian blockade; it was intended as a kind of intellectual air-lift, a demonstration of Western solidarity with the brave and battered outpost of Berlin, a hundred miles behind the Iron Curtain.

The extract which follows is the text of the address delivered (in German) to the opening session of the Congress, June 25, 1950, first printed in The Trail of the Dinosaur:

Two Methods of Action

Since the earliest days, the teachers of mankind have recommended two diametrically opposed methods of action. The first demands that we should refuse to see the world divided into black and white, heroes and villains, friends and foes; that we should distinguish nuances, and strive for synthesis, or at least compromise; it tells us that in nearly all, seemingly inescapable dilemmas there exists a third alternative which patient search may discover. In short, we should refuse the choice between Scylla and Charybdis and rather navigate like Odysseus of the nimble wits. We may call this the *"neither-nor"* attitude.

The second, opposite advice was summed up two thousand years ago, in one single phrase: "Let your communication be, Yea, yea, Nay, nay; for whatsoever is more than these, comes from evil". This we may call the *"either-or"* attitude.

Obviously humanity could not have survived without taking both methods into account. By neglecting the first advice, mankind would long ago have torn itself to pieces. By neglecting the second, man would have forsaken his dignity and moral backbone, and lost his capacity to distinguish between good and evil.

It is equally obvious that each of the two tenets has a different field of application. To enumerate these would be a tedious and pedantic undertaking, and frequently there is conflict between both methods within the same field. Our concern here is with action in the political field. And there it seems that the first method is valid for long-term planning with a certain elbow-room in space and time, and that the second is valid in immediate and vital emergencies when, in Beethoven's words, "Fate knocks at the gate of existence".

In such an emergency, the threatened individual or group or civilisation can only survive if it acts with the unhesitating assurance of an organic reflex. The nerves of living organisms function according to the so-called all-or-nothing law; they either react to a stimulus for all they are worth or do not react at all. And it is not by chance that the calculating machines called electronic brains are constructed according to the same "either-or" principle. They perform immensely complex functions, but each time a decision is required of them, they act according to the Gospel of Matthew.

In vital emergencies like the present, when man stands at a crossroads which only leaves the choice of this way or that, the difference between the very clever and the simple in mind narrows almost to vanishing point, or even turns to the latter's advantage. It is amazing to observe how in a crisis the most sophisticated often act like imbeciles. Imbued with the mental habits of the "neither-nor" attitude, of looking for synthesis or compromise – a profoundly human attitude of essential value in its proper field – they are incapable of admitting, even to themselves, that there are situations in which an unambiguous decision is vital for spiritual and physical survival. Faced with destiny's challenge, they act like clever imbeciles and preach neutrality towards the bubonic plague. mostly they are victims of a professional disease: the intellectual's estrangement from reality. And having lost touch with reality they have acquired that devilish art: they can prove everything that they believe, and believe everything that they can prove. Their logic reminds one of the German students' old nonsense-song:

> The elephant has his tail in front and his trunk is at his rear;
> But when he turns round his trunk is in front and his tail is at his rear.

Don't misunderstand me: I know that many of those who are not here with us today cherish freedom too, and are rather frightened of the fate which might befall them if everybody imitated their attitude of contemplative detachment. It is only that they haven't yet learnt that there is a time to speak in relative clauses, and a time to speak in terms of Yea and Nay. For destiny's challenge to man is always couched in simple and direct language, without relative clauses – and requires an answer in equally simple terms.

The next item is a talk to the political panel session of the Berlin Congress. It is a kind of landmark, for it shows that the pilgrim's regress had gone another stage further: when I renounced Communism more than a decade earlier, I still continued, for some years, to consider myself a Socialist, without worrying too much about a precise definition of the term; but by 1950, as the talk indicates, this was no longer the case.

An Outgrown Dilemma*

The thesis which I wish to put before you is that the antinomies "Socialism and Capitalism", "Left and Right", are rapidly becoming meaningless, and that so long as Europe remains bogged down in these false alternatives which obstruct clear thinking, it cannot hope to find a constructive solution for its problems.

* From The Trail of the Dinosaur

1

The term "Political Left" originated, as you know, with the distribution of factions in the French National Assembly after the Revolution in 1789. At the beginning of the nineteenth century it spread over the Continent and was applied to that section of a country's legislature which sat to the left of the President's chair and was traditionally associated with liberal and democratic opinions. Gradually, the word came to mean the radical or purist or extremist wing of any ideological school or movement, whether liberal and democratic or not. Later on it was used in an even more vague and metaphorical way; and the more it was drained of meaning, the stronger became its emotional appeal. At the beginning of the last war there existed about half a dozen political parties in France, all of them conservative to reactionary in their programme, all of them seated in the right wing of the Chamber of Deputies, and all of them carrying the word "Left" in their names.

I mention this development as a semantic curiosity and because of its relevance to the present situation. For to this day European Liberals and Social-Democrats refer to themselves as "the moderate Left" which, if words are to be taken seriously, must mean that they differ only in degree but not in kind from their neighbours of "the extreme Left". And "the extreme Left" is still regarded as synonymous with the Communist Party, in spite of the fact that virtually every tenet in the Communist credo is diametrically opposed to the principles originally associated with the Left. In short, the term "Left" has become a verbal fetish whose cult sidetracks attention from the real issues. It is at the same time a dangerous anachronism, for it implies the existence of a continuous spectrum between liberal progressives and the worshippers of tyranny and terror. And such is the magic power of words over the mind that European Socialists who think of themselves as "men of the Left" were unconsciously led from a fallacious verbal identification to a real feeling of solidarity with the Communists. They may feel critical or even hostile towards their "extreme" neighbours of the Communist Party; they retain nevertheless an ambivalent neighbourly feeling for them, a conviction of being, after all, "on the same side of the barricades".

A good many American liberals fell into the same emotional trap during the 'thirties and even later. The victim of the witch-hunt supplied the whip which scourged him and became an accomplice in his own perdition. However, the relative safety and prosperity of that continent made the confused American liberal gradually accessible to reality and enabled him to get out of the trap, while a major portion of the French and Italian Left, and a smaller portion of the British, exposed to the neurosis-forming climate of Europe, are still caught in it.

In the past it was always "the Left" who protested loudest against tyranny, injustice, and infringements of human rights. The failure of European "Leftists" and American liberals to lead the fight against the worst regime of terror and despotism in human history created a vacuum on the ideological battlefield. This vacuum was filled by the Christian Democrats in Italy, the Gaullists in France, by Senator McCarthy and his associates in the USA. McCarthyism represents the wages of the American liberals' sins. If today everywhere in the world the parties who claim to represent the "moderate Left" are beaten or in retreat, it is because they were found wanting on the most crucial issue of our time.

2

Europe has developed a political climate in which words can no longer be taken seriously. The ideological chaos created a seman-tic inflation and a semantic black market where words are traded at a meaning-value entirely different from their official quotation: where war is prepared by peace petitions, police states are labelled Popular Democracies, and "Leftism" means benevolent neutrality towards despotism.

At first sight the alternative "Capitalism or Socialism" appears much more concrete and meaningful than "Right or Left". But on closer inspection it will be found that the term "Socialism" has suffered a semantic decay similar to that of the "Left". German National Socialism, Russian Soviet Socialism; French Socialism which is Marxist with a pinch of salt, British Socialism which is Christian, non-Marxist, Fabianist, and heaven knows what, all derive their emotional dynamism from the fetish-power of the same word, attached to quite different meanings.

However, let us leave semantics aside, though it is an essential branch of political hygiene. If we are not too pedantic, we may hope to agree at least on some rough-and-ready definition of what Socialism really means, and on some common denominator for the aspirations of the various existing Socialist parties.

3

Let us turn first to the field of *international* politics. One of the basic elements of Socialist thought, from Spartacus's slave revolt to Thomas More's *Utopia*, from the primitive Christian communities to Marx, is the brotherhood of man. In the past, Socialists have always fought against parochialism, chauvinism, aggressive nationalism and have preached internationalism, cosmopolitanism, the abolition of ideological and political barriers among nations. But do they still?

In the Union of Soviet Socialist Republics the word "cosmopolitan" has become a term of abuse, and chauvinism has reached a hitherto unprecedented peak. At the same time at the recent Paris Congress of the French Communist Party a banner was stretched across the hall which read: "The true internationalist is he who is prepared unreservedly, unhesitatingly, and unconditionally to defend the USSR."

In the *Western* world the only great power with a Socialist Government is Great Britain. The Labour Party won the elections a few weeks after the end of the war in the still strongest country of Europe, and just at the decisive moment when it no longer needed a Socialist training to understand that Europe must unite or perish. Never before in history was Socialism offered such a chance. Yet from the moment it came to power, the Labour Government has deliberately obstructed every effort towards European unity. The non-Socialist Governments of France, Germany and Italy have proved themselves more internationally-minded than the Socialist Government in England.

Of course Britain has a particularly difficult position between the Continent and the Commonwealth; and there are always plausible arguments for avoiding decisions which would require a certain amount of historical imagination. But the essential point is that the victory of British Socialism has not abolished British insularity; it has, on the contrary, strengthened and deepened it. It was Churchill the Conservative, not Attlee the Socialist, who started the United Europe movement which led to the Council of Strasbourg; and when the movement got under way, the Labour Party's attitude to it remained consistently hostile. The reason for this was explained in a statement by the National Executive Committee of the Labour Party issued in June, 1950. "No Socialist government in Europe," the decisive phrase in the statement runs, "could submit to the authority of a [supranational] body whose policies were decided by an anti-Socialist majority."

What this amounts to is simply a mild British version of the Russian "Socialism in One Country" policy. The Russian veto in the United Nations finds its equivalent in the British veto against the political and economic unity of Europe.

It need not be emphasised that there is a world of difference between the British and the Soviet regimes. My comparison refers merely to one specific aspect; the collapse of the cosmopolitan *élan* in the Socialist movement. This process started almost a generation ago, in 1914, and has now reached a stage where we can see the paradoxical phenomenon of capitalist America being prepared to make sacrifices in national sovereignty which Socialist Russia refuses, and of British, French, and German Conservatives pursuing a more internationally-minded policy than their Socialist opposite numbers. In other words, *Socialism has lost its claim to represent the internationalist trend of humanity*. As far as the integration of our world is concerned, the Socialist-Capitalist alternative has become void of meaning.

4

Is it more meaningful when applied to *domestic* policy?

As regards political and intellectual freedom, there is no relevant difference between Socialist Britain and the capitalist United States. And in the domain of unfreedom there is little to choose between Socialist Russia and Fascist Spain. Again the real division cuts across the abstract frontiers between Socialism and Capitalism. Only one field remains where the alternative is apparently still relevant: the *economic* field.

Theoretically there is an unbridgeable gulf between nationalisation of the means of production on the one hand, and private ownership, profits, and exploitation on the other. But in fact recent developments have abolished the static trench-warfare between the classes and have transformed it into a fluid war of movement. As the question is too complex to be treated here in any systematic manner, I must confine myself to a few remarks in shorthand, as it were.

First, even Marx and Engels knew that nationalisation itself is not a panacea. It is useful to recall Frederick Engels's remark that if nationalisation were identical with Socialism, then the first Socialist institution must have been the regimental tailor. In fact, the Soviet workers do not own their nationalised factories any more than the sailors of the Royal Navy own the battleship in which they serve. The people's control over the battleships, railways, factories, coal mines, which they theoretically own, depends entirely on the political structure of the state. In Russia,

where the Trade Unions have ceased to be an instrument of the
working class and have become an instrument for the coercion of
the working class, the theoretical "owners" of the factories and of
the land have less influence over management, and work under
worse conditions, than their comrades in any Western country.
On the other hand, trust managers, factory directors, and "proletarian millionaires" (an official Russian term) form a privileged
class, just as much as and more so than in capitalist countries. To
be sure, their income is called salary and not profit, but again this
distinction is mainly abstract. Nor is, on the other hand, the
factory owner in capitalist countries any longer able to draw
unlimited profits from his enterprise or do with his workers what
he likes. I refer you to James Burnham's analysis of the relevant
changes in the meaning of the term "ownership" in recent times.

Generally speaking, nationalisation without an appropriate
change in political structure leads not to State Socialism but to
State Capitalism. The difference between the two cannot be
defined in economic terms; it is a matter of democratic controls, of
political freedom, and cultural climate. A nationalised economy
in itself may serve as a basis for a totalitarian autocracy of the
Russian type or even for a Fascist regime.

Equally problematic is the question just *how much* nationalisation makes a country socialist or capitalist? British Socialism
nationalised the railways, but France and Germany had state-
owned railways long before. The total nationalisation of all means
of production and distribution has been recognised as unworkable even in Russia. The alternative is no longer nationalisation or
private economy in the abstract; the real problem is to find the
proper balance of state ownership, control, planning, and free
enterprise. And the search for this delicate balance is again not an
abstract but an empirical pursuit. Apparently each nation has to
work out its own formula, for there are many imponderabilia
which enter into the equation.

As an example of the complex reality masked by the "Capitalism versus Socialism" slogan, one may quote food-rationing.
During and after the war, food-rationing – which means state
control of distribution – worked very satisfactorily in puritan
England under Conservative and Socialist governments alike. But
it broke down completely in Italy and France, both countries with
a highly individualistic and resourceful Latin population. Obviously, far-reaching inferences must be drawn from this fact
concerning the balance of state control and free enterprise

appropriate to each of these countries. In short, even in the purely economic sphere we are not dealing with a clear-cut alternative between Capitalism and Socialism, but with a kind of continuous rainbow spectrum whose shape and colour are largely determined by psychological and other factors not contained in Socialist theory.

5

What I have said should not be misinterpreted as an apology for Capitalism or as an attack on Socialism. My point is that this alternative is rapidly becoming as antiquated and meaningless as the dispute between Jansenists and Jesuits or the Wars of the Roses. Nor did I mean to say that it always *was* meaningless. I said it is *becoming* meaningless, because it operates with rigid nineteenth-century conceptions, and does not take into account new realities which have emerged since, and new conflicts which cut across the conventional boundaries.

It is not a novelty in history that a real dilemma which once seemed all-important is gradually drained of its meaning and becomes a pseudo-dilemma as new historical realities emerge. People lost interest in waging wars of religion when national consciousness began to dawn on them. The conflict between republicans and monarchists went out of fashion when economic problems became all-important. The examples could be multiplied. Every period seems to have its specific conflict which polarises the world and serves as an ideological compass – until history passes over it with a shrug; and afterwards people wonder what they were so excited about.

It is a further fact that some of these great ideological conflicts are never decided; they end in a stalemate. In successive centuries it looked as if the whole world would either become Islamic or Christian, either Catholic or Protestant, either republican or monarchist, either capitalist or socialist. But instead of a decision there came a deadlock and a process which one might call *the withering away of the dilemma*. The withering, or draining of meaning, always seems to be the result of some mutation in human consciousness accompanied by a shift of emphasis to an entirely different set of values – from religious consciousness to national consciousness to economic consciousness and so on.

This "and so on" poses a problem which we are unable to answer with certainty. We cannot foretell the nature of the next mutation in the consciousness of the masses, nor the values which will emerge on the next higher level. But we may assume, on the strength of past analogies, that the battle-cries of economic man will appear to his successor just as sterile as the Wars of the Roses appear to us.

Two short remarks in conclusion. First, it is necessary to qualify the statement that the apparently decisive conflicts of a given period tend to end in a stalemate and wither away. This did indeed happen in the past, but only in cases where the forces in the conflict were fairly balanced. Europe remained Christian because the Arabs never got to Paris and the Turks were beaten back at the ramparts of Vienna. There are other, less edifying examples of history solving its dilemmas. The conclusion is obvious.

In the second place, though we cannot foresee the values and spiritual climate of post-economic man, certain conjectures are permissible. While the majority of Europeans are still hypnotised by the anachronistic battle-cries of Left and Right, Capitalism and Socialism, history has moved on to a new alternative, a new conflict which cuts across the old lines of division. The real content of this conflict can be summed up in one phrase: total tyranny against relative freedom. Sometimes I have a feeling in my bones that the terrible pressure which this conflict exerts on all humanity might perhaps represent a challenge, a biological stimulus as it were, which will release the new mutation of human consciousness; and that its content might be a new spiritual awareness, born of anguish and suffering. If that is the case, then we are indeed living in an interesting time.

Manifesto of the Congress for Cultural Freedom

The following "Manifesto", which I drafted at the request of the steering committee of the Congress, was unanimously adopted at the closing session on June 30, 1950. (The words in square brackets were added to the draft by the British members of the editorial committee, Professor A. J. Ayer and Professor Hugh Trevor-Roper.) Its main purpose was to dispel the intellectual confusion created by the Soviet "peace campaigns" (such as the so-called Stockholm Peace Appeal) which served as a smoke-screen for acts of aggression – the Prague coup, the Berlin blockade, etc.

1. We hold it to be self-evident that intellectual freedom is one of the inalienable rights of man.

2. Such freedom is defined first and foremost by his right to hold and express his own opinions, and particularly opinions which differ from those of his rulers. Deprived of the right to say "no", man becomes a slave.

3. Freedom and peace are inseparable. In any country, under any regime, the overwhelming majority of ordinary people fear and oppose war. The danger of war becomes acute when governments, by suppressing democratic representative institutions, deny to the majority the means of imposing its will to peace.

Peace can be maintained only if each government submits to the control and inspection of its acts by the people whom it governs, and agrees to submit all questions immediately involving the risk of war to a representative international authority, by whose decisions it will abide.

4. We hold that the main reason for the present insecurity of the world is the policy of governments which, while paying lip-service to peace, refuse to accept this double control. Historical experience proves that wars can be prepared and waged under any slogan, including that of peace. Campaigns for peace which are not backed by acts that will guarantee its maintenance are like counterfeit currency circulated for dishonest purposes. Intellectual sanity and physical security can only return to the world if such practices are abandoned.

5. Freedom is based on the toleration of divergent opinions. The principle of toleration does not logically permit the practice of intolerance.

6. No political philosophy or economic theory can claim the sole right to represent freedom in the abstract. We hold that the value of such theories is to be judged by the range of concrete freedom which they accord the individual in practice.

We likewise hold that no race, nation, class or religion can claim the sole right to represent the idea of freedom, nor the right to deny freedom to other groups or creeds in the name of any ultimate ideal or lofty aim whatsoever. We hold that the historical contribution of any society is to be judged by the extent and quality of the freedom which its members actually enjoy.

7. In times of emergency, restrictions on the freedom of the individual are imposed in the real or assumed interest of the community. We hold it to be essential that such restrictions be confined to a minimum of clearly specified actions; that they be understood to be temporary and limited expedients in the nature of a sacrifice; and that the measures restricting freedom be themselves subject to free criticism and democratic control. Only thus can we have a reasonable assurance that emergency measures restricting individual freedom will not degenerate into a permanent tyranny.

8. In totalitarian states restrictions on freedom are no longer intended and publicly understood as sacrifices imposed on the people, but are, on the contrary, represented as triumphs of progress and achievements of a superior civilisation. We hold that both the theory and practice of these regimes run counter to the basic rights of the individual and the fundamental aspirations of mankind as a whole.

9. We hold the danger represented by these regimes to be all the greater since their means of enforcement far surpasses that of all previous tyrannies in the history of mankind. The citizen of the totalitarian state is expected and forced not only to abstain from crime but to conform in all his thoughts and actions to a prescribed pattern. Citizens are persecuted and condemned on such unspecified and all-embracing charges as "enemies of the people" or "socially unreliable elements".

10. We hold that there can be no stable world so long as mankind, with regard to freedom, remains divided into "haves" and "have-nots". The defence of existing freedoms, the reconquest of lost freedoms [and the creation of new freedoms], are parts of the same struggle.

11. We hold that the theory and practice of the totalitarian state are the greatest challenge which man has been called on to meet in the course of civilised history.

12. We hold that indifference or neutrality in the face of such a challenge amounts to a betrayal of mankind and to the abdication of the free mind. Our answer to this challenge may decide the fate of man for generations.

13. [The defence of intellectual liberty today imposes a positive obligation: to offer new and constructive answers to the problems of our time.]

14. We address this manifesto to all men who are determined to regain those liberties which they have lost, and to preserve [and extend] those which they enjoy.

*One of the offshoots of the Berlin Congress was a loose network of debating clubs in various French towns, called "Les Amis de la Liberté". The extract which follows is translated from a pamphlet written in French, under the title "Que Veulent les Amis de la Liberté?"** *

First and foremost, we want our civilisation to survive. Two conditions are essential for its survival: freedom and peace. We have put freedom first because peace is a function of freedom. A nation enslaved can at any time be whipped by its leaders into war hysteria and aggression. By isolating their countries behind an Iron Curtain or a Chinese Wall, totalitarian governments can preach pacifism to foreign peoples, and world conquest to their own.

The threat to peace came successively from countries in various degrees of enslavement: militarist Prussia, Fascist Italy, Nazi Germany, Japan, Soviet Russia. Each of these countries has made during the present century successive bids for world conquest in the name of some ideology or secular religion. Each promised some form of Thousand-Year Reich or social paradise as a distant aim. Each time, the professed aim served as a cloak for wars of conquest. Each time, millions of people were led to their destruction in the name of a phantom.

Communism in its present form has become a phantom ideology. It has as little to do with Socialism as the reign of the Borgias had with the teachings of Christ. Our civilisation can only be saved if the hypnotic power of this phantom is broken. This is not a task which any political party or group can achieve alone. It is an operation of mental hygiene which can be accomplished only by a joint effort of the educated classes – of the men in public life, in the arts and letters, in the universities and elementary schools, in the laboratories and editorial offices, in the trade unions and professional organisations – who determine the intellectual climate of the nation. If we fail, we shall become guilty of a new *trahison des clercs*, and the responsibility before history will be ours.

*English text in The Trail of the Dinosaur.

We do not pretend that our democracies are anywhere approaching an ideal state. We are defending our relative freedoms against the total unfreedom of dictatorial regimes. This is not an abstract distinction. Its validity is demonstrated by the mass exodus of persecuted people from the satellite countries to the West. Europe has become a one-way street which points from total slavery to relative freedom. The wretched masses who have left their homes, their goods and chattels, have a bitter knowledge of the reality of our time – a knowledge which a considerable proportion of our intelligentsia is lacking.

The pamphlet continues with a series of "Question and Answers", the last of which strikes a resigned note:

Question: Communism may be a phanton creed – it nevertheless has a strong emotional dynamism, the power of a secular religion. What creed or mystique can you offer which would counteract this force with equal power?

Answer: None. Don't let us have any illusions on this point. We must face our predicament with realism and honesty.

Fanatical mass movements are always at a temporary advantage against the defenders of civilisation. The invading hordes, whether Mongol, Tartar, Fascist, Nazi or Communist, have the advantage of a simple monolithic creed over a complex and divided culture. Neither Capitalist America, nor Socialist Britain, nor Christian-Democrat Italy has been capable of producing a faith with the same dynamism as the Communist phantom-creed. Ours is a defensive battle, as most battles which have saved the continuity of civilisation have been. The difficulty which results from this position is that the freedom which we are defending is taken for granted and not much appreciated by the masses – until they are deprived of it. *Habeas corpus,* civil rights, freedom of expression – nay, such elementary privileges as freedom to change one's job if one so desires, to read newspapers which express opposite opinions, and to travel freely in one's own country – all these do not add up to a militant creed. To quote Matteotti, freedom is like the air you breathe; you only become conscious of it when the rope is round your neck.

We have no panacea to offer to the manifold problems which beset the civilisation we are defending. We do not wish to embark on a crusade. We have learned the tragic lesson of our times; we are conscious of the fact that most crusades in history have ended in disaster and brought only misery and disillusionment in their wake.

To the totalitarian threat and its fanatical creed we oppose an absolute and unconditional No. But our Yes to the civilisation which we are defending leaves full scope for nuances, divergent opinions, social theories and experiment.

A more concrete – and among progressive intellectuals even more unpopular – approach to the problems posed by the Cold War is reflected in the following article (first published in the New York Times Magazine, *October 8, 1950). It was included in the original edition of* The Trail of the Dinosaur *in 1955, but omitted from the Danube edition of 1970, because it seemed to me outdated. Now, another ten years later, I am not so sure that it is:*

For a European Legion of Liberty

Western Europe is a patient in an iron lung. American economic and military aid provide it with oxygen, but it cannot live and breathe by itself. The sickness which paralyses it is not of an economic nature. The cause is both deeper and simpler: Europe has lost faith in itself.

In the larger part of Europe, that civilisation which made its greatness has already been destroyed, and human life degraded to the routine of the penitentiary. The remaining, truncated part is equally doomed – unless there is a radical change in its political and moral climate. This change, or spiritual revival, is the only product which America cannot provide for it. It must come out of Europe itself. In what form?

There is only one way, the obvious way: to replace the people's shattered national consciousness and tottering loyalties to their rulers by a European consciousness and a European loyalty.

In 1940, after the fall of Paris, Winston Churchill proposed the unification of the French and British Empires by a simple stroke of the pen. When the danger was past, the lesson was forgotten. In 1948, after Stalin's seizure of Czechoslovakia, Ernest Bevin declared that Europe must unite or perish. Since then, he and his colleagues have acted as if they had chosen the second alternative. Political federation, we have been told, is premature; it must be preceded by economic integration. But when the Schuman plan of economic integration was presented, it was declared unacceptable because it would entail a sacrifice in political sovereignty. And so it goes on.

Where can we break this vicious circle? The only political reality which has emerged after years of sterile haggling and prostration, is the North Atlantic Pact [NATO]. To the people of Europe this is still an abstract reality. A military alliance in itself is not a factor likely to ignite public imagination. But it could be made into such a factor.

A united European army could be the leaven which ultimately gives rise to a united Europe. It could be the means to by-pass the difficulties, real or imaginary, which at present block the road to political and economic integration. But on one condition only: that the problem of the European army should be approached not from a purely military, but from a psychological angle.

An army can reflect itself in the public mind as an abhorrent war-machine, or as a symbol which arouses the political libido and evokes fervent emotions. The armies of the French and American Revolutions, and the International Brigades in Spain, were such symbols. Is it very paradoxical to suggest that a European army of this type would be the most direct and logical means to restore Europe's faith in itself; to make it re-conquer its pride and dignity; and to fill its people with a new, European consciousness?

The proposal I am going to make is merely an experiment; but an experiment relatively easy to carry out, which does not run counter to any vested national interests, and which, if successful, may produce far-reaching and unexpected results.

The proposal aims at the creation of an élite force, within the framework of the Atlantic Pact and under the direct authority of its supreme command, called the Legion of Liberty. The Legion of Liberty (abbrev. "LL") is to consist of individual volunteers from the eleven West-European nations, and is to be so composed that the various nationalities are mixed together on the lowest level, i.e. that each platoon comprises soldiers from several, and if possible all, nationalities. In other words, instead of being "integrated from above" by the co-ordination of units from different national armies, the LL would be a force "integrated at the base". It would represent Pan Europa in a nutshell.

The value of such a force would be both practical and symbolic. Let us take the practical aspects first.

The example of the French Foreign Legion, the Spanish Tertio, and the International Brigades tends to show that the fighting morale of such mixed units is excellent, and often superior to that of normal units. The reason for this may be that the heterogeneous nature of such forces leaves less scope than in homogeneous units for the development of collective grudges and adverse political currents.

The language of command in the LL should be French. The language barrier presents no difficulties, as experience shows that the limited technical vocabulary of the army is picked up by the alien recruit almost as quickly as if he had to learn the terms in his own language. This the present writer can confirm from personal experiences as a soldier in the French Foreign Legion and the British Aliens' Pioneer Corps.

Recruitment of one or several LL regiments could start immediately. The only condition required is that the various governments concerned should consider service in the Legion of Liberty as equivalent to military service at home. It is hard to see what valid objection could be raised to such an arrangement.

The creation of the LL force does not interfere with existing official projects, such as the Acheson plan, or with unofficial suggestions such as Churchill's Strasbourg proposal of a European Ministry of Defence, or the Culbertson proposal of a United Nations Police Force, or the proposal of Senator Lodge for a Brigade composed of refugees from Eastern Europe.

The LL force should be modelled on the pattern of the USA "Regimental Combat Teams". That is to say, the LL regiment or regiments (depending on the number of volunteers) should be to a large extent self-supporting, with their own infantry, tank and engineer battalions, field artillery, and a small tactical air arm.

The Legion should have American equipment and European manpower.

Its non-commissioned officers and subalterns should be selected according to ability; its officers from the rank of Captain upward should be citizens of small nations.

It could be stationed anywhere in Europe, e.g. in Western Germany or in the Franco-German border provinces.

The psychological aspect of the project, which is its very essence and raison d'être, need not be discussed at length. The very name of a "Legion of Liberty" expresses its symbolic value and emotional significance.

At worst, the LL would remain a small élite corps of a few thousand men – say 4000 to 5000, the strength of a single regiment. It is hard to imagine that this number of volunteers would not be forthcoming. Even on this limited scale its symbolic value would be considerable. The young men of various nationalities would, through mutual contact, gain an inestimable experience and enlarged horizon – much more effectively than through all sorts of summer schools, student exchange projects and holidays abroad. They should acquire a European consciousness, and spread it in their home countries after their return.

At best, the Legion of Liberty would become the catalytic agent for a truly integrated European Army, and thus the pioneer of a United Europe. Every squad, platoon and company would act as incubator of the new European spirit. The condition of being a soldier would lose its odious associations with wars of national jealousy and imperialist conquest. The Legion of Liberty would discard the worn-out flags which have long ceased to represent the reality of our shrinking planet. The French *poilu* and the German *Soldat* would no longer regard themselves as the helpless victims of archaic chauvinism, or the sinister machinations of politicians. They would be soldiers of Europe, marching under the flag of Europe, to the sound of a European anthem.

"Why," wrote the President of the European Assembly, Henri Spaak, a few days ago, "why should the responsible statesmen who signed the Brussels Pact and the North Atlantic Treaty be incapable of drawing the logical conclusions from their texts? The defence of Europe means, to be sure, a good army; but it also means, and perhaps above all, the consciousness that Europe exists and that it deserves to exist."

In the original edition of The Trail of the Dinosaur *(1955), this* New York Times *piece of 1950 was reprinted with an added comment which is of some minor historical interest:*

The plan proposed in this article was taken up by a group of American politicians, including some of General Eisenhower's close advisers. As the following excerpt from the *New York Herald Tribune*, March 18, 1951) shows, it was for a while favourably discussed in Washington – and has apparently petered out since:

Eisenhower's Military Melting Pot

3 Plans Studied for Integrating Nationalities in Army
By Vic Reinemer, Washington

. . . Military leaders, now that General Eisenhower has set up his cadre in Europe, will tackle in earnest the problem of finding the best way of welding the soldiers from the North Atlantic pact countries into a cohesive and strong force.

Several types of military organisation may be considered. . . .

. . .A third proposal, favoured privately by some authorities but not widely publicised, is that the soldiers from all the Atlantic pact countries be mixed down through squad level, rather than separated in large national contingents. This may be more practicable and advantageous than it seems at first glance. Interviewed recently in Washington, officers from countries which have thus integrated soldiers from various language and cultural backgrounds, almost unanimously favoured such organisation over separation of the different groups. . . . For example, the Israeli Army includes immigrants from about fifty countries. Even now some of the recruits do not speak Hebrew, the official language. Yet they are mixed indiscriminately in the army. A ranking Israeli officer said that this "melting pot" characteristic of the army has been the main unifier of the Israeli people. . . .

The Swiss Air Force uses a technical jargon which combines the country's three main languages, German, French and Italian. A Swiss air officer who used to command a squadron which included one Italian, three French and six German speaking pilots said their diversity of ideas and temperaments made for a better staff organisation than did the relatively similar characteristics of one language and cultural group. . . .

Strained relations sometimes developed among the Allies during World War II when one national contingent suffered heavy casualties while others were comparatively unscathed. On the other hand, in a platoon or company which includes several nationalities, the common sacrifice tends to unite the troops, say men who have served in such units. . . .

The Atlantic peoples might well discover, as did the Israelis, that an army integrated on a man-to-man basis can infuse its *esprit de corps* into the entire life of the community. The creation of an Atlantic Legion could well be that big first step which would start the ball rolling.

Chapter 20

THE GOOD SAMARITANS

An Army needs a Medical Corps; and even a Cold War needs not only fighters but also Good Samaritans. At least that was what I felt when faced with the misery of fellow writers who had escaped across the Iron Curtain and were now struggling for bare survival. I also felt that the prosperous writers of the West had a special obligation to help their less fortunate colleagues – not by charitable alms, but by creating the conditions which would enable them to continue writing during the cruel period of transition before they found their feet on alien soil. Thus about the same time when I was agitating for a "Legion of Liberty", I started an organisation called Fund for Intellectual Freedom (FIF), provided the initial finances, and for two years (1950–2) devoted half of my working time to it.

The aims of the FIF were outlined in the following speech at a fund-raising dinner at Delmonico's Restaurant in New York, May 7, 1951, chaired by Reinhold Niebuhr:*

Ladies and Gentlemen,
This is a report on an experiment which a group of writers have undertaken.† Its purpose is to create the material conditions which would enable the exiled cultures of the countries under totalitarian rule to survive.

I say "exiled cultures" and not "exiled writers" or "artists" or individual refugees. For the problem with which we are faced has grown beyond the scope for individual relief. We are faced today

---

*This was the only occasion of a semi-public appeal for funds in the long history of the FIF.
†In fact, of these only Aldous Huxley, Stephen Spender and Budd Schulberg lived up to their promises of financial help.

with the calculated and systematic extermination of whole national cultures – the Russian, Ukrainian, Czech, Hungarian, Polish and so on. Culture, as we understand this term, is dependent, among other factors, on two essential conditions: freedom of expression and continuity of tradition. Both these conditions are absent in countries under totalitarian rule.

The main hope of preserving the continuity of these cultures rests today with a small number of exiled writers who have succeeded in saving their physical lives and spiritual integrity by coming over to the West. Their number is limited – I should say that there are not more than about two hundred creative writers among them. The unsatisfactory aspect of charity is that your contribution is merely a drop in an ocean. But in the case of this limited number, effective help is possible.

The refugee writers' existence is more difficult than that of refugees in other professions. Charitable organisations, overburdened by the mass misery of the displaced populations of Europe, can only supply the bare necessities to keep them above starvation level, but cannot create the conditions for creative work.

We felt, therefore, that the traditional methods of charity were insufficient and that a more positive method of help was required. Only writers can understand the specific needs of their fellow writers and provide constructive help without bureaucratic formalities, applications in triplicate and the rest. We have accordingly pledged ourselves to assign a part of our income to our refugee colleagues from Russia and the satellite dictatorships. We regard this help extended to our colleagues not as an act of charity but as a duty which can best be discharged by a method of self-taxation. Up to this day we have neither accepted cash donations nor appealed for them. The only income of the FIF is derived from the assigned percentage of our royalties or from the donation of the copyright of a book, or the stage or screen rights or translations of it. All paper work is done by voluntary workers, among whom I would particularly like to mention Mrs H. R. Knickerbocker.* We have no overhead expenses whatsoever. For legal purposes it was necessary that we should become incorporated, which we did under the name "Fund for Intellectual Freedom". This is an organisation which hates to be an organisation; it is merely a kind of bundling together of individual efforts.

---

*Widow of H. R. Knickerbocker, the writer.

So far we have spent around $20,000 to help our colleagues. We do this in two ways: by enabling individual writers to continue their creative work, and by providing outlets to publish them.

The report went on to give examples of (unnamed) refugee writers (of whom several have since acquired international fame) who were helped by providing them with typewriters (some with Cyrillic keyboards); bridging subsidies (for periods usually not less than six months) to finish a book; with the means for paying translators; with book, magazine and radio contracts, etc. The FIF also published or subsidised émigré magazines and small publishing firms in Russian (Literaturny Sovremennik), Polish (Kultura), Rumanian (Orizontori) and Hungarian (Uj Magyar Ut). These activities were carried out by volunteer workers in the two main centres for Iron Curtain refugee intellectuals – Munich and Paris. The report continues with some comments on the most ambitious of these enterprises:

The *Literaturny Sovremennik* (Literary Contemporary) is a monthly magazine, published in Munich, circulation 3000, length approximately 260 pages octavo including three-colour illustrations. This is the classic format of the so-called "fat" Russian literary magazine which from the beginning of the nineteenth century played a central part in Russian cultural life. (Most of the masterpieces of the great Russian novelists were first published in serial form in the "fat" magazines.) Hence the creation of a "fat" magazine in exile is regarded as a landmark by the new Russian emigration. I realise that another literary magazine does not seem a very exciting subject. But what it meant in this particular case will perhaps become clearer when I read you an extract from a letter by the editor of the *Literaturny Sovremennik*, Boris Yakovlev:

People say that there are no miracles, and least of all among exiles. Hence the first news that a group of you English and American authors intended to make a miracle come true and give us back our lost voice was received with sceptical smiles. They could not believe that solidarity, this word which we have heard so often misused as a political slogan, could exist in the world of facts.

. . .I started writing late: before the war, after my discharge from prison. I decided to specialise in fairy stories for children which seemed the relatively least dangerous ground. I became fairly well-known and the more attention my work attracted the more my writing deteriorated. I was looking for a new form of the socialist fairy-tale, and discussed endlessly with the editor of the State Publishing Firm for Children's Books, the problem whether it was permissible to let the ducks in my tales speak in human language, and what Darwin, Marx, Engels and Lenin would have said to that. We could reach no final conclusion, and then the war broke out. I became a prisoner of war in Germany, and when it was over, a Displaced Person. . . .

He then goes on to explain how the Russian exiles are unable to find a market for their work because they have no money to pay translators and cannot get publishers and editors to read a manus-cript in Russian. He describes how these men, who risked their lives to get out and make their voices heard, have one after the other given up writing in discouragement and despair. The letter concludes:

And now the miracle has come true. We have waited for it during twenty-five years "over there", and during five years over here – for the miracle to be permitted to write what we think, and to see what we have written published. Now it has come true. I believe our people here have deserved it. You as writers will understand no doubt what it means to us writers and poets escaped from the USSR to have for the first time in thirty years, the chance of saying what we like in print.

Yours sincerely,
B. Yakovlev

So much for our work. I said at the beginning of this report that we are providing the funds ourselves and are not appealing for dona-tions from the public. This occasion is exceptional; the reason why we are making this exception is that the response from American writers has so far been disappointing. We brought the existence of our little organisation to their knowledge through personal contacts and by communiqués in the three organs which are read by most writers in this country, the *New York Times Book Supplement*, the *Herald Tribune Book Supplement* and the *Saturday Review of Literature*. The result was as follows: one anonymous donor sent us $5. The only other letter we received came from a crank who had invented an umbrella with an electric bulb inside, which goes on when you open the umbrella. He told us that if we marketed his invention we could have 10 per cent of his royalties. Even more sad was the fate of a special appeal which Budd Schulberg sent out in aid of Ivan Bunin to twelve addres-sees: six bestselling writers and six well-known publishing firms. Bunin, after all, is not an anonymous young poet with an unpronounceable name.* The sum which Schulberg received from these twelve prosperous agencies amounted to a total of $125.

What kept the Fund for Intellectual Freedom going, in spite of this almost total lack of response, was a malicious twist of fate which is embarrassing to report, while suppressing it would deprive the story of its point. At the start of that venture, I assigned to the FIF, as my own contribution, all future royalties derived from the forthcoming New York stage production of Darkness at Noon. *I could not foresee at the time that it would run for eighteen months on Broadway, and that the royalties would amount, quite literally, to a modest fortune. Had I foreseen it, I am not sure whether I would have made the same gesture. As it turned out, it provided more than 90 per cent of the FIF's budget throughout its existence.*

The irony of it was that I happened to be rather broke at the time.

After a couple of years, the work connected with the FIF became too much of a burden, and in 1952 I handed over the administration of the fund to the International PEN Club. The PEN, in turn, transferred it in 1956 to the Congress for Cultural Freedom. Conditions by that time had changed, particularly after the new flood of refugees produced by the Hungarian Revolution, and the FIF was merged with other relief organisations.

As an added piquancy I may mention here that the Congress for Cultural freedom was at that time still mostly financed by the CIA, because the American administration had no system for channelling funds for deserving cultural institutions in Europe. Thus, while my former comrades accused me of being "on the payroll of the CIA, the opposite was true – to wit, my well-earned royalties from the stage production of Darkness at Noon *now went via the FIF into the coffers of that worthy organisation.*

To end this chapter I feel like quoting these lines from Christopher Fry:

> I apologise
> For boasting, but once you know my qualities
> I can drop back into a quite brilliant
> Humility. . . .

---

*Ivan Bunin – the first Russian to receive the Nobel Prize for Literature (in 1933) – was at the time over eighty and in urgent need of an operation. After Schulberg's appeal had failed, the FIF did what was necessary, although Bunin, as a pre-war émigré, did not qualify for aid.

Chapter 21

IN MEMORY OF
GEORGE ORWELL

*The staunchest British Left-wing opponent of the Soviet regime
during and immediately after the war was George Orwell. He
stood out like a rock in the swamp of the fellow-travelling intelligentsia of varying degrees of muddiness. It was thus almost
inevitable that we became first political allies, then friends, however different in character and background. The task of writing
his obituary, which the Observer asked me to do, was made even
more painful by the shortness of the available space.**

To meet one's favourite author in the flesh is mostly a disillusion-
ing experience. George Orwell was one of the few writers who
looked and behaved exactly as the reader of his books expected
him to look and behave. This exceptional concordance between
the man and his work was a measure of the exceptional unity and
integrity of his character.

An English critic recently called him the most honest writer
alive; his uncompromising intellectual honesty was such that it
made him appear almost inhuman at times. There was an emanation of austere harshness around him which diminished only in
proportion to distance, as it were: he was merciless towards himself, severe upon his friends, unresponsive to admirers, but full of
understanding sympathy for those on the remote periphery, the
"crowds in the big towns with their knobby faces, their bad teeth
and gentle manners; the queues outside the Labour Exchanges,
the old maids biking to Holy Communion through the mists of the
autumn morning. . . ."

*First published in the Observer, January 29, 1950; reprinted in The Trail of the
Dinosaur (1955).

Thus, the greater the distance from intimacy and the wider the radius of the circle, the more warming became the radiations of this lonely man's great power of love. But he was incapable of self-love or self-pity. His ruthlessness towards himself was the key to his personality; it determined his attitude towards the enemy within, the disease which had raged in his chest since his adolescence.

His life was one consistent series of rebellions both against the conditions of society in general and his own particular predicament; against humanity's drift towards 1984 and his own drift towards the final breakdown. Intermittent haemorrhages marked like milestones the rebel's progress as a sergeant in the Burma police, a dishwasher in Paris, a tramp in England, a soldier in Spain. Each should have acted as a warning, and each served as a challenge, answered by works of increasing weight and stature.

The last warning came three years ago. It became obvious that his life-span could only be prolonged by a sheltered existence under constant medical care. He chose to live instead on a lonely island in the Hebrides, with his adopted baby son, without even a charwoman to look after him.

Under these conditions he wrote his savage vision of 1984. Shortly after the book was completed he became bedridden, and never recovered. Yet had he followed the advice of doctors and friends, and lived in the self-indulgent atmosphere of a Swiss sanatorium, his masterpiece could not have been written – nor any of his former books. The greatness and tragedy of Orwell was his total rejection of compromise.

The urge of genius and the promptings of common sense can rarely be reconciled; Orwell's life was a victory of the former over the latter. For now that he is dead, the time has come to recognise that he was the only writer of genius among the *littérateurs* of social revolt between the two wars. Cyril Connolly's remark, referring to their common prep-school days: "I was a stage rebel, Orwell a true one," is valid for his whole generation.

When he went to fight in Spain he did not join the sham-fraternity of the International Brigades, but the most wretched of the Spanish Militia units, the heretics of the POUM. He was the only one whom his grim integrity kept immune against the spurious *mystique* of the "Movement", who never became a fellow-traveller and never believed in Moses the Raven's Sugar-candy Mountain – either in heaven or on earth. Consequently, his seven books of that period, from *Down and Out* to *Coming up for Air*, all remain fresh and bursting with life, and will remain so for decades to come, whereas most of the books produced by the "emotionally shallow Leftism" of that time, which Orwell so despised, are dead and dated today.

A similar comparison could be drawn for the period of the war. Among all the pamphlets, tracts and exhortations which the war produced, hardly anything bears re-reading today – except, perhaps, E. M. Forster's *What I Believe*, a few passages from Churchill's speeches, and, above all, Orwell's *The Lion and the Unicorn*. Its opening section, "England Your England", is one of the most moving and yet incisive portraits of the English character, and a minor classic in itself.

Animal Farm and *1984* are Orwell's last works. No parable was written since *Gulliver's Travels* equal in profundity and mordant satire to *Animal Farm*, no fantasy since Kafka's *In the Penal Settlement* equal in logical horror to *1984*. I believe that future historians of literature will regard Orwell as a kind of missing link between Kafka and Swift. For, to quote Connolly again, it may well be true that "it is closing time in the gardens of the West, and from now on an artist will be judged only by the resonance of his solitude or the quality of his despair".

The resonance of Orwell's solitude and the quality of his despair can only be compared to Kafka's – but with this difference: that Orwell's despair had a concrete, organised structure, as it were, and was projected from the individual to the social plane. And if "four legs good, two legs bad", is pure Swift, there is again this difference: that Orwell never completely lost faith in the knobby-faced yahoos with their bad teeth. Had he proposed an epitaph for himself, my guess is that he would have chosen these lines from Old Major's revolutionary anthem, to be sung to a "stirring tune, something between 'Clementine' and 'La Cucaracha' ":

> Rings shall vanish from our noses,
> And the harness from our back . . .
>
> For that day we all must labour,
> Though we die before it break;
> Cows and horses, geese and turkeys,
> All must toil for freedom's sake.

Somehow Orwell really believed in this. It was this quaint belief which guided the rebel's progress, and made him so very lovable though he did not know it.

Chapter 22

THE AGE OF LONGING

The title of this novel, set in the turmoil of post-war France, is explained in an impassioned diatribe which Jules Commanche, a former leader of the French Resistance and now a high-ranking government official, directs at the young American heroine, Hydie:

"As you know, Mademoiselle, we French have an incurable passion for analysis," said Commanche with a look which made Hydie feel that in some subtle way he was making fun of her. "We just talk and talk, and in between we are invaded once in every generation or so, and lose the best talkers in every family, and then we go on talking. For, unlike in your country, where one type does the talking, the other the fighting, with us it is the briiiiant talkers who usually do the fighting and dying. We don't go in for your strong, dumb, silent heroes. We are an incurably articulate nation. Our prototype of a hero is Cyrano de Bergerac, who makes his thrusts at the end of each strophe of a verbose poem. . . . But to come back to our political libido. When does an instinct get diverted into the wrong channels? When it is thwarted at its source, or frustrated in its object. Now the source of all political libido is faith, and its object the New Jerusalem, the Kingdom of Heaven, the Lost Paradise, Utopia, what have you. Therefore each time a god dies there is trouble in History. People feel that they have been cheated by his promises, left with a dud cheque in their pocket; and they will run after every charlatan who promises to cash it. The last time a god died was on July 14, 1789, the day when the Bastille was stormed. On that day the Holy Trinity was replaced by the three-word slogan which you find written over our town halls and post offices. Europe has not yet recovered from that operation, and all our troubles today are secondary complications, a kind of septic wound-fever. The People – and when I use that word, Mademoiselle, I always refer to people who have no bank accounts – the People have been deprived of their only asset: the knowledge, or the illusion, whichever you like, of having an immortal soul. Their faith is dead, their kingdom is dead, only the longing remains. And this longing, Mademoiselle, can express itself in beautiful or murderous forms, just like the frustrated sex instinct. For, believe me, Mademoiselle, it is very painful to forsake copulation when the mating season is on. And because it is so painful, the whole complex is repressed. Only the longing remains – a dumb, inarticulate longing of the instinct, without knowledge of its source and object. So the People, the Masses, mill around with that irksome feeling of having an uncashed cheque in their pockets and whoever tells them 'Oyez, oyez, the Kingdom is just round the corner, in the second street to the left', can do with them what he likes. The more they feel that itch, the easier it is to get at them. If you tell them that their kingdom stinks of corpses, they will answer you that it has always been their favourite scent.''

Hydie was brought up in a Catholic convent and had a strong inclination towards mysticism, until a traumatic experience made her lose her faith and turned her into another victim of the "age of longing". In Paris – where her father is a military attaché – she starts an affair with Fedya Nikitin, a young and fanatical, but physically attractive Soviet Intelligence Officer working under diplomatic cover. As she later confesses to her father, the nice, bewildered Colonel:

"I fell for him because – because he was sure of himself and had a belief, a certitude which none of you have. Because he is *real*, which none of you are.''

The climax of the affair – and actually the key to the novel – is a symbolic episode, bordering on science fiction, yet entirely within the realm of the possible:

Hydie had insisted that they celebrate New Year's Eve alone in Fedya's new bachelor flat. Though Fedya took a childish pride in the little flat, he would have preferred to dine out in a gay and noisy restaurant, but for once her wish had prevailed. She arrived early and excited, loaded with parcels of delicatessen and drinks,

and had locked herself into the kitchenette with an apron fastened
to her evening dress. Fedya sat down, resigned, in the sitting-
room and turned the radio on.

Their affair was now about four months old, and he wondered
without worrying what it was leading up to. He had his superiors'
blessing; though nothing concrete could be expected to come out
of it, one could never tell. Anyway, the fact that he was allowed to
carry on with an American colonel's daughter was a sign of their
confidence, of their knowing that Fedya could be trusted. He
smiled, humming out in his pleasant baritone voice the tune of the
"Toreador's March" which came from the portable radio set – a
white, ebony and chromium affair with luminous dials. He picked
up the evening papar, and began to read an astrologer's prophecy
of events to come in the New Year.

"The critical period," it said, "will be the end of August, when
Mars enters the second house. There will be an unusual fall of
meteors, a period of abnormal weather, and a grave epidemic of a
new variety. Whether war will break out will depend on the race
between the powers of evil and the powers of salvation. . . ."

Fedya laughed aloud and let the newspaper drop on the floor.
"What's the matter?" cried Hydie from the kitchen.

"I invite you to have a drink with me," said Fedya. "You can
cook later."

"I won't be a minute."

Fedya resumed the "Toreador's March", stamping the rhythm
out with his foot. His shoe left an imprint on the blue, fitted carpet;
he brushed over it lovingly with his fingers. The prospect of
spending a whole evening alone in the flat with his mistress filled
him with moderate boredom. He decided to get the love-making
over immediately after dinner, and then go out to some place. He
had never seen how the French bourgeoisie celebrated New
Year's Eve, and next year it might be too late for that.

"Here we are. Now for the drink," said Hydie, discarding her
apron in the kitchen door and stepping over it. She looked rather
beautiful in her black evening dress, but her face had grown thin,
with deep shadows under her eyes, and her bright manner had
something artificial about it, like the radiance of a neon-tube.

"You have trodden on that apron," said Fedya.

"Never mind, you can send it to the laundry with your things. I
have brought three with me."

She saw that he regarded this as reckless squandering and that
it made him angry. Her eyebrows twitched one or twice – a

nervous tic which she had acquired recently and which made her face appear for seconds pathetically defenceless. With a gesture which had become a habit, she rubbed Fedya's mop of hair with her palm. "I have been invited for a drink," she said.

"What shall it be?" said Fedya.

"I will get it."

She brought a bottle of champagne from the ice-box and Fedya opened it with a loud pop. This always put him into a better humour.

"Now for the New Year's toast," she said brightly.

He thought of the ritual toasts one drank at home in strict hierarchical order, but none of them seemed appropriate. He remembered how, in 1938, they had all toasted somebody whose name, as he learned the next morning, was not to be mentioned any more, and how he had afterwards suffered from diarrhoea for a whole week. This was one of those little jokes which nobody here could understand, and the memory gave him a sudden pang of homesickness. "I don't know any New Year toasts," he said.

"I don't either," said Hydie. "But I know one for Christmas." She lifted her glass and said in her clear, soft voice:

"Peace on earth, and mercy mild,
God and sinners reconciled. . . ."

She drained her glass, and poured herself a new one. Fedya smiled:

"Still the convent, yes?"

Hydie sat down in an armchair at some distance from Fedya. It was an armchair of the flowery French kind. "What have you been reading?" she asked.

He smiled. "The newspaper has a prophecy by a soothsayer. They say this newspaper is read by a million people. Every day they read it they get more stupid, and every day the proprietor of the newspaper gets more rich. Then he makes a speech at a banquet and says we must defend the freedom of the Press. You have teachers to educate the children, but you let these gangsters take charge of the uneducated masses who are just like children. What do you say?"

"You are right as usual, Professor." Her happiest moments were when she felt able to agree with him.

He shook his head, smiling:

"Why always this mocking tone? Is it necessary?"

"No. It's just one of those silly mannerisms. But you must be patient with my re-education, and you have to take into account my deformed mentality due to my social background.''

He did not know whether she was mocking or in earnest; neither did she. She rose and went back to the kitchenette. Fedya was bored, so he decided to help and followed her. In the tiny kitchenette they kept bumping into each other, and as they were both bending over the cupboard to get the plates out, her hair brushed against his face. He felt by the rhythm of her breathing that she longed to be picked up and carried to the couch, leaving the dinner to burn. His own desire sharpened; but he was hungry, and he knew that it was wiser to keep her on tenterhooks. He patted her on the back. ''Now everything is ready and we can eat,'' he said contentedly.

She had brought two bottles of vintage claret, and after the champagne it went quickly to their heads. ''How was that toast?'' Fedya asked.

''The one for Christmas? I am glad you like it.'' And, leaning across the table, she repeated softly: ''Peace on earth and mercy mild – Flesh and Spirit reconciled. . . .''

''But these were not the words. It said, 'God and sinners reconciled.' ''

''Of course. How very silly of me. . . .'' She bit her lip and fell silent. Fedya always felt uneasy when that distant look appeared in her eyes. ''You are a mystery. A great mystery,'' he cried enthusiastically. He was a little drunk and he knew that it flattered women to be called a mystery.

''I will solve the mystery for you,'' said Hydie. ''I have a woman's body, a man's brains, the aspirations of a saint and the instincts of a harlot. Does that satisfy you?''

''Ah,'' said Fedya laughing. ''How very banal.''

''You are becoming sophisticated,'' said Hydie. ''Well, I can tell you more. When I was nineteen I was sent to a psychoanalyst. My parents wanted a boy, but I was born a girl; the analyst said this was important. He also said that I had got a crush on my daddy and that this is why I fell in love with Jesus Christ. Then I went to another analyst who said I have a low self-reliance, that's why I am always acting the part which others expect me to. Then I got married to a very polite young man who made love like a bird, and he explained to me that I was frigid out of selfishness because I lacked the generosity to let myself go. Then I met you and let myself really go, and you explain to me that I am a typical product of a doomed civilisation. What does it all add up to?''

Fedya laughed; then he said in his gentle, pedagogical voice:

"At first you never wanted to talk about yourself, and now you do it all the time. You say you are no mystery but you really believe you are a very great mystery and you believe all people are great mysteries. You say 'what does it all add up to', I tell you it adds up to something very simple. There is no mystery, only reflexes, like in this radio machine." He patted tenderly the white and ebony casing. "You turn a knob, there is a reaction. You hit it, there is damage; you repair it, it is all right again. It talks, screams, it makes music – all very useful and amusing; but there is no mystery. . . ."

Hydie yawned demonstratively. "You talk exactly like Grandad," she said. "He was a president of a railway company. In between buying up other companies, he spent his spare time reading pamphlets about 'the survival of the fittest' and 'man, a machine'. You talk just like him." She cleared the plates away and brought the ice-cream with another bottle of champagne. "Anyway," she said, "this is New Year's Eve, and I intend to get tight."

Fedya opened the bottle, and after filling up their glasses he said with a mischievous smile:

"So you maintain there is a mystery, and not just reflexes?"

"Oh, shut up, darling," said Hydie. "Must you go on lecturing?"

"Yes. I wish to tell you about the dogs of Professor Pavlov."

Hydie felt her head swimming. She felt so mixed-up lately that she did not even know whether she was happy or miserable. To find out, she mixed some of the claret into the champagne, drank it and lay down on the couch, wishing that Fedya would come to her and blot everything out with his hard, crushing body . But he was still talking about Professor Pavlov and his dogs, looking at her with a curious smile through half-closed eyes. "So, you see," he was saying, "after a while when the bell rings in the laboratory, the dog salivates and drops his spittle although there is no meat. . . ." He walked slowly over to the couch. "And that explains what we are: conditions and reflexes, and the rest is superstition." He was now standing at the couch, bending over her, and her heart was pumping away violently.

"Oh, rot," she said breathlessly, waiting to be taken.

"So you don't believe it," he said, bending closer, with the same fixed smile. He slowly stretched out his arm and his hand gripped her with firm pressure under the left armpit, his thumb pressing against her nipple. It was a grip, more than a caress, which she knew only too well; he always did precisely this at the precise moment of her physical climax. "Now . . ." he said. She felt her eyeballs turn upward, the familiar, blissful convulsion, then peace.

Fedya relaxed his grip, walked back to the table and sat down, emptying his glass. "What do you think now of Professor Pavlov?" he said politely.

She gave no answer. Her mind was in a mist which she was very careful not to dispel; her body limp and relaxed. Without thinking she knew that she had suffered a humiliation past anything that a drunken customer might inflict on a prostitute, and that she would hate him for the rest of her life as she had never hated before.

A few days later she tries to kill Fedya, whom she has come to regard as a kind of Antichrist, and bungles the job. The novel ends with some reflections by Hydie, the renegade Catholic, which sound not very unlike a renegade Communist's:

. . .And those who were still alive and free today, were watching for the appearance of the Comet, and they were all sick with longing. Her thoughts travelled back to Sister Boutillot standing in the alley which led to the pond, where the autumn breeze swept the leaves towards her feet. Oh, if she could only go back to the infinite comfort of father confessors and mother superiors, of a well-ordered hierarchy which promised punishment and reward, and furnished the world with justice and meaning. If only one could go back! But she was under the curse of reason, which rejected whatever might quench her thirst without abolishing the gnawing of the urge; which rejected the answer without abolishing the question. For the place of God had become vacant, and there was a draught blowing through the world like in an empty flat before the new tenants have arrived.

The Age of Longing was written in 1949–50, in France, in the highly charged atmosphere of the post-war period when the Communists were the strongest single party in the National Assembly. I wrote it in between the essays and speeches collected in The Trail of the Dinosaur and just after I wrote my part of The God That Failed. The Age of Longing is, in a way, a dramatisation of those essays, and is the only one of my novels which I dislike (except for a few chapters). But it helped to work out of my system the bitterness towards that failed god, and the guilt of having served him. It also made me realise that to carry on in the same vein would be repetitive and might become an obsession. To go on repeating oneself may be permissible, and even necessary, for a politician; for a writer it is fatal.

Thus, at the age of forty-five I found myself changing from an active participant into a veteran of the Cold War. The change is reflected in the preface to The Trail of the Dinosaur (1955), which amounted to a kind of public vow:

This book is a farewell to arms. The last essays and speeches in it that deal directly with political questions date from 1950, and are now five years old. Since then I felt that I have said all that I had to say on these questions which had obsessed me, in various ways, for the best part of a quarter-century. Now the errors are atoned for, the bitter passion has burnt itself out; Cassandra has gone hoarse, and is due for a vocational change.

The "bitter passion" referred to the disillusioned ex-Communist's attitude to the Soviet regime, the sufferings it inflicted on the people under its rule, and the threat it represented to the rest of the world. To refer to oneself as a "hoarse Cassandra" may sound presumptuous, but so many hostile critics had called me that name so insistently that I felt justified in adopting it for once.

The "vocational change" meant a turning away from politics towards a renewed interest in science and philosophy, which was to dominate the second half of my life as a writer, and will be the subject matter of Book Two.

However, before saying farewell to politics, I must pick up the thread of that other main political involvement — Palestine — which has been temporarily lost from view, and follow it to its conclusion.

PART FIVE

BIRTH OF A NATION

Chapter 23

POMPEII IN REVERSE

Everything becomes legend, if the gentlemen
will have the goodness to wait.

NORMAN DOUGLAS

In 1926, at the age of twenty, I had set out for the Holy Land as a
romantic youth to work in a Kibbutz at the foot of Mount Gilboa;
three years later I had left Palestine, and subsequently lost interest in Zionism. However, another eight years later, after the
prison episode in Spain, I found myself back in Palestine – this
time as a special correspondent of the News Chronicle, for which I
was working at the time, to cover the Arab terror campaign
against the British Administration.

We are now in 1937, four years after Hitler's ascent to power.
My friends of the old days had undergone a profound change – I
quote from The Invisible Writing:*

In the streets of Haifa and Tel Aviv, in the settlements of Samaria
and Galilee, they went about their business with the calm, slow
motions imposed by the heat, but underneath they were all fanatics and maniacs. Every single one of them had a brother, parent,
cousin or bride in the part of Europe ruled by the assassins. It was
no longer a question whether Zionism was a good or bad idea.
They knew that the gas-chambers were coming. They were past
arguing. When provoked, they bared their teeth.

*Ch. xxxv.

When the Arab terror campaign was resumed on October 15, one of the first victims was a young orthodox Jew who had recently escaped from Germany. He was stabbed in the back on the holy Sabbath while walking through a street in Jerusalem reading his Bible. It was typical of the pointless, senseless charac- ter of the terror. Though everything here was on a smaller scale, in a sense it was even worse than Spain. There one had at least known where the enemy's frontline was, but here both camps were mixed together, and no one knew when he was going to be knifed in the back, or where the next home-made bomb was going to explode.

Mostly they exploded in crowded buses and train- compartments, or on the railway tracks. The oil pipeline from Mosul was set on fire, the airport in Lydda burnt down, British soldiers were ambushed, Jewish settlers sniped at in the fields, girls were raped, then stabbed to death. After a week, things calmed down a little; another week later it started all over again. The Jews were still holding back, swallowing their bile. It took some time for the tailors from Warsaw and the lawyers from Prague and the Talmud-students from Jerusalem to acquire a taste for throwing gelignite bombs. A year later they had acquired it, with a vengeance.

During these eight years of absence from the country, I had believed that the small and irksome Jewish question would even- tually be solved, together with the Negro question, the Armenian question and all other questions, in the global context of the Socialist revolution. So I had left the old Promised Land for the new land of promise, and had found it an even more bitter disap- pointment. Now, on my way out of the Communist Party, I had come back.

But it was not a coming full circle. It was a return on a different level of the spiral: a turn higher in maturity, but several turns lower in expectation. I no longer believed that this small and bitter country held out a messianic promise, an inspiration for mankind at large. And I also knew that I belonged to Europe, and that if Europe went down, I would rather go down with her than take refuge in a country which no longer meant anything but a refuge. This resolution was actually put to the test when, after the fall of France, instead of heading for Palestine or the USA, I made my escape to England.

On the other hand, there were six million doomed people in Germany and Eastern Europe who had no such freedom of choice, and for whom Palestine meant their only chance of survival. Whether they were welcome or not, whether the climate and culture suited them or not, were irrelevant questions when the alternative was the concentration camp and the crematorium. In this limited, resigned, and utilitarian sense, I was and still am a Zionist.

In the early days, I had been a member of Vladimir Jabotinsky's maximalist party which aimed at the transformation of the whole of Palestine into a Jewish State with an Arab minority. In the light of the intervening years, this programme had proved to be unworkable; Jews and Arabs were too profoundly divided by religion, culture and social pattern to live harmoniously together in the foreseeable future. I had thus become gradually convinced that partition of the country, as proposed by the Royal Commission of 1937 under Lord Peel, was, though not an ideal solution, yet the only possible solution. The serial that I wrote for the *News Chronicle* on my return ended with an urgent plea for carrying out the partition scheme, and a warning of the horrors which further procrastination would entail:

> The prospects for the future of the Holy Land are one colossal night-mare. Perpetual insecurity is ruining the country's economy; fear and hatred grow daily as murders and vendettas link up into an endless chain. The implacable savagery of this petty guerilla war threatens to destroy slowly but surely a historically unprecedented experiment. Britain must act, and act quickly. This is an SOS for Palestine.*

In 1937 partition could have been carried out with relatively little trouble and less bloodshed. The representative Jewish bodies were prepared to accept it. The moderate Arab leaders would have yielded to diplomatic pressure. The most influential among them, King Abdullah of Transjordan (whom I revisited in Amman during a lull in the riots), gave me an interview which, in somewhat veiled terms, amounted to an acceptance of partition. The Government of Neville Chamberlain, however, refused to implement the Royal Commission's plan, and for the next ten years British policy in Palestine was plunged into a dark night of indecision, error and prejudice. Partition was finally endorsed, after a decade of needless torment and bloodshed, by the United Nations, and implemented by force of arms in the Arab-Jewish war of 1948.

*"An SOS for Palestine", *News Chronicle*, December 15, 1937.

From 1942, when the mass-extermination of European Jews got under way, until the establishment of the State of Israel, the Palestine question became once more my main preoccupation next to the Cold War; the two haunting leitmotifs – Gulag and the Holocaust – were interwoven, running parallel in time. Thus I spent during this period altogether a year and a half in Palestine (1944–5; 1948); wrote two books (Thieves in the Night (1946) and Promise and Fulfilment (1949)), several pamphlets and numerous articles; sat on committees, and met in secret Menahem Begin when he was in hiding with a reward of five hundred pounds on his head – all the time pleading the case of partition, as the only means to end the horror and provide a haven to save those who could still be saved. "Of the various crusades in which I have been engaged," I wrote later in The Invisible Writing, "this was perhaps the most harrowing and painful; it led to an acute conflict between emotion and reason, for I have had my fill of terror and violence, and was yet compelled to explain and defend the cause of the Jewish terrorists."

Thieves in the Night was written in 1945, mostly in Jerusalem, in an atmosphere of savagery and mourning. Some extracts of the novel appear in Chapter 2 of this volume; I would like to add to these a few lines from the Postscript to the later Danube edition (published in 1965):

The central theme of the earlier trilogy – The Gladiators, Darkness at Noon, Arrival and Departure – was the ethics of revolution; the central theme of Thieves in the Night is the ethics of survival. If power corrupts, the reverse is also true: persecution corrupts the victim, though in subtler ways. In both cases the dilemma of noble ends begetting ignoble means has the stamp of inevitability.

Whatever its artistic merits and demerits, Thieves in the Night had certain political repercussions. Thus I learned that several members of the United Nations Palestine Commission of 1947 (which made the historic Recommendations for partition and the establishment of a Jewish state) had gone to the trouble of reading the book, and that it had even to some extent influenced their decisions. The Chairman of that eleven-nation Commission, Judge Sandstrom of Sweden, repeatedly teased members of the later Israeli Government by telling them that the story of Ezra's Tower had made a stronger impression on him than their official memoranda; and though this was no doubt said tongue in cheek, I was more moved by it than by the praise and abuse of literary critics.

The extracts which follow are from Promise and Fulfilment –
Palestine 1917–49:

During the siege of Jerusalem, two venerable old Jews were overheard talking.

"We can only be saved," said one, "either by a miracle or by a
natural event."

"So what is the natural event?" asked the other.

"The coming of Messiah, of course."

During the first fortnight of the life of the newborn State, it
looked as if it would share the fate of the infants under Herod
whose tender bodies were put to the sword. May 15, 1948, the date
of the official termination of the British Mandate, was the
appointed D-Day (D for Deluge), on which the armies of five
sovereign Arab Nations invaded Palestine from the north, east
and south. The days of the new State seemed to be numbered, and
speedy capitulation the Jews' only chance to avoid wholesale
massacre. Contrary to all expectations, the men of Haganah held
their ground.

*I had fervently hoped, but could never quite believe, that a Jewish
state would come into being in my lifetime; and even less that I
would be privileged to witness its birth. Needless to say, great
expectations always carry the seed of anticlimax within them –
and the eye-witness to History in the making usually finds his
spectacles clouded. The following extracts from my diary notes
(published in* Promise and Fulfilment*) illustrate this process:*

Haifa, Friday, June 4, 1948
After a bumpy flight from Cyprus, which made Mamaine feel sick
and the two returning Irgun terrorists on board look humble, a
pencilled yellow streak appears, interposed between water and
skyline: the coast of Israel. It swiftly unfolds into the golden dunes
of Acco Bay, the pine slopes of Carmel. The golden dunes are
mined. Among the pines of Carmel Arab and Jewish snipers play
hide and seek. The weathered wall of Acco's Crusader fortress had
a hole blown in it through which the friends of our terrorists made
their escape.

But none of this is written over the smiling face of the bay. The
whole sunny landscape, this levantine twin-sister of the Gulf of
Naples, strikes at once the dominant chord of all journeys into
war: it is so completely peaceful.

This intense and perverse peace, superimposed on scenes of flesh-tearing and eardrum-splitting violence, is an archetype of war-experience. Grass never smells sweeter than in a dug-out during a bombardment when one's face is buried in the earth. What soldier has not seen that caterpillar crawling along a crack in the bark of the tree behind which he took cover, and pursuing its climb undisturbed by the spattering of his tommy-gun? This intersecting of the tragic and the trivial planes of existence has always obsessed me – in the Spanish Civil War, during the collapse of France, in the London blitz.

The Dakota, with its load of terrorists, newspaper men and war-volunteers, is preparing to land. This is the moment we have all quietly dreaded since Le Bourget: the Arabs are supposed to be blockading Israel by sea and by air; a landing plane is to attacking aircraft what a pigeon is to a hawk, and the Jewish state has so far no air protection. But there are no Syrian or Egyptian planes in sight. With the relieving bump on the runway the worst is over; now one can settle down quietly to the routine of another war: to another blackout, more wailing sirens, girls in sweaty uniforms and operations according to plan.

The reflections of the sun on the ripples of the sea, the straight thin shadows of the palm-trees on the sand, register the silent comment of mineral and plant on that novelty in evolution, the human brain.

The airport. As we squeeze one by one through the small port-door of the Dakota and stumble down the wobbly step-ladder, there is a great clicking of Leicas and purring of movie-cameras. The State of Israel is exactly eighteen days old, so all events here are Historic Events and all persons arriving from abroad are Very Important Persons. Elated, we troop to the Customs.

Haifa airport is the newborn state's first and as yet only link with the world outside. The signposts with the Hebrew words for CUSTOMS, PASSPORTS, POLICE, LADIES and GENTS are freshly painted and still wet. The newly appointed Immigration Officer has as yet no uniform. Nor has the Customs Inspector; nor the Police; nor the Army. All servants of the State, civil and military, wear the same dress: khaki shirt and khaki shorts.

The newbaked officials are all affable, rattled and inefficient. Here is bureaucracy in a larval state of innocence, before it has had time to spin itself a cocoon of red tape. Soon they will learn to scan with expressionless faces the little booklet with the names black-listed by the secret police and dig for hidden shekels among the voyagers' dirty shirts, every one a little Elohim. But as yet all is in a state of virginal muddle, as on the first day of creation, before the heavens and the earth were divided, when Immigration Officers, floating on little clouds through chaos, treated the passengers to cigarettes and brandy. The one who handles our passports visibly tries to take himself seriously, but without much success. He looks at our visas; he feasts his eyes on them; they are another symbol of Israel having attained the dignity of statehood. M.'s and mine are among the ten first visas issued by the Provisional Government's Representation in Paris; they have the serial numbers five and seven. We showed them the same evening to a group of wounded Haganah men in the military hospital in Haifa. They looked at them like children at a new toy. We found later the same enraptured expression on the faces of people looking at the first Israeli pound-notes, at aeroplanes with the star of David painted on their wings, at the new flag, at the first foreign Ambassador presenting his credentials to the Government. They can't get over their amazement that these are real aeroplanes, real flags, real ambassadors.

Israel's citizens are rubbing their eyes. It does not often happen that a dream comes true.

Sunday, June 6, Tel Aviv

This morning we set out for Tel Aviv in a taxi, and as we watched the traffic on the coastal road, I thought again I was back in the Spanish Civil War. The road was teeming with trucks and requisitioned passenger buses packed with singing soldiers. Some trucks are covered with a kind of home-made armour-plating, some other makeshift contraptions are trying to look like tanks. Most of the soldiers have no rifles or kitbags. It is just like the road from Valencia to Madrid in 1936. Everything bears the sign of amateurishness, muddle and enthusiastic improvisation.

The soldiers are all young, sunburnt and visibly feeling on top of the world. So were the Spanish militianos, the Serb guerillas, the soldiers of the French Revolution. Only improvised revolutionary armies know this emotional exuberance. They fight like devils, and when they panic they run like monkeys. They are not blasé like soldiers of a regular army where grousing is a sign of self-respect and a token of reliability.

A few villages along the road are still populated by Arabs. Some of them are even working in the fields; and a little withered Arab woman is selling oranges to Jewish soldiers out of a basket on her back. War is Hecuba to her and she is Hecuba to war. But not for long. A few weeks later some Arab lads will start sniping from these villages at Jewish trucks on the road; the Jewish army will herd the villagers together, dynamite their houses, and put the young men into concentration camps; while the old ones will tie a mattress and a brass coffee-pot on the donkey, the old woman will walk ahead leading the donkey by the rein and the old man will ride on it, wrapped in his kefiye, and sunk in solemn meditation about the lost opportunity of raping his youngest grandchild.

Monday, June 7, Tel Aviv
Since we have arrived in the Capital I am even more puzzled by this feeling of unreality. We have had our first air-raids, watched people digging shelters, and read the communiqués. But to read in Biblical Hebrew that our troops have improved their positions around Mount Canaan and that all is quiet by the Sea of Galilee, is a strange experience. It is almost impossible to believe that Israel is a real state, its army a real army, and this war a real war. It is certainly the most improbable war that modern history has seen.

But there is another reason for the dreamlike character of the whole thing. What we experience here is a kind of Pompeii in reverse. In Pompeii, schoolboys playing with marbles were suddenly caught by the lava and petrified into monuments. Man-made catastrophes work the same way. Danton's lifted arm freezes in mid-air into the gesture of a bronze monument. Napoleon's liver and Cleopatra's nose belong at the same time to the trivial and historic planes. The actors do not know where exactly the two planes meet, at what point a private gesture becomes a datum of history. But in this country everybody is conscious of living through a Pompeii in reverse. They feel that everything that happens now will be preserved for eternity. Even the schoolboys playing with marbles feel a host of Maccabean spectres looking over their shoulders.

Chapter 24

AT THE CROSSROADS

I stayed in Israel throughout the War of Independence (as a special correspondent of the New York Herald Tribune, Manchester Guardian *and* Le Figaro*), then returned to France where I wrote* Promise and Fulfilment – *a history of Palestine from 1917 to 1949. I quote from the Preface:*

This book consists of three parts, "Background", "Close-up" and "Perspective". The first part is a survey of the development which led to the foundation of the State of Israel. It is written from a specific angle which stresses the part played by irrational forces and emotive bias in history.

The second part, "Close-up", is meant to give the reader a close and coloured, but not I hope technicoloured, view of the Jewish war and of everyday life in the new State.

The third part, "Perspective", is an attempt to present to the reader a comprehensive survey of the social and political structure, the cultural trends and future prospects of the Jewish State.

I lived in Palestine from my twentieth to my twenty-third year. I have since revisited the country at fairly regular intervals, and each of these visits provided an occasion to study not only developments in the country, but also my personal attitude to it. The last phase of this pilgrim's progress through a thicket of emotive and ideological entanglements is summed up in the Epilogue.

The conclusions of that epilogue seemed to me obvious at the time (and still seem so today); I did not foresee the emotional reactions and protracted polemics to which they gave rise. These led me a year later to enlarge the epilogue into an essay, "Judah at

the Crossroads". I shall quote it at some length, because I believe
that even after thirty years it has a valid message.*

Judah at the Crossroads

The martyrdom of the Jews runs like a jagged scar across the face
of human history. The resurrection of the State of Israel offers, for
the first time in two thousand years, the possibility of solving the
Jewish problem. Up to now the Jews' fate lay in the hands of the
Gentiles. At present it lies in their own hands. The wandering Jew
has arrived at a crossroads, and the consequences of his present
choice will make themselves felt for centuries to come.

When the State of Israel proclaimed its independence, Jews all
over the world rejoiced, then carried on business as usual. Their
private lives were not affected. They did not realise that this
historic event confronted them with a historic decision: either to
become citizens of the Jewish state or to abandon the claim to be
members of a distinctive Jewish nation – a claim which is the
foundation-stone of the Jewish faith.

Unlike any other religion, Judaism is inseparably wedded to the
concept of nationhood. Christianity and Islam propound doctrines which are intended for all mankind; Judaism implies membership of a historical nation, descended from a chosen race, the
seed of Abraham, Isaac and Jacob, with whom God made a special
covenant, including a promise of preferential treatment for their
offspring. "Blessed be the Lord, our God, who led our fathers out
of the bondage of Egypt" – every person who repeats that prayer
claims a racial ancestry which (whether real or imagined) automatically sets him apart from the racial and historic past of the
people in whose midst he lives. Unlike Christian festivals, which
are mainly mythological in origin, Jews commemorate landmarks
in national history: the exodus from Egypt, the Maccabean revolt,
the death of the oppressor Haman, the destruction of the Temple.
The Old Testament is first and foremost the narrative of a nation's
history; every prayer and ritual observance reinforces the Jew's
consciousness of his national identity. The oft-heard argument
that Judaism is "a religion like other religions, a purely spiritual

---

*Published in The Trail of the Dinosaur *(1955). Yet another version of it
appeared in the anthology* Next Year in Jerusalem – Portraits of the Jew in the
Twentieth Century, *ed. Douglas Villiers (London and New York, 1976), from
which I have also incorporated some passages in the text below.*

matter which has nothing to do with politics or race", is either hypocritical or based on self-deception. The Jewish faith is nationally and socially self-segregating – and was intended to be so from its tribal beginnings.

At the end of the Passover meal, for the last two thousand years, Jews all over the world have drunk a sacred toast to "next year in Jerusalem". If he takes his religion seriously, the faithful Jew is compelled to regard himself as a person not only with a national past, but also with a national future different from that of the Gentiles among whom he lives. The "Englishman of Jewish faith" becomes a contradiction in terms. As a member of the chosen race, temporarily exiled from the Promised Land, he is not an English Jew, but a Jew living in England. This refers not only to Zionists, but to any member of the Jewish community, whatever his attitude to Zionism, if he takes his religion seriously. The fact that he is naïvely unaware, or only half aware in a muddled way, of the secular and racial implications of his creed, and that he indignantly rejects "racial discrimination" if it comes from the other camp, makes the Jewish tradition only the more paradoxical.

Let us face it, racial discrimination works both ways. Even among liberal and enlightened Jews, who do not claim to belong to a "chosen race", there is a strong tendency to keep themselves to themselves in marriage, business and social life – from Whitechapel to Golders Green. This is only partly due to the pressure of hostile surroundings; an equally important bond is tradition with an ethnic and racial tinge. It is reflected in the discriminatory character of the Jewish attitude to the Gentile. That twenty centuries of persecution must leave their marks of suspicion and defensive hostility, one takes for granted; the point is too obvious to need elaboration. But the Jewish attitude to the Stranger in Israel carries an element of rejection which is older than the ghettos; it dates back to the tribal exclusiveness of the Mosaic religion. The Hebrew word "Goy" for non-Jews does not merely signify "pagan" or "unbeliever"; it does not refer to a soul capable of salvation or a body capable of being accepted into the community after acquiring the true faith. The "Goy" corresponds rather to the Greeks' "Barbarian", to our "natives" and "aborigines". It refers not to a religious, but to a racial and ethnic distinction. In spite of occasional, and somewhat half-hearted, injunctions to be kind to the Stranger in Israel, the Goy is treated in the Old Testament with a mixture of hostility, contempt and pity, as not really quite up to human standards. Later on, the word

"Goy" lost some of its tribal emotionalism, but it has never entirely lost its derogatory echo. In the ghettos of Poland, the young men sang mocking songs about the drunken Goy, which were no nobler in spirit than the anti-Semitic jingles about Kikes and Yids. A persecuted minority certainly has good excuses for repaying hostility and contempt in the same coin, but the point I wish to make is that we are faced with a vicious circle: that a religion with the secular claim of racial exclusiveness must needs create secular repercussions. The Jew's religion sets him apart and invites his being set apart. It automatically creates cultural and ethnic ghettos. The archaic, tribal element in it engenders anti-Semitism on the same archaic level. No amount of enlightenment and tolerance, of indignant protests and pious exhortations, can break this vicious circle.

"Anti-Semitism is a disease that spreads apparently according to its own laws: I believe the only fundamental cause of anti-Semitism – it may seem tautological – is that the Jew exists. We seem to carry anti-Semitism in our knapsacks wherever we go." This was said by Chaim Weizmann, first President of the resurrected Jewish State, in summing up the calvary of twenty long centuries. To expect that it will come to a spontaneous end in the twenty-first is to go against historic and psychological evidence. It can only be brought to an end by Jewry itself. But neither President Weizmann nor any of the Jewish leaders of our time had the courage to face this fact and to speak out openly.

The general distinguishing mark of the Jew, that makes him a Jew on his documents and in the eyes of his fellow-citizens, is his religion; and the Jewish religion, unlike any other, is racially discriminatory, nationally segregative, socially tension-creating. When this basic fact – supported by the evidence of the Old Testament and two thousand years of history – is firmly and uncontroversially established in our minds, and the unconscious resistances against accepting it are overcome, then the first step towards solving the problem will have been made.

We may distinguish between three categories of Jews: (a) the minority of orthodox believers, (b) the larger group of the adherents of a liberalised and diluted version of the Mosaic religion, (c) the largest group of agnostics, who, for reasons of tradition or pride, persist in calling themselves and their children "Jews".

The orthodox believers outside the State of Israel are a small and dwindling minority. The stronghold of orthodox Jewry was Eastern Europe where the Nazi fury reached its peak and wiped them almost completely off the face of the earth. The scattered survivors, and the small orthodox groups in the United States, are composed mostly of elderly people. Orthodoxy is dying out in the Western world, while the bulk of the tradition-bound communities of North Africa, the Yemen, Syria and Iraq emigrated to Israel.

Thus the remnants of orthodox Jewry outside Israel no longer carry much weight. But their position is symbolical. Since the burning down of the Temple they have never ceased to pray for the restoration of the Jewish State. Now, since their prayer has been fulfilled, there seems to be not much point in repeating it. But if prayers of this kind are no longer repeated, if the mystic yearning for the return to Palestine is eliminated from the Jewish faith, then the very foundations and essence of that faith will have gone. No obstacle prevents any longer the orthodox Jew from obtaining a visa at the Israeli Consulate, and booking a passage on the Israeli Line. The choice before him is either to be "next year in Jerusalem", or to cease repeating a vow which has become mere lip-service.

In fact the major part of Judaism's prayers, rites and symbols have become meaningless since the restoration of the Jewish State. To persist in them in the future would be as anachronistic and absurd as if Christians persisted in gathering in catacombs, or Lutherans continued reading their Bible in secret. The Proclamation of Independence of the State of Israel affirms that "it will be open to Jews from all the countries of their dispersion". On the eve of the Sabbath the ram-horn sounds again in the streets of Jerusalem to call the faithful to worship. The Lord of Israel has returned Canaan to Abraham's seed. The orthodox Jew can no longer refer to himself with the ritual phrase as living "in exile" – unless he means a self-imposed exile, based on practical considerations which have nothing to do with religion.

The orthodox position typifies in extreme form the dilemma that is inherent in any liberalised and reformed version of Judaism. I have dwelt at length on the essentially racial and national character of the Jewish religion. Any attempted reform, however enlightened, which aims at eliminating this specific content of Judaism would eliminate its very essence. Take away the "Chosen Race" idea, the genealogical claim of descent from one of the twelve tribes, the focal interest in Palestine as the stage of a glorious past, and the memories of national history perpetuated in the religious festivals; take away the promise of a return to the Holy Land – and all that remained would be a set of archaic dietary prescriptions and tribal laws. It would not be the reform of a religion but its complete emaciation.

Let us now consider the position of that vast majority of contemporary Jewry who display an enlightened or sceptical attitude towards the faith of their ancestors, yet for a number of complex motives persist in confirming their children in that faith and impose on them the "separateness" that it entails. Paradoxically, it is this type of "nondescript" Jew, unable to define his Jewishness in either racial or religious terms, who perpetuates the "Jewish question".

In discussing this central problem, I shall repeatedly quote from Isaiah Berlin's series of articles, "Jewish Slavery and Emancipation",* which has come to be regarded as a classic treatment of the subject. Berlin starts by agreeing that "there is no possible argument against those truly religious Jews to whom the preservation of Judaism as a faith is an absolute obligation to which everything, including life itself, must without hesitation be sacrificed", and later on endorses the view that for these full-blooded Jews, as it were, the only logical solution is emigration to Israel. He then turns to the "nondescript" category and says:

> . . .But it is not so clear that those who believe in the preservation and transmission of "Jewish values" (which are usually something less than a complete religious faith, but rather an amalgam of attitudes, cultural outlook, racial memories and feelings, personal and social habits) are justified in assuming without question that this form of life is obviously worth saving, even at the unbelievable cost in blood and tears which has made the history of the Jews for two thousand years a dreadful martyrology. Once . . . unreasoning faith is diluted into loyalty to traditional forms of life, even though it be sanctified by history and the suffering and faith of heroes and martyrs in every generation, alternative possibilities can no longer be dismissed out of hand.

Obviously, the "alternative possibility" for the nondescript majority who have outgrown Jewish nationalism and the Jewish religion, is to renounce both, and to allow themselves to be socially and culturally absorbed by their environment. All that I have said before leads up to this inescapable conclusion.

*Jewish Chronicle, June, 1950.

Yet the psychological resistance against it is enormous. It is rooted in the general human tendency to avoid a painful choice. But equally important emotional factors are spiritual pride, civic courage, the apprehension of being accused of hypocrisy or cowardice, the scars of wounds inflicted in the past, and the reluctance to abandon a mystic destiny, a specifically "Jewish mission".

Let me concede at once that psychologically there is every excuse for Jews being emotional, illogical and touchy on the question of renunciation – even if they are unable to say what exactly they are reluctant to renounce. But let it also be understood that, while every man has a right to act irrationally and against his own interests, he has no right to act in this way where the future of his children is concerned. I would like to make it clear at this point that my whole line of argument, and the practical conclusions derived from it, are aimed not at the present, but *at the next generation*, at the decisions which men and women who were brought up in the Jewish community must take regarding *not their own status, but the future of their children*. Once this point is clearly established, a number of objections against the process of assimilation will be automatically removed.

I shall now consider some typical objections which were raised since I first proposed the solution advocated in these lines. They are well summarised in the questions put to me by an interviewer from the London *Jewish Chronicle* after the publication of *Promise and Fulfilment* in which I had tentatively broached the subject. The interviewer was Mr Maurice Carr, and the interview, from which the following extracts are quoted, appeared in the official weekly paper of British Jewry under the headline "Arthur Koestler's Renunciation".* It opened with an introductory remark by Mr Carr:

... I was anxious to obtain [the author's comments] to the Epilogue in his book *Promise and Fulfilment* whose message may be summed up in this one brief passage:

"The existence of the Hebrew State . . . puts every Jew outside Israel before a dilemma which will become increasingly acute. It is the choice between becoming a citizen of the Hebrew nation and renouncing any conscious or implicit claim to separate nationhood."

... If that was what Arthur Koestler really meant, then it seemed to me, willy-nilly, that he was placing himself in the evil company of the

*Jewish Chronicle, May 5th, 1950.

professional anti-Semites, who, with the logic of violence, bedaub the walls with the slogan: "Jew go to Israel or into the crematorium!" . . . The ineffable quality of Jewishness, having weathered so many cataclysmic storms in the past, will no doubt resist Arthur Koestler's assault upon it.

Question When you say categorically that the Wandering Jew must decide either to become an Israeli or to renounce utterly his Jewishness, are you thinking in ultimate or immediate terms?

Answer I think that the choice must be made here and now, for the next generation's sake. The time has come for every Jew to ask himself: Do I really consider myself a member of a Chosen Race destined to return from exile to the Promised Land? In other words: Do I want to emigrate to Israel? And if not, what right have I to go on calling myself a Jew and thereby inflicting on my children the stigma of otherliness? Unless one shares the Nazis' racial theories, one has to admit that there is no such thing as a pure Jewish *race*. The primary distinguishing mark of the Jew is his *religion*. But this religion becomes meaningless if you go on praying for the Return to Zion even while you are firmly resolved to stay away. What then remains of your Jewishness? Not much more than the habit of regarding yourself, and being looked upon by others, as an outsider. You thereby condemn your children to unwholesome environmental pressures which at best create handicaps of varying severity for their inner development and public career, and at worst lead to Belsen and Auschwitz.

Q. Is your haste in proclaiming the choice between Israel and total abandonment of Jewishness attributable to the fear of new Belsens and Auschwitzes?

A. Anti-Semitism is growing. Even the British, for all their traditional tolerance, have been affected, otherwise they wouldn't have swallowed Mr Bevin's Palestine policy. But, to my mind, it is not so much the danger of pogroms as the fundamental evil of abnormal environmental pressures from which the Wandering Jew must save himself and the coming generations.

Q. Does it not occur to you that in seeking the will-o'-the-wisp of "normality" and security, runaway Jewry will be sacrificing the distinctive Jewish genius: and do you not consider, from the broadest humanist viewpoint, that such a loss of the Jewish heritage and of Jewish talents will more than outweigh any problematic gains?

A. It is undoubtedly true that the stimulus of environmental pressure has produced a greater proportion of intellectuals among Jews than among their host nations. This type of phenomenon is familiar both to the psychologist and the historian – see in particular Adler's concept of "over-compensation" and Toynbee's "challenge and response". We also know that most great men in literature, art or politics had an unhappy childhood, were lonely and misunderstood, and that their creative achievements were partly due to their reactions to these pressure-stimuli. But would you recommend parents to give their children deliberately an unhappy childhood in the hope of breeding an Einstein, a Freud, or a Heine? Of course, abolish all suffering in the world and you abolish the chance of producing outstanding personalities. But, after all, out of 1000 individuals subjected to unhealthy environmental pressure, 999 will develop thwarted characters and only one will perhaps become an outstanding personality. I reject as wholly indefensible the vague Jewish sentiment: "We must go on being persecuted in order to produce geniuses".

As for the Jewish cultural heritage, the Old Testament and Apocrypha have become the common property of mankind. The Talmud is today of interest only to a narrow specialised group. To impose a study of it, and of Biblical exegesis, on Jewish children in general is as utterly absurd and sterile as it would be to compel all Christian children to study mediaeval scholasticism. As for a *secular* Jewish culture to-day there is only Yiddish literature: but the Yiddish language was killed with the people who spoke it in Eastern Europe, and I don't suppose you would defend its survival in America any more than that of Ukrainian. The only legitimate, natural home for the preservation and future growth of a *specifically Jewish* culture is Israel.

Q. How do you reconcile your dictum "the means justify the end"* with your advice to the Wandering Jew to run away from himself? After the first cowardly step of abdication, surely the renegade Jew will have to stoop to gross deceitfulness, resolutely lying to himself, to his neighbours, and to his children about his Jewish origin. Otherwise if he chooses to be honest and disdains concealment, neither he nor his children will become thoroughgoing non-Jews. Rather will they merely become "ex-Jews". Will not then an ex-Jew be a new sort of freakish outsider, certainly spurned by the Jews, and in all probability still derided by the anti-Semites?

A. Today every Jew has the possibility to go to Israel, so it is no longer an act of cowardice to choose the alternative of renouncing one's Jewishness. It has become a free, voluntary decision which before the re-birth of Israel it was not. . . . To cling to an outworn status of "negative Jewishness" out of sheer stubbornness or from fear of being called a coward, is in itself an inverted form of cowardice for which helpless children will be made to suffer. As to the quality of honesty, that is the very thing I am advocating. It takes an equal measure of uncompromising honesty for one Jew to opt for "next year in Jerusalem" and for another Jew to decide on renunciation. He who abandons Jewishness should not conceal anything from his children; nor on the other hand need he bother the children prematurely. After

*What Mr Carr presumably meant was: "Your rejection of the tenet that the end justifies the means."

all, it is a question of tact and delicacy, rather like the problem of education on sexual matters.

Q. Of all the Jews persecuted by Hitler, none suffered such terrible despair as those who had thought to cast off all traces of their own or their father's or their grandmother's Jewishness. In one form or another, might not a similarly cruel fate – far worse than that which can ever befall a real Jew – overtake the would-be ex-Jews?

A. Whatever one does in life, there is always the chance that something will go wrong. But I am certain that by and large the Gentile world will welcome wholehearted Jewish assimilation. Individual complications may arise, especially in the first and second generations, but thereafter – what with mixed marriages – the Jewish problem will gradually disappear, to the benefit of all concerned.

Q. What religious education, if any, would you suggest for the children of ex-Jews?

A. First let me make it clear that when I advocate the renunciation of the Jewish faith by those who are unwilling to live according to its tenets (that is, to return to the Promised Land) I emphatically do *not* advocate their conversion to any other religion – unless of course they feel spiritually attracted to it. This would be contemptible hypocrisy. But I do advocate with equal emphasis that the *children* of these "ex-Jews", who are neither spiritually nor formally committed to the Jewish creed which their parents have abandoned, should be brought up like the other children of the community in which they live. Do not brand them as different; leave it to them to make their own decisions on matters spiritual when they grow up. To put it bluntly, I regard it as an outright crime for parents who neither believe in Jewish doctrine nor live up to its commandments, to impose the stigma of "otherliness" on a defenceless child.

Q. Do you not feel that there is something abject, humiliating, in such a conformist surrender by the minority to the majority? Without any belief in, say, Catholicism, the ex-Jew is to send his children to a Jesuit school. He is to bury alive his own traditions and memories, and these memories, unfortunately, include bitter persecution at the hands of those whose ranks he is now joining uninvited. Is that not asking altogether too much?

A. To take your last question first, the memory of past persecutions: surely you do not suggest that resentment should be kept rankling and old hatreds perpetuated? It is, of course, never an easy thing to break with the past, to cast off traditions and memories. But millions of American immigrants have done just that without great effort.

Q. Do you still regard yourself as a Jew? Do you wish others to consider you as being no longer a Jew?

A. In so far as religion is concerned, I consider the Ten Commandments and the Sermon on the Mount as inseparable as the root and the flower. In so far as race is concerned, I have no idea and take no interest in the question how many Hebrews, Babylonians, Roman legionaries, Christian crusaders, Hungarian nomads or Caucasian tribesmen converted to Judaism were among my ancestors. I consider it a chance occurrence that my father happened to be of the Jewish faith; but I felt that it committed me morally to identify myself with the Zionist movement, as long as there was no haven for the persecuted and the homeless. The moment that Israel became a reality I felt released from this commitment, and free to choose between living as an Israeli in Israel or a European in Europe. My whole cultural formation made Europe the natural choice. Hence, to give a precise answer to your question: I regard myself, first, as a member of the European community; secondly, as a naturalised British citizen of uncertain and mixed racial origin, who accepts the ethical values and rejects the dogmas of our Helleno-Judaeo-Christian tradition. Into what pigeon-hole others put me is their affair.

That was the end of this long interview, followed by Mr Carr's conclusion:

I do fear that a large number of lukewarm Jews are subconsciously thinking along the lines formulated by Arthur Koestler; and his "thinking aloud" on their behalf may prove extremely useful in drawing attention to an, as it were, submerged menace.

The publication of this interview aroused general indignation among the *Jewish Chronicle*'s readers. A week later the journal came out with an editorial:

The very provocative interview, published recently in *The Jewish Chronicle*, with Mr Arthur Koestler, should remind us of the fact, apparent to most Jewish women, that the home is the citadel in which to defend the Jewish faith. ... And there has yet to be found any comparable system of daily home life. The dietary laws receive daily confirmation from leading medical authorities [sic]: the Jewish housewife down the ages knew how often they protected her and her loved ones from the scourges and plagues that raged around her. Is she, then, at a time when the world so badly needs good men and women, to abandon her faith and sink her own and her family's identity, in order that boys and girls may appear like robots in uniforms indistinguishable one from another?

In subsequent issues there were more letters of protest, all of them sadly illustrative of the manner in which religious fervour degenerates, unnoticed by the believer, into racial arrogance:

In common with the vast majority of my fellow-Jews, outside as well as inside Israel, I feel myself to be just one of a grand array of comrades-in-arms, clad in spiritual armour, scattered over the wide world, and engaged in a fierce and enduring defensive action for a world of freedom, truth, and justice. This struggle began on the day about 4000 years ago, when the Children of Israel turned their backs on the slave-State of Egypt. . . . Mr Koestler seems to be unaware of the fact that the Sermon on the Mount has its origin in Rabbinic thought, that it is merely a rehash of Jewish doctrine. . . .

Another week later the paper came out with yet another editorial:

In actual fact, the dilemma which Mr Koestler poses . . . is basically false. . . . While the Holy Land must always retain its unique significance for Jewry, the message of Judaism and the mission of the Jewish people are not confined to the Holy Land but are universalistic in character. . . . The undying Messianic hopes and aspirations of our Faith forbid us to withdraw from our world-wide mission in the service of mankind. More than ever in these days are we called upon to promote, in whatever country we may dwell, the Jewish ideals of righteousness and brotherhood among the nations. It is not easy to share Mr Koestler's satisfaction that modern civilisation stands in no need of this Jewish contribution.

Apparently the official organ of British Jewry still regards "the ideal of righteousness and brotherhood" as a Jewish monopoly; it actually drove its message home with the somewhat dated quotation: "and ye shall be unto Me a kingdom of priests and a holy nation". It is precisely this kind of turgid bombast which gave rise to the legend of the Elders of Zion, and keeps suspicions of a Jewish world-conspiracy alive. But the controversy served nevertheless a useful purpose by letting the cat of racial pride out of the religious bag, and revealing the tragic contradiction of Jewish existence. For how is the world to reconcile the claim that an Englishman of Jewish faith is like other Englishmen, with the statement, printed in the same issue of the paper: "To be a Jew means that you believe that the past of Jewry is your past, its present your present, its future your future . . ."?

I shall now elaborate some of the points raised in the controversy, in the guise of an imaginary dialogue (which in this case is based on a series of actual dialogues in the past):

Question All previous attempts of Jewish communities to become completely assimilated to their host nation have ended in failure – see Germany for instance; why should it be different this time?

Answer The reason for these past failures is that so far all attempts at assimilation were half-hearted, based on the faulty assumption that Jews could become full-blooded members of their host nations *while retaining their religion. Ethnic assimilation is impossible while maintaining the Mosaic faith: and the Mosaic faith becomes untenable with ethnic assimilation.* The Jewish religion perpetuates national separateness – there is no way around that fact.

There is, on the other hand, at least one example of successful assimilation on a large scale: the Spanish Jews, who some five centuries ago embraced the Catholic faith as an alternative to expulsion, and who (with the exception of a heroically stubborn minority who continued to practise Judaism in secret until they were martyred) have been completely absorbed, racially and culturally, by the Spaniards. To quote Arnold Toynbee again: "There is every reason to believe that in Spain and Portugal today there is a strong tincture of the blood of these Jewish converts in Iberian veins, especially in the upper and middle classes. Yet the most acute psychoanalyst would find it difficult, if samples of living upper- and middle-class Spanish and Portuguese were presented to him, to detect who had Jewish ancestors."

Q. Your arguments are based on the assumption that the only, or at least the principal, distinguishing mark of the Jew is his religion. What about race, physical features, and those peculiarities of Jewish character and behaviour which are difficult to define and yet easy to sense?

A. Racial anthropology is a controversial and muddy field, but there is a kind of minimum agreement among anthropologists on at least these two points: (a) that the Biblical tribe belonged to the Mediterranean branch of the Caucasian race, and (b) that the motley mass of individuals now spread all over the world and designated as "Jews" are from the racial point of view an extremely mixed group who have only a remote connection, and in many cases no connection at all, with that tribe. The contrast between the short, wiry, dark-skinned Yemenite Jew who looks like an Arab, and his Scandinavian co-religionist is obvious.

When the fallacies of racialism have been discarded, all that survives of the Biblical race is probably a statistically very small "hard core" of genes which in segregated Jewish communities keeps "Mendeling out", as the biologist says, in curved noses and wistful irises. But even regarding such facial features it is difficult to distinguish between true heredity and environmental influence. The fairly uniform facial changes of priests living in celibacy, of actors, of convicts serving long sentences, and other types of "professional physiognomies" could easily be mistaken for racial characteristics; and the growing likeness of ageing married couples is an equally puzzling confirmation of the feature-forming power of shared environment.

As for the mental habits and peculiarities of Jews, these vary so widely from country to country that we can only regard them as the product of social, not biological inheritance. The typical Jewish abhorrence of drunkenness, for instance, is the unconscious residue of living for centuries under precarious conditions which made it dangerous to lower one's guard; the Jew with the yellow star on his back had to remain cautious and sober, and watch with amused or frightened contempt the antics of the drunken Goy. Revulsion against alcohol, recklessness and debauch was instilled from parent to child in successive generations – down to the milk-drinking Prime Minister of France* and the abstemious owners of Château Lafitte.

Jewish casuistry, hair-splitting and logic-chopping, can be traced back to the Talmudic exercises which, until recent times, dominated the Jewish child's curriculum in school; as one brilliant biographer of Marx has pointed out, the Dialectic owes as much to Hegel as to Marx's rabbinical background.† The financial and forensic genius of the Jew is obviously a consequence of the fact that until the end of the eighteenth century, and in some countries well into the nineteenth, Jews were debarred from most normal professions; the reasons why in the arts and letters Jews play an interpretative rather than a creative part have been exhaustively analysed in Isaiah Berlin's essay.

We thus have a small and somewhat hypothetical "hard core" of Jewish characteristics in the sense of biological heredity, and a vast complex of physical and mental characteristics which are of environmental origin and transmitted through social inheritance. Both the biological and social features are too complex and diffuse to identify the Jew as a Jew with anything approaching certainty; the decisive test and official identification mark remains his religion.

Q. Even if all your arguments were granted, there would still remain a deep-felt reluctance, a spiritual and aesthetic revulsion

*M. Mendès-France.
†Leopold Schwarzschild, *The Red Prussian* (London, 1948).

in Jewish parents against the idea of bringing up their children in a faith in which they themselves do not believe.

A. My plea is addressed to parents who do not believe in the Jewish religion either; to that vast majority of agnostics who accept the ethical values of our Judeo-Christian heritage and reject all rigid doctrine. The proper thing for them is to say: "If my child must be brought up in a definite religion, then let it be the same in which his playmates are brought up, and not one which sets him apart by its racial doctrine, marks him out as a scapegoat, and gives him mental complexes. What matters is that he should not start under a handicap."

Q. Your arguments betray a utilitarian approach to religious questions which seems to me cynical and improper.

A. Only because you suffer from the guilt-complex of the agnostic who is unable to hold a dogmatic belief but wishes that he could. That, I suspect, goes for all of us, children of the post-materialistic era, filled with transcendental yearnings; once more conscious of a higher, extra-sensory order of reality, and yet intellectually too honest to accept any dogmatic version of it as authentic. If you belong to this category, then surely you too regard the historical accounts of the lives of Buddha, Moses, Jesus and Mohammed as eternal symbols, as archetypes of man's trans-cendental experience and spiritual aspirations, and it makes little difference which set of symbols will be taught to your child according to the hazards of its birth. I believe that it is essential for the moral development of the child to start with some form of belief in a divine order, whose framework he will at first take for Gospel truth until the spiritual content matures into symbolic interpretation. From this point of view – which is the basis of our discussion since my argument is expressly not directed at the orthodox believer – it is quite irrelevant whether the child's imagination is centred on Moses bringing water forth from the rock, or on water turned into wine at Cana.

Allow me to reverse the charge: I find it cynical on your part to turn your child into a potential victim by teaching him to believe in the miracle of the rock but to reject the miracle of Cana, or by celebrating the Sabbath on Saturday instead of Sunday. Do you realise that this futile calendrical dispute, the Jew closing his shop on Saturday and working on Sunday, has been a major irritant and cause of martyrdom for centuries? Do you call it cynical if one deplores the holocausts of Jewish victims burnt, raped, robbed, chased and gassed in the name of a Lilliputian fanaticism regarding the question on which end to break the spiritual egg?

I must now turn to one last objection which carries more psychological weight than all the others because it is not based on logic but on the denial of logic as a guide in human affairs. Isaiah Berlin has expressed this attitude with much insight and eloquence in his essay. After explaining that he was to a large extent in agreement with my position, he continued with a "but":

> But there are . . . many individuals in the world who do not choose to see life in the form of radical choices between one course and another, and whom we do not condemn for this reason. "Out of the crooked timber of humanity," said a great philosopher, "no straight thing was ever made." Fearful thinkers, with minds seeking salvation in religious or political dogma, souls filled with terror, may wish to eliminate such ambiguous elements in favour of a more clear-cut structure, and they are, in this respect, true children of the new age which with its totalitarian systems has tried to institute just such an order among human beings, and sort them out neatly each to his own category. . . . To protest about a section of the population merely because it is felt to be an uncosy element in society, to order it to alter its outlook or get out . . . is . . . a kind of petty tyranny, and derives ultimately from the conviction that human beings have no right to behave foolishly or inconsistently or vulgarly, and that society has the right to try and rid itself by humane means, but rid itself nevertheless, of such persons although they are neither criminals nor lunatics nor in any sense a danger to the lives or liberties of their fellows. This attitude, which is sometimes found to colour the views of otherwise civilised and sensitive thinkers, is a bad attitude because it is clearly not compatible with the survival of the sort of reasonable, humane, "open", social texture in which human beings can enjoy those freedoms and those personal relationships upon which all tolerable life depends.

Isaiah Berlin is as sceptical as I am regarding the possibility of normalising the social status of Jews so long as they insist on calling themselves and being called Jews. Half of his essay is devoted to a penetrating analysis of the psychological factors inherent in the Jewish condition, which make anti-Semitism past, present and future, unavoidable. He also agrees that the rebirth of the State of Israel puts every individual Jew in a dilemma. His argument is simply that you should neither expect nor encourage people to act logically, and that unreason, however irritating or maddening, must be tolerated.

I fully agree that nothing could be more unreasonable than to expect people to behave reasonably. But if you argue that Jews have a right to be guided by irrational emotion and to behave "foolishly, or inconsistently, or vulgarly", you must grant the same right to their adversaries, and I need not enlarge upon the result. It seems to me that if you have a voice and a pen, it is incumbent on you to advocate that course of action which you believe to be in the public interest, and thereby to influence the precarious balance between reason and passion in people's minds. It also seems to me, as I said before, that people have an inalienable right to mess up their own lives, but no right to mess up the lives of their children, just because being a Jew is such a cosy mess.

To sum up: Orthodox Jewry is a vanishing minority. It is the well-meaning but confused majority which, through inertia, perpetuates the anachronism by clinging to a tradition in which it no longer really believes, to a mission which is fulfilled, a pride which has become inverted cowardice. Let them stop to think whether they have the right to place the burden of the ominous knapsack, now void of contents, on their children who have not asked for it.

These conclusions, reached by one who has been an active supporter of the Zionist movement for a quarter-century, while his cultural allegiance belonged to Western Europe, are mainly addressed to the many others in the same situation. Now that the State of Israel has become reality, they are at least free to do what they could not do before: to go their own way with the nation whose life and culture they share.

The legend of the Wandering Jew has become out of date; he must cease to be an accomplice in his own destruction. The fumes of the death chambers still linger over Europe; there must be an end to the calvary.

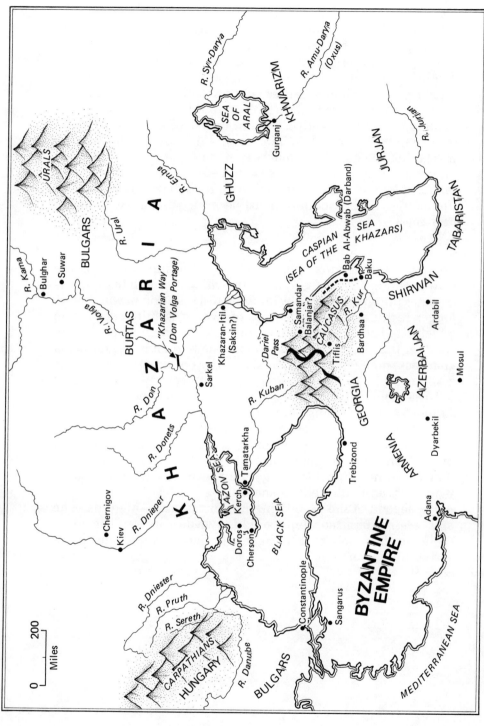

The Khazar Empire

Chapter 25

THE THIRTEENTH TRIBE

*"In Khazaria, sheep, honey and Jews exist in large quantities."
Thus the Arab geographer Muqaddasi, writing in the tenth century.* *

*Other references to the mysterious land of Khazaria sounded
equally puzzling. I first heard about that country as a schoolboy
in my native Hungary. The Khazars were supposed to have been
related to the Magyars, and were thus briefly mentioned in the
school history-books – which also mentioned the legendary tale
of a Khazar King's conversion to Judaism on the bidding of an
angel who appeared to him in a dream.*

*Later I read a treatise by Jehuda Halevi, the famous Jewish poet
and philosopher, who lived in Moorish Spain 1085–1141, and
died on a pilgrimage to the Holy Land. Al Kuzari, the Khazars,
was written a year before his death. It is a theological tract,
propounding the view that the Jewish nation is the sole mediator
between God and the rest of mankind. At the end of History, all
other nations will be converted to Judaism; and the conversion of
the Khazar King appears as a prelude or token of that ultimate
event. The treatise contains no factual information about the
Khazar country itself, which serves merely as a background for
the account of the conversion – the King, the dream, the angel –
and for long dialogues on theology. Yet later I discovered that
Halevi's tract was virtually all that people incomparably better
versed in Judaism than I knew about this crucially important
chapter in the history of world Jewry.*

*Nor did I learn more about it during all the years of involvement
in the Jewish problem. It was some fifteen years after the re-birth*

*Muqaddasi, Descriptio Imperii Moslemici, Bibliotheca Geographorum Arabica
III, 3 (Bonn).

of Israel – which I thought to be the end of the involvement – that the true significance of the Khazar problem began to dawn on me.

My interest in it was first aroused by a chance encounter with a French Orientalist – whose name I have, ungratefully, forgotten – while I was a Fellow of the Center for Advanced Study in the Behavioral Sciences in Stanford, California. He gave me a rough outline of the historical facts about the Khazars, and alleged that Jewish historians have deliberately played down the importance of the subject, because of its potentially explosive implications.

However, another ten years were to pass until I got really immersed in research into Khazar history. Our knowledge of it is mainly derived from Arab, Byzantine, Russian and Hebrew sources with corroborative evidence of Persian, Syrian, Armenian, Georgian and Turkish origin. Most of these sources I found available in translations in various specialised libraries, and there was also much information to be gathered from modern historians – Toynbee, Bury, Vernadsky, Dunlop – who had written on some aspect of Khazar history. Thus the jigsaw gradually fell into place and resulted in The Thirteenth Tribe – The Khazar Empire and its Heritage (1976).

I cannot claim to have discovered any previously unknown facts; merely to have assembled the bits of the puzzle, most of them known only to scholars with a specialised interest in Eastern mediaeval history.

I quote from the opening pages of the book:

About the time when Charlemagne was crowned Emperor of the West, the eastern confines of Europe between the Caucasus and the Volga were ruled by a Jewish state, known as the Khazar Empire (see map). At the peak of its power, from the seventh to the tenth centuries AD, it played a significant part in shaping the destinies of mediaeval, and consequently of modern, Europe. The Byzantine Emperor and historian, Constantine Porphyrogenitus (913–959), must have been well aware of this when he recorded in his treatise on court protocol* that letters addressed to the Pope in Rome, and similarly those to the Emperor of the West, had a gold seal worth two solidi attached to them, whereas messages to the King of the Khazars displayed a seal worth three solidi. "In the period with which we are concerned," wrote Bury, "it is probable

*Constantine Porphyrogenitus, *De Ceremoniis*, ed., with commentary, A. Vogt (Paris, 1935–40), Vol. I, p. 690.

that the Khan of the Khazars was of little less importance in view of the imperial foreign policy than Charles the Great and his successors".*

The country of the Khazars, a people of Turkish stock, occupied a stategic key position at the vital gateway between the Black Sea and the Caspian, where the great eastern powers of the period confronted each other. It acted as a buffer protecting Byzantium against invasions by the lusty barbarian tribesmen of the northern steppes – Bulgars, Magyars, Pechenegs, etc. – and, later, the Vikings and the Russians. But equally, or even more important both from the point of view of Byzantine diplomacy and of European history, is the fact that the Khazar armies effectively blocked the Arab avalanche in its most devastating early stages, and thus prevented the Muslim conquest of Eastern Europe. Professor Dunlop of Columbia University, a leading authority on the history of the Khazars, has given a concise summary of this decisive yet virtually unknown episode:

> The Khazar country . . . lay across the natural line of advance of the Arabs. Within a few years of the death of Muhammad (AD 632) the armies of the Caliphate, sweeping northward through the wreckage of two empires and carrying all before them, reached the great mountain barrier of the Caucasus. This barrier once passed, the road lay open to the lands of eastern Europe. As it was, on the line of the Caucasus the Arabs met the forces of an organized military power which effectively prevented them from extending their conquests in this direction. The wars of the Arabs and the Khazars, which lasted more than a hundred years, though little known, have thus considerable historical importance. The Franks of Charles Martel on the field of Tours turned the tide of the Arab invasion. At about the same time the threat to Europe in the east was hardly less acute. . . . The victorious Muslims were met and held by the forces of the Khazar kingdom. . . . It can . . . scarcely be doubted that but for the existence of the Khazars in the region north of the Caucasus, Byzantium, the bulwark of European civilization in the east, would have found itself outflanked by the Arabs, and the history of Christendom and Islam might well have been very different from what we know. †

It is perhaps not surprising, given these circumstances, that in 732 – after a resounding Khazar victory over the Arabs – the future Emperor Constantine V married a Khazar princess. In due time their son became the Emperor Leo IV, known as Leo the Khazar.

*Bury, J. B., A History of the Eastern Roman Empire (London, 1912), p. 402.
†Dunlop, D. M., The History of the Jewish Khazars (Princeton, 1954), pp. ix–x.

Ironically, the last battle in the war, AD 737, ended in a Khazar defeat. But by that time the impetus of the Muslim Holy War was spent, the Caliphate was rocked by internal dissensions, and the Arab invaders retraced their steps across the Caucasus without having gained a permanent foothold in the north, whereas the Khazars became more powerful than they had previously been.

A few years later, probably AD 740, the King, his court and the military ruling class embraced the Jewish faith, and Judaism became the state religion of the Khazars. No doubt their contemporaries were as astonished by this decision as modern scholars were when they came across the evidence in the Arab, Byzantine, Russian and Hebrew sources. One of the most recent comments is to be found in a work by the Hungarian Marxist historian, Dr Antal Bartha. His book on *The Magyar Society in the Eighth and Ninth Centuries** has several chapters on the Khazars, as during most of that period the Hungarians were ruled by them. Yet their conversion to Judaism is discussed in a single paragraph, with obvious embarrassment. It reads:

> Our investigations cannot go into problems pertaining to the history of ideas, but we must call the reader's attention to the matter of the Khazar kingdom's state religion. It was the Jewish faith which became the official religion of the ruling strata of society. Needless to say, the acceptance of the Jewish faith as the state religion of an ethnically non-Jewish people could be the subject of interesting speculations. We shall, however, confine ourselves to the remark that this official conversion – in defiance of Christian proselytizing by Byzantium, the Muslim influence from the East, and in spite of the political pressure of these two powers – to a religion which had no support from any political power, but was persecuted by nearly all – has come as a suprise to all historians concerned with the Khazars, and cannot be considered as accidental, but must be regarded as a sign of the independent policy pursued by that kingdom.

Which leaves us only slightly more bewildered than before. Yet whereas the sources differ in minor detail, the major facts are beyond dispute.

What is in dispute is the fate of the Jewish Khazars *after* the destruction of their empire, in the twelfth or thirteenth century. On this problem the sources are scant, but various late mediaeval Khazar settlements are mentioned in the Crimea, in the Ukraine, in Hungary, Poland and Lithuania. The general picture that

*Budapest, 1968, p. 35.

emerges from these fragmentary pieces of information is that of a migration of Khazar tribes and communities into those regions of Eastern Europe – mainly Russia and Poland – where, at the dawn of the Modern Age, the greatest concentrations of Jews were found. This has led several historians to conjecture that a substantial part, and perhaps the majority of eastern Jews – and hence of world Jewry – might be of Khazar, and not of Semitic origin.

The far-reaching implications of this hypothesis may explain the great caution exercised by historians in approaching this subject – if they do not avoid it altogether. Thus in the 1973 edition of the *Encyclopaedia Judaica* the article "Khazars" is signed by Dunlop, but there is a separate section dealing with "Khazar Jews after the Fall of the Kingdom", signed by the editors, and written with the obvious intent to avoid upsetting believers in the dogma of the Chosen Race:

> The Turkish-speaking Karaites [a fundamentalist Jewish sect] of the Crimea, Poland, and elsewhere have affirmed a connection with the Khazars, which is perhaps confirmed by evidence from folklore and anthropology as well as language. There seems to be a considerable amount of evidence attesting to the presence in Europe of descendants of the Khazars.

One of the most radical propounders of the hypothesis concerning the Khazar origins of Jewry is the Professor of Mediaeval Jewish History at Tel Aviv University, A. N. Poliak. His book *Khazaria* (in Hebrew) was published in 1944 in Tel Aviv, and a second edition in 1951.* In his introduction he writes that the facts demand –

> a new approach, both to the problem of the relations between the Khazar Jewry and other Jewish communities, and to the question of how far we can go in regarding this [Khazar] Jewry as the nucleus of the large Jewish settlement in Eastern Europe. . . . The descendants of this settlement – those who stayed where they were, those who emigrated to the United States and to other countries, and those who went to Israel – constitute now the large majority of world Jewry.

This was written before the full extent of the Holocaust was known, but that does not alter the fact that the vast majority of surviving Jews in the world is of Eastern European – and thus perhaps mainly of Khazar – origin. If so, this would mean that

Khazaria – The History of the Jewish Kingdom in Europe (in Hebrew) (Mossad Bialik Tel Aviv, 1951).

their ancestors came not from the Jordan but from the Volga, not from Canaan but from the Caucasus, once believed to be the cradle of the Aryan race; and that genetically they are more closely related to the Hun, Uigur and Magyar tribes than to the seed of Abraham, Isaac and Jacob. Should this turn out to be the case, then the term "anti-Semitism" would become void of meaning, based on a misapprehension shared by both the killers and their victims. The story of the Khazar Empire, as it slowly emerges from the past, begins to look like the most cruel hoax which history has ever perpetrated.

From this prelude to the book, let me proceed straight to the Summary at the end of the last chapter:

Summary

In Part One of this book I have attempted to trace the history of the Khazar Empire based on the scant existing sources.

In Part Two, Chapters V–VII, I have compiled the historical evidence which indicates that the bulk of Eastern Jewry – and hence of world Jewry – is of Khazar–Turkish, rather than Semitic, origin.

In the last chapter I have tried to show that the evidence from anthropology concurs with history in refuting the popular belief in a Jewish race descended from the Biblical tribe.

From the anthropologist's point of view, two groups of facts militate against this belief: the wide *diversity* of Jews with regard to physical characteristics, and their *similarity* to the Gentile populations amidst whom they live. Both are reflected in the statistics about bodily height, cranial index, blood-groups, hair and eye colour, etc. Whichever of these anthropological criteria is taken as an indicator, it shows a greater similarity between Jews and their Gentile host-nation than between Jews living in different countries.

The obvious biological explanation for both phenomena is miscegenation, which took different forms in different historical situations: intermarriage, large-scale proselytising, rape as a constant (legalized or tolerated) accompaniment of war and pogrom.

The belief that, notwithstanding the statistical data, there exists a recognisable Jewish type is based largely, though not entirely, on various misconceptions. It ignores the fact that features regarded as typically Jewish by comparison with Nordic people cease to appear so in a Mediterranean environment; it is unaware of the impact of the social environment on physique and countenance; and it confuses biological with social inheritance.

Nevertheless, there exist certain hereditary traits which characterise a certain type of contemporary Jew. In the light of modern population-genetics, these can to a large degree be attributed to processes which operated for several centuries in the segregated conditions of the ghetto: inbreeding, genetic drift, selective pressure. The last-mentioned operated in several ways: natural selection (e.g. through epidemics), sexual selection and, more doubtfully, the selection of character-features favouring survival within the ghetto walls.

In addition to these, social heredity, through childhood conditioning, acted as a powerful formative and deformative factor.

Each of these processes contributed to the emergence of the ghetto type of Jew. In the post-ghetto period it became progressively diluted. As for the genetic composition and physical appearance of the *pre-ghetto* stock, we know next to nothing. In the view presented in this book, this "original stock" was predominantly Turkish mixed to an unknown extent with ancient Palestinian and other elements. Nor is it possible to tell which of the so-called typical features, such as the "Jewish nose", is a product of sexual selection in the ghetto, or the manifestation of a particularly "persistent" tribal gene. Since "nostrility" is frequent among Caucasian peoples, and infrequent among the Semitic Bedouins, we have one more pointer to the dominant role played by the "thirteenth tribe" in the biological history of the Jews.

After this Summary, there are several Appendices to the book, of which the last one has the title: "Some Implications – Israel and the Diaspora". Although it repeats some of the arguments which appear in earlier essays, I shall quote it in full.

Some Implications – Israel and the Diaspora

While this book deals with past history, it unavoidably carries certain implications for the present and future.

In the first place, I am aware of the danger that it may be maliciously misinterpreted as a denial of the State of Israel's right to exist. But that right is not based on the hypothetical origins of the Jewish people, nor on the mythological covenant of Abraham with God; it is based on international law – i.e., on the United Nations' decision in 1947 to partition Palestine, once a Turkish province, then a British Mandated Territory, into an Arab and a Jewish State. Whatever the Israeli citizens' racial origins, and whatever illusions they entertain about them, their State exists *de jure* and *de facto*, and cannot be undone, except by genocide. Without entering into controversial issues, one may add, as a matter of historical fact, that the partition of Palestine was the result of a century of peaceful Jewish immigration and pioneering effort, which provide the moral justification for the State's legal existence. Whether the chromosomes of its people contain genes of Khazar or Semitic, Roman or Spanish origin, is irrelevant, and cannot affect Israel's right to exist – nor the moral obligation of any civilised person, Gentile or Jew, to defend that right. The geographical origin even of the modern Israeli's parents or grandparents tends to be forgotten in the bubbling racial melting pot. The problem of the Khazar infusion a thousand years ago, however fascinating, is irrelevant to modern Israel.

The Jews who inhabit it, regardless of their chequered origins, possess the essential requirements of a nation: a country of their own, a common language, government and army. The Jews of the Diaspora have none of these requirements of nationhood. What sets them apart, as a special category from the Gentiles amidst whom they live, is their declared religion, whether they practise it or not. Here lies the basic difference between Israelis and Jews of the Diaspora. The former have acquired a national identity; the latter are labelled as Jews only by their religion – not by their nationality, not by their race.

This, however, creates a paradox, because the Jewish religion – unlike Christianity, Buddhism or Islam – implies membership of a historical nation. The Old Testament is the narrative of a nation's history; it gave monotheism to the world, yet its credo is tribal rather than universal. Every prayer and ritual observance proclaims membership of an ancient race, which automatically separates the Jew from the racial and historic past of the people in whose midst he lives. The Jewish faith, as shown by two thousand years of tragic history, is nationally and socially self-segregating. It sets the Jew apart and invites his being set apart. It creates physical and cultural ghettos. It transformed the Jews of the Diaspora into a *pseudo-nation* without any of the attributes and privileges of nationhood, held together loosely by a system of traditional beliefs based on racial and historical premises which turn out to be illusory.

Orthodox Jewry is dying out in the Diaspora; it is the vast majority of enlightened or agnostic Jews who perpetuate the paradox by loyally clinging to their pseudo-national status in the belief that it is their duty to preserve the Jewish tradition.

It is, however, not easy to define what the term "Jewish tradition" signifies in the eyes of this enlightened majority, who reject the Chosen-Race doctrine. That doctrine apart, the universal messages of the Old Testament – the enthronement of the one and invisible God, the Ten Commandments, the ethos of the Hebrew prophets, the Proverbs and Psalms – have entered into the mainstream of the Judeo–Hellenic–Christian tradition and become the common property of Jew and Gentile alike.

After the destruction of Jerusalem, the Jews ceased to have a language and secular culture of their own. Hebrew as a vernacular yielded to Aramaic before the beginning of the Christian era; the Jewish scholars and poets in Spain wrote in Arabic, others later in German, Polish, Russian, English and French. Certain Jewish communities developed dialects of their own, such as Yiddish and Ladino, but none of these produced works comparable to the impressive Jewish contribution to German, Austro-Hungarian or American literature.

The main, *specifically* Jewish literary activity of the Diaspora was theological. Yet Talmud, Kabbala, and the bulky tomes of Biblical exegesis are practically unknown to the contemporary Jewish public, although they are, to repeat it once more, the only relics of a *specifically Jewish* tradition – if that term is to have a concrete meaning – during the last two millennia. In other words, whatever came out of the Diaspora is either not specifically Jewish, or not part of a living tradition. The philosophical, scientific and artistic achievements of individual Jews consist in contributions to the culture of their host nations; they do not represent a common cultural inheritance or autonomous body of traditions.

To sum up, the Jews of our day have no cultural tradition in common, merely certain habits and behaviour-patterns, derived by social inheritance from the traumatic experience of the ghetto, and from a religion which the majority does not practise or believe in, but which nevertheless confers on them a pseudo-national status. Obviously – as I have argued before – the long-term solution of the paradox can only be emigration to Israel or gradual assimilation to their host nations. Before the Holocaust, this process was in full swing; and in 1975 *Time* magazine reported* that American Jews "tend to marry outside their faith at a high rate; almost one-third of all marriages are mixed".

Nevertheless the lingering influence of Judaism's racial exclusiveness, though based on illusion, acts as a powerful brake by appealing to tribal loyalty. It is in this context that the part played by the "thirteenth tribe" in ancestral history becomes relevant to the Jews of the Diaspora. Yet, as already said, it is irrelevant to modern Israel, which has acquired a genuine national identity. It is perhaps symbolic that Abraham Poliak, a professor of history at Tel Aviv University and no doubt an Israeli patriot, made a major contribution to our knowledge of Jewry's Khazar ancestry, undermining the legend of the Chosen Race. It may also be significant that the native Israeli "Sabra" represents, physically and mentally, the complete opposite of the "typical Jew", bred in the ghetto.

*March 10, 1975.

POSTSCRIPT TO BOOK ONE

Before saying farewell to politics, I felt the urge to take stock of the past — of nearly fifty years of sound and fury. The result of this stock-taking was two volumes of autobiography, Arrow in the Blue *(1952) and* The Invisible Writing *(1954), which I have frequently quoted in these pages. To write one's memoirs before one has reached the age of fifty may seem a premature and somewhat presumptuous undertaking. But if one's past is worth recording at all, this should be done before its colour and fragrance have faded. Gains in distance and perspective must be balanced against losses in emotional freshness, for facts are more easily retained than feelings. Facts can be enshrined in records, emotions not.*

I shall quote one last bit from the Epilogue to The Invisible Writing:

Here this case history, which has now grown to four volumes,* comes to an end. A fitting epitaph for it was sent to me a few months ago. It is an election poster, three feet by two, put out by the Social-Democratic party of Germany, reproduced overleaf. The translation of the text reads:

1933 . . .
In those days the pyres were blazing in Germany's towns. By the order of Goebbels millions of books were burned in the flames.

The design below this text shows Goebbels hurling a book into the fire while Hitler looks on; the book shows the name "Köstler" on its cover.

*Dialogue with Death, Scum of the Earth, Arrow in the Blue *and* The Invisible Writing.

1933...

In jenen Tagen loderten in deutschen Städten die Scheiterhaufen. Auf Befehl von Goebbels wanderten Millionen Bücher in die Flammen.

1952...

In diesen Tagen lodern in der Sowjetzone wieder Scheiterhaufen. Wieder werden 9 Millionen Bücher von dieser Flamme verzehrt!

Es ist dieselbe Flamme!   Es ist derselbe Ungeist!

Es sind dieselben Methoden!

Zumeist sind es die Werke der Freiheit und des Friedens, die zu Asche werden! Wer den Frieden will, muß lernen, daß man Freiheit und Geist nicht auf den Scheiterhaufen wirft!

1952 . . .

In these days new pyres were blazing in the German towns of the Soviet zone. Again 9 million books perished in the flames.

The design shows Pieck throwing another book, again marked "Köstler", into the fire, while Stalin looks on.

Though one may object that by 1933 I had only published one book of which no large quantities were available for burning, I found the fact that this poster was being displayed in the towns of Germany nevertheless gratifying. A copy of it now hangs outside my study, framed like a professional diploma certifying that its owner has passed his examinations and is entitled to exercise his craft. For, to be burned twice in one's lifetime, is, after all, a rare distinction.

BOOK TWO
In Search of a Synthesis

Une vie d'analyse pour une
heure de synthèse!

FUESTEL DE COULANGES

PART ONE

THE ACT
OF CREATION

Chapter 26

JOKING APART

Artists treat facts as stimuli for the imagination, while scientists use their imagination to coordinate facts. The aim of this
book is, first to show that such distinctions are not fundamental, that all the creative activities of man are based on a
common pattern, and to present a unifying theory of humour,
art and discovery.   *Insight and Outlook*

*Book Two is a selection from writings after the "vocational
change" and reflects the successive stages of what one might call
an intellectual armchair odyssey.*

*The long journey started at an after-dinner coffee party at the flat
of a Hungarian psychoanalyst. It was during my last visit to my
native Budapest, in 1935, some forty-five years ago. The analyst's
name was Dr Rappaport, affectionately known among his friends
as "Rappa"; he later became a distinguished academic in the
United States. Rappa's patients were mostly writers, and he
treated most of them gratis; his late coffee parties were a favourite
attraction among intellectuals — a sort of private coffee-house for
exchanging political gossip and engaging in highbrow discussions. On one such occasion, Rappa quoted an ancient joke from
Bergson's book Le Rire* and raised the question why it should
strike one as funny. The joke was about a dignitary of Monte Carlo
who wore no less than thirty-six medals on his breast. Somebody*

*For a critique of Bergson's and Freud's theories of humour, see Insight and
Outlook, Appendix II.

asked him by what noble deeds he had earned them. "That's simple," he replied, "I got a medal for my faithful services to the Prince; I put it on a number on the roulette table, and, lucky me, the number came up."

Various subtle explanations were offered and found wanting; yet the answer seemed so obvious that I hesitated before spelling it out. It went something like this: winnings at roulette are paid out according to certain rules of the game. Decorations are awarded according to certain conventions, i.e., rules of another kind of game. Both sets of rules, or frames of reference, are logically self-consistent, but they are mutually exclusive. In our normal routines of thinking, we keep such frames of reference neatly separate. In the dignitary's reply, however, the two frames suddenly collide. As a result, the medals are no longer perceived in a single associative context, as is normally the case, but are, so to speak, "bisociated" with two incompatible contexts. It is this unexpected short-circuiting of the two contexts, defying our logical expectations, which provides the comic effect.

This suggestion was not received with much enthusiasm – understandably, as it applied to one only among the many aspects of the problem. Yet the improvised term "bisociation" turned out to be a useful conceptual tool – not only for the analysis of humour, but also in the study of scientific discovery and artistic creation – and eventually found its way into the venerable columns of the Encyclopaedia Britannica.

At the time, however, I could not pursue the subject further. For the next fifteen eventful years I was still immersed in the activities related in previous chapters. Nevertheless, in the relatively quiet intervals I kept returning, as a hobby, to the psychology of humour, and to work on a theory which was subsequently to grow into a study of creativity in general. Its aim was defined in the Preface to The Act of Creation (1964):

The first part of this book proposes a theory of the act of creation – of the conscious and unconscious processes underlying scientific discovery, artistic originality, and comic inspiration. It endeavours to show that all creative activities have a basic pattern in common, and to outline that pattern.

However, The Act of Creation – a massive tome of 750 pages – was not my first book on the subject. The first, called Insight and Outlook, was published in 1949, and although I believe that it was more or less on the right track, it was marred by an academic pedantry which was perhaps a reaction, or over-reaction, against all the political oratory still buzzing in my ears. Insight and Outlook was intended as the first of two volumes, and its preface contained the optimistic sentence: "Volume Two is in preparation and will, it is hoped, appear twelve months after the first".

The twelve months grew into fifteen years. When I started on the second volume I soon found it preferable to scrap the first and begin again at the beginning. But during those fifteen years the theory kept branching out, as theories are wont to do, and one of these branches, intended as a chapter on the Copernican revolution, grew into a self-contained opus of 620 pages: The Sleepwalkers – A History of Man's Changing Vision of the Universe (1959). It took four years to write, and although it is, so to speak, a by-product, it seems to have filled a gap in the history of science, as an abridged version of it is included in the "Science Study Series"* and widely used by students as a textbook. The following quote is from the Preface of The Sleepwalkers:

In the index to the six hundred odd pages of Arnold Toynbee's A Study of History, abridged version, the names of Copernicus, Galileo, Descartes and Newton do not occur. This one example among many should be sufficient to indicate the gulf that still separates the Humanities from the Philosophy of Nature. I use this outmoded expression because the term "Science", which has come to replace it in more recent times, does not carry the same rich and universal associations which "Natural Philosophy" carried in the seventeenth century, in the days when Kepler wrote his Harmony of the World and Galileo his Message from the Stars. Those men who created the upheaval which we now call the "Scientific Revolution" called it by a quite different name: the "New Philosophy". The revolution in technology which their discoveries triggered off was an unexpected by-product; their aim was not the conquest of Nature, but the understanding of Nature. Yet their cosmic quest destroyed the mediaeval vision of an immutable social order in a walled-in universe together with its fixed hierarchy of moral values, and transformed the European landscape, society, culture, habits and general outlook, as thoroughly as if a new species had arisen on this planet.

*Under the title The Watershed – A Biography of Johannes Kepler (New York, 1960).

This mutation of the European mind in the seventeenth century is merely the latest example of the impact of the "Sciences" on the "Humanities" – of the inquiry into the nature of Nature on the inquiry into the nature of Man. It also illustrates the wrong-headedness of erecting academic and social barriers between the two; a fact which is at last beginning to gain recognition, nearly half a millennium after the Renaissance created the *uomo universale*.

Another result of this fragmentation is that there exist Histories of Science which tell one at what date the mechanical clock made its first appearance, and Histories of Astronomy which inform one that the precession of the equinoxes was discovered by Hipparchus of Alexandria; but, surprisingly, there exists to my knowledge no modern History of Cosmology, no comprehensive survey of man's changing vision of the universe which encloses him.

The above explains what this book is aiming at. It is not a history of astronomy, though astronomy comes in where it is needed to bring the vision into sharper focus; and, though aimed at the general reader, it is not a book of "popular science" but a personal and speculative account of a controversial subject. It opens with the Babylonians and ends with Newton; the cosmology of Einstein is as yet in a fluid state, and it is too early to assess its influence on culture.

I have been interested, for a long time, in the psychological process of discovery as the most concise manifestation of man's creative faculty – and in that converse process that blinds him towards truths which, once perceived by a seer, become so heart-breakingly obvious. However, this blackout shutter operates not only in the minds of the "ignorant and superstitious masses" as Galileo called them, but is even more strikingly evident in Galileo's own, and in other geniuses like Aristotle, Ptolemy or Kepler. It looks as if, while part of their spirit was asking for more light, another part had been crying out for more darkness. The History of Science is a relative newcomer on the scene, and the biographers of its Cromwells and Napoleons are as yet little concerned with psychology; their heroes are mostly represented as reasoning-machines on austere marble pedestals, in a manner long outdated in the mellower branches of historiography – probably on the assumption that in the case of a Philosopher of Nature, unlike that of a statesman or conqueror, character and personality are irrelevant. Yet all cosmological systems, from the Pythagoreans to Copernicus, Descartes and Eddington, reflect the unconscious prejudices, the philosophical or even political bias of their authors; and from physics to physiology, no branch of Science, ancient or modern, can boast freedom from metaphysical bias of one kind or another. The progress of Science is generally regarded as a kind of clean, rational advance along a straight ascending line; in fact it has followed a zig-zag course, at times almost as bewildering as the evolution of political thought. The history of cosmological theories, in particular, may without exaggeration be called a history of collective obsessions; and the manner in which some of the most important individual discoveries were arrived at reminds one more of a sleepwalker's performance than an electronic brain's.

Thus, in taking down Copernicus or Galileo from the pedestal on which science-mythology has placed them, my motive was not to "debunk", but to inquire into the obscure workings of the creative mind. Yet I shall not be sorry if, as an accidental by-product, the inquiry helps to counteract the legend that Science is a purely rational pursuit, that the Scientist is a more "level-headed" and "dispassionate" type than others (and should therefore be given a leading part in world affairs); or that he is able to provide for himself and his contemporaries a rational substitute for ethical insights derived from other sources.

I shall return to The Sleepwalkers *in Chapter 34.*

After that book was finished, it took another three years to complete the fifteen years of apprenticeship for The Act of Creation, *which was finally published in 1964.*

Altogether thirty years had passed since Dr Rappa told that joke about the thirty-six medals. Yet humour remained for me the master-key to the understanding of the creative process. The rationale for this seemingly perverse approach will, I hope, soon become apparent; a few lines (from Janus – A Summing Up) *may serve as a prelude:*

The psychology of the creative process is, oddly enough, most clearly revealed in humour and wit. But this will appear less odd if we remember that "wit" is an ambiguous term, relating to both witticism and to ingenuity or inventiveness. "Wit" stems from *witan*, understanding, whose roots go back to the Sanskrit *veda*, knowledge. The German *Witz* means both joke and acumen; it comes from *wissen*, to know; *Wissenschaft*, science, is a close kin to *Fürwitz* and *Aberwitz* – presumption, cheek, and jest. French teaches the same lesson. *Spirituel* may either mean witty or spiritually profound; "to amuse" comes from "to muse" (a-muser), and a witty remark is a jeu d'esprit – a playful, mischievous form of discovery. The jester, the artist and the scientist all "live on their wits", and we shall see that the jester's riddles provide a convenient back-door entry, as it were, into the inner sanctum of creative originality. Hence this inquiry will start with an analysis of the comic.

In The Act of Creation that analysis occupies nearly a hundred pages. The extract which follows is a condensation of it, which I wrote for the Encyclopaedia Britannica (article on "Humour and Wit", E. B., 15th edition, 1974).

Humour and Wit

Humour, in all its many-splendour'd varieties, can be simply defined as a type of stimulation which tends to elicit the laughter reflex. Spontaneous laughter is a reflex produced by the contraction of fifteen facial muscles in a stereotyped pattern and accompanied by altered breathing. Electrical stimulation of the zygomatic major, the main lifting muscle of the upper lip, with currents of growing intensity produces facial expressions ranging from the faint smile through the broad grin, to the contortions typical of explosive laughter.* (The laughter and smile of civilised man is of course often of a conventional kind where voluntary effort deputises for, or interferes with, spontaneous reflex activity; we are concerned, however, only with the latter.)

PARADOXES OF LAUGHTER

Once we realise that laughter is a humble reflex, we are faced with several paradoxes. Motor reflexes, such as the contraction of the pupil in dazzling light, are simple responses to simple stimuli; their value in the service of survival is obvious. But the involuntary contraction of fifteen facial muscles, associated with certain irrepressible noises, strikes one as an activity devoid of any practical value, quite unrelated to the struggle for survival. Laughter is a reflex, but unique in that it has no apparent biological utility.

*Duchenne de Boulogne, Le Mécanisme de la Physionomie Humaine (Paris, 1862).

One might call it a luxury reflex. Its only purpose seems to be to provide relief from the stress of purposeful activities.

The second, related paradox of laughter is the striking discrepancy between the nature of the stimulus and that of the responses. When a blow beneath the knee-cap causes an automatic upward kick, both "stimulus" and "response" are on the same primitive physiological level. But that such a complex mental activity as reading a comic story should cause a specific reflex-contraction of the facial musculature is a phenomenon which has puzzled philosophers since Plato. There is no fixed, predictable bodily response which would tell the concert pianist whether he has succeeded in moving his audience; but when the comedian tells a funny story, laughter provides a reliable experimental test for success or failure. *Humour is the only form of communication in which a stimulus on a high level of complexity produces a stereotyped, predictable response on the physiological reflex level.* This enables us to use the response as an indicator for the presence of that elusive quality we call humour – as we use the click of the Geiger counter to indicate the presence of radioactivity. Such a procedure is not possible in any other form of art; and since the step from the sublime to the ridiculous is reversible, the study of the ridiculous may yield important clues for the study of the sublime.

THE LOGIC OF LAUGHTER

The range of laughter-provoking experiences is enormous, from physical tickling to mental titillations of the most varied and sophisticated kind. I shall attempt to demonstrate that there is unity in this variety, a common denominator of a specific and specifiable pattern which reflects the "logic" or "grammar" of humour. A few examples will help to unravel that pattern.

(a) A masochist is a person who likes a cold shower in the morning; so he takes a hot one.

(b) A pious lady, on being asked what she thought of her departed husband's whereabouts: "Well, I suppose the poor soul is enjoying eternal bliss, but I wish you wouldn't talk about such unpleasant subjects."

(c) A doctor comforts his patient: "You have a very serious disease. Of ten persons who catch it only one survives. It is lucky you came to me, for I have recently had nine patients with this disease and they all died of it."

(d) Dialogue in a film by Claude Berri:
"Sir, I would like to ask for your daughter's hand."
"Why not? You have already had the rest."
(e) A marquis at the court of Louis XV unexpectedly returned from a journey and, on entering his wife's boudoir, found her in the arms of a bishop. After a moment's hesitation the marquis walked calmly to the window, leaned out and began going through the motions of blessing the people in the street.
"What are you doing?" cried the anguished wife.
"Monseigneur is performing my functions, so I am performing his."

Is there a common pattern underlying these five stories? Starting with the last, we discover after a little reflection that the marquis's behaviour is both unexpected and perfectly logical – but of a logic not usually applied to this type of situation. It is the logic of the division of labour, governed by rules as old as human civilisation. But we expected that his reactions would be governed by a different set of rules – the code of sexual morality. It is the sudden clash between these two mutually exclusive codes of rules – or associative contexts – which produces the comic effect. It compels us to perceive the situation in two self-consistent but incompatible frames of reference at the same time; it makes us function simultaneously on two different wave-lengths. While this unusual condition lasts, the event is not, as is normally the case, associated with a single frame of reference, but *bisociated* with two.

The term "bisociation" was coined by the present writer to make a distinction between the routines of disciplined thinking within a single universe of discourse – on a single plane, as it were – and the creative types of mental activity which always operate on more than one level. In humour, both the creation of a subtle joke and the *re-creative* act of perceiving the joke, involve the delightful mental jolt of a sudden leap from one plane or associative context to another.

Let us turn to our other examples. In the film dialogue, the daughter's "hand" is perceived first in a metaphorical frame of reference, then suddenly in a literal, anatomical context.

The widowed lady who looks upon death as "eternal bliss" and at the same time "an unpleasant subject", epitomises the common human predicament of living in the "divided house of faith and reason". The simple joke carries unconscious overtones and undertones, audible to the inner ear alone.

The doctor thinks in terms of abstract statistical probabilities, the rules of which are inapplicable to individual cases; and there is an added twist because, in contrast to what naive common sense suggests, the patient's odds of survival are unaffected by whatever happened before, and are still one against ten, just as the chances of Red coming up on the roulette table are still only fifty-fifty, even if Black has come up previously nine times in a row. This is one of the profound paradoxes of the theory of probability; the mathematical joke implies a riddle.

The masochist under the shower, who punishes himself by depriving himself of his daily punishment, is governed by rules which are a *reversal* of those of normal logic. (We can also construct a pattern where *both* frames of reference are reversed: "A sadist is a person who is kind to a masochist.") However, the joker does not really believe that the masochist takes his hot shower as a punishment; he only pretends to believe it. *Irony* is the satirist's most effective weapon; it pretends to accept the opponent's method of reasoning in order to expose its implicit absurdity or viciousness.

Thus the common pattern underlying these stories is *the perceiving of a situation or idea in two self-consistent but mutually incompatible frames of reference or associative contexts*. This formula can be shown to have a general validity for all forms of humour and wit, some of which will be discussed below. But it covers only one aspect of humour – its *logical structure*. We must now turn to another fundamental aspect – the *emotional dynamics* which breathes life into that structure and makes us laugh, giggle or smile.

LAUGHTER AND EMOTION

When a comedian tells a story, he deliberately sets out to create a certain tension in his listeners, which mounts as the narrative progresses. But it never reaches its expected climax. The punchline acts as a verbal guillotine which cuts across the logical development of the story; it debunks our dramatic expectations; the tension we felt becomes suddenly redundant and is exploded in laughter, like water gushing from a punctured pipe. To put it differently, laughter disposes of emotive excitations which have suddenly become pointless and must somehow be worked off along physiological channels of least resistance; and the function of the "luxury reflex" is to provide these channels.

A glance at a caricature by Hogarth or Rowlandson, showing the brutal merriment of people in a tavern, makes one realize at once that they are working off their surplus of adrenalin by contracting their face muscles into grimaces, slapping their thighs, and exhaling in explosive puffs through the half-closed glottis. Their flushed faces reveal that the emotions disposed of through these tension-relieving safety valves are brutality, envy, sexual gloating. However, if one leafs through an album of *New Yorker* cartoons, coarse laughter yields to an amused and rarefied smile: the ample flow of adrenalin has been distilled and crystallized into a grain of Attic salt. As we move across the spectrum of humour, from its coarse to its subtle forms, from practical joke to brain-teaser, from jibe to irony, from anecdote to epigram, the emotional climate shows a gradual transformation. The emotion discharged in coarse laughter is aggression robbed of its purpose; the jokes small children enjoy are mostly scatological; adolescents of all ages gloat on vicarious sex; the sick joke trades on repressed sadism, satire on righteous indignation. There is a bewildering variety of moods involved in different forms of humour, including mixed or contradictory feelings; but whatever the mixture, it must contain a basic ingredient which is indispensable: an impulse, however faint, of aggression or apprehension. It may appear in the guise of malice, contempt, the veiled cruelty of condescension, or merely an absence of sympathy with the victim of the joke – "a momentary anaesthesia of the heart", as Bergson put it.

In the subtler types of humour the aggressive tendency may be so faint that only careful analysis will detect it, like the presence of salt in a well-prepared dish – which, however, would be tasteless without it. Replace aggression by sympathy, and the same situation – a drunk falling on his face – will no longer be comic but pathetic, and evoke not laughter but pity. It is the aggressive element, the detached malice of the comic impersonator which turns pathos into bathos, tragedy into travesty. Malice may be *combined* with affection in friendly teasing – or when we don't know whether we shall laugh or cry at the misadventures of Charlie Chaplin; and the aggressive component in civilised humans may be sublimated or no longer conscious. But in jokes which appeal to children and primitive people, cruelty and boastful self-assertiveness are much in evidence. In 1961 a survey carried out among American children aged eight to fifteen made the researchers conclude that "mortification or discomfort or hoaxing of others very readily caused laughter, while a witty or funny remark often passed unnoticed".

Similar attitudes are reflected in historically earlier forms and theories of the comic. In Aristotle's view, laughter was intimately related to ugliness and debasement. Cicero held that "the province of the ridiculous . . . lies in a certain baseness and deformity". Descartes believed that laughter was a manifestation of joy "mixed with surprise or hatred or sometimes with both". In Francis Bacon's list of the causes which give rise to laughter, the first place is given to "deformity". One of the most frequently quoted utterances on the subject is this definition in Hobbes's *Leviathan*:

> The passion of laughter is nothing else but sudden glory arising from a sudden conception of some eminency in ourselves by comparison with the infirmity of others, or with our own formerly.

However much the opinions of the theorists differ, on this one point nearly all of them agree: that the emotions discharged in laughter always contain an element of aggressiveness. But aggression and apprehension are twin phenomena; psychologists talk of "aggressive-defensive impulses". Accordingly, one of the typical situations in which laughter occurs is the moment of sudden cessation of fear caused by some imaginary danger. Rarely is the nature of laughter as an over-flow of redundant tensions more strikingly manifested than in the sudden change of expression on the small child's face from anxious apprehension to the happy laughter of relief. This seems to be unrelated to humour; yet at a closer look we find here the same logical structure as before: the wildly barking little dog was first perceived by the child in a context of danger, then as a tail-wagging puppy; the tension has suddenly become redundant, and spills over.

Kant realised that what causes laughter is "the sudden transformation of a tense expectation into nothing". Freud attempted to explain why the excess energy should be worked off in that particular way:

> According to the best of my knowledge, the grimaces and contortions of the corners of the mouth that characterise laughter appear first in the satisfied and over-satiated nurseling when he drowsily quits the breast. . . . They are physical expressions of the determination to take no more nourishment, an "enough" so to speak, or rather a "more than enough". . . . This primal sense of pleasurable saturation may have provided the link between the smile – that basic phenomenon under-

lying laughter – and its subsequent connection with other pleasurable processes of de-tension.*

In other words, the muscle-contractions of the smile, as the earliest expressions of relief from tension, would thereafter serve as channels of least resistance. Similarly, the explosive exhalations of laughter seem designed to "puff away" surplus tension, and the agitated gestures obviously serve the same function.

It may be objected that such massive reactions often seem quite out of proportion with the slight stimulations which provoke them. But we must bear in mind that laughter is a phenomenon of the trigger-releaser type, where a minute twist may open the tap for vast amounts of stored emotions, often derived from unconscious sources: repressed sadism, sexual tumescence, unavowed fear; even boredom: the explosive laughter of a class of schoolboys at some trivial incident is a measure of their pent-up resentment during a boring lecture. Another factor which may amplify the reaction out of all proportion to the comic stimulus is the social infectiousness which laughter shares with other emotive manifestations of group-behaviour.

Laughter or smiling may also be caused by stimulations which are not in themselves comic, but *signs* or *symbols* deputising for well-established comic patterns: Chaplin's boots, Groucho Marx's cigar, catch-phrases or allusions to family jokes. To discover why we laugh requires on some occasions tracing back a long, involved thread of associations to its source. This task is further complicated by the fact that the effect of such comic symbols – on a cartoon or on the stage – appears to be instantaneous, without allowing time for the accumulation and subsequent discharge of "expectations" and "emotive tensions". But here memory comes into play, acting as a storage battery whose charge can be sparked off at any time: the smile which greets Falstaff's appearance on the stage is derived from a mixture of memories and expectations. Besides, even if our reaction to a cartoon appears to be instantaneous, there is always a process in time until we "see the joke"; the cartoon has to tell a story, even if it is telescoped into a few seconds. All of which goes to show that to analyse humour is a task as delicate as analysing the chemical composition of a perfume with its multiple ingredients – some of which are never consciously perceived, while others, when sniffed in isolation, would make us wince.

*Freud, *Ges. Werke*, Vol. VI.

THE INERTIA OF EMOTION

I have discussed first the logical structure of humour; and then its emotional dynamics. Putting the two together, we may summarise the result as follows: the bisociation of a situation or idea with two mutually incompatible contexts, and the resulting abrupt transfer of the train of thought from one context to another, puts a sudden end to our "tense expectations"; the accumulated emotion, deprived of its object, is left hanging in the air, and is discharged in laughter. When the marquis rushes to the window and starts blessing the people in the street, our intellect turns a somersault and enters with gusto into the new game; but the malicious erotic feeling which the start of the story has aroused cannot be fitted into the new context; deserted by the nimble intellect, it gushes out in laughter like the air from a punctured tyre.

To put it differently: *we laugh because our emotions have a greater inertia and persistence than our reasoning processes.* Affects are incapable of keeping step with reasoning; unlike reasoning, they cannot "change direction" at a moment's notice. To the physiologist this should be self-evident since our aggressive emotions operate through the phylogenetically old, massive apparatus of the sympathetic nervous system and its allied hormones, acting on the whole body, while language and logic are confined to the neocortex at the roof of the brain. Common experience provides daily confirmation of this dichotomy. We are literally "poisoned" by our adrenal humours; it takes time to talk a person out of a mood; fear and anger show persistent after-effects long after their causes have been removed. If we could change our moods as quickly as we can jump from one idea to another, we would be acrobats of emotion; but since we are not, our thoughts and emotions frequently become dissociated. It is emotion deserted by thought that is discharged in laughter. For emotion, owing to its greater mass-momentum, is, as we have seen, unable to follow the sudden switch of ideas to a different type of logic; it tends to persist in a straight line. Ariel leads Caliban on by the nose: Ariel jumps on a branch, Caliban crashes into the tree. Aldous Huxley once wrote:

> We carry around with us a glandular system which was admirably well adapted to life in the Paleolithic times but it is not very well adapted to life now. Thus we tend to produce more adrenalin than is good for us, and we either suppress ourselves and turn destructive

energies inwards or else we do not suppress ourselves and we start hitting people.*

A third alternative is to laugh at people. There are other outlets for tame aggression such as competitive sports – or literary criticism; but they are acquired skills, whereas laughter is a gift of nature, included in our native equipment. The glands that control our emotions reflect conditions at a stage of evolution when the struggle for existence was more deadly than at present – and when the reaction to any strange sight or sound consisted in jumping, bristling, fighting or running. As security and comfort increased in the species, new outlets were needed for the disposal of emotions which could no longer be worked off through their original channels, and laughter is obviously one of them. But it could only emerge when reasoning had gained a degree of independence from the "blind" urges of emotion. Below the human level, thinking and feeling appear to form an indivisible unity; not until thinking became gradually detached from feeling could man perceive his own emotion as redundant, confront his glandular "humours" with a sense of humour, and make the smiling admission, "I have been fooled".

VERBAL HUMOUR

The foregoing discussion was intended to provide the tools for dissecting and analysing any specimen of humour. The procedure to be followed is to determine the nature of the two (or more) frames of reference whose collision gives rise to the comic effect – to discover the type of logic or "rules of the game" which govern each. In the more sophisticated type of joke the "logic" is implied and hidden; and the moment we state it in explicit form, the joke is dead. Unavoidably, the section that follows will be strewn with cadavers.

Max Eastman, in *The Enjoyment of Laughter*, remarked of a laboured pun by Ogden Nash: "It is not a pun but a punitive expedition." That goes for most puns, even for Milton's famous lines about the Prophet Elijah's ravens – which were "though ravenous taught to abstain from what they brought"; or Freud's character, who calls the Christmas season the "alcoholidays". Most puns strike one as atrocious, perhaps because they represent the most primitive form of humour: two disparate strings of

*In *Control of the Mind*, Farber and Wilson, eds. (New York, 1961).

thought tied together in an acoustic knot. But the very primitive-
ness of such bisociations based on pure sound may account for the
pun's immense popularity with children and its prevalence in
certain types of mental disorder ("punning mania").

From the *play on sounds* – puns and Spoonerisms – an ascending series leads to the *play on words* and so to the *play on ideas*.
When Groucho Marx says of a safari in Africa, "We shot two
bucks, but that was all the money we had", the joke hinges on the
two meanings of the word "buck". It is moderately funny, but
would be even less so without the reference to Groucho, which
evokes a visual image instantly arousing a high voltage of expectations. The story of the marquis and the bishop is clearly of a
superior type of humour, because it plays not on mere words, but
on ideas.

It would be quite easy – and equally boring – to draw up a list in
which jokes and witticisms are classified according to the nature
of the frames of reference whose collision creates the comic effect.
We have already come across a few, such as metaphorical versus
literal meaning (the daughter's "hand"); professional versus
common-sense logic (the statistically minded doctor); incompatible codes of behaviour (the marquis); confrontations of the trivial
and the exalted ("eternal bliss"); trains of reasoning travelling
happily joined together in opposite directions (the sadist who is
kind to the masochist). The list could be extended indefinitely; in
fact *any* two cognitive matrices can be made to yield a comic effect
of sorts by hooking them together and infusing a drop of malice
into the concoction. The frames of reference may even be defined
by such abstract concepts as "time" and "weather"; the absent-
minded professor who tries to read the temperature from his
watch or to tell the hour from the thermometer, is comic for the
same reason as it would be to watch a game of ping-pong played
with a football or a game of rugby played with a ping-pong ball.
The variations are infinite, the formula remains the same.

Jokes and anecdotes have a single point of culmination. The
literary forms of *sustained humour*, such as the picaresque novel,
do not rely on a single effect but on a series of minor climaxes. The
narrative moves along the line of intersection of contrasted planes
– e.g., the fantasy world of Don Quixote and the cunning horse-
sense of Sancho Panza – or is made to oscillate between them; as a
result tension is continuously generated and discharged in mild
amusement.

Comic verse thrives on the melodious union of incongruities –

Carroll's "cabbages and kings"; and particularly on the contrast between lofty form and flatfooted content. Certain metric forms like the hexameter or Alexandrine arouse expectations of pathos, of the heroic and exalted; to pour into these epic moulds some homely, trivial content –"Beautiful soup, so rich and green – Waiting in a hot tureen" – is an almost infallible comic device. The rolling dactyls of the first lines of a limerick which carry, instead of Hector or Achilles, a young lady from Niger for a ride, make her ridiculous even before the expected calamities befall her. Instead of a heroic mould, a soft lyrical one may also pay off: "And what could be moister – Than the tears of an oyster?"

Another type of *incongruity between form and content* yields the bogus proverb: "The rule is: jam tomorrow and jam yesterday – but never jam today". Two contradictory statements have been telescoped into a line whose homely, admonitory sound conveys the impression of a popular adage. In a similar way, *nonsense verse* achieves its effect by pretending to make sense, by forcing the reader to project meaning into the phonetic pattern of the *jabberwocky*, as one interprets the ink blots in a Rorschach test.

Satire is a verbal caricature which shows us a deliberately distorted image of a person, institution or society. The traditional method of the caricaturist is to *exaggerate* those features which he considers to be characteristic of his victim's personality and to *simplify* by leaving out everything that is not relevant for his purpose. The satirist uses the same technique; and the features of society which he selects for magnification are of course those of which he disapproves. The result is a juxtaposition, in the reader's mind, of his habitual image of the world in which he moves, and its absurd reflection in the satirist's distorting mirror. The reader is thus made to recognise familiar features in the absurd, and absurdity in the familiar. Without this double vision the satire would be humourless. If the human Yahoos were really such evil-smelling monsters as Gulliver's Houyhnhnm hosts claim, the book would not be a satire but the statement of a deplorable truth. Straight invective is not satire; it must deliberately overshoot its mark.

A similar effect is achieved if, instead of exaggerating the objectionable features, the satirist projects them by means of the *allegory* on to a different background, such as an animal society. A succession of writers, from Aristophanes through Swift and Anatole France to George Orwell, have used this technique to focus attention on deformities of society which, blunted by habit, we take for granted.

SITUATIONAL HUMOUR

The coarsest type of humour is the *practical joke*: pulling away the chair from under the dignitary's lowered bottom. The victim is perceived, first as a person of consequence, then suddenly as an inert body subject to the laws of physics: authority is debunked by gravity, mind by matter; man is degraded to a mechanism. Goose-stepping soldiers act like automatons, the pedant behaves like a mechanical robot, the Sergeant-Major attacked by diarrhoea or Hamlet getting the hiccups show man's lofty aspirations deflated by his all-too-solid flesh. A similar effect is produced by artefacts which masquerade as humans: Punch and Judy, Jack-in-the-Box, gadgets playing tricks on their masters as if with calculated malice.

From the bisociation of *man and machine*, there is only a step to the *man–animal* hybrid. Disney's creations behave as if they were human without losing their animal appearance. The caricaturist follows the reverse procedure by discovering horsey, mousey, piggish features in the human face.

This leads us to the comic devices of *imitation, impersonation and disguise*. The impersonator is perceived as himself and somebody else at the same time. If the result is slightly degrading – but only in that case – the spectator will laugh. The comedian impersonating a public personality, two pairs of trousers serving as the legs of the pantomime horse, men disguised as women and women as men – in each case the paired patterns reduce each other to absurdity.

The most aggressive form of impersonation is the *parody*, designed to deflate hollow pretence, to destroy illusion, and to undermine pathos. Wigs falling off, speakers forgetting their lines, gestures remaining suspended in mid-air: the parodist's favourite points of attack are again situated on the line of intersection between the sublime and the trivial.

Playful behaviour in young animals and children is amusing because it is an unintentional parody of adult behaviour, which it imitates or anticipates. Young puppies are droll, because their helplessness, affection and puzzled expression make them appear more "human" than full-grown dogs; because their ferocious growls strike one as impersonations of adult behaviour – like a child in a bowler hat; because the puppy's waddling, uncertain gait makes it a choice victim of nature's practical jokes; because its bodily disproportions, the huge padded paws, Falstaffian belly and wrinkled philosopher's brow give it the appearance of a caricature; and lastly because we are such very superior beings compared to a puppy. A fleeting smile can contain many logical ingredients and emotional spices.

Both Cicero and Francis Bacon regarded *deformity* as the most frequent cause of laughter. Renaissance princes collected dwarfs, hunchbanks and blackamoors for their merriment. As we have become too humane for that kind of fun, we are apt to forget that it requires a good deal of imagination and empathy to recognise in a midget a fellow-human who, though different in appearance, thinks and feels much as oneself does. In children this projective faculty is still rudimentary; they tend to mock people with a stammer or a limp, and laugh at the foreigner with an odd pro-nunciation. Similar attitudes are shown by tribal or parochial societies to any form of appearance or behaviour that deviates from their strict norms: the stranger is not really human, he only pretends to be "like us". The Greeks used the same word "bar-barous" for the foreigner and the stutterer: the uncouth, barking sounds the stranger uttered were considered a parody of human speech. Vestiges of this primitive attitude are still found in the curious fact that we accept a foreign accent with tolerance, but find the imitation of a foreign accent comic. We know that the imitator's mispronunciations are mere pretence; this knowledge makes sympathy unnecessary and enables us to be childishly cruel with a clean conscience.

Another source of innocent merriment occurs when *the part and the whole* change roles, and attention becomes focused on a detail torn out of the functional context on which its meaning depended. When the gramophone needle gets stuck, the sop-rano's voice keeps repeating the same word on the same quaver, which suddenly assumes a grotesquely independent life. The same happens when faulty orthography displaces attention from meaning to spelling, or when the beam of consciousness is directed at functions which otherwise are performed automati-cally – the paradox of the centipede. The self-conscious, awkward youth who "does not know what to do with his hands" is a victim of the same predicament.

Comedies used to be classified according to their reliance on situations, manners or characters. The last two need no further discussion; in the first, comic effects are contrived by making a situation participate simultaneously in two independent chains of events with different associative contexts, which intersect through coincidence, mistaken identity, or confusions of time and occasion. The coincidence on which they are hinged is the *deus ex machina* of both comedy and antique tragedy.

Why *tickling* should produce laughter remained an enigma in all earlier theories of the comic. As Darwin was the first to point out, the innate response to tickling is squirming and straining to withdraw the tickled part – a defence-reaction designed to escape attacks on vulnerable areas such as the soles of the feet, armpits, belly and ribs. If a fly settles on the belly of a horse, it causes a ripple of muscle-contractions across the skin – the equivalent of squirming in the tickled child. But the horse does not laugh when tickled, and the child not always. It will laugh only – and this is the crux of the matter – when it perceives tickling as *a mock attack*, a caress in mildly aggressive disguise. For the same reason people laugh only when tickled by others, not when they tickle themselves.

Experiments in Yale on babies under one year old revealed the not very surprising fact that they laughed fifteen times more often when tickled by their mothers than when they were tickled by strangers; and when tickled by strangers they mostly cried. For the mock attack must be recognised as being only pretence, and with strangers one cannot be sure. Even with its own mother there is an ever-so-slight feeling of uncertainty and apprehension, the expression of which will alternate with laughter in the baby's behaviour; and it is precisely this element of tension between the tickles which is relieved in the laughter accompanying the squirm. The rule of the game is: "Let me be just a little frightened so that I can enjoy the relief."

Thus the tickler is impersonating an aggressor, but is simultaneously known not to be one; this is probably the first situation in life which makes the infant live on two planes at once – a delectable foretaste of being tickled by the horror comic.

Humour in the visual arts reflects the same logical structures as discussed before. Its most primitive form is the distorting mirror at the fun fair which reflects the human frame elongated into a column or compressed into the shape of a toad; it plays a practical joke on the victim who sees the image in the mirror both as his familiar self and a patient lump of plasticine that can be stretched and squeezed into any absurd form. But while the mirror distorts mechanically, *the caricaturist* does it *selectively*, by the same technique of *exaggerating* characteristic features and *simplifying* the rest, which the satirist employs. Like the satirist, the caricaturist reveals the absurd in the familiar; and like the satirist he must overshoot his mark. His malice is rendered harmless by our knowledge that the monstrous pot-bellies and bow-legs he draws are not *real*; real deformities are no longer comic, they arouse pity.

The artist, painting a stylized portrait, also uses the technique of *selection, exaggeration and simplification;* but his attitude to the model is dominated by positive empathy instead of negative malice; and the features he selects for emphasis differ accordingly. In some character-studies by Leonardo, Hogarth or Daumier the passions reflected are so violent, the grimaces so ferocious, that it is impossible to tell whether they were meant as portraits or caricatures. If you feel that such distortions of the human face are not really possible, that Daumier merely pretended that they exist, then you are absolved from horror and pity and can laugh at his grotesques. But if you think that this is indeed what Daumier saw in those de-humanised faces, then you feel that you are looking at a work of art.

Humour in music is a subject to be approached with diffidence, because the language of music ultimately eludes translation into verbal concepts. All one can do is to point at some analogies: a "rude" noise, such as the blast of a trumpet inserted into a passage where it does not belong, has the effect of a practical joke; a singer or an instrument out of tune produces a similar reaction; the imitation of animal sounds, vocally or instrumentally, exploits the technique of impersonation; a nocturne by Chopin transposed into hot jazz, or a simple street song performed in the style of the Valkyrie is a marriage of incompatibles. These are primitive devices corresponding to the lowest levels of humour; higher up we come across compositions like Ravel's *La Valse* – an affectionate parody of the sentimental *Wiener Walzer*; or Haydn's Surprise Symphony or the mock-heroics of Kodály's folk opera, *Hári János*. But in comic opera it is almost impossible to sort out how much of the comic effect is derived from the book, how much from the music; and the highest forms of musical humour, the unexpected delights of a light-hearted scherzo by Mozart, defy verbal analysis – or else this would have to be so specialised and technical as to defeat its purpose. Although a "witty" musical passage, which springs a surprise on the audience and cheats it of its "tense expectations", certainly has the emotion-relieving effect which tends to produce laughter, a concert audience may occasionally smile, but will hardly ever laugh; which goes to show that the emotions evoked by musical humour are of a subtler kind than those of the verbal and visual variety.

STYLES AND TECHNIQUES IN HUMOUR

The criteria which determine whether a humorous offering will be judged good, bad or indifferent, are of course partly a matter of period taste and individual preference, partly dependent on the *style and technique* of the humorist. It would seem that these criteria can be summed up under three main headings: (a) originality, (b) emphasis, (c) economy.

The merits of *originality* are self-evident; it provides the essential element of surprise, which cuts across our expectations. But true originality is not very often met either in humour or in other forms of art. One common substitute for it is to arouse the audience by various techniques of suggestive *emphasis*. The clown's domain is the rich, coarse type of humour; he piles it on; he appeals to sadistic, sexual, scatological impulses; one of his favourite tricks is repetition of the same situation, the same key-phrase. This diminishes the effect of surprise, but helps in drawing emotion into the familiar channel – more and more liquid is being pumped into the punctured pipeline.

Emphasis on local colour and ethnic peculiarities – as in Scottish, Jewish, Cockney stories – is a further means to channel emotion into familiar tracks. The Scotsman or Cockney must of course be caricatures if the comic purpose is to be achieved – in other words, exaggeration and simplification once more appear as indispensable tools to provide emphasis.

In the higher forms of humour, however, emphasis tends to yield to the opposite kind of virtue: *economy*. Economy, in humour and art, does not mean mechanical brevity, but the implicit hint instead of the explicit statement – the oblique allusion in lieu of the frontal attack. The old-fashioned *Punch* cartoon featuring the British lion and the Russian bear "rubs it in"; the *New Yorker* cartoon poses a riddle which the reader must solve by an imaginative effort in order to "see the joke".

In humour, as in other forms of art, emphasis and economy are complementary techniques. The first forces the offering down the consumer's throat; the second tantalises, to whet his appetite.

Earlier theories – including even Bergson's and Freud's – have treated humour as an isolated phenomenon, without attempting to throw light on the obvious and intimate connections between the comic and the tragic, between laughter and crying, between artistic inspiration, comic inventiveness and scientific discovery. Yet (as we shall see) these three domains of creative activity form a continuum with no sharp boundaries between wit and ingenuity, nor between the art of discovery and the discoveries of art.

It has been said, for instance, that scientific discovery consists in seeing an analogy which nobody has seen before. When, in the Song of Songs, Solomon compared the Shulamite's neck to a tower of ivory, he saw an analogy which nobody had seen before; when William Harvey perceived in the exposed heart of a fish a messy kind of mechanical pump, he did the same; and when the caricaturist draws a nose like a cucumber, he again does just that. In fact, *all the bisociative patterns discussed above, which constitute the "grammar" of humour, are also present in science and art.* Thus the pun has its equivalent in the rhyme, but also in the problems which confront the philologist. The clash between incompatible codes of behaviour may yield comedy, tragedy or new psychological insights. The dualism of mind and inert matter is exploited by the practical joker, but also provides one of the eternal themes of literature: man as a marionette on strings, manipulated by the gods or his chromosomes. The man-beast dichotomy is reflected by Donald Duck, but also in Kafka's *Metamorphosis* and the psychologist's animal experiments. The caricature corresponds not only to the artist's character-portrait, but also to the scientist's diagrams and charts, which emphasise the relevant features and leave out the rest.

The conscious and unconscious processes underlying creativity are essentially combinatorial activities – the bringing together of previously separate areas of knowledge and experience. The humorist's game is to contrive a *collision*; the scientist's purpose is to achieve *synthesis*; the artist aims at a *juxtaposition* of the familiar and the eternal. But the transitions from one to the other are continuous: witticism blends into epigram, caricature into portrait; and whether one considers architecture, medicine, chess or cookery, there is no clear frontier where the realm of science ends and that of art begins. Comedy and tragedy, laughter and weeping, mark the extremes of a *continuous spectrum*.

SUMMARY*

Humour provides a back-door entry to the domain of creativity because it is *the only example of a complex intellectual stimulus releasing a simple and predictable bodily response* – the laughter reflex.

To describe the unitary pattern underlying all varieties of humour I have proposed the term "bisociation" – perceiving a situation or event in two mutually exclusive associative contexts. The result is an abrupt transfer of the train of consciousness to a different track, governed by a different logic or "rule of the game". This intellectual jolt deflates our expectations; the emotions they aroused have suddenly become redundant, and are flushed out along channels of least resistance in laughter.

The emotions thus involved, however complex, always contain a dominant element of the self-assertive, aggressive–defensive tendencies. They are based on the ancient adrenal–sympathetic branch of the nervous system and have a much stronger momentum and persistence than the subtle and devious processes of reasoning, with which they are unable to keep step. It is emotion deserted by thought that is discharged, harmlessly, in laughter. But this luxury reflex could only arise in a creature whose reasoning has gained a degree of independence from its biological drives, enabling him to perceive his own emotions as redundant – to realise that he has been fooled. The person who laughs is the opposite of the fanatic whose reason has been blinded by emotion – and who fools himself.

After applying the theory to various types of the comic – from physical tickling to social satire – I discussed the criteria of styles and techniques in humour: *originality* or unexpectedness; *emphasis* through selection, exaggeration and simplification; and its reverse: *economy* or implicitness which forces the audience to make a re-creative effort.

Lastly, the brief cross-references to creativity in science and art at the end of this chapter may serve as an introduction to the sections that follow.

---

*The following brief summing up of the theory is quoted from Janus (1978).

Chapter 27

THE ART OF DISCOVERY AND THE DISCOVERIES OF ART

It is technically difficult and sometimes impossible to convey a complex theory by quoting extracts from the original text. The alternative is to condense and summarise – to abstract rather than extract. I have tried to abstract the main contents of The Act of Creation *in later books (*The Ghost in the Machine *and* Janus*); and I shall, in the chapters that follow, sometimes quote these condensed versions rather than the original. The passage below is quoted from* Janus.

Creativity in science could be described as the art of putting two and two together to make five. In other words, it consists in combining previously unrelated domains of knowledge in such a way that you get more out of the emergent whole than you have put in. This apparent bit of magic derives from the fact that the whole is not merely the sum of its parts, but an expression of the relations between its parts; and that each new synthesis leads to the emergence of new patterns of relations – more complex cognitive structures on higher levels of the mental hierarchy.

Let me give a few brief examples, selected from the detailed case-histories of scientific discoveries in *The Sleepwalkers*, *The Act of Creation*, and elsewhere.

The motions of the tides were known to man from time immemorial. So were the motions of the moon. But the idea to connect the two, the idea that the tides were due to the attraction of the moon, was proclaimed for the first time by the German astronomer Johannes Kepler in the seventeenth century. By putting two and two together, he opened up the infinite vista of modern astronomy.

Lodestones – magnets – were known to the ancient Greeks as a curiosity of nature. In the Middle Ages they were used for two purposes: as mariner's compasses and as a means to attract an estranged wife back to her husband. Also well-known were the curious properties of amber which, when rubbed, acquired the power of attracting flimsy objects. The Greek for amber is *elektron*, but Greek science was no more interested in the freak phenomena of electricity than modern science is in telepathy. Nor were the Middle Ages. For some two thousand years magnetism and electricity were regarded as separate phenomena, as unrelated to each other as the tides and the moon. In 1820 Hans Christian Oersted discovered that an electric current flowing through a wire deflected a magnetic compass which happened to be lying on the table. At that historic moment the two hitherto separate contexts began to fuse into an emergent synthesis: electromagnetism – thus creating a kind of chain-reaction which is still continuing. At successive stages of it electricity and magnetism merged with radiant light, chemistry merged with physics, the humble *elektron* became an orbiting planet within the solar system of the atom, and ultimately energy and matter became unified in Einstein's single, sinister equation, $E = mc^2$.

If we go back to the beginnings of the scientific quest, there is an ancient tradition according to which Pythagoras discovered the secrets of musical harmony while watching some blacksmiths at work on his native island of Samos, and noticing that iron bars of different lengths gave out sounds of different pitch under the strokes of the hammer. This spontaneous amalgamation of arithmetic and music was probably the starting-point of the science of physics.

From the Pythagoreans, who mathematised the harmony of the spheres, to their modern heirs, who combined space and time into a single continuum, the pattern is always the same: the discoveries of science do not create something out of nothing; they combine, relate and integrate already existing but previously separate ideas, facts, associative contexts – frames of reference. This act of cross-fertilisation – or self-fertilisation within a single brain – appears to play an essential part in creativity, and to justify the term "bisociation". We have seen how the humorist bisociates mutually incompatible mental sets in order to produce a *collision*. The scientist, on the other hand, aims at synthesis, at the *integration* of previously unrelated ideas. The Latin *cogito* comes from *coagitare*, to shake together. Bisociation in humour consists of the sudden shaking together of incompatible elements which briefly collide, then separate again. Bisociation in science means combining hitherto unrelated elements in such a way that a new level is added to the hierarchy of knowledge, which contains the previously separate structures as its members.

We have seen that the two domains are continuous, without a sharp boundary: each subtle witticism is a malicious discovery, and vice versa: many great discoveries of science have been greeted with howls of laughter, precisely because they seemed to represent a marriage of incompatibles – until the marriage bore fruit and the apparent incompatibility turned out to derive from prejudice. What looked like a collision ended in fusion: witticism is paradox stated, discovery is paradox resolved. Even Galileo treated Kepler's theory of the tides as a bad joke, and one can easily imagine a contemporary caricaturist drawing a fat-faced moon sucking up the earth's oceans through a straw. But, to say it again, the step from the sublime to the ridiculous is reversible: the satires of Swift and Orwell carry deeper insights than a whole library of works on social anthropology.

The triptych on page 347 is intended to represent the three domains of creativity – humour, science and art. Its meaning will become apparent as the argument unfolds.

As we travel from the coarse toward the sophisticated types of humour, and then continue across the fluid boundary into the domain of invention and discovery (the centre panel of the triptych), we come across such hybrid cases as brain-twisters, mathematical games, logical paradoxes. The conundrums about Achilles and the Tortoise and about the Cretan Liar have for two millennia tickled philosophers and spurred logicians to creative efforts. The task has been transformed from "seeing the joke" into "solving the problem".

And as we continue the journey in the same direction across the triptych we find the same continuous transitions from the domain of science into the domain of art – like the gradual shading, without breaks or dividing lines, of one colour of the rainbow into another.

The horizontal lines across the triptych are meant to indicate the continuity of some typical bisociative patterns which are found in all three panels. These patterns are *trivalent* – they can enter the service of humour, discovery or art. We have seen, for example, that the caricaturist's cartoon, the scientist's diagram, and the artist's portrait employ the same bisociative technique of superimposing selective filters on visual perception. In the language of behaviourist psychology we would have to say that Cézanne, glancing at a landscape, receives a "stimulus", to which he responds by putting a dab of paint on, and that is all there is to it. In reality, perceiving the landscape and re-creating it on the canvas are two activities which take place simultaneously on two different planes, in two different environments. The stimulus is part of a large, three-dimensional environment, the distant landscape. The response acts on a different environment, a small two-dimensional canvas. The two are governed by different rules of organisation. There is no point-to-point correspondence between the two planes; they are bisociated as wholes in the artist's creation and in the beholder's eye.

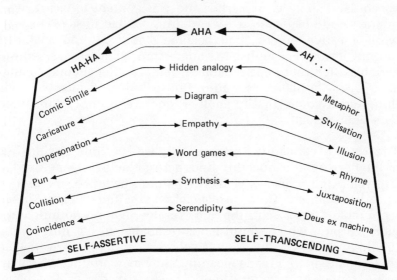

The three domains of creativity

The creation of a work of art involves a series of processes which happen virtually all at the same time and cannot be rendered in verbal terms without suffering impoverishment and distortion. The artist, as the scientist, is engaged in projecting his vision of reality into a particular medium, whether the medium is paint, marble, or words. But the product of his efforts can never be an exact representation or copy of reality, even if he naively hopes to achieve one. In the first place, he has to come to terms with the peculiarities and limitations of his chosen medium. In the second place, his own perception and world-view also have their own peculiarities and limitations imposed by the implicit conventions of his period or school and by his individual temperament. These lend coherence to his vision, but also tend to freeze into fixed formulae, stereotypes, verbal and visual clichés. The originality of genius, in art as in science, consists in a shift of attention to aspects of reality previously ignored, discovering hidden connections, seeing familiar objects or events in a new light.

In the discussion which followed a lecture at an American university on the theme of the present chapter, one of the "resident painters" remarked angrily: "I do not 'bisociate'. I sit down, look at the model and paint it."

In a sense he was right. He had found his "style", his visual vocabulary, some years earlier and was content to use it, with minor variations, to express everything he had to say. The erstwhile creative process had become stabilised into a skilled routine. It would be foolish to underestimate the achievements of which skilled routine is capable, whether in the chemical laboratory or in the painter's studio. But technical virtuosity is one thing, creative originality another; and we are only concerned here with the latter.

The trinity of caricature – diagram – stylised portrait provides one of the horizontal connecting lines across the three panels of the triptych. Some other such trivalent patterns have been mentioned in earlier chapters. Thus the bisociation of *sound and meaning* in its humblest form yields the pun. Yet the *rhyme* is nothing but a glorified pun, where sound lends resonance to meaning; while the linguist weaves them into a coherent fabric. Likewise, when *rhythm* and *metre* invade meaning, they may produce a Shakespeare sonnet or a comic limerick; while in the central panel rhythmic pulsations play a vital role in the study of biology, from the alpha waves of the brain to systole and diastole of the heart – the iambi and trochee of life. No wonder that metric verse carries echoes of the shaman's tom-tom and, to quote Yeats, "lulls the mind into a waking trance".

The triune character of other bisociative combinations appears almost over-obvious once one has realised the underlying principle, and perceives the three domains of creativity as a continuum. Thus the tracing of *hidden analogies* yields the poetic metaphor, scientific discovery or comic simile, according to the explorer's motivation. The dichotomies of *mind and matter*, of spiritual being and hairless ape, yield endless variations for scientific, artistic or comic treatment.

Less obvious is the trivalent role of *illusion*. The actor or impersonator on the stage is two people at the same time. If the result is *degrading* – Hamlet getting the hiccups in the middle of his monologue – illusion is debunked and the spectator will laugh. If he is led to *identify* with the hero, he will experience the particular state of split-mindedness known as the magic of the stage. But beside the parodist and the actor there is a third type of impersonator who purposefully employs the human faculty of being oneself and someone else at the same time: the physician or healer, who projects himself into the patient's mind and at the same time acts as a guide, magician or father-figure. Empathy – *Einfühlung* – is a nice, sober term for the rather mysterious process of entering into a kind of mental symbiosis with other selves, of stepping out of one's skin, as it were, and putting oneself into the skin of the other. It is the source of our intuitive understanding – more direct than language – of how the other thinks and feels, and is the starting point of the science and art of medical diagnosis and psychiatry.

Coincidence may be described as the chance encounter of two unrelated causal chains which – miraculously, it seems – merge into a significant event. It provides the neatest paradigm of the bisociation of previously separate contexts, engineered by fate. Coincidences are puns of destiny. In the pun, two strings of thought are tangled into an acoustic knot; in the coincidental happening two strings of events are knitted together by invisible hands.

Moreover, coincidence may serve as a classic example of the trivalence of bisociative patterns. It is the mainstay of the type of *comedy* which relies on ambiguous situations, resulting in mistaken identity or confusion of time and occasion. In the classic *tragedy* apparent chance-coincidences are the *deus ex machina* by which the gods interfere in the destiny of man – Oedipus is trapped into murdering his father and marrying his mother by mistaken identity. Lastly, lucky hazards – the gifts of *serendipity* – play a conspicuous part in the history of scientific discoveries.

On a higher level, however, the comedy of situations yields to the comedy of manners, which no longer relies for its effects on coincidence, but on the clash of *incompatible codes* of reasoning or conduct, as a result of which the hypocrisy or absurdity of one or both rule-books is exploded. Modern drama shows a similar change; destiny no longer acts from the outside, but from inside the personae; they are no longer marionettes on strings, manipulated by the gods, but victims of their own passions: "the fault, dear Brutus, is not in our stars but in ourselves".

Drama thrives on *conflict*, and so does the novel. The nature of the conflict may be explicitly stated or merely implied; but an element of it must be present, otherwise the characters would be gliding through a frictionless universe. Conflict can provide fuel for comedy or attain the dignity of tragedy, if the audience is led to accept the attitudes of both antagonists as valid, each within its own frame of reference. If the author succeeds in this, the conflict will be projected into the spectator's – or reader's – mind and experienced as a clash between two simultaneous and incompatible identifications. "We make out of our quarrels with others rhetoric, but out of our quarrels with ourselves poetry," wrote Yeats. The comedian makes us laugh at the expense of the victim; the tragedian makes us suffer as his accomplice. The psychologist is engaged in *resolving* conflict by analysing the factors which gave rise to it.

Chapter 28

ART AND EMOTION

The previous extracts dealt with the continuity of the domains of humour, science and art, and the logical affinities between them symbolised by the horizontal lines across the three panels; but as for the all-important emotional factor, only the dynamics of humour has been considered so far – which is a relatively simple matter compared to the emotional aspects of the two other panels. The following extract is from The Ghost in the Machine, *with a few paragraphs inserted from* The Act of Creation *and from* Janus.

. . .But how does one define the emotional climate of art? How does one classify the emotions which give rise to the experience of beauty? If you leaf through textbooks of experimental psychology, you won't find much of it. When behaviourists use the word "emotion", they nearly always refer to hunger, sex, rage and fear, and the related effects of the release of adrenalin. They have no explanations to offer for the curious reaction one experiences when listening to Mozart, or looking at the ocean, or reading for the first time John Donne's *Holy Sonnets*. Nor will you find in the textbooks a description of the physiological processes accompanying the reaction: moistening of the eyes, catching one's breath, followed by a kind of rapt tranquillity, the draining of all tensions. Let us call this the AH reaction – in contrast to the HA-HA reaction of laughter.

Laughter and weeping, the Greek masks of comedy and tragedy, mark the extremes of a continuous spectrum; both provide channels for the overflow of emotion; both are "luxury reflexes" without apparent utility. This much they have in common; in every other respect they are direct opposites.

Although weeping is neither an uncommon nor a trivial phenomenon, academic psychology has consistently ignored it.

Surprising as it may seem, the only mention of the subject in a recently published standard textbook of psychology for American college students, refers to the chapters on weeping in *The Act of Creation*.*

As a first step in our inquiry we must take a distinction between weeping and crying: it is a peculiarity of the English language to treat them as synonymous. *Weeping* has two basic reflex characteristics: the secretion of tears and a specific way of breathing. *Crying* is the emission of sounds signalling distress or protest. It may be combined with or alternate with weeping, but should not be confused with it. Crying is a form of communication, weeping is a private affair. And we are talking, of course, of *spontaneous* weeping, not of the contrived sobs of stagecraft, public or private.

Let us compare the physiological processes involved in laughter and weeping. Laughter is triggered by the adrenal-sympathetic branch of the autonomic nervous system, weeping by the parasympathetic branch. The first serves to energise the body, tensing it for action; the second has the opposite effect: it lowers blood pressure, slows down the pulse rate, and generally tends towards quietude and catharsis – literally the "purging" of tensions.

This physiological contrast is clearly reflected in the visible manifestations of laughter and weeping. The laugher's eyes sparkle, the corners are wrinkled, but brow and cheeks are taut and smooth, which lends the face an expression of radiance; the lips are parted, the corners lifted. In weeping, the eyes are "blinded by tears", they lose their focus and lustre; the features seem to crumble. Even when weeping for joy or in aesthetic rapture, the transfigured face reflects a serene languidness.

Watch yourself breathing when you laugh: long deep intakes of air, followed by bursts of exhalatory puffs – ha-ha-ha! In weeping, you do the opposite: short, gasping inspirations – sobs – are followed by long, sighing expirations – a-a-h, ah. . . .

In keeping with this, the emotions which overflow in the AH reaction are the direct opposites of those exploded in laughter. The latter belong to the adrenergic, aggressive-defensive type of emotions. In the present theory, these are manifestations of the *self-assertive* tendency. Their opposites I shall call the *self-transcending* emotions. [The basic polarity of these two types of

*Hilgard and Atkinson, *Introduction to Psychology* (4th ed., 1967), ch. 7 "Emotion", sub-section "Weeping".

emotion and their biological origin will be discussed at length in chapters 36–38.]

The *self-transcending* emotions show a wide range of variety. They may be joyous or sad, tragic or lyrical; their common denominator is the feeling of participation in a type of experience which transcends the narrow confines of the self.

The *self-assertive* emotions tend towards bodily activity; the self-transcending emotions are essentially passive and cathartic. The former are manifested in aggressive–defensive behaviour; the latter in empathy, rapport and identification, admiration and wonder. The shedding of tears is an outlet for an excess of the self-transcending emotions, as laughter is for the self-assertive emotions. In laughter, tension is suddenly exploded, emotion debunked; in weeping it is gradually drained away, without breaking the continuity of mood; emotion and thought remain united. The self-transcending emotions do not tend towards action, but towards quiescence. Respiration and pulse rate are slowed down; "entrancement" is a step towards the trance-like states induced by contemplative mystics; the emotion is of a quality that cannot be consummated by any specific voluntary act. You cannot take the mountain panorama home with you; you cannot merge with the infinite by any exertion of the body; to be "overwhelmed" by awe and wonder, "enraptured" by a smile, "entranced" by beauty – each of these words expresses passive surrender. The surplus of emotion cannot be worked off by any purposeful muscular activity, it can only be consummated in internal – visceral and glandular – processes.

The various causes which may lead to an overflow of tears – bereavement, joy, sympathy, self-pity, aesthetic or religious rapture – all have this basic element in common: a craving to transcend the island boundaries of the individual, to enter into a symbiotic communion with a human being, living or dead, or to surrender one's identity to God, Nature or Art. Listening to the organist playing in an empty cathedral, or looking at the stars on a summer night, may cause a welling-up of emotions which moisten the eyes, accompanied by an expansion of consciousness, which becomes quasi-depersonalised and – if the experience is very intense – leads into "the oceanic feeling of limitless extension and oneness with the universe"* – the Ah . . . reaction in its

*Romain Rolland describing the character of religious experience in a letter to Freud – who regretfully professed never to have felt anything of the sort (E. Jones, *Sigmund Freud* [London, 1953–7], Vol. 3, p. 364).

purest form. Ordinary mortals rarely ascend to such mystic heights, but they are at least familiar with the foothills.

The self-transcending emotions are the step-children of academic psychology, but they are as basic and as firmly rooted in biology as their opposites. Freud and Piaget, among others, have emphasised the fact that the very young child does not differentiate between ego and environment. The nourishing breast appears to it as a more intimate possession than the toes of its own body. It is aware of events, but not of itself as a separate entity. It lives in a state of mental symbiosis with the outer world, a continuation of the biological symbiosis in the womb. The universe is focussed on the self, and the self *is* the universe – a condition which Piaget called "protoplasmic" or "symbiotic" consciousness.* It may be likened to a fluid universe, traversed by the tidal rise and fall of physiological needs, and by minor storms which come and go without leaving solid traces. Gradually the floods recede, and the first islands of objective reality emerge; the contours grow firmer and sharper; the islands grow into continents, the dry territories of reality are mapped out; but side by side with it the liquid world coexists, surrounding it, interpenetrating it by canals and inland lakes, the vestigial relics of the erstwhile symbiotic communion – the origin of that "oceanic feeling" which the artist and the mystic strive to recapture on a higher level of development, at a higher turn of the spiral.

It is also at the origin of the sympathetic magic practised by all primitive and not so primitive people. When the medicine man disguises himself as the rain-god, he produces rain. Drawing a picture of a slain bison guarantees a successful hunt. This is the ancient unitary source out of which the ritual dance and song, the mystery plays of the Acheans and the calendars of the Babylonian priest-astronomers were derived. The shadows in Plato's cave are symbols of man's loneliness; the paintings in the Altamira caves are symbols of his magic powers.

We have travelled a long way from Altamira and Lascaux, but the artist's inspirations and the scientist's intuitions are still fed by that same unitary source – though by now we should rather call it an underground river. Wishes do not displace mountains, but in our dreams they still do. Symbiotic consciousness is never completely defeated, merely relegated underground to those primi-

---

*For a more recent treatment of this subject, see E. G. Schachtel's important work *Metamorphosis* (1963).

tive levels in the mental hierarchy where the boundaries of the
ego are still fluid and blurred – as blurred as the distinction
between the actor and the hero whom he impersonates, and with
whom the spectator identifies. The actor on the stage is himself
and somebody else at the same time – he is both the dancer and the
rain-god. Dramatic illusion is the coexistence in the spectator's
mind of two universes which are logically incompatible; his
awareness, suspended between the two planes, exemplifies the
bisociative process in its most striking form. All the more striking
because he produces physical symptoms – palpitations, sweating
or tears – in response to the perils of a Desdemona whom he knows
to exist merely as a shadow on the TV screen.

Chapter 29

SCIENCE AND EMOTION*

Many years ago, Gestalt psychologists coined the term "Aha-reaction" to indicate the euphoria which follows the moment of truth, the flash of illumination when the bits of the puzzle click into place – when the bisociated contexts fuse into a new synthesis. As we shall see in a moment, the Aha-reaction fits in very neatly between the Ha-ha and Ah reactions. The emotion exploding in the Ha-ha of laughter is aggression robbed of its purpose; the tension discharged in the Aha reaction after the penny has dropped is mainly derived from intellectual curiosity, the urge to explore and understand – which, when gratified, has a cathartic effect, akin to the Ah reaction of the aesthetic experience.

In recent years biologists have been led to recognise the existence of a primary instinct, the "exploratory drive", which is as basic as the instincts of hunger and sex, and can occasionally be even more powerful. Countless experimental zoologists – starting with Darwin himself – have shown that curiosity is an innate drive in rats, birds, dolphins, chimpanzees and men. It is the driving power which makes the laboratory rat find its way through the experimental maze without reward or punishment, and even defy punishment by traversing electrified grids instead of turning back. It makes the child take the new toy to pieces "to see what's inside", and is the prime mover behind human exploration and research.

The exploratory drive may combine with other drives such as hunger or sex. The pure scientist's proverbially "detached" and "disinterested" quest – his self-transcending absorption in the

*From Janus, ch. VII.

mysteries of nature – is in fact often combined with ambition, competitiveness, vanity. But these self-assertive tendencies must be restrained and highly sublimated to find fulfilment in the – mostly meagre – rewards for his slow and patient labours. There are, after all, more direct methods of asserting one's ego than the study of spiral nebulae.

But while the exploratory drive may be adulterated by ambition and vanity, the quest in its purest form is its own reward.

"Were I to hold the truth in my hand," Emerson wrote, "I would let it go for the positive joy of seeking." In a classic experiment, Wolfgang Köhler's chimpanzee, Sultan, discovered, after many unsuccessful efforts to rake in a banana placed outside his cage with a stick which was too short, that he could do it by fitting two hollow sticks together. His new discovery "pleased him so immensely" that he kept repeating the trick and forgot to eat the banana.

However, vanity apart, the self-assertive tendencies also enter on a deeper level into the scientist's motivation. "I am," wrote Freud, "not really a man of science . . . but a *conquistador* . . . with the curiosity, the boldness, and the tenacity that belong to that type of person." The exploratory drive aims at understanding nature, the conquistadorial element at mastering nature (including human nature). Every variety of the scientific quest has this dual motivation, although they need not be equally conscious in the individual scientist's mind. Knowledge can beget humility or power. The archetypes of these opposite tendencies are Prometheus and Pythagoras – one stealing the fire of the gods, the other listening to the harmony of the spheres. Freud's confession can be contrasted with the statements of many scientific geniuses that the only purpose of their labours was to lift a fraction of the veil covering the mysteries of nature, and their only motivation a feeling of awe and wonder. "Men were first led to the study of natural philosophy," wrote Aristotle, "as indeed they are today, by wonder." Maxwell's earliest memory was "lying on the grass, looking at the sun, and *wondering*". Einstein – the humblest of all – struck the same chord when he wrote that whoever is devoid of the capacity to wonder at the cosmic mystery, "whoever remains unmoved, whoever cannot contemplate, or know the deep shudder of the soul in enchantment, might just as well be dead for he has already closed his eyes on life". He could not foresee, when he discovered the wondrous equation which unified matter and energy, that it would turn into black magic.

Thus the ubiquitous polarity of the self-asserting and self-transcending tendencies is strikingly displayed in the domain of scientific creativity. Discovery may be called the emotionally neutral art – not because the scientist is devoid of emotion, but because his labours require a delicately balanced and sublimated blend of motivations, where the drives to exploration and domination are in equilibrium. For the same reason he is assigned the central panel of the triptych, between the jester who, exercising his wit at the expense of others, is primarily motivated by self-asserting malice, and the artist, whose creative work depends on the self-transcending power of his imagination.

The order of the three panels of the triptych seems further justified by the nature of the Aha reaction. It combines the explosive discharge of tension, epitomised in the Eureka cry which is akin to the Ha-ha reaction, with the cathartic Ah . . . reaction – that "deep shudder of enchantment" of which Einstein speaks, and which is closely related to the artist's experience of beauty and the mystic's "oceanic feeling". The Eureka cry reflects the conquistadorial, the Ah . . . reaction the mystical element, which jointly provide the hybrid motivation of the scientist's quest.

Chapter 30

CREATIVITY AND THE UNCONSCIOUS

The preceding extracts were devoted to the shared elements in the logic or "grammar" of humour, science and art; the emotive climate in each of these three domains, and its dependence on the polarity of the self-assertive and self-transcending emotions.

In the extract which follows we take a closer look at the unconscious factors in the creative act. It starts with a brief discussion of the difference (frequently ignored) between creativity and virtuosity.* The extract is taken from a paper read at the Conference on "Brain Function and Learning" of the Brain Research Institute, University of California, Los Angeles.†

Creative activity could be described as a type of learning process where teacher and pupil are located in the same individual. Creative people like to ascribe the role of the teacher to an entity they call the unconscious, which they regard as a kind of Socratic demon – while others deny its existence, and still others are prepared to admit it but deplore the ambiguity of the concept. I belong to this last group.

The first point to consider is the individual's awareness of the activity in which he is involved. It is a trivial fact of experience that awareness is not an all-or-nothing affair but a matter of degrees, a continuum which extends from the unconsciousness that results from being hit on the head, through the extra-consciousness of visceral processes, through tying one's shoelaces with an "absent mind", through fringe-conscious per-

**This subject will turn up again later, in the discussion of Zen art in ch. 51.
†First printed in the proceedings of the Conference published by the UCLA Forum in Medical Sciences, 1967, and included in Drinkers of Infinity (1968).*

ceptions and routines, up to the laser-beam of focal consciousness. These states can be arranged on a linear gradient – white
through grey to black. Bright new skills acquired by learning –
regardless whether perceptual, motor or cognitive skills – tend to
condensate into habits, and their control to migrate to the twilight
zones of awareness. I can carry on a conversation while driving
the car, and hand over control to the automatic pilot in my nervous system. Gastaut and Beck* have suggested that well-
established habits may be handed down from the cortico-reticular
level to the lymbic system or other structures in the diencephalon
[i.e., from phylogenetically new, to older levels of the brain]. But
this mechanism seems a bit too crude to account for those fine
shadings along the gradient. However that may be, let us note that
*automatised skills do not necessarily become rigid and
stereotyped*. The night-club pianist who syncopates Chopin
while carrying on a flirtation with the barmaid, displays virtuosity, although he functions semi-automatically, on the lower
reaches of the gradient of awareness.

Thus habit-formation entails a constant downward traffic along
that gradient of awareness, as on a moving escalator. But this
down-grading does not necessarily involve an impoverishment of
the skill, and does not exclude virtuosity of a kind which is often
mistaken for creativity. Watch a locksmith at work as he feels his
way with a simple bent wire in a complicated lock and snaps it
open, as if guided by some mysterious intuition. In fact his performance is controlled by certain *fixed rules* of the game which
apply to all locks in general, and a flexible *strategy*, both derived
from countless past experiences, and sent down the escalator belt.
The much-admired masters of the various Zen arts, from fencing
to caligraphic painting, have always aimed at precisely this kind
of virtuosity, confusing unconscious automatisms with unconscious inspiration. To ride a bicycle over a tightrope, or to perform
the feats of a calculating prodigy, are virtuoso achievements, but
at the opposite pole to creative originality.

So if we say that creativity relies, at certain critical moments, on
inspirations of unconscious origin, we mean some kind of
upward traffic on the escalator belt. This can be interpreted in
more than one way. "Inspiration" can be taken to mean a message
received from the unconscious conceived as an autonomic agency

*H. Gastaut and E. Beck, "Brain rhythms and learning", *New Scientist*, March 1,
1962.

– a separate compartment of the mind in which the Socratic demon does your homework for you. I believe this view to be untenable, although it was upheld not only by romantically inclined artists, but also by mathematicians like Poincaré. The very term "*the* unconscious", used as a noun, is rather confusing because it implies a structural entity, a kind of box inside which certain activities take place, whereas in fact awareness is, as we have seen, a variable *dimension* of activities. One and the same activity can be accompanied by varying degrees of awareness; even visceral functions can apparently be brought under conscious control by Yoga techniques or by Valsalva manoeuvring [slowing of the heart by voluntary effort].* The opposite kind of thing happens when on awakening you try to hang on to the remembrance of a dream which is running away like quick-sand from conscious reach. One might call this phenomenon *oneirolysis* – from "oneiros", dream, plus "lysis", dissolution – I shall return to it in a moment.

If we discard the notion of the unconscious acting as a *deus ex machina*, we can adopt an alternative, more sober interpretation. In this view the experience of sudden illumination, the apparently spontaneous creative leap appears as the result of mental events of a known and definable type, which, however, took place on the lower reaches of the gradient, below the level of focal or even peripheral awareness. The puzzling question is why these dark interludes are apparently indispensable to the wide-awake pursuits of science. The first, rough answer that suggests itself is that the particular type of mental activity which takes place in the so-called "period of incubation" does not meet the criteria of articulateness and logical decency required for admission into the focal awareness of the wide-awake state – for the very good reason that if given unrestricted access, it would play havoc with our every-day thinking routines. But under exceptional circumstances, when routine breaks down, a temporary regression to these pre-rational and pre-logical forms of mentation often just does the trick.

The paper then goes on to discuss how such regressions can become aids to creativity, but as it is couched in rather technical language, I have diluted it with passages from The Act of Creation *and* Janus:

*Cf. e.g. Ch. M. McClure in *Calif. Medicine*, Vol. 90, No. 6 (June, 1959).

All our coherent thinking, acting and planning is governed by "rules of the game", although we are mostly unaware of being controlled by them. In the artificial conditions of the psychological laboratory the rules are explicitly spelt out by the experimenter; for instance: "name opposites". Then the experimenter says "dark" and the subject promptly answers "light". But if the rule is "synonyms", the subject will respond with "black" or "night" or "shadow". Note that though the rule is fixed, it leaves the subject a choice of several answers, even in this simple game. To talk, as behaviourists do, of stimuli and conditioned responses forming chains of associations in a vacuum is meaningless: what response a particular stimulus will evoke depends (a) on the fixed rules of the game and (b) on flexible strategies guided by past experience, temperament and other factors. Thus in playing chess – or cricket – the rules are fixed, while permitting a vast number of strategic choices.

But the games we play in everyday life are more complex than those in the laboratory or on the chessboard, where the rules are laid down by explicit orders. In the normal routines of thinking and talking the rules exercise their control implicitly, from way below the level of conscious awareness. Not only the codes of grammar and syntax operate hidden in the gaps between the words, but also the codes of commonsense logic and of those more complex methods of reasoning which include our built-in, axiomatic prejudices and emotional inclinations. Even if consciously bent on defining the rules which govern our thinking, we find it extremely difficult to do so, and have to enlist the help of specialists – linguists, semanticists, psychiatrists, and so forth. We play the games of life, obeying rule-books written in invisible ink or a secret code. In *The Act of Creation* I proposed the term "matrix" as a unifying formula to designate those cognitive systems which we variously call "frames of reference", "associative contexts", "mental sets" of "universes of discourse" – that is to say, all habits, routines and skills governed by an invariant code of *rules* (which may be explicit or implicit) but capable of varied *strategies* in attacking a problem or task.

When life confronts us with a problem or task, it will be dealt with according to the same set of rules which enabled us to deal with similar situations in our past experience. It would be foolish to belittle the value of such law-abiding routines. They lend coherence and stability to behaviour, and structured order to reasoning. But when the difficulty or novelty of the task exceeds a critical limit, the matrices of daily routines are no longer adequate to cope with it. The world is on the move, and new situations arise, posing questions and offering challenges which cannot be met within the conventional frames of reference, the established rule-books. In science, such situations arise under the impact of new data which shake the foundations of well-established theories. The challenge is often self-imposed by the insatiable exploratory drive, which prompts the original mind to ask questions which nobody has asked before and to feel frustrated by dusty answers. In the artist's case, the challenge is a more or less permanent one, arising out of the limitations of his medium of expression, his urge to escape from the constraints imposed by the conventional styles and techniques of his time, his ever-hopeful struggle to express the inexpressible.

When the challenge cannot be met, the problem is *blocked* — though the subject may realise this only after a series of hopeless tries, or never at all. A blocked situation increases the stress of the frustrated drive. When all promising attempts at solving a problem by traditional means have been exhausted, thinking tends to run in circles like cats in the puzzle-box, until the whole personality becomes saturated with the problem. At this stage — the "period of incubation" — the single-mindedness of the creative obsession produces a state of receptivity, a readiness to pounce on favourable chance constellations and to profit from any casual hint. As Lloyd Morgan said: "Saturate yourself through and through with your subject, and wait." Thus in discoveries of the type in which both rational thinking and the trigger-action of chance play a noticeable part, the main contribution of the unconscious is to keep the problem constantly on the agenda while conscious attention is occupied elsewhere — like Newton watching an apple fall. Our friend, the Socratic demon, seems to have bugged all primary cortical receptor areas with hidden microphones —to make sure that no bit of information of any conceivable use to him is lost. Which is just another way of quoting Pasteur: "Fortune favours only the prepared mind."

But in other types of discovery unconscious mentation seems to intervene in more specific, active ways, and enable the mind to perform surprisingly original, quasi-acrobatic feats, which lead to revolutionary breakthroughs in science or art, open new vistas, and create a radically changed outlook. Every revolution has a destructive as well as a constructive aspect. When we speak of a "revolutionary" discovery in science or of revolutionary changes in artistic style, we imply the destructive aspect.* The destruction is wrought by jettisoning previously sacrosanct doctrines and seemingly self-evident axioms of thought, cemented into our mental habits. This is what enables us to distinguish between creative originality on the one hand, and diligent routine or virtuosity on the other. A problem solved or a task accomplished in accordance with established rules of the game leaves the matrix of the skill intact – unharmed and possibly even enriched by the experience. Creative originality, on the other hand, always involves un-learning and re-learning, undoing and re-doing. It involves the breaking up of petrified mental structures, discarding matrices which have outlived their usefulness, and re-assembling others in a new synthesis – in other words, it is a complex operation of *dissociation* and *bisociation*, involving several levels of the mental hierarchy.

All biographical evidence indicates that such a radical re-shuffling operation requires the intervention of mental processes beneath the surface of conscious reasoning, in the twilight zones of awareness. In the decisive phase of the creative process the rational controls are relaxed and the creative person's mind seems to *regress* from disciplined thinking to less specialised, more fluid ways of mentation. A frequent form of this is the retreat from articulate verbal thinking to vague, visual imagery. There is a naive popular belief that scientists arrive at their discoveries by reasoning in strictly rational, precise, verbal terms. The evidence indicates that they do nothing of the sort. In 1945, Jacques Hadamard's famous inquiry† among American mathematicians to find out their working methods produced the striking conclusion that nearly all of them (with only two exceptions) tackled their problems neither in verbal terms nor by algebraic symbols, but relied on visual imagery of a vague, hazy nature. Einstein was among them; he wrote: "The words of the language as they are written or spoken do not seem to play any role in my mechanisms of thought . . . which relies on more or less clear images of a visual

*Cf. Popper: "In order that a new theory should constitute a discovery or a step forward it should conflict with its predecessor; that is to say, it should lead to at least some conflicting results. But this means, from a logical point of view, that it should contradict its predecessor: it should overthrow it. In this sense, progress in science – or at least striking progress – is always revolutionary." (Popper in *Problems of Scientific Revolution*, ed. R. Harré [Oxford, 1975].)

†J. Hadamard, *The Psychology of Invention in the Mathematical Field* (Princeton, 1949).

and some of a muscular type. . . . It also seems to me that what you call full consciousness is a limit-case which can never be fully accomplished because consciousness is a narrow thing."* We are reminded of another great mathematician, Gauss, who complained: "I have got my solution, but I don't know how I arrived at it."

Most creative scientists, who have described their working methods, seem to have been visualisers who shared Woodworth's opinion: "Often we have to get away from speech to think clearly." Watson [founder of Behaviourist psychology] was very naive indeed; and so are those among his successors who still equate thinking with "implicit (or sub-vocal) verbal behaviour". Words crystallise thoughts, but a crystal is no longer a liquid. Verbal reasoning occupies the latest and highest level in the mental hierarchy, but it can erect a screen between the thinker and reality. Creativity often starts where language ends, that is, by regressing to pre-verbal and seemingly pre-rational levels of mental activity, which may in some respects be comparable to the dream, but closer perhaps to the transitory states between sleep and full wakefulness.

Such regression implies a temporary suspension of the "rules of the game" which control our reasoning routines; the mind in labour is momentarily liberated from the tyranny of rigid, over-precise schemata, their built-in prejudices and hidden axioms; it is led to un-learn and acquire a new innocence of the eye and fluidity of thought, which enable it to discover hidden analogies and reckless combinations of ideas which would be unacceptable in the sober, wide-awake state. The biographies of great scientists provide countless examples of this phenomenon; their virtually unanimous emphasis on spontaneous intuitions and hunches of unknown origin suggests that there always are large chunks of irrationality embedded in the creative process – not only in art, where we take it for granted, but in the exact sciences as well.

In The Act of Creation I have ventured some guesses as to how this unconscious guidance works – how a temporary regression to less sophisticated mental levels can produce the happy combination of ideas, the focal bisociation, which produces the solution of the problem. I have mentioned before the experience of awakening from sleep and trying to hang on to the remembrance of a dream which is running away, like sand through a sieve, out of conscious reach. I have called this phenomenon oneirolysis –

*In Hadamard, op. cit.

dream-dissolution. The dream itself, while it lasts (and to some extent also the drowsy daydream) drifts effortlessly from one scenario to another, in a free-wheeling manner, indifferent to contradiction, to the rules of logic and the conventional limita-tions of space, time or cause; it establishes bizarre connections and churns out analogies between cabbages and kings which disintegrate when the sleeper awakes and which he cannot describe in precise verbal terms – except by saying that something reminded him of something, but he no longer knows what or why. Now in the throes of the creative obsession, when all levels of the mental hierarchy, including the unconscious strata, are saturated with the problem, the phenomenon of oneirolysis may be reversed into a kind of *oneirosynthesis*, in which those vaguely sensed connections form a nascent analogy. It may be a hazy, tentative affair, like Einstein's "images of a visual or muscular type", or Faraday's "lines of force" surrounding magnets which he saw in vivid hallucinations; and its shape may be changing from camel to weasel like Hamlet's cloud. The unconscious reaches of fertile minds must be teeming with such nascent analogies, hidden affinities, and the cloudy "forms of things unknown". But we must also remember that clouds form and dissolve again; and cloudbursts are rare events. False inspira-tions, alas, carry the same spontaneous convincingness as the legitimate ones which they outnumber a thousandfold; the acid test of verification comes *after* the act.

The French have an expression for which I can find no English equivalent: *reculer pour mieux sauter* – draw back to take a running jump. The process I have been discussing follows a similar pattern: a temporary *regression* to more primitive and uninhibited levels of ideation, followed by a creative *forward leap*. Disintegration and reintegration, dissociation and bisocia-tion reflect the same pattern. Cogitation in the creative sense is co-agitation, the shaking together of the previously separate; but the fully conscious, rational mind is not the best cocktail shaker. It is invaluable in our daily routines, but the revolutionary break-throughs in science and art always represent some variation of *reculer pour mieux sauter*.

We might call it an archetypal pattern, which is reflected in the death and resurrection (or "withdrawal and return") motive in mythology. Joseph is thrown into a well, Jonah is reborn out of the belly of the whale, Jesus is resurrected from the tomb.

Lastly, as we shall see later, *reculer pour mieux sauter*, draw-back-to-leap, plays a crucial part not only in mental creativity, but also in the creative evolution of higher life-forms. We shall see that biological evolution may be described as a series of escapes from the blind alleys of stagnation, over-specialisation and maladjustment, by an undoing and re-forming process which is basically analogous to the phenomena of mental evolution and in some respects foreshadows them. But before moving on towards those wider vistas, there are still some loose ends to be tied up relating to creativity in science and art.

Chapter 31

ON TRUTH AND BEAUTY

In the previous sections I have been at pains to stress that the artist and scientist do not inhabit separate universes, merely different regions of a continuous spectrum. After emphasising the affinities, it remains to discuss the differences – some apparent, some real – between the opposite ends of the continuum. The most evident contrast is reflected in the different criteria of excellence which we are supposed to apply to scientific theories and to works of art: in the first case objective truth supported by hard evidence, in the second case subjective judgements based on vague aesthetic considerations. But this is, as I have tried to show, a vastly over-simplified view. I have discussed it in The Act of Creation and in various essays, and welcomed the opportunity to do so once more for an audience of professional writers – the International Congress of the PEN Club in August, 1976. The theme of the Congress was "The Truth of Imagination", and I was asked to give the opening address, from which the extracts that follow are taken.*

The theme of this Congress is a rather obscure passage in a letter from Keats to Benjamin Bailey, written in 1817, which says:

> I am certain of nothing but of the holiness of the
> Heart's affections and the truth of Imagination. . . .

This, frankly, does not seem to make much sense. Nor does it help much to find an echo of that passage in the famous last lines of the Ode on a Grecian Urn, written two years later:

> Beauty is truth, truth beauty – that is all
> Ye know on earth, and all ye need to know.

*Unavoidably, some passages overlap with the contents of earlier chapters, and I have excised repetitions as far as possible – except where these would have amounted to a mutilation of the text.

No doubt there is beauty in these lines, but do they speak the truth? I happen to believe that they do, but the relationship between truth and beauty, or more generally between science and art, is an old and tricky problem.

The Pythagoreans, who started the scientific adventure, regarded the cosmos as a large musical box, where the musical intervals corresponded to the distances between the planetary orbits, thus providing the mathematical foundation of the harmony of the spheres. Far from being materialists, they regarded all matter as a dance of numbers, and modern physics, after dematerialising matter, has reverted to a similar attitude.

According to a popular misconception, the scientist's reasoning processes are strictly logical and lacking in the sensuous and visual quality of the poetic imagination. In fact an inquiry among American mathematicians revealed that nearly all of them, including Einstein, thought in terms of visual images, and not of precise verbal concepts. One of the greatest physicists of all time, Michael Faraday, visualised the tensions surrounding magnets as curves in space which he called "lines of force" and which, in his imagination, were as real as if they consisted of solid tubes. He literally saw the universe patterned with these curving lines and shortly after suffered an attack of schizophrenia. There is a strong affinity between the curves of force which crowd Faraday's universe and the giddy vortices in Van Gogh's skies.

However, science, as the hoary cliché goes, aims at truth, art at beauty. There seems to be a crack in Keats's Grecian urn and its message to sound somewhat hollow; but if we look closer, the crack tends to disappear. The artist and the scientist each projects his experience of reality into his chosen medium of expression. The criteria by which we judge scientific and artistic achievement vary of course according to the medium; but they show continuous gradations from the *relatively* objective methods of verifying a scientific theory by experiment, to the *relatively* subjective criteria of aesthetic value. But the emphasis is on "relative". Thus the same experimental data can in most cases be interpreted in more than one way – which is why the history of science echoes with as many venomous controversies as the history of literary criticism – which ought to be a comfort to all of us.

In fact the progress of science is strewn, like an ancient desert trail, with the bleached skeletons of discarded theories which once seemed to possess eternal life. The progression of art involves equally agonising reappraisals of accepted values, criteria of relevance, frames of perception. In the last two centuries alone Europe saw the rise and fall of classicism; romanticism and *Sturm und Drang*; naturalism; surrealism and Dada; the socially conscious novel; the existentialist novel; the *nouveau roman*. In the history of painting, the changes were even more drastic. But the same zigzag course characterises the progress of science, whether you turn to the history of medicine, or psychology, or the fundamental changes in physics from the Aristotelian to the Newtonian to Einstein's conception of the cosmos. The poet, the painter, the scientist, each superimposes his more or less ephemeral vision on the universe; each constructs his own biassed model of reality by selecting and highlighting those aspects of experience which he considers significant and ignoring those which he considers irrelevant.

I do not wish to exaggerate: there is certainly a considerable difference, in precision and objectivity, between the methods of judging a theorem in physics and a work of art. But I must emphasise once more that there are continuous transitions between them. Moreover, the process of judging comes always *post factum*, after the creative act; whereas the decisive phase of the act itself is always a leap into the dark, a dive into the twilight zones of consciousness; and the diver is more likely to come up with a handful of mud than with a coral. False inspirations and crank theories are as abundant in the history of science as are bad works of art; yet they command in the victim's mind the same forceful conviction, the same euphoria, as the happy finds which are *post factum* proven right. In this respect the scientist is in no better position than the artist: while in the throes of the creative process, guidance by truth is as uncertain and subjective as guidance by beauty.

We can now venture a step farther: every valid scientific discovery gives rise, in the connoisseur, to the experience of beauty, because the solution of a vexing problem creates harmony out of dissonance; and vice versa, the experience of beauty can only occur if the intellect endorses the validity of the operation – whatever its nature – designed to elicit the experience. A virgin by Boticelli and a mathematical theorum by Poincaré do not betray any similarity between the motivations or aspirations of their respective creators; the first seemed to aim at "beauty", the second at "truth". But it was Poincaré himself who wrote that what guided him in his unconscious gropings towards the "happy combinations" which yield new discoveries was "the feeling of mathematical beauty, of the harmony of number, of forms, of geometric elegance. This is a true aesthetic feeling that all mathematicians know." Many outstanding scientists have made similar confessions. "Beauty is the first test; there is no permanent place in the world for ugly mathematics," G. H. Hardy wrote in his classic *A Mathematician's Apology*. The doyen of English physicists, Paul Dirac, went even further with his famous pronouncement: "It is more important to have beauty in one's equations than to have them fit experiment." It was a shocking thing to say, but he got the Nobel nevertheless.

Let us now turn to the opposite end of the spectrum. The novelist or poet does not create in a vacuum; his world-view is confined – whether he realises it or not – to the philosophical and scientific panorama of his time. John Donne was a mystic, but he instantly realised the significance of Galileo's telescope:

> Man has weav'd out a net, and this net throwne
> Upon the Heavens, and now they are his owne.

Newton had a comparable impact on literature; so of course had Darwin, Marx, Fraser of the Golden Bough, Freud or Einstein. Painters and sculptors, too, have always been guided, and often obsessed, by scientific or pseudo-scientific theories: the Golden Section of the Greeks; the geometry of perspective and foreshortening; Dürer's and Leonardo's "ultimate laws of perfect proportion"; Cézanne's doctrine that all natural form can be reduced to spheres, cylinders and cones, and so forth. The counterpart of the mathematician's apology which puts beauty before logical method is Seurat's pronouncement: "They see poetry in what I have done. No, I apply my *method*, and that is all there is to it."

Both sides seem to lean over backward: the scientist by confessing his dependence on intuitive hunches which guide his theorising – while the artist values, or over-values, the abstract principles which impose discipline on his intuition. The two factors complement each other; the proportions in which they combine depend foremost on the medium in which the creative drive finds its expression.

Every great artist has an element of the explorer in him; the poet does not "manipulate words" as the behaviourist would have it, he explores the emotive and descriptive potentialities of language; the painter is engaged, throughout his life, in learning to see (and in teaching others to see the world the way he does). Thus the creative drive can be canalised into a variety of directions. It is a blend of curiosity and wonder – where curiosity refers to its intellectual, and wonder or awe to its emotional aspect. Jointly they motivate the scientist's and the artist's voyages of exploration. Johannes Kepler, the astronomer, wrote of the sensation of "marvelous clarity" which enraptured him when he discovered the laws of planetary motion; and that experience is shared by every writer when a stanza suddenly falls into what seems to be its predestined pattern, or when the felicitous image unfolds in the mind. Experiences of this kind always combine intellectual satisfaction with emotional release – that quasi-mystical "oceanic feeling". Art is a school of self-transcendence; at its best, it expands individual consciousness into cosmic awareness, as science endeavours to explain particular phenomena by laws of a general order; to reduce a particular puzzle to the great universal puzzle.

To say it again: intellectual illumination and emotional catharsis are the essence of the aesthetic experience. The first constitutes the moment of truth, the second provides the experience of beauty. The two are *complementary aspects of an indivisible process*. The experience of truth, however subjective, must be present for the experience of beauty to arise; and conversely, the solution of any of nature's riddles, like that of a noble chess problem, makes one exclaim, "How beautiful!"

Thus to heal the crack in the Grecian urn and make it acceptable in this age, we would have to improve on Keats's wording and translate it into computer jargon: beauty is a function of truth, truth a function of beauty. They can be separated by analysis, but in the lived experience of the creative act – and its recreative echo in the beholder – they are as inseparable as emotion is inseparable from thought. Both signal – one in the language of the brain, the other of the bowels – the moment of the Eureka cry when, in the words of Carlyle, "the infinite is made to blend itself with the finite, to stand visible, as it were, attainable here".

To conclude this chapter, let us have a glance at a diagram in The Act of Creation *which was meant to illustrate, in a simplified way, the continuity of the "two cultures". The vertical axis represents the dimension of "Objective Truth", verifiable by experiment, the horizontal axis represents the subjective experience of "Beauty"; the former governed by the intellect, the latter by the emotions. The chart shows neighbouring provinces of science and art arranged in a continuous series. As we move downwards along the*

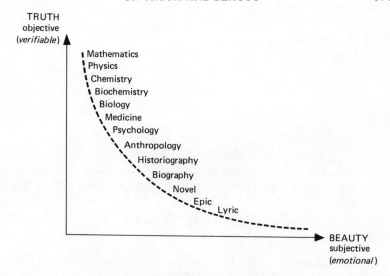

sloping curve, "objective verifiability" steadily diminishes, while the subjective, emotional factor increases. Yet even in the highest ranges of the curve, the realm of pure mathematics, we find disturbing logical paradoxes which cannot be resolved,* and mathematicians yearning for "beauty in the equations". As we descend from mathematics to sub-atomic physics, the interpretations of empirical data become more and more controversial; and so we can move further down the slope, from the so-called exact sciences like chemistry through biology, then through medicine – which is, alas, a much less exact science – through such hybrid domains as psychology and biography to the biographical novel and lastly into pure fiction. Similar graded series lead from construction engineering through architecture and interior design to the hybrid "arts and crafts" and finally to the representative arts; here one variable of the curve could be called "utility", the second "beauty". The point of this game is to show that regardless of what scale of values you choose to apply, you move through a continuum, without encountering a crack in the Grecian urn – or a precipice between the two cultures.

*Mathematics had its logical foundations shaken by paradoxes like Gödel's theorem; or earlier on by Cantor's theory of infinite aggregates (as a result of which Cantor was barred from promotion in all German universities, and the mathematical journals refused to publish his papers).

Chapter 32

EVOLUTIONS AND REVOLUTIONS IN SCIENCE AND ART

A brief comparison of the history of science and the history of art yields further proof of the affinities between the two cultures — affinites mostly hidden from the eye because art historians tend to ignore science, and vice versa. The text below is extracted from "The Cheltenham Lecture", given at the Cheltenham Festival of Literature, 1969,* plus a few insertions from Janus.

1 Historical Parallels

In Solzhenitsyn's novel *The First Circle* some prisoners are having an argument about the progress of science. One of them, Gleb Nerzhin, exclaims in a passionate outburst:

"Progress! Who wants progress? That's just what I like about art — the fact that there can't be any 'progress' in it."

He then discusses the tremendous advances in technology during the previous century and concludes with the taunt: "But has there been any advance on *Anna Karenina?*"

The opposite attitude was taken by Sartre in his essay "What is Literature?", where he compared novels to bananas which you can enjoy only while they are fresh. *Anna Karenina*, in this view, must have rotted long ago.

Solzhenitsyn's hero reflects the traditional view that science progresses in a cumulative manner, brick upon brick, the way a tower is built, whereas art is timeless, a dance of coloured balls on the jets of a fountain — a playing of variations on eternal themes.

---

*Printed in The Heel of Achilles *under the title* "Literature and the Law of Diminishing Returns".

To a limited extent, this conventional view is of course justified. In the great discoveries of science, the fusion of previously separate contexts (electricity and magnetism, matter and energy, etc.) results in a new synthesis, which in its turn will merge with others on a higher, emergent level of the hierarchy. The evolution of art does not, generally, show this overall pattern. The creative act which produces a poetic metaphor consists of an emotive *juxtaposition*, rather than an intellectual *fusion* of two contexts. But once again, this difference is relative, not absolute. If you accept Gleb Nerzhin's view *in toto*, then it is pointless to search for objective criteria of "progress" in literature, painting or music; art, then, does not evolve, it merely formulates and reformulates the same archetypal experiences in the costumes and styles of the period; and although the vocabulary is subject to changes – including the visual vocabulary of the painter – the statement contained in a great work of art remains valid and unmarked by time's arrow, untouched by the vulgar march of progress.

But at a closer look this view turns out to be historically untenable. For one thing, there are periods in which a given art-form shows a definite, cumulative evolution, comparable to scientific progress. To quote our leading art historian, Sir Ernst Gombrich:

> In antiquity the discussion of painting and sculpture inevitably centred on [the] imitation [of nature] – mimesis. Indeed it may be said that the progress of art towards that goal was to the ancient what the progress of technology is to the modern: the model of progress as such. Thus Pliny told the history of sculpture and painting as the history of inventions, assigning definite achievements in the rendering of nature to individual artists: the painter Polygnotus was the first to represent people with open mouth and with teeth, the sculptor Pythagoras was the first to render nerves and veins, the painter Nikias was concerned with light and shade. The history of these years [*ca.* 550 to 350 BC] as it is reflected in Pliny or Quintilian was handed down like an epic of conquest, a story of inventions. . . . In the Renaissance it was Vasari who applied this technique to the history of the arts of Italy from the thirteenth to the sixteenth century. Vasari never fails to pay tribute to those artists of the past who made a distinct contribution, as he saw it, to the mastery of representation. "Art rose from humble beginnings to the summit of perfection" [Vasari says] because such natural geniuses as Giotto blazed the trail and others were thus enabled to build on their achievements.*

Art and Illusion (London, 1962), pp. 9, 120.

Here then, we have at least a partial refutation of Nerzhin's thesis
that there is no progress in art. "If I could see further than others,"
said Newton, "it is because I stood on the shoulders of giants."
Leonardo said much the same. "It is a wretched pupil," he wrote,
"who does not surpass his master." Dürer and others expressed
similar opinions. What they evidently meant was that during the
period of explosive development which started with Giotto
around the year 1300, each successive generation of painters had
discovered new tricks and techniques – foreshortening, perspective, the treatment of light, colour and texture, the capture of
movement and facial expression – inventions which the pupil
could take over from the master and use as his base-line for new
departures.

As for literature, it need hardly be emphasised that the various
schools and fashions of the past were not static, but evolved
during their limited life-span toward greater refinement and
technical perfection – or decadence. We take it for granted that
today's physicists know more about the atom than Democritus;
but then Joyce's *Ulysses* also knows more about human nature
than Homer's *Odysseus*. There is hardly a writer, past or present,
who did not or does not sincerely believe his style and technique
of writing to be closer to reality, intellectually and emotionally,
than those of the past. Let us face it: our reverence for Homer or
Goethe is sweetened by a dash of condescension not unlike our
attitude to infant prodigies: how clever they were for their age!

Thus we can safely reject as a gross over-simplification Gleb
Nerzhin's view that science is cumulative like a brick-layer's
work, while art is timeless. The history of art, too, shows cumulative progress – in certain periods, though not in others. In the
history of European painting, for instance, there are two outstanding periods in which we find rapid, sustained, cumulative progress in representing Nature, almost as tangible as the progress in
engineering. The first stretches roughly from the middle of the
sixth to the middle of the fourth century BC, the second from the
beginning of the fourteenth to the middle of the sixteenth century.
Each lasted for about six to eight generations, in the course of
which each giant did indeed stand on the shoulders of his pre-
decessors, and could take in a wider view. It would of course be
silly to say that these were the *only* periods of cumulative progress. But it is nevertheless true that in between these periods of
rapid evolution there are much longer stretches of stagnation or
decline. Besides, there are the lone giants, who seem to appear

from nowhere and cannot be fitted into any neat pyramid of acrobats balancing on each other's shoulders.

The conclusion seems to be obvious. Our museums and libraries demonstrate that there *is* a cumulative progression in every art-form – in a limited sense, in a limited direction, during limited periods. But these short, luminous trails sooner or later peter out in twilight and confusion, and the search for a new departure in a new direction is on.

However, contrary to popular belief, the evolution of science does not show a more coherent picture. Only during the last three hundred years has its advance been continuous and cumulative; but those unfamiliar with the history of science – and they include the majority of scientists – tend to fall into the mistaken belief that the acquisition of knowledge has always been a neat and tidy ascent on a straight path towards the ultimate peak.

In fact, neither science nor art has evolved in a continuous way. Whitehead once remarked that Europe in the year 1500 knew less than Archimedes who died in 212 BC. In retrospect there was only one step separating Archimedes from Galileo, Aristarchus of Samos (who fathered the heliocentric system) from Copernicus. But that step took nearly two thousand years to be made. During that long period, science was hibernating. After the three short glorious centuries of Greek science, roughly coinciding with the cumulative period of Greek art, comes a period of suspended animation about six times as long; then a new furious awakening, so far only about ten generations old.

Progress, then, in science as in art, is neither steady nor absolute, but – to say it again – a progression in a limited sense during limited periods in limited directions; not along a steady curve, but in a jagged, jerky, zigzag line.

A Chinese proverb says that there is a time for fishing and a time for drying the nets. If you take a kind of bird's-eye view of the history of any branch of science, you will find a rhythmic alternation between long periods of relatively peaceful evolution and shorter bursts of revolutionary change. Only in the peaceful periods which follow after a major breakthrough is the progress of science continuous and cumulative in the strict sense. It is a period of consolidating the newly conquered frontiers, of verifying, assimilating, elaborating and extending the new synthesis: a time for drying the nets. It may last a few years or several generations; but sooner or later the emergence of new empirical data, or a change in the philosophical climate, leads to stagnation, a hardening of the matrix into a closed system, the rise of a new orthodoxy. This produces a crisis, a period of fertile anarchy in which rival theories proliferate – until the new synthesis is achieved and the cycle starts again; but this time aiming in a different direction, along different parameters, asking a different kind of question.

It is thus possible to detect a recurrent pattern in the evolution of both science and art. As a rule the cycle starts with a passionate rebellion against and rejection of the previously dominant school or style with a subsequent breakthrough towards new frontiers: call this *phase one*. The *second phase* in the cycle has a climate of optimism and euphoria; in the footsteps of the giants who spearheaded the advance, their more pedestrian followers and imitators move into the newly opened territories to explore and exploit its rich potentials. This, as said before, is the phase *par excellence* of cumulative progress in elaborating and perfecting new insights and techniques in research, and new styles in art. The *third phase* brings saturation, followed by frustration and deadlock. The *fourth* and last phase is a time of crisis and doubt – epitomised in John Donne's complaint on the fall of Aristotelian cosmology: " 'Tis all in pieces, all coherence gone." But it is also a time of wild experimentation (Fauvism and Dada and its equivalents in science) and of creative anarchy – *reculer pour mieux sauter* – which prepares and incubates the next revolution, initiating a new departure – and so the cycle starts again.

2 The Law of Infolding

Let me, briefly, dwell on the *first phase* of the cycle.

The French Revolution demolished the Bastille and used its huge stones to pave the Place de la Concorde. In other words, revolutions are both destructive and constructive. Old restraints and conventions are discarded, aspects of human experience previously neglected or repressed are suddenly highlighted, there is a shift of emphasis, a reshuffling of data, a reordering of the hierarchy of values and of the criteria of relevance. This is what happened at each of the turning-points of narrative prose styles – classicism to romanticism, naturalism, and so on. This is what happened in the succession of dramatic changes in the artist's perception of the human body, from Egyptian painting to Picasso; or in the novelist's view of the relation between the sexes; or the painter's attitude to nature. Throughout the Renaissance, for instance, and up to the late Venetians, landscapes were conceived merely as more or less stereotyped backdrops for the human figures on the stage. Art historians appear to agree that Giorgione's "Tempest" is the first European painting in which nature claims to be seen in her own right – the violent thunderstorm in the background competes for our attention with the bucolic scene in the foreground.

This does not mean that artists who painted before Giorgione were blind to nature, or that poets before the romantic movement were lacking in emotion. But their vision and response were different from ours, molded by the *Zeitgeist*, just as successive schools of philosophers put different interpretations on the same data. To Homer, a storm at sea signified the fury of Poseidon, and the dawn was painted by the rosy fingers of Aurora; to Virgil, nature appeared tame and bucolic; it took quite a series of revolutionary shifts of emphasis and reshuffling of data until people learnt to see an apple through Cézanne's eyes, or a snow-covered plain through the eyes of Verlaine. And the adjective "revolutionary" is no exaggeration, although in retrospect these revolutions seem quite tame. Verlaine, for instance, does not seem to have been unduly audacious when he compared the uncertain colour of the snow to luminous sand covering the "interminable boredom of the plain," and the sky to dull copper in which the moon "lived and died". To-day French schoolchildren have to learn this poem by heart. But when it was published, a famous writer and critic attacked Verlaine in the shrill voice of the literary fishwife:

> How can the moon live and die in a copper heaven? And how can snow shine like sand? How can the French attribute such importance to this versifier who is far from skilful in form and most contemptible and commonplace in subject-matter?

The fishwife was Count Leo Tolstoy; the source of the quotation is his once-celebrated essay, "What is Art?"

If we try to define what these revolutions in different ages and in different art forms have in common, I would suggest that the one obvious feature they all share is a radical *shift in selective emphasis*. The artist, as the scientist, is engaged in projecting his vision of reality into a particular medium. But the product of his efforts can never be an exact copy of reality. In the first place, he is up against the peculiarities and limitations of his medium: the

painter's canvas does not have the micro-structure of the human
retina, stone lacks the plasticity of living tissue, words are symbols which do not smell, or bleed. In the second place, the artist's
perception and outlook on the world also has its peculiarities and
limitations imposed by the implicit conventions of his time. The
two factors interact: there is continuous feedback from language
to thought, from the clay under the sculptor's fingers to the image
he is trying to materialise. The dynamic tension between the
biased mind and the obstinate medium compels the artist to make
decisions at every step he takes (though the decision-making need
not be conscious): to select and emphasise those features of reality
which he considers to be significant and to ignore those which he
considers irrelevant. Some aspects of experience defy representation, some can only be rendered in a simplified or distorted way,
some only at the price of sacrificing others.

The term "selective emphasis" thus always involves three
related factors: *selection, exaggeration* and *simplification.* * They
are at work in every province of art: in the narrative of events,
historic or fictitious; in the visual representation of landscape or
human figure, in portrait and caricature. But selective emphasis
also operates in the scientist's laboratory. Every geographical
map, every statistical diagram, every theoretical model of man or
the universe is a deliberately schematised caricature of reality,
based on the technique of selecting and highlighting the relevant
features, simplifying or ignoring others according to the criteria
of relevance of that particular discipline or school of thought.
In psychology, for instance, one finds radically different criteria
of relevance among nineteenth-century introspectionists,
contemporary behaviourists, Freudians, Jungians and existential
psychologists, with corresponding contrasts in selective
emphasis, resulting in radically different portraits of man; and the
same considerations apply to the history of medicine. In physics,
the paradigm of exact science, there are radical shifts from Aristotelian anthropomorphism to Newtonian mechanism, from the
deterministic to the probabilistic approach, from forces to fields.
Even a cursory glance at the history of science makes one realise
that its criteria of relevance are liable to changes as striking as the
changes of style in art; and comparison between the two domains
makes the history of art appear a little less confusing by showing
us at least a dim outline of a more comprehensible pattern.

*See above, e.g. Chapter 26.

Thus the recurrent revolutionary upheavals in the content and style of literary productions can be described as shifts in the criteria of relevance and in selective emphasis.

The *second phase* in the historic cycle is, as already mentioned, the exploration of the new subject-matter, the elaboration of the new styles and techniques, which need not further detain us here. For it is the *third* phase in the cycle which is of special interest to (and the main headache of) every practitioner of our profession: the phase of saturation and subsequent frustration of the writer and his audience. I quoted Tolstoy's indignant outcry against Verlaine's moon dying in a copper sky; today it is hard to understand what Tolstoy got so excited about. Yesterday's daring metaphors are today's clichés. Yesterday's obscenities are today's banalities, the bourgeois is no longer *épatable*; stark sex, like the moon deprived of its mystery, turns out to be all craters and pimples.

These are inevitable consequences of a fundamental property of the nervous system. Seasoned ambulance crews no longer turn a hair at the sight of mangled casualties, and even the inmates of Auschwitz developed a degree of emotional immunity. There exists a phenomenon which psychologists call habituation. You do not hear the ticking of the clock in your room, but you hear that it has suddenly stopped. You do not feel the pressure of the chair against your back; but you do feel it when you shift your position. Nerve cells in the retina do not signal sameness, they only signal contrast. And habituation is not confined to man. Dr Horn at Cambridge has recently found single nerve cells in the mid-brain of a rabbit which responded promptly to a tone sounded at a frequency of 1000 cycles per second, but ceased to respond after several repetitions of the stimulus. Habituation to the 1000-cycle tone does not, however, prevent a strong response of the same cell when an only slightly different, 900-cycle tone is sounded. Dr Horn presented examples of similar phenomena in animals as different as locusts, squids and cats.*

If even a squid can be that blasé, how can the writer hope to fight the law of diminishing returns? The recurrent cycles of stagnation, crisis, revolution and new departure seem to be mainly caused by the progressive habituation of both artist and audience to any well-established technique, style or subject-matter, and its resulting loss of emotional appeal, of evocative power. This loss,

*New Scientist, August 7, 1969.

unfortunately, is unavoidable, because once the new style has become stablised and familiar, the reader no longer needs to exert his imagination to assimilate the message; he is deprived of the effort of re-creation and degraded to a mere consumer. There can be little doubt that the bulk of all literature, probably from Greece onwards, but certainly since the invention of the printing press, consisted of inferior consumer goods, written in the long periods of stagnation within the recurrent cycle. But this huge mass of pulp has decayed and vanished from sight; only samples of exceptional quality have survived and provide the material of the history of literature.

Any new art form, however revolutionary it seemed at first, grows after a while tired and stale; it loses its power over the audience. The staleness lies of course not in the form itself, which may be enduring, but in the consumer's jaded palate. The history of art could be written in terms of the artist's struggle against the deadening effects of saturation. It is not his fault if he is fighting a losing battle. He may produce cheesecake or he may produce caviare, he is nevertheless helpless against the fundamental process of habituation which operates in the rabbit's brain as in the reader's nervous system. Its effect on the artist is a growing sense of frustration, and the growing realisation – which may be conscious or not – that the conventional techniques of his time have become inadequate as a medium of communication and self-expression.

Two opposite methods seem to have been tried over and again to improve communication with the audience: screaming and whispering. The first tries to impress the message on the audience by an overly direct appeal to the emotions, through tear-jerkers, melodramatics or more refined derivations of it; it tries to provide spicier fare for jaded appetites and to cover impotence by flamboyant gestures and mannerisms. In the visual arts one finds some or all of these symptoms cropping up in the successive periods of decline of Egyptian, Greek and Roman sculpture, in the manneristic styles of the late Baroque, in the choicer horrors of the Victorian age, and so on. The general trend in periods of decadence is towards the over-emphatic and the over-explicit, and need not concern us further.

The opposite method to counteract the law of diminishing returns in the evolution of art is of much greater interest. Instead of relying on the emphatic and the explicit, it tends towards economy and implicitness. It is usual to credit the French Symbolist movement – Mallarmé, Verlaine, Rimbaud – with having initiated the shift from explicit statement to implicit suggestion, and the French Impressionist school with a parallel achievement in painting. However, this movement from the obvious to the oblique can be observed in the most varied periods and art forms as an effective antidote to satiety and decadence. Nevertheless it is worth quoting a passage in which Mallarmé outlines the programme of the Symbolist movement:

> It seems to me that there should be only allusions. The volatile image of the dreams they evoke, these make the song: the Parnassians [the classicist movement of Leconte de Lisle, Heredia, et al.] who make a complete demonstration of the object thereby lack mystery; they deprive the [reader's] mind of that delicious joy of imagining that it creates. To name the thing means forsaking three-quarters of a poem's enjoyment – which is derived from unravelling it gradually, by happy guesswork; to suggest the thing creates the dream.*

Yet this technique was not invented by the symbolists; it is as old as art itself. It starts with mythology. The *Bhagavad Gita* is an allegory which every Hindu scholar and mystic interprets after his own fashion; Genesis is studded with archetypal symbols; Christ speaks in parables, the Oracle in riddles, Orpheus on fiddles. The purpose is not to obscure the message; on the contrary, it is to make it more luminous by compelling the recipient to act as a fluorescent screen, to work out the implications by his own effort, to re-create it. "Implicit" is derived from the Latin *plicare*, and means "folded in", like a roll of parchment. The implicit message has to be unfolded by the reader; he must unravel it, fill the gaps, solve riddles. But as time goes by, the reader learns to see through the tricks, the diguises become transparent, he is deprived, as Mallarmé has it, "of that delicious joy of imagining that he creates". So the writer or poet will strive towards even more disciplined economy and more subtle implications; the parchment will be rolled in even tighter.

I once called this "the law of infolding";† it seems to be the most effective reply to the law of diminishing returns. It runs like a kind of *leitmotif* through the history of literature. The Homeric epics were originally broadcast by travelling bards who impersonated their heroes by voice and acting, which is the most direct and

*S. Mallarmé, *Enquête sur l'Evolution Littéraire* (1888).
†*The Act of Creation.*

emphatic method of narration. Later on, around the seventh century BC, the epics were consolidated in their present form, to be
recited on festive occasions; by now, however, they were folded
into rolls of parchment. The bard impersonated; the written word
had to be deciphered. A pair of quotation marks are sufficient to
symbolise the human voice, and printer's ink is generally more
effective in arousing emotion than a histrionic recital. Histrionics
are left to the stage and screen, but they are also subject to the law
of infolding. Victorian melodrama has become a parody of its own
genre, and films not more than twenty years old which moved us
at the time appear now – exceptions always granted – surprisingly
dated, obvious, overacted, overexplicit. And the background
music is simply incredible.

The writer's best friend is his pair of scissors. In his advice to a
younger writer, Hemingway wrote: "The more bloody good stuff
you cut out, the more bloody good your novel will be. . . ." The
law of infolding demands that the reader should never be given
something for nothing; he must be made to pay in emotional
currency by exerting his imagination. Otherwise one gets the
dreaded "so what?" reaction. "Caroline felt her heart go out to
Peter." So what? Let it go out. The German word for composing
poetry is *dichten* – to compress. But compression can also operate
in semantic space, by squeezing several meanings, or levels of
meaning, into a single statement. Freud thought that this was the
essence of poetry; Empson's "seven types of ambiguity" are variations on the same theme.

Needless to say, the techniques of infolding can be used in a
fraudulent manner to create deliberate obscurity. Though it has
been said that the Venus of Milo would lose much of her attraction
if her arms were restored, it is unlikely that her creator broke them
off in cold blood. But who can draw the line between deliberate
cheating and the tricks of the unconscious? Much of the *nouveau
roman* and of *Last Year in Marienbad* reminds one of a way of
playing poker where you hide your cards not only from your
opponent but from yourself. This can sometimes be a winning
strategy – but what does "winning" mean in this context?

There are many other fields where one can watch the law of
infolding at work. Humour has travelled a long way from the
Punch cartoon to the *New Yorker*'s sophisticated riddles.
Metaphors have a way of shrivelling into dehydrated clichés; they
are replaced by fresh supplies of a less obvious and explicit kind.
Rhythm and metre have evolved from simple, repetitive pulses

into intricate patterns, in which the erstwhile beat of the tom-tom is implied, but no longer pounded out. Rhyme, as the most explicit form of euphony, is folding in – or up.

In the contemporary visual arts the process is too obvious to need stressing. Only a forger could, in our day, paint in the style of Vermeer (however perfect his technique) because to paint like Vermeer, the artist would have to forget that he has ever seen a Manet or Cézanne. So he has to be either a forger or a Rip Van Winkle who has slept since the seventeenth century. But it would be a mistake to believe that the trend towards the implicit is found only in modern painting. Leonardo invented the technique of the *sfumato* or veiled form, such as the blurred contours at the corners of the Mona Lisa's eyes, which have never lost their fascination; and Titian in his old age invented the technique of what Vasari called "the crudely daubed strokes and blobs" which, looked at from close quarters, cannot be deciphered and which let the picture unfold only when you step back; Rembrandt went through a similar progression, from the neat and meticulous to the loose and suggestive brushstroke in his rendering of embroideries. The examples could be multiplied. It could be said, for instance, that in the peak periods of Chinese painting the picture consisted of what was left out. I cannot resist quoting just one phrase from a seventeenth-century Chinese manual (which I owe to Gombrich): "Figures even though painted without eyes, must seem to look ; without ears, must seem to listen. . . . That is truly giving expression to the invisible. . . ."

To make a last cross-reference to science, even there the law of infolding operates. Aristotle firmly believed that all possible discoveries and inventions had already been made in his time; Bacon and Descartes thought that it would take just one more generation to solve all the mysteries of the universe; even nineteenth-century scientists held such optimistic beliefs. Only recently did we begin to realise that the unfolding of the secrets of nature was accompanied by a parallel process of infolding, because the more precise knowledge the physicist acquired, the more ambiguous and elusive were the mathematical symbols he had to use; he can no longer make an intelligible model of reality, he can only allude to it by abstract equations.

To sum up – I have tried to point to a recurrent pattern in the history of science and art which, broadly speaking, both seem to move through cycles of revolution – consolidation – saturation –

crisis and new departure. Revolutions are characterised by shifts in selective emphasis; the period of consolidation is one of cumulative progress; the third period is a constant struggle against the law of diminishing returns, and one of the effective antidotes is indicated by the law of infolding. I must ask your indulgence for so much law-making and speculation; but if the Creator had a purpose in equipping us with a neck, he surely meant us to stick it out.

In Janus there are some further comments which may serve as a footnote to the present chapter:

These recurrent cycles in the history of science are in some respects analogous to the successive stages in the process of individual discovery, according to the schema proposed by Helmholtz and Graham Wallas:* conscious preparation – unconscious incubation – illumination – verification and consolidation. But while the individual's process of discovery is concluded at the last of these stages, on the historical scale the last stage of one cycle merges into the first stage of the next.

   A more recent theory which has strong affinities with the conception of historic cycles, formulated in *The Act of Creation* and summarised above, is Thomas Kuhn's much-quoted essay *The Structure of Scientific Revolutions*.† Kuhn calls the cumulative phases of the cycle "normal science" and refers to the revolutionary breakthroughs as "paradigm changes". In spite of the different terminology, there are some striking similarities between Kuhn's schema and the one proposed in *The Act of Creation*, though they were developed independently from each other. Both represent radical departures from George Sarton's venerable theory which asserts that the history of science is the only history which displays cumulative progress, and that, accordingly, the progress of science is the only yardstick by which we can measure the progress of mankind.

   In fact, however, as we have seen, the progress of science on the charts of history does not appear as a continuously ascending curve, but as a zigzag line, not unlike the history of art. This does not mean, of course, that there is no advance; only that both are advancing on an unpredictable, often erratic course.

*G. Wallas, *The Art of Thought* (London, 1945).
†Chicago, 1962.

In the course of the last hundred years, history has accelerated like a rocket taking off, and has produced new discoveries at a breath-taking rate — but also more crises, about-turns and undoing-redoings than ever before. This is in evidence in all branches of science and art — in painting and literature, physics and brain-research, genetics and cosmology. In every field the demolition squads were as feverishly active as the construction workers, but we see only what the latter have built, and tend to forget the once proud citadels of orthodoxy that were destroyed. No doubt in the next few decades we shall witness even more spectacular feats of undoing-redoing. Some speculative hunches on this subject will be found in later chapters.

As an afterthought, the diagram below may serve to sum up the remarks in earlier chapters about the styles, techniques and methods of representation which are found to be instrumental in all types of creative activity:

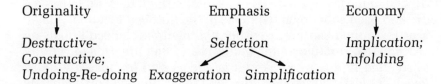

Originality   Emphasis   Economy

Destructive-   Selection   Implication;
Constructive;   Infolding
Undoing-Re-doing Exaggeration Simplification

We had glimpses of the schema reflected in the techniques of humour, in literature, painting and in science.

Originality, selective emphasis, and economy are certainly not the only criteria of literary excellence, but they proved to be a kind of handy mariner's compass for the critic at sea; and the "law of infolding" appears to be equally valid – and tantalising – in science as in art.

Chapter 33

THE TRAGIC AND THE TRIVIAL

On some previous occasions I used the metaphor of the Tragic and the Trivial planes of existence. The next extracts (from The Act of Creation, ch. xx) will show that it has a bearing on the creative process.

The metaphor of the two planes was not a literary construct, but the outcome of a painful private experience. During the war, in 1942, I made friends with a young fighter pilot, Richard Hillary. * He had been shot down in flames in the Battle of Britain when he was not quite twenty. His earlier photographs showed him as an extremely attractive young man; when I met him, his burnt and shrivelled hands were like birds' claws and his face a clumsy mask of plastic surgery where even the eyelids were artificial. He was given a job in the Ministry of Information, published a book, The Last Enemy, which instantly became a bestseller, had an attractive mistress, and led a pleasant life in London. Yet after a couple of years of this, he fooled the Medical Board into certifying him fit for active service, returned to flying, and crashed to his death a few months later while training to become a night fighter.

His letters from this last period described a kind of double existence he was leading on the aerodrome. During the day, his burnt body suffered agonies from the intense cold; he was bored, frightened, irritated. But at night – as he wrote in a letter – "I have only to step into an aeroplane – that monstrous thing of iron and steel just watching for its chance to down me – and all fear goes. I am at peace again. I feel the elusive touch of those Circles of Peace travelling past in the air."

*Cf. "In Memory of Richard Hillary" in The Yogi and the Commissar. Hillary was the model for Andrew in Arrival and Departure.

We discussed this dualism of experience; he summed up what I was trying to say in a letter to a third person:

K. has a theory for this. He believes there are two planes of existence which he calls vie tragique and vie triviale. Usually we move on the trivial plane, but occasionally in moments of elation or danger, we find ourselves transferred to the plane of the vie tragique, with its non-commonsense, cosmic perspective. When we are on the trivial plane, the realities of the other appear as nonsense – as overstrung nerves, and so on. When we live on the tragic plane, the joys and sorrows of the other are shallow, frivolous, trifling. But in exceptional circumstances, for instance, if one has to live through a long stretch of time in physical danger, one is placed, as it were, on the intersection line of the two planes; a curious situation which is a kind of tightrope-walking on one's nerves. . . . I think he is right.

Right or not, since Hillary's death the metaphor never lost its power over me.

Evidently, not all excursions from the trivial to the tragic plane are irreversible and fatal. On the contrary, they can be creative and life-enhancing. There exist countless variations on this theme in mythology, variously known as the Night Journey or the Death and Rebirth motif, which all share the same basic, archetypal pattern:

Under the impact of some overwhelming experience, the hero is made to realise the shallowness of his life, the vanity and futility of his daily pursuits, caught in the trivial routines of existence. This realisation may come to him as a sudden shock caused by some catastrophic event, or as the cumulative effect of a slow spiritual maturation, or through the trigger action of some apparently banal experience which assumes an unexpected significance. The hero then suffers a crisis which shakes the very foundations of his being; he embarks on the Night Journey, is suddenly transferred to the Tragic Plane – from which he emerges purified, enriched by new insights, regenerated on a higher level of integration.

The Night Journey may take the form of a visit to the underworld (Orpheus, Odysseus); or the hero is cast to the bottom of a well (Joseph), buried in a grave (Jesus), swallowed by a fish (Jonah); or he retires alone into the desert, as Buddha, Mahomet, Christ, and other prophets and founders of religions did at the crucial turn in their lives. In tribal societies, the pattern is symbolically enacted in the initiation-rites which precede the turning points in the life of the individual, such as puberty or marriage. He is made to undertake a minor Night Journey: segregated from the community, he must fast, endure physical hardships and various ordeals, so that he may experience the essential solitude of man, and establish contact with the Tragic Plane. A similar purpose is served by the symbolic drowning and rebirth of baptism; in fasts and other purification rituals; in the initiation ceremonies of religious or masonic orders, even of university societies. Illumination must be preceded by the ordeals of incubation.

Freudians and Jungians alike emphasise the intimate relation between the symbolism of the Night Journey, and the unconscious craving for a return to the womb. The connection is no more far-fetched than our references to "mother earth", "mother ocean", or "mother church". Mythology is full of these symbols – the metaphors of the collective unconscious. However bewildering they may appear to the waking mind, they are familiar to the dreamer, and recur constantly in the sleep of people who have little else in common. The Night Journey is the antipode of Promethean striving. One endeavours to steal the bright fire of the gods; the other is a sliding back towards the pulsating darkness, one and undivided, of which we were part before our separate egos were formed.

Thus the Night Journey is a regression in which consciousness becomes unborn – to become reborn in a higher form of synthesis. It is once more the process of *reculer pour mieux sauter*; the creative impulse, having lost its bearing in trivial entanglements, must effect a retreat to recover its vigour.

Without our regular, minor night journeys in sleep we would soon become victims of mental desiccation. Dreaming is for the aesthetically underprivileged the equivalent of artistic experience, his only means of self-transcendence, of breaking away from the trivial plane and creating his own mythology.

The Guilt of Jonah

Among the many variations of the Night Journey in myth and folklore, one of the most forceful is the story of Jonah and the whale – perhaps because in no ancient civilisation was the tension between the Tragic and Trivial planes more intensely felt than by the Hebrews. The first was represented by the endless succession of invasions and catastrophes, the exacting presence of Jehovah and of his apocalyptic prophets; the second by the rare periods of relatively normal life, which the overstrung spiritual leaders of the tribe condemned as abject. Jonah had committed no crime which would warrant his dreadful punishment; he is described as a quite ordinary and decent fellow with just a streak of normal vanity – for he is, justifiably, "very angry" when, at the end of the story, God does not raze Nineveh as Jonah had prophesied at His bidding, and thus makes Jonah appear an impostor or fool.

Now this very ordinary person receives at the beginning of the story God's sudden order to "go to Nineveh, that great city, and cry against it" – which is a rather tall order, for Jonah is no professional priest or prophet. It is quite understandable that he prefers to go on leading his happy and trivial life. So, instead of responding to the call from the Tragic Plane, he buys a passage on a ship to Tarshish; and he has such a clean conscience about it, that while the storm rages and the sailors cry "every man unto his god" and throw the cargo into the sea, Jonah himself is fast asleep. And therein – in his normality, complacency, in his thick-skinned triviality and refusal to face the storm, and God, and the corruption of Nineveh; in his turning his back on the tragic essence of life – precisely therein lies his sin, which leads to the crisis, to the Night Journey in the belly of the whale, in "the belly of hell":

> The waters compassed me about, even to the soul: the depth closed me round about, the weeds were wrapped about my head . . . *yet hast thou brought up my life from corruption, O Lord my God*. When my soul fainted within me I remembered the Lord: and my prayer came in unto thee. . . . *They that observe lying vanities forsake their own mercy*.

The story sounds in fact like an allegory of a nervous breakdown and subsequent spiritual conversion. Jonah might serve as a symbol for Dimitri Karamazov, or any of the countless heroes of fiction who progress through crisis to awakening. For I must repeat that Jonah's only crime was to cling to the Trivial Plane and to cultivate his little garden, trying to ignore the uncomfortable, unjust, terrible voice from the other plane. Melville understood this when, in the great sermon in *Moby Dick*, he made his preacher sum up the lesson of Jonah and the whale in this unorthodox moral:

> Woe to him who seeks to pour oil upon the waters when God has brewed them into a gale! Woe to him who seeks to please rather than to appal! Woe to him whose good name is more to him than goodness! Woe to him who, in this world, courts not dishonour!

And the author of the Jonah story himself must have been aware of its vast implications, of the impossibility of treating all men who lead an ordinary life as harshly as Jonah – for the story ends with an unusual act of clemency by the otherwise so vengeful desert-god, which comes as a curious anticlimax full of ironical tolerance for the inadequacy of man:

> Then said the Lord – And should I not spare Nineveh, that great city, wherein are more than six score thousand persons that cannot discern between their right hand and their left hand: and also much cattle?

The ordinary mortal moves virtually all his life on the Trivial Plane; only on a few dramatic occasions – during the storms of puberty, when in love, or confronted with death – does he fall suddenly through a manhole, and is transferred to the Tragic Plane. Sudden catastrophes – famines, wars, and plagues – may shift a whole population frm the Trivial to the Tragic Plane; but they soon succeed in banalising even tragedy itself, and carry on, business as usual. During the Spanish Civil War, one of my fellow prisoners, a youth suffering from appendicitis, was put on a milk diet two days before his execution.

The force of habit, the grip of convention, hold us down on the Trivial Plane; we are unaware of our bondage because the bonds are invisible, their constraints acting below the level of awareness. They make us run, most of the time, in the grooves of habit – reducing us to the status of skilled automata which behaviourism proclaims to be the true condition of man. But, glory be, man is not a flat-earth dweller all the time – only most of the time. His need for self-transcendence is as basic as his need for self-assertion.

Life on the Trivial Plane is a state of unnoticed confinement – but also a condition of emotional and intellectual stability. The belly of the whale cannot be made into a permanent residence. Neither emotionally, nor intellectually, can we afford to live for more than brief transition periods on the Tragic Plane. Emotionally, it would mean the journey of no return of Blake; intellectually, it would mean the abdication of reason. Eternity, infinity, do not lend themselves to logical manipulation. They are too inhuman and elusive to cope with, unless they are made to blend with some experience in the tangible world of the finite. The absolute becomes emotionally effective only if it is bisociated with something concrete – dovetailed, as it were, into the familiar. This is what both artist and scientist are aiming at, though not always consciously. Both are gifted – or cursed – with the faculty of perceiving trivial events *sub specie aeternitatis* surrounded by a halo of mystery, and conversely to perceive the cosmic mystery in mortal terms, to draw it into the orbit of man. The *locus in quo* of human creativity is always on the line of intersection between the two planes. The scientist discovers the working of eternal laws in the ephemeral grain of sand, or in the contractions of a dead frog's leg hanging on a washing-line. The artist carves out the image of the god which he saw hidden in a piece of wood. The jester deflates the god: "Don't be so proud – I have known you from a plum-tree."

Needless to say, not all novels are "problem novels", subjecting the reader to a sustained barrage of existential conundrums. But indirectly and implicitly every great work of art has some bearing on man's ultimate problems. Even a humble daisy has a root, and a work of art, however light-hearted or serene, is ultimately nourished through its delicate capillaries by the archetypal substrata of experience.

By living on both planes at once, the creative artist or scientist is able to catch an occasional glimpse of eternity looking through the window of time. Whether it is a mediaeval stained-glass window or Newton's formula of universal gravity, is a matter of temperament and taste.

Chapter 34

GRAVITY AND THE HOLY GHOST

Earlier on I mentioned The Sleepwalkers *as an off-shoot of* The Act of Creation *and quoted from its Preface, but to avoid breaking the continuity of the argument, I have relegated the excerpts which follow to the end of this section.*

One of the central characters in the book is the founder of modern astronomy, Johannes Kepler (1571–1630) – an endearing, wayward genius, half mystic, half scientist:

Johannes Kepler, Keppler, Khepler, Kheppler or Keplerus was conceived on 16 May, AD 1571, at 4.37 a.m., and was born on 27 December at 2.30 p.m., after a pregnancy lasting 224 days, 9 hours and 53 minutes. The five different ways of spelling his name are all his own, and so are the figures relating to conception, pregnancy and birth, recorded in a horoscope which he cast for himself. The contrast between his carelessness about his name and his extreme precision about dates reflects, from the very outset, a mind to whom all ultimate reality, the essence of religion, of truth and beauty, was contained in the language of numbers (*The Sleepwalkers*, p. 225).

As mentioned before, a biography of Kepler, extracted from The Sleepwalkers, *was published under the title* The Watershed *in the American "Science Study Series" for college students. In his Foreword, the editor, John H. Durston, pointed out that "over the centuries science has made great use of Kepler's works but ignored the man. Few of his contemporaries tried, or cared, to understand him, and his famous laws, resurrected by Isaac Newton, were all of him that seemed to have escaped the grave. But time, happily, has a way of redressing balances. In this biography, for which the world had to wait three hundred and thirty years, Kepler the man emerges as a rich, if outlandish, character, deserving of immortality.''*

I have tried to convey the essence of his achievement in my article on Kepler in the Encyclopaedia of Philosophy* *and in a more popular form in the following lecture† – condensed from* The Sleepwalkers:

When Newton died in 1727, Alexander Pope, the most fashionable poet at that time, wrote this oft-quoted epitaph:

> Nature and Nature's Laws lay hid in night:
> God said let Newton be, and all was light.

Pope certainly voiced the mood of the Age of Reason, of that Pan-European New Philosophy which was emerging out of the Scientific Revolution of the previous century, and whose cornerstone was the Newtonian cosmology. It was this new view of the universe which lent the whole movement its characteristic mixture of humility and arrogance. The humility came from the realisation that our earth is not the centre of the world and that humanity is reduced to the condition of "so many ants crawling on a flying balloon". This metaphor, devised by one of Galileo's critics,‡ with intent to ridicule, had now become sober reality. But there was arrogance to compensate for man's hurt pride. The tiny ants had huge brains which, aided by the polished lenses of the telescope, enabled them to encompass all infinity.

The Newtonian edifice provided the framework for the philosophy of the Age of Enlightenment. Once that edifice was completed, it looked like an entirely rational construction. But it was not built by rational, logical steps. One of its chief architects was a German mystic, Johannes Kepler. The tortuous road by which he arrived at his famous three laws of planetary motion – the cornerstones of modern astronomy – is characteristic of the great convulsions and confusions of thought during the transition from the mediaeval to the scientific world-view. I shall try briefly to retrace his development, because it forms a little-known, but symbolic prologue to the Century of Enlightenment – its birthpangs, as it were.

*New York, 1967.
†Delivered at the Symposium on "The Scientific and Artistic Achievements of the Century of Enlightenment" at the Cini Foundation, Venice, September, 1967; reprinted in Drinkers of Infinity.
‡Monsignor Querengo.

"If I could see further than others," Newton once remarked, "it was because I stood on the shoulders of giants." The principal giants were Copernicus, Galileo and Kepler.

Canon Copernick had died in 1543 at the age of seventy: the first printed copy of his book *On the Revolutions of the Heavenly Spheres* was handed to him on his deathbed. Its first thirty pages outlined the theory of the heliocentric universe; the rest of the book, describing the motions of the earth, moon and planets, is so confusing and unreadable that it became an all-time worst-seller. There are indications that even Galileo did not read all through it. Its first edition of a thousand copies never sold out, and it had altogether four reprints in four hundred years. A contemporary astronomical work, Christoph Clavius' *The Treatise on the Sphere*, had nineteen reprints within fifty years – Copernicus' book one.

I mention this curiosity to show that the Copernican theory attracted very little attention in Europe for the next two generations. It was not put on the Index of the Holy Office until 1616 – that is, seventy-three years after its publication (and then only for four years, "pending corrections"). New ideas, like infectious diseases, need a period of incubation before their full impact makes itself felt. Kepler was the first astronomer to raise his voice in public in favour of the Copernican theory. His *Mysterium Cosmographicum*, published in 1597 – fifty-four years after Copernicus' death – initiated the controversy. Galileo entered the scene fifteen years later.

Kepler was twenty-five when he wrote the *Mysterium*, and at that time he knew very little of astronomy. He had started as a hopeful student of theology at the Lutheran University of Tübingen, but a chance opportunity brought him as a teacher of mathematics to the provincial school of Gratz in Austria. In an autobiographical sketch, which he also wrote at twenty-five, he described the varied interests of his student-years; they ranged from the writing of comedies and Pindaric odes, to compositions "on unusual subjects, such as the resting place of the sun, and the sources of rivers, the sight of Atlantis through the clouds, the heavens, the spirits, the genii, the nature of fire, and other things of the same kind". In this varied menu of preoccupations one also finds the following remark: "I often defended the opinions of Copernicus in the disputations of the students, and I composed a careful disputation on the first motion which consists in the rotation of the earth [around its axis]; then I added to this the motion of the earth around the sun *for physical, or if you prefer, metaphysical reasons.*"

I have emphasised the last phrase because it can be found verbatim repeated in various passages in his works, and contains the *leitmotif* of his quest – which was eventually to lead him to the laws of planetary motion, and provide the mathematical foundations of the Newtonian universe.

Kepler became acquainted with Copernicus's book through one of his teachers in Tübingen, a certain Michael Maestlin, who possessed a copy of it – although Maestlin himself, like everybody else (including Galileo) taught the traditional, earth-centred Ptolemaic astronomy. Six years later, in the Preface to the *Mysterium Cosmographicum*, Kepler wrote:

> I was so delighted with Copernicus . . . that I proceeded to ascribe to the earth the apparent motions of the sun *for physical, or if you like it better, for metaphysical reasons* – as Copernicus had done for mathematical reasons.

He then proceeded to explain his metaphysical reasons for preferring a heliocentric to a geocentric world. Surprising though it may seem, they were based on a supposed analogy between the stationary sun, the stars and interstellar space on the one hand, and God the Father, the Son and the Holy Ghost on the other. "I shall pursue this analogy in my future cosmographical work," he promised. And twenty-five years later, when he was over fifty, he reaffirmed his belief in it: "It is by no means permissible to treat this analogy as an empty comparison; it must be considered by its Platonic form and archetypal quality as one of the primary causes."

He believed in this to the end of his life; it was one of the axioms of faith on which his edifice was built. But gradually his cherished analogy underwent a significant change. In a letter to Maestlin of the period in which the *Mysterium Cosmographicum* was written, he explained:

> The sun in the middle of the moving stars, himself at rest and yet the source of motion, carries the image of God the Father and Creator. He distributes his motive force through a medium which contains the moving bodies, even as the Father creates through the Holy Ghost.

It should be noted that at this point the "moving bodies", that is, the planets, are brought into the picture. The sun has become their "source of motion"; the Holy Ghost no longer merely fills the space between the motionless sun and the motionless stars: it has now become an active agent, a *vis motrix*, which drives the nimble planets in their orbits. Nobody before had suspected the existence of such a force emanating from the sun – except perhaps the Pythagoreans. But for the last two thousand years astronomy had been concerned not with the *causes* of the heavenly motions but with their *description* in purely geometrical terms, divorced from all physical considerations.

I would like to suggest that the passages I have just quoted reflect the first hesitant introduction of physical causation into man's vision of the skies – the first intimation of the forthcoming synthesis of cosmography and physics. I shall return to this point in a moment; but first let us follow the gradual transformation of the Holy Ghost into a physical force.

In the twentieth chapter of the *Mysterium*, Kepler attacks the problem of the mathematical relation between a planet's distance from the sun and the speed of its motion. This again was a question which nobody before him had raised, because it implied a causal connection of a physical nature between the sun and the planets – and such an idea, as I said, was completely strange to mediaeval cosmology. Now, the greater their distance from the sun, the slower the planets move (both regarding angular and tangential velocity). This phenomenon, says Kepler, allows only the following two explanations:

> Either the souls (*animae*) which move the planets are the less active the farther the planet is removed from the sun, or there exists only *one moving soul in the centre of all the orbits*, that is, the sun, which drives the planet the more vigorously the closer the planet is, but whose force is quasi-exhausted when acting on the outer planets because of the long distance and the weakening of the force which it entails.

Twenty-five years later, commenting on this passage, he wrote:

> If we substitute for the word "soul" the word "force" then we get just the principle which underlies my physics of the skies in the *Astronomia Nova*. . . . Once I firmly believed that the motive force of a planet was a soul. . . . Yet as I reflected that this cause of motion diminishes in proportion to distance, just as the light of the sun diminishes in proportion to distance from the sun, I came to the conclusion that this force must be something substantial – "substantial" not in the literal sense but . . . in the same manner as we say that light is something substantial, meaning by this an unsubstantial entity emanating from a substantial body.

The twenty-five years that separate these two quotations mark the transition from *anima motrix* to *vis motrix*, from a universe animated by purposeful intelligences to one moved by inanimate, "blind" forces devoid of purpose. For the rest of his life Kepler struggled with this new concept of "force" emerging from the womb of animism (its very name, *virtus*, or *vis*, betrays its origin) without ever coming to terms with it. At first he was not aware of the difficulties inherent in it. While he was working on his *magnum opus*, the *Astronomia Nova*, he wrote with youthful optimism to a friend:

> My aim is to show that the heavenly machine is not a kind of divine, live being, but a kind of clockwork (and he who believes that a clock has a soul, attributes the maker's glory to the work), in so far as nearly all the manifold motions are caused by a most simple, magnetic, and material force, just as all motions of the clock are caused by a simple weight. And I also show how these physical causes are to be given numerical and geometrical expression.

Kepler had defined the essence of the Scientific Revolution. But it turned out to be easier to talk about a "most simple, magnetic, material force" than to form a concrete idea of its working. Kepler's efforts to visualise the nature of the "moving force" (that is, gravity) emanating from the sun are not only of interest from the historian's point of view; they also illuminate the philosophical difficulties that were inherent in the concept of force from its very beginning. Since no English, French or Italian translation of the *Astronomia Nova* exists as far as I know, a few further quotations may be in order. First, Kepler wondered whether the mysterious force which moves the planets might be the *light* of the sun. But this could not be; so he went on:

> Though the light of the sun cannot itself be the moving force . . . it may perhaps represent a kind of vehicle, or tool, which the moving force uses. But the following considerations seem to contradict this. Firstly, the light is arrested in regions that lie in shade. If then the moving force were to use light as a vehicle, then darkness would bring the planets to a standstill. . . .
>
> This kind of force, just as the kind of force which is light . . . is propagated through the universe . . . but it is nowhere received except where there is a moveable body, such as a planet. The answer to this is: although the moving force has no substance, it is aimed at substance, i.e. at the planet-body to be moved. . . .
>
> Who, I ask, will pretend that light has substance? Yet nevertheless it acts and is acted upon in space, it is refracted and reflected, and it has

quantity, so that it may be dense or sparse, and can be regarded as a plane where it is received by something capable of being lit up. For, as I said in my *Optics*, the same thing applies to light as to our moving force; it has no present existence in the space between the source and the object which it lights up, although it has passed through that space in the past; it "is" not, it "was", so to speak.

Thus Kepler's intuitive gropings brought him closer to our contemporary, rather surrealistic concepts of electromagnetic and gravitational *fields* than to the classic, Newtonian concept of force; the modern scientist will find here an echo of his own perplexities. And that may be the reason why Kepler, having hit on the concept of universal gravity, subsequently discarded it – as Galileo was to discard it.

The most precise pre-Newtonian formulations of gravity are to be found in the Preface to the *Astronomia Nova*. Kepler started by refuting the Aristotelian doctrine according to which all "earthy" matter is heavy because it is its nature to strive towards the centre of the world – that is, the earth, whereas all "fiery" matter strives by its nature towards the periphery of the universe and is therefore light. Kepler explained that "heaviness" and "lightness" are not absolute properties:

> Matter that is less dense, either by nature or through heat, is relatively lighter . . . and therefore less attracted [to the earth] than heavier matter. . . . Supposing the earth *were* in the centre of the world, heavy bodies would be attracted to it, not because it is in the centre, but because it is a material body. It follows that regardless of where we place the earth, heavenly bodies will always seek it. . . .
>
> There is a mutual bodily tendency between cognate [i.e. material] bodies towards unity or contact (of which kind the magnetic force also is), so that the earth draws a stone much more than the stone draws the earth. . . .
>
> If the earth and the moon were not kept in their respective orbits by a spiritual or some equivalent force, the earth would ascend towards the moon 1/54 of the distance, and the moon would descend the remaining 53 parts of the interval, and thus they would unite. But this calculation presupposes that both bodies are of the same density.
>
> If the earth ceased to attract the waters of the sea, the seas would rise and flow into the moon. . . .
>
> If the attractive force of the moon reaches down to the earth, it follows that the attractive force of the earth, all the more, extends to the moon and even farther. . . .
>
> If two stones were placed anywhere in space near to each other, and outside the reach of force of a third cognate body, then they would

come together, after the manner of magnetic bodies, at an intermediate point, each approaching the other in porportion to the other's mass.

In the same passage is to be found the first approximation to a correct theory of the tides, which Kepler explained as "a motion of the waters towards the regions where the moon stands in the zenith". In a work written at the same time – *Somnium – A Dream of the Moon* (an early exercise in science fiction) – he furthermore postulated that the sun's attraction, too, influences the tides – that is, that the gravitational force of the sun reaches as far as the earth.

But here we are faced with another paradox. In the Preface to the *Astronomia Nova*, Kepler, as we have just seen, had grasped the essence of gravity, and even the idea that its force is proportionate to mass; yet in the rest of the book, and in all his subsequent works, *he seems to have completely forgotten it.* The force that emanates from the sun in the Keplerian universe is not a force of attraction but a tangential force, a kind of vortex or "raging current which tears all the planets, and perhaps all the celestial ether, from West to East".

To the question of what made Kepler drop gravity no answer is found anywhere in his profuse writings. Everything points to some unconscious psychological blockage; and we may gather hints about its nature in the writings of the other pioneers of the Scientific Revolution. Thus Galileo indignantly rejected Kepler's suggestion that the tides were due to the moon's attraction, and called it an occult superstition. In the *Dialogue on the Two Great World Systems* he says that Kepler "despite his open and penetrating mind, lent his ear and his assent to the moon's dominion over the waters, to occult properties [that is, gravity] and such like fancies (*fanciullezze'*)".

Descartes was equally repelled by the idea of a non-mechanical force acting at a distance, and, like Kepler, substituted for it vortices in the ether. As for Newton, his attitude is summed up in his famous third letter to Bentley:

It is inconceivable, that inanimate brute matter should, without the mediation of something else, which is material, operate upon, and affect other matter without mutual contact. . . . And this is one reason why I desired you would not ascribe innate gravity to me. That gravity should be innate, inherent, and essential to matter, so that one body may act upon another, at a distance through a vacuum, without the mediation of anything else, by and through which their action and

force may be conveyed from one to another, is to me so great an
absurdity, that I believe no man who has in philosophical matters a
competent faculty of thinking, can ever fall into it. . . .

Kepler, Galileo, and Descartes did not fall into the philosophical
abyss; their thinking was much too "modern" – that is, mechanistic – for that. The notion of a "force" that acts without an intermediary agent and pulls at immense stellar objects with ubiquitous
ghost fingers appeared to them mystical and unscientific, a
lapse into that Aristotelian animism from which they had just
broken loose. Universal gravity, *gravitatio mundi*, smacked of the
anima mundi of the ancients. Newton overcame the obstacle and
made the concept of gravity respectable by invoking the ubiquitous ether, whose attributes, however, were equally paradoxical,
so that eventually the whole concept of the ether had to be abandoned. But Newton himself refused to speculate on the manner in
which gravity worked* and even to surmise whether the ether
was a "spiritual" or a "corporeal" agency. Thus the natural
philosophy of the Age of Reason did not rest on quite such solid
and reasonable foundations as Pope and his optimistic contemporaries thought.

   Yet Newton was able to provide a precise mathematical equation for the mysterious agency to which the word gravity referred.
That equation was essentially derived from combining the results
of Galileo's studies of free fall and the motion of projectiles with
Kepler's three laws of planetary motion. There is no need, in this
town of Venice, to enlarge on the genius of Galileo, and the
importance of his contribution. But Galileo was a modern, who
belongs to the Century of Enlightenment, though he did not live to
see it; whereas in Kepler all the contradictions of his age seem to
have become incarnate – the age of transition from the mediaeval
to the modern world-view. One half of his divided personality
belonged to the past; he was a mystic, given to theological speculation, astrology, and number-lore. However, he was also an
empiricist with a scrupulous respect for observational data, who
unhesitatingly threw out his earlier theory of planetary motions,
the product of five years of dogged labour, because certain
observed positions of Mars deviated from those that the theory
demanded by a paltry eight minutes arc. This new-found respect

---

*His famous pronouncement "hypothesis non fingo" refers to this problem, and
to this problem alone, though it is often quoted out of context as a positivistic
slogan.

for "hard obstinate facts" was to determine, to a large extent, the climate of European thought during the next three centuries. It provided Kepler with the necessary discipline and put a restraint on his exuberant fantasy; but the primary motivation of his researches was mysticism of a Pythagorean brand. Throughout his life he was obsessed by certain mystic convictions, each of which had the power of an *idée fixe*. But far from interfering with his reasoning powers, these irrational obsessions were harnessed to his rational pursuits and provided the drive for his tireless labours. From a subjective point of view, Kepler's fundamental discoveries were in fact merely by-products of his chimerical quest. I have tried to show how a mystically inspired conviction – which was our starting point – led him to the revolutionary step of projecting physical causation into the skies, to heal the millennial rift between earthly physics and heavenly geometry, and thus to become the founder of modern astronomy. His *Astronomia Nova*, where the First and Second Planetary Laws are found, actually bears the provocative title:

A NEW ASTRONOMY BASED ON CAUSATION OR A PHYSICS OF THE SKY

Another of his obsessions was the belief that the planets' motions were governed by musical harmonies (the Pythagorean "music of the spheres"); the book containing his Third Law is called *Harmonice Mundi*. Columbus was not the only genius who set out for India and landed in America.

In such crooked ways does the tree of science grow. The curious detours by which Kepler and other pioneers of the Scientific Revolution arrived at their destination may serve as a cautionary tale to scientists and philosophers to remind them of the vast chunks of irrationality embedded in their rational pursuits. The philosophers and encyclopaedists of the *secolo dei lumi* thought that they were living in a solid, rational universe. In fact it was a universe held together by a mysterious force which, like the Holy Ghost, was acting at a distance, in defiance of all the laws of mechanics; and was justifiably rejected by Galileo and other modern-minded thinkers.

This, however, is only one example of the contradictions built into the arrogant rationalism of the Enlightenment. Like the re-pressed complexes of the Freudians, they were to erupt after a period of latency, with a shattering effect on all established norms, from astronomy to the representative arts.

Chapter 35

THE SENSE OF WONDER*

In one of his essays – *The Cutting of an Agate* – William Butler Yeats voiced one of the silliest popular fallacies of our times:

> Those learned men who are a terror to children and an ignominious sight in lovers' eyes, all those butts of a traditional humour where there is something of the wisdom of peasants, are mathematicians, theologians, lawyers, men of science of various kinds.

It is a fallacy of relatively recent origin. Tillyard† and Marjorie Nicolson‡ have shown how profoundly the Pythagorean revival had influenced Shakespeare and transformed the Elizabethan world-picture. Perhaps the greatest experience of Milton's youth was peering for the first time through a Galilean telescope:

> Before [his] eyes in sudden view appear
> The secrets of the hoary Deep – a dark
> Illimitable ocean, without bound,
> Without dimension. . . .

And we remember John Donne's excitement caused by Kepler's discoveries:

> Man hath weav'd out a net, and this net throwne
> Upon the Heavens, and now they are his owne. . . .

The sense of wonder was shared by mystic, poet, and scientist alike; their falling apart dates only from the end of the nineteenth century. I have discussed the scientist's motivational drive; the present chapter provides illustrations from the lives of a few outstanding men.

---

*From The Act of Creation, *Appendix II: Some Features of Genius.*
†*The Elizabethan World Picture* (London, 1946).
‡*Science and Imagination* (New York, 1956).

ARISTOTLE ON MOTIVATION

The mental image that one tries to form of a white-clad, sandalled member of the Pythagorean Brotherhood, living around 530 BC in Croton, southern Italy, is necessarily hazy. But at least we know that the Brotherhood was both a scientific academy and a monastic order; that its members led an ascetic communal life where all property was shared, thus anticipating the Essenes and the primitive Christian communities. We know that much of their time was spent in contemplation, and that initiation into the higher mysteries of mathematics, astronomy, and medicine depended upon the purification of spirit and body, which the aspirant had to achieve by abstinences and examinations of conscience. Pythagoras himself, like St Francis, is said to have preached to animals; the whole surviving tradition indicates that his disciples, while engaged in number-lore and astronomical calculations, firmly believed that a true scientist must be a saint, and that the wish to become one was the motivation of his labours.

The Hippocratics followed a materialist philosophy; yet that wonderfully precise ethical commandment, the Hippocratic Oath, prescribed not only that the physician should do everything in his powers to help the sick, but also that he should refrain, in the patient's house, "from any act of seduction, of male or female, bond or free" – a truly heroic act of self-denial. The motivation of Greek science in general was summed up in a passage by Aristotle, from which I have briefly quoted before (my italics):

> Men were first led to study [natural] philosophy, as indeed they are today, by wonder. At first they felt wonder about the more superficial problems; afterwards they advanced gradually by perplexing themselves over greater difficulties; e.g., the behaviour of the moon, the phenomena of the sun, and the origination of the universe. Now he who is perplexed and wonders believes himself to be ignorant. Hence even the lover of myths is, in a sense, a philosopher, for a myth is a tissue of wonders. Thus if they took to philosophy to escape ignorance, it is patent that they were pursuing science for the sake of knowledge itself, and not for utilitarian applications. This is confirmed by the course of historical development itself. *For nearly all the requisites both of comfort and social refinement had been secured before the quest for this form of enlightenment began.* So it is clear that we do not seek it for the sake of any ulterior application. Just as we call a man free who exists for his own ends and not for those of another, so it is with this which is the only free man's science: it alone of the sciences exists for its own sake.*

*Quoted by B. Farrington, Greek Science (London, 1953), pp. 130–31.

It is amusing to note Aristotle's belief that applied science and technology had completed their tasks long before his time – as the italicised lines and other passages in his writings clearly indicate. His statement is somewhat biased, because it does not take into account the utilitarian element in the origin of geometry: land-surveying, and of astronomy: calendar-making. Nevertheless, his summing up of the motives which drove the Greek men of science seems to be by and large true. Archimedes, the greatest of them, was compelled by necessity to invent a whole series of spectacular mechanical devices – including the water screw, and some engines of war which brought him all the fame and glory an inventor can dream of. Yet such was his contempt for these practical inventions that he refused to have a written record of them. His passions were mathematics and pure science; his famous words, "give me but a firm spot on which to stand and I will move the earth" reflect a metaphysical fantasy, not an engineer's ambitions. When Syracuse fell in 212 BC to the Roman general Marcellus, the sage, in the midst of the turmoil and massacre, was calmly drawing geometrical figures in the sand; according to tradition, his last words were – after being run through the body by a Roman soldier: "Pray, do not disturb my circles." Apocryphal or not, that tradition symbolises the Greek attitude to science as a quest transcending the mortal self.

THE LEADERS OF THE REVOLUTION

After the long dark interlude which came to an end with the Pythagorean Renaissance in Italy around AD 1500, four men stand highlighted on the stage of history: Copernicus, Tycho, Galileo, Kepler. They were the pioneers of the Scientific Revolution, the men on whose shoulders Newton stood: what do we know about their personal motives – which ultimately changed the face of this planet?

We know least about Copernicus (1473–1543); as a person, he seems to have been a pale, insignificant figure, a timid Canon in the God-forsaken Prussian province of Varmia; his main ambition, as far as one can tell, was to be left alone and not to incur derision or disfavour. As a student in Italy, he had become acquainted with the Phythagorean idea of a sun-centred universe, and for the next thirty or forty years he elaborated his system in secret. Only in the last year before his death, at the age of seventy, did he agree, under pressure of his friends and superiors, to publish it; the first printed copy of his book *On the Revolutions of the Heavenly Spheres* reached him on the day of his death. It is one of the dreariest and most unreadable books that made history, and remained practically unnoticed for the next fifty years, until Kepler took the idea up (the Church turned against it only eighty years after Copernicus' death).

Copernicus was neither an original nor even a progressive thinker; he was, as Kepler later remarked, "interpreting Ptolemy rather than nature". He clung fanatically to the Aristotelian dogma that all planets must move in perfect circles at uniform speeds; the first impulse of his long labours originated in his discontent with the fact that in the Ptolemaic system they moved in perfect circles but not at uniform speed. It was the grievance of a perfectionist – in keeping with his crabbed, secretive, stingy character (which every Freudian would gleefully identify as the perfect "anal" type). Once he had taken the Ptolemaic clockwork to pieces, he began to search for a useful hint how to put it together again; he found it in Aristarchus's heliocentric idea which at that time was much in the air.* It was not so much a new departure as a last attempt to patch up an outdated machinery by reversing the arrangement of its wheels. As a modern historian has said, the fact that the earth moves is "almost an incidental matter in the system of Copernicus which, viewed geometrically, is just the old Ptolemaic pattern of the skies, with one or two wheels interchanged and one or two of them taken out".†

For "four times nine years", as he later confessed, Copernicus had worked in secret on his book, hugging it to his aching heart – it was the timid Canon's only refuge from a life of frustrations. It was his version of the harmony of the spheres.

Tycho de Brahe (1546–1601) was an irascible, boastful Danish nobleman, truculent and quixotic, born with a silver spoon in his mouth – to which a silver nose was added later, for his own had been sliced off in a duel with another noble Danish youth, who had the temerity to claim that he was the better mathematician of the two. Devotion to science could hardly assume more heroic

---

*The Aristarchian system and the motion of the earth had been discussed or taught by Copernicus' forerunners, the astronomers Peurbach and Regiomontanus, by his teachers Brujewski and Novara, and his colleagues at the University of Bologna, Calcagnini, Ziegler, etc. (cf. *The Sleepwalkers*, pp. 205–10).
†H. Butterfield, *The Origins of Modern Science* (London, 1949), p. 29.

proportions. But with Tycho everything was on a heroic scale: his figure (he kept, perhaps for the sake of contrast, a dwarf as a court jester); his eating and drinking, which led to his premature death from a burst bladder – because, with quixotic courtesy, he refused to leave the dinner table to pass water (even his pet animal, a temperamental elk, died of drinking too much beer); his quarrels with the kings he entertained, with the fellow astronomers whom he slandered, and with retainers whom he put in chains. On an even more gigantic scale were his observatories and instruments – the likes of which the world had never seen – built on his island in the Sund.

At fourteen Tycho had witnessed a partial eclipse of the sun, and "it struck him as something divine that men could know the motions of the stars so accurately that they were able a long time beforehand to predict their places and relative positions".* From then onward his course was set, and he became the "Phoenix of Astronomy" – against the resistance of his family who thought such plumage unworthy of a nobleman. The decisive revelation for him was the *predictability* of astronomical events – in contrast to the unpredictability of a child's life among the headstrong Brahes (Tycho had been kidnapped from his cot and brought up by his Uncle Joerge, a squire and admiral). His passion for astronomy began much earlier than Copernicus's and Kepler's, and took a direction almost opposite to theirs: it was not a passion for theory-making but for exact observation. Unlike those two, he was neither frustrated nor unhappy, merely irritated by the triviality of a Danish nobleman's existence among "horses, dogs, and luxury".

He took to astronomy not as an escape or metaphysical lifebelt but rather as a hobby – which then turned into the only thing held sacred by that Gargantuan heathen.

"You cannot help it, Signor Sarsi, that it was granted to me alone to discover all the new phenomena in the sky and nothing to anybody else".† The most conspicuous feature in the character of Galileo (1564–1642) and the cause of his tragic downfall was vanity – not the boisterous and naive vanity of Tycho, but a hypersensitivity to criticism combined with sarcastic contempt for others: a fatal blend of genius plus arrogance minus humility.

*J. L. E. Dreyer, *Tycho de Brahe* (Edinburgh, 1890), p. 14.
†Galileo, *Il Saggiatore, Opere*, VI, p. 323.

There seems to be not a trace here of mysticism, of "oceanic feeling"; in contrast to Copernicus, Tycho, and Kepler, even to Newton and Descartes who came after him, Galileo is wholly and frighteningly modern in his consistently mechanistic philosophy. Hence his contemptuous dismissal in a single sentence of Kepler's explanation of the tides by the moon's attraction: "He [Kepler] has lent his ear and his assent to the moon's dominion over the waters, to occult properties and such like *fanciullezze*".* The occult little fancy he is deriding is Kepler's anticipation of Newtonian gravity.

Where, then, in Galileo's personality is the sublime balance between self-asserting and self-transcending motives which I suggested as the true scientist's hallmark? I believe it to be easily demonstrable in his writings on those subjects on which his true greatness rests: the first discoveries with the telescope, the foundations of mechanics, and of a truly experimental science. Where that balance is absent – during the tragic years 1613–33, filled with poisonous polemics, spurious priority claims, and impassioned propaganda for a misleadingly oversimplified Copernican system – in that sad middle period of his life Galileo made no significant contribution either to astronomy or to mechanics. One might even say that he temporarily ceased to be a scientist – precisely because he was entirely dominated by self-asserting motives. The opposite kind of imbalance is noticeable in Kepler's periods of depression, when he entirely lost himself in mystic speculation, astrology, and number-lore. In both these diametrically opposed characters, unsublimated residues of opposite kind temporarily dominated the field, upsetting the equilibrium and leading to scientific sterility.

But in the balanced periods of Galileo, the eighteen happy years in Padua in which most of his epoch-making discoveries in the study of motion were made, and in the last years of resignation, when he completed and revised the *Dialogue Concerning Two New Sciences* – in these creative periods we seem to be dealing with a different kind of person, patiently and painstakingly experimenting and theorising on the motions of the pendulum; on the free fall and descent along an inclined plane of heavy bodies; on the flight of projectiles; the elasticity, cohesion, and resistance of solid bodies, and the effects of percussion on them; on the buoyancy of "things which float on the water", and a hundred

---

Dialogue on the Great World Systems, p. 469.

related matters. Here we have a man absorbed in subjects much
less spectacular and conducive to fame than the wonders of the
Milky Way and the arguments about the earth's motion – yet
delighting in his discoveries, of which only a select few friends
and correspondents were informed; delighting in discovery for
discovery's sake, in unravelling the laws of order hidden in the
puzzling diversity of phenomena.

That order was for Galileo, as it was for Kepler, a mathematical
order: "The book of nature is written in the mathematical language. Without its help it is impossible to comprehend a single
word of it".* But unlike Kepler and the Pythagoreans, Galileo did
not look at the "dance of numbers" through the eyes of a mystic.
He was interested neither in number-lore nor in mathematics for
its own sake – almost alone among the great scientists of his
period, he made no mathematical discoveries. Quantitative
measurements and formulations were for Galileo simply the most
effective tools for laying bare the inherent *rationality of nature*.
The belief in this rationality (and in the rationality of nature's
creation, the human mind) was Galileo's religion and spiritual
salvation – though he did not realise that it was a religion, based
on an act of faith. In his best and happiest moments, Galileo is
transformed from a scientist into a poet. In the midst of his formidable polemical onslaught on the Platonist "dualism of
despair" – which contrasted the perfect, immutable, crystalline
heavens to the earthy corruption of generation and decay – his
imagination and language suddenly grow wings:

> *Sagredo:* I cannot without great wonder, nay more, disbelief, hear it
> being attributed to natural bodies as a great honour and perfection that
> they are impassible, immutable, inalterable, etc.: as, conversely, I hear
> it esteemed a great imperfection to be alterable, generable, mutable, etc. It
> is my opinion that the Earth is very noble and admirable by reason of
> the many and different alterations, mutations, generations, etc., which
> incessantly occur in it. And if, without being subject to any alteration,
> it had been all one vast heap of sand, or a mass of jade, or . . . an
> immense globe of crystal, wherein nothing had ever grown, altered, or
> changed, I should have esteemed it a wretched lump of no benefit to
> the Universe, a mass of idleness. . . . What greater folly can be
> imagined than to call gems, silver, and gold noble and earth and soil
> base? . . . If there were as great a scarcity of earth as there is of jewels
> and precious metals, there would be no king who would not gladly
> give a heap of diamonds and rubies . . . to purchase only so much earth

*Il Saggiatore, op. cit., p. 232.

as would suffice to plant a jessamine in a little pot or to set a tangerine in it, that he might see it sprout, grow up, and bring forth goodly leaves, fragrant flowers, and delicate fruit. . . . These men who so extol incorruptibility, inalterability, etc., speak thus, I believe, out of the great desire they have to live long and for fear of death, not considering that, if men had been immortal, they would not have had to come into the world. These people deserve to meet with a Medusa's head that would transform them into statues of diamond and jade that so they might become more perfect than they are.*

About Kepler I have said enough to show that mysticism was the mainspring of his fantastically laborious life – starting with the analogy between God the Father and the Sun, continued in his lifelong conviction that the universe was built around the frames of the five Pythagorean solids, and that the planetary motions were regulated by the laws of musical harmony. But his mystic convictions, and the disarmingly child-like streak in his character, did not prevent him from casting horoscopes for money – however much he despised himself for it; from indulging in naive snobbery, and quarrelling like a fish-wife with the overbearing Tycho. His vanity had a perverse twist: he was very proud of himself when his astrological forecasts of a cold spell and an invasion by the Turks came true; but towards his real discoveries he was completely indifferent, and he was astonishingly devoid of professional jealousy. He naively expected the same of other astronomers; and when Tycho's heirs delayed publication of his priceless collection of observational data, Kepler simply stole the material to put it to proper use – his ethics did not include respect for private property in Urania's domains.

When Kepler had completed the foundations of modern astronomy by his Third Law, he uttered a long Eureka cry:

The heavenly motions are nothing but a continuous song for several voices (perceived by the intellect, not by the ear); a music which, through discordant tensions, through sincopes and cadenzas, as it were (as men employed them in imitation of those natural discords), progresses towards certain pre-designed, quasi six-voiced clausuras, and thereby sets landmarks in the immeasurable flow of time. It is, therefore, no longer surprising that man, in imitation of his creator, has at last discovered the art of figured song, which was unknown to the ancients. Man wanted to reproduce the continuity of cosmic time within a short hour, by an artful symphony for several voices, to obtain

*Dialogue on the Great World Systems, pp. 68–9.

a sample test of the delight of the Divine Creator in His works, and to partake of His joy by making music in the imitation of God.*

Here we have the perfect union of the two drives: the vain-glorious ego purged by cosmic awareness — *ekstasis* followed by *katharsis*.

NEWTON, MONSTER AND SAINT

From the end of the seventeenth century onward the scene becomes too crowded for a systematic inquiry into individual motivations; however, I have said enough to suggest the basic pattern — and though the character of the times changed, that pattern remained essentially the same.

Look at Newton, for instance: he has been idolised and his character bowdlerised to such an extent (above all in the Victorian standard biography by Brewster) that the phenomenal mixture of monster and saint out of which it was compounded was all but lost from sight. On the one hand he was deeply religious and believed — with Kepler and Bishop Ussher — that the world had been created in 4004 BC; that the convenient design of the solar system — for instance, all planetary orbits lying in a single plane — was proof of the existence of God, who not only created the universe but also kept it in order by correcting from time to time the irregularities which crept into the heavenly motions — and by preventing the universe from collapsing altogether under the pressure of gravity. On the other hand, he fulminated at any criticism of his work, whether justified or not, displayed symptoms of persecution mania, and in his priority fight with Leibnitz over the invention of the calculus he used the perfidious means of carefully drafting in his own hand the findings, in his own favour, of the "impartial" committee set up by the Royal Society.

Here is pettiness on a heroic scale — combined with a heroic vision of the universe worked out in minute detail: in other words, the mixture as before.

THE MYSTICISM OF FRANKLIN

As we move on into the eighteenth century, the towering genius of Benjamin Franklin sticks out of it like his lightning rod. Printer, journalist, pamphleteer, politician, wire-puller, diplomat, and statesman; pioneer of electricity, founder of the physics of liquid surfaces, discoverer of the properties of marsh gas, designer of the

*J. Kepler, *Harmonice Mundi*, cap. 7.

chevaux de frise which halted the advance of the British fleet on the Delaware, inventor of bifocal spectacles and of improved fireplaces, advocate of watertight bulkheads on ships and of chimney-shafts for the ventilation in mines – the list could be continued. And yet this "first civilised American", as one of his biographers called him, for all his incomparable clarity of thought and lucidity of style, had formed his metaphysical outlook at the age of sixteen when he read a book by Tryon, a member of the group of British Pythagoreans. The members of his sect were chiefly known for their vegetarianism because, like the ancient Brotherhood, they believed in the transmigration of souls and wished to avoid the risk of feasting on some reincarnation of a human being. Franklin became a convert to vegetarianism and believed in transmigration to the end of his life. At the age of twenty-two he composed an epitaph for himself; at the age of eighty-four, the year of his death, he ordered that it should appear, unchanged, on his tomb. It reads:

The Body Of
BENJAMIN FRANKLIN
Printer
(Like the Cover of an Old Book
Its Contents Torn Out
And Stript of its Lettering and Gilding)
Lies Here, Food for Worms.
But the Work Shall Not Be Lost
For It Will (As He Believed) Appear Once More
In a New and More Elegant Edition
Revised and Corrected
By The Author

His conviction that souls are immortal, that they cannot be destroyed and are merely transformed in their migrations led him, by way of analogy, to one of the first clear formulations of the law of the conservation of matter. The following quotations will make the connection clear:

> The power of man relative to matter seems limited to the dividing it, or mixing the various kinds of it, or changing its form and appearance by differing compositions of it, but does not extend to the making or creating of new matter, or annihilating the old.

This was written when he was seventy-eight. The following was written one year later:

I say that when I see nothing annihilated, and not even a drop of water wasted, I cannot suspect the annihilation of souls, or believe that He will suffer the daily waste of millions of minds ready made that now exist, and put Himself to the continual trouble of making new ones. Thus finding myself to exist in the world, I believe I shall, in some shape or other, always exist.

The argument seems to indicate that what one might call the principle of the "conservation of souls" was derived from that of the "conservation of matter". But in fact it was the other way round. As Kepler had transformed the Holy Trinity into the trinity of Sun — Force — Planets, so in Franklin's case, too, a mystical conviction gave birth, by analogy, to a scientific theory. And could there be a more charming combination of man's vanity with his transcendental aspirations than to pray for a "more elegant, revised, and corrected edition" of one's proud and humble self?

THE FUNDAMENTALISM OF FARADAY

The nineteenth-century landscape is crowded with giants; I shall briefly comment on four of them. In the physical sciences Faraday and Maxwell are probably the greatest: Einstein, who ought to know, has put them on a par with Galileo and Newton. To these let me add, from the biological sciences, Darwin and Pasteur, to make up a foursome.

Faraday, whom Tyndall described as "the great mad child", was the most inhuman character of the four: the son of a sectarian blacksmith, self-taught, with a passionate temperament which was denied all human outlets except religion and science. This was probably the cause of the protracted episode of mental disorder, comparable to Newton's, which began when he was forty-nine. (Characteristic of the coyness of science historians is the *Encyclopaedia Britannica*'s reference to Faraday's clinical insanity: "In 1841 he found that he required rest, and it was not till 1845 that he entered on his second great period of research.")

At thirty, shortly after his marriage — which remained childless — Faraday joined an extreme fundamentalist, ascetic sect, the "Sandemanians", to which his father and his young wife belonged, and whose services he had attended since infancy. The Sandemanians considered practically every human activity as a sin — including even the Victorian virtue of saving money; they washed each other's feet, intermarried, and refused to proselytise; on one occasion they suspended Faraday's membership because he had to dine, by royal command, with the Queen at Windsor, and thus had to miss the congregation's Sunday service. It took many years before he was forgiven and re-elected an Elder of the sect.

In his later years Faraday withdrew almost completely from social contacts, refusing even the presidency of the Royal Society because of its too wordly disposition. The inhuman self-denials imposed by his creed made Faraday canalise his ferocious vitality into the pursuit of science, which he regarded as the only other permissible form of divine worship.

THE METAPHYSICS OF MAXWELL

James Clerk Maxwell was of an altogether different, balanced, and happy disposition. In his case, too, religious belief became a spur to scientific activity, but in more subtle ways. He was a double-faced giant: he completed the classical edifice of the Newtonian universe, but he also inaugurated the era of what one might call the "surrealistic" physics of the twentieth century.

As Kepler had embraced the Copernican system "for physical or if you prefer, metaphysical reasons", so Maxwell confessed that the theories of his later period were formed "in that hidden and dimmer region where Thought weds Fact. Does not the way to it pass through the very den of the metaphysician, strewed with the remains of former explorers and abhorred by every man of science?"

The metaphysician in Maxwell had by that time long outgrown the crude materialism of mid-nineteenth-century science, and its equally crude forms of Christianity. Maxwell's religious beliefs were conceived in symbolic, almost abstract, terms; they compared to Faraday's fundamentalist creed as his abstract equations of the electromagnetic field compare with the lines of force which to Faraday were "as real as matter".

There is a characteristic passage in one of his letters to his wife:

"I can always have you with me in my mind – why should we not have our Lord always before us in our minds. . . . If we had seen Him in the flesh we should not have known Him any better, perhaps not so well."

It was the time when Berthelot proclaimed: "The world today has no longer any mystery for us"; when Haeckel had solved all his *Welträtsel* and A. R. Wallace, in his book on *The Wonderful Century*, declared that the nineteenth century had produced "twenty-four fundamental advances, as against only fifteen for all the rest of recorded history". Maxwell was well aware of the limitations of a rigidly deterministic outlook; it was he who, in his revolutionary treatment of the dynamics of gases, replaced mechanical causation by a statistical approach – a decisive step towards quantum physics and the principle of indeterminism. Moreover, he was fully aware of the far-reaching implications of this approach.

Already at the age of twenty-four he had realised the limitations of materialist philosophy. Twenty years later, at the height of his fame, he gave full rein to his hobby, satirical verse, to ridicule the shallow materialism of the Philistines. The occasion was the famous presidential address by John Tyndall to the British Association meeting in Belfast. Tyndall, a generous soul but a narrow-minded philosopher, attacked the "theologians" and extolled the virtues of the brave new materialist creed. Maxwell's satire is still valid today:

> In the very beginning of science,
>   the parsons, who managed things then,
> Being handy with hammer and chisel,
>   made gods in the likeness of men;
> Till Commerce arose, and at length
>   some men of exceptional power
> Supplanted both demons and gods by
>   the atoms, which last to this hour.
>
> From nothing comes nothing, they told us,
>   nought happens by chance but by fate;
> There is nothing but atoms and void,
>   all else is mere whims out of date!
> Then why should a man curry favour
>   with beings who cannot exist,
> To compass some petty promotion
>   in nebulous kingdoms of mist? . . .
>
> First, then, let us honour the atom,
>   so lively, so wise, and so small;
> The atomists next let us praise, Epicurus,
>   Lucretius, and all;
> Let us damn with faint praise Bishop Butler,
>   in whom many atoms combined
> To form that remarkable structure,
>   it pleased him to call – his mind.

And thus in the nineteenth century's most advanced scientific mind we meet once again, in a sublimated and rarified form, the ancient belief in the indestructibility of the numinous.

THE ATHEISM OF DARWIN

Dr Robert Darwin was an atheist who chose for his son Charles the career of a country clergyman – simply because this seemed to be the most gentlemanly occupation for a youth so obviously devoid of any particular ambition and intellectual excellence. Charles himself fully agreed with this choice. As a student at Cambridge he had read *Pearson on the Creeds*, and had come to the conclusion that he did not "in the least doubt the strict and literal truth of every word in the Bible".* Even during the voyage of the *Beagle* he amused the officers by his naive orthodoxy, and he was deeply shocked when one of his shipmates expressed doubts concerning the Biblical account of the Flood. Such a rigid fundamentalist belief could not be reconciled with speculations about the origin of species; his loss of faith coincided with his conversion to the evolutionary theory. For a while he fought a rearguard action against his doubts by day-dreaming about the discovery of old manuscript texts which would confirm the historical truth of the Gospels; but this did not help much. In the months following his return from the voyage the new theory was born and his faith in religion was dead.

Before the great turning point in his life, he had not only been an orthodox believer, but at least on one occasion, in the grandeur of the Brazilian forest, he had also felt that quasi-mystical, "deep inward experience" that there must be more in man than "the mere breath of his body".† But after the turning point such experiences did not recur – and he himself wondered sometimes whether he was not like a man who had become colour-blind. At the same decisive period, when he was about thirty, Darwin suffered, in his own words, a "curious and lamentable loss of the higher aesthetic tastes". An attempt to re-read Shakespeare bored him "to the point of physical nausea".‡ He preferred popular novels of the sentimental kind – so long as they had a happy ending. In his autobiography he complained:

> But now for many years I cannot endure to read a line of poetry. My mind seems to have become a kind of machine for grinding general laws out of a large collection of facts, but why this should have caused the atrophy of that part of the brain on which the higher tastes depend,

---

*G. Himmelfarb, *Darwin and the Darwinian Revolution* (New York, 1959), p. 26.
†Ibid., p. 317.
‡Ibid., p. 119.

I cannot conceive. The loss of these tastes is a loss of happiness, and
may possibly be injurious to the intellect, and more probably to the
moral character, by enfeebling the emotional part of our nature.

The concept of "religious experience" did not mean to Darwin
what it did to Maxwell – the intuition of an "unknown reality
which held the secret of infinite space and eternal time"; it meant
to him believing the story told in Genesis, and also in eternal
hellfire. In his youth he had believed in the "strict and literal truth
of every word in the Bible"; later on he considered himself an
atheist because he did not believe in the Tower of Babel. Neither
attitude has much relevance to the unconscious, inner motivation
of his work. More relevant is the fact that the kind of undefinable
intuition which he had experienced in the Brazilian forest went
out of his life at the same time as the "atrophy of the higher tastes"
set in. This was at the time when he made his basic discovery. The
remaining forty odd years were spent on the heroic labours of its
elaboration.

Darwin was, like Copernicus, essentially a one-idea man. Each
had his "nuclear inspiration" early in life, and spent the rest of his
life working it out – the ratio of inspiration to perspiration being
heavily in favour of the second. Both lacked the many-sidedness,
that universality of interest and amazing multitude of achievement in unrelated fields of research which characterised Kepler,
Newton, Descartes, Franklin, Faraday, Maxwell, and hundreds of
lesser but equally versatile geniuses. It is perhaps no concidence
that both Darwin and Copernicus, after the decisive turning point
when their course was set, led a life of duty, devotion to task,
rigorous self-discipline, and spiritual desiccation. It looks as if the
artesian wells of their inspiration had been replaced by a mechanical water supply kept under pressure by sheer power of will.

In Darwin's case, the magnitude of this power must be measured against the handicap of forty years of chronic ill health,
which also afflicted his large family. The sense of duty which kept
him going became his true religion. After the publication of the
Origin and the *Descent*, he became one of the most celebrated
personalities in Europe, but he continued to lead the same rigorously scheduled life, without allowing himself to bask in the sun,
without getting spoilt or distracted from his work.

His last years were spent in churning out a number of technical
books and papers; his very last book was called *The Formation of
Vegetable Mould through the Action of Worms*. He had started

this research on earthworms at twenty-eight, after his return from the voyage of the *Beagle*; now, after this momentous detour, he finished it at the age of seventy-two, one year before his death. It is a measure of the enormous vogue which Darwin enjoyed that the worm book, in spite of its unprepossessing title, sold eight thousand five hundred copies in the first three years after publication – which would be quite a respectable success for a novel in our own days.

On one occasion in his late years Darwin was asked to state his opinion on religion. He answered that while the subject of God was "beyond the scope of man's intellect", his moral obligations were nevertheless clear: "Man can do his duty."

It has been said that Darwin's philosophising was "painfully naive". Yet his life bore witness, not to his philosophical rationalisations, but to his transcendental beliefs – he was a *croyant malgré lui*. The proof is in the closing passages of his two great books:

It is interesting to contemplate a tangled bank, clothed with many plants of many kinds, with birds singing in the bushes, with various insects flitting about, and with worms crawling through the damp earth, and to reflect that these elaborately constructed forms, so different from each other, and dependent upon each other in so complex a manner, have all been produced by laws acting around us. . . . Thus, from the war of nature, from famine and death, the most exalted object which we are capable of conceiving, namely, the production of the higher animals, directly follows. There is grandeur in this view of life, with its several powers, having been originally breathed by the creator into a few forms or into one; and that, whilst this planet has gone cycling on according to the fixed law of gravity, from so simple a beginning endless forms most beautiful and most wonderful have been, and are being evolved.*

Man may be excused for feeling some pride at having risen, though not through his own exertions, to the very summit of the organic scale; and the fact of his having thus risen, instead of having been aboriginally placed there, may give him hope for a still higher destiny in the distant future. But we are not here concerned with hopes or fears, only with the truth as far as our reason permits us to discover it; and I have given the evidence to the best of my ability. We must, however, acknowledge, as it seems to me, that man with all his noble qualities, with sympathy which feels for the most debased, with benevolence which extends not only to other men but to the humblest living creature, with his god-like intellect which has penetrated into the

The Origin of Species (6th ed., London, 1873), p. 429.

movements and constitution of the solar system – with all these exalted powers – Man still bears in his bodily frame the indelible stamp of his lowly origin.*

Here is humility and wonder, and a sense of participation which transcends not only the individual self but the collective pride of *homo sapiens.*

THE FAITH OF PASTEUR

Louis Pasteur's character and life is an almost perfect illustration of ambition, pride, vanity, self-righteousness, combined with self-sacrifice, charity, humility, romanticism, and religion, to make a happy balance of opposites. At the height of his fame, Pasteur related with evident relish that at an official reception the Queen of Denmark and the Queen of Greece had broken etiquette by walking up to him to pay their homage. But he also spent several months every year for five years in the mountains of Cevennes, to find a cure for an epidemic disease of silkworms. When he had found its cause, and saved the French silk manufacturing industry from ruin, the Minister of Agriculture sent him for examination three lots of eggs which a famous silkworm breeder was distributing throughout the country, ignoring Pasteur's recommendations of his method to obtain healthy strains. Pasteur replied:

> M. le Ministre – These three samples of seed are worthless. . . . They will in every instance succumb to corpuscle disease. . . . For my part I feel so sure of what I affirm, that I shall not even trouble to test, by hatching them, the samples which you have sent me. I have thrown them into the river.

In his polemics against scientific adversaries he used the same impassioned language – the style sometimes reminds one of Galileo. But, unlike Galileo, he engaged in controversy only after he had established his case beyond all possible doubt in his experimental laboratory, and had hardened it by countless painstaking repetitions. As a result, again unlike Galileo, he was invariably, and to his opponents infuriatingly, proven right. He even wrote an article in the Galilean dialogue style for a wine-growers' trade journal. The dialogue was meant to be a report of Pasteur's conversation with the mayor of Volnay, M. Boillot – which resulted in the conversion of M. Boillot to the Pasteurisation of Burgundy wines. This epic dialogue starts with:

*The Descent of Man (1913 ed.), pp. 946–7.

Pasteur Do you heat your wines, M. Maire?
M. Boillot No sir. . . . I have been told that heating may effect unfavourably the taste of our great wines.
Pasteur Yes, I know. In fact it has been said that to heat these wines is equivalent to an amputation. Will you be good enough, M. Maire, to follow me into my experimental cellar?

For the next two pages M. Boillot is shown what's what. He has to taste the treated and untreated wines of a score of vintages and vineyards, until he capitulates and admits the superior quality of the pasteurised wines – including those which came from his own vineyards:

M. Boillot I am overwhelmed. I have the same impression as if I were seeing you pouring gold into our country.
Pasteur There you are, my dear countrymen, busy with politics, elections, superficial reading of newspapers but neglecting the serious books which deal with matters of importance to the welfare of the country. . . . And yet, M. Maire, had you read with attention, you could have recognized that everything I wrote was based on precise facts, official reports, *degustations* by the most competent experts, whereas my opponents had nothing to offer but assertions without proof.
M. Boillot . . . Do not worry, Monsieur. From now on I shall no longer believe those who contradict you and I shall attend to the matter of heating the wines as soon as I return to Volnay.*

Pasteur had grown up in the Arbois; he was a connoisseur of wine, and he despised beer. But after the defeat of France by the Prussians in 1871, he considered it his patriotic duty to improve the quality of French beer – with the declared intention to produce a "*bière de la revanche*", superior to the Germans' cherished national drink. He even invaded, armed with his microscope, the sacred premises of Whitbread's in London; his laconic account of that historic visit makes one appreciate the drama that took place.

Pasteur was reverently handed two casks of the famed brew. He put a drop of one under the microscope and – "I immediately recognised three or four disease filaments in the microscopic field. These findings made me bold enough to state in the presence of the master-brewer, who had been called in, that these beers would rapidly spoil . . . and that they must already be somewhat defective in taste, on which point everyone agreed, although after long hesitation. I attributed this hesitation to the natural reserve of a manufacturer whom one compels to declare

*R. Dubos, *Louis Pasteur* (Boston, 1950), p. 72.

that his merchandise is not beyond reproach. When I returned to the same brewery less than a week later, I learned that the managers had made haste to acquire a microscope." It was not the least of the miracles that Pasteur achieved.

Silkworms, wine, beer – and before that, studies on the souring of milk, the turning of wine into vinegar, of vinegar into acid, of beet-sugar into alcohol. "Louis . . . is now up to his neck in beet-juice," Madame Pasteur complained in a letter. Each of these campaigns was conducted with the same crusading zeal, the same showmanship, the same patience and precision in method. Pasteur's father had been a sergeant in the Napoleonic army; after Waterloo he had become a tanner in the Arbois. He had probably heard the Emperor's famous speech at the Pyramids: "Soldiers, from these summits forty centuries look down upon you." Louis Pasteur, crouching with his microscope on top of one of the gigantic vats at Whitbread's, may have spoken the same words to the awe-stricken master-brewers.

And that is hardly an exaggeration, for in Pasteur's work we see clearly how the trivial by a short step can lead to the momentous, and how the two are inextricably mixed up in the scientist's mind and motives. One of the landmarks of science is the publication, in 1877, of Pasteur's book with the unprepossessing title, *Etudes sur la Bière, ses Maladies, Les Causes qui les Provoquent. Procédé pour la Rendre Inalterable* . . . followed, almost as an afterthought, by . . . *Avec une Théorie Nouvelle de la Fermentation*. It contains the first complete statement of Pasteur's revolutionary discovery that yeast and all other agents which cause fermentation and putrefaction, are *living beings* of very small size – that is, micro-organisms, germs. In a similar way, his work on the silkworms had confirmed that contagious diseases were caused by microbes of different varieties. The principles of sterilisation and partial sterilisation ("pasteurisation"); of immunisation, of antisepsis and asepsis; our knowledge of the causative agents of disease and of the general conditions which determine the organism's receptivity for those agents; lastly, the "domestication" of microbes and their use as antibiotics – all this grew out of Pasteur's often far-fetched researches into some specific technical problem, undertaken for apparently trivial motives.

Yet there were other motivational factors at work which lent urgency and drive to each of these technical research projects, from the earliest (*On the Turning of Milk*) onward: the intuitive vision of a grand unitary design underlying all biochemical transformations, a design which embraced not only the utilisation of energy by living organisms in health and disease, but also – as we shall see in a moment – the secret of the origin of life. And finally, each particular project – whether it was concerned with silk-worms, wine, or the inoculation of cattle against anthrax – though carried through with consummate showmanship and a Gallic flourish, was nevertheless a crusade for the public benefit; the resulting self-gratification was no more than a delicious by-product. Through the same interaction of the trivial and monu-mental which led to Pasteur's intellectual triumphs, the proponent of the *bière de la revanche* became the greatest benefactor of mankind since Hippocrates.

I have mentioned Pasteur's hope to discover "the secret of life". This is to to be taken quite literally.

The earliest discovery of Pasteur, and for him the most exciting in all his life, was the asymmetry of molecules as a specific characteristic of living organisms – in other words, the fact that the molecules of living matter come in two varieties which, though chemically identical, are in their spatial structure like mirror images to each other – or like right and left gloves. "Left-handed" molecules rotate polarised light to the left, "right-handed" molecules to the right; life substances are thus "optically active". Why this should be so we still do not quite know; but it remains a challenging fact that "no other chemical characteristic is as distinctive of living organisms as is optical activity".

"I am on the verge of mysteries, and the veil which covers them is getting thinner and thinner. The night seems to me too long. . . . Life as manifested to us is a function of the asymmetry of the universe. . . . The universe is asymmetrical; for, if all the bodies in motion which compose the solar system were placed before a glass, the image in it could not be superimposed upon the reality. . . . Terrestrial magnetism . . . the opposition between positive and negative electricity, are but resultants of asymmetrical actions and movements. . . . Life is dominated by asymmetrical actions. I can even imagine that all living species are primordially in their structure, in their external forms, functions of cosmic asymmetry."*

These intoxicating speculations caused Pasteur to embark on a series of fantastic experiments, aiming at nothing less than the

*R. Dubos, *Pasteur and Modern Science* (New York, 1960), p. 36.

creation of life by means of imitating the asymmetric action of nature in the laboratory, using powerful magnets and all kinds of optical tricks. It was this alchemist's dream which gave birth to the "grand design" which I have mentioned and which – like a blue-print drawn in invisible ink – remained the secret inspiration behind his researches. Luckily, circumstances compelled him to descend from the monumental to the trivial level: Pasteur had to give up trying to create life and had to get "up to his neck in beet-juice". He had been appointed Professor of Chemistry in Lille; and no sooner was he installed than Monsieur Bigo, an industrialist engaged in the production of alcohol from beet-sugar, came to consult him about certain difficulties encountered in the process. Since this was one of the main industries of the region, Pasteur embarked on the task with patriotic fervour – it was the first in the series of this type of venture, long before the silkworms, the wine, and the beer.

In examining the fermented juice of the beet, he found in it a component, amyl alcohol, which turned out to be optically active. Therefore its molecules must be asymmetrical; but according to the grand design, asymmetry is the privilege and secret of life; therefore fermentation came from the activity of living things, of microbes. At this point the chain-reaction set in which fused the germ theory of fermentation to the germ theory of disease. Thus did the alchemist's pipe-dream give birth to modern medicine – as Kepler's chimerical quest for the harmonies led to modern astronomy.

Here, I believe, is the clue to the scientist's ultimate motivation – the equivalent of the meeting of the Tragic and the Trivial planes in the artist's mind. Peering through his microscope or polariscope, in a never-ending series of dreary, technical, specialised investigations of amyl acid, tartaric acid, butyric acid, Pasteur was attending on one level to the business in hand – the beets of Mr Bigo; on another he was scanning the secret of life "through veils getting thinner and thinner". But since the actual experiments of creating life had failed, Pasteur, in his later years, reversed his opinions and embarked on another celebrated controversy to prove that the alleged "spontaneous generation" of micro-organisms (without progenitors, out of fermenting or putrefying matter) was a legend. Among his unpublished writings there is a passage written when he was approaching sixty:

I have been looking for spontaneous generation for twenty years without discovering it. No, I do not judge it impossible. But what allows you to make it the origin of life? You place matter before life and you decide that matter has existed for all eternity. How do you know that the incessant progress of science will not compel scientists . . . to consider that life has existed during eternity, and not matter? You pass from matter to life because your intelligence of today . . . cannot conceive things otherwise. How do you know that in ten thousand years one will not consider it more likely that matter has emerged from life. . .?*

At the age of forty-six Pasteur suffered a stroke which left his left arm and leg permanently paralysed. Yet his greatest work was done during the following two decades, when he was an invalid and had to use his assistants' hands to carry out his experiments. In old age he would often browse in his earlier publications. "Turning the pages of his writings, he would marvel at the lands that he had revealed by dispelling the fogs of ignorance and by overcoming stubbornness. He would live again his exciting voyages, as he told Loir in a dreamy voice: 'How beautiful, how beautiful! And to think I did it all. I had forgotten it.' "†

*Dubos, Louis Pasteur, pp. 306 f.
†Ibid., p. 87.

PART TWO

OUTLINE
OF A THEORY

Chapter 36

REGRESS TO PROGRESS

The Act of Creation consists of two parts: Book One, entitled "The
Art of Discovery and the Discoveries of Art", from which the
excerpts in the previous chapters are taken; and Book Two:
"Habit and Originality", in which I endeavoured to place the
theories and speculations of Book One on a more rigorous scientific basis. As I explained at the start of Book Two:

> So far I have discussed creativity in science and art, that is to say, the
> highest forms of mental activity, with only occasional references to
> the humbler routines of existence. I started at the roof, as it were –
> what remains to be done is to build up the walls which support it. . . .
> The aim of Book Two is to show that certain basic principles operate
> throughout the organic hierarchy – from the fertilised egg to the fertile
> brain of the creative individual.

Book Two started literally with the "fertilised egg" – morphogenesis and embryology – and took the reader stepwise
through the higher echelons, through instinct and learning, perception and memory, to contemporary psychology, the controversies between Behaviourism and Gestalt, and lastly to a
tentative outline of those "basic principles which operate
throughout the organic hierarchy".

This turned out to be an ambitious undertaking; hence this
warning in the Preface (addressed as much to myself as to the
reader):

> I have no illusions about the prospects of the theory I am proposing: it
> will suffer the inevitable fate of being proven wrong in many, or most,

details, by new advances in psychology and neurology. What I am hoping for is that it will be found to contain a shadowy pattern of truth, and that it may stimulate those who search for unity in the diverse manifestations of human thought and emotion.

As it happened, in the fifteen years which have passed since the publication of The Act of Creation, no major revisions were needed in subsequent editions. Rather the opposite was the case: the search for "basic principles" which operate on all levels of the hierarchies of life – i.e., what scientists call a "General Systems Theory" – led to two further books, The Ghost in the Machine (1967) and Janus (1978), which represent further steps towards such a theory.

The first extract in this chapter may serve as an example of the process of relating a particular phenomenon to general systems theory. The particular phenomenon in this case is the temporary regression preceding a new synthesis, discussed in earlier chapters. The extract is from an address delivered at the Bicentennial Celebration held at the Smithsonian Institution in Washington, September 1965,* with addenda from The Ghost in the Machine.

Biological and Mental Evolution: an Exercise in Analogy

Allow me to take you on a ride on the treacherous wings of analogy, starting with an excursion into genetics. Creativity – the main subject of this paper – is a concept notoriously difficult to define; and it is sometimes useful to approach a difficult subject by way of contrast. The opposite of the creative individual is the pedant, the slave of habit, whose thinking and behaviour move in rigid grooves. His biological equivalent is the over-specialised animal. Take, for example, that charming and pathetic creature, the koala bear, which specialises in feeding on the leaves of a particular variety of eucalyptus tree and on nothing else; and which, in lieu of fingers, has hook-like claws, ideally suited for clinging to the bark of the tree – and for nothing else. Some of our departments of higher learning seem expressly designed for breeding koala bears.

*First published by the Smithsonian Institution in Knowledge Among Men, Eleven Essays on Science, Culture and Society (New York, 1966); reprinted in Drinkers of Infinity (1968).

Sir Julian Huxley has described over-specialisation as the principal cause why evolution in all branches of the animal kingdom – except man's – seems to have ended either in stagnation or in extinction. But, having made his point, he drew a conclusion which you may find less convincing. "Evolution," he concluded, "is thus seen as an enormous number of blind alleys with a very occasional path to progress. It is like a maze in which almost all turnings are wrong turnings."* With due respect, I think this metaphor is suspiciously close to the behaviourist's view of the rat in the maze as a paradigm of human learning. In both cases the explicit or tacit assumption is that progress results from a kind of blind man's buff – random mutations preserved by natural selection, or random tries preserved by reinforcement – and that that is all there is to it. However, it is possible to dissent from this view without invoking a *deus ex machina*, or a Socratic *daimon*, by making the simple assumption that, while random events no doubt play an important part in the picture, that is *not* all there is to it.

One line of escape from the maze is indicated by a phenomenon known to students of evolution by the ugly name of paedomorphosis, a term coined by Garstang† some forty years ago. The existence of the phenomenon is well established; but there is little mention of it in the textbooks, perhaps because it runs against the *Zeitgeist*. To put it simply, the phenomenon of paedomorphosis indicates that in certain circumstances evolution can retrace its steps, as it were, along the path which led to the dead end, and make a fresh start in a new, more promising direction. The crucial point here is the appearance of some useful evolutionary novelty in the *larval or embryonic* stage of the ancestor, a novelty that may disappear before the ancestor reaches the adult stage, but which reappears and is preserved in the *adult stage of the descendant*. The following example will make this involved process clearer.

There is now strong evidence in favour of the theory, proposed by Garstang as far back as 1928, that the chordates – and thus we, the vertebrates – are descended from the larval stage of some primitive echinoderm, perhaps rather like the sea urchin or sea cucumber (echinoderm = "prickly-skinned"). Now an adult sea cucumber would not be a very inspiring ancestor – it is a sluggish creature which looks like an ill-stuffed sausage with leathery

*J. Huxley, *Man in the Modern World* (London and New York, 1948), p. 13.
†W. J. Garstang, *Zoology* (Linnean Soc. Lond., 1922), Vol. 35, p. 81.

skin, lying on the sea bottom. But its free-floating larva is a much more promising proposition: unlike the adult sea cucumber, the larva has bilateral symmetry like a fish; it has a ciliary band – a forerunner of the nervous system – and some other sophisticated features *not found in the adult animal*. We must assume that the sedentary adult residing on the sea bottom had to rely on mobile larvae to spread the species far and wide in the ocean, as plants scatter their seeds in the wind; that the larvae, which had to fend for themselves, exposed to much stronger selective pressures than the adults, gradually became more fish-like; and that eventually they became sexually mature while still in the free-swimming, larval state – thus giving rise to a new type of animal which never settled on the bottom at all, and altogether eliminated the senile, sedentary cucumber-stage from its life history.

The beauty of the idea strikes one forcibly when one compares a photograph of an adult echinoderm, like the sea urchin, with an adult chordate like the sea squirt. Although it is a mighty step higher up on the evolutionary scale, the adult squirt looks hardly more promising than the adult urchin, but the difference between the two *larvae* is dramatic; the first looks like a floating jelly, the second is streamlined like a fish.

This speeding up of sexual maturation relative to the development of the rest of the body – or, to put it differently, the gradual retardation of bodily development beyond the age of sexual maturation – is a familiar evolutionary phenomenon, known as *neoteny*. Its result is that the animal begins to breed while still displaying larval or juvenile features; and it frequently happens that the fully adult stage is never reached – it is dropped off the life cycle.

This tendency towards a "prolonged childhood", with the corresponding squeezing out of the final adult stages, amounts to a *rejuvenation and de-specialisation* of the race – an escape from the cul-de-sac in the evolutionary maze. Neoteny, in fact, amounts to a rewinding of the biological clock when evolution is in danger of running down and coming to a standstill. Gavin de Beer has compared the classical view of evolution (such as expressed in Huxley's image of the maze) to the classical view of the universe as a mechanical clockwork.

> On this view [he wrote] phylogeny would gradually slow down and become stationary. The race would not be able to evolve any further and would be in a condition to which the term "racial sensecence" has been applied. It would be difficult to see how evolution was able to

produce as much phylogenetic change in the animal kingdom as it has, and it would lead to the dismal conclusion that the evolutionary clock is running down. In fact, such a state of affairs would present a dilemma analogous to that which follows from the view that ... the universe has been wound up once and that its store of free energy was irremediably becoming exhausted. We do not know how energy is built up again in the physical universe; but the analogous process in the domain of organic evolution would seem to be paedomorphosis. A race may become rejuvenated by pushing the adult stage of its individuals off from the end of their ontogenies, and such a race may then radiate out in all directions ... until racial senescence due to gerontomorphosis [see below] sets in again.*

Neoteny in itself is of course not enough to produce these evolutionary bursts of adaptive radiations. The "rejuvenation" of the race merely provides the opportunity for evolutionary changes to operate on the early, malleable phases of ontogeny: hence paedomorphosis, "the shaping of the young". In contrast to it, gerontomorphosis (geras = old age) is the modification of fully adult structures which are already highly specialised.† This sounds like a rather technical distinction, but it is in fact of vital importance. Gerontomorphosis cannot lead to radical changes and new departures; it can only carry an already specialised evolutionary line one more step further in the same direction – as a rule into a dead end of the maze.

It seems that this retracing of steps to escape the dead ends of the maze was repeated at each decisive evolutionary turning point. I have mentioned the evolution of the vertebrates from a larval form of some primitive echinoderm. Insects have in all likelihood emerged from a millipede-like ancestor – not, however, from adult millipedes, whose structure is too specialised, but from its larval forms. The conquest of the dry land was initiated by amphibians whose ancestry goes back to the most primitive type of lung-breathing fish; whereas the apparently more successful later lines of highly specialised gill-breathing fishes all came to a dead end. The same story was repeated at the next major step, the reptiles, who derive from early, primitive amphibians – not from any of the later forms that we know.

And lastly, we come to the most striking case of paedomorphosis: the evolution of our own species. It is now generally

*G. R. de Beer, Embryos and Ancestors (Oxford, 1940).
†The word "gerontomorphosis" was coined by de Beer as a contrast to Garstang's "paedomorphosis".

recognised that the human adult resembles more the embryo of an
ape than an adult ape. In both simian embryo and human adult,
the ratio of the weight of the brain to total body weight is disproportionately high. In both, the closing of the sutures between the
bones of the skull is retarded to permit the brain to expand. The
back-to-front axis through man's head – i.e., the direction of his
line of sight – is at right angles to his spinal column: a condition
which, in apes and other mammals, is found only in the
embryonic, not in the adult stage. The same applies to the angle
between backbone and uro-genital canal – which accounts for the
singularity of the human way of copulating face to face. Other
embryonic – or, to use Bolk's term, *foetalised* – features in adult
man are: the absence of brow-ridges; the scantness and late
appearance of body hair; pallor of the skin; retarded growth of the
teeth, and a number of other features – including "the rosy lips of
man which were probably evolved in the young as an adaptation
to prolonged suckling and have persisted in the adult, possibly
under the influence of sexual selection" (de Beer).

"If human evolution is to continue along the same lines as in the
past," wrote J. B. S. Haldane, "it will probably involve still greater
prolongation of childhood and retardation of maturity. Some of
the characters distinguishing adult man will be lost."* There is,
incidentally, a reverse of the medal which Aldous Huxley pointed
out in one of his later, despairing novels: artificial prolongation of
the absolute lifespan of man might provide an opportunity for
features of the *adult* primate to reappear in human oldsters:
Methuselah would turn into a hairy ape.† But this ghastly perspective does not concern us here.

The essence of the process which I have described is an
evolutionary *retreat* from specialised adult forms of bodily structure and behaviour, to an earlier or more primitive, but also more
plastic and less committed stage – followed by a sudden *advance*
in a new direction. It is as if the stream of life had momentarily
reversed its course, flowing uphill for a while, then opened up a
new stream-bed. It seems that this *reculer pour mieux sauter* – of

*J. B. S. Haldane, *The Future of Evolution* (London, 1932), p. 150.
†Huxley, *After Many a Summer*. Some physical characteristics in the very old
seem to indicate that the genes which could produce such a transformation are
still present in our gonads, but are prevented from becoming active by the
neotenic retardation of the biological timeclock. The obvious conclusion is that
prolongation of the human lifespan is only desirable if it can be accompanied by
techniques which exert a parallel influence on the genetic clock.

drawing back to leap, of undoing and re-doing – is a favourite gambit in the grand strategy of both *biological and mental evolution*.

The diagram on this page is from W. J. Garstang's original paper,* and is meant to represent the progress of evolution by paedomorphosis. Z to Z_9 is the progression of zygotes (fertilised eggs) along the evolutionary ladder; A to A_9 represents the adult forms resulting from each zygote. Thus the black line from Z_4 to A_4, for instance, represents ontogeny, the transformation of egg into adult; the dotted line from A to A_9 represents phylogeny – the evolution of higher forms. But note that the thin lines of evolutionary progress do not lead directly from, say, A_4 to A_5 – that would be gerontomorphosis, the evolutionary transformation of an *adult* form. The line of progress branches off from the unfinished, embryonic stage of A_4. This represents a kind of evolutionary retreat from the finished product, and a new departure towards the evolutionary novelty Z_5—A_5. A_4 could be the adult sea cucumber: then the branching-off point on the line Z_4—A_4 would be its larva; or A_8 could be the adult primate ancestor of man, and the branching-off point its embryo – which is so much more like the A_9 – ourselves.

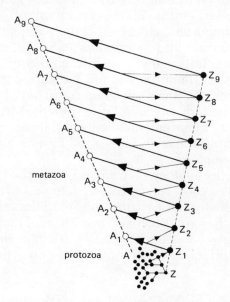

* Garstang, op.cit.

But Garstang's diagram could also represent a fundamental aspect of the evolution of *ideas*. The emergence of biological novelties and the creation of mental novelties are processes which show certain analogies. It is of course a truism that in mental evolution social inheritance through oral tradition and written records replaces genetic inheritance. But the analogy goes deeper: neither biological evolution nor mental progress follows a continuous line from A_1 to A_9. Neither of them is strictly cumulative in the sense of continuing to build where the last generation has left off. Both proceed in the zigzag fashion indicated in the diagram. The revolutions in the history of science are successful escapes from blind alleys. The evolution of knowledge is continuous only during those periods of consolidation and elaboration which follow a major break-through. Sooner or later, however, consolidation leads to increasing rigidity, orthodoxy, and so into the dead end of over-specialisation. Eventually there is a crisis and a new "break-through" out of the blind alley – followed by another period of consolidation, a new orthodoxy, and so the cycle starts again.

But the new theoretical structure which emerges from the break-through is not built on top of the previous edifice; it branches out from the point where progress has gone wrong. The great revolutionary turns in the evolution of ideas have a decidedly paedomorphic character. Only in the quiet periods of consolidation do we find gerontomorphosis – small improvements added to a fully grown, established theory.

In the history of literature and art, the zigzag course is even more in evidence: Garstang's diagram could have been designed to show how periods of cumulative progress within a given "school" and technique end inevitably in stagnation, mannerism or decadence, until the crisis is resolved by a revolutionary shift in sensibility, emphasis, style.

At first sight the analogy may appear far-fetched; I shall try to show that it has a solid factual basis. Biological evolution is to a large extent a history of escapes from the blind alleys of over-specialisation, the evolution of ideas a series of escapes from the bondage of mental habit; and the escape mechanism in both cases is based on the principle of undoing and re-doing, the draw-back-to-leap pattern.

The activities of animal and man vary from machine-like automatisms to ingenious improvisations, according to the challenge they face.* Other things being equal, a monotonous environment leads to the mechanisation of habits, to stereotyped routines which, repeated under the same unvarying conditions, follow the same rigid, unvarying course. The pedant who has become a slave of his habits thinks and acts like an automaton running on fixed tracks; his biological equivalent is the over-specialised animal – the koala bear clinging to his eucalyptus tree.

On the other hand, a changing, variable environment presents challenges which can only be met by flexible behaviour, variable strategies, alertness for exploiting favourable opportunities.

However, the challenge may exceed a critical limit, so that it can no longer be met by the organism's customary skills. In such a major crisis – and both biological evolution and human history are punctuated by such crises – one of two possibilities may occur. The first is *degenerative* – leading to stagnation, biological senescence, or sudden extinction as the case may be. In the course of evolution this happened over and again; to each surviving species there are a hundred which failed to pass the test. There are indications that our own species is facing a crisis unique in its history, and that it is in imminent danger of failing the test.

The alternative possibility of reacting to a critical challenge is *regenerative* in a broad sense; it involves major reorganisations of structure and behaviour, which result in biological or mental progress. Both are based on the same draw-back-to-leap pattern, activating creative potentials which are dormant or inhibited in the normal routines of existence. In phylogeny, the major advances are due to the activation of embryonic potentials through paedomorphosis. In mental evolution something analogous seems to happen at each major turning point. The connection between the emergence of biological novelties and of mental novelties is provided by one of the basic attributes of living things: their capacity for regeneration or *self-repair*. It is as fundamental to life as the capacity for reproduction, and in some lower organisms which multiply by fission or budding, the two are often indistinguishable.

To understand this connection, we must proceed by a series of steps from primitive to higher animals, and finally to man. Needham has called regeneration "one of the more spectacular pieces of magic in the repertoire of living organisms".† Its most impressive manifestations are found in lowly creatures like

*See *The Ghost in the Machine*, ch. VIII.
†A. E. Needham, *New Scientist* (London), November 2, 1961.

flatworms and polyps. If a flatworm is cut transversely into two parts, the head-end will grow a new tail, and the tail-end will grow a new head; even if cut into six or more slices, each slice can regenerate a complete animal.

Among higher animals, amphibians are capable of regenerating a lost limb or organ. When a salamander's leg is amputated, the muscle and skeletal tissues near the wound-surface de-differentiate and assume the appearance of embryonic cells. Around the fourth day, a blastema or "regeneration bud" is formed, similar to the "organ bud" in the normal embryo; and from then on the process follows closely the growth of limbs in embryonic development. The region of the amputation-stump has regressed to a quasi-embryonic state and displays genetic growth-potentials which are inhibited in normal adult tissues. I have compared elsewhere* the gene-complex in a specialised cell to a piano with most keys inactivated by scotch tape; regenerating tissues have the whole keyboard at their disposal. The "magic" of self-repair thus has a regressive (catabolic) and a progressive (anabolic) phase; it follows the undoing-re-doing pattern. "The trauma plays a role similar to that of fertilisation in embryonic development." The shock triggers off the creative reaction.

The replacement of a lost limb or lost eye is a phenomenon of a quite different order from that of adaptive processes in a normal environment. Regeneration could be called a *meta-adaptation* to traumatising challenges. But the power to perform such feats manifests itself only when the challenge exceeds a critical limit. The regenerative capacity of a species thus provides it with an additional safety device in the service of survival, which enters into action when normal adaptive measures fail – as the hydraulic shock-absorbers of a motor car enter into action when the limit of elasticity of the suspension springs is exceeded.

But it is more than a safety device: we have seen that the major phylogenetic changes were also brought about by a retreat from adult to embryonic forms. Indeed, the main line of development which led up to our species could be described as a series of oper-ations of *phylogenetic self-repair*: of escapes from blind alleys by the undoing and re-moulding of maladapted structures.†

*See Chapter 37.
† Evidently, self-repair by the individual animal produces no evolutionary novelty, it merely restores its capability to function normally in a stable envi-ronment; "phylogenetic self-repair", on the other hand, implies evolutionary changes in a changing environment.

As we move further up the ladder from reptile to mammal, the power of regenerating bodily structures decreases, and is superseded by the increasing powers of the nervous system to reorganise behaviour. (Ultimately, of course, these reorganisations of function must also involve structural changes of a fine-grained nature in the nervous system, and so we are still moving along a continuous gradient.) More than a century ago, the German physiologist Pflüger demonstrated that even a decapitated frog is not just a reflex automaton. If a drop of acid was put on the back of its left foreleg, it would wipe it off with the hind-leg on the same side – this is the normal spinal reflex. But if the left hind-leg was immobilised, the frog used its *right* hind-leg instead, to wipe off the acid. Thus even the headless creature – a "spinal preparation" as it is euphemistically called – proved itself capable of improvising when reflex-action was prevented.

In the first half of this century, K. S. Lashley and his collaborators, in a series of classical experiments, demolished the notion of the nervous system as a rigid mechanism. To mention one among many examples: Lashley trained rats to choose between two alternative targets always the relatively brighter one. Then he removed the rats' visual cortex, and their discriminatory skill disappeared, as one would expect. But, contrary to what one would expect, the mutilated rats were able to learn the same skill again. Some other brain area, not normally specialising in visual learning, must have taken over this function, deputising for the lost area.

Moreover, if a rat has learned to find its way through a maze, no matter what parts of its motor cortex are injured, it will still make a correct run; and if the injury renders it incapable of executing a right turn, it will achieve its aim by a three-quarter turn to the left. The rat may be blinded, deprived of smell, partially paralysed in different ways – each of which would throw the chain-reflex automaton, which it is supposed to be, completely out of gear. Yet: "One drags himself through the maze with his forepaws; another falls at every step but gets through by a series of lunges; a third rolls over completely in making each turn, yet avoids rolling into a cul-de-sac and makes an effortless run".*

Similar feats of meta-adaptation have been reported in insects, birds, chimpanzees, and so on. They also occur on the collective level. In a beehive there is normally a fixed division of labour

*K. S. Lashley, *Brain Mechanisms and Intelligence* (Chicago, 1929)

according to age group; each worker specialises in different tasks at different stages of its life. But if all building workers are taken away from the hive, their task is taken over by foragers. The foragers belong to an older age group who were builders earlier on, but lost their wax glands when they entered on their new job. So now they have to grow new wax glands – and they do. Here we have regeneration of structures and reorganisation of functions on a heroic scale.

As we arrive at the top of the ladder, we find in man the faculty of physical regeneration reduced to a minimum, but compensated by his unique powers to re-mould his patterns of behaviour – to meet critical challenges by creative responses.

Even on the level of elementary perception, learning to see through spectacles which turn the world upside down testifies to these powers. The effect at first is thoroughly upsetting: you see your body upside-down, your feet planted on a floor which has become the ceiling of the room. Or, with left-right inverters, you try to move away from a wall, and bump into it. Yet after a certain time, which may mean several days, the subject becomes adjusted to living in an inverted world, which then appears to him more or less normal again. The retinal image and its projection in the visual cortex are still upside-down; but, thanks to the intervention of some higher echelons in the hierarchy, the mental image has become reorganised. At the present stage of knowledge physiology has no satisfactory explanation for this phenomenon. All one cay say is that if our orientation, our postural and motor reactions to the visual field depend on wiring circuits in the brain, living in an inverted world must entail a lot of undoing and re-doing in the wiring diagram.

Inverting spectacles are drastic gadgets; but most of us go through life wearing contact lenses of which we are unaware and which distort our perceptions in more subtle ways. Psychotherapy, ancient and modern, from shamanism down to contemporary forms of analytical or abreaction techniques, has always relied on that variety of undoing-re-doing procedure which Ernst Kris, an eminent practitioner, has called "regression in the service of the ego".* The neurotic, with his compulsions, phobias, and elaborate defence-mechanisms, is a victim of rigid, maladaptive specialisation – a koala bear hanging on for dear life to a barren telegraph pole. The therapist's aim is to induce a

*E. Kris, *Psychoanalytic Explorations in Art* (New York, 1952).

temporary regression in the patient; to make him retrace his steps to the point where they went wrong, and to come up again, metamorphosed, reborn.

The same pattern is reflected in countless variations on the death-and-resurrection motif in mythology. Goethe's *Stirb und Werde*, Toynbee's Withdrawal and Return, the mystic's dark night of the soul preceding spiritual rebirth, derive from the same archetype: draw back to leap.

There is no sharp dividing line between self-repair and self-realisation. All creative activity is a kind of do-it-yourself therapy, an attempt to come to terms with traumatising challenges. In the scientist's case the trauma may be the impact of data which shake the foundations of a well-established theory, and make nonsense of his cherished beliefs; observations which contradict each other, problems which cause frustration and conflict. In the artist's case, challenge and response are manifested in his tantalising struggle to express the inexpressible, to conquer the resistance of his medium, to escape from the distortions and constraints imposed by the conventional styles and techniques of his time.

Thus the decisive break-throughs in science, art or philosophy are successful escapes from blind alleys, from the bondage of mental habits, from orthodoxy and over-specialisation. The method of escape follows the same undoing-re-doing pattern as in biological evolution; and the zigzag course of advance in science or art repeats the pattern of Garstang's diagram.

Every revolution has a destructive and a constructive aspect. The destruction is wrought by jettisoning previously unassailable doctrines, and seemingly self-evident axioms of thought. Progress in art involves an equally agonising reappraisal of accepted values, criteria of relevance, frames of perception. I have discussed this subject in some detail in a recent book [*The Act of Creation*] and shall not dwell on it. The point I want to make here is that the creation of novelty in mental evolution follows the same pattern of *reculer pour mieux sauter*, of a temporary regression followed by a forward leap, which we have found in biological evolution. We can carry the analogy further and interpret the Aha reaction, or "Eureka!" cry, as the signal of a happy escape from a blind alley – an act of mental self-repair, achieved by the de-differentiation of cognitive structures to a more plastic state, and the resulting liberation of creative potentials – the equivalent of the release of genetic growth-potentials in regenerating tissues.

I began this lecture with a wistful remark about the treacherous wings of analogy, aware of the fact that those who trust these waxen wings usually share the fate of Icarus. But it is one thing to argue from analogy, and quite another to point to an apparent similarity which has perhaps not been paid sufficient attention, and then to ask whether that similarity has some significance or whether it is trivial and deceptive. I believe that the parallel between certain processes underlying biological and mental evolution has some significance. To say it once more: biological evolution could be described as a history of escapes from over-specialisation, the evolution of ideas as a series of escapes from the bondage of mental habit; and the escape mechanism in both cases is based on the same principles. We get an inkling of them through the phenomena of regeneration – the remoulding of structures and reorganisation of functions – which only enter into action when the challenge exceeds a critical limit. They point to the existence of unsuspected "meta-adaptive" potentials which are inhibited or dormant in the normal routines of existence, and, when revealed, make us sometimes feel that we move like sleep-walkers in a world of untapped resources and unexplored pos-sibilities.

It could be objected that I have presented a reductionist view; that it is sacrilegious to call the creation of a Brahms symphony or of Maxwell's field equations an act of self-repair, and to compare it with the mutation of a sea-squirt larva, the regeneration of a newt-tail, the relearning process in the rat or the rehabilitation of patients by psychotherapy. But I think that such a view is the opposite of sacrilegious. It points, however tentatively, at a com-mon denominator, a factor of purposiveness, without invoking a *deus ex machina*. It does not deny that trial and error are inherent in all progressive development. But there is a world of difference between the random tries of the monkey at the typewriter, and the process which I called, for lack of a better name, *reculer pour mieux sauter*. The first means reeling off all possible responses in the organism's repertory until the correct one is hit on by chance and stamped in by reinforcement. The second may still be called trial and error, but of a purposive kind, using more complex, sophisticated methods: a groping and searching, retreating and advancing towards a goal. "Purpose," to quote Herbert J. Muller,* "is not imported into Nature and need not be puzzled over as a

*H. J. Muller, *Science and Criticism* (New Haven, Conn., 1943).

strange or divine something. . . . It is simply implicit in the fact of organisation." This directiveness of vital processes is present all along the line, from conscious behaviour down to what Needham called "the striving of the blastula to grow into a chicken". How tenacious and resourceful that striving is has been demonstrated by experimental embryology, from Speeman to Paul Weiss — though its lessons have not yet been fully digested.

Thus to talk of goal-directedness or purpose in *ontogeny* has become respectable again. But in *phylogeny* the monkey still seems to be hammering away at the typewriter, perhaps because the crude alternatives that had been offered — amorphous entelechies, or the Lysenko brand of Lamarckism — were even more repellent to the scientific mind. On the other hand, in recent years the rigid, atomistic concepts of Mendelian genetics have undergone a softening process and have been supplemented by a whole series of new terms with an almost holistic ring. Thus we learn that the genetic system represents a "micro-hierarchy" which exercises its selective and regulative control on the molecular, chromosomal and cellular level; that development is "canalised", stabilised by "developmental homeostasis" or "evolutionary homeostasis"* so that mutations affect not a single unit character but a "whole organ in a harmonious way",† and, finally, that these various forms of "internal selection" create a restricted "mutation spectrum"‡ or may even have a "direct, moulding influence guiding evolutionary change along certain avenues"§ and all this happens long before external, Darwinian selection gets to work. But if this is the case, then the part played by a lucky chance mutation is reduced to that of the trigger which releases the co-ordinated action of the system; and to maintain that evolution is the product of blind chance means to confuse the simple action of the trigger, governed by the laws of statistics, with the complex, purposive processes which it sets off. Their purposiveness is manifested in different ways on different levels of the hierarchy, from the self-regulating properties of the genetic system through internal and external selection, culminating perhaps in the phenomena of phylogenetic self-repair: escapes

*H. G. Cannon, *The Evolution of Living Things* (Manchester, 1958).
†C. H. Waddington *The Listener* (London), November 13, 1952.
‡H. Spurway in *Supplemento, La Ricerca Scientifica*, Pallenza Symp., Vol. 18 (Rome, 1949).
§For a survey of literature in this field see L. L. Whyte, *Internal Factors in Evolution* (London, 1965).

from blind alleys and departures in new directions. On each level there is trial and error, but on each level it takes a more sophisticated form. Some twenty years ago, Tolman and Krechevsky* created a stir by proclaiming that the rat learns to run a maze by forming hypotheses; soon it may be permissible to extend the metaphor and to say that evolution progresses by making and discarding hypotheses.

Any directive process, whether you call it selective, adaptive or expectative, implies a reference to the future. The equifinality of developmental processes, the striving of the blastula to grow into an embryo regardless of the obstacles and hazards to which it is exposed, might lead the unprejudiced observer to the conclusion that the pull of the future is as real and sometimes more important than the pressure of the past. The pressure may be compared to the action of a compressed spring, the pull to that of an extended spring, threaded on the axis of time. Neither of them is more or less mechanistic than the other. If the future is completely determined in the Laplacian sense, then there is nothing to choose between the actions of the two springs. If it is indeterminate in the Heisenbergian sense, then indeterminacy works in both directions, and the distant past is as blurred and unknowable as the future; and if there is something like free choice operating within the air-bubbles in the stream of causality, then it must be directed towards the future and oriented by feedback from the past.

*L. Krechevsky, *Psychol. Rev.*, Vol. 39 (1932).

Chapter 37

THE HOLON

The previous chapter was meant to illustrate by a particular
example the urge to "connect, always connect" – the search for
basic principles on which a theory could eventually be built.
Such a quest can be both boring and exhilarating, for it involves
long stretches of pedestrian plodding alternating with short
flights on those treacherous "wings of analogy" – of which the
next few chapters will provide further examples. They are mainly
based on The Ghost in the Machine, which was published in 1967,
three years after The Act of Creation.

At that time I was regarded as something of a renegade by
friends and critics firmly entrenched on the pro-Art, anti-Science
side of the war between the two cultures, who were dismayed by
this apparent desertion into the enemy camp. In heartening contrast to these rather depressing attitudes was the encouragement
received from the other side of the cardboard barricades – from
(mostly American) universities and scientific bodies. Invitations
to lecture or to participate in symposia, from institutions such as
the Smithsonian, the Brain Research Institute of the University of
California, the Harvard Medical Faculty, the Nobel Foundation,
and so forth, provided invaluable opportunities for informal discussions with representatives of the main branches of contemporary science, and even to form lasting friendships. They also
enabled me to organise and edit an interdisciplinary symposium
– Beyond Reductionism: New Perspectives in the Life Sciences.

The highlight of these years of prolonged apprenticeship was
six months spent in 1964–5 as a Fellow at the Center for
Advanced Study in the Behavioral Sciences in Stanford,
California. This rather unique institution, more familiarly known
as the CASBA, annually assembles fifty Fellows elected from
varied academic disciplines from all over the world, and pro-

vides them, on its hill-top campus, with the facilities for a whole year's interdisciplinary discussions and research. This proved a most beneficial opportunity for the clarification and testing of ideas in workshops and seminars, attended by specialists in various fields, from neurology to linguistics. They provided the stimulation and the criticism which are both indispensable to keep flights of speculation under control.

The extract which follows contains the basic outline of the theoretical structure which emerged from these labours in The Ghost in the Machine, Part One; *but to keep it to manageable proportions I have mostly followed the condensed version of it in* Janus, ch ı.

"Beyond Reductionism – New Perspectives in the Life Sciences" was the title of a symposium which I had the pleasure and privilege to organise in 1968, and which subsequently aroused much controversy.* One of the participants, Professor Viktor Frankl, enlivened the proceedings by some choice examples of reductionism in psychiatry, quoted from current books and periodicals. Thus, for instance:

> Many an artist has left a psychiatrist's office enraged by interpretations which suggest that he paints to overcome a strict bowel training by free smearing. . . .
> We are led to believe that Goethe's work is but the result of pregenital fixations. Goethe's struggle does not really aim for an ideal, for

---

*It is usually referred to as the "Alpbach Symposium" after the Alpine resort where it was held. The participants were: Ludwig von Bertalanffy (*Faculty Professor, State University of New York at Buffalo*), Jerome S. Bruner (*Director, Center for Cognitive Studies, Harvard University*), Blanche Bruner (*Center for Cognitive Studies, Harvard University*), Viktor E. Frankl (*Professor of Psychiatry and Neurology, University of Vienna*), F. A. Hayek (*Professor of Economics, Nobel laureate, University of Freiburg, Germany*), Holger Hyden (*Professor and Head of the Institute of Neurobiology and Histology, University of Gothenburg, Sweden*), Bärbel Inhelder (*Professor of Developmental Psychology, University of Geneva*), Seymour S. Kety (*Professor of Psychiatry, Harvard University*), Arthur Koestler (*Writer, London*), Paul D. MacLean (*Head of the Laboratory of Brain Evolution and Behavior, NIMH, Bethesda, Maryland*), David McNeill (*Professor of Psychology, University of Chicago*), Jean Piaget (*Professor of Experimental Psychology, University of Geneva*), J. R. Smythies (*Reader in Psychiatry, University of Edinburgh*), W. H. Thorpe (*Director, Sub-Department of Animal Behaviour, Department of Zoology, University of Cambridge*), C. H. Waddington (*Professor and Chairman, Department of Genetics, University of Edinburgh*), Paul A. Weiss (*Emeritus Member and Professor, Rockefeller University, New York*).

beauty, for values, but for the overcoming of an embarrassing problem of premature ejaculation. . . .*

Now it is quite possible that some sexual (or even scatological) motivation may enter into an artist's work; yet it is absurd to proclaim that art is "nothing but" goal-inhibited sexuality, because it begs the question of what makes Goethe's art a work of genius, quite unlike other premature ejaculators'. The reductionist attempt to explain artistic creation by the action of sex-hormones is futile, because that action, though biologically vital, does not give us an inkling of the aesthetic criteria which apply to a work of art. Those criteria pertain to the level of conscious mental processes, which cannot be reduced to the level of physiological processes without losing their specifically mental attributes in the course of the operation. Reductionist psychiatry is a Procrustean host to the weary traveller.

It is easy to make fun of those latter-day orthodox Freudians who have reduced the master's teaching to a caricature. In other fields, the reductionist fallacy is more discreetly implied, less obvious and therefore more insidious. Pavlov's dogs, Skinner's rats, Lorenz's geese, each served for a while as fashionable paradigms of the human condition. Generally speaking, we are faced with two impressive strongholds of reductionist orthodoxy. One is the neo-Darwinian (or "Synthetic") theory which holds that evolution is the outcome of "nothing but" chance mutations retained by natural selection – a doctrine recently exposed to growing criticism which nevertheless is still taught as gospel truth. The other is the behaviourist psychology of the Watson-Skinner school which holds that all human behaviour can be "explained, predicted and controlled" by methods exemplified in the conditioning of rats and pigeons. By its persistent denial of a place for values, meaning and purpose in the interplay of blind forces, the reductionist attitude has cast its shadow beyond the confines of science, affecting our whole cultural and even political climate.† Its philosophy may be epitomised by a last quote from a recent college textbook, in which man is defined as "nothing but a complex biochemical mechanism, powered by a combustion system which energises computers with prodigious storage facilities for retaining encoded information."‡

*V. E. Frankl in *Beyond Reductionism* (1969) pp. 397–8.
†For a detailed critique of neo-Darwinism and Behaviourism see *The Ghost in the Machine*, Part Two, and *Janus*, Part Three.
‡Quoted by Frankl in *Beyond Reductionism*.

Now the reductionist fallacy lies not in comparing man to a "mechanism powered by a combustion system" but in declaring that he is "nothing but" such a mechanism and that his activities consist of "nothing but" a chain of conditioned responses which are also found in rats. For it is of course perfectly legitimate, and in fact indispensable, for the scientist to try to analyse complex phenomena into their constituent elements – provided he remains conscious of the fact that in the course of the analysis something essential is always lost, because the whole is more than the sum of its parts, and its attributes as a whole are more complex than the sum of the attributes of its parts. Thus the analysis of complex phenomena elucidates only a certain segment or aspect of the picture and does not entitle us to say that it is "nothing but" this or that. Yet such *nothing-but-ism* as it has been called, is still the – explicit or implied – world-view of the reductionist orthodoxy. If it were to be taken literally, man could be ultimately defined as consisting of "nothing but" 90 per cent water and 10 per cent minerals – a statement which is no doubt true, but not very helpful.

Nevertheless, reductionism proved an eminently successful method within its limited range of applicability in the exact sciences, while its antithesis, holism, never really got off the ground. Holism may be defined by the statement that the whole is more than the sum of its parts. The term was coined by Jan Smuts in the nineteen-twenties in a remarkable book* which for a while enjoyed great popularity. But holism never got a grip on academic science† – partly because it went against the *Zeitgeist*, partly perhaps because it represented more of a philosophical than an empirical approach and did not lend itself to laboratory tests.

In fact both reductionism and holism, if taken as sole guides, lead into a cul-de-sac. "A rose is a rose is a rose" may be regarded as a holistic statement, but it tells us no more about the rose than the formulae of its chemical constituents. For our inquiry we need a third approach, beyond reductionism and holism, which incorporates the valid aspects of both. It must start with the seemingly abstract yet fundamental problem of the relations between the whole and its parts – any "whole", whether it be the universe or

*J. C. Smuts, *Holism and Evolution* (London, 1926).
†Except indirectly through *Gestalt* psychology.

human society, and any "part", whether an atom or a human being. This may seem an odd, not to say perverse, way to get at a diagnosis of man's condition, but the reader will eventually realise, I hope, that the apparent detour through the theoretical considerations in the present chapter may be the shortest way out of the labyrinth.

To start with a deceptively simple question: what exactly do we mean by the familiar words "part" and "whole"? "Part" conveys the meaning of something fragmentary and incomplete, which by itself has no claim to autonomous existence. On the other hand, a "whole" is considered as something complete in itself which needs no further explanation. However, contrary to these deeply ingrained habits of thought and their reflection in some philosophical schools, "parts" and "wholes" in an absolute sense do not exist anywhere, either in the domain of living organisms, or in the universe at large.

A living organism is not an aggregation of elementary parts, and its activities cannot be reduced to reeling off a chain of conditioned responses. In its bodily aspects, the organism is a whole consisting of "sub-wholes", such as the circulatory system, digestive system, etc., which in turn branch into sub-wholes of a lower order, such as organs and tissues – and so down to individual cells, and to the organelles inside the cells. In other words, the structure and behaviour of an organism cannot be explained by, or "reduced to", elementary physico–chemical processes; it is a multi-levelled, stratified hierarchy of sub-wholes, which can be conveniently diagrammed as a pyramid or a inverted tree, where the sub-wholes form the nodes, and the branching lines symbolise channels of communication and control: see diagram on p. 448.

The point first to be emphasised is that each member of this hierarchy, on whatever level, is a sub-whole or "holon" in its own right – a stable, integrated structure, equipped with self-regulatory devices and enjoying a considerable degree of *autonomy* or self-government. Cells, muscles, nerves, organs, all have their intrinsic rhythms and patterns of activity, often manifested spontaneously without external stimulation; they are subordinated as *parts* to the higher centres in the hierarchy, but at the same time function as quasi-autonomous *wholes*. They are Janus-faced. The face turned upward, toward the higher levels, is that of a dependent part; the face turned downward, towards its own constituents, is that of a whole of remarkable self-sufficiency.

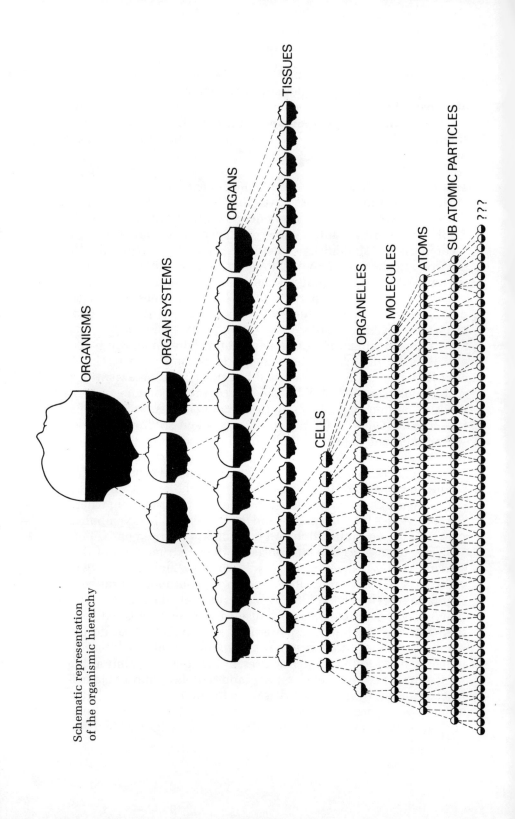

Schematic representation of the organismic hierarchy

ORGANISMS

ORGAN SYSTEMS

ORGANS

TISSUES

CELLS

ORGANELLES

MOLECULES

ATOMS

SUB ATOMIC PARTICLES

? ? ?

The heart, for instance, has its own pacemakers – actually several pacemakers, capable of taking over from each other when the need arises. Other major organs are equipped with different types of co-ordinating devices and feedback controls. Their autonomy is convincingly demonstrated by transplant surgery. At the beginning of our century, Alexis Carrell showed that a minute strip of tissue taken from the heart of a chicken embryo and put into a nutrient solution will go on pulsating for years. Since then, whole organs were shown to be capable of functioning as quasi-independent wholes when taken out of the body and kept *in vitro*, or transplanted into another body. And as we descend the steps of the hierarchy to the lowest level observable through the electron microscope, we come upon structures within each cell – organelles – which are neither "simple" nor "elementary", but systems of staggering complexity. Each of these minuscule parts of a cell functions as a self-governing whole in its own right, each apparently obeying a built-in *code of rules*. One type, or tribe, of organelles looks after the cell's growth, others after its energy supply, reproduction, communication, and so on. The mitochondria, for instance, are power plants which extract energy from nutrients by a chain of chemical reactions involving some fifty different steps; and a single cell may have up to five thousand such power plants. The activities of a mitochondrion can be switched on or off by controls on higher levels; but once triggered into action it will follow its own code of rules. It co-operates with other organelles in keeping the cell happy, but at the same time each mitochondrion is a law unto itself, an autonomous unit which will assert its individuality even if the cell around it is dying.

Science is only just beginning to rid itself of the mechanistic preconceptions of the nineteenth century – the world as a billiard table of colliding atoms – and to realise that hierarchic organisation is a fundamental principle of living nature; that it is "the essential and distinguishing characteristics of life"* and that it is "a real phenomenon, presented to us by the biological object, and not the fiction of a speculative mind"†. It is at the same time a conceptual tool which on some occasions acts as an Open Sesame.

*H. H. Pattee in *Towards a Theoretical Biology*, ed. C. H. Waddington (Edinburgh, 1970).
†P. A. Weiss in *Beyond Reductionism*, p. 193.

All complex structures and processes of a relatively stable character display hierarchic organisation, regardless whether we consider galactic systems, living organisms and their activities, or social organisations. The tree diagram with its series of levels can be used to represent the evolutionary branching of species into the "tree of life"; or the stepwise differentiation of tissues in the development of the embryo. Anatomists use the tree diagram to demonstrate the locomotor hierarchy of limbs, joints, individual muscles, and so down to fibres, fibrils and filaments of contractile proteins. Ethologists use it to illustrate the various sub-routines involved in such complex instinctive activities as a bird building a nest; but it is also an indispensable tool to the new school of psycholinguistics started by Chomsky. It is equally indispensable for an understanding of the processes by which the chaotic stimuli impinging on our sense organs are filtered and classified in their ascent through the nervous system into consciousness. Lastly, the branching tree illustrates the hierarchic ordering of knowledge in the subject-index of library catalogues – and the personal memory stores inside our skulls.

The universal applicability of the hierarchic model may arouse the suspicion that it is logically empty. I hope to show that this is not the case, and that the search for the fundamental properties, or laws, which all these varied hierarchies have in common amounts to more than a play on superficial analogies – or to riding a hobby horse. It should rather be called an exercise in General Systems Theory – that relatively recent interdisciplinary school, founded by von Bertalanffy, whose purpose is to construct theoretical models and discover general principles which are universally applicable to biological, social and symbolic systems of any kind – in other words, a search for common denominators in the flux of phenomena, for unity-in-diversity.

Yet the whole conception of multi-levelled hierarchies went against the materialist *Zeitgeist*, because it implied that mental phenomena cannot be "reduced" to the blind dance of atoms; that the mind of man is different not only in degree, but in kind, from the conditioned responses of Pavlov's dogs and Skinner's rats, which the dominant school in psychology considered as the paradigms of human behaviour. Harmless as the word "hierarchy" sounded, it turned out to be subversive. It did not even appear in the index of most modern textbooks of psychology or biology.

Yet there have always been voices in the wilderness, insisting that the concept of hierarchic organisation was an indispensable prerequisite – a *conditio sine qua non* – of any methodical attempt to bring unity into the diversity of science, and might eventually lead to a coherent philosophy of nature. The present chapter is meant to convey the outlines of a theory, based on hierarchic principles, in order to provide a platform or runway for the more speculative flights that follow.

To say it once more: if we look at any form of stable social organisation, from the insect state to the Pentagon, we shall find that it is hierarchically structured; the same applies to the individual organism and (less obviously) to its innate and acquired skills. However, to prove the validity and significance of the model, it must be shown that there exist specific principles and laws which apply (a) to all levels of a given hierarchy, and (b) to hierarchies in different fields. Some of these principles might appear self-evident, others rather abstract; taken together, they form the stepping stones for a new approach to some old problems.

"A good terminology," someone has said, "is half the game." To get away from the traditional misuse of the words "whole" and "part", one is compelled to operate with such awkward terms as "sub-whole", or "part-whole", "sub-structures", "sub-skills", "sub-assemblies", and so forth. To avoid these jarring expressions, I proposed some years ago* a new term to designate those Janus-faced entities on the intermediate levels of any hierarchy, which can be described either as wholes or as parts, depending on the way you look at them from "below" or from "above". The term I proposed was the *holon*, from the Greek *holos* = whole, with the suffix *on*, which, as in proton or neutron, suggests a particle or part. Thus the concept of the holon is intended to provide the missing link between the atomistic and holistic approaches.

The holon seems to have filled a genuine need, for it is gradually finding its way into the terminology of various branches of science, from biology to communication theory. It was particularly gratifying to discover that it has also insinuated itself into other languages: in Professor Raymond Ruyer's much discussed book *La Gnose de Princeton*† there is a chapter entitled: "*Les accolades domaniales et les holons*" – with a footnote which says:

*In *The Ghost in the Machine*.
†Paris, 1974.

"If I am not mistaken, the word originated with Koestler." New words are like parvenus: once their humble origin is forgotten, they have made it.

Unfortunately, the term "hierarchy" itself is rather unattractive and often provokes an emotional resistance. It is loaded with military and ecclesiastic associations, or evokes the "pecking hierarchy" of the barnyard, and thus conveys the impression of a rigid, authoritarian structure, whereas in the present theory a hierarchy consists of autonomous, self-governing holons endowed with varying degrees of flexibility and freedom. Encouraged by the friendly reception of the holon, I shall occasionally use the terms "holarchic" and "holarchy", but without undue insistence.

We have seen that biological holons, from organisms down to organelles, are self-regulating entities which manifest both the independent properties of wholes and the dependent properties of parts. This is the first of the general characteristics of all types of holarchies to be retained; we may call it the *Janus principle*. In social hierarchies it is self-evident: every social holon – individual, family, clan, tribe, nation, etc. – is a coherent whole relative to its constituent parts, yet at the same time part of a larger social entity. A society without holarchic structuring would be as chaotic as the random motions of gas molecules colliding and rebounding in all directions.*

Not quite as obvious at first glance is the hierarchic organisation of our skilled activities. Yet the skill of driving a motor-car does not consist in the conscious activation of individual muscles by the driver's brain, but in the triggering of sub-routines like steering, accelerating, braking, changing gears, etc., each of which represents a quasi-autonomous pattern of activities – a *behavioural holon* which is so self-reliant that once you have mastered the skill of driving one particular car, you can drive any car.

Or, take the skill of communicating ideas by speech. The sequence of operations starts at the apex of the hierarchy with the *intention* of conveying the idea or message. But that idea is as often as not of a pre-verbal nature; it may be a visual image, a feeling, a vague impression. We are familiar with the frustrating

---

*However, the situation is somewhat obscured by the fact that complex societies are structured by *several* interlocking hierarchies – see below.

experience of knowing what we want to say, but not knowing how to express it; and this refers not only to the search for the right word, but preceding that, to the structuring of the intended message and arranging it in a sequential order; processing it according to the laws of grammar and syntax; and lastly, activating co-ordinated patterns of muscle contractions in the tongue and vocal chords. Thus speaking involves the stepwise concretisation, elaboration and articulation of originally inarticulate mental contents. Although these operations follow each other very fast and to a large extent automatically, so that we are not consciously aware of them, they nevertheless require a succession of different activities on different levels of the mental hierarchy. And each of these levels has its own laws: the laws of enunciation, the rules of grammar and syntax, the canons of semantics, etc.

From the listener's point of view, the sequence of operations is reversed. It starts at the lowest level – the perceptual skills of recognising phonemes (speech sounds) in the air-vibrations reaching the ear-drums, amalgamating them into morphemes (syllables, prefixes, etc.) and so forth, through words and sentences, finally reconstituting the speaker's message at the apex of the hierarchy.

Let us note that nowhere on the upward or downward journey through the linguistic holarchy do we encounter hard and indivisible "atoms of language". Each of the entities on various levels – phonemes, morphemes, words, sentences – is a whole relative to its parts, and a subordinate part of a more complex entity on the next higher level. For instance, a morpheme like /men/ is a linguistic holon which can be put to many uses – menace, mental, mention, mentor, etc.; and which particular meaning it will assume depends on the context on the higher level.

Psycholinguists use the branching tree as a convenient model for this step-by-step process of spelling out an implicit thought in explicit terms, of converting the potentialities of an amorphous idea into the actual motion-patterns of the vocal chords. This remarkable process has been compared to ontogenesis – the development of the embryo. First, there is the fertilised egg, which contains all the potentialities defining the finished product, the "idea", as it were, of the future individual: these potentials are then "spelt out" in successive stages of differentiation. It may also be compared to the process by which a military action is carried out: the order "Eighth Army will advance in the direction of Tobruk", issued from the apex of the hierarchy by the General in Command, is concretised, articulated and spelt out in more detail at each of the successive lower echelons.

Generally speaking, the performance of any purposeful action, whether instinctive, like the nest-building of birds, or acquired as most human skills are, follows the same pattern of spelling out a general intent by the stepwise activation or triggering of functional holons – sub-routines on successively lower levels of the hierarchy. This rule is universally applicable to all types of "output hierarchies", regardless whether the "output" is a human baby, a sentence spoken in English, the playing of a piano sonata or the action of tying one's shoelaces. (For input hierarchies, as we shall see later, the reverse sequence holds.)

The next point to emphasise is that every level in a holarchy of any type is governed by a set of fixed, *invariant rules*, which account for the coherence, stability, and the specific structure and function of its constituent holons. Thus in the *language* hierarchy we found on successive levels the rules which govern the activities of the vocal chords, the laws of grammar and above them the whole semantic hierarchy concerned with meaning. The codes which govern the behaviour of *social* holons, and lend them coherence, are written and unwritten laws, traditions, belief-systems, fashions. The development of the *embryo* is governed by the "genetic code". Turning to *instinctive activities*, the web which the spider weaves, the nest which the blue tit builds, and the courting ceremony of the greylag goose all conform to fixed, species-specific patterns, produced according to certain "rules of the game". In *symbolic operations*, the holons are rule-governed cognitive structures (or "matrices") variously called "frames of reference", "associative contexts", "universes of discourse", "algorithms", etc., each with its specific "grammar" or canon. We thus arrive at a tentative definition: the term "holon" may be applied to any structural or functional sub-system in a biological, social or cognitive hierarchy, which manifests rule-governed behaviour and/or structural *Gestalt*-constancy.* Thus organelles and homologous organs are evolutionary holons; morphogenetic fields are ontogenetic holons; the ethologist's "fixed action-patterns" and the sub-routines of acquired skills are

---

*The "or" is necessary to include configurations in symbolic hierarchies – which do not manifest "behaviour" in the usual sense.

behavioural holons; phonemes, morphemes, words, phrases are linguistic holons; individuals, families, tribes, nations are social holons.*

The set of fixed rules which govern a holon's structure and function we shall call its *code* or *canon*. However, let us note at once that while the canon imposes constraints† and controls on the holon's activities, it does not exhaust its degrees of freedom, but leaves room for more or less flexible strategies, guided by the contingencies of the environment. This distinction between *fixed (invariant) codes* and *flexible (variable) strategies* may sound at first a little abstract, but it is fundamental to all purposeful behaviour; a few examples will illustrate what is meant.

The common spider's web-making activities are controlled by a fixed inherited canon (which prescribes that the radial threads should always bisect the laterals at equal angles, thus forming a regular polygon); but the spider is free to suspend his web from three, four or more points of attachment — to choose his strategy according to the lie of the land. Other instinctive activities — birds building nests, bees constructing their hives, silkworms spinning their cocoons — all have this dual characteristic of conforming to an *invariant code* or rule-book which contains the blueprint of the finished product, but using amazingly *varied strategies* to achieve it.

---

*Various authors have pointed to certain affinities between the concept of the holon and Ralph Gerard's "org". Thus D. Wilson in *Hierarchical Structures*: "Koestler (1967) elects to designate these 'Janus-faced' entities by the term *holon*. . . . We note that Gerard uses the term org to designate the same concept (Gerard, 1957)." This of course amounts to a veiled hint at plagiarism. The two quotations from Gerard that follow indicate the similarities and differences between his org and the *holon* (my italics): "Those *material* systems or entities which are individuals at a given level but are composed of subordinate units, lower level orgs" (*Science*, Vol. 125 [1957], pp. 429–33). The limitation to "material systems" is made more explicit in the second quotation, where he defines the org as "that sub-class of systems composed of material systems, in which matter enters into the picture; this excludes formal systems, for example" (*Hierarchical Structures*, ed. L. L. Whyte, A. G. Wilson and D. Wilson [New York, 1969], p. 228). Thus the term "org" cannot be applied to behavioural or linguistic or cognitive hierarchies where the concept of the holon proved especially useful. Orgs, as defined by Gerard, represent a sub-category of holons confined to material systems.

†"Constraint" is a rather unhappy scientific term (reminiscent of the straitjacket) which refers to the rules which govern organised activity.

Passing from the instinctive activities of the humble spider to sophisticated human skills like playing chess, we again find a code of fixed rules which define the *permissible* moves, but the choice of the *actual* move is left to the player, whose strategy is guided by the environment – the distribution of the chessmen on the board. *Speech*, as we saw, is governed by various canons on various levels, from semantics through grammar down to phonology, but on each of these levels the speaker has a vast variety of strategic choices: from the selection and ordering of the material to be conveyed, through the formulation of paragraphs and sentences, the choice of metaphors and adjectives, right down to enunciation – the selective emphasis placed on in-dividual vowels. Similar considerations apply to the pianist improvising variations on a theme. The fixed "rule of the game" in this case is the given melodic pattern, but he has almost infinite scope for the strategic choices in phrasing, rhythm, tempo or transposition into a different key.* A lawyer's activities are very different from a pianist's but the lawyer, too, operates within fixed rules laid down by statute and precedent, while he disposes of a vast range of strategies in interpreting and applying the law.

In ontogenesis – the development of the embryo – the distinction between "rules" and "strategies" is at first sight less obvious, and requires a slightly longer explanation.

The apex of the hierarchy in this case is the fertilised egg; the axis of the tree represents time: and the holons on successive levels represent successive stages in the differentiation of tissues into organs. The growth of the embryo from a shapeless blob to a "roughed in" form and through various stages of increasing articulation has been compared to the way in which a sculptor carves a figure out of a block of wood – or, as already mentioned, to the "spelling out" of an amorphous idea into articulate phonemes.

The "idea" to be spelt out in ontogeny is contained in the genetic code, housed in the double helix of nucleic acid strands in the chromosomes. It takes fifty-six generations of cells to produce a human being out of a single, fertilised egg-cell. The cells in the growing embryo are all of identical origin, and carry the *same* set of chromosomes, i.e., the same hereditary potential. In spite of

---

*Incidentally, transposition of a musical theme into a different key on the piano, where the sequence of finger movements is totally different, amounts to a complete refutation of the behaviourists' chain-response theory.

this, they develop into such diverse products as muscle cells, kidney cells, brain cells, toe-nails. How can they do this if they are all governed by the same set of laws, by the same hereditary canon?

This is a question which, as W. H. Thorpe recently wrote, "we are not yet within sight of being able to answer".* But at least we can approach it by a rough analogy. Let the chromosomes be represented by the keyboard of a grand piano – a very grand piano with a few thousand million keys. Then each key will represent a gene or hereditary disposition. Every single cell in the body carries a complete keyboard in its nucleus. But each specialised cell is only permitted to sound one chord or play one tune, according to its speciality – the rest of the keyboard having been sealed off by scotch-tape.†

But this analogy immediately poses a further problem: quis custodiet ipsos custodes – who or what agency decides which keys the cell should activate at what stage and which keys should be sealed off? It is at this point that the basic distinction between fixed codes and adaptable strategies comes in once again.

The genetic code, defining the "rules of the game" of ontogeny, is located in the nucleus of each cell. The nucleus is bounded by a permeable membrane, which separates it from the surrounding cell-body, consisting of a viscous fluid – the cytoplasm – and the varied tribes of organelles. The cell-body is enclosed in another permeable membrane, which is surrounded by body-fluids and by other cells, forming a tissue; this, in turn, is in contact with other tissues. In other words, the genetic code in the cell-nucleus operates within a hierarchy of environments like a nest of Russian dolls.

Different types of cells (brain cells, kidney cells, etc.) differ from each other in the structure and chemistry of their cell-bodies. These differences are due to the complex interactions between the genetic keyboard in the chromosomes, the cell-body itself, and its external environment. The latter contains physico-chemical factors of such extreme complexity that Waddington coined for it the expression "epigenetic landscape". In this landscape the cell moves like an explorer in unknown territory. To quote another geneticist, James Bonner, each embryonic cell must be able to "test" its neighbour-cells "for strangeness or similarity, and in

---

*W. H. Thorpe, Animal Nature and Human Nature (Cambridge, 1974), p. 35.
†This sealing-off process also proceeds stepwise, as the hierarchic tree branches out into more and more specialised tissues.

many other ways".* The information thus gathered is then transferred – "fed back" – via the cell-body to the chromosomes, and
determines which chords on the keyboard should be sounded,
and which should be temporarily or permanently sealed off; or, to
put it differently, which rules of the game should be applied to
obtain the best results. Hence the significant title of Waddington's
important book on theoretical biology: *The Strategy of the
Genes.*†

Thus ultimately the cell's future depends on its position in the
growing embryo, which determines the strategy of the cell's
genes. This has been dramatically confirmed by experimental
embryology: if the tail-bud of a newt embryo was grafted into a
position where a leg should be, it grew not into a tail, but into a leg
– surely an extreme example of a flexible strategy within the rules
laid down by the genetic code. At a later stage of differentiation
the tissues which form the rudiments of future adult organs – the
"organ-buds" or "morphogenetic fields" – behave like autonomous, self-regulating holons in their own right. If at this stage half
of the field's tissue is cut away, the remainder will form, not half
an organ, but a complete organ. If the growing eye-cup is split into
several parts, each fragment will form a smaller, but normal eye.

These self-regulating properties of holons within the growing
embryo ensure that whatever accidental hazards arise during
development, the end-product will be according to norm. In view
of the millions and millions of cells which divide, differentiate,
and move about, it must be assumed that no two embryos, not
even identical twins, are formed in exactly the same way. The
self-regulating mechanisms which correct deviations from the
norm and guarantee, so to speak, the end-result, have been compared to the homeostatic feedback devices in the adult organism –
so biologists speak of "developmental homeostasis". The future
individual is potentially predetermined in the chromosomes of
the fertilised egg; but to translate this blueprint into the finished
product, billions of specialised cells have to be fabricated and
moulded into an integrated structure. It would be absurd to
assume that the genes of that one fertilised egg should contain
built-in provisions for each and every particular contingency
which every single one of its fifty-six generations of daughter-cells
might encounter in the process. However, the problem becomes a

*J. Bonner, *The Molecular Biology of Development* (Oxford, 1965), p. 136.
†C. H. Waddington, *The Strategy of the Genes* (London, 1957).

little less baffling if we replace the concept of the "genetic blue-print", which implies a plan to be rigidly copied, by the concept of a genetic *canon of rules* which are fixed, but leave room for alternative choices, i.e., adaptive strategies guided by feedbacks and pointers from the environment.

Needham once coined a phrase about "the striving of the blas-tula to grow into a chicken". One might call the strategies by which it succeeds the organism's "pre-natal skills". After all, the development of the embryo and the subsequent maturation of the new-born into an adult are continuous processes; and we must expect that pre-natal and post-natal skills have certain basic prin-ciples in common with each other and with other types of hierarchic processes.

The foregoing section was not intended to describe embryonic development, only one aspect of it: the combination of *fixed rules and variable strategies*, which we also found in instinctive skills (such as nest-building, etc.) and learnt behaviour (such as lan-guage, etc.).

Ontogeny and phylogeny, the development of the individual and the evolution of species, are the two grand *hierarchies of becoming.*

Motor-car manufacturers take it for granted that it would make no sense to design a new model from scratch; they make use of already existing sub-assemblies – engines, batteries, steering sys-tems, and try to improve one or the other. Compare the front wheels of the latest model with those of an old vintage car or horse-cart – they are based on the same principles. Compare the anatomy of the forelimbs of reptiles, birds, whales and man – they show the same structural design of bones, muscles, nerves and blood-vessels and are accordingly called "homologous" organs.

The functions of legs, wings, flippers and arms are so different that one would expect them to have quite different designs. Yet they are merely modifications, strategic adaptations of an already existing structure – the forelimb of the common reptilian ances-tor. Once Nature has taken out a patent on a vital component or process, she sticks to it with amazing tenacity: the organ or device has become a stable *evolutionary holon*. It is as if she felt compel-led to provide unity in variety. Geoffroy de St Hilaire, one of the pioneers of modern biology, wrote in 1818: "Vertebrates are built upon one uniform plan – e.g., the forelimb may be modified for running, climbing, swimming, or flying, yet the arrangement of the bones remains the same".* That basic design is part of the invariant *evolutionary canon*. Its adaptation for swimming or flying is a matter of *evolutionary strategy*.

This principle holds all along the line, through all the levels of the evolutionary hierarchy down to the organelles inside the cell, and the DNA chains in the chromosomes. The same standard models of organelles function in the cells of mice and men; the same ratchet-device using a contractile protein serves the motion of amoebae and of the concert-pianist's fingers; the same four chemical molecules constitute the basic alphabet in which heredity is encoded throughout the animal and plant kingdoms – only the words and phrases formed by them are different for each creature.

If evolution could only create novelties by starting each time afresh from the "primeval soup", the four thousand million years of the earth's history would not have been long enough to produce even an amoeba. In a much quoted paper on hierarchic structures, H. J. Simon concluded: "Complex systems will evolve from simple systems much more rapidly if there are stable intermediate forms than if there are not. The resulting complex forms in the former case will be hierarchic. We have only to turn the argument around to explain the observed predominance of hierarchies among the complex systems Nature presents to us. Among possible complex forms, hierarchies are the ones that have the time to evolve".†

We do not know what forms of life exist on other planets, but we can safely assume that wherever there is life, it is hierarchically organised.

Neglect of the hierarchic concept, and the failure to make a categorical distinction between *rules* and *strategies* of behaviour, has caused much confusion in academic psychology.‡ Since its

*G. de St Hilaire, *Philosophie Anatomique* (Paris, 1818).
†H. J. Simon in *Proc Am. Philos. Soc.* Vol. 106, No. 6 (December, 1962).
‡It is interesting to note the intense reluctance of some psychologists – even those who have outgrown the cruder forms of behaviourist S-R theory – to come to grips with reality. Thus Professor G. Miller writes in an article on psycholinguistics: "As psychologists have learnt to appreciate the complexities of language, the prospect of reducing it to the laws of behaviour so carefully studied in lower animals [he means Skinner's rats] has grown increasingly remote. We have been forced more and more into a position that non-psychologists probably take for granted, namely, that language is rule-governed behaviour characterised by

primary concern for the last fifty years was the study of rats in confined spaces ("Skinner boxes"), this failure is hardly surprising. Yet to any spectator of a game of football it is at once obvious that each player obeys rules which determine what he is *allowed* to do, and uses his strategic skills to choose what he *will* do. In other words, *the code defines the rules of the game, strategy decides the course of the game.* The examples cited in previous sections indicate that this categorical distinction between rules and strategies is universally applicable to innate and acquired skills, to the hierarchies which make for social coherence, as well as to the hierarchies of becoming.

The nature of the code which regulates behaviour varies of course according to the nature and level of the hierarchy concerned. Some codes are innate — such as the genetic code, or the codes which govern the instinctive activities of animals; others are acquired by learning — like the kinetic code in the circuitry of my nervous system which enables me to ride a bicycle without falling off, or the cognitive code which defines the rules of playing chess.

It seems that life in all its manifestations, from morphogenesis to symbolic thought, is governed by rules of the game which lend it order and stability but also allow for flexibility; and that these rules, whether innate or acquired, are represented in coded form on various levels of the hierarchy, from the genetic code to the structures in the nervous system associated with language and thought.

Let us now turn from codes to *strategies.* To repeat it once more: the code defines the permitted moves, strategy decides the choice of the actual move. The next question is: how are these choices made? We might say that the chess-player's choice is "free" in the sense that it is not determined by the rule-book. In fact the number of choices confronting a player in the course of a game of forty moves (while calculating the potential variations which each move might entail two moves ahead) is astronomical. But though his choice is "free" in the above sense of not being determined by

---

enormous flexibility and freedom of choice. Obvious as this conclusion may seem, it has important implications for any scientific theory of language. If rules involve the concepts of right and wrong, they introduce a normative aspect that has always been avoided in the natural sciences. ... To admit that language follows rules seems to put it outside the range of phenomena accessible to scientific investigation" (*Encounter* [London], July, 1964). What a very odd notion of the purpose and methods of "scientific investigation"!

the rules, it is certainly not *random*. The player tries to select a "good" move, which will bring him nearer to a win, and to avoid a bad move. But the rule-book knows nothing about "good" or "bad" moves. What guides the player's choice of a hoped-for "good" move are strategic precepts of a much higher complexity than the simple rules of the game. The rules a child can learn in half an hour; whereas the *strategy* is distilled from past experience, the study of master games and specialised books on chess theory. Generally we find on successively higher levels of the hierarchy increasingly complex, more flexible and less predictable patterns of activity with more degrees of freedom (a larger variety of strategic choices); while conversely every complex activity, such as writing a letter, branches into sub-skills which on successively lower levels of the hierarchy become increasingly mechanical, stereotyped and predictable.* The original choice of subjects to be discussed in the letter is vast; the next step, phrasing, still offers a great number of strategic alternatives but is more restricted by the rules of grammar; the rules of spelling are fixed with no elbow-room for flexible strategies, and the muscle-contractions which move the pen or depress the keys of the typewriter are fully automatised.

If we descend even further down into the basement of the hierarchy, we come to visceral processes which are self-regulating, controlled by homeostatic feedback devices. These, of course, leave little scope for strategic choices; nevertheless, my conscious self can interfere to some extent with the normally unconscious, automated functioning of my respiratory system by holding my breath or applying some Yoga technique. Thus the distinction between rules and strategies remains valid even on this basic physiological level. But the relevance of this distinction will only become fully apparent in later chapters when we turn to such fundamental problems as free will versus determinism.

As already mentioned, the purpose of this chapter is not to provide a manual of hierarchies, but to convey some idea of the conceptual framework on which this inquiry is based, and to give the reader the "feel" of holarchic thinking as opposed to the current reductionist and mechanistic trends. To conclude this summary survey, I must mention, however briefly, a few more principles which all hierarchic systems have in common.

*Cf. the ethologist's "fixed action patterns".

One obvious point is that hierarchies do not operate in a vacuum, but interact with others. This elementary fact has given rise to much confusion. If you look at a well-kept hedge surrounding a garden like a living wall, the rich foliage of the entwined branches may make you forget that the branches originate in separate plants. The plants are vertical, *arborising* structures. The entwined branches form horizontal *networks* at numerous levels. Without the individual plants there would be no network. Without the network, each plant would be isolated, and there would be no hedge. *"Arborisation"* and *"reticulation"* (net-formation) are complementary principles in the architecture of organisms and societies. Thus the circulatory system controlled by the heart and the respiratory system controlled by the lungs function as quasi-autonomous, self-regulating hierarchies, but they interact on various levels. In the subject-catalogues in our libraries the branches are entwined through cross-references. In cognitive hierarchies – universes of discourse – arborisation is reflected in the "vertical" denotation (classification) of concepts, reticulation in their "horizontal" connotations in associative nets.

The complementarity of arborisation and reticulation yields (as we shall see in Chapter 39), relevant clues to the complex problem of how memory works.

I have repeatedly referred to the "apex" of the hierarchy. Some hierarchies do indeed have a well-defined apex or peak, and a definite bottom level – e.g., a small business enterprise with a single proprietor and a stable work force. But the grand holarchies of existence – whether social, biological or cosmological – tend to be "open-ended" in one or both directions. A laboratory chemist, analysing a chemical compound, is engaged in a stepwise operation, where the apex of his tree – the sample to be analysed – is on the molecular level of the hierarchy, branching into chemical radicals, branching into atoms. For his particular purpose this hierarchy of a limited number of levels is sufficient. But from a broader point of view, which takes into account sub-atomic processes, what appears to the chemist as a complete tree turns out to be merely a branch of a more comprehensive hierarchy. Just as holons are, by definition, sub-wholes, so all branches of a hierarchy are sub-hierarchies, and whether you treat them as "wholes" or "parts" depends on the task in hand. The chemist need not bother about the so-called elementary particles which, as somebody remarked, have a disconcerting tendency not to remain elementary for very long, and seem to consist ultimately – or penultimately – of patterns of concentrated energy or stresses in the universal foam of space-time. Our laboratory chemist can safely ignore these surrealistic developments in modern quantum physics; but he must not forget – under the penalty of mental dehydration – that his tidy little hierarchic tree extends only through a very limited number of levels in the great open-ended hierarchies of being.

The same applies at the other end of the scale to the astronomer faced with the wheels-within-wheels display of solar systems, galaxies, galactic clusters and the possibility of parallel universes in hyper-space.

Chapter 38

BEYOND EROS AND THANATOS

We must now turn to one of the most fundamental characteristics of holarchic organisation, which I have so far only mentioned in passing. The chapter which follows is condensed from The Ghost in the Machine, *ch.* III, *and* Janus, *ch.* II.

The holons which constitute a living organism or a social body are, as we have seen, Janus-like entities: the face turned towards the higher levels in the holarchy is that of a subordinate part in a larger system; the face turned towards the lower levels shows a quasi-autonomous whole in its own right.

This implies that every holon is possessed of two opposite tendencies or potentials: an *integrative tendency* to function as part of the larger whole, and a *self-assertive tendency* to preserve its individual autonomy.

The most obvious manifestation of this basic polarity is found in *social* holarchies. Here the autonomy of the constituent holons is jealously guarded and asserted on every level – from the rights of the individual to those of clan or tribe, from administrative departments to local governments, from ethnic minorities to sovereign nations. Every social holon has a built-in tendency to preserve and defend its corporate identity. This *self-assertive tendency* is indispensable for maintaining the individuality of holons on all levels, and of the hierarchy as a whole. Without it, the social structure would dissolve into an amorphous jelly or degenerate into a monolithic tyranny. History provides many examples of both.

At the same time the holon is dependent on, and must function as an integrated part of the larger system which contains it: its *integrative or self-transcending tendency*, resulting from the holon's partness, must keep its self-assertive tendency in check.

Under favourable conditions, the two basic tendencies – *self-assertion and integration* – are more or less equally balanced, and the holon lives in a kind of dynamic equilibrium within the whole – the two faces of Janus complement each other. Under unfavourable conditions the equilibrium is upset, with dire consequences.

We thus arrive at a basic polarity between the *self-assertive tendency* and the *integrative tendency* of holons on every level, and, as we shall see, in every type of hierarchic system. This polarity is a fundamental feature of the present theory and one of its *leitmotifs*. It is not a product of metaphysical speculation, but is in fact *implied* in the model of the multi-levelled holarchy, because the stability of the model depends on the equilibration of the dual aspects of its holons, as wholes and as parts. This polarity or *coincidencia oppositorum* is present in varying degrees in all manifestations of life. Its philosophical implications will be discussed in later chapters; for the time being let us note that *the self-assertive tendency is the dynamic expression of the holon's wholeness, its integrative tendency the dynamic expression of its partness.**

As far as the holons in social hierarchies are concerned, the polarity is obvious – shouting at us from the headlines of the daily newspaper. But in less obvious ways the dichotomy of self-assertion versus integration is ubiquitous in biology, psychology, ecology and wherever we find complex hierarchic systems – which is practically everywhere around us. To paraphrase Gertrude Stein again: a whole is a part is a whole. Each sub-whole is a "sub" and a "whole". In the living animal or plant, as in the body social, each part must assert its individuality, for otherwise the organism would lose its articulation and disintegrate; but at the same time the part must submit to the demands of the whole – which is not always a smooth process.

We have seen earlier on that each part of the living creature, from complex organs down to the organelles inside the cell, has its intrinsic rhythm and pattern of activity, governed by its own built-in code of rules, which makes it function as a quasi-independent unit. On the other hand, these autonomous activities of the holon are controlled by higher levels of the hierarchy which make it function as a subordinate part. In a healthy organism as in a healthy society, the two tendencies are in equilibrium on every

*For "integrative tendency" I shall occasionally use as synonyms "participatory" or "self-transcending" tendency.

level of the hierarchy. But when exposed to stress, the self-asserting tendency of the affected part of the organism or society may get out of hand – i.e., the part will tend to escape the restraining controls of the whole. This can lead to pathological changes – such as malignant growths with an untrammelled proliferation of tissues which have escaped genetic restraint. On a less extreme level, virtually any organ or function may get temporarily and partially out of control. In rage and panic the sympathico-adrenal apparatus takes over from the higher centres which normally co-ordinate behaviour; when sex is aroused, the gonads seem to take over from the brain. The idée fixe, the obsession of the crank, are cognitive holons running riot. There is a wide range of mental disorders in which some subordinate part in the cognitive hierarchy exerts a tyrannical rule over the whole, or in which some chunks of the personality seem to have "split off" and lead a quasi-independent existence. The most frequent aberrations of the human mind are due to the obsessional pursuit of some part-truth, treated as if it were the whole truth – a holon masquerading as the whole.

No man is an island; he is a holon. Looking inward, he experiences himself as a unique, self-contained, independent whole; looking outward as a dependent part of his natural and social environment. His self-assertive tendency is the dynamic manifestation of his individuality; his integrative tendency expresses his dependence on some larger whole to which he belongs, his part-ness. When all is well, the two tendencies are more or less evenly balanced. In times of stress and frustration, the equilibrium is upset, manifested in emotional disorders. The emotions derived from the frustrated self-assertive tendencies are of the well-known, adrenergic, *aggressive-defensive* type: hunger, rage and fear, including the possessive components in sexual and parent-child relations. The emotions derived from the integrative tendency, which have been to a large extent neglected by academic psychology, we have called the *self-transcending* type of emotions. They arise, as we have seen, out of the human holon's need to belong, to transcend the narrow boundaries of the self and to be part of a more embracing whole – which may be a community, a religious creed or political cause, Nature, Art, or the *anima mundi*.

When the need to belong, the urge towards self-transcendence, is deprived of adequate outlets, the frustrated individual may lose his critical faculties and surrender his identity in blind worship or

fanatical devotion to some cause, regardless of its merits. It is one
of the ironies of the human condition that its ferocious destructiveness derives not from the self-assertive, but from the integrative potential of the species. The glories of science and art, and the
holocausts of history caused by misguided devotion, were both
nurtured by the self-transcending type of emotions. For the code
of rules which defines the corporate identity, and lends coherence
to a social holon (its language, traditions, standards of conduct,
systems of belief) represents not merely negative constraints
imposed on its activities but also positive precepts, maxims and
moral imperatives. When the social hierarchy is in equilibrium,
each of its holons operates in accordance with its code of rules,
without attempting to impose it on others; in times of stress and
crisis, a social holon may get over-excited and tend to assert itself
to the detriment of the whole, just like any over-excited organ or
obsessive idea.

The dichotomy of wholeness and partness, and its dynamic manifestation in the polarity of the self-assertive and integrative tendencies are, as already said, inherent in every multi-levelled
hierarchic system, and implied in the conceptual model. We find
it reflected even in inanimate nature: wherever there is a relatively
stable dynamic system, from atoms to galaxies, its stability is
maintained by the equilibrium of opposite forces, one of which
may be centrifugal — i.e., inertial or separative, the other cen-
tripetal, i.e., attractive or cohesive, which binds the parts together
in the larger whole, without sacrifice of their identity. Newton's
first law — "Every body continues in its state of rest or uniform
motion in a straight line unless compelled by a force to change
that state" — sounds like a proclamation of the self-assertive tendency of every speck of matter in the universe; while his Law of
Gravity reflects the integrative tendency.*

  We may venture a step further, and regard the Principle of
Complementarity as an even more basic example of our polarity.
According to this principle, which dominates modern physics, all
elementary particles — electrons, photons, etc. — have the dual

---

*In a science-fiction play, written many years ago, I had a visiting maiden from
an alien planet explain the central doctrine of its religion: ". . . We worship
gravitation. It is the only force which does not travel through space in a rush; it is
everywhere in repose. It keeps the stars in their orbits and our feet on our earth. It
is Nature's fear of loneliness, the earth's longing for the moon; it is love in its
pure, inorganic form" (*Twilight Bar*, [1945]).

character of corpuscles and waves: according to circumstances they will behave either as compact grains of matter, or as waves without substantial attributes or definable boundaries. From our point of view, the corpuscular aspect of the electron – or any elementary holon – manifests its wholeness and self-assertive potential, while its wave-character manifests its partness and integrative potential.*

Needless to say, the manifestations of the two basic tendencies appear on different levels of the hierarchy in different guises, according to the specific codes – or "organising relations" – characteristic of that level. The rules which govern the interactions of sub-atomic particles are not the same rules which govern the interactions between atoms as wholes; and the ethical rules which govern the behaviour of individuals are not the same rules which govern the behaviour of crowds or armies. Accordingly, the manifestations of the polarity of self-assertive and integrative tendencies, which we find in all phenomena of life, will take different forms from level to level. Thus, for example, we shall find the polarity reflected as:

integration	↔ self-assertion
partness	↔ wholeness
dependence	↔ autonomy
centripetal	↔ centrifugal
co-operation	↔ competition
altruism	↔ egotism

Let us further note that the self-assertive tendency is by and large *conservative* in the sense of tending to preserve the individuality of the holon in the here and now of existing conditions; whereas the integrative tendency has the dual function of co-ordinating the constituent holons of a system in its present stage, *and* of generating new levels of complex integrations in evolving hierarchies – whether biological, social or cognitive. Thus the self-assertive tendency is present-orientated, concerned with self-maintenance, while the integrative tendency may be said to work both for the present and towards the future.

As the polarity of the self-assertive and the integrative tendencies plays a crucial role in our theory and will keep cropping up in later

*Another instance of the polarity of inanimate nature is reflected in Mach's Principle, which connects terrestrial inertia with the total mass of the universe.

chapters, a brief comparison with Freud's metaphysical system, which achieved such immense popularity, may be of some interest.

Freud postulated two basic *Triebe* ("drives", or loosely, "instincts") which he conceived as mutually antagonistic universal tendencies inherent in all living matter: Eros and Thanatos, or libido and death-wish. A close reading of the relevant passages (in *Beyond the Pleasure Principle, Civilisation and its Discontents*, etc.) reveals, surprisingly, that both his drives are *regressive*: they both aim at the restoration of a past primeval condition. Eros, through the lure of the Pleasure Principle, tries to re-establish the erstwhile "unity of protoplasm in the primordial slime", while Thanatos aims even more directly at a return to the inorganic state of matter through the annihilation of self and other selves.

Freud took a rather dim view of the working of Eros. According to this view, pleasure is always derived from "the diminution, lowering, or extinction of psychic excitation" and "un-pleasure* from an increase of it". The organism tends towards stability; it is guided by "the striving of the mental apparatus to keep the quantity of excitations present in it as low as possible or at least constant. Accordingly, everything that tends to increase the quantity of excitation must be regarded as adverse to this tendency, that is to say, as unpleasurable."†

Now this is of course true, in a broad sense, in so far as the frustration of elementary needs like hunger is concerned. But it passes in silence a whole class of experiences to which we commonly refer as "pleasurable excitement". The preliminaries of love-making cause an increase in sexual tension and should, according to the theory, be unpleasant – which they decidedly are not. It is curious that in the works of Freud there is no answer to be found to this embarrassingly banal objection. The sex-drive in the Freudian system is essentially something to be disposed of – through the proper channels or by sublimation; pleasure is derived not from its pursuit, but from getting rid of it.‡

Unlust, dysphoria, as distinct from physical pain.
†Freud, *Jenseits des Lustprinzips* (1920). pp. 3–5.
‡One might argue that in Freud's universe there is no place for amorous love-play because Freud, like D. H. Lawrence, was basically a puritan with a horror of frivolity, who treated sex *"mit tierischem Ernst"*. Ernest Jones says in his biography: "Freud partook in much of the prudishness of his time, when allusions to lower limbs were improper." He then gives several examples – such as Freud "sternly forbidding" his fiancée to stay "with an old friend, recently married, who as she delicately put it, 'had married before her wedding' " (*Sigmund Freud*, Vol. I, p. 142).

Freud's concept of Thanatos – the *Todestrieb* – is as puzzling as his Eros. On the one hand, the death-wish "works silently, within the organism towards its disintegration" by catabolic processes, breaking down living into lifeless matter. (This aspect of it may in fact be equated with the Second Law of Thermodynamics* – the gradual dispersion of matter and energy into a state of chaos.) But, on the other hand, Freud's death-instinct, which works so quietly *within* the organism, appears, when projected outward, as active destructiveness or sadism. How these two aspects of Thanatos can be harmonised and causally connected is difficult to see. For the first aspect is that of a physico-chemical process which tends to reduce living cells to quiescence and ultimately to dust; while the second aspect shows a co-ordinated, violent aggression of the whole organism against other organisms. The process by which the silent sliding towards senescence and disintegration is converted into the infliction of violence on others is not explained by Freud; the only link he provides is the ambiguous use of words like "death-wish" and "urge to destruction".

Not only is the connection between these two aspects of the Freudian Thanatos missing, but each in itself is highly questionable. Taking the second aspect first, nowhere do we find in nature destruction for destruction's sake. Animals kill to devour, not to destroy; and even when they fight in competition for territory or mates, the fight is ritualised like a fencing bout and is hardly ever carried to a lethal end. To prove the existence of a primary "destructive instinct", it would have to be shown that destructive behaviour regularly occurs *without* external provocation, as hunger and the sex-drive make themselves felt regardless of the absence of external stimuli. To quote Karen Horney (once an eminent, but critical psychoanalyst):

> Freud's assumption implies that the ultimate motivation for hostility or destructiveness lies in the impulse to destroy. Thus he turns into its opposite our belief that we destroy in order to live: we live in order to destroy. We should not shrink from recognising error, even in an age-old conviction, if new insight teaches us to see it differently, but this is not the case here. If we want to injure or to kill, we do so because we are or feel endangered, humiliated, abused; because we are or feel rejected or treated unjustly; because we are or feel interfered with in wishes which are of vital importance to us.†

*Incidentally, this famous law applies only to so-called "closed systems" in physics, and not to living organisms; but this is a relatively recent discovery which Freud could not have known.
†K. Horney, *New Ways in Psychoanalysis* (London, 1939).

It was, after all, Freud himself who taught us to seek out in apparently wanton, unprovoked acts of destructiveness, by disturbed children or adults, the hidden motive – which usually turns out to be a feeling of being rejected, jealousy, or hurt pride. In other words, cruelty and destructiveness are to be regarded as *pathological extremes of the self-assertive tendency when frustrated or provoked beyond a critical limit* – without requiring the gratuitous postulate of a death-instinct, for which there is not a trace of evidence anywhere in biology.

Turning once more to the other aspect of Freud's Thanatos, the outstanding characteristic of living substance is, as already mentioned, that it seems to ignore the Second Law of Thermodynamics. Instead of dissipating its energy into the environment, the living animal extracts energy from it, eats environment, drinks environment, burrows and builds in environment, sucks information out of noise and meaning out of chaotic stimuli. "Neither senescence nor natural death are necessary, inevitable consequences of life," as Pearl summed it up;* the protozoa are potentially immortal; they reproduce by simple fission, "leaving behind in the process nothing corresponding to a corpse". In many multicellular animals, too, senescence and natural death are absent; they reproduce by fission or budding, again without leaving any dead residue behind. "Natural death is biologically a relatively new thing";† it is the cumulative effect of some, as yet little understood, deficiency in the metabolism of cells in complex organisms – an epiphenomenon, and not a basic law of nature.

Thus Freud's primary drives, sexuality and the death-wish, cannot claim universal validity; both are based on biological novelties which appear only on a relatively high level of evolution: sex as a new departure from asexual reproduction and sometimes (as in some species of flatworms) alternating with it; death as a consequence of imperfections arising with growing complexity. In the theory proposed here there is no place for a "destructive instinct" in organisms; nor for regarding sexuality as the *only* integrative force in human or animal society. Eros and Thanatos are relatively late arrivals on the stage of evolution; a host of creatures which multiply by fission (or budding) are ignorant of both. In our view, *sexuality is only one out of the many manifesta-*

*Pearl in *Encyclopaedia Britannica*, 14th ed., Vol. VIII, pp. 110f.
†Ibid.

tions of the integrative tendency, aggressiveness an extreme form of the self-assertive tendency; while Janus appears as the symbol of the two irreducible properties of living matter: wholeness and partness, and their precarious equilibrium in the hierarchies of nature.

To say it once more, this generalised schema is not based on metaphysical assumptions but is built in, as it were, into the architecture of complex systems – physical, biological or social – as a necessary precondition of the coherence and stability of their multilevelled assemblies of holons. Not by chance did Heisenberg call his autobiographical account of the genesis of modern physics *The Part and the Whole.** Where indeed in micro-physics do we find the ultimate "elementary" parts which do not turn out to be composite wholes? Where in the macro-world of astrophysics do we locate the boundaries of our universe in multi-dimensional space-time? Infinity yawns both at the top and bottom of the stratified hierarchies of existence, and the dichotomy of self-assertive wholeness and self-transcending partness is present on every level, from the trivial to the cosmic.

Emotions can be described as mental states accompanied by intense feelings and associated with bodily changes of a widespread character – in breathing, pulse, muscle tone, glandular secretions of hormones such as adrenalin, etc. They have also been described as "over-heated drives". They can be classified, in the first place, according to the *nature of the drive* which gives rise to them: hunger, sex, curiosity, protection of the offspring, and so on. In the second place, a conspicuous feature of all emotions is the feeling of *pleasurableness* or *unpleasurableness*, the "hedonic tone", attached to them. In the third place, there is the polarity between the *self-assertive* and *self-transcending* tendencies which enter into every emotion. We thus arrive at a three-dimensional conception of human emotions. Let us take a closer look at each, and particularly at those features which distinguish it from other theories.

One of the difficulties inherent in the subject is that we rarely experience a pure emotion: sex may be combined with curiosity and with virtually any other drive. The point is too obvious to need further discussion.

---

*Der Teil und das Ganze in the German original. In the English translation this was changed to Physics and Beyond.

The second variable, the pleasure-unpleasure scale of "hedonic tone", also gives rise to ambiguous, "mixed feelings". Earlier on I quoted Freud's dictum that pleasure is always derived from "the diminution, lowering or extinction of psychic excitation and unpleasure from an increase of it". This view (which was held throughout the first half of our century by the major schools in psychology, including American behaviourism* and Continental psychoanalysis) is no doubt true for the frustration of "over-heated" primitive drives which arise, for instance, from the pangs of starvation; but it is palpably untrue for that class of complex emotions, which we call pleasurable excitement, thrill, arousal, suspense. Reading an erotic passage in a book leads, in Freud's words, to an "increase in psychic excitation" and should therefore be unpleasant; in fact it arouses a complex emotion in which *frustration is combined with pleasure.*

The answer to this paradox lies in the important part played by *imagination* in human emotions. Just as an imagined stimulus in an erotic reverie is sufficient to arouse physiological impulses, so, vice versa, imagined satisfaction may lead to a pleasurable experience – the "internalised" consummation of those components in the complex drive which can be lived out in fantasy.

Another gateway through which imagination enters into the emotional drive is *anticipation* of its reward. When one is thirsty, the sight of the publican pouring beer into one's glass is pleasurable, although it "increases psychic excitation". Stevenson saw deeper than Freud when he wrote that to travel hopefully is better than to arrive.

Romantic lovers have always been aware of this. Longing is a bitter-sweet emotion with painful and pleasurable components. Sometimes the imagined presence of the beloved person can be more gratifying than the real one. Emotions have a many-coloured spectrum of components, each with its own hedonic tone. To ask whether to love is pleasurable or not is like asking whether a Rembrandt painting is bright or dark.

We can now turn to the third source of ambivalence in our emotions. The first, we remember, was the biological origin of the drive, the second the pleasure-unpleasure tone attached to it, the third is the polarity of self-assertion versus self-transcendence which is manifested in all our emotions.

---

*Where Thorndike's "Law of Effect", which asserted the same fallacy, reigned as supreme dogma.

Take love first – an ill-defined but heady cocktail of emotions with countless variations. (Sexual, platonic, parental, oedipal, narcissistic, patriotic, botanistic, canine-directed or feline-orientated, as the textbooks would say.) But whatever its target and method of wooing, there is always present an element of self-transcending devotion in varying proportions. In *sexual* relationships, domination and aggression are blended with empathy and identification; the outcome ranges from rape to platonic worship. *Parental love* reflects, on the one hand, a biological bond with "one's own flesh and blood" which transcends the boundaries of the self; while domineering fathers and over-protective mothers are classic examples of self-assertiveness. Less obvious is the fact that even *hunger*, an apparently simple and straightforward biological drive, can contain a self-transcending component. Everyday experience tells us that appetite is enhanced by congenial company and surroundings. On a less trivial level, ritual commensality is intimately related to magic and religion among primitive people. By partaking of the flesh of the sacrificed animal, man or god, a process of transubstantiation takes place; the virtues of the victim are ingested and a kind of mystic communion is established which includes all who participated in the rite. Transmitted through the Orphic mystery cult, the tradition of sharing the slain god's flesh and blood entered in a symbolic guise into the rites of Christianity. To the devout, Holy Communion is the supreme experience of self-transcendence; and no blasphemy is intended by pointing to the continuous tradition which connects ritual feeding with transubstantiation as a means of breaking down the ego's boundaries.

Other echoes of this ancient communion survive in such rites as baptismal and funeral meals, symbolic offerings of bread and salt. We can only conclude that even while eating, man does not live by bread alone: that *even the apparently simplest act of self-preservation may contain an element of self-transcendence.*

And vice versa, such admirably altruistic pursuits as caring for the sick or poor, protecting animals against cruelty, serving on committees and joining protest marches, can serve as wonderful outlets for bossy self-assertion, even if unconscious. Professional do-gooders, charity tigresses, hospital matrons, missionaries and social workers are indispensable to society, and to inquire into their motives, often hidden to themselves, would be ungrateful and churlish.

I am aware that this chapter may have seemed to oscillate between the over-obvious and the speculative; yet one of the tests of a speculative theory is that, once grasped, it appears self-evident.

There is a further difficulty inherent in the subject. The postulate of a universal self-assertive tendency needs no apology; it has an immediate appeal to commonsense, and has many forerunners – such as the "instinct of self-preservation", "survival of the fittest", and so forth. But to postulate as its counterpart an equally universal integrative tendency, and the dynamic interplay between the two as the key to a general systems theory, smacks of old-fashioned vitalism and runs counter to the philosophical climate of our time, epitomised in books like Monod's *Chance and Necessity* or Skinner's *Beyond Freedom and Dignity*.

But climates are liable to change. . . .

PART THREE

APPLYING THE THEORY

Chapter 39

MEMORY

The extracts in the previous section were meant to convey the outlines of a theory. In the three chapters of the present section I shall attempt to show its applicability to some widely different problems – i.e., the problems of memory, free will and group mentality.

The extract which follows is from a paper read at the symposium on "The Pathology of Memory" organised by the Department of Psychiatry, Massachusetts General Hospital,* with addenda from The Ghost in the Machine, *ch. IV, and* Janus, *ch. I.*

In Stevenson's novel *Kidnapped*, Alan Breck makes the casual remark: "I have a grand memory for forgetting, David." He speaks for all of us, and not only those afflicted with aphasia or senility. Painful as it is, we have to admit that a large proportion of our memories resembles the dregs in a wine glass, the dehydrated sediments of experiences whose flavour has gone – or, to change the metaphor, they are like dusty abstracts of past events on the shelves of a dimly lit archive. Fortunately this applies only to one type or category of memories, which I shall call *abstractive memory*. But there is another category, derived from our capacity to recall past episodes, or scenes, or details of scenes, with almost hallucinatory vividness. I shall call this the *spotlight* type of memory, and I shall contend that "abstractive memory" and

*Ed. George A. Talland and Nancy C. Waugh, Academic Press (New York and London, 1969).

"spotlight memory" are different classes of phenomena, based on different neural mechanisms.

Take abstractive memory first. The bulk of what we can remember of our life history, and of the knowledge we have accumulated in the course of it, is of the abstractive type.

The word "abstract" has, in common usage, two main connotations: it is the opposite of "concrete", in the sense that it refers to a general concept rather than a particular instance; in the second place, an "abstract" is a condensation of the essence of a longer document. Memory is abstractive in both senses. I watch a television play. The exact words of each actor are forgotten within a few seconds; only their abstracted meaning is retained. The next morning I can only remember the sequence of scenes which constituted the story. A month later, all I can remember is that the play was about a gangster on the run. Much the same happens to the mnemonic residues of books one has read, and to whole chapters of one's own life-story. The original experience has been stripped of detail, skeletonised, reduced to a colourless abstract before being confined to the memory store. The nature of that store is still a complete mystery in brain-research, but it is obvious that if stored knowledge and experience are to be retrievable (for otherwise they would be useless), they must be ordered like a thesaurus or a library subject-catalogue, with headings and sub-headings but also with a wealth of cross-references to assist the process of retrieval (the former representing arborisation, the latter the reticulation of the hierarchic structure).

If we pursue for a moment the metaphor of a library representing our memory stores, we arrive at rather depressing conclusions. Quite apart from the countless volumes that are left to rot away or fall to dust, there is also a hierarchy of librarians at work who ruthlessly condense long texts into short abstracts and then make abstracts of the abstracts.

This process of sifting and abstracting actually starts long before a lived experience is confined to the memory store. At every relay station in the perceptual hierarchy through which the sensory input must pass before being admitted to consciousness it is analysed, classified and stripped of irrelevant detail.* This

*The psychologist distinguishes on the lower levels of the hierarchy lateral inhibition, habituation, and efferent control of the receptors; on the higher levels the mechanisms responsible for the visual and auditory constancy phenomena, and the scanning and filtering devices that account for pattern recognition and enable us to abstract universals.

enables us to recognise the letter R in an almost illegible scrawl as "the same thing" as a huge printed R in a newspaper headline, by a sophisticated scanning process which disregards all details and abstracts only the basic geometrical design – the "R-ness" of the R – as worth signalling to higher quarters. This signal can now be transmitted in a simple code, like a message in Morse, which contains all the relevant information – "it's an R" – in a condensed, skeletonised form; but the wealth of calligraphic detail is of course irretrievably lost, as the inflections of the human voice are lost in the Morse message. The wistful remark "I have a memory like a sieve" may be derived from an intuitive grasp of these filtering devices which operate all along the input channels and storage channels of the nervous system.

Yet even the chosen few among the multitude of potential stimuli incessantly bombarding our receptor organs which have succesfully passed all these selective filters and have attained the status of consciously perceived events, must submit, as we have seen, to further rigorous stripping procedures before being admitted to the permanent memory store; and as time passes, they will suffer further decay. Memory is a prize example of the law of diminishing returns.

This retrospective impoverishment of lived experience is unavoidable; "abstractive" memory implies the sacrifice of particulars. If, instead of abstracting generalised concepts, like "R" or "tree" or "dog", our memories consisted of a collection of all our particular experiences of R's and trees and dogs encountered in the past – a storehouse of lantern slides and tape-recordings – it would be a chaotic jumble, completely useless for mental guidance, for we would never be able to identify an R or understand a spoken sentence. Without hierarchic order and classification, memory would be bedlam (or the parroting of sequences learned by rote, and reinforced by conditioning, which is the behaviourist's model – or caricature – for remembering).

To say it again: the loss of particulars in abstractive memory is unavoidable. Fortunately this is not the whole story, for there are several compensating factors which, at least in part, make up for the loss.

In the first place, the abstractive process can acquire a higher degree of sophistication by learning from experience. To the novice, all red wines taste alike, and all Japanese males look the same. But he can be taught to superimpose more delicate perceptual filters on the coarser ones, as Constable trained himself to discriminate between diverse types of clouds and to classify them into sub-categories. Thus we learn to abstract finer and finer nuances – to make the trees of the hierarchies of perception grow new shoots, as it were.

Moreover, it is important to realise that abstractive memory is not based on a single hierarchy but on several interlocking hierarchies pertaining to different sensory realms such as vision, hearing, smell. What is less obvious is that there may exist several distinct hierarchies with different criteria of relevance operating within the same sense modality. I can recognise a melody regardless of the instrument on which it was played; but I can also recognise the sound of an instrument regardless of the melody played on it. We must therefore assume that melodic pattern and instrument sound (timbre) are abstracted and stored independently by separate filtering hierarchies *within the same sensory modality but with different criteria of relevance*. One abstracts melody and disregards timbre, the other abstracts the timbre of an instrument and disregards melody as irrelevant. Thus not all the detail discarded as irrelevant by one filtering system is irretrievably lost, because it may have been retained and stored by another filtering hierarchy with different criteria of relevance.

The recall of an experience would then be made possible by the co-operation of several interlocking hierarchies, which may include different sense modalities, for instance, sight and sound or odour, or different branches within the same modality. You may remember the words of the aria "Your Tiny Hand is Frozen", but have lost the tune. Or you may remember the tune after having forgotten the words. And you may recognise the unique timbre of Caruso's voice on a gramophone record, regardless of the words and the tune he is singing. But if two, or all three of these features have been abstracted and stored, the recall of the original experience will have more dimensions and be the more complete.

The process could in some respects be compared to multicolour printing by the superimposition of several colour-blocks. The painting to be reproduced – the original experience – is photographed through different colour-filters on blue, red and yellow plates, each of which retains only those features that are "relevant" to it: i.e., those which appear in its own colour, and ignores all other features; then they are recombined into a more or less faithful reconstruction of the original input. Each hierarchy would then have a different "colour" attached to it, the colour symbolising its *criteria of relevance*. Which memory-forming hierarchies will be active at any given time depends, of course, on the subject's general interests and momentary state of mind.

Although this hypothesis represents a radical departure from both the behaviourist and the *Gestalt* schools' conceptions of memory, some modest evidence for it can be found in a series of experiments carried out in co-operation with Professor J. J. Jenkins in the psychological laboratory of Stanford University;* and more tests on these lines can be designed without much difficulty.

The "colour printing" hypothesis may provide part of the explanation of the complex phenomena of memory and recall, but it is based solely on the *abstractive* type of memory which by itself cannot account for the extreme vividness of the *spotlight* type of memory mentioned at the beginning of this chapter. It is a method of retention based on principles which seem to be the exact opposite of memory formation in abstractive hierarchies. It is characterised by the recall of scenes or details with almost hallucinatory clarity. They are rather like photographic close-ups, in contrast to abstractive memory's aerial panorama seen through a haze. The emphasis is on detail, which may be a fragment, torn from its context, that survived the decay of the whole to which it once belonged – like the single lock of hair on the shrivelled mummy of an Egyptian princess. It may be auditory – a line from an otherwise forgotten poem, or a chance remark by a stranger overheard in a bus; or visual – a wart on Nanny's chin, a hand waving farewell from the window of a departing train; or even refer to taste and smell, like Proust's celebrated *madeleine* (the French pastry, not the girl). Though often trivial from a rational point of view, these spotlighted images add texture and flavour to memory, and have an uncanny evocative power. This suggests that, although irrelevant by logical criteria, they have some

---

*Koestler and Jenkins, "Inversion Effects in the Tachistoscopic Perception of Number Sequences" in *Psychon. Sci.*, Vol. 3 (1965). This is a rather technical paper of possible interest to experimental psychologists, which the general reader can safely ignore. The gist of the experiment was to show to each subject for a fraction of a second only (by means of an apparatus called a tachistoscope) a number of seven or eight digits, and then let him try to repeat the sequence. The results of several hundred experiments show that a highly significant number of errors (approximately 50 per cent) consisted in the subject *correctly identifying* all numbers in the sequence, but *inverting the order* of two or three neighbouring digits. This seems to confirm that the identification of individual digits, and the determination of their sequential order, are carried out by different branches of the perceptual hierarchy.

special *emotive* significance (on a conscious or unconscious level) that caused them to be retained.

Nobody, not even computer designers, thinks all the time in terms of abstractive hierarchies. Emotion colours most of our perceptions, and there are indications that our emotive reactions also involve a hierarchy of levels – including archaic structures in the brain which are phylogenetically much older than the structures concerned with abstract conceptualisations. One might speculate that in the formation of "spotlight memories" these older levels in the hierarchy play a dominant part.

There are some further considerations in favour of such a hypothesis. First, from the neurophysiologist's point of view, they receive strong support from the Papez-MacLean theory of emotions.* Second, from the standpoint of the communication-theorist, abstractive memory *generalises and schematises*, while spotlight memory *particularises and concretises* – which is a much more primitive method of storing information.† Third, from the standpoint of the psychologist, abstractive memory would be related to insightful learning and spotlight memory to a process resembling imprinting. But imprinting in Konrad Lorenz's geese is restricted to a critical period of a few hours, and apparently results in a very coarse and vague imprint. On the human level, imprinting may take the form of eidetic imagery. According to Jaensch‡ and Kluever,§ a considerable proportion of children have the eidetic faculty – they are able to "project" a photographically accurate, coloured image of a previously fixated picture onto a blank screen and to repeat this after long intervals, sometimes even years. Penfield and Roberts'‖ experiments, evoking what is claimed to be total recall of past scenes by electrical stimulation of the patient's temporal lobes, may be a related phenomenon.

---

*See below, Part Four.

†The term "information" in modern communication-theory is used in a more general sense than in common parlance. Information includes anything from the colour and taste of an apple to the Ninth Symphony of Beethoven. Irrelevant inputs convey no information and are called "noise" – on the analogy of a noisy telephone line.

‡E. R. Jaensch, *Eidetic Imagery* (London, 1930).

§H. Kluever in *A Handbook of Child Psychology*, ed. C. Murchison (Worcester, Mass., 1933).

‖ W. Penfield and L. Roberts, *Speech and Brain Mechanisms* (Princeton, 1959).

But though apparently quite common in children, eidetic memory tends to vanish with the onset of puberty, and is rare among adults. Children and primitives live in a world of visual imagery. In William Golding's novel *The Inheritors*, the author makes his Neanderthalers say, instead of "I have thought of something", "I have a picture in my head." The eidetic child's way of "imprinting" pictures on the mind may represent a phylogenetically and ontogenetically earlier form of memory formation – which is lost when abstractive, conceptual thinking becomes dominant.

To sum up, abstractive memory, operating through multiple interlocking hierarchies, strips down the input to bare essentials according to each hierarchy's criteria of relevance. *Recalling* the experience requires dressing it up again. This is made possible, up to a point, by the co-operation of the hierarchies concerned, each of which contributes those aspects it has deemed worth preserving. The process is comparable to the superimposition of colour-plates in printing. Added to this are "spotlight" memories of vivid details which may include fragments of eidetic imagery, and carry a strong emotive charge. The result of this exercise in re-creating the past is a kind of collage, with glass eyes and a strand of genuine hair stuck on to the hazy, schematised picture.

It may also happen that fragments of different origin are mistakenly incorporated into the collage – included in the recall of experiences to which they do not belong. For memory is a vast archive of abstracts and curios, which are all the time being rearranged and revalued by the archivist; the past is constantly being re-made by the present. But most of the making and re-making is not consciously experienced. The canons of perception and memory operate instantaneously and unconsciously; we are always playing games without awareness of the rules.

Chapter 40

FREE WILL

As mentioned before, scientific conferences provided welcome occasions for exposing the concept of the holarchy to expert criticism and testing its validity the hard way. One of these occasions was a conference at the Rockefeller Foundation's Villa Serbellone in Bellagio on "Mind in Nature"; it provided an opportunity for attempting to apply the hierarchic way of thinking to the hoary problem of Free Will versus Determinism. The paper read there overlaps with some earlier excerpts in this volume; to keep repetitions to a minimum, I have relied on its condensed version in Janus.

In some respects Mind in Nature,* as the editors of the proceedings pointed out, continued where Beyond Reductionism had left off – i.e., searching "for ways of thinking that explain without explaining away".

"If Cleopatra's nose had been shorter," remarked Pascal, "the history of the world would have been different." And if his contemporary, Descartes, had kept a poodle, the history of philosophy would have been different. The poodle would have taught Descartes that contrary to his doctrine, animals are not machines, and hence the human body is not a machine, forever separated from the mind, which he thought to be located in the pineal gland.

A diametrically opposite view is summed up in an unforgettable aphorism of Bergson's: "The unconsciousness of a falling stone is something quite different from the unconsciousness of a growing cabbage."

Bergson's attitude is close to panpsychism: the theory that some rudimentary kind of sentience is present throughout the animal

* Ed. John B. Cobb Jr and David Ray Griffin, University Press of America (Washington, 1977).

kingdom and even in plants. Some speculatively inclined modern physicists would attribute a psychic element even to sub-atomic particles. Thus panpsychism postulates a continuum extending from the growing cabbage to human self-awareness, while Cartesian dualism regards consciousness as an exclusive possession of man, and places a kind of Iron Curtain between matter and mind.

Panpsychism and Cartesian dualism mark opposite ends of the philosophical spectrum. I shall not go into the various elaborations to which they have given rise – interactionism, parallelism, epiphenomenalism, identity-hypothesis, and so forth; instead I shall attempt to show that the concept of the multi-levelled holarchy is well suited to shed some new light on this very old problem. It is a conceptual tool which provides an alternative to the mechanistic, linear chaining of events torn from their multi-levelled context – like a thread extracted from a Persian carpet and suspended in a vacuum. One might say that hierarchical thinking relates to linear causality as the theory of algebraic functions relates to elementary arithmetic.

As we shall see, the hierarchic approach replaces the panpsychist's continuously ascending curve from cabbage to man by a whole series of discrete steps – a staircase instead of a slope; and it replaces the Cartesian single wall separating mind from body by a series of swing-gates, as it were.

To start with, everyday experience tells us that consciousness is not an all-or-nothing affair but a *matter of degrees*. There are levels of consciousness which form ascending series from the unconsciousness under an anaesthetic, through the drowsiness induced by milder drugs, through the performance of complex routines like tying one's shoelaces automatically with an "absent mind", through full awareness and self-awareness to the self's awareness of its awareness of itself – and so on, without hitting a ceiling.

In the downward direction we are also faced with a multiplicity of levels of consciousness or sentience which extend far below the human level. Ethologists who have a close *rapport* with animals generally refuse to draw a line indicating the lower limit of consciousness on the evolutionary ladder, while neurophysiologists talk of the "spinal consciousness" in lower vertebrates and even of the "protoplasmic consciousness" of protozoa. To mention a single example: Sir Alister Hardy has given us a vivid description of *Foraminifera* – single-celled miniature sea-animals related to amoeba, which build elaborate microscopic "houses" out of the needle-like speculae of dead sponges – houses which Hardy calls "marvels of engineering skill"* Yet these primitive protozoans have neither eyes nor a nervous system and are but a gelatinous mass of flowing protoplasm. Thus the hierarchy appears to be open-ended both in the upward and downward direction.

To quote an eminent ethologist, W. H. Thorpe:

> The evidence suggests that at the lower levels of the evolutionary scale consciousness, if its exists, must be of a very generalised kind, so to say unstructured; and that with the development of purposive behaviour and a powerful faculty of attention, consciousness associated with expectation will become more and more vivid and precise.†

However, it is essential to realise that these gradations in the "structuring, vividness and precision" of consciousness are found not only along the evolutionary ladder, and in members of the same species at different stages of their ontogeny, but also within adult individuals when confronted by different situations. I am referring to the deceptively trivial fact that one and the same activity – driving a car – can be either performed *automatically*, without conscious awareness of one's own actions, or accompanied by varying *degrees of awareness*. Driving along a familiar road with little traffic on it, I can hand over to the "automatic pilot" in my nervous system and think about something else. In other words, the task of controlling and co-ordinating my driving performance has been shifted from a higher to a lower level in my mental hierarchy. Vice versa, overtaking another car requires an *upward* shift of control to the level of semi-conscious routine; and overtaking in a tricky situation requires a further shift to full awareness of what I am doing.

There are several factors which determine how much, if any, conscious attention is paid by a person to the activity in which he is engaged. The most important of these factors in the present context is habit-formation. While learning a skill we must concentrate on every detail of what we are doing. We learn laboriously to recognise and name the printed letters of the alphabet, to ride a bicycle, to hit the right key on the piano or typewriter. But with increasing mastery and practice, the typist can let his fingers "look after themselves"; we read, write, drive "automatically",

*Sir A. Hardy, The Living Stream (London, 1965), p. 229.
†W. H. Thorpe in Brain and Conscious Experience, ed. Sir J. Eccles (New York, 1966).

which is another way of saying that the rules which govern the exercise of the skill are now applied unconsciously. This condensation of learning into habit may be looked upon as a process *which transforms mental into mechanical activities* – mind-processes into machine-processes. It starts with infancy and never stops.

This tendency towards the progressive automatisation of habits has a positive side: it conforms to the principle of parsimony. By manipulating the wheel of the car mechanically, I am able to carry on a conversation; and if the rules of grammar and syntax did not operate automatically I could not attend to meaning. But on the other hand the progressive mechanisation of habits and routines threatens to turn us into automata. Man is not a machine, but most of the day we behave like machines – or sleepwalkers, without mentally attending to the activities we are engaged in. This applies not only to manipulative routines – wielding knife and fork at table, lighting a cigarette or signing a letter – but also to mental activities: one can read a whole paragraph in a boring book "absent-mindedly" without taking in a single word. Karl Lashley once quoted a colleague of his, a professor of psychology, who told him: "When I have to give a lecture I turn my mouth loose and go to sleep."

Thus consciousness may be described, somewhat perversely, as that special attribute of an activity which *decreases in direct proportion to habit formation.* (This is less paradoxical than it sounds, if one remembers that Norbert Wiener, following in Schroedinger's footsteps, defined information as "essentially a negative entropy".)

The condensation of learning into habit is accompanied by a dimming of the light of awareness. We expect therefore that the opposite process will take place when routine is disturbed by running into some unexpected obstacle or problem: that this will cause an instantaneous switch from "mechanical" to "minding" or "mindful" behaviour. Let a kitten suddenly cross the road on which you have been driving absent-mindedly, and your previously absent mind will return in a flash to take over control, i.e., to make an instant decision whether to run over the kitten or risk the safety of your passengers by slamming on the brakes. What happens in such a crisis is a sudden transfer of control of an ongoing activity to a higher level of the multi-levelled hierarchy, because the decision to be made is beyond the competence of the automatic pilot and must be referred to "higher quarters". In the present theory this sudden *shift of the control* of behaviour from a lower to a higher level of the hierarchy – analogous to the physicist's quantum jump – is the essence of conscious decision-making and of the subjective experience of free will.

The opposite process, as we have seen, is the mechanisation of routines, the enslavement to habit. We thus arrive at a dynamic view of a continuous two-way traffic up and down the mind-body hierarchy. The automatisation of habits and skills implies a steady *downward* motion as on a moving escalator, thus making room in the upper strata for more sophisticated activities – but also threatening to turn us into automata. Each downward step is a transition from the mental to the mechanical; each upward shift in the hierarchy produces more vivid and structured states of consciousness.

These alternations between robot-like and numinous behaviour are, as I said, a matter of everyday experience. On some rare occasions, however, creative people experience a quick oscillation – *a reculer pour mieux sauter* – from the over-articulated, over-specialised strata in the cognitive hierarchy down to more primitive and fluid levels, and up again to a re-structured upper level.

Classical dualism knows only a single mind-body barrier. The holarchic approach on which the present theory is based implies a *pluralistic instead of a dualistic view*: the transformation of physical events into mental events, and vice versa, is effected not by a single leap over a single barrier, but by a whole series of steps up or down through the swing-gates of the multi-levelled hierarchy.

As a concrete example, let us remember how we convert airwaves arriving at the ear-drum, which are physical events, into ideas, which are mental events. It isn't done "in one go". In order to decode the message which the air-pulsations carry the listener must perform a rapid series of "quantum jumps" from one level of the language hierarchy to the next higher one: phonemes have no meaning and can only be interpreted on the level of morphemes; words must be referred to their context, sentences to a larger frame of reference. Active speech – the spelling out of a previously unverbalised idea or image – involves the reverse process: it converts mental events into the mechanical motions of the vocal cords. This again is achieved by a whole intermediate series of rapid but distinct steps, each of which triggers off linguistic routines of a more and more automatised type: the structuring of the intended message into a linear sequence, processing it according to the silent dictates of grammar and syntax; and lastly, innervating the entirely mechanical motion-patterns of the organs of speech. Noam Chomsky's psycholinguistic hierarchy was anticipated in *A Midsummer Night's Dream*:

> As imagination bodies forth
> The forms of things unknown, the poet's pen
> Turns them to shapes and gives to airy nothing
> A local habitation and a name.

Let me repeat: each downward step in the stepwise conversion of airy nothings into the physical motions of the vocal cords entails a transfer of control to more automatised automatisms; each step upwards leads to more mentalistic processes of mentation. Thus the mind-body dichotomy is not localised along a single boundary or interface, as in classical dualism, but is present on every intermediary level of the hierarchy.

On this view, the categorical distinction between mind and body fades away, and instead of it *mental and mechanical* become *complementary attributes* of processes on every level. The dominance of one of these attributes over the other – whether the activity of knotting my tie is performed mindfully or mechanically – depends on the flow of traffic in the hierarchy, whether the shifts of control proceed in an upward or downward direction through the swing-gates. Thus even the lower, visceral reaches of the hierarchy, regulated by the autonomic nervous system, can apparently be brought under mental control through Yoga practices or biofeedback methods. And vice versa – to say it once more – when I am sleepy or bored, I can perform the supposedly mental activity of reading a paper – without "taking in" a single word.

We are in the habit of talking of "mind" as if it were a thing, which it is not – nor is matter, for that matter. Mentating, thinking, remembering, imagining are *processes* in a reciprocal or complementary relationship to mechanical processes. At this point of the argument modern physics provides us with a pertinent analogy: the so-called "Principle of Complementarity", which is fundamental to its whole theoretical structure. It states, put into non-technical language, that the elementary constituents of matter – electrons, protons, neutrons, etc. – are ambiguous, Janus-faced entities which under certain conditions behave like solid corpuscles, but under other conditions behave like waves in a non-substantial medium. Werner Heisenberg, Nobel laureate and one of the pioneers in sub-atomic physics, commented:

> The concept of Complementarity is meant to describe a situation in which we can look at one and the same event through two different frames of reference. These two frames mutually exclude each other, but they also complement each other, and only the juxtaposition of these contradictory frames provides an exhaustive view. . . . What we call Complementarity accords very neatly with the Cartesian dualism of matter and mind.*

Although this refers to classical dualism and not the plurality of levels proposed here, the analogy retains its attractiveness. The knowledge that an electron will behave as a particle or a wave, depending on the experimental set-up, makes it easier to accept that man too will, according to circumstances, function as an automaton or a conscious being.

Another Nobel laureate, Wolfgang Pauli, thought along similar lines:

> The general problem of the relationship between mind and body, between the inward and the outward, cannot be said to have been solved. . . . Modern science has perhaps brought us nearer to a more satisfactory understanding of this relationship by introducing the concept of complementarity into physics itself.†

One might add to these quotations almost any amount of similar pronouncements by the pioneers of contemporary physics. It is evident that they regard the parallel between the two types of complementarity – body/mind and corpuscle/wave – as more than a superficial analogy. It is, in fact, a very deep analogy, but in order to appreciate what it implies, we must try to get some inkling of what the physicist means by the "waves" which constitute one of the two aspects of matter. Commonsense, that treacherous counsellor, tells us that to produce a wave, there must be something that waves – a vibrating piano-string, or undulating water, or air in motion. But the conception of "matter-waves" excludes by definition any medium with material attributes as a carrier of the wave. Thus we are faced with the task of imagining the vibration of a string but without the string, or the grin of the Cheshire cat but without the cat. We may, however, derive some comfort from the analogy between the two complementarities.

*W. Heisenberg, *Der Teil und das Ganze* (Munich, 1969), p. 113.
†W. Pauli in *Naturerklärung und Psyche, Studien aus dem CG Jung-Institut, Zurich IV*, ed. Jung and Pauli (1952), p. 164.

The contents of consciousness that pass through the mind, from the perception of colour to thoughts and images, are un-substantial "airy nothings", yet they are somehow linked to the material brain, as the unsubstantial "waves" of physics are some-how linked to the material aspects of the sub-atomic particles.

It seems that the dual aspect of man reflects the dual aspect of the ultimate constituents of the universe.

The "spelling out" of an intention – whether it is the verbal articulation of an idea or just the stubbing out of a cigarette – is a process which triggers successive sub-routines into action – func-tional holons from arithmetical skills down to mechanical muscle-contractions: in other words, it is a process of *particular-isations* of a general intent. Vice versa, the referring of decisions to higher levels is an *integrative* process which tends to produce a higher degree of co-ordination and wholeness of the experience. How does the problem of free will fit into this schema?

We have seen that all our bodily and mental skills are governed by *fixed rules* and more or less *flexible strategies*. The rules of chess define the permissible moves, strategy determines the choice of the actual move. The problem of free will then boils down to the question how such choices are made. The chess player's choice may be called "free" in the sense that it is not determined by the rules. But though his choice is free in the above sense, it is certainly not random. On the contrary, it is guided by considerations of a much greater complexity – involving a higher level of the hierarchy – than the simple rules of the game. Com-pare the game of noughts and crosses with the game of chess. In both cases my strategic choice of the next move is "free" in the sense of not being determined by the rules. But noughts and crosses offer only a few alternative choices guided by relatively simple stategies, whereas the chess player is guided by considera-tions on a much higher level of complexity with an incomparably larger variety of choices – that is, *more degrees of freedom.**
Moreover, the strategic considerations which guide his choice again form an ascending hierarchy. On the lowest level are tacti-cal precepts such as occupying the centre squares of the chess-board, avoiding loss of material, protecting the king – precepts which every duffer can master, but which the master is free to

*The term "degrees of freedom" is used in physics to denote the number of independent variables defining the state of a system.

overrule by shifting his attention to higher levels of strategy where material may be sacrificed and the king exposed in an apparently crazy move which, however, is more promising from the viewpoint of the game as a whole. Thus in the course of the game decisions have to be constantly referred to higher echelons with more degrees of freedom, and each shift upward is accompanied by a heightening of awareness and the experience of making a free choice. Generally speaking, in these sophisticated domains the constraining code of rules (whether of chess or of the grammar of speech) operates more or less automatically, on unconscious or preconscious levels, whereas the strategic choices are aided by the beam of focal awareness.

To repeat: the degrees of freedom in the hierarchy increase with ascending order, and each upward shift of attention to higher levels, each handing over of a decision to higher echelons, is accompanied by *the experience of free choice*. But is it merely a subjective experience fraught with illusion?

I do not think this to be the case. After all, freedom cannot be defined in absolute, only in relative terms, as freedom *from* some specific constraint. The ordinary prisoner has more freedom than one in solitary confinement; democracy allows more freedom than tyranny; and so on. Similar gradations are found in the multi-levelled hierarchies of thought and action, where with each step upwards to a higher level *the relative importance of the constraints decreases and the number of choices increases*. But this does not mean that there is a highest level free from all constraints. On the contrary, the present theory implies that the hierarchy is *open-ended* towards infinite regress, both in the upward and downward direction. We tend to believe that the ultimate responsibility rests with the apex of the hierarchy – but that apex is never at rest, it keeps receding. The self eludes the grasp of its own awareness.

Facing downward and outward, a person is aware of the task in hand, an awareness that fades with each step down in the dimness of routine, the darkness of visceral processes, the various degrees of unawareness of the growing cabbage and the falling stone, and finally dissolves in the ambiguity of the Janus-faced electron.

But in the upward direction the hierarchy is also open-ended and leads into the infinite regress of the self. Looking upwards, or inwards, man has a feeling of wholeness, of a solid core to his personality from which his decisions emanate, and which in Penfield's words, "controls his thinking and directs the searchlight of his attention". But this metaphor of the great neurosurgeon is deceptive. When a priest chides a penitent for indulging in sinful thoughts, both priest and penitent tacitly assume that behind the agency which switches on the sinful thoughts, there is another agency which controls the switchboard, and so on *ad infinitum*.

The ultimate culprit, the self which directs the searchlight of my attention, can never be caught in its focal beam. The experiencing subject can never fully become the object of his experience; at best he can achieve successive approximations. If learning and knowing consist in making oneself a private model of the universe, it follows that the model can never include a complete model of itself, because it must always lag one step behind the process which it is supposed to represent. With each upward-shift of awareness towards the apex of the hierarchy – the self as an integrated whole – it recedes like a mirage. "Know thyself" is the most venerable and the most tantalising command. Total awareness of the self, the identity of the knower and the known, though always in sight is never achieved. It could only be achieved by reaching the peak of the hierarchy which is always one step removed from the climber.

This is an old conundrum, but it seems to blossom into new life in the context of the open-ended holarchy. Determinism fades away not only on the sub-atomic quantum level, but also in the upward direction, where on successively higher levels the constraints diminish, and the degrees of freedom increase, *ad infinitum*. At the same time the nightmarish concept of predictability and predestination is swallowed up in the infinite regress. Man is neither a plaything of the gods, nor a marionette suspended on his chromosomes. To put it more soberly, similar conclusions are implied in Sir Karl Popper's proposition that no information-processing system can embody within itself an up-to-date representation of itself, *including that representation.*[*] Somewhat similar arguments have been advanced by Michael Polanyi[†] and Donald MacKay.[‡]

Some philosophers dislike the concept of infinite regress because it reminds them of the little man inside the little man inside the little man. But we cannot get away from the infinite.

[*]Sir K. Popper in *Br. J. Phil. Sci*, Pt I and II (1950).
[†]M. Polanyi, *The Tacit Dimension* (New York, 1966).
[‡]D. M. MacKay in *Brain and Conscious Experience*, Sir J. Eccles, ed. (New York, 1966).

What would mathematics, what would physics be without the infinitesimal calculus? Self-consciousness has been compared to a mirror in which the individual contemplates his own activities. It would perhaps be more appropriate to compare it to a Hall of Mirrors where one mirror reflects one's reflection in another mirror, and so on. Infinity stares us in the face, whether we look at the stars or search for our own identities. Reductionism has no use for it, but a true science of life must let infinity in and never lose sight of it.

The problem of Free Will versus Determinism has haunted philosophers and theologians from time immemorial. Ordinary mortals are rarely bothered by the paradox concerning the agency which directs one's thinking, and of the agency behind that agency, because, paradoxical or not, they take it for granted that "I" am responsible for my actions. In *The Ghost in the Machine* I invented a short parable to illustrate the point. It took the form of a dialogue at high table at an Oxford college between an elderly don of strictly deterministic persuasion, and a young Australian guest of uninhibited temperament. The Australian exclaims: "If you go on denying that I am free to make my own decisions, I'll punch you in the nose!"

The old man gets red in the face: "I deplore your unpardonable behaviour."

"I apologise. I lost my temper."

"You really ought to control yourself."

"Thank you. The experiment was conclusive."

It was indeed. "Unpardonable", "ought to", and "control yourself" are all expressions which imply that the Australian's behaviour was *not* determined by his chromosomes and upbringing, that he was free to choose whether to behave politely or rudely. Whatever one's philosophical convictions, in everyday life it is impossible to carry on without the implicit belief in personal responsibility; and responsibility implies freedom of choice. The subjective experience of freedom is as much a given datum as the sensation of colour, or the feeling of pain.

Yet that experience is constantly being eroded by the formation of habits and mechanical routines, which tend to turn us into automata. When the Duke of Wellington was asked whether he agreed that habit was man's second nature he exclaimed: "Second nature? It is ten times nature." Habit is the denial of creativity and the negation of freedom; a self-imposed strait-jacket of which the wearer is unaware.

Another enemy of freedom is passion, or more specifically, an excess of the self-asserting emotions. When these are aroused, the control of behaviour is taken over by those primitive levels in the hierarchy which are correlated to the "old brain". The loss of freedom resulting from this downward shift is reflected in the legal concept of "diminished responsibility", and in the subjective feeling of acting under a compulsion – expressed by colloquialisms such as: "I couldn't help it", "I lost my head", "I must have been out of my mind".

It is at this point that the moral dilemma of judging others arises. Ruth Ellis was the last woman to be hanged in England – for shooting her lover "in cold blood", as it was said. How am I to know, and how could the jury know, whether and to what extent her responsibility was "diminished" when she acted as she did, and whether she could "help it"? Compulsion and free will are philosophical concepts at opposite ends of a scale, but there is no pointer attached to the scale which I could read. In dilemmas like this the safest procedure is to apply two different standards: to ascribe a minimum of free will to the other, and a maximum to oneself. There is an old French saying: *Tout comprendre c'est tout pardonner* – to understand all is to forgive all. In the light of the above, this should be altered to: *Tout comprendre, ne rien se pardonnner*: understand all – forgive yourself nothing.

It may be difficult to live up to, but at least it is a safe maxim.

Chapter 41

THE GROUP MIND

In The Gladiators, *the lawyer and philosopher, Fulvius of Capua,
is engaged in writing a history of the Slave Revolt. Bitterly disappointed with the irrational behaviour of the Capuan slaves, he
pens the title of his next chapter:*

ON THE CAUSES WHICH INDUCE MAN TO ACT CONTRARY TO
HIS OWN INTERESTS

But as soon as he had written this, he realised that it was incorrect; he
remembered the numerous cases he had conducted in the Courts,
recalled the tenacity and artfulness of his clients guarding their interests, ever ready to hound their neighbours to dungeon or scaffold for
the sake of one stolen goat.

*Through his window comes the hubbub of a marching crowd:
slaves off to the ramparts to fight "in serene enthusiasm" for their
tormentors and against their liberators. He crosses out his previous heading and writes instead:*

ON THE CAUSES WHICH INDUCE MAN TO ACT CONTRARY TO THE
INTERESTS OF OTHERS WHEN ALONE, AND TO ACT CONTRARY TO
HIS OWN INTERESTS WHEN ASSOCIATED IN GROUPS OR CROWDS

A long while he brooded over this first phrase, but nothing more
occurred to him.

*The lawyer Fulvius, and his bewildered creator, had good reason
to brood over this question. Almost exactly two thousand years
after the suicidal folly of the ignorant slaves of Capua, the well-
educated citizens of the mightiest nation in Europe voted with
"serene enthusiasm" a maniac into power who brought unprecedented disaster on their heads. The closer one looked at history,
the more clearly the suicidal pattern repeated itself. And the more*

one listened to politicians and social scientists, the clearer it
became that they had no explanations to offer for the paranoid
trend running through human history, and no basic remedy for
man's predicament.

The Sleepwalkers and The Act of Creation were devoted to art
and discovery, the creative side of the human mind. But the voice
of the little Roman lawyer kept repeating his unanswered question and refused to be silenced. So in the latter part of The Ghost
in the Machine, the emphasis shifted from the creative to the
destructive and self-destructive aspect of the human condition.
To quote from the Preface:

In a previous book, The Act of Creation, I discussed art and
discovery, the glory of man. The present volume ends with a
discussion of the predicament of man, and thus completes a cycle.
The creativity and pathology of the human mind are, after all, two
sides of the same medal coined in the same evolutionary mint.
The first is responsible for the splendour of our cathedrals, the
second for the gargoyles that decorate them to remind us that the
world is full of monsters, devils and chimeras. They reflect the
streak of insanity which runs through the history of our species,
and which indicates that somewhere along the line of its ascent to
prominence something has gone wrong. Evolution has been compared to a labyrinth of blind alleys, and there is nothing very
strange or improbable in the assumption that man's native
equipment, though superior to that of any other living species,
nevertheless contains some built-in error or deficiency which
predisposes him towards self-destruction.

Since we are dealing with the two sides of the same medal, it is
perhaps not surprising that certain manifestations of man's creative side should yield essential clues to the understanding of his
pathological side. I am referring in particular to his power to
create illusion, and his proneness to succumb to it, as exemplified by the magic of the stage. The extracts which follow* will
make this clearer.

You watch a filmed version of The Moor of Venice. You com-
miserate with Desdemona: as a result the perfidious Iago makes
your blood boil. Yet the psychological process which causes the

*The extracts in this chapter are compiled from The Ghost in the Machine, Part
Three, and Janus, Part One.

boiling is quite different from facing a real opponent. You know that the people on the screen are merely actors, or rather electronic projections – and anyway the whole situation is no personal concern of yours. The adrenalin in your bloodstream is not produced by a primary biological drive or hypothetical killer-instinct. Your hostility to Iago is a *vicarious* kind of aggressivity, devoid of self-interest and derived from a previous process of empathy and identification. This act of identification *must come first*; it is the trigger or catalyst of your hatred of Iago.

To recapitulate: we are faced with a process in two steps. At the first step, the self-transcending impulses of empathy, participation, indentification *inhibit* the self-assertive tendencies, purge us of our self-centred worries and desires. This leads to the second step: the process of loving identification may *stimulate* – or trigger off – the surge of hatred, fear, vengefulness, which, though experienced on behalf of another person, or group of persons, nevertheless increases the pulse rate. The physiological processes which these vicarious emotions activate are essentially the same whether the threat or insult is directed at oneself or at the person or group with whom one identifies. They belong to the self-assertive category, although the self has momentarily changed its address – by being, for instance, projected into the guileless heroine on the stage; or the local soccer team; or "my country, right or wrong".

It is a triumph of the imaginative powers of the human mind that we are capable of shedding tears over the death of Anna Karenina, who only exists as printer's ink on paper, or as a shadow on the screen; and capable of manufacturing large quantities of adrenalin to provide the hero on the stage with the required vigour to fight his adversaries.

Art is a school of self-transcendence. So is a voodoo session or a Nazi rally.

*   *   *

From the dawn of civilisation, there has never been a shortage of inspired reformers. Hebrew prophets, Greek philosophers, Chinese sages, Indian mystics, Christian saints, French humanists, English utilitarians, German moralists, American pragmatists, Hindu pacifists, have denounced wars and violence and appealed to man's better nature, without much success. The reason for this failure may be the common fallacy among reformers of putting all the blame on man's selfishness, greed and alleged destructiveness; that is to say, on the *self-assertive tendency* of the individual. Nothing could be more mistaken, as the historical evidence shows.

No historian would deny that the part played by crimes committed for personal motives is very small compared to the vast populations slaughtered in unselfish loyalty to a jealous god, king, country, or political system. The crimes of Caligula shrink to insignificance compared to the havoc wrought by Torquemada. The number of people killed by robbers, highwaymen, gangsters and other asocial elements is negligible compared to the masses cheerfully slain in the name of the true religion, the sacred cause. Heretics were tortured and burned alive not in anger but in sorrow, for the good of their immortal souls. The Russian and Chinese purges were represented as operations of social hygiene, to prepare mankind for the golden age of the classless society. The gas chambers and crematoria worked towards the advent of a different type of millennium. To say it once more: throughout human history, the ravages caused by excesses of individual self-assertion are quantitatively negligible compared to the numbers slain *ad majorem gloriam* out of a self-transcending devotion to a flag, a leader, a religious faith or political conviction. Man has always been prepared not only to kill, but also to die for good, bad, or completely hair-brained causes. What can be a more valid proof for the reality of the urge towards self-transcendence?

Thus the historical record confronts us with the paradox that the tragedy of man originates not in his aggressiveness but in his devotion to transpersonal ideals; not in an excess of individual self-assertiveness but in a malfunction of the integrative tendencies in our species. But how did this paradox arise?

Among the various pathogenic factors to be discussed, the first that comes instantly to mind is the protracted period of infancy in homo sapiens:

The human infant is subjected to a longer period of helplessness and total dependence on the adults who rear it than the young of any other species. This protracted experience may be at the root of the adult's ready submission to authority, and his quasi-hypnotic suggestibility by doctrines and ethical commandments – his urge to *belong*, to identify himself with a group, or its leader, or its system of beliefs.

We can distinguish three overlapping factors in these

pathogenic manifestations: *submission* to the authority of a father-substitute; unqualified *identification* with a social group; uncritical *acceptance of its belief-system*. All three are reflected in the gory annals of our history.

The leader-follower relationship can embrace a whole nation, as in the case of the Hitler cult; or a small sect of devotees; or be confined to a duet as in the hypnotic rapport, or the psychotherapist's couch, or in the Father Confessor's curtained box. The common element is the act of *surrender*.

When we turn to the second and third factors mentioned above – the unqualified identification of an individual with a social group and its system of beliefs – we have a wide variety of social aggregations which can be designated as "groups", and described in terms of "group-mentality" or *Massenpsychologie*. But this branch of psychology tended to concentrate its attention on extreme forms of group behaviour such as the outbreaks of mass-hysteria in the Middle Ages, or Le Bon's classic studies of the behaviour of the heroic and murderous mobs unleashed by the French Revolution (which Freud and others took as their text). This tendency to focus attention on the dramatic manifestations of mass-psychology made them overlook the more general principles underlying group mentality and its dominant influence on human history, past and present. Thus they failed to realise that a person need not be physically present in a crowd to be affected by the group-mind; emotive identification with a nation, Church or political movement can be quite effective without physical contact. One can be a victim of group-fanaticism even in the privacy of one's bathroom.

Nor does every group need a personal leader or father-figure in whom authority is vested. Religious and political movements need leaders to get under way; once established they still benefit from efficient leadership; but the primary need of a group, the factor which lends it cohesion as a social holon, is a credo, a shared system of beliefs, and the resulting code of behaviour. This may be represented by human authority, or by a symbol – the totem or fetish which provides a mystic sense of union among the members of the tribe; by sacred icons or the regimental flag to which soldiers in battle were supposed to hang on even at the price of their lives. The group-mind may be governed by the conviction that the group represents a Chosen Race whose ancestors made a special covenant with God; or a Master Race whose forebears were blond demi-gods; or whose Emperors were descended from the sun. Its credo may be based on the conviction that observance of certain rules and rites qualifies one for membership in a privileged élite in after-life; or that manual work qualifies one for membership in the élite class of history. Critical arguments have little impact on the group-mind, because identification with a group always involves a certain sacrifice of the critical faculties of the individuals which constitute it, and an enhancement of their emotional potential by a kind of group-resonance or positive feedback.

Let me repeat that in the present theory the term "group" is not confined to a crowd assembled in one place, but refers to any social holon, governed by a set code of rules (language, traditions, customs, beliefs, etc.) which defines its corporate identity, lends it cohesion and a "social profile". As an autonomous holon, it has its own pattern of functioning and is governed by its own code of conduct, which cannot be "reduced" to the individual codes which govern the behaviour of its members when acting as individuals and not as parts of the group. The obvious example is the conscript who as an individual is forbidden to kill, as a disciplined member of his unit is in duty bound to do so. Thus it is essential to distinguish between the rules which govern individual behaviour and those which guide the behaviour of the group as a whole.

The group, then, is to be regarded as a quasi-autonomous holon, not simply as a sum of its individual parts; and its activities depend not only on the interactions of its parts, but also on the group's interactions, as a whole, with other social holons. These interactions will again reflect the polarity of the holon's self-assertive and integrative tendencies, oscillating between competition and/or co-operation with other groups. In a healthy social holarchy the two tendencies are in equilibrium; but when tensions arise, this or that social holon may impose upon its rivals or usurp the role of the whole. History provides a never-ending list of such tensions, confrontations and conflicts.

All that has been said points to the conclusion that in the group-mind the self-assertive tendencies are more dominant than on the level of the average individual; and that, by identifying himself with the group, the individual adopts a code of behaviour different from his personal code. The individual – pace Lorenz – is not a killer, the group is; and by identifying with it, the individual is transformed into a killer. The paradox derives from the fact that the act of identification with the group is a self-

transcending act, yet it reinforces the *self-assertive* tendencies of the group. Identification with the group is an act of devotion, of loving submission to the interests of the community, a partial or total surrender of personal identity and of the self-assertive tendencies of the individual. In our terminology, *he relinquishes his "wholeness" in favour of his "partness"* in a larger whole on a higher level of the holarchy. He becomes to some extent depersonalised, i.e., unself-ish in more than one sense. He may become indifferent to danger; he feels impelled to perform altruistic, even heroic actions to the point of self-sacrifice, and at the same time to behave with ruthless savagery towards the enemy – real or imagined – of the group. But his brutality is impersonal and unselfish; it is exercised in the interest, or supposed interest of the whole; he is prepared not only to kill, but also to die in its name. Thus the self-assertive behaviour of the group is based on the self-transcending behaviour of its members; or to put it simply, *the egotism of the group feeds on the altruism of its members*.

The "infernal dialectics" of this process is reflected on every level of the various social holarchies. Patriotism is the noble virtue of subordinating individual interests to the interests of the nation; yet it gives rise to chauvinism, the militant expression of those higher interests. Loyalty to the clan produces clannishness; *esprit de corps* blossoms into arrogant cliquishness; religious fervour into zealotry; the Sermon on the Mount into the Church militant.

Both the historical record and the headlines of the daily paper testify to the infernal dialectics in man's condition. It is not, as the facile catch-phrase goes, his "innate aggressiveness" (i.e., his self-assertive tendency) which transforms harmless citizens into killers, but their self-transcending devotion to a cause. It is *the integrative tendency acting as a vehicle or catalyst* which induces the change of morality, the abrogation of personal responsibility, the replacement of the individual's code of behaviour by the code of the "higher component" in the hierarchy. In the course of this fatal process, the individual becomes to a certain extent depersonalised; he no longer functions as an autonomous holon or part-whole, but merely as a part. Janus no longer has two faces – only one is left, looking upward in holy rapture or in a moronic daze. To quote Professor Stanley Milgram's remarkable book *Obedience to Authority*:*

---

*(New York, 1974). Milgram's highly original experiments on blind obedience are described at length in *Janus*, pp. 83–90.

This is a fatal flaw nature has designed into us, and which in the long run gives our species only a modest chance of survival.

It is ironic that the virtues of loyalty, discipline, and self-sacrifice that we value so highly in the individual are the very properties that create destructive organisational engines of war and bind men to malevolent systems of authority. . . .*

Throughout recorded history, human societies have always been fairly successful in restraining the *self-assertive* tendencies of the individual – until the howling little savage in its cot became transformed into a more or less law-abiding and civilised member of society. The same historical record testifies to mankind's tragic inability to induce a parallel sublimation of the *integrative tendency*. Yet, to say it again, both the glory and the pathology of the human condition derive from our powers of self-transcendence, which are equally capable of turning us into artists, saints or killers, but more likely into killers. Only a small minority is capable of canalising the self-transcending urges into creative channels. For the vast majority, throughout history, the only fulfilment of its need to belong, its craving for communion, was identification with clan, tribe, nation, Church, or party, submission to its leader, worship of its symbols, and child-like acceptance of its emotionally saturated system of beliefs. Thus we are faced with a contrast between the mature restraint of the self-assertive tendency and the immature vagaries of the integrative tendency, strikingly revealed whenever the group-mind takes over from the individual mind.

To put it in the simplest way: the individual who indulges in an excess of aggressive self-assertion incurs the penalties of society – he outlaws himself, he contracts *out* of the hierarchy. The true believer, on the other hand, becomes more closely knit *into it*; he enters the womb of his Church or party, or whatever social holon to which he surrenders his identity.

This leads us to a basic distinction between primitive or infantile forms of *identification*, and mature forms of *integration* into a social holarchy. In a well-balanced holarchy, the individual retains his character as a social holon, a part-whole who, *qua* whole, enjoys autonomy within the limits of the restraints imposed by the interests of the group. He remains an autonomous whole in his own right, and is even expected to assert his holistic attributes by originality, initiative and, above all, personal responsibility. The same considerations apply to the social

*Milgram, op. cit., p. 188.

holons on the higher levels of the hierarchy – clans and tribes, ethnic and religious communities, professional groups and political parties. They, too, ought ideally to display the virtues implied in the Janus principle: to function as autonomous wholes and at the same time to conform to the national interest; and so on, upwards, level by level, to the world community at the apex of the pyramid. An ideal society of this kind would possess "*hierarchic awareness*", every holon on every level being conscious both of its rights as a whole and its duties as a part.

Needless to say, the mirror of history, past and present, confronts us with a different picture.

Those dramatic manifestations of mass-hysteria which so much impressed Freud and Le Bon I have only mentioned in passing, because I meant to focus attention on the process of "normal" group-formation and its devastating effects on the history of our species. This "normal" process, as we have seen, involves identification with the group, and acceptance of its beliefs. An important side-effect of the process is to deepen the *split between emotion and reason*. For the group-mind is dominated by a system of beliefs, traditions, moral imperatives, with a high emotive potential regardless of its rational content; and quite frequently its explosive power is enhanced by its very irrationality. Faith in the group's credo is an emotional commitment; it anaesthetises the individual's critical faculties and rejects rational doubt as something evil. Moreover, individuals are endowed with minds of varying complexity, while the group must be single-minded if it is to maintain its cohesion as a holon. Consequently, the group-mind must function on an intellectual level accessible to all its members: single-mindedness must be simple-minded. The overall result of this is the *enhancement* of the emotional dynamics of the group and simultaneous *reduction* of its intellectual faculties: a sad caricature of the ideal of hierarchic awareness.

I mentioned earlier the *paranoid streak* which runs through our History. Enlightened people may be quite willing to admit that such a streak existed among the head-hunters of Papua or in the Aztec kingdom, where the number of young men, virgins and children sacrificed to the gods amounted to between 20,000 and 50,000 *per annum*. "In this state of things," commented Prescott,

... it was beneficially ordered by Providence that the land should be delivered over to another race, who would rescue it from the brutish superstitions that daily extended wider and wider. . . . The debasing institutions of the Aztecs furnish the best apology for their conquest. It is true, the conquerors brought along with them the Inquisition. But they also brought Christianity, whose benign radiance would still survive, when the fierce flames of fanaticism should be extinguished. . . .*

Prescott must have known, though, that shortly after the Mexican conquest, the "benign radiance" of Christianity manifested itself in the Thirty Years War, which killed off a goodly proportion of Europe's population. And so on to Auschwitz and Gulag. Yet even clear-sighted people who recognise the mental disorder underlying these horrors are apt to dismiss them as phenomena of the past. It is not easy to love humanity and yet to admit that the paranoid streak, in different guises, is as much in evidence in contemporary history as it was in the distant past, but more potentially deadly in its consequences; and that it is not accidental but inherent in the human condition.

The symptoms vary with time, but the underlying pattern of the disorder is the same: the split between faith and reason, rational thought and irrational beliefs. Religious beliefs are derived from ever-recurrent archetypal motifs, which seem to be shared by all mankind and evoke instant emotive responses.† But once they become institutionalised as the collective property of a specific group, they degenerate into rigid doctrines which, without losing their emotive appeal, are potentially offensive to the critical faculties. To paste over the split, various forms of double-think have been designed at various times – powerful techniques of self-deception, some crude, some extremely sophisticated. The same fate has befallen the secular religions which go by the name of political ideologies. They too have their archetypal roots – the craving for Utopia, for an ideal society; but when they crystallise into movements and parties, they can become distorted to such an extent that the actual policy they pursue is the direct opposite of their professed ideal. This apparently inevitable tendency of both religious and secular ideologies to degenerate into their own caricatures is a direct consequence of the characteristics of the group-mind: its need for intellectual simplicity combined with emotional arousal.

*O. Prescott, The Conquest of Mexico (New York, 1964), p. 62.
†See, for instance, William James's The Varieties of Religious Experience, still a classic in this field. A more recent treatment is offered by Sir Alister Hardy in The Divine Flame and The Biology of God.

PART FOUR

THE URGE TO SELF-DESTRUCTION

Chapter 42

AFTER HIROSHIMA

As the nineteen-sixties were drawing to a close, it became increasingly difficult not to give in to despair regarding the future of mankind. The 1969 Nobel Symposium in Stockholm provided an opportunity to summarise some of the more alarming conclusions reached in The Ghost in the Machine. *This chapter is based on a paper read at that symposium (with some additions from* The Ghost in the Machine, *Part Three, and* Janus, *Part One).*

If I were asked to name the most important date in the history of the human race, I would answer without hesitation, August 6, 1945. The reason is simple. From the dawn of consciousness until August 6, 1945, man had to live with the prospect of his death as an *individual*; since the day when the first atomic bomb outshone the sun over Hiroshima, mankind as a whole has had to live with the prospect of its extinction as a *species*.

We have been taught to accept the transitoriness of personal existence, while taking the potential immortality of the human race for granted. This belief has ceased to be valid. We have to revise our axioms.

It is not an easy task. There are periods of incubation before a new idea takes hold of the mind; the Copernican doctrine which so radically downgraded man's status in the universe took nearly a century until it penetrated European consciousness. The new downgrading of our species to the status of mortality is even more difficult to digest.

It actually looks as if the novelty of this outlook had worn off even before it had properly sunk in. Already the name Hiroshima has become a historical cliché like the Boston Tea Party. We have returned to a state of pseudo-normality. Only a small minority is conscious of the fact that ever since it unlocked the nuclear Pandora's Box, our species has been living on borrowed time.

Every age had its Cassandras, yet mankind managed to survive their sinister prophecies. However, this comforting reflection is no longer valid, for in no earlier age did a tribe or nation possess the necessary equipment to make this planet unfit for life. They could inflict only limited damage on their adversaries – and did so, whenever given a chance. Now they can destroy the entire biosphere.

The trouble is that an invention, once made, cannot be disinvented. The nuclear weapon has come to stay; it has become part of the human condition. Man will have to live with it permanently: not only through the next confrontation-crisis and the one after that; not only through the next decade or century, but forever – that is, as long as mankind survives. The indications are that it will not be for very long.

There are two main reasons which point to this conclusion. The first is technical: as the devices of nuclear warfare become more potent and easier to make, their spreading to young and immature as well as old and arrogant nations becomes inevitable, and global control of their manufacture impracticable. Within the foreseeable future they will be made and stored in large quantities all over the globe among nations of all colours and ideologies, and the probability that a spark which initiates the chain-reaction will be ignited sooner or later, deliberately or by accident, will increase accordingly, until, in the long run, it approaches certainty. One might compare the situation to a gathering of delinquent youths locked in a room full of inflammable material who are given a box of matches – with the pious warning not to use it.

The second main reason which points to a low life-expectancy for homo sapiens in the post-Hiroshima era is the paranoid streak revealed by his past record. A dispassionate observer from a more advanced planet who could take in human history from Cro-Magnon to Auschwitz at a single glance, would no doubt come to the conclusion that our race is in some respects an admirable, in the main, however, a very sick biological product; and that the consequences of its mental sickness far outweigh its cultural achievements when the chances of prolonged survival are considered. The most persistent sound which reverberates through man's history is the beating of war drums. Tribal wars, religious wars, civil wars, dynastic wars, national wars, revolutionary wars, colonial wars, wars of conquest and of liberation, wars to prevent wars, follow each other in a chain of compulsive repetitiveness as far as man can remember his past, and there is every reason to believe that the chain will extend into the future. In the first twenty years of the post-Hiroshima era, between the years 0 and 20 p.H. – or 1946–66 according to our outdated calendar – forty wars fought with conventional weapons were tabulated by the Pentagon;* and at least on two occasions – Berlin 1950 and Cuba 1962 – we have been on the brink of nuclear war. If we discard the comforts of wishful thinking, we must expect that the focal areas of potential conflict will continue to drift across the globe like high-pressure regions over a meteorological chart. And the only precarious safeguard against the escalating of local into total conflict, mutual deterrence, will, by its very nature, always remain dependent on the restraint or recklessness of fallible key individuals and fanatical regimes. Russian roulette is a game which cannot be played for long.

The most striking indication of the pathology of our species is the contrast between its unique technological achievements and its equally unique incompetence in the conduct of its social affairs. We can control the motions of satellites orbiting distant planets, but cannot control the situation in Northern Ireland. Man can leave the earth and land on the moon, but cannot cross from East to West Berlin. Prometheus reaches out for the stars with an insane grin on his face and a totem-symbol in his hand.

I have said nothing about the added terrors of biochemical warfare; nor about the population explosion, pollution, and so forth, which, however threatening in themselves, have unduly distracted the public's awareness from the one central, towering fact: that since the year 1945 our species has acquired the diabolic power to annihilate itself; and that, judging by its past record, the chances are that it will use that power in one of the recurrent crises in the not-too-distant future. The result would be the transformation of space-ship earth into a Flying Dutchman, drifting among the stars with its dead crew.

If this is the probable outlook, what is the point of going on with our piecemeal efforts to save the panda and prevent our rivers

*Time (New York) January 29, 1965.

from turning into sewers? Or making provisions for our grand-children? Or, if it comes to that, of going on writing this book? It is not a rhetorical question, as the general mood of disenchantment among the young indicates. But there are at least two good answers to it.

The first is contained in the two words "as if" which Hans Vaihinger turned into a once-influential philosophical system: "The Philosophy of As If".* Briefly, it means that man has no choice but to live by "fictions"; *as if* the illusory world of our senses represented ultimate Reality; *as if* he had a free will which made him responsible for his actions; *as if* there was a God to reward virtuous conduct, and so on. Similarly, the individual must live *as if* he were not under sentence of death, and humanity must plan for its future *as if* its days were not counted. It is only by virtue of these fictions that the mind of man fabricated a habitable universe, and endowed it with meaning.†

The second answer is derived from the simple fact that although our species now lives on borrowed time, from decade to decade as it were, and the signs indicate that it is drifting towards the final catastrophe, we are still dealing in probabilities and not in certainties. There is always a hope of the unexpected and the unforeseen. Since the year zero of the new calendar, man has carried a time-bomb fastened round his neck, and will have to listen to its ticking – now louder, now softer, now louder again – until it either blows up, or he succeeds in de-fusing it. Time is running short, history is accelerating along dizzy exponential curves, and reason tells us that the chances of a successful de-fusing operation before it is too late are slender. All we can do is to act *as if* there was still time for such an operation.

But the operation will require a more radical approach than UNO resolutions, disarmament conferences and appeals to sweet reasonableness. Such appeals have always fallen on deaf ears, from the time of the Hebrew prophets, for the simple reason that *homo sapiens* is not a reasonable being – for if he were, he would not have made such a bloody mess of his history.

The first step towards a possible therapy is a correct diagnosis of

---

*H. Vaihinger, *Die Philosophie des Als Ob* (1911, English tr. C. K. Ogden, London, 1924).
†Vaihinger's (1852–1933) philosophy should not be confused either with Phenomenalism or with American Pragmatism, though it has affinities with both.

what went wrong with our species. There have been countless attempts at such a diagnosis, invoking the Biblical Fall, or Freud's "death wish", or the "territorial imperative" of contemporary ethologists. None of these carried much conviction, because none of them started from the unpleasant hypothesis that *homo sapiens* may be an aberrant biological species, an evolutionary misfit, afflicted by an endemic disorder which sets it apart from all other animal species – just as language, science and art set it apart in a positive sense.

Evolution has made many mistakes; the fossil record is a waste-basket of the Chief Designer's discarded models. The evidence from man's past history and from contemporary brain-research both strongly suggest that at some point during the last explosive stages of the biological evolution of *homo sapiens* something went wrong; that there is a flaw, some potentially fatal engineering error built into our native equipment – more specifically, into the circuits of our nervous system – which would account for the streak of paranoia running through our history. This is the hideous but plausible hypothesis which any serious inquiry into man's condition has to face. The best intuitive diagnosticians – the poets – have kept telling us that man is mad and has always been so; but anthropologists, psychiatrists, and students of evolution do not take poets seriously and keep shutting their eyes to the evidence staring them in the face. This unwillingness to face reality is of course in itself an ominous symptom. It could be objected that a madman cannot be expected to be aware of his own madness. The answer is that he can, because he is not entirely mad the entire time. In their periods of remission, schizophrenics have written astonishingly lucid reports of their illness.

I shall now venture to propose a summary list of some of the outstanding pathological symptoms reflected in the disastrous history of our species, and then proceed from the symptoms to a discussion of their possible causes. I have confined the list of symptoms to four main headings.

1. In one of the early chapters of Genesis, there is an episode which has inspired many great paintings. It is the scene where Abraham ties his son to a pile of wood and prepares to cut his throat and burn him, out of sheer love of God. We are here faced with a striking phenomenon to which anthropologists have paid far too little attention: human sacrifice, the ritual killing of children, virgins, kings and heroes to placate and flatter gods con-

ceived in nightmare dreams. It was a ubiquitous ritual, which
persisted from the prehistoric dawn to the peak of pre-Columbian
civilisations, and in some parts of the world to the beginning of
our century. From South Sea islanders to the Scandinavian Bog
People, from the Etruscans to the Aztecs, these practices arose
independently in the most varied cultures, as manifestations of a
delusionary streak in the human psyche to which the whole
species was and is apparently prone. To dismiss the subject as a
sinister curiosity of the past, as is usually done, means to ignore
the universality of the phenomenon, the clues that it provides to
the paranoid element in man's mental make-up and its relevance
to his ultimate predicament.

2. *Homo sapiens* is virtually unique in the animal kingdom in
his lack of instinctive safeguards against the killing of con-
specifics – members of his own species. The "Law of the Jungle"
knows only one legitimate motive for killing: the feeding drive,
and only on condition that predator and prey belong to different
species. *Within* the same species competition and conflict between individuals or groups are settled by symbolic threat-
behaviour or ritualised duels which end with the flight or
surrender-gesture of one of the opponents, and hardly ever
involve lethal injury. The inhibitory forces – instinctive taboos –
against killing or seriously injuring con-specifics are as powerful
in most animals, including the primates, as the drives of hunger,
sex or fear. Man is alone (apart from some controversial phenomena among rats and ants) in practising intra-specific murder on
an individual and collective scale, in spontaneous or organised
fashion, for motives ranging from sexual jealousy to quibbles
about metaphysical doctrines. Intra-specific warfare in perma-
nence is a central feature of the human condition. It is embel-
lished by the infliction of torture in its various forms, from
crucifixion to electric shocks.*

3. The third symptom is closely linked to the two previous
ones: it is manifested in the chronic, quasi-schizophrenic split

*"Torture today is so widespread an instrument of political repression that we
can speak of the existence of 'Torture States' as a political reality of our times.
The malignancy has become epidemic and knows no ideological, racial or
economic boundaries. In over thirty countries, torture is systematically applied
to extract confessions, elicit information, penalise dissent and deter opposition
to repressive governmental policy. Torture has been institutionalised . . ." (Victor Jokel, Director, British Amnesty, in "Epidemic: Torture", Amnesty International, London n.d., *c.* 1975).

between reason and emotion, between man's rational faculties and his irrational, affect-bound beliefs.

4. Finally, there is the striking disparity between the growth-curves of science and technology on the one hand and of ethical conduct on the other; or, to put it differently, between the powers of the human intellect when applied to mastering the environment and its inability to maintain harmonious relationships within the family, the nation and the species at large. Roughly two and a half millennia ago, in the sixth century BC, the Greeks embarked on the scientific adventure which eventually carried us to the moon; that surely is an impressive growth-curve. But the sixth century BC also saw the rise of Taoism, Confucianism and Buddhism – the twentieth of Hitlerism, Stalinism and Maoism: there is no discernible growth-curve. As von Bertalanffy has put it:

> What is called human progress is a purely intellectual affair . . . not much development, however, is seen on the moral side. It is doubtful whether the methods of modern warfare are preferable to the big stones used for cracking the skull of the fellow-Neanderthaler. It is rather obvious that the moral standards of Laotse and Buddha were not inferior to ours. The human cortex contains some ten billion neurons that have made possible the progress from stone axe to airplanes and atomic bombs, from primitive mythology to quantum theory. There is no corresponding development on the instinctive side that would cause man to mend his ways. For this reason, moral exhortations, as proffered through the centuries by the founders of religion and great leaders of humanity, have proved disconcertingly ineffective.*

The list of symptoms could be extended. But I think that the four points I mentioned indicate the essence of the human predicament. They are of course inter-dependent; thus human sacrifice can be regarded as a sub-category of the schizophrenic split between reason and emotion, and the contrast between the growth-curves of technological and moral achievement can be regarded as a further consequence of it.

So far we have moved in the realm of facts, attested by the historical record and the anthropologist's research into prehistory. As we turn from *symptoms* to *causes* we must have recourse to more or less speculative hypotheses, which again are interrelated, but pertain to different disciplines, namely, neurophysiology, anthropology and psychology.

*L. von Bertalanffy in *Scientific Monthly*, January, 1956.

The neurophysiological hypothesis is derived from the so-called Papez-MacLean theory of emotions, supported by some thirty years of experimental research.* I have discussed it at length in *The Ghost in the Machine*, and shall confine myself here to a summary outline, without going into physiological details.

The theory is based on the fundamental differences in anatomy and function between the archaic structures of the brain which man shares with the reptiles and lower mammals, and the specifically human neocortex, which evolution superimposed on them – without, however, ensuring adequate co-ordination. The result of this evolutionary blunder is an uneasy coexistence, frequently erupting in acute conflict, between the deep ancestral structures of the brain, mainly concerned with instinctive and emotional behaviour, and the neocortex which endowed man with language, logic and symbolic thought. MacLean has summed up the resulting state of affairs in a technical paper, but in an unusually picturesque way:

> Man finds himself in the predicament that Nature has endowed him essentially with three brains which, despite great differences in structure, must function together and communicate with one another. The oldest of these brains is basically reptilian. The second has been inherited from the lower mammals, and the third is a late mammalian development, which . . . has made man peculiarly man. Speaking allegorically of these three brains within a brain, we might imagine that when the psychiatrist bids the patient to lie on the couch, he is asking him to stretch out alongside a horse and a crocodile.†

If we substitute for the individual patient mankind at large, and for the psychiatrist's couch the stage of history, we get a grotesque, but essentially truthful picture of the human condition.

In a more recent series of lectures on neurophysiology, MacLean offered another metaphor:

> In the popular language of today, these three brains might be thought of as biological computers, each with its own peculiar form of subjectivity and its own intelligence, its own sense of time and space and its own memory, motor and other functions. . . .‡

---

*Dr Paul D. MacLean is head of the Laboratory of Bran Evolution and Behavior, National Institute of Mental Health, Bethesda, Maryland.

†P. D. MacLean in *J. of Nervous and Mental Disease*, Vol. 135, No. 4 (October, 1962).

‡P. D. MacLean in *A Triune Concept of the Brain and Behavior*, ed. T. J. Boag and D. Campbell (Toronto, 1973).

The "reptilian" and "paleo-mammalian" brains together form the so-called limbic system which, for the sake of simplicity, we may call the "old brain", as opposed to the neocortex, the specifically human "thinking cap". But while the antediluvian structures at the very core of our brain, which control instincts, passions and biological drives, have been hardly touched by the nimble fingers of evolution, the neocortex of the hominids expanded in the last half a million years at an explosive speed which is without precedent in the history of evolution – so much so that some anatomists compared it to a tumorous growth.

This brain explosion in the second half of the Pleistocene seems to have followed the type of exponential curve which has recently become so familiar to us – population explosion, information explosion, etc. – and there may be more than a superficial analogy here, as all these curves reflect the phenomenon of the acceleration of history in various domains. But explosions do not produce harmonious results. The result in this case seems to have been that the rapidly developing thinking cap, which endowed man with his reasoning powers, did not become properly integrated and co-ordinated with the ancient emotion-bound structures on which it was superimposed with such unprecedented speed.

Thus the brain explosion gave rise to a mentally unbalanced species in which old brain and new brain, emotion and intellect, faith and reason, were at loggerheads. On one side, the pale cast of rational thought, of logic suspended on a thin thread all too easily broken; on the other, the raging fury of passionately held irrational beliefs, reflected in the holocausts of past and present history.

If neurophysiological evidence had not taught us the contrary, we would have expected it to reveal an evolutionary process which gradually transformed the primitive old brain into a more sophisticated instrument – as it transformed the forelimb of the reptilian ancestor into the bird's wing, the flipper of the whale, the hand of man. But instead of *transforming* old brain into new, evolution *superimposed* a new, superior structure on an old one with partly overlapping functions, and without providing the new brain with clear-cut power of control over the old.

To put it crudely: evolution has left a few screws loose between the neocortex and the hypothalamus. MacLean has coined the term *schizophysiology* for this endemic shortcoming in the human nervous system. He defines it as:

a dichotomy in the function of the phylogenetically old and new cortex that might account for differences between emotional and intellectual behaviour. While our intellectual functions are carried on in the newest and most highly developed part of the brain, our affective behaviour continues to be dominated by a relatively crude and primitive system, by archaic structures in the brain whose fundamental pattern has undergone but little change in the whole course of evolution from mouse to man.*

The hypothesis that this type of schizophysiology is part of our genetic inheritance, built into the species as it were, could go a long way towards explaining some of the pathological symptoms listed before. The chronic conflict between rational thought and irrational beliefs, the resulting paranoid streak in our history, the contrast between the growth-curves of science and ethics, would at last become comprehensible and could be expressed in physiological terms. And any condition which can be expressed in physiological terms should ultimately be accessible to remedies – as will be discussed later on. For the moment let us note that the origin of the evolutionary blunder which gave rise to man's schizophysiological disposition appears to have been the rapid, quasi-brutal *superimposition* (instead of *transformation*) of the neocortex on the ancestral structures and the resulting *insufficient co-ordination* between the new brain and the old, and *inadequate control* of the former over the latter.

It should be emphasised once more that to the student of evolution there is nothing improbable in the assumption that man's native equipment, though superior to that of any animal species, nevertheless contains some serious fault in the circuitry of that most precious and delicate instrument, the nervous system. When the biologist speaks of evolutionary "blunders", he does not reproach evolution for having failed to attain some theoretical ideal, but means something quite simple and precise: some obvious deviation from Nature's own standards of engineering efficiency, which deprives an organ of its effectiveness – like the monstrous antlers of the Irish elk, now defunct. Turtles and beetles are well protected by their armour, but it makes them so top-heavy that if in combat or by misadventure they fall on their back, they cannot get up again, and starve to death – a grotesque construction fault which Kafka turned into a symbol of the human predicament.

*P. D. MacLean in *Am. J. of Medicine*, Vol. XXV, No. 4 (October, 1958), pp. 611–26.

But the greatest mistakes occurred in the evolution of the various types of brain. Thus the invertebrates' brain evolved around the alimentary tube, so that if the neural mass were to evolve and expand, the alimentary tube would be more and more compressed (as happened to spiders and scorpions, which can only pass liquids through their gullets and have become blood-suckers). Gaskell, in *The Origin of Vertebrates*, commented:

> At the time when vertebrates first appeared, the direction and progress of variation in the Arthropoda was leading, owing to the manner in which the brain was pierced by the oesophagus, to a terrible dilemma – either the capacity for taking in food without sufficient intelligence to capture it, or intelligence sufficient to capture food and no power to consume it.*

And another great biologist, Wood Jones:

> Here, then, is an end to the progress in brain building among the invertebrates. ... The invertebrates made a fatal mistake when they started to build their brains around the oesophagus. Their attempt to develop big brains was a failure. ... Another start must be made.†

The new start was made by the vertebrates. But one of the main divisions of the vertebrates, the Australian marsupials (who, unlike us placentals, carry their unfinished newborn in pouches) again landed themselves in a cul-de-sac. Their brain is lacking a vital component, the *corpus callosum* – a conspicuous nerve tract which, in placentals, connects the right and left cerebral hemispheres.‡ Now recent brain research has discovered a fundamental division of functions in the two hemispheres which complement each other rather like Yin and Yang. Obviously the two hemispheres are required to work together if the animal (or man) is to derive the full benefit of their potentials. The absence of a *corpus callosum* thus signifies *inadequate co-ordination* between the two halves of the brain – a phrase which has an ominously familiar ring. It may be the principal reason why the evolution of the marsupials – though it produced many species which bear a striking resemblance to their placental cousins – finally got stuck on the evolutionary ladder at the level of the koala bear.

The marsupials and the arthropoda may serve as cautionary tales, which make it easier to accept the possibility that *homo*

*W. H. Gaskell, *The Origin of Vertebrates* (1908), pp. 65–7.
†F. Wood Jones and S. D. Porteus, *The Matrix of the Mind* (London, 1929), pp. 27–8.
‡More precisely, the higher (non-olfactory) functional areas.

sapiens, too, might be a victim of faulty brain design. We, thank God, have a solid *corpus callosum* which integrates the right and left halves, horizontally; but in the vertical direction, from the seat of conceptual thought to the spongy depths of instinct and passion, all is not so well. The evidence from the physiological laboratory, the tragic record of history on the grand scale, and the trivial anomalies in our everyday behaviour, all point towards the same conclusion.

Another approach to man's predicament starts [as already mentioned] from the fact that the human infant has to endure a longer period of helplessness and total dependence on its parents than the young of any other species. The cradle is a stricter confinement than the kangaroo's pouch; one might speculate that this early experience of dependence leaves its life-long mark, and is at least partly responsible for man's willingness to submit to authority wielded by individuals or groups, and his suggestibility by doctrines and moral imperatives. Brain-washing starts in the cradle.

The first suggestion the hypnotist imposes on his subject is that he should be open to the hypnotist's suggestions. The subject is being conditioned to become susceptible to conditioning. The helpless infant is subjected to a similar process. It is turned into a willing recipient of ready-made beliefs.* For the vast majority of mankind throughout history, the system of beliefs which they accepted, for which they were prepared to live and to die, was not of their own making or choice; it was shoved down their throats by the hazards of birth. *Pro patria mori dulce et decorum est*, whichever the *patria* into which the stork happens to drop you. Critical reasoning played, if any, only a secondary part in the process of adopting a faith, a code of ethics, a *Weltanschauung*; of becoming a fervent Christian crusader, a fervent Moslem engaged in Holy War, a Roundhead or a Cavalier. The continuous disasters in man's history are mainly due to his excessive capacity and urge to become identified with a tribe, nation, Church or cause, and to espouse its credo uncritically and enthusiastically, even if its tenets are contrary to reason, devoid of self-interest and detrimental to the claims of self-preservation.

*Konrad Lorenz talks of "imprinting", and puts the critical age of receptivity just after puberty (*On Aggression* [London, 1966]). He does not seem to realise that in man, unlike his geese, susceptibility for imprinting stretches from the cradle to the grave.

We are thus driven to the unfashionable conclusion that the trouble with our species is not an excess of *aggression*, but an excess capacity for fanatical *devotion*. Excepting a small minority of mercenary or sadistic disposition, wars are not fought for personal gain, but out of loyalty and devotion to king, country or cause. Homicide committed for personal reasons is a statistical rarity in all cultures, including our own. Homicide for unselfish reasons, at the risk of one's own life, is the dominant phenomenon in history.

At this point I must insert two brief polemical remarks:

Firstly, when Freud proclaimed *ex cathedra* that wars were caused by pent-up aggressive instincts in search of an outlet, people tended to believe him because it made them feel guilty, although he did not produce a shred of historical or psychological evidence for his claim. Anybody who has served in the ranks of an army can testify that aggressive feelings towards the enemy hardly play a part in the dreary routines of waging war. Soldiers do not hate. They are frightened, bored, sex-starved, homesick; they fight with resignation, because they have no other choice, or with enthusiasm for king and country, the true religion, the righteous cause – moved not by hatred but by *loyalty*. To say it once more, man's tragedy is not an excess of aggression, but an excess of devotion.

The second polemical remark concerns another theory which recently became fashionable among anthropologists, purporting that the origin of war is to be found in the instinctive urge of some animal species to defend at all costs their own stretch of land or water – the so-called "territorial imperative". It seems to me no more convincing than Freud's hypothesis. The wars of man, with rare exceptions, were not fought for individual ownership of bits of space. The man who goes to war actually *leaves* the home which he is supposed to defend, and does his shooting far away from it; and what makes him do it is not the biological urge to defend his personal acreage of farmland or meadows, but his devotion to symbols derived from tribal lore, divine commandments and political slogans. Wars are not fought for territory, but for words.

This brings us to the next item in our inventory of the possible causes of the human predicament. Man's deadliest weapon is *language*. He is as susceptible to being hypnotised by slogans as he is to infectious diseases. And when there is an epidemic, the

group-mind takes over. It obeys its own rules, which are different
from the rules of conduct of individuals. The main catalyst of that
transformation is the hypnotic power of the word. The words of
Adolf Hitler were the most powerful weapons of destruction at his
time. Even before the printing press was invented, the words of
Allah's chosen Prophet unleashed an emotive chain-reaction
which shook the world from Central Asia to the Atlantic coast.
Without words there would be no poetry – and no war. Language
is the main factor in our superiority over brother animal – and, in
view of its explosive emotive potentials, a constant threat to
survival.

This apparently paradoxical point is illustrated by recent
field-observations of Japanese monkey-societies which have
revealed that different tribes of a species may develop surprisingly different habits – one might almost say, different cultures.
Some tribes have taken to washing potatoes in the river before
eating them, others have not. Sometimes migrating groups of
potato-washers meet non-washers, and the two groups watch
each other's strange behaviour with apparent bewilderment. But
unlike the inhabitants of Lilliput, who fought holy crusades over
the question at which end to break the egg, the potato-washing
monkeys do not go to war with the non-washers, because the poor
creatures have no language which would enable them to declare
washing a divine commandment and eating unwashed potatoes a
deadly heresy.

Obviously the quickest way to abolish war would be to abolish
language, and Jesus seems to have been aware of this when he
said: "Let your communication be Yea, yea, Nay, nay, for anything beyond that cometh from the devil." And in a sense mankind *did* renounce language long ago, if by language we mean a
method of communication for the whole species. The Tower of
Babel is a timeless symbol. Other species do possess a single
method of communication – by signs, sounds or by secreting
odours – which is understood by all members of that species.
When a St Bernard meets a poodle they understand each other
without needing an interpreter, however different they look.
Homo sapiens, on the other hand, is split into some 3000 language
groups. Each language – and each dialect thereof – acts as a
cohesive force within the group and a divisive force between
groups. It is one of the reasons why the disruptive forces are so
much stronger than the cohesive forces in our history. Men show a
much greater variety in physical appearance and behaviour than

any other species (excepting the products of artificial breeding); and the gift of language, instead of bridging over these differences, erects further barriers and enhances the contrast. We have communication satellites which can convey a message to the entire population of the planet, but no *lingua franca* which would make it universally understood. It seems odd that, except for a few valiant Esperantists, neither UNESCO nor any international body has as yet discovered that the simplest way to promote understanding would be to promote a language that is understood by all.

The last item on my list of factors which could account for the pathology of our species is the *discovery of death* – or rather its discovery by the intellect and its rejection by instinct and emotion. It is yet another manifestation of man's split mind, perpetuating the divided house of faith and reason. Faith is the older and more powerful partner, and when conflict arises, the reasoning half of the mind is compelled to provide elaborate rationalisations to allay the senior partner's terror of the void. Yet not only the naive concept of "eternal bliss" (or eternal torment for the wicked) but also the more sophisticated parapsychological theories of survival present problems which are apparently beyond the reasoning faculties of our species. There may be millions of other cultures on planets that are millions of years older than ours, to whom death no longer is a problem; but the fact remains that, to use computer jargon, we are not "programmed" for the task. Confronted with a task for which it is not programmed, a computer is either reduced to silence, or it goes haywire. The latter seems to have happened, with distressing repetitiveness, in the most varied cultures. Faced with the intractable paradox of consciousness emerging from the pre-natal void and drowning in the post-mortem darkness, their minds went haywire and populated the air with the ghosts of the departed, gods, angels and devils, until the atmosphere became saturated with invisible presences which at best were capricious and unpredictable, but mostly malevolent and vengeful. They had to be worshipped, cajoled and placated by elaborately cruel rituals, including human sacrifice, Holy Wars and the burning of heretics.

For nearly two thousand years, millions of otherwise intelligent people were convinced that the vast majority of mankind who did not share their particular creed or did not perform their rites, were consumed by flames throughout eternity by order of a loving god.

Similar nightmarish fantasies were collectively shared by other cultures, testifying to the ubiquity of the paranoid streak in the race.

There is, once again, another side to the picture. The refusal to believe in the finality of death made the pyramids rise from the sand; it provided a set of ethical values, and the main inspiration for artistic creation. If the word "death" were absent from our vocabulary, the great works of literature would have remained unwritten. To say it once more: the creativity and pathology of man are two faces of the same medal, coined in the same evolutionary mint.

To sum up, the disastrous history of our species indicates the futility of all attempts at a diagnosis which do not take into account the possibility that *homo sapiens* is a victim of one of evolution's countless mistakes. The example of the arthropods and marsupials, among others, shows that such mistakes do occur and can adversely affect the evolution of the brain.

I have listed some conspicuous symptoms of the mental disorder which appears to be endemic in our species: (a) the ubiquitous rites of human sacrifice in the prehistoric dawn; (b) the persistent pursuit of intra-specific warfare which, while earlier on it could only cause limited damage, now puts the whole planet in jeopardy; (c) the paranoid split between rational thinking and irrational, affect-based beliefs; (d) the contrast between mankind's genius in conquering Nature and its ineptitude in managing its own affairs – symbolised by the new frontier on the moon and the minefields along the borders of Europe.

It is important to underline once more that these pathological phenomena are specifically and uniquely human, and not found in any other species. Thus it seems only logical that our search for explanations should also concentrate primarily on those attributes of *homo sapiens* which are exclusively human and not shared by the rest of the animal kingdom. But however obvious this conclusion may seem, it goes against the prevailing reductionist trend. "Reductionism" is the philosophical belief that all human activities can be "reduced" to – i.e., explained by – the behavioural responses of lower animals – Pavlov's dogs, Skinner's rats and pigeons, Lorenz's greylag geese, Morris's hairless apes; and that these responses in turn can be reduced to the physical laws which govern inanimate matter. No doubt Pavlov and Lorenz provided us with new insights into human nature –

but only into those rather elementary, non-specific aspects of human nature which we share with dogs, rats or geese, while the specifically and exclusively human aspects which define the uniqueness of our species are left out of the picture. And since these unique characteristics are manifested both in the creativity and pathology of man, scientists of the reductionist persuasion cannot qualify as competent diagnosticians. That is why the scientific establishment has so pitifully failed to define the predicament of man. If he is really an automaton, there is no point in putting a stethoscope to his chest.

The diagnostic approaches that I have briefly outlined, were: (a) the explosive growth of the human neocortex and its insufficient control of the old brain; (b) the protracted helplessness of the newborn and its consequent uncritical submissiveness to authority; (c) the twofold curse of language as a rabble-rouser and builder of ethnic barriers; (d) lastly, the discovery of, and the mind-splitting fear of death.

To neutralise these pathogenic tendencies does not seem an impossible task. Medicine has found remedies for certain types of schizophrenic and manic-depressive psychoses; it is no longer Utopian to believe that it will discover a combination of benevolent enzymes which provide the neocortex with a veto against the follies of the archaic brain, correct evolution's glaring mistakes, reconcile emotion with reason, and catalyse the breakthrough from maniac to man. Still other avenues are waiting to be explored and may lead to salvation in the nick of time, provided that there is a sense of urgency – and a correct diagnosis of the condition of man, based on a new approach to the sciences of life.

Chapter 43

ALTERNATIVES TO DESPAIR*

The Sleepwalkers, The Act of Creation *and* The Ghost in the Machine *form a trilogy on the evolution, creativity and pathology of the human mind. As I was writing the last chapter of* The Ghost in the Machine, *I strongly felt that it should not end on a note of despair. However, the only alternative to it which seemed to offer some hope – the "benevolent enzyme" – was of a nature which, I knew, would alienate even sympathetic readers. Hence the apologetic tone of the closing chapter of* The Ghost in the Machine, *and its "Plea to the Phantom Reader".*

As long as we believed that our species was potentially immortal, with an astronomical lifespan before it, we could afford to wait patiently for that evolutionary change in human nature which, gradually or suddenly, would make love and sweet reason prevail. But man's biological evolution came to a virtual standstill in Cro-Magnon days, 50,000 to 100,000 years ago. We cannot wait another 100,000 years for the unlikely chance mutation which will put things right; we can only hope to survive by *inventing techniques which supplant biological evolution.* That is to say, we must search for a cure for the schizophysiology endemic in our nature, which led to the situation in which we find ourselves. If we fail to find that cure, the old paranoid streak in man, combined with his new powers of destruction, must sooner or later lead to his extinction. But I also believe that the cure is not far beyond the reach of contemporary biology; and that with the proper concentration of efforts it might enable man to win the race for survival.

I am aware that this sounds over-optimistic, in contrast to the pessimistic views expressed in previous chapters, of the pros-

*From The Ghost in the Machine, *ch.* xviii, *with addenda from* Janus, *ch.* v.

pects ahead of us. Yet I do not think that these fears are exaggerated, and I do not think that the hope for a rescue is entirely Utopian. It is not inspired by science fiction, but based on recent advances in neuro-chemistry and related fields. They do not yet provide a cure for the mental disorder of our species, but they indicate the area of research that may eventually produce the remedy.

Yet I have learned from painful experience that any proposal which involves "tampering with human nature" is bound to provoke strong emotional resistances. These are partly based on ignorance and prejudice, but partly on a justified revulsion against further intrusions into the privacy and sanctity of the individual by social engineering, character engineering, various forms of brain-washing, and other threatening aspects of overt or covert totalitarianism. It hardly needs saying that I share this loathing for a nightmare in whose shadow most of my life was spent. But on the other hand it has to be realised that ever since the first cave-dweller wrapped his shivering frame into the hide of a dead animal, man has been, for better or worse, creating for himself an artificial environment and an artificial mode of existence without which he no longer can survive. There is no turning back on housing, clothing, artificial heating, cooked food; nor on spectacles, hearing aids, forceps, artificial limbs, anaesthetics, antiseptics, prophylactics, vaccines and so forth. We start tampering with human nature almost from the moment a baby is born, by the universal practice of dropping a solution of silver nitrate into its eyes as a protection against *opthalmia neonatorum*, a form of conjunctivitis often leading to blindness, caused by bacilli which lurk in the mother's genital tract. This is followed later by preventive vaccinations, compulsory in most civilised countries, against smallpox and other infectious diseases. To appreciate the value of these tamperings with the course of nature, let us remember that the epidemics of smallpox among American Indians were one of the main reasons why they lost their lands to the white man. It also decimated the population of Europe in the beginning of the seventeenth century – its ravages only equalled, perhaps symbolically, by the massacres, in the name of true religion, of the Thirty Years War.

A less well-known form of tampering, pertinent to our subject, is the prevention of goitre and the variety of cretinism associated with it. When I was a child, the number of people in Alpine mountain valleys with monstrous swellings in the front of their necks, and of cretinous children in their families was quite frightening. On recent trips, revisiting the same regions half a century later, I cannot remember having come across a single cretinous child. Thanks to the progress of biochemistry, it has been discovered that this type of cretinism was caused by a malfunction of the thyroid gland. This in turn was due to the shortage of iodine in the nutrients of the mountainous areas affected. Without sufficient iodine, the gland is unable to synthesize the required quantities of thyroid hormones, with tragic consequences for the mind. Thus iodine in small quantities was added by the health authorities to the common table salt, and goitrous cretinism in Europe became virtually a thing of the past.

Obviously, our species does not possess the biological equipment needed to live in environments with iodine-poor soil, or to cope with the micro-organisms of malaria and smallpox. Nor does it possess instinctual safeguards against excessive breeding: ethologists tell us that every animal species they have studied – from flower beetles through rabbits to baboons – is equipped with such instinctual controls, which inhibit excessive breeding and keep the population density in a given territory fairly constant, even when food is plentiful. When the density reaches a critical limit, crowding produces stress which affects the hormonal balance and interferes with lifespan and reproductive behaviour. Thus there is a kind of feedback mechanism which adjusts the rate of breeding and keeps the population at a more or less stable level. The population of a given species in a given territory behaves in fact as a self-regulating social holon.

But in this respect, too, man is a biological freak, who, somewhere along the way, lost this instinctual control-mechanism. It seems almost as if in human populations the ecological rule were reversed: the more crowded they are in slums, ghettoes and poverty-stricken areas, the faster they breed. What prevented the population from exploding much earlier in history was not the kind of automatic feedback control which we observe in animals, but the death-harvest of wars, epidemics, pestilence and infant mortality. These were factors beyond the control of the masses; but nevertheless conscious attempts to regulate the birthrate through contraception and infanticide are on record from the very dawn of history. (The oldest recipes to prevent conception are contained in the so-called Petri Papyrus, dating from about 1850 BC.) Birth control through infanticide was also common from ancient Sparta to quite recently among Eskimos. Compared to these cruel methods, the modern ways of directly "tampering with Nature" by intra-uterine coils and oral contraceptives are certainly preferable. Yet they interfere in a radical and permanent manner with the vital physiological processes of the oestrous cycle. Applied on a world-wide scale they would amount to the equivalent of an artificially induced adaptive mutation.

There is no end to the list of beneficial "tamperings with human nature", compared to which the abuses and occasional follies of medicine and psychiatry shrink to relative insignificance. What the sum total of these tamperings amounts to is in fact *correcting* human nature, which without these correctives would in its *biological* aspect hardly be viable, and which in its *social* aspect, after countless disasters, is heading for the ultimate catastrophe. Having conquered the worst of the infectious diseases which assail the body of man, the time has come to look for methods to immunise him against the infectious delusions which from time immemorial have assailed the group-mind and made a blood-bath of his history. Neuropharmacology has given us lethal nerve-gases, drugs for brain-washing, others to induce hallucinations and delusions at will. *It can and will be put to beneficial use.* Let me quote a single example of the type of research pointing in that direction:

In 1961 the University of California San Francisco Medical Centre organised an international symposium on *Control of the Mind*. At the first session, Professor Holger Hyden of Gothenburg University made headlines in the Press with his paper – "Biochemical Aspects of Brain Activity". Hyden is one of the leading authorities in that field. The passage which created the sensation is quoted below (the reference to me is explained by the fact that I was a participant at the symposium):

> In considering the problem of control of the mind, the data give rise to the following question: would it be possible to change the fundamentals of emotion by inducing molecular changes in the biologically active substances in the brain? The RNA,* in particular, is the main target for such a speculation, since a molecular change of the RNA may lead to a change in the proteins being formed. One may phrase the question in different words to modify the emphasis: do the experimental data presented here provide means to modify the mental state by specifically induced chemical changes? Results pointing in that direction have been obtained; this work was carried out using a substance called tricyano-aminopropene.

*Ribonucleic acid, a key substance in the genetic apparatus.

... The application of a substance changing the rate of production and composition of RNA and provoking enzyme changes in the functional units of the central nervous system has both negative and positive aspects. There is now evidence that the administration of tricyano-aminopropene is followed by an *increased suggestibility* in man. This being the case, a defined change of such a functionally important substance as the RNA in the brain could be used for conditioning. The author is not referring specifically to tricyano-aminopropene, but to any substance inducing changes of biologically important molecules in the neurons and the glia and affecting the mental state in a negative direction. It is not difficult to imagine the possible uses to which a government in a police-controlled state could put this substance. For a time they would subject the population to hard conditions. Suddenly the hardship would be removed, and at the same time, the substance would be added to the tap water and the mass-communications media turned on. This method would be much cheaper, and would create more intriguing possibilities than to let Ivanov treat Rubashov individually for a long time, as Koestler described in his book. On the other hand, a counter-measure against the effect of a substance such as tricyano-aminopropene is not difficult to imagine either.*

The last sentence is formulated with caution, but the implications are clear. However shocking this may sound, if our sick species is to be saved, salvation will come, not from UNO resolutions and diplomatic summits, but from the biological laboratories. It stands to reason that a biological malfunction needs a biological corrective.

It would be naive to expect that drugs can present the mind with gratis gifts, and put into it something which is not already there. Neither mystic insights, nor philosophical wisdom, nor creative power can be provided by pill or injection. The biochemist cannot *add* to the faculties of the brain – but he can *eliminate* obstructions and blockages which impede their proper use. He cannot put additional circuits into the brain, but he can improve coordination between existing ones and enhance the power of the neocortex – the apex of the hierarchy – over the lower, emotion-bound levels and the "blind passions" engendered by them. Our present tranquillisers, barbiturates, stimulants, anti-depressants and combinations thereof are merely a first step towards more sophisticated aids to promote a balanced state of mind, immune

*H. Hyden in *Control of the Mind*, ed. S. M. Farber and R. H. L. Wilson (New York, 1961).

against the sirens' song, the barking of demagogues and false Messiahs. Not the Pop-Nirvana procured by LSD or the *soma* pills of *Brave New World*, but a state of dynamic equilibrium in which the divided house of faith and reason is reunited and hierarchic order restored.

I first published these hopeful speculations – as the only alternative to despair that I could (and can) see – in the concluding chapter of *The Ghost in the Machine*. Among the many negative criticisms which it brought in its wake, the one most frequently voiced accused me of proposing the manufacture of a little pill which would suppress all feeling and emotion and reduce us to the equanimity of cabbages. This charge, sometimes uttered with great vehemence, was based on a complete misreading of the text. What I proposed was not the castration of emotion, but *reconciling* emotion and reason which through most of man's schizophrenic history have been at loggerheads. Not an amputation, but a process of harmonisation which assigns each level of the mind, from visceral impulses to abstract thought, its appropriate place in the hierarchy. This implies reinforcing the new brain's power of veto against that type of emotive behaviour – *and that type only* – which cannot be reconciled with reason, such as the "blind" passions of the group-mind. If these could be eradicated, our species would be safe.

There are blind emotions and visionary emotions. Who in his senses would advocate doing away with the emotions aroused while listening to Mozart, or looking at a rainbow?

Any individual living today who asserted that he had made a pact with the devil and had intercourse with succubi would be dispatched to a mental home. Yet not so long ago, belief in such things was taken for granted and approved by "common sense" – i.e., the consensus of opinion, i.e., the group-mind. Psychopharmacology is playing an increasing part in the treatment of mental disorders in the clinical sense, such as individual delusions which affect the critical faculties and are *not* sanctioned by the group-mind. But we are concerned with a cure for the paranoid streak in what we call "normal people", which is revealed when they become victims of group-mentality. As we already have drugs to increase man's suggestibility, it will soon be within our reach to do the opposite: to reinforce man's critical faculties, counteract misplaced devotion and that militant enthusiasm, both murderous and suicidal, which is reflected in history books and the pages of the daily paper.

But who is to decide which brand of devotion is misplaced, and which beneficial to mankind? The answer seems obvious: a society composed of autonomous individuals, once they are immunised against the hypnotic effects of propaganda and thought-control, and protected against their own suggestibility as "belief-accepting animals". But this protection cannot be provided by counter-propaganda or drop-out attitudes; they are self-defeating. It can only be done by "tampering" with human nature itself to correct its endemic schizophysiological disposition. History tells us that nothing less will do.

Assuming that the laboratories succeed in producing an immunising substance conferring mental stability – how are we to propagate its global use? Are we to ram it down people's throats, whether they like it or not?

Again the answer seems obvious. Analgesics, pep pills, tranquillisers, contraceptives have, for better or worse, swept across the world with a minimum of publicity or official encouragement. They spread because people welcomed their effects. The use of a mental stabiliser would spread not by coercion but by enlightened self-interest; from then on, developments are as unpredictable as the consequences of any revolutionary discovery. A Swiss canton may decide, after a public referendum, to add the new substance to the iodine in the table salt, or the chlorine in the water supply, for a trial period, and other countries may imitate their example. There might be an international fashion among the young. In one way or the other, the simulated mutation would get under way. It is possible that totalitarian countries would try to resist it. But today even Iron Curtains have become porous; fashions are spreading irresistibly. And should there be a transitional period during which one side alone went ahead, it would gain a decisive advantage because it would be more rational in its long-term policies, less frightened and less hysterical. In conclusion, let me address this plea to the phantom reader:

Every writer has a favourite type of imaginary reader, a friendly phantom but highly critical, with whom he is engaged in a continuous, exhausting dialogue. I feel sure that my friendly phantom-reader has sufficient imagination to extrapolate from the recent breath-taking advances of biology into the future, and to concede that the solution outlined here is in the realm of the possible. What worries me is that he might be repelled and disgusted by the idea that we should rely for our salvation on molecular chemistry instead of a spiritual rebirth. I share his distress, but I see no alternative. I hear him explain: "By trying to sell us your Pills, you are adopting that crudely materialistic attitude and naive scientific *hubris* which you pretend to oppose." I still oppose it. But I do not believe that it is "materialistic" to take a realistic view of the condition of man; nor is it *hubris* to feed thyroid extracts to children who would otherwise grow into cretins. . . . Like the reader, I would prefer to set my hopes on moral persuasion by word and example. But we are a mentally sick race, and as such deaf to persuasion. It has been tried, in vain, from the age of the prophets to Albert Schweitzer; and Swift's anguished cry: "Not die here in a rage, like a poisoned rat in a hole," has acquired an urgency as never before.

Nature has let us down, God seems to have left the receiver off the hook, and time is running out. To hope for salvation to be synthesised in the laboratory may seem materialistic, crankish or naive; it reflects the ancient alchemist's dream to concoct the *elixir vitae*. What we expect from it, however, is not eternal life, but the transformation of *homo maniacus* into *homo sapiens*.

This is the only alternative to despair which I can read into the shape of things to come.

*   *   *

While the allegedly rational community of scientists and sociologists stubbornly refuses to admit – ignoring the evidence from past and present history – that mankind may be an evolutionary misfit, poets and seers have always taken man's insanity for granted or attributed it to the malice of the gods. Reading the Gospels from this angle, the motives of Jesus seemed to become more intelligible if one interpreted his voluntary martyrdom as an act of protest against the indifference of the Almighty towards the tragic madness of his creation. I thought this a reasonable hypothesis and was for a long time haunted by it; it finally took shape in fictional form: a short story called "The Misunderstanding". It is reprinted in the next chapter.

Chapter 44

THE MISUNDERSTANDING

A Short Story*

The bones of the earth are sticking out of this barren hill. The ancient rocks have faces that sneer at me. The roots of the dead olive trees are like snakes in the white dust waiting to bite into my sandals, to trip me up under my load. Fast vultures sail over our procession, not doves. My blood has dried on the thorns and the black flies have clustered into another crown round my head. Three starved dogs are following us at a distance. Verily a procession fit for a king.

Father, if you see me, how can you bear it? Almighty you, who made the sun stand still, can you not shift that timber on my shoulder by an inch to get its splintered edge away from my collar-bone to the muscle? It would hurt less on the muscle; I am a healer, I know. But I cannot lay hands on my own body, not even to shift that piece of timber, because it might slip. If I fall, they will flog me again, and I might cry out. Or I might pass water. They say when one is hoisted up one passes water and they laugh. Even my bowels might open. A father cannot let it happen to his son.

You teased Abraham when you bid him to cut his firstborn's throat, but you only stopped him in the last minute. Your sense of humour makes my sweat run cold. This ugly play is being performed before empty seats, for your benefit alone. Its only purpose is to make you listen, to wake you up.

When did you fall asleep, or start to look away? When David went after Absalom? Or earlier on, when Cain slew Abel? You have made a rotten hash of Adam's seed, almighty you. Often when the night lay heavily on me while the others slept like

*First printed in Encounter, London, under the title "Episode" (December, 1968).

stones in the moonlight, I wondered whether you yourself were
the deaf and dumb spirit who possessed that boy they brought to
me when we came down from the mountain. Was it you, disguised as a demon, who seized that boy, and tore him, and shook
him with convulsions, so that he had to throw himself into the fire
and into water, to make an end of himself? Are you the one who is
playing these games with Adam's seed? Or are you only absent-
minded and asleep? Soon I shall know when this stake and I
change places, when instead of me carrying it, it will carry me.
That will be the test, your trial. Then I shall know.

I have been flogging myself, harder than the soldiers flogged
me, into believing that you were only absent-minded, preoccupied with matters more important than your creation – though
what they could be beats me, harder than the soldiers beat me.
Perhaps you were also absent-minded when you went into my
mother, that tearful woman who keeps getting in my way. If that is
the case, and you are only distracted or asleep, I shall pull your
sleeve in my pain until you wake up and my purpose is achieved.
But if you are that deaf and dumb spirit, then pulling your sleeve
will be the gesture of a fool, and dying will be hard. They say it
takes three days to die in this way, unless they break your bones to
speed it up. It will be hard, and my bowels will open from my lofty
height upon this orphaned world, and it will all have been a
mockery – you, a mirage formed by desert vapours, and my tearful
mother an adulteress.

Speak, damn you, speak to me as you did on that night on the
mountain, and don't pretend you have more important business
to attend to. Have I not told those innocents that you have numbered every hair on their heads, and that not even a sparrow can
fall to the ground without your will? Does not Adam's seed count
for more than a host of sparrows? Do you feel that burning splinter
in my shoulder-bone? Shift it an inch, you can shift mountains
with your breath.

The path is getting steeper, we are approaching the top. Soon I
shall know the answer. The soldiers curse me without conviction,
they keep stumbling and kicking at stones, they are afraid of you, a
vicious desert god. The three dogs are still behind us; when I was
born, I was visited by three Kings. There is still time, you know,
to change my mind; the Governor said so, he will arrange a pardon
if I recant. I could recant even when already up. But by then my
arms will be broken and roped to the crossbar. The soldiers say

that in earlier times it was done with nails, but it was not safe because the man might come loose and fall down. The pain I can perhaps bear, though they all howl like wolves when they are hoisted up, but the healing power will have gone from my broken hands. They were good hands. They healed the sick, raised the dead, cleansed the lepers, cast out devils. And verily, I did these things, no one can deny it. Father, I have worked miracles for you, now it is your turn.

The path is getting less steep, I can glimpse the top. But the stones roll under my feet to taunt me, the roots keep tripping me up, they have to push and whip me on like a reluctant mule. My royal crown of flies bothers me more than the pain in the bone. The sun is a sword of flame but my eyes are clouded by mist. On the swaying hill-top the women are waiting, three weeping willows. I shall not speak to them, but they will watch what is done to me and witness my defilement. I was never drawn to their hungry flesh. They want the bridegroom to be cradled in his mother's womb, or in another womb, but it is the same. When the dead rise again there will be no marrying. The pain is so strong that I feel it no longer, but if I fall they will beat me until I hate them and you will have another excuse for looking away.

If a father turns his back, how shall the son know whether he exists? I know that you exist, but I know your shape no more than that of the filthy spirit which threw the boy into convulsions. In a place high in the mountains there was a village idiot whom the heathens worshipped, a bald, hunchbacked dwarf cavorting in the dust and feeding on dogs' excrement which the alderman served him on golden plates. Now I seem to be falling, falling, but ever so slowly, going down. The stake is gone, it did not break my spine, now they can beat me to their hearts' content, my brow enjoys its dustbath in the sand, all is blessed peace. They are standing around me, discussing what is to be done, and I am lying prone in white dust and bliss. There is a stranger with them now, a farm boy with round eyes, they are putting that yoke of timber on his naked back. See now I am up again, and had to make no effort, they did it for me, ever so gently. And I am walking again, supported on both sides, walking on air as I walked that day on the lake. Then I was holding up that foolish fisherman of little faith, but now I am being held up by the gentle soldiers who are as brothers to me. So did Abraham carry his son to the place of sacrifice, and both were frightened until you called off the joke. I could not be sure that this was also meant as a joke and I was a little frightened, but now I know. The joke was played by both of us, so half the fault was mine, and I must explain to you just once more why I did it. I have tried to explain it before, but you would not listen. *I wanted to die in order to wake you up.* That was the only reason. For I thought that you were asleep, or absent-minded or otherwise engaged, and therefore unaware of the abominations and desolation of the world you made. How else could I explain to myself that you have allowed these goings on, that you allowed in your lovingness, allowed in your omniscience, that you let pass in your omnipotence, that men should become worse than beasts, worse than all that crawls and creeps, that the breath you blew into Adam's nostrils should become a stink of dragons, and his seed a pollution of the earth? So I had to decide on this course to wake you up. My prayers had been of no avail. I could cure the sick and cast out a few devils, but that universal sickness of mind that has befallen your creation, that was your responsibility. And you did nothing about it. You were asleep. Once I even heard you snore through the sobs of a youth whom the soldiers put to torture.

So I had to decide on this course, to die in this ugly and painful way, to bring you back to your senses. Is there a father who could not be made to repent by the suicide of his son? Could he watch with eyes of stone while they break his arms and hoist him up to let him rot like a vegetable tied to a stick? I knew that you could not let it pass. You would have to intervene, and then you would clean up this whole mess in your holy wrath, as I cleaned the moneylenders out of the temple. And then there would be no more butchers and no more lambs.

That is how I planned it; but I could not tell it to those blockheads of little faith. They would not have understood. Because these men chose their path for the love of me, father, not for the love of you. They saw me cure the sick and feed the starving, and this they approved of and understood. But they never understood your devious ways. They were not allowed to make themselves any likeness or graven image of you, and that was a great mistake. They were told that no man can see your face and live, and that was another great mistake. For men cannot love nor understand that which has no shape nor substance, and which has no likeness in their own world. So I had to tell them parables by which to provide the likenesses and images that were missing. I told them that the wine was my blood and the bread my substance, and they swallowed both, and felt that their god was inside them. I could not tell them that I had to decide on this course to make you sit up and remind you of your responsibilities, because that would have made them love you even less. Instead I told them the parable of Jonah, who was three days and three nights in the belly of the whale, and told them I would lie three days and three nights in the heart of the earth. I repeated the parable of Jonah several times to rub it into their thick heads, and in the end they swallowed that too and would have me rise again as Jonah rose from the deep and Joseph rose from the well. They have eyes but you hide from them, they have ears but you do not speak to them. So they must live by parables.

Only one man understood my plan, the Governor. He wondered why I stayed silent instead of refuting the false accusations, but then he understood. He looked through my eyes which to him were like open windows, then turned his back and rinsed his hands, which also was a parable to indicate that this business could only be settled between you and me. So be it.

Here then is the place; we have arrived. I don't like these preparations. The soldiers who supported me no longer look kind. They sweat and breathe hard. They are measuring my length. From crown to sandals. They seem to mean business. Now is the time, now is the time, father, to call it off, to stop this frightening make-believe. Abraham is drawing his knife on his son. These men are pressing me down against the stake. It cannot be, they cannot do this to me, it cannot be borne. A voice is howling like a wolf's, it cannot be mine. And the women look on. The sponge in my mouth is bitter and soothing, dimming the world, a mouthful of sleep. It cannot be true that this is happening to me. These broken hands are not mine. This filth comes not out of me. This rising higher and higher up in white flames of pain happens not to me. I am rising and sinking, turning on a wheel, riding in the belly of the whale. The sun has turned black and darkness fills the air, I must not faint. I must look into his eyes if he has eyes to see. Eli, eli, how can you bear watching this? Thou dumb spirit, vapour of the desert, ignoble absence, thou art not, hast never been. Only a parable. And my own death another parable; they will remember it and twist its meaning. They will torture and kill in the name of a parable. They will fight insane wars for its correct interpretation. They will slay children for the love of a metaphor and burn women alive in praise of an allegory. And thus will your will be done, not mine.

CAMPAIGNS AND CAUSES

Chapter 45

REFLECTIONS ON HANGING

*More down-to-earth "alternatives to despair" than the specula-
tive hopes outlined in chapter 43 offered themselves in the guise
of various involvements which cynics might describe as compulsive do-gooding. The trilogy which started with* The Sleepwalkers
and ended with The Ghost in the Machine *took more than ten
years to write, but nobody who has led a politically active life can
sit for ten years at his desk in scholarly quietude. Thus from time
to time there were bursts of hectic activity, and the one in which I
became most deeply involved was the National Campaign for the
Abolition of Capital Punishment, which was founded by the late
Victor Gollancz, Canon John Collins (President of Christian
Action) and myself on a Sunday afternoon in the summer of 1955.
It took fifteen years to achieve its aim.*

*At that first meeting it was decided to launch the campaign
with a pamphlet which I was to write. It actually grew into a book,*
Reflections on Hanging, *but it achieved its purpose of reaching a
mass audience by being serialised in the Sunday Observer in five
long instalments and in a shorter version in Picture Post, with its
vast middle-brow readership, mostly in favour of hanging; an
abridged version, co-authored by C. H. Rolf, was later published
as a Penguin Special.**

---

*Hanged by the Neck – An Exposure of Capital Punishment in England *(London,
1961).*

The motives for writing the book (and for taking an active part in the campaign) were explained in the Preface:

In 1937, during the Civil War in Spain, I spent three months under sentence of death as a suspected spy, witnessing the executions of my fellow prisoners and awaiting my own. These three months left me with a vested interest in capital punishment – rather like "half-hanged Smith", who was cut down after fifteen minutes and lived on. Each time a man's or a woman's neck is broken in this peaceful country, memory starts to fester like a badly healed wound. I shall never achieve real peace of mind until hanging is abolished.

I have stated my bias. It colours the arguments in the book; it does not affect the facts in it, and most of its content is factual. My intention was to write it in a cool and detached manner, but it came to naught; indignation and pity kept seeping in. This is perhaps just as well, for capital punishment is not merely a problem of statistics and expediency, but also of morality and feeling. Fair pleading requires that one's facts and figures should be right, that one should not distort or quote out of context; it does not exclude having one's heart and spleen in it.

Some of the Learned Friends who helped with the material for this book, warned me against offending certain venerable prejudices and traditional susceptibilities concerning judges and juries, the notion of a fair trial, the handling of the prerogative of mercy, and so on. I have disregarded their warnings because appeasement never pays, and because I believe that the case for abolition has been weakened by lack of outspokenness. Others advised silence regarding the physiological facts about executions, past and present. That amounts to saying that the Queen of Spain has no legs and the hanged man has no neck. We hang on an average one person each month; if this thing is done in the name of the people, they have a right to know what is being done.

The reason why, twenty years ago, I made the acquaintance of the condemned cell was the hopeful belief in the salvation of mankind by world revolution; this book aims, more modestly, at saving thirteen wretches a year the pain and terror of going through the same experience. Apart from that, there is also a larger issue involved, for the gallows is not merely a machine of death, but the oldest obscene symbol of that tendency in mankind which drives it towards moral self-destruction.

London, October 3, 1955

Although its immediate purpose was to make propaganda for the abolition campaign, writing the book required a good deal of research into the historical background, in the course of which I became more and more fascinated by the sheer lunacy of English Criminal Law relating to the death penalty and the way it was practised over the past two centuries. Here was a practically unknown chapter of cultural history, unparalleled in absurdity, which threw yet another lurid sidelight on the pathology of the human mind. The following extracts from Reflections on Hanging *may convey a taste of it. (The reasons for the relative length of the extracts I have explained in the prefatory remarks to this volume.)*

1 The Jack-in-the-Box

Great Britain is that peculiar country in Europe where people drive on the left side of the road, measure in inches and yards, and hang people by the neck until dead. To most Britons it never occurs that there may be something odd about this custom. Every nation takes its traditions for granted, and hanging is as much part of the British tradition as counting in shillings and pence. Generations of children have squeaked with delight at the appearance of the puppet hangman in the Punch and Judy show. Four executioners are included in the *Dictionary of National Biography*; Jack Ketch, Calcraft, and "William Boilman"* were as popular figures in their time as film-stars are today. There seems to be a jolliness about the procedure as if the victim twitching at the end of the rope were not a real person but a dummy burnt on Guy Fawkes' Day. The present hangman, Pierrepoint, runs a public house called "Help the Poor Struggler"; his former assistant, Allenby, ran one called "The Rope and the Anchor";† and the present Lord Chief Justice‡ delighted a Royal Academy banquet with the story of a judge who, after passing sentence of death on three men, was welcomed by a band playing the Eton Boating Song's refrain: "We'll all swing together".

It all goes to show that hanging has a kind of macabre cosiness, like a slightly off-colour family joke, which only foreigners,

*Nickname for the executioner, derived, according to Macaulay, from the custom of publicly boiling the entrails of traitors after they were disembowelled alive.
†Charles Duff, *A New Handbook on Hanging* (London, 1954).
‡Lord Goddard.

abolitionists and other humourless creatures are unable to share.
On November 2, 1950, Mr Albert Pierrepoint was called to testify
as a witness before the Royal Commission on Capital Punishment.
He was asked how many people he had hanged in his career as an
executioner, and answered: "Some hundreds."*

> Q. Have you had any awkward moments?
> A. No, I have only seen one in all my career.
> Q. What happened?
> A. He was rough. It was unfortunate; he was not an Englishman, he
> was a spy, and he kicked up rough.

The acting Under-Sheriff for the County of London, Mr H. N.
Gedge, was also examined by the Commission on the unpleasant
character who had kicked up rough, and confirmed Mr Pierrepoint's view:

> Yes. He was a foreigner, and I personally have noticed that English
> people take their punishment better than foreigners.

There you are. Hanging is all right for Englishmen; they actually
seem to like it; it is only the foreigners who cause trouble. They
appreciate neither the clean fun, nor the ritual aspect of the
procedure, nor the venerable tradition behind it.

The scaffold and the executioner are memories of the past in all
Western European democracies except France. The death-penalty
has also been abolished in several North American States, in
virtually the whole of Central and South America, and in a
number of Asiatic and Australian states; making altogether
thirty-six countries, the major portion of the civilised world.

The British are a proverbially disciplined and law-abiding
people – more so than the average of abolitionist nations, which
include hot-tempered Latin Americans and Germans who had
been exposed to the brutalising influence of the Nazi regime. Yet
the defenders of capital punishment claim that this nation, unlike
others, cannot afford to dispense with the services of the hangman
as protector and avenger of society. They say that the example of
other nations proves nothing, because conditions in this country
are "different"; foreigners may be deterred from crime by the
threat of long-term imprisonment, the British criminal can only
be deterred by the gallows. This paradoxical belief is so deeply
rooted in the pro-hanging party that they do not even see it as a

*Royal Commission on Capital Punishment, 1949–53, Minutes of Evidence,
8402.

paradox. Many of them hate the idea of hanging and admit that the practice is repellent and evil, yet they believe it to be a necessary evil. This belief in the irreplaceable deterrent value of the death-penalty has been proved to be a superstition by the long and patient inquiries of the Parliamentary Select Committee of 1930 and the Royal Commission on Capital Punishment of 1948; yet it pops up again and again. Like all superstitions, it has the nature of a Jack-in-the-box; however often you hit it over the head with facts and statistics, it will solemnly pop up again, because the hidden spring inside it is the unconscious and irrational power of tradi-tional beliefs. Hence all arguments are wasted unless we go back to the origins of that tradition, and unearth the elements in the past which exert such a strong influence on our present beliefs.

It will be an excursion into a strangely neglected and little-known chapter of English history, which is very curious indeed – a forensic Wonderland where the March Hare wears a wig.

2 The "Bloody Code"

At the beginning of the nineteenth century the criminal law of this country was commonly known as the Bloody Code. It was unique in the world inasmuch as it listed between 220 and 230 offences to be punished by death, from the stealing of turnips to associating with gipsies, to damaging a fishpond, to writing threatening let-ters, to impersonating out-pensioners at Greenwich Hospital, to being found armed or disguised in a forest, park or rabbit warren, to cutting down a tree, to poaching, forging, picking pockets, shoplifting, and so on, through 220-odd items.

We are not talking of the Dark Ages, but of the nineteenth century, up to Queen Victoria's reign, when everywhere in the civilised world offences against property were being removed from the list of capital crimes. In 1810, Sir Samuel Romilly said in the House of Lords that "there was no country on the face of the earth in which there had been so many different offences accord-ing to law to be punished with death as in England".* Twenty years later Sir Robert Peel complained to the House of Commons: "It is impossible to conceal from ourselves that capital punish-ments are more frequent and the criminal law more severe on the whole in this country than in any country in the world."† And the

*Hansard, 1810, Vol. XV, col. 366.
†Hansard, April 1, 1830, col. 1179.

greatest nineteenth-century authority at law, Sir James Stephen, talked of "the clumsiest, most reckless, and most cruel legislation that ever disgraced a civilised country". *

This state of affairs was the more puzzling as in some other respects British civilisation was ahead of the rest of the world. Foreign visitors were amazed to find the highways dotted with gibbets, creaking and groaning with the bodies of criminals. The gallows and the gibbet were such common objects in the English countryside that in early guide-books they were used as land-marks for the traveller; for instance:

> By the Gallows and Three Windmills enter the suburbs of York. . . .
> You pass through Hare Street . . . and at 13′4 part for Epping Forest,
> with the gallows to the left. . . . You pass Penmeris Hall, and at 250′4
> Hildraught Mill, both on the left, and ascend a small hill with a gibbet
> on the right. . . . You leave Frampton, Wilberton and Sherbeck, all on
> the right, and by a gibbet on the left, over a stone bridge.†

Between London and East Grinstead alone, three gallows stood at different points on the highway, in addition to several gibbets where the dead criminal's body was suspended in chains "till his corpse rot". Sometimes a criminal was "hung in chains" alive, and died only after several days. Sometimes the corpse was drenched in tar to make it last longer. Sometimes the skeleton was left hanging after decay of the body was completed. The last gibbeting took place in 1832 in Saffron Lane, near Leicester, when the body of James Cook, a book-binder, was suspended thirty-three feet high, his head shaved and tarred, but had to be taken down after a fortnight to stop the merrymaking of the Sunday crowds.‡

"Hanging days" were, during the eighteenth and up to half-way through the nineteenth century, the equivalent of national bank holidays, only more frequent. We read, for instance, that in George III's reign, working hours for the poor "were inordinately long, and there were very few holidays except just at Easter, Whitsuntide and Christmas, and on the eight 'Hanging Days' at Tyburn".§

---

*Quoted from Leon Radzinowicz, *A History of English Criminal Law and its Administration from 1750*, Vol. I. (London, 1948), p. 24.
†W. Andrews, *Bygone Punishments* (London, 1899), p. 39.
‡Ibid, p. 75.
§ B. Williams, *The Whig Supremacy, 1714–60* (Oxford, 1945).

Yet this was the age of romantic sensibility, when women swooned at the slightest provocation, and bearded men shed happy tears in each other's arms.

The victims were hanged singly or in batches of up to twenty. Frequently the prisoners were drunk, and the executioner too:

> This day Will Summers and Tipping were executed here for house-breaking. At the tree, the hangman was intoxicated with liquor, and supposing that there were three for execution, was going to put one of the ropes round the parson's neck, as he stood in the cart, and was with much difficulty prevented by the gaoler from so doing.

Whether drunk or not, public hysteria frequently caused the hangman to lose his nerve and bungle his job. The volumes of the *Newgate Calendar* abound in examples of people who had to be hanged twice, and even three times. These horrors continued through the nineteenth century. The whole process was carried out in such uncertain, haphazard and barbaric ways that not only were victims found to be alive fifteen minutes and more after the onset of strangling, but there are also authenticated cases of people reviving in the dissecting hall.

It is unavoidable, in discussing capital punishment, to go into these ghoulish technicalities in order to make people realise what exactly we are talking about. For these are not entirely matters of the distant past. Official hypocrisy, taking advantage of the fact that executions are no longer public, pretends that modernised hanging is a nice and smooth affair which is always carried out "expeditiously and without a hitch", as prison governors were instructed to say. But the hanging of the Nuremberg war criminals in 1946 was as terribly bungled, and the hanging of Mrs Thompson in 1923 was a butchery as revolting as any reported in the *Newgate Calendar*. Her executioner attempted suicide a short time later, and the prison chaplain stated that "the impulse to rush in and save her by force was almost too strong". Yet Government spokesmen tell us that all executions are smooth and nice, and Government spokesmen are honourable men.

There was little discrimination of sex or age. Children were not liable to the death-penalty if under seven years, and fully liable over fourteen; between seven and fourteen they could be and were hanged if there was "strong evidence of malice" because malice was held "to supply age".* Here are a few cases:

*Radzinowicz, op. cit., p. 12.

In 1801, Andrew Brenning, aged thirteen, was publicly hanged for breaking into a house and stealing a spoon. In 1808 a girl aged seven was publicly hanged at Lynn.* In 1831, a boy of nine was publicly hanged at Chelmsford for having set fire to a house, and another aged thirteen at Maidstone.† Three years later the Lord Chancellor, Lord Eldon, in opposing any mitigation of the law, had the temerity to state that "he had been His Majesty's adviser for twenty-five years and so far as his knowledge extended, mercy had never been refused in any instance where it ought not to have been withheld".‡

Similar statements about mercy "never being refused" where there is a "scintilla of doubt" were made in the 1948 debate on capital punishment, and on later occasions after Bentley, Evans, Rowland, etc., had been hanged.

Let me repeat: we are not talking about the Dark Ages, but about the Period of Enlightenment, when all over Europe criminal legislation was rapidly being humanised. Influenced by the teachings of Beccaria, Montesquieu and Voltaire, capital punishment was abolished in Austria for the first time as far back as 1781 by Joseph II.§ His brother, the Grand Duke of Tuscany, followed suit in 1786‖ and promulgated a penal code which proclaimed the readaptation of offenders to normal life as the main object of all punishment. Catharine the Great of Russia issued her famous "Instruction" in 1767¶ which abolished capital punishment, and declared that: "It is Moderation which rules a People and not Excess of Severity."

This shocking contrast between England and the Continent was mainly due to the fact that hanging was regarded by the Bloody Code as a cure-all for every offence, from stealing a handkerchief upward. Yet these comparisons refer to the eighteenth century only. During the first third of the nineteenth, in the period between the Napoleonic Wars and the beginning of Victoria's reign, the contrast is even more staggering. The oldest democracy in Europe, which had never suffered the brutalising effects of foreign invasion, became distinguished, in Sir James Stephen's

---

* G. Gardiner and N. Curtis-Raleigh, "The Judicial Attitude to Penal Reform", *The Law Quarterly Review* (April, 1949), p. 8.
† Ibid.
‡ Ibid.
§ Radzinowicz, op. cit., pp. 290f.
‖ Ibid pp. 291f.
¶ Ibid pp. 295f.

words, by "the most reckless and most cruel legislation that ever disgraced a civilised country".

How did this fantastic situation come about? The answer can only be traced in its outlines, but it is of the greatest relevance to the present situation.

3 Historic Origins of the Bloody Code

The situation round 1800 was not a heritage of the dark past, but the result of a deliberate turning-back of the clock. Three main causes seem to have been at work to make English criminal law during the eighteenth century develop in a direction opposite to that of the rest of the world: (a) England's lead in the Industrial Revolution; (b) the Englishman's dislike of authority, which prevented the creation of an effective police force; (c) the peculiarity of English Common Law, which led to the emergence of a class of men with the authority of oracles, opposed to any departure from precedent and to any concession to the moving times.

Medieval Common Law imposed the death-penalty only on a few grave offences, such as murder, treason, arson and rape. Under the Tudors and Stuarts the law became more rigorous, but at the beginning of the eighteenth century there were as yet no more than fifty capital offences. At the beginning of the nineteenth, there were nearly five times as many. The development of the Bloody Code was simultaneous with, and largely caused by, the Industrial Revolution, which transformed the nation as thoroughly as if it had been put through a cement-mixing machine. It gave England the lead in the western world, but at the same time produced social evils whose distant echoes are still felt in our day.

"For fifty years that great change was left uncontrolled by the community which it was transforming."* Towns were growing like squalid mushrooms, without any machinery of administration, local government and public security. The ancient order of society was disintegrating, but nobody had any experience or any clear idea how to cope with the resulting social chaos, and particularly with the new town proletariat of wage-earners, uprooted from their rural existence, transformed into a race of shiftless slum-dwellers. The spreading of extreme poverty with its concomitants of prostitution, child labour, drunkenness and law-

*Trevelyan, British History in the Nineteenth Century and After (London, 1943), p. xiv.

lessness, coincided with an unprecedented accumulation of wealth as an additional incentive to crime. All foreign visitors agreed that never before had the world seen such riches and splendour as displayed in London residences and shops – nor so many pickpockets, burglars and highwaymen. "One is forced to travel even at noon as if one was going to battle," Horace Walpole wrote in 1752. It was this general feeling of insecurity, often verging on panic, which led to the enactment, by the dozen, of capital statutes, making any offence from poaching and stealing from the value of one shilling upward punishable by death. And each statute branched out like a tree to cover any similar or related offences.

This process went on for over a hundred years, and was only brought to an end when Robert Peel, in 1829, created the modern police force. Had that been done a century earlier, the whole shame and terror could have been avoided. The reason why it was not done was, paradoxically, the Englishman's love of freedom, and his dislike of regimentation: the fear that a regular police force, once established, would be used to curtail his individual and political freedom.

Faced by the choice between the cop and the hangman, England chose the hangman. He was a familiar figure from the past; the cop was a new-fangled innovation of foreign countries, and a much too dangerous experiment. As all other curiosities in this chapter, I mention this not for curiosity's sake, but because it is directly relevant to the controversy of our day. The last-ditch stand of the defenders of capital punishment is made precisely on the same issue which started the whole disaster: to wit, that if hanging were abolished, the police would have to carry arms to cope with the emboldened criminal. To this day, the idea of allowing cops to wear a revolver is more abhorrent to the Englishman's sensibilities than the continuance of hanging.

The panicky character of the emergency legislation of the eighteenth century is strikingly illustrated by the so-called "Waltham Black Act". It set the example and the pace of the whole development. In 1722, the Hampshire landowners were worried by a band of poachers who went around with their faces blackened to make recognition more difficult. They were following yet another and even more ancient tradition: that of the Roberdsmen, the followers of Robert, or Robin, Hood. The gentlemen of Hampshire appealed to Parliament, not knowing that they were going to make British history; and Parliament enacted a statute "for the more effectual punishing wicked and evil disposed Persons going armed in Disguise, and doing Injuries and Violence to the Persons and Properties of His Majesty's Subjects, and for the more speedy bringing of Offenders to Justice".

The Roberdsmen vanished from Hampshire, but the Waltham Black Act came to stay. It was enacted to meet a local and temporary emergency for a limited period of three years; and it stayed for 101 years, till 1823; and all the time it was ramifying. For it was so vaguely and generally worded that the judges could apply it to an unlimited range of offenders and offences, each time creating a precedent on which further convictions could be based. Altogether, the Waltham Black Act, by budding and ramification, created over 350 new capital crimes. These referred to: persons either armed and having their faces blackened; or armed and otherwise disguised; or being merely otherwise disguised; or being *neither blackened nor disguised*; or principals in the second degree; or accessories after the act. The offences included: offences against red or fallow deer, thefts of hares, conies and fish, destroying the heads of fishponds, cutting down "a tree planted in any avenue, garden, orchard or plantation for ornament, shelter or profit", offences against cattle, setting anything on fire, shooting at any person, sending a letter demanding money if unsigned or signed by a fictitious name, and so on and so forth through 350-odd items.

I have tried to trace the origins of this madness which cast the shadow of the gallows over every hamlet, forest and borough of the land. But collective madness and panic last, as a rule, only a short time. This was the age when Beccaria's, Voltaire's and Montesquieu's teachings fell everywhere on fertile ground, except in England; and in England itself there were Jeremy Bentham, the Mills, Eden and Howard, Romilly, Selborne and other enlightened men, conscious of the national shame, who fought it with the power of the word and the pen. What, then, was the cause, and which were the forces that kept the madness going and resisted all attempts to stop it, all measures of reform, until the mid-nineteenth century? The answer is as simple as it is shocking: the judges of England.

4 The Oracles

In the fifteenth and sixteenth centuries, most European countries adopted written codes based on the Roman Law, in replacement of their old customary "common law" or "folk-law". Two hundred years later, a second wave of codification swept over Europe in the wake of the *Code Napoléon*. England alone has adhered to this day to common law, defined by Blackstone as "not set down in any written statute or ordinance, but depending on immemorial usage for support".* The validity and application of these usages are to be determined by the judges – "the depositories of the law, the living oracles, who must decide in all cases of doubt, and who are bound by oath to decide according to the law of the land".† Their judgements are preserved as records, and "it is an established rule to abide by former precedents. . . . The most extraordinary deference paid to precedents is the source of the striking peculiarities of the English Common Law."‡

The benefits of the Common Law as a bulwark of the Britons' political and personal freedom were enormous, and are an essential part of English history. But these benefits were heavily paid for. Dislike of regimentation by the police was a major cause for the prevalence of the hangman; dislike of law by code and statute left English legislation at the mercy of the wigged oracles, who, since precedent must be their only guidance, by the very nature of their calling had their minds riveted on the past. They not only administered the law; they made it. It was the judges who interpreted the Waltham Black Act in such a way that it finally branched into over 350 capital offences; under whose guidance Parliament enacted more and more capital statutes which they could interpret and expand; and who fought tooth and nail against the repeal of any of them.

In 1813, when Romilly's Bill for the abolition of the death-penalty for shoplifting was for the third time defeated by the House of Lords (see below), the later Chief Justice Common Pleas, Lord Wynford, stated the judges' attitude in an unusually frank manner. The text of his speech was *Nolumus leges Angliae mutari* – "We do not wish the laws of England to be changed." The shoplifting act which reformers wished to abolish, he said, had been passed in Cromwell's day, "in the best period of our history, and there was no reason for hazarding an experiment". He would vote for the bill if it could be shown that a single individual had suffered under the existing law, but the humanity of judges was

---

Encyclopaedia Britannica (1955), article on "Common Law", Vol. IV, p. 122.
†Ibid.
‡Ibid., p, 123.

proverbial.* This, at a time when children from the age of seven upward were being publicly strangled.

The motto "We do not wish the laws of England to be changed" referred, however, only to mitigations, not to aggravations, of the law. There is no known example of a protest coming from the judges against adding new capital offences to the statute, and a considerable number of death statutes were moved by themselves. It was a one-way process, which made every aggravation of the law irreversible.

The decisive struggle for the repeal of the Bloody Code took place between 1808, when Romilly brought in his first Reform Bill, and Queen Victoria's ascent to the throne in 1837. At the beginning of this legal Thirty Years' War, the number of capital statutes was 220-odd; at its end, they were reduced to fifteen.

The stubborn determination of the die-hards and hang-hards may be gathered from a single example: Romilly's Bill to abolish the death-penalty for shoplifting to the value of five shillings and over, was passed by the Commons and defeated by the Lords no less than six times: in 1810, 1811, 1813, 1816, 1818 and 1820. It was only passed, long after Romilly's death, in 1832. In the first House of Lords Debate on the bill, on May 30, 1810, Chief Justice Lord Ellenborough made two speeches which, later on, became famous:

> I trust your lordships will pause before you assent to an experiment pregnant with danger to the security of property, and before you repeal a statute which has so long been held necessary for public security. I am convinced with the rest of the Judges, public expediency requires there should be no remission of the terror denounced against this description of offenders. Such will be the consequences of the repeal of this statute that I am certain depredations to an unlimited extent would immediately be committed. . . .
>
> My Lords, if we suffer this Bill to pass, we shall not know where to stand; we shall not know whether we are upon our heads or our feet. . . .

The resistance began to break down only when Peel came to the Home Office and created the modern police force in 1829. Ten years later, capital offences were at long last reduced to the number of fifteen; and in 1861 to four (murder, treason, arson in dockyards and piracy). This is where the matter rests until this day.

*Gardiner and Curtis-Raleigh, op. cit., p. 13.

*The narrative goes on to relate, at considerable length, the truly
fanatical resistance of the judges to any mitigation of other forms
of punishment – from "drawing, hanging and quartering" for
treason (which was only abolished in 1814) to the pillory and the
cat-o'-nine-tails. They were also adamant in denying (until 1836)
prisoners on a capital charge the right to be defended by Counsel
(remember that some of those charged were children under ten);
and in denying those sentenced to death the right to appeal:*

The judges were equally determined in their opposition to the
establishment of a Court of Criminal Appeal – which they succeeded in postponing by a modest *seventy years*. During this time
the question had come before Parliament no less than *twenty-
eight times.*

Before the Court of Criminal Appeal was established in 1907,
there existed no body to which prisoners wrongfully sentenced to
death could appeal; their only hope was the Royal pardon. The
1866 Royal Commission had considered the question, but the four
judges who gave evidence, Lords Cranworth, Bramwell, Martin
and Wensleydale, unanimously opposed it, on the grounds that it
would "worry prosecutors", that "a Court of Appeal is not what
one may call a natural thing", and because "people in England are
never convicted, except, in my judgment, upon the very clearest
evidence. . . ."*

Of course, there were always kind and understanding judges on
the lower rungs of the hierarchy. There were exceptions even at
the top, such as Lord Brougham (Lord Chancellor 1830–4), and
Lord Denman (Chief Justice 1832–50), who sided with the reformers. But the core of resistance against reform, around which the
reactionary forces rallied, was the authority of the oracles. Robed
with the august symbols of tradition, they lent to the public
strangling of ten-year-olds a halo of respectability, and led this
gentle nation through two centuries of gore. . . .

The terror of the French Revolution preserves in retrospect the
grandeur of a tragic but essential chapter of history. The terror of
the Bloody Code was wanton and purposeless, alien to the character of the nation, imposed on it, not by fanatical Jacobins, but by a
conspiracy of wigged fossils. They quoted the Bible to defend
drawing and quartering, and they quoted each other's quotations,

*Ibid., pp. 20f.

and became more and more estranged from reality. Solicitors and counsel, prison chaplains and gaolers know criminals as individuals, and know that they are human. The judges only meet the accused in court, as a case, not as a human being. All the great oracles had a blind belief in the gallows as the only deterrent from crime, though the only criminals they had occasion to see were those who had obviously not been deterred. They were like physicians who would justify their favourite cure by the example of patients who have not been cured by it. Yet they must go on believing in their magic deterrent, for if they renounced that belief, they would stand condemned for those they have condemned, before their own conscience.

From Coke to Stephen and beyond, they all show the same curious trend to inhumanity because, though posing as experts, they knew little of human nature and the motives of crime.* Victims of their professional deformity, ignorant of the forces of heredity and social environment, hostile to any social and psychological explanation, the criminal was for them nothing but a bundle of depravity, who cannot be redeemed and must be destroyed. Like all who believe in terror as the only protection of society, they were frightened men. Their grotesque outcries against any relaxation of the terror statutes were caused by an irrational but genuine fear. From the psychiatrist's point of view, the horrors of the Bloody Code, the hanging of children, the saturnalia of the public executions, were symptoms of hysteria. But psychiatrists are considered by the oracles as their hereditary enemies, not only because they might see through the accused, but also, perhaps, through the judge.

In his *Lives of the Chief Justices*, Lord Campbell quotes a judge at Stafford Assizes who, having sentenced to death a prisoner for passing on a forged one pound note, exhorted him as follows to prepare for his journey to another world:

---

*Thus, for instance, Sir Travers Humphreys (better known as Mr Justice Humphreys) writes in his memoirs, *A Book of Trials* (1953):

"John George Haigh belonged to what is perhaps the largest class of murderers, that is, murderers for gain."

Yet according to Home Office statistics, during the years 1900 to 1949, 1210 persons were convicted for murder in England and Wales. Out of these, 161 were committed for gain, 837 were *crimes passionels* and the rest were miscellaneous, or committed during a quarrel. These statistics (see R. C. Report, p. 330), were available to the illustrious judge when he published his memoirs.

And I trust that, through the merits and mediation of our blessed Redeemer, you may there experience that mercy which a due regard to the credit of the paper currency of the country forbids you to hope for here.*

The words convey a complete mental picture of the early nineteenth-century oracle: the nasal voice half-choked with phlegm, the august hrrumph, the corkscrew-braided tea doily warming the bald pate and making its wearer forget the ailing prostate; add it together, and you have the awe-inspiring majesty of the Capital Law.

English law is based on tradition and precedent. I hope that this – necessarily sketchy – excursion into the past may have dispelled some of the unconscious preconceptions which cloud the issue, and will help the reader to consider the problem of capital punishment against its historical background, with an unprejudiced mind.

The next chapter, on "The Hangman's Protection – or Capital Punishment as a Deterrent", struck a more sober note, and was based mainly on statistics:

In the most recent Parliamentary debates to date – February 10 and July 22, 1955 – the present Home Secretary, Major Lloyd George, again patiently trotted out the three customary reasons why the Government opposed abolition: that the death-penalty carried a unique deterrent value; that no satisfactory alternative punishment could be designed; and that public opinion was in favour of it.

At present I am only concerned with the first and main argument. To give it a fair hearing, we must set all humanitarian considerations and charitable feelings aside, and examine the effectiveness of the gallows as a deterrent to potential murderers from a coldly practical, purely utilitarian point of view. This is, of course, a somewhat artificial view, for in reality "effectiveness" can never be the only consideration; even if it were proved that death preceded by torture was more effective, we would refuse to act accordingly. However, it will be seen that the theory of hanging as the best deterrent can be refuted on its own purely utilitarian grounds, without calling ethics and charity to aid.

*Quoted from Gardiner and Curtis-Raleigh, op. cit., p. 13.

A deterrent must logically refer to a "deterree" – if the reader will forgive me for adding a verbal barbarity to the barbarous subject. So the first question is: who are the hypothetical deterrees, who will be prevented from committing murder by the threat of hanging, but not by the threat of long-term imprisonment? The fear of death is no doubt a powerful deterrent; but just how powerful is it?

The gallows obviously failed as a deterrent in all cases where a murder has actually been committed. It is certainly not a deterrent to murderers who commit suicide – and one-third of all murderers do.* It is not a deterrent to the insane and mentally deranged; nor to those who have killed in a quarrel, in drunkenness, in a sudden surge of passion – and this type of murder amounts to 80 to 90 per cent of all murders that are committed. It is not a deterrent to the type of person who commits murder because he desires to be hanged; and these cases are not infrequent. It is not a deterrent to the person who firmly believes in his own perfect method – by poison, acid bath, and so on – which, he thinks, will never be found out. Thus the range of hypothetical deterrees who can only be kept under control by the threat of death and nothing short of death, is narrowed down to the professional criminal class. But both the abolitionists and their opponents agree that "murder is not a crime of the criminal classes";† it is a crime of amateurs, not of professionals. None of the points I have mentioned so far is controversial; they are agreed on by both sides.

If the death-penalty were a more effective deterrent than lesser penalties, then its abolition for a given category of crime should be followed by a noticeable increase in the volume of that crime, precisely as the hanging party says. But the facts tell a different story. After the great reform of the eighteen-thirties, the crime-rate did not rise; it fell. And yet the era of reform coincided with one of the most difficult periods in English social history. As if History herself had wanted to make the task of the abolitionists more difficult, the repeal of the death-penalty for offences against property during the eighteen-thirties was immediately followed by the "hungry forties". The great experiment of mitigating the rigour of the law could not have been carried out under more unfavourable circumstances. Yet half-way through the experiment, when the number of capital offences had been reduced to fifteen, His

*Viscount Templewood, The Shadows of the Gallows (London, 1951), p. 76.
†Royal Commission Report on Capital Punishment, 1949–53, Appendix 6, p. 5.

Majesty's Commissioners on Criminal Law, 1836, summed up their report as follows:

> It has not, in effect, been found that the repeal of Capital Punishment with regard to any particular class of offences has been attended with an increase of the offenders. On the contrary, the evidence and statements to be found in our appendix go far to demonstrate that . . . the absolute number of the offenders has diminished.*

And at the conclusion of this most dangerous experiment in the history of English criminal law, Sir Joseph Pease was able to state in the House of Commons that "the continual mitigation of law and of sentences has been accomplished with property quite as secure, and human life quite as sacred".†

To clinch the argument, there was the formidable statistical evidence available from the thirty-six countries which had abolished the death-penalty not only for crimes against property but also for murder in the course of the last hundred years.

The evidence has been studied by criminologists and Departments of Justice all over the world, and summarised with previously unequalled thoroughness by the British Parliamentary Select Committee of 1929–30 and the Royal Commission on Capital Punishment of 1948–53. The report and evidence of the first fills some 800 closely printed pages; the report of the second, plus its Minutes of Evidence, nearly 1400 pages of quarto and folio. The conclusion of the Select Committee is summed up as follows:

> Our prolonged examination of the situation in foreign countries has increasingly confirmed us in the assurance that capital punishment may be abolished in this country without endangering life or property, or impairing the security of Society.‡

The conclusions of the Royal Commission were essentially the same.

The defenders of capital punishment are well aware that the statistical evidence is unanswerable. They do not contest it; they ignore it. When pressed in debate, they invariably fall back on one of two answers: (a) "statistics lie" or "do not prove anything"; (b) that the experience of foreign countries has no bearing on conditions in Britain. . . .

*Report of the Select Committee on Capital Punishment, 1929–30, p. 38.
†Ibid., p. 445.
‡Ibid., p. 453.

To sum up: the experience of the civilised world proves as conclusively as the most rigorously sifted evidence can ever prove, that the gallows is no more effective than other, non-lethal, deterrents.

The next part of the book is a detailed analysis of the Law relating to the death penalty as it stood in 1955. It starts with a tour de force – "Reflections on the Hanging of a Pig – or What is Criminal Responsibility?" – intended as a reductio ad absurdum of the principles on which the Law was based:

In Mangin's *L'Homme et la Béte** there is an engraving, entitled: "Infliction of the Death Penalty on a Sow". The sow, dressed in human clothes, legs pinioned, is held down on the scaffold by the executioner, who is fixing the noose round its throat. Facing the sow is the town clerk, reading the sentence from a scroll; at the foot of the scaffold is a jostling crowd, much of the same kind as the crowds which used to assemble around the Tyburn Tree. Mothers are lifting up their children to give them a better view; and a stern worthy is pointing his finger at the screaming sow, obviously explaining: "She is only getting what she deserves."

Animals guilty of killing a human being were, in the Middle Ages, and in isolated cases up to the nineteenth century, tried by lawful procedure, defended by counsel, sometimes acquitted, more often sentenced to be hanged, burned or buried alive. The sow on the engraving had killed a baby, and was hanged in 1386 at Falaise; a horse which had killed a man was hanged at Dijon in 1389; another sow, with a litter of six, was sentenced for the murder of a child at Savigny in 1457, but the baby pigs were reprieved "in lack of positive proof of complicity".

A further capital crime for animals besides homicide (with or without malice aforethought) was sexual intercourse with a human being. In such cases both partners in crime, man and animal, were burned alive together, according to the Lex Carolina. The last recorded case was the burning of Jacques Ferron in 1750 at Vanvres for sodomy with a she-ass; but the animal was acquitted after the Parish Priest and several leading citizens had testified that she was "the victim of violence and had not participated in the crime of her own free will".† Capital punishment of animals

*Paris, 1872.
†E. P. Evans, *The Criminal Prosecution and Capital Punishment of Animals* (London, 1906), p. 150.

fell gradually into abeyance in the eighteenth century; the last recorded case is the trial and execution of a dog for having participated in a robbery and murder, in Délémont, Switzerland, 1906.*

Why do we find the hanging of an animal even more revolting than the hanging of a human being? The question deserves some reflection.

Let us look at the problem from the point of view of the protection of society. We know that hanging pigs won't deter other pigs from attacking babies left carelessly lying around; properly penning up the pigs is a quite sufficient protection of society. But this answer won't hold good, because experience proves that executing the human criminal is also no more effective as a deterrent than penning him up; thus once the belief in deterrence falls, hanging a man is just as pointlessly cruel as hanging a horse. Why, then, are we more horrified by the idea of strangling a horse? Because it is a helpless creature? A woman pinioned or strapped to a chair and hoisted to the rope is just as helpless.

We must try another approach. Let us put it this way: "The poor dumb creature did not know what it was doing, it is not responsible for its acts; and hence the proceedings of the court are an absurd farce." Now at last we seem to be getting somewhere. But are we really? For if you have ever seen the guilty look in your dog's eye after he stole a chop or chewed up your slippers, you know that the jury would have no choice but to find him criminally responsible according to the so-called M'Naghten rule: that he knew the nature of his act, and knew that it was wrong.

A pig, of course, is less intelligent than a dog, and may be said to be lacking, comparatively, in moral sense. But feeble-mindedness and lack of moral sense do not abolish criminal responsibility, nor are they sufficient grounds for pleading "guilty but insane". Nor would a plea of diminished responsibility help, because a creature can have his responsibilty diminished in Scotland but cannot have it diminished in England or Wales. Hence counsel for the defence of the animal must try another line. His last hope is to get the charge reduced from murder to manslaughter. In the case of the horse who kicked its master to death, "provocation" might perhaps do the trick, for the horse had been nervous and irritable ever since it was shocked by a blunderbuss in the battle of Cherbourg, and witnesses testified that its nasty master had fired off a

*Ibid., p. 334.

firecracker in front of its nose to tease it. So the fool had only himself to blame if the horse went off its head. But that won't do either; firstly because provocation is not a mitigating circumstance if committed by mere word or gesture.* And secondly, because the provocation must be such as to satisfy the jury (a) that it deprived the accused of his self-control, and (b) that it *would also have deprived any other reasonable man (or horse) of self-control.* Thus a creature "who is mentally deficient or mentally abnormal or is 'not of good mental balance' or who is 'unusually excitable or pugnacious' is *not* entitled to rely on provocation which would not have led an ordinary person to act as he did".† This nicety of the law referring to provocation is usually called "the test of the reasonable man".‡ It states expressly that when the jury has to decide whether the provocation was sufficient to deprive a reasonable man of his self-control, they ought *not to* "take into account different degrees of mental ability".§ That means that the jury, in assessing the effect of provocation, must not consider the living individual before them but an abstract ideal being. This fantastic ruling was approved by the Court of Criminal Appeal (in 1940), and again by the House of Lords (in 1942).‖ Accordingly, the firecracker let off in front of the shell-shocked horse, which made the creature go off its head, does not justify a plea of provocation because a reasonable horse wouldn't have gone off its head; nor calling a survivor from a Nazi concentration camp a filthy Jew, because a reasonable person wouldn't turn a hair.

As a last resort, Counsel might try to argue that the poor horse did not act with "malice aforethought"; if he could prove that, the charge would be reduced from murder to manslaughter. But how could he prove that? For, to quote the 1953 Royal Commission Report on Capital Punishment, "in the phrase 'malice aforethought' neither of the two words used is used in its ordinary sense. . . . It is now only an arbitrary symbol. For the malice may have in it nothing really malicious; and need never be really aforethought, except in the sense that every desire must necessar-

---

*Except "in cirumstances of a most extreme and exceptional character". There has been no recent case in which mere words or gesture have been accepted as sufficient provocation.
†Royal Commission Report on Capital Punishment, 1949–53, p. 141.
‡Ibid., p. 128.
§Ibid., p. 137.
‖Ibid.

ily come before – though perhaps only an instant before – the act which is desired. The word aforethought in the definition has thus become either false or else superfluous."*

And yet this meaningless phrase is still the *basic criterion* of murder. "The statement of the modern law most commonly cited as authoritative is that given in 1877 by Sir James Stephen in his *Digest of the Criminal Law*: 'Malice aforethought means any one or more of the following states of mind preceding or coexisting with the act . . . by which death is caused, and *it may exist where the act is unpremeditated.*' "†

The short and long of the matter is: if animals were still prosecuted in our courts, the jury, according to the law as it stands, would have no choice but to bring in a verdict of guilty against the pig, the horse and the cow.

Subsequent chapters of the book deal with the problem of free will versus determinism, as it affects the death-penalty. The crucial concept of "criminal responsibility" in the Law is based on the tacit assumption that the accused chose to commit the act out of his own free will, and was not compelled to do so by heredity, environment and other determinant factors – for if this were the case, he could not be held responsible. The result is a deadly labyrinth of paradoxes (like the definition of "malice aforethought"); whether the accused will get out of it depends largely on the skill of opposing Counsels.

The remaining chapters deal with "alternatives to hanging" and the appalling record of people hanged as a result of judicial error:

Innocent men have been hanged in the past and will be hanged in the future unless either the death-penalty is abolished or the fallibility of human judgement is abolished and judges become supermen.

Let us go back to the last Royal Commission appointed by Queen Victoria in 1864. The chief witness on the question of judicial error was Sir Fitzroy Kelly, the former Attorney-General and Solicitor-General, whose testimony was summed up in the Commission's report as follows:

*Ibid., p. 74.
†Ibid.

After careful consideration and examination, he has come to the conclusion that it is not in any way reasonably to be doubted that in many instances innocent men have been capitally convicted, and in certain numbers of instances have been actually executed.*

These were the cases where the innocence of the victims was virtually proven; but, Kelly continued, "There is presumptive ground for believing that [other] innocent persons have suffered death for want of having influential or wealthy friends to procure an investigation of their case."† He added that the Sheriff of London, Mr Wilde, "had given him the names and particulars of the cases of five persons who *in a single year* were erroneously convicted and sentenced to death".‡

That, one may say, was a long time ago, and justice has improved since. But the law and court procedure have remained *substantially the same.*§ In 1864 the possibility of judicial error was as pompously and categorically denied by the Law Lords and Home Secretaries as it is today. In 1864, before Kelly gave the evidence just quoted, Lord Wensleydale "was not aware of a capital case in which he thought the verdict ill-founded"; in 1948, Sir Maxwell Fyfe stated with the same assurance that "there is no practical possibility" of justice miscarrying: "the Honourable and Learned Member is moving in a realm of fantasy when he makes that suggestion". A couple of years later we hanged Timothy Evans‖ – who was subsequently declared not guilty as charged by the Home Secretary responsible for his execution.

Every country and every age has its famous cases of men convicted by judicial error. Once a man is dead, the chances of proving that he was innocent are virtually nil. It is an axiom of the law that the burden of proof should lie with the prosecution; but when you try to vindicate a man, and a dead man to boot, it is up to the defence to establish positive proof of his innocence. And since it needs a near-miracle for a judicial error to be detected, it is not unreasonable to assume that the number of undetected errors may be greater than we believe. There is a long row of cases, stretching

*Capital Punishment Commission, 1866, Minutes, 1054–5.
†Ibid., 1063–74.
‡Ibid., 1060–3.
§The only differences relevant to this chapter are that since 1896 the accused man has been allowed to give evidence from the witness box (which is often a doubtful blessing); and the establishment of the Court of Criminal Appeal.
‖For an account of the Evans case see *Ten Rillington Place* (London, 1961), by Ludovic Kennedy.

from Queen Victoria's day to ours, in which judicial error was either admitted, or all but technically proved. [There follows a selected list of about a dozen cases.]

No doubt judge and jury always try, according to their lights, to give a man a fair trial. If judicial errors nevertheless continue to occur with monotonous regularity, this cannot be due to accident; *the probablity of error is inherent in the judicial procedure.* I shall now briefly examine some of the main sources of error and uncertainty in murder trials. They fall under the following headings: (a) fallibility of witnesses; (b) fallibility of experts; (c) coincidence; (d) to (h) fallibility of juries, judges, appeal judges and Home Secretaries; (i) carelessness of solicitors and counsel; (j) unworkability of the M'Naghten rules defining insanity.

The book then describes the procedure under each heading and some examples of actual miscarriages of justice resulting from it. To quote a single example, under heading (b): in murder trials both sides call, as a rule, their own experts, and it is up to the jury to decide which side to believe. How is a jury of laymen to decide which of the conflicting expert evidence to accept, which to reject?

In 1953 Mrs Merrifield was convicted and hanged for the poisoning of another woman by arsenic. The pathologist giving evidence for the prosecution said the victim had been poisoned. The pathologist for the defence said she had died a natural death. The case is the more remarkable because the pathologist for the defence whom the jury did not believe was Professor Webster, chief of the Forensic Laboratory in Birmingham for twenty years, who during that period had been the *prosecution's* witness in every murder case of the Midlands Circuit. We are left to infer that Professor Webster was a sufficiently reliable expert to secure a conviction, but not reliable enough to secure an acquittal even by "reasonable doubt". . . . One shudders at the discovery how much of one's notion of a "fair trial" was built on illusion.

In 1938, a Gallup poll on the question whether the death-penalty should be maintained or not, showed 50 per cent "ayes" in favour of hanging, and 50 per cent "nays" and "don't knows". Nine years later, in a similar poll, "ayes" in favour of hanging had increased to 68 per cent. Another eight years later, in July, 1955, the *Daily Mirror* arranged a new poll which revealed a complete reversal of

public opinion: 65 per cent voted against the death-penalty —
about the same proportion which previously had voted for it.

Such wild fluctuations of public opinion are unusual in a country where the floating vote amounts only to a small fraction of the
total, and General Elections are decided by narrow margins. There
is, no doubt, a steady, gradual increase in the number of people
who favour a more humane administration of the law; but this
slowly mounting tide does not account for the violent gales which
blow now in one direction, now in the other. When the vision of
the gibbet appears on the nation's horizon, opinion swings and
twists like the body suspended from it; eyes bulge and reason is
strangled. If the last victim happens to arouse pity, up go the
"nays" of mercy like a flight of doves; if he is a cool customer like
Christie, up go the "ayes" like a swarm of vultures. Let us agree
that this is not a dignified or desirable state of affairs.

Public opinion is still the strongest passive support of the
hang-hards. The main reasons for this are ignorance, prejudice
and repressed cruelty.

The public's ignorance of the facts and arguments of the issue is
fostered by official spokesmen and other oracles. The public is
made to believe that only the hangman can protect them against
"the hardened robber"; that it is quite impossible for an innocent
to be hanged; that no mentally sick person is hanged; that all the
burglars of the realm are impatiently waiting for Abolition D-Day
to arm themselves with guns, and that the day of the hanging
judges is past. Once the smoke-screen is dispelled, people will
realise that hanging is simply a stupid and cruel relic of the past,
much more stupid and cruel than they ever imagined.

Ignorance can be cured, but not callousness. Those who feel
strongly that this nation should continue to break people's necks
or strangle them to glory, display a curious mixture of insensitiv-
ity and sentimental traditonalism which makes them impervious
to reasoned argument. They believe that legal murder prevents
illegal murder, as the Persians believed that whipping the sea will
calm the storm. They will say that England cannot do without
hanging, and when you point to the example of other countries
which get along perfectly well without it, they will say that
foreigners are different. They will say that English justice makes
hanging by legal error impossible, and when you quote the names
of people who were hanged in error, they will answer that you
cannot expect any system to be perfect. They will say that hanging
is the most humane method of execution, and if you quote cases of

women dragged to the drop in a free-for-all fight, they will answer
that mentioning such matters is in bad taste.

Samuel Romilly said that cruel punishments have an inevitable
tendency to produce cruelty in people. The image of the gallows
appeals to latent sadism as pornography appeals to latent sexual
appetites. Newspaper editors cannot be expected to stop making
the most of hanging, so long as hanging exists. In countries from
which the death-penalty has vanished, this dirty sensationalism
has vanished too, and murder trials do not get more publicity in
the press than cases of burglary or fraud now get in this country.
For the fascination of the murder trial, and its appeal to unconscious cruelty, lies in the fact that a man is fighting for his life like
a gladiator in the arena, and in the thrilling uncertainty whether
the outcome will be thumbs up or thumbs down. One only wonders why the bookmakers and tote do not come in.

Moral deterrent, public example, reverence for human life –
what bloody hypocrisy! So long as there are bull-fights there will
be *aficionados*, and so long as there are gladiators there will be a
circus audience. There is a poisoned spray coming from the Old
Bailey which corrupts and depraves; it can only be stopped by
abolishing its cause, the death-penalty itself. Tradition has a
hypnotic effect which commands blind belief, an instinctive
recoil from any new departure as a "dangerous experiment", and
unwillingness to listen to reasoned argument. This is why the
principal defenders of hanging have always been the most
tradition-bound bodies of the nation: the House of Lords, the
Bishops Bench, the upper ranks of the gowned and wigged profession. Yet in spite of their power and influence over the public
mind, chunk after chunk of sacred tradition has been wrenched
from their hands: the pillory and the ducking chair, the stake and
the gibbet, the cat-o'-nine-tails; and within the next few years the
strangling cord will be wrested from them too.

For despite the inertia of man's imagination and its resistance to
reason and fact, people are beginning to realise that the deliberate
taking of life by the State is unjustifiable on religious or
philosophic or scientific grounds; that hanging by mistake will go
on as long as capital punishment will go on, because the risk is
inherent in its nature; that the vast majority of murderers are
either mentally sick and belong to the mental sick ward, or victims of circumstance, who can be reclaimed for human society;
and that the substitution of the life sentence for the death-penalty
exposes the peaceful citizen to no greater risk than that of being

killed by lightning in a bus queue, and considerably less than the risk of being a passive accomplice in the execution of an innocent or a mentally deranged person.

It is not only a question of the thirteen individual lives which we offer annually as a sacrifice to the stupid moloch of prejudice. The gallows is not only a machine of death, but a symbol. It stands for everything that mankind must reject, if mankind is to survive.

Chapter 46

KEEPING THE SPARK ALIVE

The strong public response to the serialisation of Reflections on Hanging in the Observer induced the Home Office to make a rather unusual move. On the eve of the second reading of the ill-fated Abolition Bill of 1956, the Under-Secretary of State, Lord Mancroft, accused me in the House of Lords of having deliberately misquoted official documents. As he had got all his facts and figures wrong – due, presumably to a too hurried briefing by his Department – the accusations were easy to refute; thus, after my reply, published in the next issue of the Observer (March 11, 1956), the Under-Secretary (and two other Peers who had seconded him) were obliged to apologise in the House of Lords and to withdraw all their allegations – which was a considerable moral victory for the Campaign. The Press Council found even these apologies not strong enough and administered stern rebukes to the offenders. I mention this episode as a typical example of how vindictiveness combines with ignorance of facts among the defenders of hanging. (A similar incident – accusation, retraction and Press Council rebuke of the Home Secretary – took place in the House of Commons.)

Sidney Silverman's Abolition Bill of 1956, after passing through its three stages in the Commons, was thrown out by the House of Lords; not until 1965 was the death penalty suspended, and finally abolished in 1970. During the later stages of the Campaign, I frequently wrote in the Observer under the pen-name Vigil, which was less controversial than my own. The following article by Vigil* is a sample of that judicious and dispassionate worthy's comments on one of the murderous inanities of the Law, already mentioned in the extracts from the book, but worth some further comment because of its sheer incredibility.

*The Observer, January 22, 1956. Reprinted in Drinkers of Infinity (1968).

The Unreasonable Murderer

Clarence William Ward is due to be hanged in Armley Gaol next Thursday at 9 a.m. He is aged thirty-one and officially described as a "lorry driver's mate" – that is, the man next to the driver in the coal delivery van who hauls down the sacks of coal on his shoulders and empties them into the chute.

Ward was sentenced to death at Leeds Assizes on December 14 last for murdering eighteen-month-old Margaret Walker, the illegitimate child, by another man, of the mistress with whom he lived. At his trial he was described by Chief Inspector Byrne as a man of subnormal mentality, and Margaret as a backward child who at eighteen months could not walk, stand or crawl. Giving evidence, the mother, Miss Walker, said that Ward had "spent hours" trying to teach Margaret to walk.

Ward said in evidence that on the day of the crime he came home tired from work and plagued by gastric ulcers; he started to repair Margaret's bed while the child kept crying; he lost his temper and shook it by using his "full force", but was not aware of it at the time. When he realised that the child was dead, he persuaded its mother to help him bury it in a slagheap, where the body was discovered nearly twenty months later, in September, 1955.

This humdrum tragedy may turn out to be of considerable legal significance owing to the subsequent ruling of the Court of Criminal Appeal. Ward appealed on the grounds that the Judge, Mr Justice Pilcher, had misdirected the jury regarding the test to be applied to decide whether Ward was guilty of murder or manslaughter. The Judge had instructed the jury that the test was what a "reasonable man would have thought or contemplated" (while committing the act); whereas Counsel for the appellant submitted that the test was "what went on in that particular man's head at that particular moment". There was, he submitted, no reported case and no authority for the application of the "test of the reasonable man" in cases of this type.

The Court of Criminal Appeal dismissed the appeal on January 11. Lord Chief Justice Goddard, giving the judgement of the Court, endorsed the Judge's direction to the jury that the only test which could be applied in these cases was "what would a reasonable man contemplate? If the act was one which any reasonable man must have known would cause death or grievous bodily harm, then it did amount to murder."

Since precedent has been the basis of Common Law from time immemorial, and still is, it is to be expected that the Court's ruling against Ward will be quoted time and again in the future in cases where the vital (and deadly) distinction between murder and manslaughter is involved. The law of the realm, put into lay language, will now be on the following lines:

If A kills B in a frenzy of jealousy, or as a result of anger or nervous stress, the Judge will be justified in directing the jury to find the culprit guilty of murder and not manslaughter, because (cf. *Regina v. Ward*, January 11, 1956) "the test must be applied to all alike and the only test which could be applied in these cases was – what would a reasonable man contemplate?"

The ruling is not an entirely new departure, because the "test of the reasonable man" has for a long time served to assess the gravity of *provocation*. The law on this point as it presently stands says that provocation can be regarded as a mitigating circumstance, reducing murder to manslaughter, only if it is shown that the provocation not only deprived the accused person of his self-control, *but was also sufficient to deprive a "reasonable man" of his self-control*. This means that if the accused is mentally abnormal or for some other reason abnormally susceptible to provocation, he must still be judged *as if* he were an ordinary, reasonable, average Englishman.

So much then for provocation. But Ward did not plead that he was provoked; his defence was that he had killed the baby unintentionally, i.e. without malice aforethought. His appeal was based on the submission that Mr Justice Pilcher had "imported", in the absence of any authority and precedent, the "test of the reasonable man" *as a test for malice aforethought* or murderous intent. The ruling of the Court of Criminal Appeal has now sanctioned this importation.

Henceforth, it would seem that in the light of this interpretation a man can be convicted of murder if, while deprived of self-control, he commits an act which a reasonable person would have foreseen would be likely to result in death. All this will make the already ambiguous and hazy distinction between murder and manslaughter even more hazardous for the jury – and for the accused.

Some jurors will probably regard the test of the "reasonable man" as begging the question, because murder of this type is always committed in an unreasonable state of mind. Ward, for instance, killed apparently in a state of frenzy. The reasonable man *ex hypothesi* is never in a state of frenzy. Ward was suffering from ulcers. Does the "reasonable man" have ulcers? The issue from the common sense point of view is that at the moment when A committed the murder he was *not* a reasonable man. The issue from the Common Law point of view is that at the moment he committed the crime he *ought* to have been a reasonable man.

The law of murder, as it stands today, demands that a man standing trial for his life should not be judged as an individual person, but by standards of a fictitious being, of an abstract idea of rationality. It is in the name of these somewhat antiquated assumptions that Clarence William Ward is scheduled to be hanged on January 26.

Ward was reprieved on January 23. A few days later, an editorial in the Manchester Guardian *suggested that Vigil's article had influenced the outcome. It is not an exaggeration to say that it was one of the happiest days in Vigil's life.*

Another of Vigil's exploits deserves perhaps to be mentioned, because it owed its effect to its very obviousness. This was a pamphlet distributed by the Campaign to all Members of Parliament on the eve of one of the debates on the 1956 Abolition Bill. It was called "Patterns of Murder – A Survey of Men and Women Executed in England, Scotland and Wales during the Five Years 1949–53" – and it summarised the individual case histories of the altogether eighty-five men and women hanged during that period. No such survey had been available before to the legislators or public; the purpose of the exercise was to refute the constantly repeated reassurances by Home Office spokesmen that only cold-blooded murderers for gain were actually hanged, all others reprieved even if found guilty:

Patterns of Murder

The list printed below is a complete record of all murderers executed in the five years 1949–53, with a brief description of their crime. It is intended to fill a conspicuous gap, for no such record for any period past or present has hitherto been published by the Home Office. Statistical summaries do not mention individual cases, and provide no answer to the question: Who are the people whom we hang? The absence of any concrete information on this fundamental point has given the debate on capital punishment a somewhat abstract, unrealistic character and has led to serious misconceptions regarding the type of murderer who is executed. An attempt to supply this missing element of information is made below. Even in this necessarily compressed form it will enable the reader to form an independent opinion on the Home Secretary's statements.

There follows the macabre list. Samples:

James Farrell, aged eighteen, killed his girl friend, aged fourteen. Defence: insanity. Farrell's mother had been in a mental home for the past three and a half years. Hanged on March 3, 1949.

Dennis Neville, labourer, twenty-two, killed his girl-friend of twenty-one after she told him she was with child by another man. Discharged from the Army with 20 per cent disability pension because of "anxiety state of psycho-neurosis". After his discharge his father was killed in a brawl and his brother killed in action. Two defence psychiatrists testified to schizophrenia. Hanged on June 2, 1949.

Benjamin Roberts, a miner, twenty-three, found his girl-friend in the arms of another man. Shot her, then shot himself in the head with a double-barrelled sporting gun. Was nursed back to life and hanged on December 14, 1949, in defiance of a Jury recommendation to mercy.

And so it goes on. The conclusions occupy six pages of the pamphlet, of which the first three paragraphs are quoted below:

1 The record confirms the statement by Sir John Macdonell, based on the statistics of 1885–1905, and endorsed by the Royal Commission fifty years later, that murder "is not generally the crime of the so-called criminal classes, but is in most cases rather an incident in miserable lives".*

2 *Prima facie*, about seventy cases, i.e., over 80 per cent, seem to belong to the category of *crime passionnel* and/or crimes of the disordered mind. Murders for financial gain *without* a marked trait of mental abnormality number twelve in all, and in most of these cases the psychiatric aspect was not discussed. Even these are almost throughout unpremeditated and committed in an affray or panic to avoid detection or arrest. Of the so-called

*Royal Commission Report, p. 330.

"cold-blooded premeditated murder for gain" by a sane person, there is only one example.

3 By far the most prevalent cause of murder is insanity and mental disorder, ranging from the certifiably insane to epileptics, psychopaths, and borderline cases of varying kinds.

*   *   *

Having served its purpose at home, Reflections on Hanging continued to serve the abolitionist cause in foreign translations. Thus the USA edition carried a "Preface for Americans" by Edmond Cahn, Professor of Law, New York University; the French edition was co-authored by Albert Camus, and new translations still keep coming in, a quarter-century after the book was written, from countries where the death penalty is a subject of renewed debate.

However, the ordeal which the vast majority of the prison population has to endure is not the fear of execution, but boredom, depression, the slow death of the spirit. In 1960, while working on The Act of Creation, the obvious idea occurred to me that creative activity could provide an antidote to mental deterioration in the case of at least some of the prisoners. This eventually led to the founding of the Prisoner Award Scheme named after me, which has been in existence since 1962.

The story of the Award does not strictly belong in a volume of selected writings, but as a footnote to Reflections on Hanging – of which it was an indirect offshoot – a few lines on it may perhaps be justified. The Award is based on an annual competition in the creative arts (literature, musical composition, arts and crafts) "open to prisoners of both sexes in HM Prisons, Borstals and Special Hospitals, except for petty offenders serving short sentences". The prizes are awarded by a panel of judges, who have included among others J. B. Priestley, Sir Victor Pritchett, Lord Clark, Julian Trevelyan, Sir Hugh Casson and Sir Arthur Bliss, Master of the Queen's Musick. Their names have provided some reflected glory inside the prison walls.

The first competition brought in about 300 entries from prisoners all over the country. The prize-winning entries in the arts and crafts are shown at annual exhibitions, and sold to private buyers on the prisoners' behalf. The average quality of the entries might be described as on a decent amateur level; but there have been a few works of exceptional merit submitted every year. Some of the prize-winners succeeded, after their release, in becoming professional painters or writers, although they had never painted or written before their imprisonment. But these success-stories, which have occasionally hit the newspaper headlines, are no more than an occasional windfall, while the primary purpose of the Award is a more modest one: to make serving the sentence a little more bearable to the prisoner; perhaps even to enable him to gain something positive from it by discovering some latent potential within himself. This seems to be a realistic approach (which does not exclude a secret wish-dream of one day discovering a Picasso in the Maximum Security Ward).

Chapter 47

THE LION AND THE OSTRICH

The "campaigns and causes" which I have mentioned (and some others not mentioned in this volume) were non-political. The only relapse into politics after the "vocational change" to which I must plead guilty was occasioned by a series of articles which the Observer published in January-February, 1963, under the general heading "What's Left For Patriotism?" The article which follows concluded the series.

To be born into this world as a British citizen involves neither effort nor act of choice. To become British by naturalisation involves both. But although I was naturalised many years ago, I felt rather awkward when, in the *Observer's* announcement of this series, I found myself advertised in London tube stations as a "patriotic Briton".

To get up my courage – and also because the episode leads straight into the subject – I must recall November, 1940. After the collapse of France, I found myself stranded with thousands of others in Portugal, trying to get to England and into her Army – the last hope of Europe. The United States, still neutral at the time, kindly offered me an entry permit on their emergency quota for "persecuted intellectuals"; the British Home Office refused to let me in.

Nevertheless, with the unlawful help of the British Consul at Lisbon, Sir Henry King, and *The Times* correspondent Walter Lucas, I managed to get on board a British transport plane. On arrival I was sent to Pentonville prison, where I did a stretch of six weeks as an illegal entrant. After that I was permitted to join the Army, more precisely, the Pioneer Corps – the only army unit then open to alien volunteers – and to "Dig for Victory", as the posters invitingly said. Thus Pentonville was my prep school, the Aliens' Pioneer Corps my Eton.

My company was employed on a vital defence job, and we were of course "too keen" as foreigners notoriously are. So we asked our British CO to do away with the ritual tea-breaks – which, what with downing tools, marching fifteen minutes to the cook-hut and back, mornings and afternoons, cost nearly two hours of our working time. The CO appreciated our laudable zeal and explained that we had to have our tea-breaks whether we liked it or not because the British Pioneer Companies, plus the local trade unions, would raise hell if we did not. That was about six months after Dunkirk.

While digging for victory, and later in the Ambulance Service, I came to know intimately the lower strata of the working classes, and found them different in several fundamental respects from workers on the Continent. Sharing the loneliness of the long-distance runners* in NAAFI canteens and at the snooker table in the ambulance station, I soon learned that the world is divided between "Them" and "us". The "T" is capitalised, the "u" is not, because "us" had nothing to do with class-consciousness in the Marxian sense – as it existed in the militant Socialist parties of Europe. Politics hardly entered into this attitude; instead of the fierce class-hatred which had scorched the Continent with revolutions and civil wars, there was a kind of stale, resentful fatalism. I learned to conform to our unwritten Rules of Life: Go slow; it's a mug's game anyway; if you play it, you are letting your mates down; if you seek betterment, promotion, you are breaking ranks and will be sent to Coventry. My comrades could be lively and full of bounce; at the working site they moved like figures in a slow-motion film, or deep-sea divers on the ocean-bed. The most cherished rituals of our tribal life were the tea-and-bun breaks – serene and protracted like a Japanese tea ceremony. Another fascinating tribal custom was the punctuation of every sentence with four-letter words used as adjectives, without reference to meaning, compulsive like hiccups. It was not swearing; these strings of dehydrated obscenity served as a kind of negative status symbol.

Some of my buddies came from the slums; some of them had been taught as children to use cupboard drawers for chamber-pots. The majority were a decent lot, with untapped human potentialities buried under the tribal observances. In the Libyan desert,

---

*An allusion to Alan Sillitoe's classic short story about working class delinquents in a Borstal institution.

or as rear-gunners in Flying Fortresses, they would have been magnificent. But then in the RAF and among the Desert Rats, the deadly gulf was at least temporarily bridged by shared danger and hardship, by that *esprit de corps* which is patriotism in miniature; and above all by an awareness of playing a man's game instead of a mug's game. The same bloke who unhesitatingly risked his life at Alamein to "keep Britain free" would not lift a finger at Dagenham to save Britain from bankruptcy.

The steep rise of wages, the improved conditions of housing, schools, health services during the post-war years; the advent of the TV set and the washing-machine have lent the upper strata of the working classes the external trappings of middle-class life. But the internal rift shows no sign of healing; on the contrary, it has deepened and hardened into a cold class war. The frontier between Britain's two civilisations – I almost said "two nations" – is not hermetically closed; exceptionally gifted young people do cross the line; but for the bulk of the population the frontier persists.

One side embraces the whole complex social pyramid of the upper and middle classes with its endless intricate sub-divisions, but with certain basic aspirations and values in common; a collective image of "gracious living" which everybody tries to emulate or imitate, even at the price of making fools of themselves. The other side will have none of it. It has its back resolutely turned on "their" style of life, standards of value, codes of behaviour. "Competition for jobs, for promotion or privileged positions – the serious concerns of the middle-class adult, are disapproved of. . . . In their own sector of society and increasingly as they get older and hardened to their class position, success must be devalued as improper, as bought by sycophancy or by cheating".*

The British working class has become an immensely powerful, non-competitive enclave in our competitive society. It has evolved its own image – a combination of Dickens and Coronation Street, of Z-Cars, "Saturday Night and Sunday Morning"; of "I'm All Right, Jack" and "The Angry Silence" – that nightmare story of one Tom Dobson, an expert welder whom his mates treat as dead because, after three wildcat strikes, he refuses to toe the line.

British social history since the end of the war differs fundamentally from that of other European countries. In the late forties, Italy

*Tom Burns, "The Cold Class War", *New Statesman*, April 7, 1956.

and France, for instance, seemed on the verge of civil war, and the Communists were the strongest single party in both countries. The rising curve of prosperity led to a corresponding decline of revolutionary fervour; moreover, the trade unions split up into Socialist, Christian-Democrat and Communist unions, which turned trade union politics into a truly democratic game.

In this country class relations evolved in the opposite direction. Communist influence in the unions was negligible at the end of the war; it increased with growing prosperity and full employment; today it is the dominant factor in industrial relations, and its disruptive effects are more strongly felt in this country than anywhere else in Europe. The nation gets only episodic glimpses of the true state of its affairs and believes that these are isolated incidents; in fact, they are the result of a planned, centralised and extremely well-organised campaign. Penetration of the trade unions "to hasten the inevitable collapse of the doomed capitalist system" has been the foremost aim of the Communist movement everywhere in the world; it has been reasserted as a programme from Lenin onward in thousands of Party brochures, Party resolutions, training courses; it is one of the cornerstones of the whole doctrine. In his cautionary tale *When the Kissing had to Stop*, Constantine FitzGibbon got hold of the wrong end of the stick. It is unthinkable that Guy Burgess and John Gollan should take over Whitehall by a political *putsch* supported by the Red Army. The real danger, if the present drift continues, is a situation patterned on the 1926 General Strike, but with more disastrous consequences.

Marxian dialectics is as much double-Dutch to the British working class as it is to the rest of the British electorate. The unofficial strikers are not Communists but unconscious tools. The rise in living standards has given the workers an increased awareness of the fact that they still live on the dark side of the moon – that they do not "belong" to a society run by Them, whose values they repudiate. They are not anti-patriotic but a-patriotic. They feel let down not only by the Establishment but also by the Labour Party and their own trade union bosses. In 1946, it was Mr Attlee's Socialist Government which had to call in the Army to maintain London's food supply during the unauthorised strike of the transport workers. The *Tribune* wrote at the time: "The leaders of this mammoth union (the TGWU) were clearly out of touch with the men they were supposed to represent. They seemed to know next to nothing of the mood of their members."

Symbolic of the prevailing mood are incidents like the following from my private "This England" file:

A thousand railwaymen at Eastleigh, Southampton, carriage works of British Railways stopped work for two hours yesterday because they may no longer be able to have their hair cut by railway employees, in railway time, and on railway premises (*The Times*, July, 1958).

Equally typical is the monotonous series of strikes resulting from internecine quarrels between rival unions: firemen against footplate men, drillers against welders, and so on. In 1956 the Merseyside dispute between joiners and metal-workers about who should drill the holes in aluminium sheets led to a strike which lasted six months and attracted national attention. It was regarded as a kind of music hall joke, an endearing quaintness of characters out of Dickens. Two years later, *The Times* reported that four hundred men had to be dismissed as redundant, eleven thousand were threatened by the same fate, that production on three vessels and a submarine had to be postponed indefinitely because the boiler-makers and the drillers could not agree who was entitled "to use five stud-welding guns designed to weld nuts and thimbles to metal plates". It then transpired that the use of this quick and efficient method had been prevented by this dispute between the two unions for the last *twelve years*.

To be sure, strikes are no rarity on the Continent either; but in no other country has the national output been crippled on such frivolous and irresponsible grounds. In this oldest of all democracies, class relations have become more bitter, trade union politics more undemocratic than in de Gaulle's France or Adenauer's Germany. The motivation behind it is neither Communism, Socialism nor enlightened self-interest; but a mood of disenchantment and cussedness. Its origins can be traced back to the period after the "Socialist landslide" of 1945 when the Labour Party had the unique chance of breaking down the psychological class barriers – and missed it. Its "Work and Want" posters gave the impression that the whole nation was living in a Borstal.

This is one side of the picture. It needed stressing because it is usually passed over in embarrassed silence, symptomatic of the guilt feelings of middle-class intellectuals. If I have been outspoken, it is because my sympathies are with Alan Sillitoe's heroes rather than with Evelyn Waugh's. The other side of the picture is sufficiently well known and more frankly discussed: the

unimaginativeness and lack of adaptability of the British entre-
preneur, the old-fashioned methods of management, the shortcomings of technological education.

The combined result of all this can be summed up in a few
disconcerting figures. In the five-year period 1950–5, British
exports increased by 6 per cent, those of the Common Market by
76 per cent. In the next five years, 1955–60, British exports rose by
13 per cent, Common Market exports by 63 per cent (OECD Report
on United Kingdom, April, 1962). Over the whole decade
1950–60 "no industrial nation had a slower growth of per capita
output than Britain" (*Time*, October 19, 1962). Last year, for
instance, the gross product of French national income increased
by 6 per cent, Britain's by less than 2 per cent; and over the whole
period since 1950, the growth of the national income of EEC
countries was twice as fast as ours. Statistics are influenced by
many factors; but the total trend is unmistakable. It is reflected in
some recent surveys, according to which 45 per cent to 60 per cent
of young people under twenty-five would like to emigrate if they
could.

In his preface to the English translation of *Das Kapital*, Engels
wrote in 1886 that Marx, "after a life-long study of the economic
history and conditions of England", had been "led to the conclusion that, at least in Europe, England is the only country where the
inevitable social revolution might be effected entirely by peaceful
and legal means".

It is one of the few Marxian predictions that has come true. The
continuity of tradition, and the knack of combining it with
piecemeal reforms, is perhaps the most impressive feature in this
country's history. The bourgeoisie, instead of stringing up the
aristocrats on lamp-posts, intermarried with them and gave rise to
a dynamic upper middle class. Continuity triumphed even over
the decline of the Empire. The declines and falls of the past were
catastrophic events; for the first time in history we saw an Empire
gradually dissolving with a certain dignity and grace.

But the price for avoiding bloody revolutions such as every
major European country has suffered since 1789, is beginning to
make itself felt. Complacency has spread like dry rot; "keen",
"smart", "clever" have become pejorative terms. Once upon a
time England was "the workshop of the world"; if the Persians
wanted a railway engine or the Turks a tooling machine, they had
to await their turn or lump it. Today, as a German industrialist
remarked, "if the Persians want to build a railway, we give them a

seven-months' delivery date and seven years' credit; der British gives them a seven-years' delivery date and seven months' credit". Britain is only just beginning to emerge from the delusion that she still lives in Queen Victoria's day; sooner or later she must face her moment of truth.

The same arrested development is reflected in the relations between social classes. The working class insists on perpetuating its proletarian status, while everywhere else it is in the process of merging into the middle classes. The other half of the nation forms a politely camouflaged caste society with a pecking hierarchy which is a unique anachronism in modern Europe. Englishmen take it for granted that a person's social background can be detected by his drawls and aitches; they are incredulous when told that in France, for instance, regional dialects apart, the vocabularly and pronunciation of the educated worker, shopkeeper or industrialist are indistinguishable. The reason is simple; the educational system is uniform; it is based on competitive selection; rank and wealth confer no educational advantages; access to the two pinnacles of learning, the *Ecole Normale Superieure* and the *Ecole Polytechnique*, is exclusively based on the candidate's merits. These two schools produce the nation's political and intellectual élite; and the only accent which commands respect and even envy is the characteristic enunciation of the *normalien*.

The first decisive step towards a true democracy is to provide equal educational opportunities for all. This alone would enable the nation to speak the same language – both in the metaphorical and in the literal sense. Does that imply that the Public School system ought to go? I am sorry to say, yes. I am not such a fool nor such a barbarian as to underestimate what the system has done to make the nation great. But its function is fulfilled; and unequal educational opportunities, placing privilege before merit, is the original sin which tears a nation apart and delivers it to the rule, not of a meritocracy but of a mediocracy.

The breaking-down of these anachronistic class barriers is, I believe, the most urgent task confronting British patriotism. It ought to be accompanied by the breaking down of the outer barriers which separate England from Europe. To go it alone is unthinkable; and "Europe or the Commonwealth" is a spurious alternative. Geographically and historically this island belongs to Europe. Economically, Commonwealth trade is decreasing, trade with Europe increasing. Our cultural heritage comes from

Europe, not from Ghana, Pakistan or Australia. Our holidays, if we can afford it, are spent in Europe, not in New Zealand. If your friends assert that the Commonwealth is more real to them than Europe, and closer to their hearts, ask them which exactly are the African and Asian countries which belong to the family; you will be surprised.

In 1940, good old John Bull alone represented Europe; today he is a European *malgré lui*, but European nevertheless. The regrettable suspension of the negotiations about British entry into the Common Market has not altered my belief in the historic necessity of a united Europe, including these European isles.

I realise that I have not explained why I love this country, why I live here, and why, though I still feel at times a stranger in Britain, I feel thoroughly British when abroad. To explain all this would have been easier and more gratifying, but out of character for an anglicised European. When all is said, one loves one's country not *because* of this or that – but rather in spite of all.

Impressed by the lively polemics to which this Observer *article gave rise, the editors of* Encounter *magazine invited me to act as guest editor of a special issue devoted to the state of Britain. It appeared in July, 1963 under the title "Suicide of a Nation?", and was published later in book form (Hutchinson, 1963). The cover design showed the traditional coat of arms, in which, however, the unicorn had been replaced by an ostrich; the reason for this innovation was explained in the Preface:*

A chimaera, in Greek mythology, was a monster with a lion's head, a goat's trunk, and a serpent's tail. The Englishman strikes one as a much more attractive hybrid between a lion and an ostrich. In times of emergency he rises magnificently to the occasion. In between emergencies he buries his head in the sand. This attitude is not only soothing, but also guarantees that a new emergency will soon arise and provide a new opportunity for turning into a lion and rising magnificently to the occasion. . . .

Here is one more quote from the Epilogue to "Suicide of a Nation?" referring to a sadly significant, specifically British, phenomenon:

. . . Two vivid memories come to mind. First, a scene in *Modern Times* where Charlie Chaplin, after several hours spent at the moving assembly belt going through the same sequence of three or four jerky motions, keeps on repeating them like a wound-up automaton after the belt has stopped moving. The second is a televised interview with two young Merseyside workers, occasioned by one of those demarcation disputes about who should drill the holes. Asked by the interviewer why they were opposed to young people learning more than one skill, to acquiring more knowledge, flexibility, and all-round understanding of the production process in which they were engaged, the two lads rigidly, stubbornly, repeated: "Because that would lead to unemployment. We don't want to be pushed about. We remember 1929. . . ."

They did not, of course, remember 1929, only what their elders had told them, and their union leaders had taught them. It was the sacred doctrine that the man who lays the cold-water pipes must not be allowed to lay the hot-water pipes, the man who makes the cable must not be allowed to make the casting for the cable, a doctrine which holds up as an ideal the narrowing of man's potentialities, his rigid specialisation in a single, mechanised, automatic routine – his reduction to a robot. Chaplin's nightmare has become the boilermaker's wish-dream.

There is no English word for *abrutissement* – the blunting of talents and sensibilities to a chronic state of bemusement and brutishness. Our archaic system of apprenticeship, preparing for a rigidly demarcated existence (the equivalent of a life-sentence to a single type of job), seems to be expressly designed to produce that *abrutissement*, or Borstal mentality, which Alan Sillitoe has so shatteringly exposed. But there is another important factor which contributes to the massive inertial resistance of the British working class: the doctrine of non-competitiveness, a series of unwritten but constantly reiterated Maxims of Life. Go slow or you are letting your mates down and we shall all be landed on the dole. . . .

About the effects of all this on the national economy no more need be said; what needs pointing out is the psychologically demoralising effect on the young workman of this process of conditioning not to work to full capacity in the natural rhythm of his muscles, not to take a pride in his job, not to have ambitions in life – a kind of deliberate castration of the human spirit. Once more we find the ideal of the *uomo universale* reversed. "The most striking conclusion," wrote Geoffrey Gorer, discussing a recent book on the life of coal-miners, "is how remarkably little high wages and secure employment have modified old habits and ways of life."

PS 1980. Since Suicide of a Nation? was published in 1963, the downward trend has accelerated, while the underlying causes which it attempted to indicate have become more visible. The ostrich's tail displays occasionally a nervous twitch – but there is no sign to date of the lion rising to the occasion.

Chapter 48

THE RIGHT TO DIE

At the same time as this volume goes to press the Voluntary Euthanasia Society* is preparing a pamphlet on "Self-Deliverance" for which I wrote the preface printed below.

The Society's aims are defined as follows:

> To create a public opinion favourable to the view that an adult person, suffering from a severe illness for which no relief is known, should be entitled by law to the mercy of a painless death if, and only if, that is his expressed wish: and to promote legislation to this effect.

It is perhaps fitting that this should be the author's last do-gooding cause: having campaigned for the right to live of those condemned to death, it seems appropriate to campaign for the right to die with dignity of those condemned on mistaken humanitarian principles to a painful and degrading prolongation of life. (It is significant that some of the most vociferous defenders of capital punishment are also the most ardent opponents of voluntary euthanasia.)

The pamphlet is intended to serve as a technical "Guide to Self-Deliverance" by drugs and other methods for those determined to terminate an intolerable existence. It will not be on sale to the general public and only available to individuals who have been members of the Society for at least six months.

Here, then, is the text of the preface.

When people talk of "the fear of death", they often fail to distinguish between two types of fear which may be combined in experience but are separate in origin. One is the fear of the state of death (or non-existence); the other is fear of the process of dying, the

*It has recently been renamed EXIT – The Society for the Right to Die with Dignity.

agony of the transition to that state. The aim of this booklet – and of the Society which, after much soul-searching, decided to publish it – is to overcome the second of these fears. For the first, we must obviously rely on whatever consolations religion, philosophy or parapsychology have to offer.

However, the division is not as clear cut as that, because the two fears are interwoven. Mystics of all denominatons have always claimed that a strong faith in afterlife deprives not only the grave of its victory, but also death of its sting. Listen to Pope's "Dying Christian to his Soul":

> Vital spark of heav'nly flame:
> Quit, oh quit this mortal frame:
> Trembling, hoping, ling'ring, flying,
> Oh the pain, the bliss of dying.

In other words, the mystic's faith can produce a form of euthanasia – a peaceful death of the body. The sceptic may call it a placebo-effect: it makes no difference. But now we come to the crucial point: this connection is reversible. If the agnostics among us could be assured of a gentle and easy way of dying, they would be much less afraid of being dead. This is not a logical attitude, but fear is not governed by logic. We tend to be guided by first impressions – of persons, landscapes, countries. An unknown country to which the only access leads through a torture chamber is frightening. And vice versa, the prospect of falling peacefully, blissfully asleep, is not only soothing but can make it positively desirable to quit this pain-racked mortal frame and become unborn again. For after all, reason tells us – when not choked by panic – that before we were born we were all dead, and that our post-mortem condition is no more frightening than the pre-natal twilight. Only the process of transition, of getting unborn, makes cowards of us all. The whole concept of death as a condition would be more acceptable if dying would be less horrendous and squalid. Thus euthanasia is more than the administration of a lethal analgesic. It is a means of reconciling man with his destiny.

*   *   *

We are in dire need of such reconciliation and acceptance, for (apart from other obvious shortcomings) our species suffers from two severe biological handicaps imposed at the entry and exit gates of existence. Animals appear to give birth painlessly or with a minimum of discomfort. But owing to some quirk of evolution, the human foetus is too large for the birth-canal and its hazardous passage entails protracted agony for the mother and – presumably – a traumatic experience for the newborn. Hence we need mid-wives to aid us to be born. A similar situation prevails at the exit-gate. Animals in the wild, unless killed by a predator, seem to die peacefully and without fuss, from old age – I cannot remember a single description to the contrary by a naturalist, ethologist or explorer. The conclusion is inescapable: we need midwives to aid us to be unborn – or at least the assurance that such aid is available. Euthanasia, like obstetrics, is the natural corrective to a biological handicap.

*   *   *

If active euthanasia were legal in this country (as it is for certain cases in the Netherlands), the justification – or need – for this booklet would be debatable. But as the progress toward legalisation will be slow, a matter of years or even decades, the publication of a practical guide to "auto-euthanasia" will, we hope, bring peace of mind to many who would otherwise despair. There is only one prospect worse than being chained to an intolerable existence: the nightmare of a botched attempt to end it. I know that I am speaking in the name of many (some of them personal friends) who tried and failed – or who don't dare to try for fear of failure.

As matters stand, assisted suicide, in whatever form, places a heavy burden of responsibility on doctors, relatives, and other "accomplices" in the eyes of the law. If this booklet succeeds in lifting some of this burden, it will have fulfilled its purpose.

PART FIVE

HOW TO FAIL AS A MYSTIC

Chapter 49

YOGA UNEXPURGATED

In 1958, having finished The Sleepwalkers, *I felt the need for a break – a breath of fresh air in a different intellectual climate. The outcome of that escapade was* The Lotus and the Robot *(1960), and the motivation for it is explained in the Preface to the book:*

Rome was saved in AD 408 by three thousand pounds of pepper imported from India as part of the ransom the Senate paid to Alaric the Goth; ever since, when Europe found itself in an impasse or in a questing mood, it has turned yearningly to the land of culinary and spiritual spices. The greatest influence during the Dark Ages was Augustine, who was influenced by Plotinus, who was influenced by Indian mysticism. Long before Aldous Huxley found in Yoga a remedy for our Brave New World, Schopenhauer called the Upanishads the consolation of his life; and the first generation of the Nuclear Age seems to have found a like solace in Zen. On the whole, the West's receptiveness to the voice of the East was limited to periods of spiritual emergency, to moods of futility and despair; its attitude to Asia was either that of the conqueror armed with his gun-and-gospel truth, or that of the pilgrim in sackcloth and ashes, anxious to prostrate himself at the guru's feet.

I travelled in India and Japan (in 1958–9) in the mood of the pilgrim. Like countless others before, I wondered whether the East had any answer to offer to our perplexities and deadlocked problems. I chose those two countries because they are at opposite ends of the spectrum: one the most tradition-bound, the other the most modern of the great countries of Asia. I did not hope for any ready-made answer, but was anxious to look at the predicament of the West from a different perspective, a different spiritual latitude. I went on my pilgrimage not so much with an open, as with an equally split, mind. What emerged is a mixture of pedantic detail and sweeping generalisations.

Part One of the book, devoted to India, starts with four "portraits of contemporary saints", of whom only one is still remembered today: Acharya Vinoba Bhave, "the marching saint", Gandhi's appointed spiritual heir. Vinoba was the founder of the Bhoodan movement which aimed at solving India's problems by persuading rich landowners to give away substantial portions of their land to the poor. By the time I joined Vinoba and his devoted band of followers on their trek across a god-forsaken part of Rajasthan, he had been on the march for eight years, had covered the equivalent of the length of the equator and collected nearly eight million acres of land. It seemed an impressive figure, but most of the donated land was uncultivatable, or else the potential recipients lacked the equipment to cultivate it. The obvious conclusion was that the Bhoodan movement could "at best be called a partial success, at worst a noble failure".*

The other three "contemporary saints" portrayed in the book were fascinating objects of study. The lesson I learnt from my encounters with them was —
a lesson childishly obvious once one has learnt it, which saved me

---

I was nevertheless so impressed even by its partial success that on my return to London I organised a "Friends of Bhoodan" Committee (jointly chaired by Arnold Toynbee and Jayaprakash Narayan). Its purpose was to finance and assist a pilot-project in Orissa — which, needless to say, came to nought because the leaders of Bhoodan, though advanced in saintliness, were hopeless as organisers.

To quote Cynthia Koestler (my secretary since 1949 and my wife since 1965): "Arthur was a great admirer of Jayaprakash Narayan, whom he had met in India. He told me he was a 'prince among Indians'. He now invited him to come and stay with him in London, an invitation which included his return air fare. J.P. accepted. He came at the beginning of December and stayed for three weeks. The visit was a disappointment for Arthur. Among other things he hoped that an urban Bhoodan movement could be set up to do something about the homeless who sleep in the streets of Bombay and Calcutta. Hopes were high, but that was all, and as usually happens with Indian projects, nothing came of it" (in Astride the Two Cultures — Arthur Koestler at 70, ed. Harold Harris, Hutchinson, 1975).

a lot of doubt and uncertainty. I never again tried to decide whether a holy man, a Yogi or Swami was a saint or a charlatan, but rather to find out the relative percentage of the genuine and the other elements in him. It saved me from disappointment and cynicism, for nobody is a saint for twenty-four hours a day; not even in India; not even Ghandi, who always travelled in a third-class carriage but did not object to having air-conditioning installed, and the carriage to himself.

The next chapter, "Yoga Unexpurgated", starts with an outline of its purpose:

The word Yoga means Union. The aim of all Yoga practices, as defined in the *Yoga Sutras of Patanjali*, is the ultimate absorption of the subject in his "real self", in "pure consciousness without object". When this is attained, individual consciousness merges into cosmic consciousness, and the real self dissolves in the universal self – "as sparks issued from the same fire are destined to return to it", or "as the dewdrop, trembling on a lotus, slips into the shining sea". Then the Yogi's detached alone-ness becomes transformed into the experience of all-oneness; both expressions are derived from the same root, and the Sanskrit word *atma* covers both.

Patanjali's *Yoga Sutras*,* which probably date from the second or third century BC, are a profoundly seductive, if somewhat obscure treatise on a mystic philosophy of even earlier origin. Yoga began apparently in the form of Raja Yoga – as a journey towards the primal verities, the Royal Union with the Absolute, by way of meditation. But it was gradually superseded by Hatha Yoga – literally "forced Union" – a discipline with its main emphasis on physiological techniques. Hatha Yoga is at least a thousand years old, and seems to have remained basically unchanged throughout that period. It is the only form of Yoga still practised on a large scale, taught by individual gurus or approved Yoga institutes, and propagated in the Western world. But of the doctrine on which it is based only bowdlerised versions are made available to Western sympathisers. These give the impression that Hatha Yoga is merely a superior system of gymnastic exercises, designed to relax the body and mind by adopting a suitable

*Patanjali's *Yoga Sutras*, tr. V. Raghavan, *The Indian Heritage* (UNESCO, 1956).

posture, a natural way of breathing, and thus to facilitate a meditative attitude. At the same time, it is usually denied that there is
anything "mysterious" or "occult" about its doctrines.

In fact, every Indian-born practitioner of Hatha Yoga, from the
Himalayan hermit to the Bombay insurance clerk who spends an
hour a day at a Yoga institute, knows that Hatha Yoga does
promise the attainment of supernatural powers; and he also
knows that every posture and exercise has both a symbolic meaning and a physiological purpose related to the tenets of *ayurvedic*
medicine, and not considered a fit subject for discussion with
foreigners.

The following summary of Hatha Yoga doctrines and practices
is based partly on the primary sources, and partly on information
obtained from various Indian Yoga Institutes, Research Centres
and individual practitioners. The primary sources are: the *Hatha
Yoga Pradipika*, apparently the first standard work on the subject,
probably written in the twelfth century, but based on a much older
tradition; the *Siva Samhita* and the *Gheranda Samhita*, which are
compendia of a somewhat later date. All three have been translated into English, but are rather difficult to obtain.*

*I was lucky to gain access, with the help of scholarly friends and
librarians, to these and other original sources; they acted as
eye-openers on the history and background of Yoga as still practised in contemporary India.*

Cleansing Practices (dhoutis and bastis)

The eight steps, or limbs, of Yoga according to Patanjali are: (1)
and (2) abstentions and observances (such as non-violence, chastity, avoidance of human company, dietary rules); (3) postures; (4)
controlled breathing; (5) and (6) sense-withdrawal and concentration; (7) meditation; (8) samadhi – the complete absorption of the
mind in the atma.

---

*Pancham Sinh (tr.), *Hatha Yoga Pradipika*, 2nd ed. Allahabad (Lalit Mohan
Basu, The Panini Office, 1932).
Rai Bahadur Srisa Chandra Vidyarnava (tr.), *Siva Samhita*, 2nd ed. Allahabad
(Sudhindra Nath Basu, The Panini Office, 1923).
Sris Chandra Vasu (tr.), *Gheranda Samhita* (The Tatva-Vivechaka Press, Bom-
bay, 1895).

The *Hatha Yoga Pradipika* opens with the statement that its purpose is to serve "as a staircase" for those aspirants who, confused by the multiplicity of methods recommended by various sects, are unable to master Raja Yoga. The steps of the staircase are bodily exercises. In the original system of Patanjali, these were contained under headings (3) and (4); posture and breathing, and were discussed only briefly, in general terms. In the *Hatha Yoga Pradipika*, however, no less than eighty-four postures are mentioned, most of them consisting of twists and contortions, and the control of breathing is carried to the gruesome length to be presently described.

Before he is allowed to practise the advanced techniques, the adept must learn to master the various cleansing practices. Foremost among these are purifications of the alimentary tract. The stomach is cleansed by three principal methods: (a) by thrusting a stalk of cane slowly down the gullet and drawing it out; (b) by swallowing as much tepid water as the stomach will hold and vomiting it up; (c) by swallowing a cloth about four inches wide and twenty-two and a half feet long, and then pulling it out. The last method is considered the most effective, and is still vigorously practised, for instance, at the approved Yoga Health Centre at Santa Cruz, Bombay. It takes about a month or two to learn to swallow the seven-and-a-half yards of surgical gauze in about ten minutes, and it is supposed to "cleanse the waste matter coating the walls of the stomach".

I must now enter upon the painful subject of the Hindu obsession with the bowel functions, which permeates religious observances and social custom. I quote from the *Gheranda Samhita*:

14 Dhouti is of four kinds, and they clear away the impurities of the body. . . .

VATASARA-DHOUTI
16 Contract the mouth like the beak of a crow and drink air slowly, and fill the stomach slowly with it, and move it therein, and then slowly force it out through the lower passage.
17 The Vatasar is a very secret process, it causes the purification of the body, it destroys all diseases and increases the gastric fire.

VARISARA-DHOUTI
18 Fill the mouth with water down to the throat, and then drink it slowly; and then move it through the stomach forcing it downwards expelling it through the rectum.
19 This process should be kept very secret. It purifies the body. And

by practising it with care one gets a luminous or shining body.
20 The Varisara is the highest Dhouti. He who practises it with ease purifies his filthy body and turns it into a shining one.

AGNISARA or FIRE PURIFICATION
21 Press in the naval knot or intestines towards the spine for one hundred times. This is Agnisar or fire process . . .

BAHISKRITA-DHOUTI
24 . . . standing in navel-deep water, draw out the Sakti-nadi (long intestines), wash the Nadi with hand, and so long as its filth is not all washed away, wash it with care, and then draw it in again into the abdomen. . . .*

The reverse procedures are known under the term basti or "Yoga enemas". Jala-basti consists in squatting in a tub of water navel-high and sucking the water up through the rectum. At a more advanced stage, the adept also learns to suck liquids up through his penis (vajroli mudra). These achievements presuppose, of course, considerable training, particularly the exercises known as uddiyama and nauli (the isolation and independent control of the straight and traverse abdominal muscles) and asvini mudra (control of the anal sphincter and of certain visceral muscles). By these methods it becomes possible to reverse peristalsis, and to create suctional effects in the digestive and urinary tracts.

The remarkable thing is that these techniques are still recommended and practised in precisely the same form in which the *Gheranda Samhita* and *Hatha Yoga Pradipika* taught them a millennium ago. Thus in *Yoga Hygiene Simplified*,† a booklet published by the above-mentioned Yoga Institute in Santa Cruz, it is asserted that practice of the methods just described leads to results "which could not be accomplished by any modern device known to science".

The Vital Breath

Pranayama occupies a central position in the doctrine of Yoga. Prana means "life breath", in the physical sense of air, and in the wider sense of vital spirit, comparable to the Greek *pneuma* and the Hebrew *ruakh*.

*pp. 2–4.
†Bombay, 1957.

Originally the control of breathing, like that of bodily posture, was meant to facilitate a peaceful, meditative state of mind. By the time the *Hatha Yoga Pradipika* came to be written, it had become not only an all-cure for every form of disease, but also a means for acquiring supernatural powers.

The opening passage of the chapter on breathing in the *Pradipika* is significant: "When the breath moves, the mind also moves. When the breath ceases to move, the mind becomes motionless. The body of the Yogi becomes stiff as a stump. Therefore one should control the breath."

"Control" means, chiefly, holding the breath locked in the body as long as possible to induce the trance state of samadhi. This is achieved by various mudras and bandhas (locks, seals, restraints), which serve to seal all bodily orifices. Some examples of these are:

Jalandhara mudra, or chin lock. It consists in contracting the throat and pressing the chin firmly into the jugular notch, while simultaneously contracting the abdominal muscles and drawing in the anus. The eyes and mind are focused on the space between the eyebrows. "This causes the mind to swoon and give comfort. For by thus joining the mind with the atma, the bliss of Yoga is certainly obtained."*

Maha mudra and maha bandha ("the great binding") consist in a combination of the chin lock, the drawing in of the abdominal viscerae towards the spine, and the drawing of air into the small intestines by contractions of the anal sphincter. The air is kept locked in by pressure of the heel of the left foot against the anus and perineum. I ought to remark here that in most of the advanced postures the left foot is used for the same definite purpose, that is, for sealing the anal orifice, with simultaneous pressure on the genitals.

One of the most important practices is khecari mudra, because it is supposed to confer the gift of levitation. It is described at great length by the *Hatha Yoga Pradipika*; a shorter version is given in the *Gheranda Samhita*:

> Cut the lower tendon of the tongue, and move the tongue constantly; rub it with fresh butter, and draw it out (to lengthen it) with an iron instrument. By practising this always, the tongue becomes long, and when it reaches the space between the eyebrows, then Khecari is accomplished. Then (the tongue being lengthened) practise turning it upwards and backwards so as to touch the palate, till at length it

Gheranda Samhita, Vol. V, p. 82.

reaches the holes of the nostrils opening into the mouth. Close those holes with the tongue (thus stopping aspiration), and fix the gaze on the space between the eyebrows. This is called Khecari. By this practice there is neither fainting, nor hunger, nor thirst, nor laziness. There comes neither disease, nor decay, nor death. The body becomes divine.*

This technique is often called the King of the Mudras. It is still actively practised. The best documented report of a European initiated into the higher techniques of Yoga is *Hatha Yoga, a Report of a Personal Experience* by Dr Theos Bernard.† His account of learning khecari mudra is as follows:

The process itself is simple enough. I started by "milking" the tongue. This was accomplished by washing it and then catching hold of it with a linen towel. . . . I pulled it straight out and then from side to side as far as it would go. This I did regularly twice a day for ten minutes. After a couple of weeks I noticed that the fraenum was beginning to give way because of being drawn over the incisor teeth; but I wanted to encourage the process, so I resorted to a razor blade. Each morning I delicately drew the blade across the fraenum until blood appeared. There was no pain, and the bleeding stopped before I finished milking the tongue. The following morning the wound had begun to heal and a light tissue was beginning to form, which I scraped off; then I repeated the process of the preceding day. . . .

Success depends upon the amount of time spent in practice. I was able to accomplish it in about four months by working an average of ten minutes a day. . . . To elongate the tongue so that it can be placed between the eyebrows requires several years,‡ but it is not necessary to achieve this goal at once. It is sufficient to acquire the ability to swallow the tongue and to use it to direct the breath into the desired nostril or shut it off completely.

Dr Bernard further reports that blocking both cranial holes of the nose seemed to inhibit the breathing reflex. He had progressed to a state of proficiency where he could hold his breath for four minutes, but that was his limit. At this stage he learned khecari mudra, which enabled him to hold it for five minutes in ten consecutive breathing cycles; while "for a single aspiration I

---

*Ibid., Vol. III, pp. 25–8.
†London, 1950, Dr Bernard studied under various gurus in India and Tibet (he was killed in Tibet in 1947). The thirty-six plates in his book showing him performing the various *asanas* are probably the best photographic demonstrations on Yoga.
‡Op. cit., pp. 67f.

could hold my breath several minutes longer". However, to acquire supernatural powers, the texts prescribe a suspension of at least an hour and a half.

The Vital Fluid (bindu)

Apart from breath control, khecari, the king of the mudras serves another, more important purpose related to one of the traditional ideas of Yoga and Hindu medicine. It is the belief that a man's vital energy is concentrated in his seminal fluid, and that this is stored in a cavity in the skull. It is the most precious substance in the body – variously called bindu, soma-rasa, nectar, vital fluid, etc. – an elixir of life both in the physical and mystical sense, distilled from the blood; it is supposed to take forty drops of blood and forty days to make one drop of semen. A large store of bindu of pure quality guarantees health, longevity and supernatural powers; it is also held responsible for that radiant glow of the body, ascribed to Yogis and all Brahmacharis – men living in continence. Conversely, every loss of it is a physical and spiritual impoverishment. Losses occur not only in sexual intercourse, but also through suspicious discharges of the ears, nose, and other body openings; they all consist of spoiled bindu.

By blocking his windpipe, gullet and nostrils through khecari mudra, the adept is supposed to prevent the loss of vital fluid through its dripping down into the lower centres, and to absorb it back through his tongue.

An even more drastic procedure, serving the same purpose, is vajroli mudra, which I have briefly mentioned before.

> Even one who lives a wayward life, without observing any rules of Yoga, but performs vajroli, deserves success and is a Yogi. Two things are necessary for this, and these are difficult to get for the ordinary people – (1) milk* and (2) a woman behaving as desired. By practising to draw in the bindu discharged during cohabitation, whether one be a man or a woman, one obtains success in the practice of vajroli. By means of a pipe, one should blow [i.e., draw] air slowly into the passage in the male organ. By practice, the discharged bindu is drawn up. One can draw back and preserve one's own discharged bindu. The Yogi who can protect his bindu thus, overcomes death; because death comes by discharging bindu, and life is prolonged by its preservation. By preserving bindu, the body of the Yogi emits a pleasing smell.†

*Milk is believed by Hindus to be an aphrodisiac.
†Hatha Yoga Pradipika, Vol. III, pp. 82–90.

The pipe mentioned in the quotation is used in the first stage of the training, until the adept has learnt to aspire fluids through the urethra, as he has previously learnt to do through the colon. To Hindus brought up in the traditions of *ayurvedic* medicine – which applies to the vast majority of the nation – the procedure may seem complicated, but perfectly logical. Thus in *Hatha Yoga Simplified*, published by the Yoga Institute, Santa Cruz,* the author explains that sexual intercourse in itself is not harmful; only the loss of vital fluid which it entails. Therefore vajroli mudra is to be highly recommended.

The author is the head of an Institute which enjoys Government support.

Let me add that this preoccupation with continence in the strictly physiological, seminal meaning, is not restricted to Yogis, but to be found in every region and in every social stratum in India.

*Bombay, 1958.

Chapter 50

MAHATMA GANDHI:
A REVALUATION

Probing these secret and degenerate aspects of Indian mysticism seemed to throw a new light on the enigmatic figure of Mahatma Gandhi, in whose person all the paradoxes of India appeared to be epitomised. The following essay* is partly based on passages referring to Gandhi in The Lotus and the Robot.

"It takes a great deal of money to keep Bapu living in poverty. . . . "†
Bapu means "father" in Gujerati, and was used all over India as a title of respect and affection for Gandhi. That flippant remark was made by Mrs Sarojini Naidu, poet, politician and one of Bapu's intimates (she sometimes called him Mickey Mouse); but she could hardly have been aware at the time of the almost prophetic significance of her words. They actually referred to her loyal efforts to collect money for Gandhi's campaign for *khadi*, homespun cloth. Like all his crusades, it was intended to serve both practical and symbolic purposes. Its practical aspect was the boycott of foreign goods, primarily of English textiles – combined with the fantastic hope of solving India's economic problems by bringing back the hand-loom and the spinning-wheel. At the same time the spinning-wheel became an almost mystical symbol of the return to the Simple Life, and the rejection of industrialisation.

> The call of the spinning-wheel, Gandhi wrote in *Young India*, is the noblest of all. Because it is the call of love. . . . The spinning-wheel is the reviving draught for the millions of our dying countrymen and

*First published in the Sunday Times, October 5, 1969, commemorating the centenary of Gandhi's birth.
†Geoffrey Ashe, Gandhi: A Study in Revolution (London, 1968), p. 267.

countrywomen. . . . I claim that in losing the spinning-wheel we lost our left lung. We are therefore suffering from galloping consumption. The restoration of the wheel arrests the progress of the fell disease. . . .*

The wheel was a lifelong obsession which reached its climax in the late nineteen-twenties between two imprisonments. It spread among his followers and ran through the successive stages of a fashion, a cult, a mystique. He designed India's national flag with a spinning-wheel in its centre. He persuaded Congress to resolve that all its members should take up spinning and pay their membership dues in self-spun yarn; office-holders had to deliver 2000 yards of yarn per month. When Congress met in session, its seasoned politicians would listen to the debates while operating their portable spinning-wheels – *tricoteuses* of the nonviolent revolution. Schools introduced spinning courses; the plain white cloth and white cap became the uniform of the Indian patriot; Nehru called it "the livery of freedom," while Gandhi praised the wheel as "the sacrament of millions" and "a gateway to my spiritual salvation". At the same time he organised public bonfires of imported cloth, threw his wife's favourite sari into the flames, and got himself arrested.

One of the few Indian intellectuals who dared to protest against the *khadi* mystique was the poet laureate, Rabindranath Tagore. He was a lifelong admirer of Gandhi, fully aware of his greatness, but also of his crankiness. I shall quote him at some length, because he seems to have realised in a single intuitive flash the basic flaw in Gandhian leadership. In 1921, after a prolonged absence, Tagore had returned to India full of expectations "to breathe the buoyant breeze of national awakening" – and was horrified by what he saw:

> What I found in Calcutta when I arrived depressed me. An oppressive atmosphere seemed to burden the land. . . . There was a newspaper which one day had the temerity to disapprove, in a feeble way, of the burning of foreign cloth. The very next day the editor was shaken out of his balance by the agitation of his readers. How long would it take for the fire which was burning cloth to reduce his paper to ashes? . . .
>
> Consider the burning of cloth. . . . What is the nature of the call to do this? Is it not another instance of a magical formula? The question of using or refusing cloth of a particular manufacture belongs mainly to

*The Gandhi Reader: A Source-Book of his Life and Writings, ed. Homer A. Jack (London, 1958), pp. 229–30.

economic science. The discussion of the matter by our countrymen should have been in the language of economics. If the country has really come to such a habit of mind that precise thinking has become impossible for it, then our very first fight should be against such a fatal habit, the original sin from which all our ills are flowing.*

Tagore had smelt a holy rat in the khadi mystique. The boycott of English textiles could be justified as a measure of economic warfare in a nation's struggle for independence. But this did not apply to other countries, and to call all foreign cloth "impure" was indeed an appeal to magic-ridden minds. If it were advantageous for India's economy to forsake foreign imports and produce all the textiles it needs, that would still leave the question open whether a return to manufacturing methods predating the industrial revolution was feasible – even if it should be deemed desirable in the name of an idealised Simple Life. But this problem, too, was bypassed by calling the wheel a "sacrament" and a "gateway to salvation". In his reply to Tagore, Gandhi went even further in what one might be tempted to call sanctimonious demagogy – if one were not aware of the pure intentions behind the muddled thinking. Rejecting Tagore's accusation that the khadi cult was begotten by mysticism and not by reasoned argument, Gandhi wrote:

> I have again and again appealed to reason, and let me assure him that if happily the country has come to believe in the spinning-wheel as the giver of plenty, it has done so after laborious thinking. . . . I do indeed ask the poet to spin the wheel as a sacrament. . . . It was our love of foreign cloth that ousted the wheel from its position of dignity. Therefore I consider it a sin to wear foreign cloth. . . . On the knowledge of my sin bursting upon me, I must consign the foreign garments to the flames and thus purify myself, and thenceforth rest content with the rough khadi made by my neighbours. On knowing that my neighbours may not, having given up the occupation, take kindly to the spinning-wheel, I must take it up myself and thus make it popular.†

Khadi did indeed become a fashionable cult among his ashramites and among active members of Congress – but never among the anonymous millions for whom it was intended. The attempt to make the half-starved masses of the rural population self-supporting by means of the spinning-wheel as a "giver of plenty" proved to be a dismal and predictable failure. The spinning-wheel

*Ibid., pp. 223, 225 and 226.
†Ibid., pp. 228–31.

found its place on the national flag, but not in the peasants' cottages.

A few years ago, a Member of Parliament in New Delhi said to me wistfully: "Yes, I do wear khadi, as you see – a lot of us in the Congress Party feel that we have to. It costs three times as much as ordinary cotton."

It took a great deal of money, and an infinitely greater amount of idealism and energy, "to keep Bapu in poverty". It is impossible to dismiss the khadi crusade as a harmless folly. On the contrary, the wheel as an economic panacea and the gateway to salvation was a central symbol of Gandhi's philosophy and social programme.

His first book, Hind Swaraj or Indian Home Rule, was written in 1909, when he was forty. He had already achieved international fame as leader of the Indian community in South Africa and initiator of several nonviolent mass movements against racial discrimination. The book was reprinted in 1921 with a new introduction by Gandhi in which he said: "I withdraw nothing of it." In 1938, he requested that a new edition should be printed at a nominal price available to all, and wrote yet another introduction, in which he affirmed: "After the stormy thirty years through which I have since passed, I have seen nothing to make me alter the advice expounded in it." Hind Swaraj may thus be regarded as an authoritative expression of opinions to which he clung to the end of his life, and as a condensed version of Gandhian philosophy. It extols the virtues of Indian civilisation, and at the same time passionately denounces the culture of the West.

> I believe that the civilisation India has evolved is not to be beaten in the world. Nothing can equal the seeds sown by our ancestors. Rome went, Greece shared the same fate, the might of the Pharaohs was broken; Japan has become westernised; of China nothing can be said; but India is still, somehow or other, sound at the foundation. The people of Europe learn their lessons from the writings of the men of Greece or Rome, which exist no longer in their former glory. In trying to learn from them, the Europeans imagine that they will avoid the mistakes of Greece and Rome. Such is their pitiable condition. In the midst of all this India remains immovable and that is her glory. . . . India, as so many writers have shown, has nothing to learn from anybody else, and this is as it should be. . . . Indian civilisation is the best and the European is a nine-days wonder. . . . I bear no enmity towards the English, but I do towards their civilisation.*

*Ibid., pp. 107–8 and 120.

His rejection of Western culture in all its aspects was deeply felt, violently emotional, and supported by arguments verging on the absurd. The principal evils of the West were railways, hospitals and lawyers:

> Man is so made by nature as to require him to restrict his movements as far as his hands and feet will take him. If we did not rush about from place to place by means of railways and such other maddening conveniences, much of the confusion that arises would be obviated. . . . God set a limit to a man's locomotive ambition in the construction of his body. Man immediately proceeded to discover means of overriding the limit. . . . I am so constructed that I can only serve my immediate neighbours, but in my conceit, I pretend to have discovered that I must with my body serve every individual in the Universe. In thus attempting the impossible, man comes in contact with different religions and is utterly confounded. According to this reasoning, it must be apparent to you that railways are a most dangerous institution. Man has gone further away from his Maker.*

If this line of argument were accepted, not only the Great Indian Peninsular Railway would stand condemned, but also Gandhi's favourite book, the *Bhagavad Gita*. For its hero is the noble Arjuna, who drives a chariot (with Vishnu as his passenger) in flagrant transgression of God's will that he should only move as far as his own feet will take him. Gandhi himself had to spend an inordinate proportion of his life in railway carriages "rushing from place to place", faithful to the tradition that the leader should remain in touch with the masses. It was not the only paradox in his life; in fact, every major principle in Gandhi's Back-to-Nature philosophy was self-defeating, stamped with a tragic irony. (Even as president of Congress, he always insisted on travelling third class; but he had a special coach to himself.)

Lawyers fare no better in Gandhi's programme than railways:

> Men were less unmanly if they settled their disputes either by fighting or by asking their relatives to decide them. They became more unmanly and cowardly when they resorted to the Courts of Law. It is a sign of savagery to settle disputes by fighting. It is not the less so by asking a third party to decide between you and me. The parties alone know who is right and therefore they ought to settle it.†

It should be remembered that Gandhi's first step towards leadership was achieved by his successful settling of a lawsuit as an

---

*Sir C. Sankavan Nair, *Gandhi and Anarchy* (Madras, 1922) pp. 4–5.
†Ibid., p. 6.

attorney in Pretoria; and his successes in negotiating with the British were as much due to the charisma of the "naked fakir" – to quote Churchill – as to the legal astuteness of the "Middle Temple lawyer".

Perhaps the main asset in the complex balance-sheet of the British Raj was the introduction of modern medicine to India. But in Gandhi's accounting, hospitals fare worst:

> How do diseases arise? Surely by our negligence or indulgence. I over-eat, I have indigestion, I go to a doctor, he gives me medicine. I am cured. I over-eat again, and I take his pills again. Had I not taken the pills in the first instance, I would have suffered the punishment deserved by me, and I would not have over-eaten again. . . . Hospitals are institutions for propagating sin. Men take less care of their bodies, and immorality increases.*

And in a letter to a friend, also written when he was forty:

> Hospitals are the instruments that the devil has been using for his own purpose, in order to keep his hold on his kingdom. They perpetuate vice, misery and degradation and real slavery.†

He tried to live up to his convictions by experimenting all his life with nature-cures, *ayurvedic* remedies, and an endless succession of vegetarian and fruitarian diets. But he was assailed at various times by fistulae, appendicitis, malaria, hook-worm, amoebic dysentery and high blood-pressure, and suffered two nervous breakdowns in his late sixties. Each time he was seriously ill he started on nature-cures, refusing Western medication and surgery; each time he had to capitulate and submit to drugs, injections, operations under anesthesia. Once more his principles proved to be self-defeating in the most painful way. Yet while his belief that diseases are caused by "negligence, indulgence or vice" was naive to a degree, its correlate, the belief in the power of mind over body, was a source of strength which carried him through his heroic fasts.

About schools and "literary education" in general he was as scornful as about hospitals, railways and law courts.

> What is the meaning of education? It simply means knowledge of letters. It is merely an instrument and an instrument may be well used or abused. . . . We daily observe that many men abuse it and very few make good use of it; and if this is a correct statement, we have proved that more harm has been done by it than good. . . .

*Ibid., pp. 6–7.
†Ibid., p. 18.

To teach boys reading, writing and arithmetic is called primary education. A peasant earns his bread honestly. He has ordinary knowledge of the world. He knows fairly well how he should behave towards his parents, his wife, his children and his fellow villagers. He understands and observes the rules of morality. But he cannot write his own name. What do you propose to do by giving him a knowledge of letters? Will you add an inch to his happiness? Do you wish to make him discontented with his cottage or his lot?

Now let us take higher education. I have learned Geography, Astronomy, Algebra, Geometry, etc. What of that? In what way have I benefited myself or those around me? . . .

I do not for one moment believe that my life would have been wasted, had I not received higher or lower education. . . . And, if I am making good use of it, even then it is not for the millions. . . .

Our ancient school system is enough. . . . To give millions a knowledge of English is to enslave them. The foundation that Macaulay laid of education has enslaved us. . . . Hypocrisy, tyranny, etc., have increased; English-knowing Indians have not hesitated to cheat or strike terror into the people. . . .*

Gandhi tried to live up to his principles, and never sent his sons to school. He intended to teach them himself, but did not find the time. They never had a chance to learn a profession. In his own words:

I will not say that I was indifferent to their literary education, but I certainly did not hesitate to sacrifice it in these higher interests, as I regarded them. My sons have therefore some reason for grievance against me. . . . Had I been able to devote at least one hour to their literary education, with strict regularity, I should have given them, in my opinion, an ideal education. But it has been my regret that I failed to ensure for them enough training in that direction. . . . But I hold that I sacrificed their literary training to what I genuinely believed to be a service to the Indian community. . . . All my sons have had complaints to make against me in this matter. Whenever they come across an MA or a BA, or even a matriculate, they seem to feel the handicap of a want of school education. Nevertheless I am of opinion that, if I had insisted on their being educated somehow at schools, they would have been deprived of the training that can be had only at the school of experience, or from constant contact with the parents. . . .†

*M. K. Gandhi, *Hind Swaraj or Indian Home Rule* (Ahmedabad, reprinted 1946), pp. 63–6.
†C. F. Andrews, *Mahatma Gandhi: His Own Story* (London, 1930, 2 vols.), ʃ 94–5.

I shall return presently to the effects this contact had on Gandhi's sons. In the public domain, his hostility to intellectuals with an English education who "enslaved India" did not prevent him from adopting as his political successor young Jawaharlal Nehru, a product of Harrow and Cambridge. If Western civilisation was poison for India, Gandhi had installed the chief poisoner as his heir.

From his early thirties, two ideas of overwhelming, obsessive power were uppermost in Gandhi's mind and dominated his life: *satyagraha* and *brahmacharya*. *Satyagraha* means, broadly, non-violent action; *brahmacharya*, sexual abstinence; but both terms, as we shall see, had for him much wider spiritual implications. The two were inextricably interwoven in his teaching, and more bizarrely in his private life. Significantly it was in the same year – 1906, when he was thirty-seven – that he took his vow of chastity for life, and started his first nonviolent campaign.

Gandhi's negative attitude to sex was reminiscent of, and partly inspired by, Tolstoy's, but was more violent and baffling. A partial explanation of its origins may perhaps be the famous episode, related in his autobiography, of his father dying while he had intercourse with his wife. He was sixteen then (having married at fourteen), and had spent the evening, as usual, ministering to his sick father – massaging his feet – when his uncle relieved him. What could be more natural than that he should join his young wife? A few minutes later, however, a servant knocked at the door, announcing the father's death – which apparently nothing had presaged:

> I ran to my father's room. I saw that, if animal passion had not blinded me, I should have been spared the torture of separation from my father during his last moments. I should have been massaging him, and he would have died in my arms. . . .
>
> This shame of my carnal desire even at the critical hour of my father's death . . . was a blot I have never been able to efface or forget. . . . It took me long to get free from the shackles of lust, and I had to pass through many ordeals before I could overcome it.*

How much this episode contributed to Gandhi's attitude to sex is a matter of speculation. But the effects of that attitude on his own sons are on record. He refused to send them to school because he wanted to mould them in his own image; and since he had

*Gandhi, *My Experiments with Truth* (London, 1949), pp. 167–8.

renounced sex, he expected them to do the same. When Harilal, the eldest son, wanted to marry at the age of eighteen, Gandhi refused permission and disowned him "for the present". Harilal had the courage to marry nevertheless – he had achieved a degree of independence from his father by living with relatives in India while Gandhi still lived in South Africa. When his wife died in the influenza epidemic of 1918, Harilal, who was now thirty, wanted to remarry; but again Gandhi objected. From that point onward, Harilal began to disintegrate. He became an alcoholic, associated with prostitutes, embraced the Moslem faith and published an attack on his father under the pen-name "Abdullah". When he became involved in a shady business transaction, a solicitor wrote a letter of complaint to Gandhi. Gandhi published the lawyer's letter in his paper, Young India (June 18, 1925), together with his own reply, which amounted to placing Harilal on a public pillory:

> I do indeed happen to be the father of Harilal M. Gandhi. He is my eldest boy, is over thirty-six years old and is father of four children. His ideas and mine having been discovered over fifteen years ago to be different, he has been living separately from me. . . . Harilal was naturally influenced by the Western veneer that my life at one time did have. His commercial undertakings were totally independent of me. . . . He was and still is ambitious. He wants to become rich, and that too easily. . . . I do not know how his affairs stand at the moment, except that they are in a bad way. . . . Men may be good, not necessarily their children.*

Father and son hardly ever met again. On her deathbed, Gandhi's wife, Kasturbai, asked for her first-born. Harilal came, drunk, and had to be removed from her presence; "she wept and beat her forehead".

He was also present at Gandhi's cremation. Although it is the duty and privilege of the eldest son to light his father's funeral pyre, he kept, or was kept, in the background. He died a month later in a hospital from tuberculosis. His name is rarely mentioned in the voluminous Gandhi literature.

Harilal may have been a difficult case under any circumstances, but the second son, Manilal, was not; he remained a loyal and devoted son to the end. Nevertheless, the way Gandhi treated him was just as inhuman – there is no other word for it. At the age of twenty, Manilal committed the unforgivable sin of losing his virginity to a woman. When Gandhi discovered this, he made a

*Ibid., p. 26.

public scene, went on a penitential fast, and decreed that he would never allow Manilal to marry. He even managed to persuade the guilty woman to shave her hair. A full fifteen years had to pass until Gandhi relented, on Kasturbai's entreaties, and gave his permission for Manilal to marry – by which time Manilal was thirty-five. But in the meantime he had been banished from Gandhi's presence and ashram, because he had lent some money, out of his own savings, to his disgraced brother Harilal. When Gandhi heard about it, he made a scene accusing Manilal of dishonesty, on the grounds that the ashramites' savings were the property of the ashram. Manilal was sent into exile with instructions to become a weaver's apprentice, and not to use the name Gandhi. "In addition to this," Manilal later told Louis Fischer, "Father also contemplated a fast, but I sat all night entreating him not to do so, and in the end my prayer was heeded. I left my dear mother and my brother Devadas sobbing. . . ."* After a year as a weaving apprentice and a publisher's assistant, Gandhi ordered him to Natal to edit *Indian Opinion*. Apart from visits, Manilal remained an exile to the end of Gandhi's life.

In fairness, Gandhi's treatment of his two eldest sons must be seen in the context of the traditional Hindu "joint family household", over which the father holds unrestricted sway. To go against his decision is unthinkable; as long as Bapu is alive, the sons are not regarded as having attained fully adult status. But even against this background Gandhi's relentless tyranny over his sons was exceptional – he rode them like the djinn of the Arab legend, whom, in the guise of an old man, his young victim cannot get off his shoulders. "I was a slave of passion when Harilal was conceived," he was wont to say. "I had a carnal and luxurious life during Harilal's childhood." Quite clearly he was visiting his own sins on his sons. By his efforts to prevent them from marrying, he was trying to deprive them of their manhood, convinced that he had a right to do so, since he had voluntarily renounced his own.

Gandhi almost invariably refers to the act of love as an expression of man's "carnal lust" or "animal passion", and to woman's role in the act as that of a "victim" or "object". He did know, of course, that women too have a sexual urge, but had a simple answer to that: "Let her transfer her love . . . to the whole of humanity, let her forget she ever was or ever can be the object of

*Louis Fischer, *The Life of Mahatma Gandhi* (London, 1951), p. 230.

man's lust."* Intercourse, he taught, was only permissible for the purpose of procreation; if indulged in for "carnal satisfaction", it is a "reversion to animality". Accordingly, he unconditionally rejected birth control, even within the limits permitted by the Catholic Church. When Dr Margaret Sanger, the pioneer of family planning, visited Gandhi in 1936, she talked about the catastrophic consequences of the population explosion in India and elsewhere, and appealed for his help, pleading that "there are thousands, millions, who regard your word as that of a saint". But throughout their conversation "he held to an idea or a train of thought of his own, and, as soon as you stopped, continued it as though he had not heard you. ... Despite his claim to open-mindedness, he was proud of not altering his opinions. ... He agreed that no more than three or four children should be born to a family, but insisted that intercourse, therefore, should be restricted for the entire married life of the couple to three or four occasions."†

As a solution to India's population problem this was about as realistic as the return to the spinning-wheel. Yet it was deeply rooted in Gandhi's religious beliefs. If *khadi* was the gateway to salvation, *brahmacharya* was "the conduct that leads to God" – which is what the word literally means. Thus, to quote his secretary and biographer Pyarelal, *"Brahmacharya* was the *sine qua non* for those who aspire to a spiritual or higher life"‡ – and thus for all ashramites, married or not. How deeply he felt about this is illustrated by an episode in Gandhi's first ashram – Phoenix Settlement in South Africa:

> Once when I was in Johannesburg I received the tidings of the moral fall of two of the inmates of the ashram. News of an apparent failure or reverse in the [political] struggle would not shock me, but this news came upon me like a thunderbolt. The same day I took the train for Phoenix. Mr Kallenbach insisted on accompanying me. He had noticed the state I was in. On the way my duty became clear to me. I felt that the guardian or the teacher was responsible, to some extent, at least, for the lapse of his pupil. ... I also felt that the parties to the guilt could be made to realise my distress and the depth of their fall only if I did some penance for it. So I imposed upon myself a fast for seven days and a vow of having only one meal for a period of four months and a

*Nirmal Kumar Bose, *My Days with Gandhi* (Calcutta, 1953), p. 203.
†Margaret Sanger, *An Autobiography* (New York, 1938), pp. 470–1.
‡Pyarelal, *Mahatma Gandhi: The Last Phase* (Ahmedabad, 1965, 2 vols.), pp. 570 and 579.

half. Mr Kallenbach tried to dissuade me, but in vain. He ultimately
accepted the propriety of the penance and insisted on joining me. . . .
My penance pained everybody, but it cleared the atmosphere.
Everyone came to realise what a terrible thing it was to be sinful.*

This episode – including the reaction of the unfortunate Mr Kallenbach – gives one a foretaste of the curious atmosphere that
prevailed in Gandhi's later ashrams. Whereas in politics Gandhi
always tended towards compromise, in the matter of
brahmacharya he became more fanatical as the years went by. He
used his proverbial fascination for women to persuade them to
take the vow, whether their husbands agreed or not, wrecking
several marriages in the process, and causing lasting unhappiness
in others (among them is the sad case of a personal friend). One
might say that the young women who came under his spell were
seduced by Gandhi into chastity.

Sexual abstinence may procure spiritual benefits to communities of monks or nuns segregated from the opposite sex and
carefully sheltered from temptation. But Gandhi had designed for
himself a very special and arduous road to *brahmacharya*; he felt
compelled to expose himself to temptation in order to test his
progress in self-control. He regarded these tests – which continued to the very end when he was nearly eighty – as a pioneering
venture, another "Experiment with Truth" (as he called his autobiography). The experiments started with his own wife after he
had taken the vow, and were then continued with other, younger
women. In a letter to Bose, justifying these practices, Gandhi
wrote:

I am amazed at your assumption that my experiment implied any
assumption of woman's inferiority. She would be, if I looked upon her
with lust with or without her consent. I have believed in woman's
perfect equality with man. My wife was "inferior" when she was the
instrument of my lust. She ceased to be that when she lay with me
naked as my sister. If she and I were not lustfully agitated in our minds
and bodies, the contact raised both of us.

Should there be a difference if it is not my wife, as she once was, but
some other sister? I do hope you will acquit me of having any lustful
designs upon women or girls who have been naked with me. A or B's
hysteria had nothing to do with my experiment, I hope. They were
before the experiment what they are today, if they have not less of it.

* Andrews, op. cit., p. 186.

The distinction between Manu and others is meaningless for our discussion. . . .*

The Manu mentioned in this letter was the granddaughter of a cousin, the last of the guinea pigs in the quest for *brahmacharya*. She had lost her mother in childhood, and Kasturbai had looked after her. On Kasturbai's death Gandhi took over. "I have been a father to many, but to you I am a mother,"† he wrote to her; strange as this may sound, he meant her to take that literally – so much so that Manu actually wrote a book with the title *Bapu: My Mother*. As a "budding girl of eighteen", in Gandhi's words, she claimed to be free from sexual feelings. Pyarelal explains in his biography:

> Manu apparently did not feel any embarrassment. She returned his ministrations by nursing him through illnesses and fasts; in her diary she recorded, in between two political messages, the effects of the enema she had administered to him, and the admonitions he addressed to her from his bathtub: "While bathing, Bapu said these words to me with great affection, and also caressed my back."‡

For Gandhi, however, this was a crucial experiment. If it succeeded "it would show that his quest for truth had been successful. *His sincerity should then impress itself upon the Moslems, his opponents in the Moslem League and even Jinnah*, who doubted his sincerity." The italics are by the faithful Pyarelal, who knew more intimately than any other contemporary the ways and twists of his Master's thought. Gandhi sincerely believed that he was an instrument of God, who "gives me guidance to react to the situations as they arise".§ But the instrument must be pure, free from carnal desire; and to attain that freedom he had to go through his experiment in *brahmacharya*. It "put him in touch with the infinite";|| at the same time it was to solve the Hindu-Moslem problem, put an end to the mutual massacres, persuade the Moslem League of his *bona fides*, and make them renounce their claim for an independent Pakistan.

From the Mahatma's point of view all this was perfectly logical. In his own mind, his public, political activities and his intimate Experiments with Truth were inseparable; *satyagraha* and

*Bose, op. cit., p. 133.
†Ibid., p. 177.
‡Manuben Gandhi, *Last Glimpses of Bapu* (Delhi, Agra and Jaipur, 1962), p. 303.
§T. A. Raman, *What Does Gandhi Want?* (Oxford, New York and Toronto, 1943), p. 49.
||Bose, op. cit., p. 176.

brahmacharya were mutually interdependent. For *satyagraha* means not only nonviolent action, but action powered by an irresistible soul-force or truth-force (*sat* – truth, *agraha* – firmness). At the stage he had reached in the last two years of his life, everything depended for him on the crucial experiment with Manu; and this may explain why he so stubbornly insisted that she share his bed, in defiance of everybody's advice.

It also explains why, while the fate of India was being decided in the dramatic months June–July, 1947, Gandhi chose to treat the Indian public to a series of six articles* – on *brahmacharya*. He had been touring the Moslem villages of East Bengal, attempting to quell the riots by his personal influence. Most of the time, his only companions on the pilgrimage were Manu, Bose and a stenographer. Several of his collaborators, including intimate friends, protested against the Manu experiment (though they must have known of previous ones), expressed their disapproval to Gandhi, and some of them actually left him. A public scandal was avoided, but Gandhi felt deprived of their unconditional admiration, utterly lonely and dejected. Even Bose left, after long discussions in which he had in vain tried to convince Gandhi of the psychological ill-effects of the experiment on both parties concerned – without ever doubting the sincerity of their motives; but he returned to serve Gandhi a few months later. The ill-timed *Harijan* articles, which made the public gasp, were Gandhi's reply to the dissidents.

He also wrote to Acharya Kripalani, the president of Congress: "This is a very personal letter, but not private. Manu Gandhi, my granddaughter . . . shares the bed with me. . . . This has cost me dearest associates. . . . I have given the deepest thought to the matter. The whole world may forsake me, but I dare not leave what I hold is the truth for me. . . . I have risked perdition before now. Let this be the reality if it has to be." † And he requests that the Acharya discuss the matter with other Congress politicians – in the midst of the negotiations about Independence.

I have dwelt at some length on Gandhi's struggle to attain chastity for two reasons; because it provides an essential – by his own testimony, the most essential – key to his personality; and because it became a part of the Gandhian heritage which had a lasting influence on the social and cultural climate of the country.

*In the weekly magazine *Harijan*.
†Pyarelal, op. cit., p. 581.

After Gandhi's death, however, the Indian Establishment attempted to suppress the facts of his last Experiment with Truth. An example of this conspiracy of silence is the story of the book by Nirmal Kumar Bose, *My Days with Gandhi*, which I have repeatedly quoted. Professor Bose, a distinguished anthropologist and expounder of Gandhi's philosophy, had written two earlier books, *Studies in Gandhism* and *Selections from Gandhi*. He had been the Mahatma's companion during the pilgrimage in East Bengal, and in *My Days with Gandhi* devoted a chapter to the repercussions of the Manu experiments, without going into details about the experiment itself. It is a discreet, affectionate and respectful work; yet not only was it rejected by all publishers whom Bose approached, but strenuous attempts were made "from very high quarters in the country" to prevent its publication.

Five years after Gandhi's death, Bose decided to publish the book on his own. It is unobtainable in India, and the most recent biographer of Gandhi, Geoffrey Ashe, remarks: "It has become common knowledge that one important memoir was partly suppressed. I had some difficulty in locating what may be the only copy in England."* Not even the British Museum has a copy of it. My own book (*The Lotus and the Robot*), in which I quoted Bose, was also banned in India on the grounds that it contained "disrespectful remarks about Gandhiji".†

Ironically, three years after Bose, the first volume of Pyarelal's monumental, authorised biography of Gandhi was published, confirming all the facts that Bose had mentioned (but without mentioning Bose).

In the Western world Gandhi's obsession with *brahmacharya* could have been shrugged off as a harmless personal quirk. In India it struck deep, archetypal chords. There is a hidden message running through Gandhi's preaching of chastity – hidden, that is, from the Western reader, but obvious to every Hindu. It relates to the physiological benefits of sexual restraint [as discussed in the previous chapter]. According to the doctrines of traditional Hindu (*ayurvedic*) medicine, man's "vital force" is concentrated in his seminal fluid. All his powers, both mental and physical, derive from this precious secretion – a kind of elixir of life – variously called *bindu*, *soma-rasa* or "vital fluid". Every expenditure of

*Ashe, op. cit., p. viii.
†See below.

vital fluid causes physical weakening and spiritual impoverishment. Conversely, the storing up of *bindu* through continence provides for increased spiritual powers, health and longevity (Gandhi hoped to live to the age of 125). It also produces that smooth skin with a radiant glow which all true saints were said to possess – including the Mahatma. Various semi-secret Hatha Yoga practices are designed to preserve the vital fluid even during intercourse.

Gandhi was a firm believer in *ayurvedic* medicine, and himself practised it on his family and intimates. Numerous passages in his writings show that he also believed in the crucial importance of preserving the "vital fluid". Thus in his pamphlet "Key to Health" he wrote:

> It is said that an impotent man is not free from sexual desire. . . . But the cultivated impotence of the man whose sexual desire has been burnt up and whose sexual secretions are being converted into vital force is wholly different. It is to be desired by everybody.*

Or:

> Ability to retain and assimilate the vital liquid is a matter of long training. Once achieved, it strengthens body and mind. The vital liquid capable of producing such a wonderful being as man cannot but, when properly conserved, be transmuted into matchless energy and strength.†

Hinduism has a notoriously ambivalent attitude towards sex. On the one hand, the cult of the *lingam*, the erotic temple carvings, the *Kama Sutra* and the "Sex Pharmacies" with their flowering trade in aphrodisiacs; on the other, prudery, hypocrisy, lip-service to the ideal of chastity combined with anxiety about the loss of the vital fluid and its debilitating effects. "Spermal anxiety" appears to be common among Hindus; and with it goes unconscious resentment against Woman, who is its cause. The Hindu Pantheon has no Eros and no Cupids – only Kama, the prime force of lust.

Gandhi's lifelong struggle to overcome his own "carnal lust" and "animal passion"; his public *mea culpa* when he confessed to a "lust dream" followed by a penance of six weeks' silence; his endorsement of the power of the "vital fluid" – all this made him the living symbol of the guilt-ridden Hindu attitude to sex, and encouraged the worshipful masses to persist in it.

*Pyarelal, op. cit., p. 581.
†Fischer, op. cit., p. 263.

Another, minor but significant feature of the Gandhian heritage is the widespread hypochondria about diet and digestion. In a country riddled with amoebic dysentery, hook-worm and other scourges, this is not surprising. But Gandhi's lifelong preoccupation with experimental diets was again primarily linked with the quest for chastity. When he took the vow, he wrote: "Control of the palate is the first essential in the observance of the vow. . . . The brahmacharya's food should be limited, simple, spiceless and if possible uncooked. . . . Six years of experiment have shown me that the brahmacharya's ideal food is fresh fruit and nuts."* Even milk he thought was an aphrodisiac to be avoided – which seems difficult to reconcile with the pamphlet he wrote on "How to Serve the Cow".†

One of Gandhi's biographers, Louis Fischer, called him "a unique person, a great person, perhaps the greatest figure of the last nineteen hundred years". Others compared him to Christ, Buddha and St Francis. The claims to immortality were mainly based on his use of nonviolence as a political weapon in a world sick of violence. The partial success of his early passive resistance, civil disobedience and non-cooperation campaigns; the unarmed marches against armed police and troops; the first sit-downs, the cheerful courting of imprisonment, the public fasts – all this was something completely new in politics, something unheard of; it was a message of hope, almost a revelation; and the amazing thing was that it seemed to work. The lasting merit of Gandhi was, not that he "liberated India" – as John Grigg‡ and others have pointed out, independence would have come much earlier without him – but to have made the world realise that the conventional methods of power-politics are not the only conceivable ones; and that under certain circumstances nonviolence – ahimsa – might be substituted for them. But the emphasis is on the limiting clause; and the tragedy of Gandhism is the narrow range of applicability of the method. It was a noble game which could only be played against an adversary abiding by certain rules of common decency instilled by long tradition; in Soviet Russia or Nazi Germany it would have amounted to mass suicide.

Like most inventors of a new philosophical system, Gandhi at first believed in its universal validity. The earliest shock of disap-

*Fischer, op cit., p. 263.
†M. K. Gandhi, "How to Serve the Cow" (Ahmedabad).
‡John Grigg, "A Quest for Gandhi", Sunday Times, September 28, 1969.

pointment came in 1919, when the first nationwide civil disobedience campaign degenerated into violent rioting all over the
country. Gandhi suspended the action, went on a penitential fast,
and confessed to having committed a "Himalayan blunder" by
starting the campaign before his followers had been sufficiently
trained in the spirit and methods of *satyagraha*.

The next year he launched a new non-cooperation movement
jointly with the Moslems. Again it led to nationwide riots, culminating in the massacre of Chauri Chaura; again he suspended
the campaign and went on a fast.

His most successful movement was the civil disobedience
campaign in 1930–1 against the salt laws, highlighted by the
spectacular "march to the sea". This time, too, there was widespread rioting, but the campaign was allowed to continue until a
compromise settlement was reached with the Viceroy.

The later *satyagraha* movements (1932–4, 1940–1 and 1942–3)
ended inconclusively. In terms of tangible results this was not an
impressive record. But the general impact on politicians, intellectuals and the world at large was momentous; it turned Gandhi into
a living legend. It was further dramatised by his eighteen public
fasts and altogether six and a half years of detention – the first in a
black hole in Johannesburg, the last in the Aga Khan's palace.

But Gandhi's methods of using nonviolence had their
Himalayan inconsistencies, and the advice he proffered to other
nations was often quite irresponsible by any humane standard.
Although he repeated over and again that only people far
advanced on the spiritual trail were able to practice nonviolent
resistance, he did not hesitate to recommend it as a universal
panacea. Thus in December, 1938, after the first nationwide pogrom in Germany, he wrote: "I make bold to say that, if the Jews can
summon to their aid soul-power that comes only from nonviolence, Herr Hitler will bow before the courage which he will
own is infinitely superior to that shown by his best stormtroop-
ers."* And in 1946, when the incredible news of six million
gassed victims became known: "The Jews should have offered
themselves to the butcher's knife. They should have thrown
themselves into the sea from cliffs. . . . It would have roused the
world and the people of Germany."†

There was only one mitigating circumstance to utterances like
this: Gandhi's notorious ignorance of international affairs.

Harijan, February 17, 1939.
†Ashe, op. cit., p. 341.

At the outbreak of the Second World War he declared his moral support for the Allied cause. After the fall of France, he praised Pétain for his courage to surrender, and on July 6, 1940 published an "Appeal to Every Briton" to follow the French example (on his insistence, the text of this appeal was transmitted by the Viceroy to the British War Cabinet):

> . . . I do not want Britain to be defeated nor do I want her to be victorious in a trial of brute strength. . . . I want you to fight Nazism without arms or with non-violent arms. I would like you to lay down the arms you have, being useless for your humanity. You will invite Herr Hitler and Signor Mussolini to take what they want of the countries you call your possessions. Let them take possession of your beautiful island, with your many beautiful buildings. You will give all these, but neither your souls, nor your minds. If these gentlemen choose to occupy your homes, you will vacate them. If they do not give you free passage out, you will allow yourself, man, woman and child, to be slaughtered, but you will refuse to owe allegiance to them.*

It would have taken a great deal of corpses to keep Bapu in nonviolence.

He had similar advice to offer to Czechs, Poles, Finns and Chinese. On the last day of his life, a few hours before he was assassinated, a correspondent of *Life* magazine asked him: "How would you meet the atom bomb . . . with nonviolence?"

He replied: "I will not go into shelter. I will come out in the open and let the pilot see I have not a trace of ill-will against him. The pilot will not see our faces from his great height, I know. But the longing in our hearts – that he will not come to harm – would reach up to him and his eyes would be opened."†

This statement, and many earlier ones on similar lines, give the impression that Gandhi's faith in nonviolence was absolute ("I know of no single case in which it has failed," he wrote in his "Appeal to Every Briton"). In fact, however, on a number of critical occasions he betrayed his own principles in a quite blatant way. There was first the episode, not to be taken too seriously, when, in 1918, he acted as a recruiting sergeant for the British Army. In a speech in the Kheda district he said:

> To bring about [Dominion status in the Empire] we should have the ability to defend ourselves, that is, the ability to bear arms and to use

*Raman, op. cit., p. 24.
†*The Essential Gandhi: An Anthology*, ed. Louis Fischer (London, 1963), p. 334.

them. . . . If we want to learn the use of arms with the greatest possible despatch, it is our duty to enlist ourselves in the army.*

Three years later, he asserted:

Under Independence I too would not hesitate to advise those who would bear arms to do so and fight for the country.†

Later on he explained these lapses by saying that they did not imply any lack of faith in nonviolence, but merely that "I had not yet found my feet. . . . I was not sufficiently sure of my ground."‡ But this excuse can hardly be applied to the climactic events in the last two years of his life – the Hindu-Moslem massacres which led to Partition, and the fighting in Kashmir which signalled the ultimate shipwreck of nonviolence. During his pilgrimage through the terror-stricken villages of East Bengal when he saw "only darkness all round", he confessed to Bose that "for the time being" he had "given up searching for a non-violent remedy applicable to the masses". A few days later, he wrote: "Violence is horrible and retarding, but may be used in self-defence." Yet another few days later, in a letter: "Non-violent defence is the supreme self-defence, being infallible."§

He was at the end of his tether.

Gandhi had strenuously opposed Partition; he called it "the vivisection of India which would mean the vivisection of myself". At the historical meeting of Congress, on June 14–15, 1947, which was to decide for or against Partition, the president, Acharya Kripalani, Gandhi's lifelong friend, made a memorable speech which signified the future Indian government's farewell to the ideals of nonviolence. Unlike Mark Antony, he started by praising Gandhi, and then proceeded to bury him. He expressed his appreciation of Gandhi's pilgrimages in Bengal and Bihar, trying to bring about Hindu-Moslem reconciliation as an alternative to Partition, but denied the efficacy of the method: "Unfortunately for us today, though [Gandhi] can enunciate policies, they have to be in the main carried out by others, and these others are not converted to his way of thinking. It is under these painful circumstances that I have supported the division of India."||

*Ibid., p. 125.
†Louis Fischer, op. cit., p. 371.
‡The Essential Gandhi, p. 125.
§Bose, op. cit., pp. 104 and 107.
||Ibid., pp. 244–5.

To everybody's surprise, Gandhi in his own speech suddenly urged acceptance of Partition on the grounds that "sometimes certain decisions, however unpalatable they may be, have to be taken". Three months later, independent India and independent Pakistan were confronting each other in Kashmir. Gandhi commented that he had been "an opponent of all warfare. But if there was no other way of securing justice from Pakistan, if Pakistan persistently refused to see its proved error and continued to minimise it, the Indian Union would have to go to war against it. War was no joke. No one wanted war. That way lay destruction. But he could never advise anyone to put up with injustice."*

He had been lavish with his advice to Britons, Frenchmen, Czechs, Poles, Jews, to lay down their arms and surrender to injustices infinitely more terrible than those committed by Pakistan. As on earlier critical occasions, when the lofty ideal clashed with hard reality, realism carried the day and the Yogi succumbed to the Commissar. He had believed in and practised nature medicine, but when critically ill had always called in the practitioners of Western science which he held in such contempt. Nonviolence had worked like magic on the British, but did not work on Moslems. Was it really the panacea for mankind as he had thought? A fortnight before his death, commenting on Deputy Premier Sirdar Patel's decision to send troops into Kashmir, Gandhi confessed to Bose:

> When power descended on [Patel], he saw that he could no longer successfully apply the method of nonviolence which he used to wield with signal success. I have made the discovery that what I and the people with me termed nonviolence was not the genuine article, but a weak copy known as passive resistance.†

To another interviewer – Professor Stuart Nelson – he repeated that "what he had mistaken for satyagraha was not more than passive resistance, which was a weapon of the weak. . . . Gandhiji proceeded to say that it was indeed true that he had all along laboured under an illusion. But he was never sorry for it. He realised that if his vision had not been clouded by that illusion, India would never have reached the point which it had done today."‡

*Ibid., p. 251.
†Ibid., p. 4n.
‡Ibid., pp. 270–1.

Yet that, too, may have been no more than an illusion. India had reached the point of independence not because of *ahimsa*, but because the British Empire had gone into voluntary self-liquidation. The spinning-wheel was preserved on India's national flag, but the Gandhian mystique played no part in the shaping of the new state, though it continued to pay lip-service to it. The armed conflicts with Pakistan, and later with China, produced outbreaks of chauvinism and mass hysteria which suggested that the Mahatma's pacifist apostolate had left hardly any tangible effects; and the bloody riots between Maharatis and Gandhi's own Gujeratis added a bitterly ironic touch to the picture. When Gandhi's adopted spiritual heir, Vinoba Bhave, "the marching saint", was asked whether he approved of armed resistance against the Chinese frontier intrusion, he replied in the affirmative, using Gandhi's erstwhile excuse that the masses were not yet ripe for nonviolent resistance.

Gandhi himself foresaw these developments in moments when his vision was not "clouded by illusion". The principles by which he hoped to shape India, laid down forty years earlier in *Hind Swaraj*, had turned out to be self-defeating. In the midst of the celebrations, their – and his – defeat was complete. It was sealed by an assassin, who was not one from the enemy camp, but a devout Hindu.

J. F. Horrabin has described a meeting with Gandhi at St James's Palace, where the Round Table Conference of 1931 was held:

> We chatted for some minutes in a small ante-room. Then, catching sight of a clock, he remembered another appointment, apologised, and hurried away. I watched him disappear down one of the long corridors of the Palace; his robes tucked in, his slippers twinkling as he ran. Dare I say it? – I am sure, at least, that no friend of his will misunderstand me if I do – I was irresistibly reminded of one of those Chaplin films which end with the little figure hurrying away to the horizon, gradually lost to sight in the distance.*

That remark, far from being disrespectful, leads straight to the secret of Gandhi's immense power over his countrymen, and the love they bore him. Chaplin was the symbol of the little man in a bowler hat in the industrialised society of the West. Gandhi was the symbol of the little man in a loincloth in poverty-stricken India. He himself was fully aware of this. When J. P. Patel once

---

Incidents of Gandhi's Life, ed. Chandrashanker Shuhla (Bombay, 1949), p. 85.

asked him "what it was in him that created such a tremendous following in our country", he replied, "It's the man of our country who realises when he sees me that I am living as he does, and I am a part of his own self."*

Nehru, the westernised progressive, often regarded Gandhi as a political liability, but he was nevertheless under his spell, precisely because Gandhi to him was, in his own words, "the soul of India".

The soul and the loincloth went together; they were inseparable. When Gandhi had tea with George V and Queen Mary at Buckingham Palace, wearing sandals, loincloth and a shawl on his shoulders, it was more than just showmanship. It was an event which instantly turned into legend, spreading to the remotest villages of India. One version of it was given years later by the vice-chancellor of Poonah University, who accompanied Gandhi to the gates of Buckingham Palace: "He went to see the King dressed in a poor man's costume, with half his legs visible. The King said, 'Mr Gandhi, how is India doing?' He said, 'Look at me and you will know what India is like.' " Every villager with naked legs who felt that Gandhi was "a part of his own self", thought himself for a moment equal to the King of England. Perhaps Gandhi's greatest gift to his people was to arouse in them, after centuries of lethargy, the first stirrings of self-respect.

But he also gave his blessing to their attitudes, derived from a petrified tradition, to sex, food, paternal authority, medicine, industry and education; and he confirmed them in that "illusion-haunted, magic-ridden slave-mentality" which Tagore has castigated as "the original sin from which all our ills are flowing". Even where he opposed tradition, he did it on the traditional principle of the identity of opposites: the Untouchables became Harijans, Children of God; the sources of defilement were turned into objects of worship, and latrine-cleaning became a sacrament for all pious ashramites – though for nobody else.

Gandhi exerted such a powerful influence over the minds of the masses that many believed him to be an Avatar, a reincarnation of Krishna. One cannot help feeling that had he crusaded for family-planning instead of the impossible demand for married continence, India might be a different country now. He was most

*Talking of Gandhiji: Four Programmes for Radio First Broadcast by the British Broadcasting Corporation, script and narration by Francis Watson, production by Maurice Brown (London, New York and Toronto, 1957), p. 14.

eloquent about the poverty-stricken life of the Indian villager and his inability to feed the exorbitant numbers of his offspring; but the only remedy he had to propose was chastity and the spinning-wheel.

He was unwilling to listen to the reasoned arguments of critics. In the words of T. A. Raman, a distinguished Indian journalist: "Almost the most marked trait of Gandhi's character is that evidenced by the virtual impossibility of reasoning with him. By definition he is a man of faith, and men of faith have little use for the slow processes of reasoning."

It is equally futile to argue with intellectuals, who adhere to the Gandhi cult and pay lip-service to a philosophy easy to eulogise and impossible to realise. It is this attitude which lends the contemporary Indian scene its twilight air of unreality and sanctimonious evasion of vital issues. Bapu still casts his saintly-sickly spell over it, but its power is waning as more people realise that, whether we like it or not, spinning-wheels cannot compete with factories, and that the most vital fluid is the water from large irrigation dams for the country's parched fields.

When all is said, the Mahatma, in his humble and heroic ways, was the greatest living anachronism of the twentieth century; and one cannot help feeling, blasphemous though it may sound, that India would be better off today and healthier in mind, without the Gandhian heritage.

*   *   *

The publication of The Lotus and the Robot *had a rather curious aftermath, which I described later in the Preface to the Danube edition (1966):*

Six years have passed since I returned the corrected proofs of "The Lotus" to the printers, with considerable misgivings. I was worried about the effect the book would have on the friends I had made in India and Japan, afraid that its outspokenness might hurt or incense them. To my relief, the Asian mail brought almost unanimous approval and encouragement – until the day when two newspaper cuttings arrived. One was a review from the *Statesman*, a leading Indian journal, the other a news item from *The Times*. I quote the first with some embarrassment because authors are not supposed to quote the praise bestowed on them (they leave that to their publishers); but the reader will see the point in a moment:

"This is a book . . . hard yet compassionate. It is completely different from all the other books which have been written about Asia. No one with any pretensions to intelligence should miss it." – *Statesman* (Calcutta).

Now for the news item:

"Delhi, May 9, 1962 – The Indian Government has banned the import of Mr Arthur Koestler's book *The Lotus and the Robot* because it contains "objectionable remarks about Gandhi", Mr Lal Bahadur Shastri, the Home Minister, stated in Parliament today – Reuter" – *The Times* (London).

The result conformed to the familiar pattern: protests in the press, questions in the Indian Parliament, increased circulation of the book on the black market. I have every reason to be grateful to Mr Shastri, who later became Prime Minister, proved his devotion to the doctrine of nonviolence by going to war with Pakistan, and died while trying to make peace. I mention this episode because it rather neatly confirms what I have said in the book about the influence of Gandhi's heritage on contemporary India. Besides, I cannot help feeling a perverse satisfaction that after all my books have been banned in Communist countries, and some of them in Catholic Ireland, one has now been banned in India. For writers of pornography it is easy to collect such accolades; essayists have to work harder for them.

Chapter 51

A TASTE OF ZEN

The second part of The Lotus and the Robot *starts with a discussion of contemporary Japanese culture, that fascinating marriage of opposites – "the Spartan and the Sybarite sharing the same bed". The concluding chapters, from which the following extracts are taken, are devoted to the history and practice of Zen-Buddhism – not in California, but in its own habitat.*

Zen is to religion what a Japanese "rock-garden" is to a garden. Zen knows no god, no afterlife, no good and no evil, as the rock-garden knows no flowers, herbs or shrubs. It has no doctrine or holy writ; its teaching is transmitted mainly in the form of parables as ambiguous as the pebbles in the rock-garden which symbolise now a mountain, now a fleeing tiger. When a disciple asks "What is Zen?", the master's traditional answer is "Three pounds of flax" or "A decaying noodle" or "A toilet stick" or a whack on the pupil's head. Zen cannot be debunked because its method is self-debunking. In its mondos and koans, ambiguity reaches its metaphysical peak; it is the ultimate evasion. And for precisely that reason it played a vital part in maintaining the balance of extremes in Japanese life.

Taken at face value and considered in itself, Zen is at best an existentialist hoax, at worst a web of solemn absurdities. But within the framework of Japanese society, this cult of the absurd, of ritual leg-pulls and nose-tweaks, made beautiful sense. It was, and to a limited extent still is, a form of psychotherapy for a self-conscious, shame-ridden society, a technique of undoing the strings which tied it into knots; in a word, Zen was the *tanki* (as the Japanese call their tranquilliser pills) of feudal Japan.

In the supposedly oldest Zen poem, attributed to Seng-Ts'an (sixth century AD), men are admonished:

Saunter along and stop worrying
If your thoughts are tied you spoil what is genuine . . .
The wise person does not strive;
The ignorant man ties himself up . . .
If you work on your mind with your mind,
How can you avoid an immense confusion? . . .

If you want to get the plain truth,
Be not concerned with right and wrong.
The conflict between right and wrong
Is the sickness of the mind.*

From its earliest beginnings – supposedly in sixth-century China – the great masters of Zen denied that it aimed at moral improvement: "If a man seeks the Buddha, that man loses the Buddha".† According to tradition, it was a fierce-looking Indian monk, Bodhidharma, who brought Buddhism to China in the sixth century. When the Emperor asked him how much merit he, the Emperor, had acquired by supporting the new creed, Bodhidharma shouted at him: "None whatsoever." The Emperor, rather shaken in his enthusiasm, then wanted to know just what the sacred doctrine of the creed was. Again Bodhidharma shouted, "It is empty, there is nothing sacred."

That interview set the tone for the Zen tradition, which makes a special point of being rude, abrupt, direct and sarcastic – precisely those things which, according to the Japanese code of manners, must be avoided like the plague. The founding father himself, Bodhidharma, a favourite subject of Zen painting, is invariably portrayed as a snarling tough, with eyes menacingly bulging out of his head yet at the same time twinkling with sarcastic glee. Once he fell asleep while meditating, and got so furious about it that he promptly sawed off his offending eyelids. These dropped to the ground and became the seeds of the first tea-plants – hence the saying that Zen and tea "taste the same". Another leg-pull story has it that the ferocious Bodhidharma persisted in meditation so long that his legs fell off.

The tradition of deliberate rudeness has been maintained to this day, and there are endless stories to illustrate it.

A monk asked Tosu (T'ou-tzu), a Zen master of the T'ang period: "I understand that all sounds are the voice of the Buddha. Is this right?"

*Quoted by Alan W. Watts, The Way of Zen (London, 1957), pp. 89 and 115.
†Ibid., p. 125.

The master said, "That is right." The monk then proceeded: "Would not the master please stop making a noise which echoes the sound of a fermenting mass of filth?" The master thereupon struck the monk.

The monk further asked Tosu: "Am I in the right when I understand the Buddha as asserting that all talk, however trivial or derogatory, belongs to ultimate truth?" The master said, "Yes, you are in the right." The monk went on, "May I then call you a donkey?" The master thereupon struck him.*

The reason why the master struck him was not the monk's rudeness – which was in the right tradition of Zen-teasing – but because he was too logical – which is the one unforgivable sin in a Zen monastery. Dr Suzuki, the sensei (teacher or scholar) of Zen senseis, comments – with a lucidity which is quite unusual in his voluminous writings:

> The masterful Tosu knew, as all Zen masters do, the uselessness of making any verbal demonstration against such a "logician". For verbalism leads from one complication to another; there is no end to it. The only effective way, perhaps, to make such a monk as this one realise the falsehood of his conceptual understanding is to strike him and so let him experience within himself the meaning of the statement, "One in All and All in One". The monk was to be awakened from his logical somnambulism. Hence Tosu's drastic measure.†

The whackings and teasings are a mild form of shock therapy to jolt the student out of his mental habits and to hammer it into his head that he must act spontaneously, without thinking, without self-consciousness and hesitation. This is the main purpose of the mondo – the brief, sharp dialogue between master and pupil – and the koan – the logically insoluble riddle which the pupil must try to solve. The master may ask: "A girl is walking down the street. Is she the younger or the older sister?" The correct answer is apparently, for the pupil to put on a mincing walk, that is, to become the girl, and thereby to demonstrate that what matters is the experience of being and not its verbal description; the "suchness" of existence and not concepts like "older" or "sister".

> The truth is [says Dr Suzuki], as Tosu declares in the following:
> A monk asks, "What is the Buddha?"
> Tosu answers, "The Buddha."
> Monk: "What is the Tao?"
> Tosu: "The Tao."

*Daisetz T. Suzuki, Zen and Japanese Culture (London, 1959), p. 33.
†Suzuki, op. cit., p. 34.

Monk: "What is Zen?"
Tosu: "Zen."*

What is a rose? Is a rose, is a rose.

"In fact," Dr Suzuki informs us, "there is no other way of illuminating the monk's mind than affirming that what is is."

And what was was, perhaps.

There are said to exist some one thousand seven hundred koans, divided into various categories. In the Rinzai sect of Zen, the disciple is supposed to pass through a series of about fifty koans of increasing difficulty before his graduation as a fully Enlightened One, and the process is supposed to take about thirty years – but this need not be taken by the letter. In the classic system of Hakuin, there are five graded categories of koan; but certain Zen abbots, whom I visited in Kyoto, mentioned a different classification: according to his character, the pupil would be given either "keen knife-edge" koans or "gentle spring-wind" koans or "iron ox" koans. A list of "correct" answers has never been published since this would destroy their purpose; but most of the koans are of a type which admits of no logically correct answer, only of a symbolic rejoinder in the spirit of Zen.

The oldest-known koans are the "Three Barriers of Hung-Lun", an eleventh-century Zen master:

> *Question* Everybody has a place of birth. Where is your place of birth?
> *Answer* Early this morning I ate white rice gruel. Now I'm hungry again.
> *Question* How is my hand like the Buddha's hand?
> *Answer* Playing the lute under the moon.
> *Question* How is my foot like a donkey's foot?
> *Answer* When the white heron stands in the snow it has a different colour.†

The first answer seems to mean that the circumstances of birth and death are mere ripples in the flow of appearances, as unimportant as the eternal cycle of hunger and satiety. The second means, perhaps: do not try to reason, but serenade the moon and you are the Buddha. The third I leave to the reader to meditate upon.

Some of the koans and mondos have an archetypal ring. When Yao-shan was asked, "What is the Tao?" he pointed upwards to

*Ibid.
†Watts, op. cit., p. 106.

the sky and downwards to the water-jug before him. When pressed for an explanation, he replied, "A cloud in the sky and water in the jug." Zen's arch-enemy, the thousand-armed hydra which it fights to destroy, is rational thinking – verbal concepts, definitions, the operations of logic, classification by categories. The more extravagant koans are designed to reduce these to absurdity, to undermine the pupil's confidence in his powers of conscious reasoning, and thus to clear away the obstacles to satori – the sudden flash of intuitive understanding which illuminates the path to Enlightenment. Hence the distrust of words, considered to be the germ-carriers of abstract thought:

> Those who know do not speak
> Those who speak do not know
>
> When you are silent "It" speaks
> When you speak "It" is silent.*

The philosophy of Zen is traditionally summed up in four sentences, attributed to the Second Patriarch – the pupil of Bodhidharma:

> Unteachable and unorthodox†
> Not founded on words and letters
> Pointing directly into the human mind
> Seeing into one's nature and attaining Buddha-hood.

The main emphasis in the quatrain is on the rejection of "words and letters", and on the "direct pointing" at the intuitive faculties. Hence the deliberately absurd answer to the question, "What is the Buddha?": "Three pounds of flax."

That answer is attributed to T'ung-shan, who lived in the ninth century, and a later authority comments that "none can excel it as regards its irrationality which cuts off all passages to speculation". The three pounds of flax remind one of the koan discussed by the mediaeval schoolmen: "If God had chosen to be incarnated in the form of an ass or a pumpkin, could a pumpkin work miracles or be crucified?" – and of Erasmus's comment: "They are Folly's servants." There is something of that Erasmian attitude in Zen's contempt for the vanity of all endeavours to approach the Absolute with the yardsticks of logic.

*Watts, op. cit., p. 106.
†This at least is my interpretation of Alan Watt's interpretation of the four ideograms which constitute the first sentence. Watt's rendering is: "Outside teaching; apart from tradition" (op. cit., p. 88).

Thus some koans do make "sense" by their direct appeal to intuitions beyond verbal thought, while others are meant to destroy the self-imposed restraints and imaginary fetters which prevent the spontaneous exercise of the imaginative powers. Once one has entered into the spirit of the game, the answers to certain types of koan become fairly obvious. For instance, if a Zen master suddenly barked at me, "Stop that ship on the distant ocean", I should answer without turning a hair: "Don't worry, I have just dropped an iceberg in front of it" – the idea being that if I am free to imagine a ship, what is there to prevent me from imagining an iceberg?

The whole teaching of Zen seems to be directed against the inhibitions and restraints imposed by the Japanese code of behaviour. Against the Spartan self-discipline demanded by the code, stands Po-chang's famous definition of Zen: "When hungry, eat, when tired, sleep." The traditional dread of unforeseen situations is neutralised by springing surprises and shocks on the disciple and encouraging him to reciprocate in equally eccentric fashion: the koan technique is designed to bring out just that side of a person which the social code condemns: "the unexpected man". In the social code, "self-respect" is practically synonymous with cautious and circumspect behaviour, designed to avoid adverse comment; Zen bullies the pupil into throwing caution to the wind, and teaches him to respond spontaneously, "without even the thickness of a hair between impulse and act". Social conditioning leads to numbing self-consciousness and blushing; Zen aims at the annihilation of "the self-observing self". It proclaims to be the philosophy of no-mind (Wu-hsin), of no-thought (Wu-mien), no-striving (Wu-wei), no-affectation (Wu-shih), and of "going ahead without hesitation". In the words of Yün-men: "When walking, just walk, when sitting, just sit, above all, don't wobble." The cramped victim of Japanese education is given by the founder of the Rinzai sect this kindly advice concerning the path towards self-realisation: "Clear every obstacle out of your way.... If on your way you meet the Buddha, kill the Buddha. When you meet your ancestor, kill your ancestor. When you meet your father and mother, kill your father and mother. When you meet your kin, kill your kin. Only thus will you attain deliverance. Only thus will you escape the trammels and become free."*

*There are several versions of this famous injunction: the above is Yukio Mishima's (The Temple of the Golden Pavilion, tr. Ivan Morris [New York, 1959], p. 258).

Another Zen command expresses the same idea in a less fierce image: "Let your mind go and become like a ball in a mountain stream."

Thus Zen-spontaneity became the ideal antidote to the Confucian rigidity of the social order. It was a marriage between extreme opposites, which is so characteristic of Japanese culture. But in this case the partners were destined for each other from childhood, as it were. Both came from China, where Confucianism and Taoism had from ancient times played complementary parts in the nation's life: the former determining law, order, book-learning and convention, the latter pointing to the intuitive Way – the Tao – towards the inner man and ultimate reality: the cloud in the sky and the water in the jug. Zen owes as much to Taoism as to Buddhism, and perhaps more: it has certainly remained closer to the philosophy of Lao-Tse than to any Buddhist sect in other countries.

Zen was introduced into Japan in the late twelfth century – more than five centuries after Confucianism and earlier forms of Buddhism. It took immediate roots; but it became radically transformed in the process, and the flower was characteristically Japanese. By a feat of mental acrobatics, of which perhaps no other nation would be capable, the gentle, non-violent doctrine of the Buddha became the adopted creed of the ferocious samurai. A little later it also became the dominant influence in painting, landscape-gardening, flower arrangement, tea ceremony, firefly-hunting and similar nipponeries on the one hand – of swordsmanship, wrestling, Judo, archery, dive-bombing on the other. How was this possible? The secret is not in the Buddha's smile but in a simple formula applicable to all these diverse activities, the panacea of Zen: trust your intuition, short-circuit reflection, discard caution, act spontaneously. It is amazing what wonders this prescription can achieve, especially in a people tied in knots, conditioned to the reverse set of principles.

To make the formula take effect on the unconscious, nonverbal levels at which it was aimed, verbal admonitions were, obviously, not enough. Apart from methods of developing the technical skills appropriate in each branch of activity, a mystic ritual and a special terminology were needed. Key-words in that terminology are satori, the sudden flash of insight which brings on Awakening or Enlightenment; the state of muga, which occurs when the split between the acting self and the self-observing self disappears, and the act becomes effortless, automatic, entranced – so that the painter or swordsman no longer feels that *he* is wielding the brush or making the thrust, but that a mysterious "It" has taken charge.* Lastly, a man who has completed his training and reached final Enlightenment, will continue to live zestfully and apparently unchanged, but he will *"live as one already dead"* – that is, detached and indifferent to success or failure.

Satori is a wonderfully rubbery concept. There are small satoris and big satoris. They occur when one solves a koan, or during meditation, but also through looking at peach-blossom or watching a pebble hit a bamboo. The mondos, in which the disciple who asked a too rational question is whacked on the head, usually end with the line: "at that moment he had his satori". Facing two famous Zen abbots in the Daitokuji Temple in Kyoto, I asked them how long a satori lasts. The first answered promptly: "One second." The second added as promptly: "It might go on for days."

Mr Christmas Humphreys, QC, President of the Buddhist Society in London, who, like most modern exponents of Zen, is a pupil of Dr Suzuki's, informs us in his book on Zen† that he had his first satori during a lesson in Judo: "on the night when, without 'thought' or feeling, I leapt to opportunity and in the fraction of time that my opponent was off his balance, threw him directly, cleanly, utterly"; but his greatest satori he had in a Turkish bath. By modern Zen standards I would be quite justified to claim that I have satori on each of the rare occasions when I manage to write down a sentence which says exactly what I mean.

Thus the phenomena covered by the term satori range from the mental click vulgarly described as "the penny has dropped", through flashes of inspiration of a higher (artistic or mystic) order, to that lasting change of character which creates a "living Buddha" – in our language, a well-balanced or integrated personality.

The accent is always on insight gained by intuition as opposed to cognition, and on tapping the resources of the unconscious; and satori could be simply translated by the word "intuition" which is equally elastic and covers the same range of phenomena. There is not more to it, but also not less. The rest is pseudomystical verbiage.

Though Zen derives from Yoga and cultivates the use of Sans-

Muga is the Japanese rendering of *Wu-mien* – No-thought.
†*Zen Buddhism* (London, 1949), p. 89.

krit terms, it aims in the opposite direction. Samadhi is the elimination of the conscious self in the deep sleep of Nirvana; satori is the elimination of the conscious self in the wide-awake activities of intuitive living. The Yogi strives to drown himself in the universal unconscious; the Zen practitioner strives to bring the submerged "It" from the depths to the surface. To make the point quite clear: *literally* speaking, samadhi means "deep sleep", satori means "awakening". *Mystically* speaking, "deep sleep" means entering into Real Life, whereas the Awakened one "lives like one already dead". But *cynically* speaking, it is less risky and more pleasant to choose the Zen path – to live in Nirvana rather than be dead in Nirvana. And, however sincere the Chinese Zen Patriarchs' intentions were when they reversed the direction of Indian Buddhism, the Zen way of the samurai, of the modern Flower Masters and gay abbots, seems to be more inspired by that cynical truth – not in their conscious minds, God forbid, but in the intuitive depths of their such-ness.

Leaving the mumbo-jumbo aside, the special training techniques in any branch of "applied Zen" show remarkable psychological insight and produce some remarkable results. Japanese wrestling, for instance, is fascinating to watch because, though the wrestlers often weigh over three hundred pounds and attain six and a half and even seven feet, which by Japanese standards makes them into giants, their movements are quick as lightning, and the contest has something of the eerie quality of a mongoose fighting a snake.

The bout itself lasts usually less than a minute, but the preliminaries take fifteen minutes and used to take up to forty-five. The purpose of these preliminary rituals is for the contestants to limber up, both mentally and physically. They approach each other, sprinkle salt on the ground by way of purification, throw water over their shoulders and perform a curious balancing act on one leg, then turn their backs and go into a kind of brooding meditation, waiting for *muga*. Part of all this may be showmanship, but one recognises the genuine element when, the psychological moment having suddenly arrived, the two inert mountains of flesh leap at each other with lightning speed, as the mongoose leaps at the cobra's throat, as if "It" has taken possession of them; after a few turns and twists of breathtaking nimbleness, which look as if no force were being used at all, one of the mountains crashes on the floor or is thrown clear of the ring.

The main emphasis in "applied" Zen training is on complete indifference towards success and failure. The "It" will only enter into action when straining and striving have ceased and the action becomes "effortless" and automatic. The formula is, of course, quite misleading because the athlete *will* use the last ounce of his strength to win; what the training really aims at is to relieve the *mental* strain, and the resulting cramped style. But in a culture haunted by the fear of failure, the contestant must be hypnotised into the belief that he does not care about the outcome, that he is not competing but performing a mystic ritual. Hence the invariably ritualistic setting, and the mystic language employed in archery or fencing or flower arrangement, to which Western enthusiasts, unacquainted with the psychological background, are so susceptible. Mr Christmas Humphreys, who had an Awakening because he had thrown an opponent in Judo, is a rather endearing case. But it is distressing when a book like Dr Eugen Herrigel's Zen *and the Art of Archery,** which manages to combine the more ponderous kind of Germanic mysticism with the more obvious kind of Zen hocus-pocus, is taken seriously by the public in the West.

In spite of its remarkable achievements, Zen began to develop certain degenerative symptoms at an early stage. They seem to have started at the spiritual core of the movement, the monasteries. When St Francis Xavier arrived in Japan in 1549 – some two hundred years after the beginning of the great Zen vogue – he made friends with a scholarly and enlightened Zen abbot named Ninjitsu.

> Ninjitsu one day took Xavier to the meditation hall of his monastery, where the monks were engaged in their usual exercises of Zazen, which consists of kneeling motionless in concentrated thought upon one subject for the purpose of clearing the mind of all extraneous matters and thus approaching an intuitive grasp of truth. Xavier asked what these men were doing, and Ninjitsu replied: "Some are counting up how much they took from the faithful last month; some are considering where they can get better clothing and treatment for themselves; others are thinking of their recreations and pastimes. In short, none of them is thinking of anything that has any sense whatever."†

I was reminded of that passage during a talk with an equally amiable Zen abbot in Kyoto, who, having passed through his final

*London, third impression, 1959.
†G. B. Sansom, *An Historical Grammar of Japanese* (London, 1928), p. 122.

satori and graduated as a Buddha "living like one already dead", had just bought himself a television set. In Mishima's novel there is another abbot, whom his devoted pupil catches out leaving a cinema, dressed in European clothes, in the company of a geisha. Their attitudes to the vanities of the world seem to be like that of the alcoholic who affirms that he is cured, and that he no longer drinks because he needs it but just for fun.

Although the practice of Zazen – sitting motionless on the wooden platform of the meditation hall – plays a dominant part in monastic routine, Zen and meditation somehow do not seem to fit together. It is the practice of a mystic technique without mystic content; if there is no God, no Moral Law, no doctrine, no teaching, what is there left to meditate about – except repeating a-rose-isarose-isarose, as a means of self-hypnosis?

Yet the more dubious the object of meditation, the more rigorously it was enforced by disciplinary measures which one might call barbaric, were it not for the Japanese love of Spartan methods. The monitor in the meditation hall carries a massive staff with a sharp end, and if a disciple fidgets or becomes drowsy, he whacks him with a sharp blow across the shoulder blades.

Zazen meditation, unlike Yoga, holds no promise of supernatural rewards. At the risk of being repetitive, I must again mention that while both Yoga and Zazen aim at penetrating beyond the captive mind, the "beyond" means in one case trance-sleep and death, in the other case a more intense awareness of the Now and Here. Thus Yoga is a challenge to existence; Zen, a challenge to conventionality. The Yogi practises physical contortions to make his body acquiesce in its own annihilation; Zen uses the mental contortions of the koan to stun reason and force it to abdicate. And just as in Hatha Yoga the asanas and mudras have become physical substitutes for true meditation, thus in Rinzai Zen the koans and mondos fill the spiritual vacuum.

This brings me back, for almost the last time, to Professor Suzuki and the question whether he and his disciples are trying to fool the reader or themselves.

The slow decline of monastic life, the voiding of Zen's spiritual core, was bound to affect the arts which had fallen under its sway. Its original impact on Japanese life had been immensely liberating and stimulating – as witnessed, for instance by the Sumi-e style of landscape painting, which had grown under Zen influence in China under the Sung dynasty and had followed Zen to Japan; or by the Haiku type of poetry; or in the Zen-inspired schools of pottery. The flourishing of the Zen arts coincided approximately with the European Renaissance, and lasted to the end of the seventeenth century. It created a style of art, and a style of life of unique flavour, a golden age whose golden fallout still lingers over the islands.

The gradual degeneration of Zen art seems to have been caused by a curious misconception inherent in Zen psychology. I mean the confusion between two different types of uninhibited "spontaneous" responses: the spontaneous flash of creative originality, and the pseudo-spontaneity in exercising a skill which has became automatic. Both are immediate and unpremeditated; but the former is an improvisation sprung up from the creative depths of the psyche, the latter is a stereotyped reaction, either innate or impressed through learning by rote.* In other words, the confusion is between intuitive response and conditioned reflex.

In a culture which rigorously suppresses the manifestation of emotions, and regards self-control as the highest of virtues, spontaneity acquires a magic aura, even if it amounts to no more than shouting in pain. Hakuin is revered as the author of the koan system in its modern form, but perhaps even more because he shouted in pain on his deathbed. In his youth, he was shocked by the story that an earlier master, Yen-t'ou, screamed when he was killed by a robber; but when Hakuin had his satori he saw in a flash that yelling in pain was a triumph of Zen, a spontaneous manifestation of "It". Since Japanese women in labour are not supposed to utter a single moan, Hakuin's satori must indeed have been a revelation to him.† In this, as in similar Zen stories, it is imposs-

---

*See above, Chapter 30.
†To utter emotional shouts in a sword fight is an even older specifically Zen invention, which became an esoteric cult. The traditional shout is "Katsu", and Dr Suzuki has explained its meaning:

" 'Katsu!' is pronounced 'Ho!' in modern Chinese. In Japan when it is actually uttered by the Zen people, it sounds like 'Katz!' or 'Kwatz!' – tz like tz in German 'Blitz'. It is primarily a meaningless ejaculation. Since its first use by Baso Doichi . . . it came to be extensively used by the Zen masters. Rinzai distinguishes four kinds of 'Katz!' (1) Sometimes the 'Katz!' is like the sword of Vajrarapa (which cuts and puts to death anything dualistic appearing before it); (2) sometimes it is like the lion crouching on the ground; (3) sometimes it is like the sounding pole or a bundle of shading grass; (4) sometimes it serves no purpose whatever. . . . In Zen, what is most significant among these four 'Katz!' is the fourth, when the cry ceases to serve any kind of purpose, good or bad, practical or impractical. Someone remarks that Rinzai with all his astuteness omits a fifth 'Katz!' . . ." (op. cit., p. 66).

ible to say whether the "It" is meant to convey a divine inspiration, or the natural, uninhibited play of physiological reactions: "When walking, walk, when sitting, sit, but above all don't wobble."*

Once more: in a culture where the native hue of resolution is sicklied o'er, this would be sound advice – if only it were left at that. The purpose of the koan is to make the cramped pupil answer without hesitation and reflection – but at this point the dreadful confusion sets in. Since it would need a genius to produce an intuitively inspired answer to every koan, the pupil soon learns instead the type of answer that is expected of him – the "pointing" gesture, the absurd non-sequitur, the rude leg-pull, etc. – and the mondo becomes a game after a stereotyped pattern, another automatic skill. When the second Patriarch whacked the third Patriarch over the head and called the Buddha a noodle, they probably meant to give a new turn to mystic thought, not to create a Punch and Judy routine.

The same basic confusion, the same substitution of a ready-made formula for original intuition bedevilled all forms of applied Zen. The inspired "It" ceded to the mechanical knack. The perfect swordsman, says Dr Suzuki, "becomes a kind of automaton so to speak, as far as his own consciousness is concerned.† In archery, fencing, wrestling or Judo, this automatic skill of the no-mind is, of course, infinitely preferable to self-conscious wobbling. But in poetry and painting, dancing or landscape gardening, the substitution leads to lingering death by paralysis.

The Haiku is a typical example of what happened to other Zen arts. It is a poem of seventeen syllables in three lines. It was derived from the classic form of Japanese poetry, the Waka – a succession of five-syllable and seven-syllable lines without rhyme, rhythm, stress or meter. The Waka could go on without limits, as it presumably did in early folk poetry; but from the tenth century onward, its most practised form was the Tanka – 31 syllables in lines of 5, 7, 5, 7, 7. Out of this the Haiku developed by chopping off the two last lines, leaving 5, 7, 5 syllables as its unalterable structure. Its form resembles a truncated limerick, but

---

*Next in importance among Zen slogans after Wu-mien (no-mind) is Wu-shih – i.e. that "nothing special" is to be gained by it; at the same time Wu-shih also means "natural, unaffected".
†Suzuki, op. cit., p. 94.

without rhyme or rhythmic pattern. Its content is a kind of lyrical epigram – a mood caught in a butterfly net.

> With the evening breeze
> The water laps against
> The heron's legs

At its best, the Haiku is allusive and elusive like the best koans – like "the sound of a single hand clapping". It has "It":

> In the dense mist
> What is being shouted
> Between hill and boat?

> The sea darkens;
> The voices of the wild ducks
> Are faintly white

> You light the fire;
> I'll show you something nice –
> A great ball of snow!

But these inspired vignettes of the great Haiku masters of the sixteenth and seventeenth centuries are few and far between the mechanical turnings-out of a genre whose knack is all too easy to learn. The proof is that out of the hundreds of Haikus in Mr Blyth's classic three-volume collection* it is always the same half-dozen favourites – by Basho, Buson, or Moritake† – that are quoted as samples. Nevertheless the seventeen-syllable Haiku and the thirty-one-syllable Tanka have remained for the last five hundred years the *only* forms of popular poetry in Japan. In 1956, the magazine *Haiku Research* estimated that there were at least four million Haiku poets practising the art – if that is the proper word for the tireless permutations of crows perching on a branch, frogs leaping into a pond, drops sliding off bamboo-leaves, and autumn leaves rustling in the ditch. Its stereotyped imagery and fixed number of syllables leave no scope for individuality, style, or for critical evaluation. The inquisitive Mr Enright once asked some Japanese professors of literature, "how they could tell a good Haiku from a bad Haiku. 'We cannot,' replied one of them, 'the trouble is that we don't know what standards to apply. But perhaps you, from Cambridge. . . .' He smiled politely. Another suggested with a strangled cough, 'All Haiku are good, perhaps?' "‡

*R. H. Blyth, *Haiku* (Tokyo 1949, 1950, 1952).
†Moritake 1472–1549; Basho 1644–94; Buson 1716–84.
‡D. J. Enright, *The World of Dew* (Tokyo-Vermont, 1959), p. 63.

The same degenerative process, due to the same causes, can be seen in the Zen schools of painting, from the truly "spontaneous", powerful work of Seshu – who used not only the brush, but fistfuls of straw dipped in ink to impart to his landscapes their violent motion – through the gradual hardening of the arteries in the Zenga, Haigu and Calligraphic styles, into mannerism and aridity.

A surprisingly large number of Japanese have the knack of drawing surprisingly pretty bamboos – and rocks, trees, cranes and butterflies; the only trouble is that the bamboos and butterflies all look the same. Zen started as a de-conditioning cure and ended up as a different type of conditioning. The cramp of self-critical watchfulness was relieved by the self-confident ease of exercising an automatic skill. The knack became a comfortable substitute for "It". The autumn leaves still rustle in the ditch, but originality has gone down the drain. The water still laps against the heron's legs, but the muse lies drowned at the bottom of the ancient pond.

Religious feeling is deader in Japan, and has been dead for a longer time, than in any of the great existing civilisations.

At the start of this discussion of Zen, I quoted a few lines attributed to Seng-Ts'an, who lived in the sixth century AD, and was the Third Patriarch – that is, second in succession to the Bodhidharma. They are from his work *Hsin-hsin Ming*, which is regarded as the oldest Zen poem and one of its basic texts:

> Be not concerned with right and wrong
> The conflict between right and wrong
> Is the sickness of the mind.

Fourteen centuries later, the last Patriarch reaffirms the unbroken continuity of Zen's ethical relativism:

> Zen is . . . extremely flexible in adapting itself to almost any philosophy and moral doctrine as long as its intuitive teaching is not interfered with. It may be found wedded to anarchism or fascism, communism or democracy, atheism or idealism.*

The difference between the two statements is in their historical setting, and in their degrees of concreteness. The first comes from a sixth century Buddhist-Taoist mystic, who looks with a smiling shrug at the sententious pedantries of Confucian society. The

*Suzuki, op. cit., p. 63.

second could come from a philosophically minded Nazi journalist, or from one of the Zen monks who became suicide pilots.

I have stressed the point, and must stress it again in concluding,
that the vivifying influence of Zen, its historical and spiritual
raison d'être, came from its function as a complement and antidote to Confucianism – from the division of labour between the
rigid and demanding social code of the latter, and the relaxing,
amoral spontaneity of Zen. The great Zen masters were, after all,
sages with a shrewd knowledge of character; they knew that the
cosmic nihilism of their doctrine was like arsenic – in small doses
a stimulant, in large doses poison. Their wisdom found an unexpected confirmation several centuries later, when Zen was
exported overseas and let loose among intellectuals with a
decidedly non-Confucian background. They tried hard to obey its
command: "let your mind go and become like a ball in a mountain
stream"; the result was a punctured tennis-ball surrounded by
garbage, bouncing down the current from a burst water main.

To revert to the old koan: Zen in itself, without its historic
counterpart, is like the sound of one-hand clapping. Whether a
religion, or a philosophy, deserves that name if it represents only
one-hand clapping, is a problem for historians and semanticists.
Perhaps the credos based on the materialism of the nineteenth
century, or on the catechism of the Council of Trent issued in
1566, could be called equally one-handed. But the fact remains
that Zen philosophy and Zen art had been declining for a century
or more when the old social system, and with it the backbone of
the Confucian code, was destroyed by the Meiji reform a hundred
years ago. State Shinto was created to fill the religious vacuum;
and when that synthetic Baal, too, collapsed after the last war,
neither Zen, nor the older forms of Buddhism were able to offer an
alternative to provide guidance in the chaos of values. They were
unable, and even unwilling to do so, because of the ethical relativism of their tradition, their denial of a universal moral law, and a
misguided tolerance which had become indistinguishable from
passive complicity.

This impartial tolerance towards the killer and the killed, a
tolerance devoid of charity, makes one sceptical regarding the
contribution which Zen Buddhism has to offer to the moral recov-
ery of the world. Once a balm for self-inflicted bruises, it has
become a kind of moral nerve-gas – colourless and without smell,
but scented by all the pretty incense sticks which burn under the
smiling Buddha statues. For a week or so I bargained with a Kyoto

antique dealer for a small bronze Buddha of the Kamakura period; but when he came down to a price which I was able to afford, I backed out. I realised with a shock that the Buddha smile had gone dead on me. It was no longer mysterious, but empty.

On this resigned note ends The Lotus and the Robot – *followed by a somewhat truculent Epilogue.*

Lilies that fester smell far worse than weeds: both India and Japan seem to be spiritually sicker, more estranged from a living faith than the West. They are at opposite ends of the Asian spectrum, whose centre is occupied by the vastness of China, one of the world's oldest cultures; yet it proved even less resistant against the impact of a materialistic ideology. The Chinese nation which had held fast for two and a half millennia to the teachings of Confucius, Lao-Tse and the Buddha, succumbed to the atheistic doctrine formulated by the son of a German lawyer, and has become the most accomplished robot state this side of science fiction. To look to Asia for mystic enlightenment and spiritual guidance has become as much of an anachronism as to think of America as the Wild West.

Asians have a tendency to lay the blame for this decline on the soul-destroying influence of the West, and Western intellectuals are inclined to accept the blame. "As pupils we were not bad, but hopeless as teachers" – Auden's *mea culpa* might serve as a motto for the Western guilt complex towards Asia. Like other complexes, it consists of a mixture of fact and fantasy. The factual elements belong to a chapter of history – imperialist expansion and colonial exploitation – which, as far as Asia is concerned, is now closed. It was, no doubt, an ugly chapter of predatoriness combined with hypocrisy. But, of course, the history of Asiatic nations is an equally unedifying tale of invasions, conquests and oppression – right up to the Moslem-Hindu massacres after Independence; and it could be cynically argued that the seafaring invaders of modern times were merely returning the visit of the Mongol invaders of Europe in earlier days. If the past were admitted to weigh on its conscience, every nation would be compelled to commit hara-kiri. Instead of nursing a guilt-complex derived from the crimes of our forebears, the duty of the West is to give material help to the "underprivileged" Asian nations; and that is now being done on a larger scale than ever before in history.

Let us turn, then, to another aspect of the complex: the psychological ravages which our materialistic civilisation is supposed to have caused among the spiritual values of the traditional Asiatic cultures.

An apparent digression might help to clarify the problem. On a similar scale, but in a more concentrated form, a similar process is now taking place closer to us. One might call it the coca-colonisation of Western Europe, and in this respect I feel the same resentment as the Asian traditionalist. I loathe processed bread in cellophane, processed towns of cement and glass, and the Bible processed as a comic-strip; I loathe crooners and swooners, quizzes and fizzes, neon and subtopia, the Organisation Man and the *Reader's Digest*. But who coerced us into buying all this? The United States do not rule Europe as the British ruled India; they waged no Opium War against us to force their revolting "coke" down our throats. Europe bought the whole package because it wanted it. The Americans did not americanise us – they were merely one step ahead on the road towards a global civilisation with a standardised style of living which, whether we like it or not, is beginning to emerge all over the world. For we live in a state of cultural osmosis where influences percolate across the porous frontiers, native traditions wane, and the movement towards a uniform, mechanised, stereotyped culture-pattern has become irresistible. What makes it irresistible are the new media of mass-communication; and what makes the emerging pattern so vulgar is the emergence of the under-privileged classes with their undeveloped tastes as consumers of mass-culture. The result is that inevitable levelling-down of standards to the lowest common denominator, which accompanied every revolution in the past.

But this process of cultural osmosis started long before the media of mass-communication were invented – it started with Alexander, it continued in the Mogul invasion of India, and it gained a new impetus with the opening up of sea communications. European rule in Asian countries was based on force, but its cultural influence was not. They bought our culture because they wanted it; because their own cultures had lost their vigour, and succumbed to European influence – as Europe succumbed in the twentieth century to American influence. The Japanese bought European Renaissance learning from the Dutch traders in Nagasaki; then nineteenth-century Science during the Meiji reform; then the robot civilisation after the Second World War. The Indian élite became anglicised because Hindu philosophy, science and literature had come to a standstill a long time ago, and had nothing to offer to them. We ruled by rape, but influenced by seduction. And a saint who lets herself be seduced willingly and asks for more, cannot be much of a saint.

The native customs and crafts were certainly damaged in the process. There is a tribe in Assam, the Khasis, who used to weave beautiful coloured fabrics; they also used to sacrifice little boys to the gods by pushing a two-pronged stick up their nostrils and into the brain. Now they buy hideous mass-produced textiles – and sacrifice no more little boys. It would have been better if they had accepted one half of the offer without the other. But these patterns of living hang together; they go, as the Americans say, by package deal. The Indian Government is now trying to revive the native crafts, but meets with little response. The reason, *mutatis mutandis*, is the same as in Europe: the produce of the cotton mills is cheaper than homespun *khadi*. It is, of course, also much uglier, and again for the same reason: the law of the lowest common denominator in taste. But this, too, may be a transitory phenomenon: some Indian factories are beginning to turn out remarkably attractive fabrics, printed in the traditional designs; and, sentimentality apart, only a few among the weavers, potters and cabinet-makers of the past were great artists.

If the Western cultural imports into Asia provide often no more than cheap, superficial frills, the reason is that the uneducated Asiatic masses are inevitably attracted by the trashiest influence and wares – as the previously under-privileged classes in Europe are attracted by the lures of coca-colonisation. If we are "hopeless as teachers" both at home and abroad, it is because literacy, culture-hunger and leisure-time are increasing even more rapidly than the birth-rate. There have never been, relatively speaking, fewer creative talents facing a vaster audience of consumers.

All this does not prove that the material poverty of Asia is a sign of its spiritual superiority in the present or in the past. Materialism as a philosophy is less than two centuries old in Europe and now on the wane; "materialism" in the sense of a mechanical, mindless sort of living is less than half a century old, though still on the increase. Before that, religion had been the dominant chord in European philosophy, art and social life, as far back into the past as historical comparisons are meaningful.

Asian history has been as bloody and cruel as ours; and the Buddhist-Hindu version of tolerance without charity produced as much suffering and misery as a Christian charity without tolerance did. Nonviolence was an abstract command, like turning the other cheek, until quite recent times when Gandhi's genius forged it into a political weapon. The great Hindu epics, the *Ramayana* and *Mahabharata*, are as full of savagery and gore as the Old Testament, and the first three chapters of the *Bhagavad Gita* – the nearest Hindu equivalent to the Gospels – are devoted to an eloquent refutation of the doctrine of nonviolence. The Lord Krishna in person appears on the battle-field as the charioteer of his friend Arjuna, and persuades him to drop his pacifist scruples – mainly on the grounds that the indestructible atma is embodied in both the slayer and the slain, who are One; therefore Arjuna must obey the law of Karma Yoga and fight. "There is no higher good for a Kashatriya (member of the warrior class) than a righteous war. The truly wise mourn neither for the living nor for the dead."

Gandhi himself was never an integral pacifist; he endorsed the Congress Resolution of 1940 that India would enter the war if granted Independence, and he gave his agreement to the invasion of Kashmir. Similarly, Vinoba Bhave in 1959 advocated armed resistance against Chinese infiltration in the Himalayas "because India is not yet spiritually prepared for a wholly non-violent resistance". Pacifism is a philosophy which, unfortunately, only appeals to pacifists. There is always that child bashed about by a brute, a Czechoslovakia or a Himalayan province invaded; and the dilemma between active intervention and passive complicity has never been solved, either by the East or by the West.

"You have developed the head; the heart did not keep pace. With us it was the opposite – it was with the development of the heart that we have been concerned in India." When Vinoba said that to me, I accepted it as a truism, as most guilt-ridden Westerners do. The first half of the statement is certainly true; but what evidence is there for the second? If "heart" refers to charity, the Oriental attitude to the sick and the poor is notoriously indifferent, because caste, rank, wealth and health are pre-ordained by the laws of Karma. Welfare work in the slums and care of the poor in general was, and still is, the monopoly of the Christian missions in Asia. Gandhi's crusade for the Untouchables and Vinoba's crusade for the landless are modern developments under Western influence – Gandhi himself acknowledged that he was inspired by Christianity, Tolstoy, Ruskin and Thoreau.

If by "heart" Vinoba meant religion, it has been in steady

decline for the last fifteen hundred years. Buddhism, Confucianism and Taoism were all founded in the sixth pre-Christian century; their spiritual message is confined to the ancient texts and to
the monumental works of art which they inspired. Religious
thought in the East retained its archetypal character; it does not
show that evolutionary progression, that combination of a firm
basic doctrine with social plasticity, which lent Western monotheism its unique continuity and ethos. Each of the great Eastern
religions represents a way of life rather than a self-contained
metaphysical doctrine; and when that way of life is altered by
changing circumstances, as in India and Japan, the spiritual values crumble away. The Sankaracharya* insisted on the rigorous
observance of the Hindu rites – because if the observances go,
nothing of Hinduism is left. A Hindu who breaks caste, eats meat
and forsakes his *lotha*, ceases, by definition, to be a Hindu. The
industrial revolution in England caused a more violent uprooting
of traditions than India is experiencing at present; yet the Church
of England weathered the storm, while Hinduism is foundering.
The only live religious tradition in India in the last thousand years
was carried on by exceptional individuals – by its great swamis,
from Sankara to Vinoba. But their contribution lay more in their
personality than in their teaching, and they rarely left written
works of value on which their successors could build.

In other words, I think that our cherished habit of contrasting the
contemplative and spiritual East with the crude materialism of
the West is based on a fallacy. The contrast is not between spiritu-
ality and materialism, but between two basically different
philosophies; so different, in fact, that Haas, the German Orientalist, who wrote a thoughtful and stimulating book on the question,† suggested a new word for the Eastern approach to life:
"philousia" as opposed to Western "philosophy". For all the
historical evidence goes to show that the East is less interested in
factual knowledge – *sophia* – of the external world than in *ousia* –
essential Being; that it prefers intuition to reason, symbols to
concepts, self-realisation through the annihilation of the ego to
self-realisation through the unfolding of individuality. Obviously
the two attitudes ought to complement each other like the principles of masculine logic and feminine intuition, the *yin* and *yang*

*One of the four "Contemporary Saints" in The Lotus and the Robot, Part One.
†William S. Haas, The Destiny of the Mind (London, 1956).

in Taoist philosophy. And in the history of European thought they did indeed complement each other – either by simultaneously competing for supremacy or alternating in dominance. In every chapter of European history we can trace this creative polarity on various levels – the Dionysian and the Apollonian principles; the materialism of the Ionian philosophers and the mysticism of the Eleatics; Plato, Plotinus and Augustine negating the world of the senses, Aristotle, Albert and Aquinas reasserting it; Schopenhauer's Indian pessimism confronted by Nietzsche's arrogant superman; Jung's psychology of archetypes by Adler's psychology of power – through the ages the fertile opposition of yin and yang is reformulated under different aspects.

In the history of the great Asiatic cultures, the emphasis lay much more consistently on one side only – on the intuitive, subjective, mystical, logic-rejecting side. This attitude apparently arose out of the equally consistent refusal to recognise the independent reality of the external world. As a result, conceptual thinking could not develop, and yin had it all to herself against yang.

Thus the hubris of rationalism is matched by the hubris of irrationality, and the messianic arrogance of the Christian crusader is matched by the Yogi's arrogant attitude of detachment towards human suffering. Mankind is facing its most deadly predicament since it climbed down from the trees; but one is reluctantly brought to the conclusion that neither Yoga, Zen, nor any other Asian form of mysticism has any significant advice to offer.

The chapter on Zen appeared, before the publication of The Lotus and the Robot *in the October, 1960, issue of* Encounter. *It led to a controversy; among those who participated in it was C. G. Jung. The following extract is a summary of the controversy.**

Jung's long letter is one of his last appearances in print. The key passage said: "In the main I fully agree with Koestler's rather unfavourable opinion [of contemporary Zen and Yoga practices]. His is a meritorious as well as a needful act of debunking, for which he deserves our gratitude. The picture he is drawing of Yoga and Zen is, as the view of the Western mind, rational, distant, and – as it were, unprejudiced and correct."

From the chapter "Polemics and Rejoinders" in Drinkers of Infinity *(1968).*

Professor Gershon Scholem of the University of Jerusalem came up with a startling disclosure concerning one of the foremost prophets of the Zen cult in the West, which should be preserved for the record:

> With reference to the article by Arthur Koestler, in your October issue, I think I ought to make a remark illustrating his point concerning the amoralism of Zen teaching. Koestler goes in for a lengthy criticism of Eugen Herrigel's Zen and the Art of Archer and some other texts by Zen adherents. About one he says that what he quoted could "come from a philosophically minded Nazi-journalist". It has obviously escaped Koestler's attention that Eugen Herrigel, who wrote this widely discussed treatise, had in fact become a member of the Nazi Party after his return from Japan and having obtained whatever Zen illumination he might have got there. This fact has been carefully hushed up by the circle of his admirers after the war and it is thus small wonder that Koestler did not hear about it. Herrigel joined the Nazi Party after the outbreak of the war and some of his former friends in Frankfurt, who broke with him over this issue, told me in 1946 about his career as a convinced Nazi. He was known to have stuck it out to the bitter end. This was not mentioned in some biographical notes on Herrigel published by his widow, who built up his image as one concerned with the higher spiritual sphere only. . . .

By sheer concidence, Encounter also published, in the middle of the Zen dispute, "The Strangled Cry" – a critical revaluation of Darkness at Noon by my old friend John Strachey.* This explains my rejoinder in winding up the controversy:

In the November issue of Encounter, John Strachey accused me, rather flatteringly, of having started the "retreat from rationalism". In the December issue, Mr Christmas Humphreys, QC, accused me of the opposite crime, of being too much of a rationalist to share in the "intuitive delights" of Zen. I am not complaining; falling between two stools may be preferable to settling down, if both of them smell of dry rot.

That Western rationalism has acquired that smell is evident, and tacitly agreed by all participants in this controversy. It seems equally obvious, and inevitable, that a culture threatened by strontium clouds should yearn for the Cloud of Unknowing. My point was that the simple abdication of reason in favour of a spurious mysticism does not resolve the dilemma; and I have tried

*"The Strangled Cry", Encounter (November, 1960). Reprinted, with other essays, as a book under the same title (London, 1962).

to prove that both Yoga and Zen, *as practised today*, are spurious and degenerate. I am grateful to Professor Jung for his authoritative endorsement of this diagnosis, and not only for personal reasons; his statement will help to dispel the fog. . . . Why must the Master [Professor Suzuki] and his pupils write book after book to explain that Zen cannot be explained, that it is "literally beyond thought, beyond the reach of thought, beyond the limits of the finest and most subtle thinking" – in a word, that it cannot be put into words? We know that not only mystical experience defies verbalisation; there is a whole range of intuitions, visual impressions, bodily sensations, which also refuse to be converted into verbal currency. Painters paint, dancers dance, musicians make music, instead of explaining that they are practising no-thought in their no-minds. Inarticulateness is not a monopoly of Zen; but it is the only school which made a philosophy out of it, whose exponents burst into verbal diarrhoea to prove constipation.

In mediaeval Japan and earlier in China, Zen fulfilled a vital function as a deliberately amoral and illogical antidote to the rigours of a hierarchic, cramped, self-conscious society. In the form in which it is taught and practised today, Zen spells intellectual and moral nihilism. The first, because the emphasis is not on marrying intuition to reason, but on castrating reason. And the second, because its moral detachment has degenerated into complacency towards, and complicity with, evil. As the Master himself tells us:

> Zen is . . . extremely flexible in adapting itself to almost any philosophy and moral doctrine as long as its intuitive teaching is not interfered with. It may be found wedded to anarchism or fascism, communism or democracy. . . .*

It is time for the Professor to shut up and for the Western intelligentsia to recognise contemporary Zen as one of the sick jokes, slightly gangrened, which are always fashionable in ages of anxiety.

Debunking is not an inspiring job. When John Donne wrote, *"Tis all in pieces, all cohesion gone"*, he was uttering an earlier "strangled cry". He also wrote, *"With a strong sober thirst, my soule attends"*; and that thirst cannot be quenched by counterfeit spirits.

*D. T. Suzuki, *Zen and Japanese Culture* (London, 1959), p. 63.

PART SIX

A GLANCE THROUGH THE KEYHOLE

Chapter 52

BEYOND MATERIALISM

Evidently Eastern mysticism did not provide the answers – nor did the vogue of various half-baked cults in subsequent years.

Thus when I finished The Lotus and the Robot, *I went back in a chastened mood to Western science, to holarchies and holons, and man's urge to self-destruction. I also participated in various congresses and symposia which provided much stimulation; yet at the same time I could not help realising that some of these occasions amounted to little more than vanity fairs, frequented by an international set of celebrities – I called it the academic call-girl circuit:*

"It becomes a habit, maybe an addiction. You get a long-distance telephone-call from some professional busybody at some foundation or university – 'sincerely hope you can fit it into your schedule – it will be a privilege to have you with us – return fare economy-class and a modest honorarium of. . . .' Or maybe no honorarium at all, and in the end you are out of pocket. I am telling you, it's an addiction."

The quotation is from a satirical novel, The Call-Girls (1972), *on which I worked on and off during what one may call my own call-girl period. It is about an interdisciplinary symposium of high-powered scientists, called "Approaches to Survival". Their task is to diagnose the human condition, to analyse man's urge to self-destruction, and to propose the remedies. At an early stage of the proceedings, a cable is read out, addressed to the participants by a high-ranking personality in the government of the United States:*

"Am instructed to convey informally Mr President's keen and agonised interest in outcome of your deliberations on quote approaches to survival unquote period. In these critical days when future destiny of mankind at stake the dedicated efforts of highpowered minds assembled at your conference may signify long over-due commencement of opening new avenues towards hopeful future period. Please communicate soonest possible conclusions reached by your conference which will be given earnest consideration on highest level period. Cordially. Signed. ..."

Needless to say, the symposium leads nowhere except to mutual incrimination and ends in chaos, with the hurried departure of the participants amid rumours that the Third World War has already started.

While the characters in the novel are fictitious, the theories which they propound, and the remedies they suggest are authentic in the sense that they reflect current trends in science, from anthropology to behaviourism. The novel is actually called a tragi-comedy, and is dedicated "to Messieurs Bouvard et Pecuchet", Flaubert's immortal pair of learned clowns who epitomise the follies of the savants of his time.

This does not mean that I had become cynical about science; only rather sceptical regarding its powers of providing "alternatives to despair" – its competence to answer the ultimate questions concerning "the meaning behind it all"; to make the invisible writing legible to our myopic eyes. Thus the last stage of this pilgrim's regress, not surprisingly perhaps, led from physics to metaphysics, from psychology to parapsychology. I say not surprisingly, because theoretical physics has always been my favourite science, and the type of physics concerned with sub-atomic and supra-galactic phenomena is both the most poetic and the most "occult" of sciences. To quote from The Challenge of Chance *(1973):*

An impressive number of eminent physicists, from Einstein downward, have shown an inclination to flirt with parapsychology — as witnessed by the list of past presidents of the SPR – the British Society for Psychical Research; and, as in other subversive movements, the number of fellow-travellers exceeds by far that of card-carrying members. Thus, for instance, the discoverer of the electron, Sir Joseph J. Thomson, was one of the earliest members of the Society. Now why should physicists in particular show this proneness to infection by the ESP virus? The answer is hinted at in the autobiographical writings and metaphysical speculations of some of the greatest among them. The dominant chord that echoes through them is a pervasive feeling of frustration, caused by the realisation that science can elucidate only certain aspects, or levels, of reality, while the ultimate questions must always elude its grasp – vanishing into infinite regress like images reflected in a hall of mirrors.

Although I have no special psychic gifts, I have had my share of experiences which I believe to have been telepathic. I shall quote only a single example, which had a strong influence on my subjective attitude towards extra-sensory perception – long before I became acquainted with the mass of objective evidence for its reality, provided by Rhine's work at Duke University, and his successors.* The episode is recorded in The Invisible Writing,† *and in a condensed version in* The Challenge of Chance:

In 1937, during the Spanish Civil War, I was imprisoned for three months by the Franco regime as a suspected spy and threatened with execution. In such situations one tends to look for metaphysical comforts, and one day I suddenly remembered a certain episode in Thomas Mann's novel *Buddenbrooks*. One of the characters, Consul Thomas Buddenbrook, though only in his forties, knows that he is about to die. He was never given to religious speculations, but now he falls under the spell of a "little book" – which for years had stood unread in his library – in which he finds explained that death is not final, merely a transition to another, impersonal kind of existence, a reunion with cosmic oneness. ". . . There clung to his senses a profound intoxication, a strange, sweet, vague allurement . . . he was no longer prevented from grasping eternity. . . ."

Remembering that passage gave me the comfort I needed. I

**Cf.*, e.g., *"An ABC of ESP"* in The Roots of Coincidence (1972).
†*Ch.* xxxiv.

knew, by the way, that the "little book" to which Consul Budden-brook owes his revelation was Schopenhauer's essay *Uber den Tod und sein Verhältnis zur Unzerstörbarkeit unseres Wesens an sich – On Death and its Relation to the Indestructibility of our Essential Selves.*

The day after I was set free, I wrote Thomas Mann a letter in which I thanked him for the comfort that I had derived from that passage, explaining the circumstances under which I had remembered it. I had not met him before; it was the first fan letter I had ever written. It was dated from the Rock Hotel, Gibraltar, May 16 or 17, 1937. The title of Schopenhauer's essay was expressly mentioned in my letter.

Thomas Mann's answer reached me a few days later in London. It was a handwritten letter, which was lost, together with all my manuscripts and files, during my flight from occupied France in 1940. I cannot, of course, remember it verbatim, but its content was not easy to forget. Mann explained that he had read the Schopenhauer essay in 1897 or 1898, while he was writing *Buddenbrooks*, and that he had never wanted to read it again because he did not want to weaken its original strong impact. The day before, however, sitting in his garden, he felt a sudden impulse to read the essay once more, after nearly forty years. He went indoors to fetch the volume from his library; at that moment there was a ring at the door and the postman handed him my letter.

Since Thomas Mann's reply was lost, there is no direct evidence for this episode. But indirect evidence is provided by the fact that I published this story in *The Invisible Writing* in 1954, when Mann was still alive. I could not have dared to do so if it had not been veridical.

I never lost my somewhat guilty interest in telepathy, odd coinci-dences, and related, even more shocking phenomena. I joined the SPR in 1952, and participated in a few experiments with incon-clusive results. But it was only twenty years later that I felt the urge to write on the subject (owing to some experiences which were subjectively important, but of little evidential value). The Roots of Coincidence appeared in 1972, with a motto I borrowed from a radio broadcast by Max Beerbohm:

> *Ladies and gentlemen, I am afraid my subject is rather an exciting one and as I don't like excitement, I shall approach it in a gentle, timid, roundabout way.*

The Roots of Coincidence *was followed by* The Challenge of
Chance *(1973), co-authored by Sir Alister Hardy and Robert Harvie; and by some lectures included in* The Heel of Achilles *(1974).
These texts are summarised in the last two chapters of* Janus; *what
follows is an abridged version of them:*

"Half of my friends accuse me of an excess of scientific pedantry;
the other half of unscientific leanings towards preposterous subjects such as extra-sensory perception (ESP), which they include
in the domain of the supernatural. However, it is comforting to
know that the same accusations are levelled at an élite of
scientists, who make excellent company in the dock." Thus the
opening paragraph of *The Roots of Coincidence.* Since this was
written, the "élite" of scientists has apparently grown into a
majority. In 1973 the *New Scientist*, that much respected English
weekly, sent out a questionnaire to its readers, inviting them to
express their opinions on the subject of extra-sensory perception.
Out of the 1500 readers – nearly all of them scientists and
engineers – who answered the questionnaire, 67 per cent
regarded ESP either as an "established fact" or "a likely possibility".*

Even earlier, in 1969, the American Association for the
Advancement of Science (the equivalent of the British Association) approved the application of the Parapsychology Association
to become affiliated to that august body. Two previous applications had been rejected; the approval of the third was a sign of the
changing intellectual climate; and for parapsychology the ultimate seal of respectability.

Accordingly, it seems to me unnecessary to recapitulate here
the progress of parapsychology, from spiritistic seances in dark-
ened Victorian drawing-rooms to a modern empirical science
employing computerised statistics and sophisticated electronic
equipment. In the pages that follow I shall no longer be concerned
with the question whether telepathy and kindred phenomena
exist – which, in view of the large body of accumulated evidence, I
have come to take for granted† – but the implications of these
phenomena for our world-view.

That world-view, in so far as the educated layman is concerned,

New Scientist, January 25, 1973.
†Some of this evidence is discussed in *The Roots of Coincidence, The Challenge
of Chance* and *The Heel of Achilles.*

A GLANCE THROUGH THE KEYHOLE

places parapsychology and physics at opposite ends of the spectrum. Physics is regarded as the queen of the exact sciences, with direct access to the immutable laws of nature which govern the material universe. In contrast to this, parapsychology deals with subjective, capricious and unpredictable phenomena which manifest themselves in apparently lawless ways, or in direct contradiction to the laws of nature. Physics is, as the academic jargon has it, a "hard-nosed" science, completely down-to-earth, whereas parapsychologists float somewhere in nebulous Cloud-cuckoo-land.

This view of physics was indeed perfectly legitimate and immensely productive during the roughly two centuries when the term "physics" was practically synonymous with Newtonian mechanics. To quote a contemporary physicist, Fritjof Capra:

> Questions about the essential nature of things were answered in classical physics by the Newtonian mechanistic model of the universe which, much in the same way as the Democritean model in ancient Greece, reduced all phenomena to the motions and interactions of hard indestructible atoms. The properties of these atoms were abstracted from the macroscopic notion of billiard balls, and thus from sensory experience. Whether this notion could actually be applied to the world of atoms was not questioned.*

Or, in Newton's own words:

> It seems probable to me that God in the beginning formed matter in solid, massy, hard, impenetrable, movable particles, of such sizes and figures, and with such other properties, and in such proportion to space, as most conduced to the end for which he formed them; and that these primitive particles being solids, are incomparably harder than any porous bodies compounded of them; even so very hard, as never to wear or break in pieces; no ordinary power being able to divide what God himself made one in the first creation.†

If you leave out the references to God, the above quotation, dating from AD 1704, still reflects the implicit credo of our educated layman. Of course he knows that the formerly indivisible atoms can be split (with sinister results); but he believes – if he gives any thought to the matter – that *inside* the atomic nucleus there are other, truly indivisible billiard balls called protons, neutrons, etc. However, if he were sufficiently interested, he would also dis-

*F. Capra, *The Tao of Physics* (London, 1975), p. 52.
†Quoted by Capra, op. cit., p. 57.

cover that the giant atom-smashers have made mincemeat of protons, neutrons, etc.; that on this sub-microscopic level the criteria of reality are fundamentally different from those we apply on our macro-level; for inside the atom our concepts of space, time, matter and causality are no longer valid, and physics turns into metaphysics with a strong flavour of mysticism. As a result of this development, the unthinkable phenomena of parapsychology appear somewhat less preposterous in the light of the unthinkable propositions of relativity and quantum physics.

One such proposition I have already mentioned: the Principle of Complementarity which turns the so-called "elementary building-blocks" of physics into Janus-faced entities that behave under certain circumstances like hard little lumps of matter, but in other circumstances as waves propagated in a vacuum. As Sir William Bragg put it, they seem to be waves on Mondays, Wednesdays and Fridays, and particles on Tuesdays, Thursdays and Saturdays. We have seen that some of the pioneers of quantum physics, as well as their contemporary successors, regarded the Principle of Complementarity as a fitting paradigm for the mind–body dichotomy. This was cheering news to parapsychologists; we must remember, however, that Cartesian dualism recognises only the two realms of mind and matter, whereas the present theory* proposes a series of levels, equipped with "swing-gates", opening now this way, now that. Both in our daily behaviour and on the sub-atomic level, the gates are kept swinging all the time.

The concept of matter-waves, launched in the nineteen-twenties by de Broglie and Schrödinger, completed the process of the *dematerialisation of matter*. It had started much earlier, with Einstein's magic formula $E = mc^2$† which implies that the mass of a particle must not be conceived as some stable material but as a concentrated pattern of energy, locked up in what appears to us as matter. The "stuff" of which protons and electrons are made is rather like the stuff of which dreams are made, as a glance at the illustration on. p. 652 suggests. It is an example of the type of events which take place all the time in the physicists' bubble chambers, where high-energy "elementary" particles collide and annihilate each other or create new particles which give rise to a new chain of events. (The particles in question are of course

*See above, Chapter 40.
†Where E stands for energy, m for mass, and c for the velocity of light.

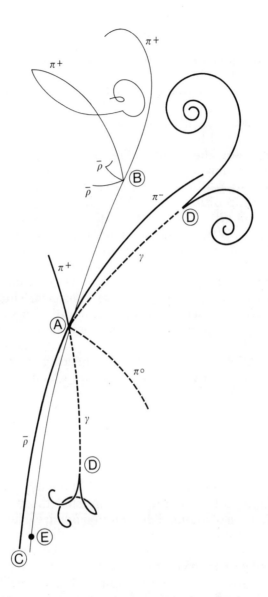

Diagram tracing a bubble-chamber photograph of subatomic events, from a Photo CERN – courtesy of European Organisation for Nuclear Research, Geneva. The caption (which leaves non-physicists none the wiser) reads: "interaction in the heavy liquid bubble chamber, Gargamelle. At A an incident antiproton which enters the chamber at C (see plan) annihilates a resident proton giving rise to a +ve and −ve pion, a neutral pion, and two gamma rays each of which converts (at D) into an electron positron pair. A second event is recorded where a particle entering at E interacts at B and produces two antiprotons and two +ve pions one of which collides subsequently twice with resident particles."

infinitesimally small and many have a lifetime much shorter than a millionth of a second; yet they leave tracks in the bubble chamber comparable to the visible trails which invisible jet-planes leave in the sky. The length, thickness and curvature of the tracks enables the physicists to decide which of the two-hundred-odd "elementary particles" has caused it, and also to identify "particles" previously unknown.)

The fundamental lesson which the bubble chamber and other sophisicated instruments teach the physicist is that on the sub-atomic level our concepts of space, time, matter and conventional logic no longer apply. Thus two particles may collide and break into pieces, but these pieces may turn out to be bigger than the original particles – because the kinetic energy liberated in the course of the collision has been transformed into "mass". Or a photon, the elementary unit of light, which has no mass, can give birth to an electron–positron pair which *does* have mass; and that pair might subsequently collide, and by the reverse process trans-form itself into a photon. The fantastic events in the bubble chamber have been compared to the dance of Shiva, with its rhythmic alternations of creation and destruction.*

All this is a long way from the beguilingly simple Rutherford–Bohr model of the beginning of our century, that represented atoms as miniature solar systems, in which negatively charged electrons circle like planets around a positively charged nucleus. Alas, the model ran into one paradox after another. The electrons were found to behave quite unlike planets – they kept jumping from one orbit into another without passing through the space between them – as if the earth were instantaneously transferred into the orbit of Mars in a single jump, ignoring space. It actually became as meaningless to ask at what exact point in space the electron was at a given moment, as it was meaningless to try to pin down a wave. As Bertrand Russell has put it:

> The idea that there is a hard little lump there, which *is* the electron or proton, is an illegitimate intrusion of common sense notions derived from touch.†

The atomic *nuclei* in the model did not fare better than the orbit-ing "planets". The nuclei turned out to be compounds of parti-cles, held together by other particles and forces which defy any visual model or representation in terms of our sensory experience.

*Capra, op. cit.
†B. Russell, *An Outline of Philosophy* (London, 1927), p. 52.

In earlier books* I have discussed some of the notorious paradoxes of quantum physics: Thomson's experiments which made the same electron appear to go through two minute holes in a screen at the same time (which, Sir Cyril Burt commented, "is more than a ghost can do"); the paradox of "Schrödinger's cat", which can be shown to be both alive and dead at the same time; Feynman's diagrams in which particles are made to move for a brief instant backward in time (which earned him the Nobel Prize in 1965); and the "Einstein–Podolsky–Rosen paradox" (or EPR paradox) to which I shall briefly return. The situation has been summed up by Heisenberg himself, one of the chief architects of quantum theory:

> The very attempt to conjure up a picture of elementary particles and think of them in visual terms is wholly to misinterpret them . . .†
>
> Atoms are not things. The electrons which form an atom's shells are no longer things in the sense of classical physics, things which could be unambiguously described by concepts like location, velocity, energy, size. When we get down to the atomic level, the objective world in space and time no longer exists.‡

Werner Heisenberg will probably be remembered as the great iconoclast who put an end to causal determinism in physics – and thereby in philosophy – by his celebrated "Principle of Indeterminacy" which is as fundamental to modern physics as Newton's Laws of Motion were to classical mechanics. I have tried to convey its meaning by a rather simplistic analogy.§ A certain static quality of many Renaissance paintings is due to the fact that the human figures in the foreground and the distant landscape in the background are both in sharp focus – which is optically impossible: when we focus on a close object the background gets blurred, and vice versa. The Principle of Indeterminacy implies that in studying the sub-atomic panorama the physicist is confronted with a similar predicament (though of course for quite different reasons). In classical physics a particle must at any time have a definite location and velocity; on the sub-atomic level, however, the situation turns out to be radically different. The more accurately the physicist is able to determine the location of an electron, for instance, the more uncertain its velocity becomes; and vice

*The Roots of Coincidence, The Challenge of Chance, and Life After Death.
†Quoted by Sir C. Burt in Science and ESP, ed. J. R. Smythies (London, 1967), p. 80.
‡W. Heisenberg, Der Teil und das Ganze (Munich, 1969), pp. 63–4.
§The Roots of Coincidence, p. 51.

versa, the more exactly he is able to determine the particle's velocity, the more blurred, i.e., indeterminate, its location becomes. This indeterminacy is not caused by the imperfection of our techniques of observation, but by the inherently dual nature of the electron as both "particle" and "wavicle", which makes it both practically *and theoretically* impossible to pin down. But this implies that down on the sub-atomic level the universe at any given moment is in a quasi-undecided state, and that its state in the next moment is to some extent indeterminate or "free". Thus if an ideal photographer with a perfect camera took a picture of the total universe at any given moment, the picture would be to some extent fuzzy, owing to the indeterminate state of its ultimate constituents.* Because of this fuzziness, physicists' statements about sub-atomic processes can only refer to probabilities, not to certainties; in the micro-world the laws of probability supplant those of causality: "nature is unpredictable" – to quote Heisenberg once more.

Thus for the last fifty years, since the advent of quantum theory, it has become a commonplace among physicists of the dominant school (the so-called Copenhagen School) that the strictly deterministic, mechanistic world-view can no longer be upheld; it has become a Victorian anachronism. The nineteenth-century model of the universe as a mechanical clockwork is a shambles and since the concept of matter itself has been dematerialised, *materialism can no longer claim to be a scientific philosophy.*

I have quoted some of the giants (most of them Nobel laureates)† who were jointly responsible for dismantling the antiquated clockwork, and attempted to replace it by a more sophisticated model, sufficiently flexible to accommodate logical paradoxes and wild theories previously considered unthinkable. During this half century countless new discoveries have been made – by radio-telescopes scanning the skies and in the bubble chambers recording the sub-atomic dance of Shiva – but no satisfactory model and no coherent philosophy has yet emerged comparable to that of classical, Newtonian physics. One might describe this post-Newtonian era as one of the periods of "creative anarchy"

*It can be shown that however short the exposure time, the Indeterminacy Principle will still blur the picture.
†The frequent mention of Nobel awards is intended as a reassurance that the strange theories quoted in this chapter were propounded not by cranks but by physicists of international renown.

which recur in the history of every science when the old concepts have become obsolete, and the breakthrough leading to a new synthesis is not yet in sight. At the time of writing, theoretical physics itself seems to be immersed in a bubble chamber, with the weirdest hypotheses criss-crossing each other's tracks. I shall mention a few, which seem pertinent to our theme.

First, there have been some eminent physicists, among them Einstein, de Broglie, Schrödinger, Vigier, and David Bohm, who were unwilling to accept the indeterminacy and acausality of sub-atomic events. (Einstein's famous phrase: "God does not play dice with the world" reflects this attitude.) They were inclined to believe in the existence of a sub-stratum below the sub-atomic level, which ruled and determined those seemingly indeterminate processes. This was called the theory of "hidden variables" – which, however, has been abandoned even by its staunchest supporters because it seemed to lead simply nowhere.

But although unacceptable to the physicist, the "hidden variables" provided a fertile field for metaphysical and parapsychological theorisings. Theologians proposed that Divine Providence might work from within the fuzzy gaps in the matrix of physical causality ("the god of the gaps"). Sir John Eccles, Nobel laureate in physiology, proposed that the quantum inde-terminacy of "critically poised" neurons in the brain made room for the exercise of free will. This was originally meant to apply to the action of individual minds on their "own" brains. In the concluding sections of his book, however, Eccles includes ESP and PK (psychokinesis) in his theory. He accepts the experimental results of Rhine and his school as evidence for a generalised "two-way traffic" between mind and matter, and of direct com-munication channels between mind and mind. The theory is not worked out in detail, but it is indicative of current trends of thought among enlightened neurophysiologists – from the late Sir Charles Sherrington to Penfield and Gray Walter, whom I have quoted in earlier works.

It is also interesting to note that Penfield, the neurologist, revived an unduly neglected hypothesis by Eddington, the astronomer, which postulated that matter "in liaison with mind" displays specific properties not otherwise found in the realm of physics – a proposition not far removed from panpsychism. Another astronomer, V. A. Firsoff, suggested that "mind was a universal entity or interaction of the same order as electricity or gravitation, and there must be a *modulus of transformation*, analogous to Einstein's famous equation $E = mc^2$".*

In other words, as matter can be transformed into physical energy, so physical energy must be transformed into psychic energy, and vice versa.

In recent years, there has been a spate of such theories, intended to bridge the gap between quantum physics and parapsychology, which sound like science fiction – but the same remark applies, as we have seen, to the basic propositions of modern physics itself.

Lifting our sights from the bubble-chamber to the starry skies, our commonsense notions of space, time, and causality turn out to be as inadequate as when we try to apply them to the sub-atomic domain. In the relativistic universe space is curved and the flow of time is speeded up or slowed down according to the time-keeper's state of motion. Moreover, if parts of the universe are furnished with galaxies of anti-matter,† which many astronomers believe to be the case, there is a fair chance that in these galaxies the flow of time is reversed.

Switching back from macrocosmos to microcosmos, we remember that in Feynman's diagrams, particles are supposed to move for a short while backwards in time. Heisenberg himself endorsed this hypothesis:

The only consolation [when faced with the paradoxes of quantum theory] is the assumption that in very small regions of space-time of the order of magnitude of the elementary particles, the notions of space and time become unclear, i.e., in very small intervals even the concepts "earlier" and "later" can no longer be properly defined. Of course nothing is altered in space-time on the large scale, but we must bear in mind the possibility that experiment may well prove that small-scale space-time processes may run in reverse to the causal sequence.‡

Thus our medium-sized world with its homely commonsense notions of space, time and causality appears to be sandwiched in between the macro- and micro-realms of reality, to which those parochial notions do not apply. As Sir James Jeans wrote: "The history of physical science in the twentieth century is one of progressive emancipation from the purely human angle of vis-

*V. A. Firsoff, *Life, Mind and Galaxies* (Edinburgh and London, 1967), pp. 102–3.
†Anti-matter consists of atoms in which the electric charges of their constituents are reversed.
‡W. Heisenberg, *The Physicist's Conception of Nature* (London, 1958), pp. 48–9.

ion.* On the macrocosmic scale of large distances and high speeds, relativity played havoc with that vision. On the microcosmic scale, relativity combined with quantum theory had the same effect. The physicist's concept of time is totally different today from what it was during Queen Victoria's reign. One of the most eminent among contemporary astronomers, Sir Fred Hoyle, has put it in his provocative way:

> You're stuck with a grotesque and absurd illusion, the idea of time as an ever-rolling stream. . . . There's one thing quite certain in this business: the idea of time as a steady progression from past to future is wrong. I know very well we feel this way about it subjectively. But we're the victims of a confidence trick.†

But if the irreversibility of time is derived from a "confidence trick" – that is, from a subjective illusion – we are no longer justified in excluding on a priori grounds the theoretical possibility of precognitive phenomena such as veridical dreams. The logical paradox that predicting a future event may prevent it or alter its course, is at least partly circumvented by the indeterminateness of the future in modern physics, and the probabilistic nature of all forecasts.

The revolution in physics which thus transformed our worldview took place in the nineteen-twenties. But in the second half of our century it took an even more surrealistic turn. At the time of writing, the universe appears to be pock-marked with so-called "black holes". The term was coined by John A. Wheeler, Professor of Physics at Princeton University, and a leading figure among contemporary physicists.‡ Black holes are hypothetical pits or sumps in distant space into which the mass of a burnt-out star which has suffered gravitational collapse is sucked at the speed of light, to be annihilated and vanish from our universe. The loci at which these apocalyptic events take place are referred to as "singularities" in the continuum; here, according to the equations of general relativity, the curvature of space becomes infinite, time is frozen, and the laws of physics are invalidated. The universe is turning out to be a very odd place indeed, and we do not need ghosts to make our hair stand on end.

---

*Sir J. Jeans, The Mysterious Universe (Cambridge, 1937).
†Sir F. Hoyle, October the First is Too Late (London, 1966).
‡Wheeler's book, Geometrodynamics, published in 1962, is considered a modern classic.

One might be tempted to ask the naive question where the matter which has fallen into the black hole "goes" (for not all of it can have been converted into energy). Wheeler has a tentative answer to that: it might emerge in the shape of a "white hole" somewhere *in another universe*, located in superspace (his italics):

> The stage on which the space of the universe moves is certainly not space itself. Nobody can be a stage for himself; he has to have a larger arena in which to move. The arena in which space does its changing is not even the space-time of Einstein, for space-time is the history of space changing with time. The arena must be a larger object: *super-space*. . . . It is not endowed with three or four dimensions – it's endowed with an *infinite* number of dimensions. Any single point in superspace represents an entire, three-dimensional world; nearby points represent slightly different three-dimensional worlds.*

Superspace – or hyperspace – has been an old stand-by of science fiction, together with the notion of parallel universes and reversed or multidimensional time. Now, thanks to radio-telescopes and particle-accelerators, they are acquiring academic respectability. The stranger the hard, experimental data, the stranger the theories which attempt to account for them.

Wheeler's version of superspace has some remarkable features:

> The space of quantum geometrodynamics can be compared to a carpet of foam spread over a slowly undulating landscape. . . . The continual microscopic changes in the carpet of foam as new bubbles appear and old one disappear symbolise the quantum fluctuations in the geometry. . . .†

Another remarkable attribute of Wheeler's superspace is multiple connectivity. This means – put into simple and over-simplified language – that regions which in our homespun three-dimensional world are far apart, may be brought temporarily into direct contact through tunnels or "holes" in superspace. They are called wormholes. The universe is supposed to be criss-crossed with these wormholes, which appear and disappear in immensely rapid fluctuations, resulting in ever-changing patterns – a cosmic kaleidoscope shaken by an invisible hand.

An essential feature of modern physics is its increasingly *holistic* trend, based on the insight that the whole is as necessary for the

*Quoted by L. B. Chase in *University, A Princeton Quarterly* (Summer, 1972).
†J. A. Wheeler in *Batelle Recontres* (1967).

understanding of its parts as the parts are necessary for understanding the whole. An early expression of this trend, dating from
the turn of the century, was "Mach's Principle", endorsed by
Einstein. It states that the inertial properties of terrestrial matter
are determined by the total mass of the universe around us. There
is no satisfactory causal explanation as to *how* this influence is
exerted, yet Mach's Principle is an integral part of relativistic
cosmology. The metaphysical implications are fundamental – for
it follows from it not only that the universe as a whole influences
local, terrestrial events, but also that local events have an
influence, however small, on the universe as a whole.
Philosophically-minded physicists are acutely aware of these
implications – which remind one of the ancient Chinese proverb:
"If you cut a blade of grass, you shake the Universe".

Bertrand Russell flippantly remarked that Mach's Principle,
though formally correct, "savours of astrology", while Henry
Margenau, Professor of Physics at Yale, commented in an address
to the American Society for Psychical Research:

> Inertia is not intrinsic in the body; it is induced by the circumstance
> that the body is surrounded by the whole universe. . . . We know of no
> physical effect conveying this action; very few people worry about a
> physical agency transmitting it. As far as I can see, Mach's Principle is
> as mysterious as your unexplained psychic phenomena, and its for-
> mulation seems to me almost as obscure. . . .*

Switching once more from macro- to microcosmos, we are confronted with the famous "Einstein–Podolsky–Rosen paradox". It
has been the subject of controversy ever since Einstein formulated
it in 1933, and has recently been given a more precise expression
by J. S. Bell, a theoretical physicist at CERN. "Bell's Theorem"
states that when two particles have interacted and then flown off
in opposite directions, interference with one particle will
instantly affect the other particle, regardless of the distance between them. The correctness of Bell's experimental results is not in
dispute, but its interpretation poses a major problem because it
seems to imply a sort of "telepathy" between the particles in
question. This is how David Bohm, Professor of Theoretical Physics at Birkbeck College, University of London, has summed up the
situation (his italics):

---

*H. Margenau in *Science and ESP*, ed. J. R. Smythies (London, 1967), p. 218.

Thus, one is led to a new notion of *unbroken wholeness* which denies the classical idea of analysability of the world into separately and independently existent parts. . . .*

These quotations (which could be multiplied indefinitely) do not represent solo voices, but rather a chorus of eminent physicists, aware of the revolutionary implications of quantum theory and of the new cosmology – which are bound to transform man's image of the universe even more radically than the Copernican revolution had done. But, as already said, the general public is slow in becoming aware of this change. The dogmas and taboos of nineteenth-century science contained within a rigid framework of causality and determinism, still dominate the habits of thought of the educated public which prides itself on its rational outlook, and feels compelled to deny the existence of ESP-type phenomena which seemingly contradict the "Laws of Nature". In fact our physicists have been engaged, over the last fifty years, in ruthlessly discarding previously sacrosanct "Laws of Nature" and replacing them with obscure mental constructs which cannot be represented in three-dimensional space, and whose quasi-mystical implications are hidden in technical jargon and mathematical formalism.

Curiously enough, during the same period parapsychology took on a more "hard-nosed" appearance by relying more and more on statistical methods, rigorous controls, mechanical gadgets and electronic computers. Thus the climate in the two camps seemed to be changing in opposite directions: Rhine's successors are sometimes accused of drab pendantry, while Einstein's successors have been accused of flirting with ghosts in the guise of particles which have no mass, no weight, nor any precise location in space. These convergent trends are certainly significant, but that does not mean that physics will provide explanations for the phenomena of parapsychology in the near or even in the distant future. What both have in common is an attitude defying commonsense and defying "Laws of Nature" previously considered as inviolable. Both are provocative and iconoclastic. And, to say it once more, the baffling paradoxes of physics make the baffling phenomena of parapsychology appear a little less preposterous. If distant regions of the universe can be

*D. Bohm and B. Hiley, "On the Intuitive Understanding of Non-Locality as Implied by Quantum Theory" (Preprint, Birkbeck College, Univ. of London, 1974).

brought into contact through wormholes in superspace, is telepathy still unthinkable? Such analogies can be treacherous – but it is encouraging to know that if the parapsychologist is out on a limb, the physicist is out on a tightrope.

There exists a type of phenomenon, even more mysterious than telepathy or precognition, which has puzzled man since the dawn of mythology: the seemingly accidental meeting of two unrelated causal chains in a coincidental event which appears both highly improbable and highly significant. Any theory which attempts to take such phenomena seriously must necessarily involve an even more radical break with our traditional categories of reasoning than the pronunciamentos of Einstein, Heisenberg or Feynman. It is certainly no coincidence that it was Wolfgang Pauli, another Nobel laureate in physics, who collaborated with C. G. Jung on the latter's famous essay: "Synchronicity: An Acausal Connecting Principle". Jung coined the term "synchronicity" for "the simultaneous occurrence of two or more meaningfully but not causally connected events",* and he claimed that the acausal factor behind such events is to be regarded as *"equal in rank to causality as a principle of explanation"*.†

"I have often come up against the phenomena in question," Jung wrote about puzzling coincidences, "and could convince myself how much these inner experiences meant to my patients. In most cases they were things which people do not talk about for fear of exposing themselves to thoughtless ridicule. I was amazed to see how many people have had experiences of this kind and how carefully the secret was guarded."‡

Apparently the Swiss are more secretive by nature than the British, for, ever since I wrote *The Roots of Coincidence* I have been inundated with coincidences in readers' letters. The most revealing among these were written by people who started by solemnly affirming that to attribute significance to coincidence is sheer nonsense, yet could not resist the urge to tell their own favourite believe-it-or-not story. Could it be that inside every hard-nosed sceptic there is a soft-nosed mystic crying to be let out?

*C. G. Jung, *The Structure and Dynamics of the Psyche*, Collected Works, Vol. VIII, tr. R. F. C. Hull (London, 1960), p. 318.
†Ibid., p. 435.
‡Ibid., p. 420.

Jung's essay on "synchronicity", published in 1952,* was partly based on Paul Kammerer's book *Das Gesetz der Serie*,† published in 1919. Kammerer was a brilliant Viennese experimental biologist of Lamarckian persuasion who was accused of faking his results, and committed suicide in 1926, at the age of forty-five.‡ He was throughout his life fascinated by coincidences and, from the age of twenty to forty, kept a log-book of them – as Jung also did.

Kammerer defined his concept of "seriality" as the concurrence in space or recurrence in time of *meaningfully but not causally connected events*. His book contains exactly one hundred selected samples, classified with the meticulousness of a biologist devoted to taxonomy. He regarded single coincidences as merely the tips of the iceberg which happened to catch the eye among the ubiquitous manifestations of "seriality". He thus reversed the sceptic's argument that we tend to see significances everywhere because out of the multitude of random events we only remember those few which *are* significant. At the end of the first, classificatory part of his book, Kammerer concluded:

> So far we have been concerned with the factual manifestations of recurrent series, without attempting an explanation. We have found that the recurrence of identical or similar data in contiguous areas of space or time is a simple empirical fact which has to be accepted and which cannot be explained by coincidence – or rather, which makes coincidence rule to such an extent that the concept of coincidence itself is negated.§

In the second part of his book, Kammerer develops his theory that coexistent with physical causality there is an acausal principle active in the universe which tends towards unity-in-variety. In some respects it is comparable to that other mysterious force, universal gravity; but whereas gravity acts indiscriminately on all matter, this hypothetical factor acts selectively to make like and like converge in space and time – it correlates by affinity or some sort of selective resonance, like tuning forks vibrating on the same

---

*Published in one volume together with Pauli's essay "*Der Einfluss Archetypischer Vorstellungen auf die Bildung Naturwissenschaftlicher Theorien bei Kepler*"(Jung–Pauli, *Naturerklärung und Psyche*, 1952).
†There is no English translation.
‡See my biography of Kammerer, *The Case of the Midwife Toad*, which to my regret I had to exclude from this selection, for reasons explained in the Preface.
§P. Kammerer, *Das Gesetz der Serie* (Stuttgart, 1919) p. 93.

wave-length. By what means this acausal agency interferes with the causal order of things we cannot know since it operates outside the known laws of physics. In space it produces confluential events related by affinities of form and function; in time, similarly related series:

> We thus arrive at the image of a world-mosaic or cosmic kaleidoscope, which, in spite of constant shufflings and rearrangements, also takes care of bringing like and like together. . . .*

One need not be a professional gambler to feel attracted by Kammerer's Law of Seriality. Most languages have a phrase or proverb for it – "*Das Gesetz der Serie*" is a cliché in German, the equivalent of "It never rains but it pours". Some people seem to become coincidence-prone as others become accident-prone. At the end of his book Kammerer expresses his belief that seriality is

> . . . ubiquitous and continuous in life, nature and cosmos. It is the umbilical cord that connects thought, feeling, science and art with the womb of the universe that gave birth to them.†

The main difference between Kammerer's "seriality" and Jung's "synchronicity" is that the former emphasises serial happenings in time (though he also includes simultaneous coincidental events), whereas the latter's emphasis is on simultaneous events (but also includes precognitive dreams which may have occurred several days before the event). Kammerer based his theory partly on the analogy with gravity, partly on the periodic cycles in biology and cosmology. Some of his excursions into physics contain naive errors; other passages show tantalising flashes of intuition – so much so that Einstein commented favourably on the book; he called it "original and by no means absurd".‡ Jung, on the other hand, used Pauli quasi as a tutor in theoretical physics, but in the end made little use of it; his explanations of the "acausal factor" were utterly obscure, invoking the collective unconscious and its archetypes. This was sadly disappointing but it helped to turn synchronicity into a cult-word. It was for the first time that the hypothesis of acausal factors at large in the universe was given the joint stamp of respectability by a psychologist and a physicist, both of international renown.

*Ibid., p. 165.
†Ibid., p. 456.
‡Quoted by H. Przibram in *Monistische Monatshefte* (November, 1926).

The belief in connections beyond physical causality did not, of course, originate with Kammerer or Jung. Its immediate ancestry can be traced back to Schopenhauer, who had considerable influence over both Freud and Jung. Schopenhauer taught that physical causality was *only one* of the principles ruling the world; the other was a metaphysical entity, a kind of universal consciousness, compared to which individual consciousness is "as a dream compared to reality". He wrote:

> Coincidence is the simultaneous occurrence of causally unconnected events. . . . If we visualise each causal chain progressing in time as a meridian on the globe, then we may represent simultaneous events by the parallel circles of latitude. . . . All the events in a man's life could accordingly stand in two fundamentally different connections.*

This idea of unity-in-diversity can be followed all the way back to the Pythagorean "Harmony of the Spheres",† and the Hippocratics' "sympathy of all things": "there is one common flow, one common breathing, all things are in sympathy". The doctrine that everything in the universe hangs together, partly by mechanical causes, but mainly by hidden affinities (which also account for apparent coincidences), provided not only the foundation for sympathetic magic, astrology and alchemy; it also runs as a *leitmotif* through the teachings of Taoism and Buddhism, the neo-Platonists, and the philosophers of the early Renaissance. It was neatly summed up by (among many others) Pico della Mirandola, AD 1550:

> Firstly there is the unity in things whereby each thing is at one with itself, consists of itself, and coheres with itself. Secondly, there is the unity whereby one creature is united with the others and all parts of the world constitute one world.‡

In the terms of the theory outlined in previous chapters, the first half of the above quotation reflects the working of the *self-assertive*, the second of the self-transcending or *integrative* tendency, on a universal level.

We may also compare Pico's statement with the consensus of contemporary physicists: "It is impossible to separate any part of the universe from the rest." The essence of both quotations, separated by four centuries, is a holistic view of the universe which transcends physical causality.

*A. Schopenhauer *Sämtliche Werke*, Vol. VIII (Stuttgart, 1859).
†For the influence of this conception on Elizabethan philosophy and poetry, see *The Sleepwalkers*, Part One, ch. II.
‡Pico della Mirandola, *Opera Omnia* (Basle, 1557), p. 40.

One of the best-kept secrets of the universe relates to the question how the sub-atomic micro-world of particles, which are at the same time wavicles, which defy strict determinism and mechanical causation – how this ambiguous "undulating carpet of foam" gives rise to the solid, orderly macro-world of everyday experience ruled by strict causality.

The modern scientist's answer is that this seemingly miraculous feat of creating order out of disorder must be seen in the light of the theory of probability or the "law of large numbers". But this law is not explainable by physical forces; it hangs, so to speak, in the air. A few examples will illustrate the point.

The first two are classic cases quoted from Warren Weaver's book on the theory of probability.* The statistics of the New York Department of Health show that in 1955 the average number of dogs biting people reported per day was 75·3; in 1956, 73·6; in 1957, 73·5; in 1958, 74·5; in 1959, 72·4. A similar statistical reliability was shown by cavalry horses administering fatal kicks to soldiers in the German army of the last century; they were apparently guided by the so-called Poisson equation of probability theory. Murderers in England and Wales, however different in character and motives, displayed the same respect for the laws of statistics: since the end of the First World War, the average number of murders over successive decades was: 1920–9, 3·84 per million of the population; 1930–9, 3·27 per million; 1940–9, 3·92 per million; 1950–9, 3·3 per million; 1960–9, approx 3·5 per million.

These bizarre examples illustrate the paradoxical nature of probability, which has puzzled philosophers ever since Pascal initiated that branch of mathematics – and which von Neumann, the greatest mathematician of our century, called "black magic". The paradox consists of the fact that the theory of probability is able to predict with uncanny precision the overall result of a large number of individual events, each of which is in itself unpredictable. In other words, we are faced with *a large number of uncertainties producing a certainty*, a large number of random events creating a lawful total outcome.

But paradoxical or not, the law of large numbers *works*; the mystery is *why and how* it works. It has become an indispensable tool of physics and genetics, of economic planners, insurance companies, gambling casinos, and opinion polls – so much so that

*W. Weaver, *Lady Luck and the Theory of Probability* (New York, 1963).

we take the black magic for granted. Thus when faced with such bizarre examples of probability-lore as the dogs or cavalry horses, we may be mildly puzzled or amused, without realising the universal nature of the paradox and its relevance to the problem of chance and design, freedom and necessity.

In nuclear physics we find striking analogies to the unpredictable dogs producing predictable statistics. A classic example is radioactive decay, where totally unpredictable radioactive atoms produce exactly predictable overall results. The point in time at which a radioactive atom will suddenly disintegrate is totally unpredictable both experimentally and theoretically. It is not influenced by chemical or physical factors like temperature or pressure. In other words, it does not depend on the atom's past history, nor on its present environment; in the words of Professor Bohm, "it does not have any causes", it is "*completely arbitrary* in the sense that it has no relationship whatsoever to anything else that exists in the world or that ever has existed" (italics in the original).* And yet it *does* have a hidden, apparently acausal relationship with the rest of the world, because the so-called "half-life" period of any grain of a radioactive substance (i.e. the time required for half of the atoms in the grain to disintegrate) is rigorously fixed and predictable. The half-life of uranium is four and a half million years. The half-life of radium A is 3·825 days. The half-life of thorium C is 60·5 minutes. And so on, down to millionths of seconds.

However, there may be fluctuations in the rate of decay of the grain; at some stages on the road to the half-life date there might be an excess or a deficit of decayed atoms which threatens to upset the time-table. But these deviations from the statistical mean will soon be corrected, and the half-life date rigorously kept. By what agency is this controlling and correcting influence exerted, since the decay of individual atoms is unaffected by what goes on in the rest of the grain? How do the dogs of New York know when to stop biting and when to make up the daily quota? How are the murderers in England and Wales made to stop at four victims per million? By what mysterious power is the roulette ball induced, after a glut of "reds", to restore the balance in the long run? By "the laws of probability" (or "the law of large numbers") we are told. But that law has no physical powers to enforce its dictates. It is impotent – and yet virtually omnipotent.

*D. Bohm, *Quantum Theory* (London, 1951).

It may seem that I am labouring the point out of sheer perversity, but this paradox is indeed vital to the problem of causality. Since the causal chains which lead to the decay of individual atoms are ostensibly independent from each other, we must either assume that the fulfilment of the statistical prediction that my sample of thorium C will have a half-life of 60·5 minutes is itself due to blind chance – which is absurd; or we must take the plunge and opt for some alternative hypothesis on the speculative lines of an "acausal connecting agency", which is complementary to physical causality in the sense in which particle and wavicle, "mechanical" and "mental" complement each other. Such an agency would operate in different guises on different levels: in the shape of "hidden variables" filling in the gaps in causality on the sub-atomic level; co-ordinating the activities of the physically independent thorium C atoms to make them respect the half-life date; bringing like and like together in the "confluential events" of seriality and synchronicity; and perhaps generating the "psi-field" of the parapsychologist.

This may sound like a tall proposition, but is in fact no taller than the paradoxical phenomena on which it is based. We live submerged in a universe of "undulating quantum foam" which ceaselessly creates weird phenomena by means transcending the classical concepts of physical causation. The purpose and design of this acausal agency is unknown, and perhaps unknowable to us; but intuitively we feel it somehow to be related to that striving towards higher forms of order and unity-in-variety which we observe in the evolution of the universe at large, of life on earth, human consciousness, and lastly science and art. One ultimate mystery is easier to accept than a litter-basket of unrelated puzzles.

In his classic essay *What is Life?* Erwin Schrödinger (one of the greatest physicists of our century) took a similar line. He called the connecting link between the totally unpredictable sub-atomic events and their exactly predictable collective result "the 'order from disorder' principle". He frankly admitted that it is beyond physical causation:

> The disintegration of a single radioactive atom is observable (it emits a projectile which causes a visible scintillation on a fluorescent screen). But if you are given a single atom, its probable lifetime is much less certain than that of a healthy sparrow. Indeed, nothing more can be said about it than this: as long as it lives (and that may be for thousands of years) the chance of its blowing up within the next second, whether

large or small, remains the same. This patent lack of individual determination nevertheless results in the exact exponential law of decay of a large number of radioactive atoms of the same kind.*

Robert Harvie, co-author (with Sir Alister Hardy and myself) of *The Challenge of Chance*, commented on this passage by Schrödinger:

> Orthodox quantum theory attempts to resolve this paradox by asserting the probabilistic nature of matter at the microscopic level. But a further paradox remains – that of probability itself. The laws of probability describe *how* a collection of single random events can add up to a large-scale certainty, but not *why*.
>
> The "order from disorder" principle seems to be irreducible, inexplicably "just there". To ask why is akin to asking "Why is the universe?" or "Why has space three dimensions?" (if indeed it has).†

In the present theory, the "order from disorder" principle is represented by the Integrative Tendency. We have seen that this principle can be traced all the way back to the Pythagoreans. After its temporary eclipse during the reign of reductionist orthodoxies in physics and biology, it is once more gaining ascendancy in more sophisticated versions. I have mentioned the related concepts of Schrödinger's negentropy, Szent Györgyi's syntropy, Bergson's *élan vital*, etc.; one might add to the list the German biologist Woltereck who coined the term "anamorphosis" – which von Bertalanffy adopted – for Nature's tendency to create new forms of life, and also L. L. Whyte's "morphic principle", or "the fundamental principle of the development of pattern". What all these theories have in common is that they regard the morphic, or formative, or syntropic tendency, Nature's striving to create order out of disorder, cosmos out of chaos, as ultimate and irreducible principles beyond mechanical causation.‡

The present theory is even more hazardous by explicitly suggesting that the integrative tendency operates in *both causal and acausal* ways, the two standing in a complementary relationship analogous to the particle–wave complementarity in physics. It is accordingly supposed to embrace not only the acausal agencies operating on the sub-atomic level, but also the phenomena of parapsychology and "confluential events". We have seen that

---

*E. Schrödinger, *What is Life?* (Cambridge, 1944), p. 83.
†Hardy, Harvie and Koestler, *The Challenge of Chance*, p. 133.
‡Although most of them do not expressly invoke acausal factors, these are implied in regarding the formative tendency as "irreducible".

ESP and "synchronicity" often overlap, so that a supposedly paranormal event can be interpreted either as a result of ESP or as a case of "synchronicity". But we are perhaps mistaken when we try to make a categorical distinction between the two. Classical physics has taught us that there are various manifestations of energy, including kinetic, potential, thermal, electrical, nuclear and radiant energy which can be converted into one another by suitable procedures, like interchangeable currencies. The present theory suggests that in a similar way telepathy, clairvoyance, precognition, psychokinesis and synchronicity are merely *different manifestations under different conditions of the same universal principle* – i.e., the integrative tendency operating through both causal and acausal agencies. How this is done is beyond our understanding; but at least we can fit the evidence for paranormal phenomena into the unified design.

Among the basic requirements for the validation of a scientific experiment are its repeatability and predictability. Paranormal events, however, whether produced in the laboratory or spontaneously, are unpredictable, capricious and relatively rare. This is one of the reasons why sceptics feel justified in rejecting the results of some forty years of rigorously controlled laboratory experiments in ESP and PK, in spite of the massive statistical evidence which, in any other field of research, would be considered as sufficient proof for the reality of the phenomena.

But the criterion of repeatability applies only when the experimental conditions are essentially the same as in the original experiment; and with sensitive human subjects the conditions are never quite the same in terms of mood, receptivity, or emotional rapport between subject and experimenter. Besides, ESP phenomena nearly always involve unconscious processes beyond voluntary control. And if the phenomena are in fact triggered by acausal agencies, it would be naive to expect that they can be produced at will.

There is, however, another explanation for the apparent rarity and capriciousness of paranormal phenomena, which is of special interest in our context. It was, I believe, originated by Henri Bergson and has been taken up by various writers on parapsychology. Thus, for instance, H. H. Price, former Wykeham Professor of Logic in Oxford:

It looks as if telepathically received impressions have some difficulty in crossing the threshold and manifesting themselves in consciousness. There seems to be some barrier or repressive mechanism which tends to shut them out from consciousness, a barrier which is rather difficult to pass, and they make use of all sorts of devices for overcoming it. . . . Often they can only emerge in a distorted and symbolic form (as other unconscious mental contents do). It is a plausible guess that many of our everyday thoughts and emotions are telepathic or partly telepathic in origin, but are not recognised to be so because they are so much distorted and mixed with other mental contents in crossing the threshold of consciousness.*

The Cambridge mathematician, Adrian Dobbs, commenting on the extract I have just quoted, went straight to the heart of the matter:

This is a very interesting passage. It evokes the picture of either the mind or the brain as containing an assemblage of selective filters, designed to cut out unwanted signals on neighbouring frequencies, some of which get through in a distorted form, just as in ordinary radio reception.†

Cyril Burt, former Professor of Psychology, University College, London, took up the same idea:

Our sense organs and our brain operate as an intricate kind of filter which limits and directs the mind's clairvoyant powers, so that under normal conditions attention is concentrated on just those objects or situations that are of biological importance for the survival of the organism and its species. . . . As a rule, it would seem, the mind rejects ideas coming from another mind as the body rejects grafts coming from another body.‡

At this stage, the reader may have experienced a feeling of *déjà vu*, because earlier on I discussed some other "filter-theories" related to the mechanisms of perception and memory. In fact, the hypothesis that there is a filtering apparatus which protects us against "unwanted" ESP signals is merely an extrapolation from what we know about normal, sensory perception. We remember William James's famous "blooming, buzzing multitude of sensations" which are constantly bombarding our sensory receptors, and particularly the eyes and ears. Our minds would be engulfed by chaos if we were to attend to each of these millions of stimuli impinging on them. Thus the central nervous system, and the

---

*Quoted by A. Dobbs in *Science and ESP*, p. 239.
†Ibid.
‡Sir C. Burt, *Psychology and Psychical Research. The Seventeenth W. H. Myers Memorial Lecture* (London, 1968), pp. 50 and 58–9.

brain, have to function as a multilevelled hierarchy of scanning, filtering and classifying devices "which eliminate a large proportion of the sensory input as irrelevant 'noise', and assemble the relevant information into coherent patterns before it is presented to consciousness". By analogy, a similar filtering apparatus might protect our rational minds against the "blooming, buzzing multitude" of messages, images, intuitions and coincidental happenings in some sort of psycho-magnetic field surrounding us.

Chapter 53

COSMIC HORIZONS*

Approaching the end of this journey, it might be useful to look back at earlier chapters in which I discussed the sudden rise of the human neocortex, and its growth at a speed without precedent in the history of evolution. We have seen that one of the consequences of this explosive process was the chronic conflict between the new brain which endowed man with his reasoning powers, and the archaic old brain, governed by instinct and emotion. The outcome was a mentally unbalanced species, with a built-in paranoid streak, mercilessly revealed by its past and present history.

But the brain explosion in the late Pleistocene also led to other consequences – less dramatic, but no less far-reaching. The crucial point is, that in creating the human brain, evolution has wildly overshot the mark.

> An instrument has been developed in advance of the needs of its possessor. . . . Natural selection could only have endowed the savage with a brain a little superior to that of the ape, whereas he possesses one very little inferior to that of the average member of our learned societies. . . .

This was written by no less an authority than Alfred Russell Wallace, who co-fathered (if the expression is permitted) with Darwin the theory of evolution by natural selection.† Darwin instantly realised the potentially disastrous implications of the argument, and wrote to Wallace: "I hope you have not murdered completely your own and my child." But he had no satisfactory answer to Wallace's criticism, and his disciples swept it under the carpet.

*From Janus, ch. xiv.
†The first public unveiling of the theory was a joint communication to the Linnean Society by Darwin and Wallace in 1858.

Why was that criticism so important? There were two reasons. The first is merely of historical interest, in that Wallace's objection demolishes one of the cornerstones of the Darwinian edifice. Evolution in Darwinian and neo-Darwinian theory must proceed in very small steps, each of which confers some minimal selective advantage on the mutated organism – otherwise the whole conception makes no sense, as Darwin himself kept reiterating. But the rapid evolution of the human cerebrum, which some anthropologists have compared to a "tumorous overgrowth", could by no stretch of the imagination be fitted into this theory. Hence Darwin's agonised response, and the subsequent conspiracy of silence.

The second, and by far the more important, aspect of Wallace's criticism, he himself does not seem to have fully realised. He emphasised that the "instrument" – the human brain – had been "developed in advance of the needs of its possessor". But the evolution of the human brain not only overshot the needs of prehistoric man, it is also the only example of evolution *providing a species with an organ which it does not know how to use*; a luxury organ, which will take its owner thousands of years to learn to put to proper use – if he ever does.

The archaeological evidence indicates that the earliest representative of *homo sapiens* – Cro-Magnon man who enters the scene a hundred thousand years ago or earlier – was already endowed with a brain which in size and shape is indistinguishable from ours. But, however paradoxical it sounds, he hardly made any use of that luxury organ. He remained an illiterate cave-dweller and, for millennium after millennium, went on manufacturing spears, bows and arrows of the same primitive type, while the organ which was to take man to the moon was already there, ready for use, inside his skull. Thus the evolution of the brain overshot the mark by a time factor of astronomical magnitude. This paradox is not easy to grasp; in *The Ghost in the Machine* I tried to illustrate it by a bit of science fiction which I called "the parable of the unsolicited gift":

> There was once a poor, illiterate shopkeeper in an Arab bazaar, called Ali, who, not being very good at doing sums, was always cheated by his customers – instead of cheating them, as it should be. So he prayed every night to Allah for the present of an abacus – that venerable contraption for adding and subtracting by pushing beads along wires. But some malicious djin forwarded his prayers to the wrong branch of the heavenly Mail Order Department, and so one morning, arriving at

the bazaar, Ali found his stall transformed into a multi-storey, steel-framed building, housing the latest IBM computer with instrument panels covering all the walls, with thousands of fluorescent oscillators, dials, magic eyes, *et cetera*; and an instruction book of several hundred pages – which, being illiterate, he could not read. However, after days of useless fiddling with this or that dial, he flew into a rage and started kicking a shiny, delicate panel. The shocks disturbed one of the machine's millions of electronic circuits, and after a while Ali discovered to his delight that if he kicked that panel, say, three times and afterwards five times, one of the dials showed the figure eight. He thanked Allah for having sent him such a pretty abacus, and continued to use the machine to add up two and three – happily unaware that it was capable of deriving Einstein's equations in a jiffy, or predicting the orbits of planets and stars thousands of years ahead.

Ali's children, then his grandchildren, inherited the machine and the secret of kicking the same panel; but it took hundreds of generations until they learned to use it even for the purpose of simple multiplication. We ourselves are Ali's descendants, and though we have discovered many other ways of putting the machine to work, we have still only learned to utilise a very small fraction of the potentials of its millions of circuits. For the unsolicited gift is of course the human brain. As for the instruction book, it is lost – if it ever existed. Plato maintains that it did once – but that is hearsay.*

When biologists talk of "mental evolution" superseding biological evolution as a specific characteristic in man and absent in animals, they generally fail to see the crux of the problem. For the learning potential in animals is inevitably limited by the fact that they, unlike man, make full use – or nearly full use – of all organs of their native equipment, including their brains. The capabilities of the computers inside the reptilian or lower mammalian skull are exploited almost to the full and thus leave no scope for cumulative learning and "mental evolution". Only in the case of *homo sapiens* has evolution anticipated his needs by a time factor of such magnitude that he is only beginning to utilise some of the unexploited, unexplored potentials of the brain's estimated ten thousand million neurons and their virtually inexhaustible synaptic cross-connections. The history of science, philosophy and art is, from this point of view, the slow process of the mind learning by experience to actualise the brain's potentials. The new frontiers to be conquered are in the convolutions of the cerebral cortex.

The Ghost in the Machine, pp. 297f.

The reasons why this process of *learning to use our brains* was so slow, spasmodic and beset with reverses, can be summed up in a simple formula: the old brain got in the way of, or acted as a brake on, the new. The only periods in European history in which there was a truly cumulative growth of scientific knowledge were the three great centuries of Greece before the Macedonian conquest, and the four centuries from the Renaissance to the present. The organ to generate that knowledge was there inside the skulls of men all the time during the dark interregnum of two thousand years; but it was not allowed to generate that knowledge. For most of the time of recorded human history, and the much longer stretches of pre-history, the marvellous potentialities of the unsolicited gift were only allowed to manifest themselves in the service of archaic, emotion-based beliefs, saturated with taboos; in the magically motivated paintings of the Dordogne caves; in the translation of archetypal imagery into the language of mythology; in the religious art of Asia and the Christian Middle Ages. The task of reason was to act as *ancilla fidei*, the hand-maid of faith – whether it was the faith of sorcerers and medicine men, theologians, scholastics, dialectical materialists, devotees of Chairman Mao or King Mbo-Mba. The fault was not in our stars, but in the horse and crocodile which we carry inside our skulls.

The historical consequences of man's split personality have been discussed at length in earlier chapters; my purpose in bringing the subject up once more is to point out a quite different consequence of this condition, which raises basic philosophical problems. To stay for another moment with our metaphor: Ali's descendants were so impressed by and delighted with the apparently inexhaustible capabilities of the computer (in those brief, happy periods when it was allowed to operate unimpeded) that they fell victim to the understandable illusion that the computer was *potentially omniscient*. This illusion was a direct consequence of evolution's overshooting the mark. In other words, the brain's powers of learning and reasoning turned out to be so enormous compared to those of other animals, and also compared to the immediate needs of its possessors, that they became convinced its untapped potentials were inexhaustible, and its powers of reasoning *unlimited*. There was indeed no reason to believe that problems existed to which the computer had no answer, because it was not "programmed" to answer them. One might call this attitude the "rationalist illusion" – the belief that it is only a question of time before the ultimate mysteries of the universe are solved, thanks to the brain's unlimited reasoning powers.

This illusion was shared by most of Ali's successors, including the most eminent among them. Aristotle thought that nearly everything worth discovering about the ways of the universe had already been discovered and that there were no unsolved problems left. Descartes was so carried away by the success of applying mathematical methods to science that he believed he would be able to complete the whole edifice of the new physics by himself. His more cautious contemporaries among the pioneers of the scientific revolution thought it might take as much as two more generations to wrest its last secret from Nature. "The particular phenomena of the arts and sciences are in reality but a handful," wrote Sir Francis Bacon. "The invention of all causes and sciences would be a labour of but a few years". Two centuries later, in 1899, the eminent German biologist and apostle of Darwin, Ernst Haeckel, published his book *Die Welträtsel* – *The Riddles of the Universe* (which, as I have mentioned before, became the bible of my youth). The book enumerated seven great riddles, of which six were "definitively solved" – including the structure of matter and the origin of life. The seventh – the subjective experience of the freedom of will – was but "an illusion having no real existence" – so there were no more unsolved riddles left, which was nice to know. Sir Julian Huxley probably shared this opinion when he wrote: "In the field of evolution, genetics has given its basic answer, and evolutionary biologists are free to pursue other problems".*

The philosophy of reductionism was a direct offspring of the rationalist illusion. "The invention [i.e., discovery] of all causes and sciences would be a labour of but a few years". Replace "years" by "centuries" and you get the essence of the reductionist credo that the potentially omniscient brain of man will eventually explain all the riddles of the universe by reducing them to "nothing but" the interplay of electrons, protons and quarks. Dazzled by the benefits derived from the unsolicited gift, it did not occur to the beneficiaries that although the human brain's powers were in some respects immense, they were nevertheless severely limited in other respects, concerned with ultimate meanings. In other words, while evolution "overshot" its target, it also griev-

Evolution as a Process, ed. Sir J. Huxley, Sir A. Hardy and E. B. Ford (New York, 1954), p. 12.

ously *undershot* it with respect to the ultimate, existential questions, for which it was not "programmed". These ultimates include the paradoxa of infinity and eternity ("If the universe started with the Big Bang, what was before the Bang?"); the curvature of space according to relativity; the notion .of parallel and inter-penetrating universes; the phenomena of parapsychology and of acausal processes; and all questions related to ultimate meanings (of the universe, of life, of good and evil, etc.). To quote, once more, the physicist, Professor Henry Margenau of Yale:

> An artifact occasionally invoked to explain precognition is to make time multidimensional. This allows a genuine backward passage of time, which might permit positive intervals in one time direction to become negative ("effect before cause") in another. In principle, this represents a valid scheme, and I know of no criticism that will rule it out as a scientific procedure. If it is to be acceptable, however, a completely new metric of space-time needs to be developed. . . .*

But we are not "programmed" for such a new metric; we are not able to visualise spatial dimensions added to length, width and height; nor time flowing from tomorrow towards yesterday. We are unable to visualise such phenomena, not because they are impossible but because the human brain and nervous system are not programmed for them.

The limitations of our programming – of our native equipment – are even more obvious in our sensory receptor organs. The human eye can perceive only a very small fraction of the spectrum of electromagnetic radiations; our hearing is restricted to a range of sound frequencies narrower than the dog's; our sense of smell is desultory and our capacity of spatial orientation cannot compare with the migrating bird's. Until about the thirteenth century man did not realise that he was surrounded by magnetic forces; nor does he have any sensory awareness of them; nor of the showers of neutrinos which penetrate and traverse his body in millions: nor of other known or unknown fields and influences operating inside and around him. If the *sensory* apparatus of our species is programmed to perceive only an infinitesimally small part of the cosmic phantasmagoria, then why not admit that its *reasoning* faculties may be subject to equally severe limitations in programming – i.e., that they are unable to provide answers to the ultimate questions of "the meaning of it all"? Such an admission would neither belittle the mind of man, nor discourage him from

*H. Margenau in *Science and ESP*, pp. 223–4.

putting it to full use – for creative minds will always try to do just that, "as if" the answers were just around the corner.

To admit the *inherent limitations* of man's reasoning power automatically leads to a more tolerant and open-minded attitude toward phenomena which seem to defy reason – like quantum physics, parapsychology and acausal events. Such a change of attitude would also put an end to the crude reductionist maxim that what cannot be explained cannot exist. A species of humans without eyes, such as the citizens of H. G. Wells's *Country of the Blind*, would reject our claim of being able to perceive distant objects without contact by touch, as occult nonsense. There is a Chinese proverb which tells us that it is useless to speak about the sea to a frog that lives at the bottom of a well.

We have heard a whole chorus of Nobel laureates assert that matter is merely energy in disguise, that causality is dead, determinism is dead. If that is so, they should be given a public funeral in the olive groves of Academe, with a requiem of electronic music. It is indeed time to get out of the strait-jacket which nineteenth-century materialism, combined with reductionism and the rationalist illusion, imposed on our philosophical outlook. Had that outlook kept abreast with the revolutionary messages from the bubble chambers and radio-telescopes, instead of lagging a century behind them, we would have been liberated from that strait-jacket a long time ago.

Once this simple fact is recognised, we might become more receptive to bizarre phenomena inside and around us which a one-sided emphasis on mechanical determinism made us ignore; might feel the draught that is blowing through the chinks of the causal edifice; include paranormal phenomena in our revised concepts of normality; and realise that we have been living in the Country of the Blind – or at the bottom of a well.

The consequences of such a shift of awareness are unforeseeable. In the words of Professor H. H. Price "psychical research is one of the most important branches of investigation which the human mind has undertaken", and "it may transform the whole intellectual outlook upon which our present civilisation is based".* These are strong words coming from an Oxford Professor of Logic, but I do not think they overstate the case.

It is possible that in this particular field of psychic endowment we are – together with our other handicaps – an under-privileged

*H. H. Price in *Hibbert J.*, Vol. XLVII (1949), pp. 105–13.

species. The grand design of evolutionary strategy does not exclude the existence of biological freaks, like the koala bear, nor of self-destructive races, like our paranoid selves. If this is the case, we have to live "as if" it were not so, and try to make the best of it – as we are trying to make the best of our suspended death-sentences *qua* individuals.

The limitations of Ali's computer may condemn us to the role of Peeping Toms at the keyhole of eternity. But at least we can try to take the stuffing out of the keyhole, which blocks even our limited view.

In earlier chapters of this book I stressed the fact that our present situation is without precedent in history. To say it once more: in all previous generations man had to come to terms with the prospect of his death as an individual; the present generation is the first to face the prospect of the death of our species. *Homo sapiens* arrived on the scene about a hundred thousands years ago, which is but the blinking of an eye on the evolutionary time-scale. If he were to vanish now, his rise and fall would have been a brief episode, unsung and unlamented by other inhabitants of our galaxy. We know by now that other planets in the vastness of space are humming with life; that brief episode would probably never have come to their notice.

Only a few decades ago it was generally thought that the emergence of life out of inanimate chemical compounds must have been an extremely improbable, and therefore extremely rare event, which may have occurred only once, on this privileged planet of ours, and nowhere else. It was further thought that the formation of solar systems, such as ours, was also a rare event, and that planets capable of supporting life must be even rarer. But these assumptions, flavoured by "earth-chauvinism", have been refuted by the rapid advances of astrophysics. It is now generally accepted by astronomers that the formation of planetary systems, including inhabitable planets, is "a common event";* and that organic compounds, potentially capable of giving rise to life, are

*Professor Carl Sagan (Center for Radiophysics and Space Research, Cornell University), at the CETI Congress, 1971. CETI (Communication with Extraterrestrial Intelligence) was jointly sponsored by the US National Academy of Sciences and the Soviet Academy of Sciences and attended by leading scientists from both countries. Its proceedings (published by the MIT Press, 1973) represent a landmark in the study of the problems of extraterrestrial life, and of the possible methods of establishing contact with alien life-forms.

present both in our immediate neighbourhood, on Mars, and in the interstellar dust-clouds of distant nebulae. Moreover, a certain class of meteorites was found to contain organic materials whose spectra are the same as those of pollen-like spores in pre-Cambrian sediments.* Sir Fred Hoyle and his Indian colleague, Professor Chandra Wickranashinghe, proposed (in 1977) a theory, which regards "pre-stellar molecular clouds such as are present in the Orion nebula, as the most natural 'cradles' of life. Processes occurring in such clouds lead to the commencement and dispersal of biological activity in the Galaxy. . . . It would now seem most likely that the transformation of inorganic matter into primitive biological systems is occurring more or less continually in the space between the stars."†

As for the pollen-like structures in meteorites, the authors hold it to be possible that they "represent primitive interstellar 'protocells' in a state of suspended animation".‡ At present "some hundred tons of meteoritic material enter the earth's atmosphere every day; but in earlier geological epochs the accumulation rate may have been much higher". Part of this material may have originated in the "cradles of life" – the dust-clouds pre-dating the formation of stars.

Thus the doctrines of "terrestrial chauvinism" have become untenable, like so many other cherished beliefs of nineteenth-century science. We are not alone in the universe – not the only spectators in the theatre, surrounded by empty seats. On the contrary, the universe around us is teeming with life, from primitive "proto-cells", floating in interstellar space, to millions of advanced civilisations far ahead of us – where "far" might mean the distance we have travelled from our reptilian or amoebic ancestry.

I find this perspective comforting and exhilarating. In the first place, it is nice to know that we are not alone, that we have company out there among the stars – so that if we vanish, it does not matter too much, and the cosmic drama will not be played out before an empty house. The thought that we are the only conscious beings in this immensity, and that if we vanish, consciousness would vanish from it, is unbearable. Vice versa, the knowledge that there are billions of beings in our galaxy, and in other galaxies, infinitely more enlightened than our poor sick selves,

*New Scientist, April 21, 1977.
†Ibid.
‡Ibid.

may lead to that humility and self-transcendence which is the source of all true religious experience.

This brings me to a perhaps naive, but I think plausible consideration regarding the nature of extraterrestrial intelligences and civilisations. Terrestrial civilisation (from the start of agriculture, written language, etc.) is, at a generous estimate, around 10,000 years old. To make guesses about the nature of extraterrestrial civilisations a few *million* years older than ours is of course totally beyond our mental capacities. On the other hand, it is entirely reasonable to assume that sooner or later – within, say, its first 10,000 years – every one of these civilisations would have discovered thermo-nuclear reactions – i.e., met the anno Hiroshima of its own calendar. From this point onward natural selection (or rather, the "selective weed-killer", as I have called it) takes over on a cosmic scale. The sick civilisations engendered by biological misfits (such as *homo sapiens* seems to be) will sooner or later act as their own executioners and vanish from their polluted planet. Those civilisations which survive this and other tests of sanity will grow, or have already grown, into demi-gods. More soberly speaking, it is a comforting thought that only the "goodies" among these civilisations will survive, whereas the "baddies" will annihilate themselves.

It is nice to know that the universe is a place reserved for goodies and that we are surrounded by them. The established religions take a less charitable view of the cosmic administration.

EPILOGUE

I have repeatedly referred to my life up to 1940 as "a typical case-history of a Central European member of the educated middle class born in the first years of our century". It was typical, in the first place, because of the historic events which affected all members of that class: the First World War and its turbulent aftermath; the rise of National Socialism and the rival lure of the Great Soviet Experiment which seemed to provide the only alternative to it; the repercussions of the Spanish Civil War; the mass-migration of the Central European intelligentsia to Western Europe, America, Palestine and Auschwitz; the surrender of Europe to the Swastika, and lastly the Second World War.

But this first half of the author's life was also fairly typical in a different sense: his intellectual formation and ideological commitments. These were by and large dominated by three symbolic figures — a trinity which, though secular, had an aura of holiness: Marx, Freud and Einstein. Marx, a bearded Lorelei, beckoning from the treacherous rock of Utopia; Freud, reducing man's spiritual aspirations to the secretions of his sex glands; Einstein being venerated in the hopeful belief that Science would provide the answers to all ultimate questions and explain the meaning of life. Each of the three deities shrank eventually into a God that Failed; together they left in their wake a *Götterdämmerung*, then a yawning vacuum. The generations which succeeded mine, with their rapidly changing cult-figures and attempts to create a counter-culture by flower-power, drugs or bombs, were and still are free-wheeling in that vacuum.

"In my youth I regarded the universe as an open book, printed in the language of physical equations, whereas now it appears to me as a text

written in invisible ink, of which in our rare moments of grace we are
able to decipher a small fragment."

This confession was written when, approaching the age of fifty,
I felt the need for that "vocational change" which is reflected in
the transition from Book One to Book Two, from the quest for
Utopia to the search for glimpses of a new synthesis. It started
with an analysis of humour which led, through a back-door, as it
were, to a theory of creativity in science and art. The theory
pointed to certain processes underlying human creativity which
seemed to have general validity both in biological and mental
evolution. The next step from here led to the rudiments of a
general systems theory, based on the concept of the holon, and its
applications to such hoary problems as free will, memory, and the
irrationality of the group mind.

A parallel line of argument led from the creativity to the pathology of the human mind, and the resulting tendency of our species
towards self-destruction, ending with the timid proposal of an
"alternative to despair".

In the concluding chapters I have tried to show that the contemporary versions of Eastern mysticism had no remedies to offer
for mankind's tragic predicament. But there are some indications
that a new form of mysticism – or cosmic consciousness – might
emerge from the infinite vista recently revealed to us of the sub-
atomic and extra-galactic worlds; and there is some comfort in the
thought that in the universe we are not alone, but surrounded by
our elders and betters.

Here the guided omnibus tour ends, and another metaphor
takes over, which sums up the author's feelings at the end of the
journey.

*   *   *

". . . And the whole earth was of one language, and they used few
words. And they found a plain in the land of Shinar; and they
settled there. And they said one to another, Go to, let us make
bricks, and burn them hard. And they had brick for stone, and
slime they had for mortar. And they said, Go to, let us build us a
city and a tower whose top may reach unto heaven and make a
name for ourselves. And the Lord came down to see the city and
the tower, which the children of man builded; and the Lord said,
Behold, they are one people, and they have all one language, and

now they have started to do this; henceforward nothing they have a mind to do will be beyond their reach. Go to, let us go down and confound their language, that they may not understand one another's speech."*

The sorry end of the tale is known to all of us, but there is more than one interpretation for it. Perhaps the Lord, in his infinite malice, made not only the previously single language shared by all the children of man split up into Babylonian, Hebrew, Egyptian and so forth – that difficulty could have been overcome with the help of a few clever translators; but, realising that an undertaking of the magnitude and complexity of the offending tower needed specialists of all sorts, He fiendishly endowed them each with a special terminology and set of beliefs, which made it quite impossible for the engineers to understand what the priests were talking about, for the brick-burners to share the architects' vision, for the philosophers to agree on the function of the tower and for the poets to overcome their revulsion against such a monstrous desecration of the pastoral environment. The higher the tower grew, the more violent the disputes between the builders became, until all communication between them broke down, and even the purpose of their brave endeavour was forgotten, and vanished in the mist.

The parable of the tower sounds in some respects like the sequel to the parable of the Fall, the latter representing man's moral, the former his intellectual predicament. We seem to be compelled to shape facts and data, as we know them, into hard bricks, and stick them together with the slime of our theories and beliefs. And thus we continue to Go to, and carry bricks to Babel, although we know that the tower will never be completed, and that even its existing parts might be smitten by lightning and destroyed at any time.

It is a frustrating job, but it is also fun – part of the human tragicomedy. Carrying bricks to Babel is neither a duty, nor a privilege; it seems to be a necessity built into the chromosomes of our species.

*Genesis, XI I have taken the liberty of combining the text in the Authorised Version with that in the New English Bible.

CHRONOLOGY

This Chronology is merely intended to complement the Bibliography by enabling the reader to get his bearings on the author's whereabouts at various periods of his life, and the circumstances in which the books quoted in this volume were written.

1905   Born in Budapest; father Hungarian, mother Viennese
1922–26   Student, Vienna Polytechnic
1926–29   Palestine – worked in Kibbutz, later as Middle East correspondent
1929–30   Foreign correspondent in Paris
1930–32   Science editor, and foreign editor, Berlin. Member of the Graf Zeppelin polar expedition
1932   Joined Communist Party
1932–33   Travels in Soviet Russia and Central Asia
1933–40   Paris. Anti-Fascist activities
1936–37   War correspondent in Spain. Captured by Nationalists. Three months in prison
1938   Break with Communist Party
1939–40   Interned in French concentration camp
1940–41   Joined French Foreign Legion. Escaped to Britain
1941–42   Served in British Pioneer Corps
1942–45   Worked for Ministry of Information and as a night ambulance driver
1945   Special correspondent in Palestine
1945–47   Lived on sheep farm, Blaenau Ffestiniog, North Wales
1948   War correspondent, Arab–Jewish War. Became naturalised British subject
1948–52   Double residence: "Island Farm", New Jersey, USA, and "Verte Rive", near Fontainebleau, France
1952   Returned to England
1952–80   Mainly in England; travels in India, Japan, Australia and South Pacific; lectures at European and American universities

BIBLIOGRAPHY

Up to and including *Dialogue with Death*, the author's books were written in German; beginning with *Scum of the Earth*, all his books were written in English.

1933   *Von Weissen Nächten und Roten Tagen*
1937   *Menschenopfer Unerhört*
           Spanish Testament
1939   *The Gladiators*
1941   *Darkness at Noon*
           Dialogue with Death (abridged version of *Spanish Testament*)
           Scum of the Earth
1943   *Arrival and Departure*
1945   *The Yogi and the Commissar and Other Essays*
           Twilight Bar: An Escapade in Four Acts
1946   *Thieves in the Night*
1949   *Insight and Outlook: An Inquiry into the Common Foundations of Science, Art and Social Ethics*
           Promise and Fulfilment: Palestine 1917–1949
1951   *The Age of Longing*
1952   *Arrow in the Blue*
1954   *The Invisible Writing*
1955   *The Trail of the Dinosaur and Other Essays*
1956   *Reflections on Hanging*
1959   *The Sleepwalkers: A History of Man's Changing Vision of the Universe*
1961   *The Lotus and the Robot*
           (With C. H. Rolph) *Hanged by the Neck: An Exposure of Capital Punishment in England*
1963   (Editor) *Suicide of a Nation? An Inquiry into the State of Britain Today*
1964   *The Act of Creation*

1967   *The Ghost in the Machine*
       Article on "Johannes Kepler" in *Encyclopaedia of Philosophy*
       (New York)
1968   *Drinkers of Infinity: Essays 1955–1967*
1969   (Editor, with J. R. Smythies) *Beyond Reductionism: New Per-
       spectives in the Life Sciences*: The Alpbach Symposium
1971   *The Case of the Midwife Toad*
1972   *The Roots of Coincidence*
       The Call-Girls
1973   (With Sir Alister Hardy and Robert Harvie) *The Challenge of
       Chance*
1974   *The Heel of Achilles: Essays 1968–1973*
       Article on "Humour and Wit" in *Encyclopaedia Britannica* (15th
       edition)
1976   *The Thirteenth Tribe*
       (With Arnold Toynbee and Others) *Life after Death*
1978   *Janus – A Summing Up*

INDEX